JUST GO DOWN
TO THE ROAD

A Memoir of Trouble and Travel

Syncopations: New Yorkers, Beats and Writers in the Dark
This Is the Beat Generation
Paris Interzone: Richard Wright, Lolita, Boris Vian and
    Others on the Left Bank
Talking at the Gates: A Life of James Baldwin
Gate Fever: Voices from a Prison
Invisible Country: A Journey Through Scotland
Thom Gunn in Conversation
The Picador Book of Blues and Jazz (editor)
The New Edinburgh Review Anthology (editor)

JUST GO DOWN
TO THE ROAD

JAMES CAMPBELL

This edition published in Great Britain in 2021 by
Polygon, an imprint of Birlinn Ltd.

Birlinn Ltd
West Newington House
10 Newington Road
Edinburgh
EH9 1QS

www.polygonbooks.co.uk

1

ISBN 978 1 84697 529 5
eBook ISBN 978 1 78885 282 1

British Library Cataloguing-in-Publication Data
A catalogue record for this book is available on request from the British Library.

Text design by Studio Monachino
Printed and bound by CPI Group (UK) Ltd, Croydon CR0 4YY

To Vera

CONTENTS

PART ONE

THIS LAND IS MY LAND

1

THEFT

I was fourteen when I was caught stealing books the first time. The year was 1965. The scene of the crime was a bookshop in West George Street, in the centre of Glasgow, long since disappeared, and the loot consisted of three *MAD* books. My friend Bruce Dryden and I were experts on the subject. We used to create our own versions of *MAD* comics in class, with stories and drawings, while poor Mr Donald – Ducky Donald – tried to interest us in the risqué parts of *The Merchant of Venice*. The school, King's Park Secondary, was among the first so-called comprehensives in Glasgow – but really it was only socially comprehensive. Pupils were streamed academically from A to G, with rough types included from insalubrious Southside areas such as Toryglen and Castlemilk, beyond the catchment area of the old King's Park Senior Secondary at which my elder sisters had thrived. The social experiment did not appeal to my parents. I had started out, aged twelve, in the A stream but was relegated to B in the second year, making my way down towards Bruce, one of those feared Toryglen natives.

It goes without saying that I wasn't at school, as I should have been, when I furtively slipped the three slim volumes inside my duffel coat. Not furtively enough, and as I approached the door I felt a hand on my shoulder.

The manager of the bookshop was a kindly soul, but he had to do his duty. He had already taken my name – "James Gunning" – and address (totally fictional). Now he offered me a choice: he could inform the police, the school, or my father.

The first I wasn't terribly keen on; as for the third – was there a gentle alternative, such as having my fingernails extracted? We settled on the middle course. The man who had become my courteous keeper lifted the receiver from the phone on his desk and dialled the number of King's Park Secondary, getting through to the headmaster with what now seems remarkable ease. He explained the situation and they arrived at a gentlemanly solution to the regrettable affair. I was to leave the shop as a boy on parole and return to Fetlar Drive, Simshill, where the school was, reporting to the headmaster directly. The manager might even have hinted to the headmaster that there was no need to mention it to the parents. He replaced the receiver and in my persona as James Gunning I thanked him and left the three *MAD* books behind, to be reshelved. I can't remember exactly what I thought as I stepped into the open air of West George Street, but it was probably along the lines of, "So that's how you get out of it".

The next time it happened, Bruce and I were in the large Boots at the corner of Union Street and Argyle Street, a famous Glasgow landmark, popular with young folk hopeful of romance ("See you at seven, under the clock at Boots"). We were doggin' off school again, not a rare occurrence (by now I had reached the C stream). Boots, which had once run a lending library, also stocked books for sale, and Bruce was a proper reader. It was from Bruce that I first learned of the natural evolution of a book from hardback to paperback. He informed me where to look in 007 novels for details involving Pussy Galore or some similar heroine, to which we had recently become susceptible: in the final paragraph, he said (I discovered that this wasn't always so).

He had other advanced tastes, Micky Spillane novels being one of them. On the first floor among the bookshelves at Boots, he constructed a little pile of novels featuring the detective Mike

Hammer. Five, to be exact. My memory is precise, because the number of books taken was to feature in a Scottish legal case. I was flicking through a copy of *Peyton Place*, the televised version of which, with Mia Farrow and Ryan O'Neal, I was currently following.

"If you want it, put it on the pile," Bruce said in a low voice. Not low enough. Again, the words are precise: they were offered as evidence in court.

I did as suggested, and Bruce sheltered the lot inside the off-white shortie raincoat he wore – so much more *in* than my duffel. We went downstairs and got as far as the front door – the door beyond which lay great, garrulous, Dear Green Glasgow, Bruce's home in tough Toryglen, mine in toffier King's Park.

That hand on the shoulder again. It made a deep impression. It steered us away from freedom – a book-filled freedom – and down to a windowless room in a basement we had never imagined existed. Two plain-clothes policemen arrived and discussed matters with the Boots store detectives as if we weren't there. We gave our names and addresses. Bruce Dryden of Edinbeg Avenue, Toryglen. And James Gunning of . . . somewhere or other.

The policemen looked into my school haversack which, in addition to being plastered with inky tributes to the Rolling Stones and the Pretty Things, contained my inadequate C-stream jotters. One of the detectives pointed out the name on the cover, which was not the name I had just given him. That was easy to deal with. "This is *his* bag", I explained, referring to someone who was putatively me, Jim Campbell. "I'm taking it home for him."

The policeman fixed me with a look which remains perfectly formed in memory.

"Oh. I see."

We were taken in an unmarked car to the City of Glasgow

Police Headquarters in St Andrew's Square, where our identities –
ha-ha, though I wasn't feeling that way at all – were registered at the
front desk. Then we were escorted down a corridor and locked in a
cell. It was by then approaching 4 o'clock, the hour at which school
would be getting out. Soon my mother would be expecting to hear
her hungry and surly son at the front door of our nice house in
Kingshill Drive, the first "bought" house either of my parents had
ever lived in, a satisfying stage in a difficult journey, the fulfilment
of which would be the further education and success of their four
children. My elder twin sisters were already well on the way.

The cell was bare and dim, though light enough to read
the graffiti, which brought a brief amusement. Bruce added to
it, probably something witty. We kept each other's spirits up
with *MAD*-type jokes, and were served bacon sandwiches on
"doorstep" white bread, dripping with butter, unforgettably
good, and large mugs of milky tea. The detective returned.

Name? James Gunning.

Address? Something or other.

He left, closing the cell door heavily behind him.

What can I plead in mitigation? We were fourteen. It was just
a few books – value one guinea, as Scottish legal history must
somewhere record (six paperbacks at 3s 6d each, amounting to 21s).
And we were readers, or at least Bruce was. My interests tended
towards music. I know it was a Thursday and that we languished
in the cell deep into the evening, because we were missing *Top of
the Pops*, the era of the Animals, the Byrds, the Righteous Brothers,
of "Little Red Rooster" and "This Old Heart of Mine".

The detective came again. Name. Address. It was getting on
towards nine. This time I asked *him* a question: When do we get
out? That same look he had given me in the basement at Boots.
"When someone calls for you."

Even a person with my interrupted education could tell there was a problem. Excuse me . . . well . . . you see . . .

He wasn't pleased at having had his time wasted. (Come to think of it, two plain-clothes detectives had just spent six hours with a pair of zealous readers in a Glasgow famous for violent crime.) My father was likewise noticeably not pleased, when he turned up at St Andrew's Square – the first time in recognized family history – to certify the reality of what had become by then my alternative identity – i.e., me.

Bruce Dryden stepped forward straight away and made a declaration which stays with me as the epitome of honour and decency. "Mr Campbell, I just want to say . . ." It was he, not I, who had taken the six books. "Jim didn't steal anything." He hadn't mentioned his intention to do this during our hours in the cell.

By the time the court papers were served, in person at the door of the house by a uniformed policeman – another moment of profound mortification for my poor mother – I had left school and embarked on a six-year apprenticeship in a jobbing printing firm in Ingram Street, in Glasgow's Townhead district, second in notoriety only to the Gorbals. My journeyman, or master printer, was not impressed to learn that the new boy was due in court at the same St Andrew's Square one Tuesday – only a ten-minute walk from Ingram Street – and was required to take the afternoon off (wages docked accordingly).

The charge was theft, of books to the value of one pound and one shilling. Bruce was to plead guilty. I intended to plead not guilty, although a policewoman advised my mother that this might mean going to trial by jury and hiring a lawyer, with all the costs that that would entail. Bruce had been heard to say, "If you want it, put it on the pile", and the defendant had been observed doing just that. It might be better to plead guilty now and accept the punishment – a plea bargain, in effect. "Although that could leave you with a criminal record," my mother said, unable to decide which was the less dreadful course. Future difficulties with employers were sketched. "And if you ever want to go to America . . ."

I stuck to my plea.

After much hanging around among hard-edged types of our own age, and their seasoned guardians, the case came before the judge in the Juvenile Court. Bruce was fined one pound – a shilling less than the value of the books. The second defendant was admonished. James Gunning's misdeed in the basement at Boots and later at the police station was not mentioned. He vanished from the record. Until now.

Sign on the wall at Central Police Headquarters, St Andrew's Square, where the two juvenile book thieves went for trial.

2

A CONFESSION

While I remained at school, Bruce was still my best friend and, as our brush with the law had proved, a loyal one. Toryglen was an area at least two notes below King's Park on the social octave. My mother would have disapproved of him, had I brought him home, but I wasn't encouraged to invite friends from households lower down than ours. There was only one official prediction of the future family outcome and it was upward-looking. Bruce would not have been greeted warmly, even without the regrettable business at Boots and the aftermath in the court at St Andrew's Square.

He had an older brother, from whom he had absorbed certain advanced notions in relation to sex, clothes, alcohol and up-to-date tastes in pop music. In short, he was more switched on than I was, and naturally I was attracted to this, even when the lights dimmed and the setting grew dark enough to make me feel uncomfortable. There was some joshing in the school playground among his Toryglen associates, about stripping the lead off the roofs of houses and selling it to scrap-metal merchants in Govanhill and the Gorbals. Bruce himself didn't take part in this, but he and his brother, and his brother's cavalier friends, were part of the background against which the activity took place. They could swerve to try to avoid it, but somewhere on the journey would bump up against it. Some of these future thieves and burglars in the making were, like us, fourteen years old. St Andrew's Square awaited them.

It was out of this context, so feared by my mother – the fortune teller – that our next escapade was born. Had it been executed as intended, it would have been far worse in its consequences than anything that happened at Boots or in the cell with its graffiti archive, or later on in the court and its chilling anterooms. It is the hardest confession for me to make. We planned a mugging or, to be more precise, a bag-snatching. We would target a woman in the streets near Victoria Road, grab her handbag, then make a run for the main road, hopping on to the first bus that came along.

If I say it was originally Bruce's idea, it is not to excuse myself. And why were we doing this? Not for the money, or not principally, because I doubt if we expected to get away with much. It was the pure thrill of an act that was outsiderish, both adventurous and rebellious, something that would jolt us out of the stillness of a dark Southside Glasgow evening. It was the will to step beyond ordinary life, to be in another zone, just for a few moments, to drink an otherworldly potion, be the absorbing agent of an alien force. That it was a wicked force we must have vaguely known, but that did not prevent us from going ahead with the plan.

Bruce and I met on a Friday evening outside a café in Queen's Park, a decent, more traditional district than the newer development of King's Park, about twenty minutes' walk away. There was life on Victoria Road, pubs filled with the noise and smoke and beery smell of pay day – not a single one in the officially "dry" area of King's Park – and on the wide pavements you could mix with men and women of various sorts, boulevarding up and down, from this pub to that, from the Albert Bar to the Victoria, then on to the oddly named Queen's Park Café further north, before reaching the Star Bar at Eglinton Toll. On Friday and Saturday nights there were dances at the Plaza close to the Toll, said to be a rough-house. We were too young to be a part of it, but we enjoyed being watchers, outsiders, palms against the beating heart.

The streets behind Victoria Road were residential and mostly quiet, lined with late-nineteenth-century sandstone tenements. There we stand, at a corner, two school-blazered lads for whom shaving is in the future – whatever future we might choose. Though ignorant of it at the instant of coming together that evening, we are in the act of choosing the future right here, right now. Did we whisper between ourselves, like real thieves in fear of being overheard – the "real" being borrowed from films or the collective myth of *Oliver Twist*? The lead thieves at school apart, I had never encountered a committed robber. We must have hesitated in advance of our act – a meaningless act, practically motiveless, committed only in order to draw a breath that would light up the inner cave: on this night *I am*.

I see the two of us, from above, as if caught in a screen shot, on a street corner to the west of Victoria Road. Night can't hide us. While I know that muscles were tense, I know equally that I was unaware that this was a night on which the course of my life might be determined. On the surface, I had little or no conception of "future". There was only the stretch of limbs, the utterances of lips and tongue. The present moment. Here on a Friday after school, in Queen's Park.

A woman walks towards us on one of the streets parallel to Victoria Road, perhaps Westmoreland Street or Annette Street. We would have not wanted to go too far from Victoria Road and the getaway bus of safety – a hypothetical, perhaps non-existent bus, on which our lives depended. A middle-aged, well-dressed woman, of a sort familiar to me. She wears a hat, suggesting that she is on her way to visit a friend or a sister, a Friday-night routine, always setting out at about this time.

There might have been an appointment at the hairdresser's in the afternoon. Her husband could be enjoying his Friday night in the pub, as my father often did (not far from here, in the Albert Bar). Or perhaps she is a widow. Tailored coat, gloves to match, proper choice of bag.

She draws closer to the loitering boys. She doesn't fear these streets, overseen as they are by lighted windows. The knights of that great communal Glasgow are her invisible protectors. I see spectacles beneath the hat brim, and a smile in the eyes, though her heart registers the merest hesitation. This is a nice district. The Gorbals is a mile to the north, and the tribes of Glasgow by and large remain on their reservations. When they do go hunting, it is not for her. As it happens, she could rely on them for protection from hostile strays.

The boys seem to await her approach. They're probably looking for a street – she knows all the streets – or a café or youth club. Or they want to know which bus will take them from Victoria Road to – wherever they have to get to. She can help.

To their "Excuse me . . ." she replies, "Yes", a response not posed as a question but as assurance. Goodwill, assistance, friendliness – the famous Glasgow semaphore.

What happened next I remember only vaguely, though I do recall the crucial moment. I was not the one who did the talking, but I was there. Was a distant figure seen walking towards our trio from the further reach of Allison Street? Was there a sudden, shared shaming, on the part of the two villains, of the devil that had possessed them?

Bruce asked for directions – or for the number of a bus – and with a few maternal words she set us on the right course. The Glasgow coat-of-arms ought to be composed of a great big affirmative, rather than the negatives of tree that never grew, bird that never flew, fish that never swam. "Just go down to the road . . . you'll see the stop." There is pleasure in assisting two well-spoken boys.

We thanked her and turned in the direction to which she had pointed, walking slowly, smothering our shame in giggles – a shame not shown to one another, but mine admitted to myself, in relief. The embodiment of good nature continued on her way, tossing a farewell over her shoulder as she went.

That pedestrian who approached from the direction of Allison Street – if indeed he existed – whose suspected presence interrupted us: if he had taken a different route, or left by his front door a minute later . . . we would have run towards Victoria Road . . . jumped on a bus. That is, if we had managed to reach the bus stop. Our excited state would have aroused attention of a sort we had not foreseen. The victim would have shouted or screamed. The streets of Glasgow are full of heroes.

Much later, I read Per Petterson's novel *Out Stealing Horses*. Near the end, there is this passage. It comes after the narrator (the author in light disguise) has drawn back from hitting a stranger on the mouth in a street in a Swedish town. "If I had punched the man in Karlstad, my life would have been a different life, and I a different man. And it would be foolish to maintain, as so many men do, that it would have come to the same thing. It would not. I have been lucky. I have said that before. But it's true."

3

REPORT CARD

I

By the time of my third year at King's Park Secondary – school motto: "Video meliora petoque"; I see and aim for better things – I had proved myself to be better than any of my classmates in one subject: doggin' it; playing truant; a previous generation called it hooky. There were various strategies one could employ. You could just not turn up, offering an excuse retrospectively, or bringing a forged note purporting to be from a parent, which would outline some minor malady. You might declare yourself suddenly "not well" and ask to be allowed to go home – sore tummies were neither verifiable nor deniable – taking immediately to the great, green liberty of King's Park, across the main road, or else skipping on to a bus into town (fare-dodging, naturally), to browse in the big Argyle Street shops: Fraser's or Lewis's (the Polytechnic), or in the Boots at the corner of Union Street, where it all went wrong in the books department. If Bruce's parents were known to be out, we might spend half the day at his house in Toryglen, a lush-carpeted, soft sofa-ed domain that gave me a bright and comfortable feeling of living in one of the TV sitcoms I liked. Once, we broke into the drinks cabinet, using water from the tap to make up the depleted measures in the Gordon's and Johnnie Walker bottles.

When too many sore-tummy declarations ran the risk of technical interference from a doctor, it seemed safer to resort to the dentist. From a surgery near the school someone stole a stack of dental appointment cards and put them up for sale at threepence each. With date and time filled in, one of these could be presented to a sceptical teacher, providing a pass from the horrors of Algebra or Physics.

Most of the teachers regarded me with sentiments that fluctuated on the spectrum of exasperation, from baffled to benign. I had one acknowledged minor talent beyond my doggin' skill: English composition. If we had to do it in class, I could whip up something imaginative and amusing on a suggested topic in the duration of an ordinary period, forty minutes. There was a pleasure not to be found elsewhere in the confined spaces of school in feeling the story unfold under my hand, one invention rolling neatly into another, the creative spark heartened by a reassurance that it saved us from the insupportable labour of actually learning anything. Mr Donald – Ducky Donald – more than once had me stand to read aloud my composition in class, encouraging a merry reaction from fellow pupils. I see now that he was doing it to try to draw me into the fold of diligent scholars.

Other aspects of the English curriculum could be negotiated with a minimum of effort: the mechanics of grammar, spelling, parsing, parts of speech, the ability to précis; all these had been drummed into me at Croftfoot Primary, and from there flowed into my present written work in a natural way. It came as easily to me as kicking a ball. My twin sisters, Jean and Phyllis, were the unchallenged stars of the Art class – their individual technical competence enhanced by their twin-ness – and their status cast a genial light on me there, too. I wasn't particularly good at drawing and painting, but I wasn't bad. The same could be said for Physical Education and Religious Instruction: *not bad*. As for everything else: *bad*.

At the conclusion of my first year among the elect, in the A class, reserved for brainy types, poor overall results led to relegation to the B stream. This meant dropping Latin, at which I had gained a respectable 67 per cent in the inaugural exam. "Amo, amas, amat", Mr Forgie had us repeat over and over. "Ama*bo*, ama*bas*, ama –" . . . "No, you're not," old Forgie would insist, patrolling the aisles between the rows of desks, sergeant-major fashion. "You are many disgusting things, but you are not a *bo* or a *bas*."

"Am*a*bo, am*a*bas, am*a*bat."

"That's better. Campbell, greet your fellow citizen, Miss Wells, in the forum, and ask if the shepherds have guided their flocks to safety for the night."

"Safety from what, sir?"

"From boys like you, Campbell."

Much laughter. "From wolves, of course."

I did so. Aileen Wells was an old Croftfoot Primary comrade. She and I were two out of only three from a class of over forty to be selected for the A stream at the new, bigger, more competitive King's Park. She replied: "Salve, civis. Gratias ago tibi, quia doluisti."

Even down among the Bs, I hadn't yet teamed up with Bruce, who was with the Cs. Few boys or girls from Castlemilk or Toryglen made it into A or even B. Their brightness glowed with a different amplitude. One of the attractive characters seen swaggering about the playground was Big George, the son of Greek immigrants, with rocky Mediterranean features and dark curly hair, the kind of charismatic figure around whom others cluster at every school. He lived in Toryglen, naturally. When Mr Forgie, chief belter at King's Park Secondary, summoned George for some infringement or other and told him to hold out

The playground at King's Park Secondary School, mid-1960s. The school was proposed as one of Glasgow's first comprehensives, though pupils were streamed from A to G. *Courtesy of Glasgow School of Art Archives.*

his hands in preparation for two or four or perhaps six strokes of the belt – never one, three or five – he said: "This hurts me more than it hurts you, Kavouras." To which Big George replied (or said he did): "I wouldnae want that. Let's swap places, well."

But the C stream was not far away. At the end of second year, it was suggested that I might repeat the entire course, which would mean dropping down to be among a younger lot and losing close contact with all my pals. If there was a hierarchy in the school, it was based not on social class or talent but on seniority. There was something humiliating about the idea, whereas there was nothing shameful about having failed in just about every subject in the exams and bullying weaker boys at lunchtime to yield up their homework so that we could copy it in time for the afternoon bell. It would also have meant going through the hell of second-year Chemistry and Physics all over again, as well as other subjects my brain couldn't cope with.

It couldn't cope with much. Exam marks came at the end of term: 30-something for French, 20-something for History, even lower for Geography, Maths and Physics. Only in English did I dimly glow. In Art, it was borderline.

Of course the results were far too low to be shown to my parents. There was nothing to be gained by it. My father would have punished me – not with violence, to which he resorted only in fits of impatience, but with something much worse, something that really hurt: being kept in at night. The idea was that if I could be confined to my room each evening after school for a week, instead of running off to the park to pursue in earnest the things that mattered – in the past, a ball; in the present, increasingly, a girl – I would buckle down to my subjunctives and dates and tectonic shifts and memorize the Periodic Table, ultimately performing at the level of what was alleged to be my potential. How had I got into the A stream in the first place, anyway, along with nice Aileen Wells and that swot Alan Buckley? Nobody knew. By an oversight, perhaps.

So I took the only route available to someone in my predicament: I altered the report card results to resemble something more acceptable. I used a black Biro pen. Twenty-something became 40-something – hardly a show-off improvement, but enough to evade the threat of incarceration. Thirty-six for French might have become, by two deft strokes, 86, but that would be to invent an achievement I could never live up to; 66 would do, and even that was stretching credulity.

When my father had signed the card, making much of his reluctance to do so, insisting in his look-sharpish Navy-discipline voice that I must "do better give yourself a shake boy-o pull up your socks young fellamalad", I restored the marks to their original state with the help of that modern miracle-worker, the ink rubber. The task was thus completed. No one was harmed by it. No one was exactly happy, but at least life could carry on without unpleasant interruption. The long, light, after-school evenings patrolling the streets or playing football in King's Park were my intake of oxygen. I lived for them and by them.

"He's no daft," Dad would say in lighter moments. "He only acts like it." He would also say (over and again), "If you had 20 per cent more brains, you'd be an idiot", which itself took some brains to work out. And if I said something meant to be funny: "You're a bit of a wit. A half."

These remarks were supposed to be good-humoured – ill humour was expressed in other terms – but they represented his genuine feelings. They exhibited just a fraction of an overall frustration. Harry Campbell was himself a wit, a party man, gifted with an abundance of that Glasgow humour that Billy Connolly would soon make famous all over the world, handsome and intelligent and staunchly dutiful, much liked by neighbours and family friends. He had left school at the age of fourteen to work as a barrow boy in Glasgow's Fruit Market in Townhead. He and my mother, Ina – a neighbour in Shawlands but a pupil at a different school – met a year or two later in "the crowd", as she liked to put it, "that we went around with" in the years leading up to their envelopment in the Second World War. Her family – pedigree Protestant Scottish Lowland working class – was none the less a rung higher on the social ladder than his, which had the taint of emerald Irish in the background.

Her father, Jimmy Beveridge, was the janitor at the school she attended, Shawlands Academy, though the word "janitor" barely describes the position of responsibility he held and the work he did, everything from odd-job carpentry and interior decoration to organizing rugby matches and the annual school sports day. It's a guess, but I imagine that the headmaster regarded Jimmy as the man who was running the school. The families visited each other during holidays in Scottish resorts, such as Dunoon, Helensburgh and Rothesay. Grandpa had a cine camera for making short, silent films, to which he gave titles: "Doon the Water", for example, a film about pleasure steamers on the River Clyde. In one of them, the headmaster, dressed in three-piece suit and tie, can be seen on holiday, smiling broadly, with his wife and our grandmother beside him.

The job came with a house next to the school, in which my mother and her younger sister Rona were raised. They were intensely respectable, and I see her father as an essential Scottish type: a man of energy and all-round geniality from a modest background, with no feelings of inferiority, no trade or training but a multifarious artisanal talent and – a strange word to use of a church-going, self-educated Scot born almost within the lifetime of Robert Louis Stevenson – modernity.

After joining up as a teenager and serving in the Highland Light Infantry during the First World War, surviving close-up engagement by the breadth of a collarbone, Grandpa worked as an adaptable builder in different parts of Scotland, going wherever the next job took him. He cut and shaped and piled the stones one on top of the other in the construction of the Gleneagles Hotel in Perthshire in the early 1920s, and my mother retained memories of the family living in the nearby village of Blackford just after the hotel opened in 1924. In later life, she chose to return to live in a place that was within walking distance of Blackford. He measured and sawed and hammered our bunk beds, our toys – a fort, a farmyard and a garage ("Jim's") for me – and was on call whenever Mum required practical advice. "Och, I'll ask Dad about it", she would say, when the other dad – ours – looked as if he wasn't up to the job. In the 1930s, Grandpa owned various cameras, a gypsy caravan near Helensburgh for weekends away, and a car in which to drive to get there. During the 1950s and 60s, he worked in a garage opposite the school in his free hours, and in my mental snapshots never looks happier than when something needed fixing on his Austin A40 or Wolseley Eight, with its opening windscreen. He could probably have built you a car – or a house – if you had said you needed one.

Our dad lacked these skills. He also lacked Grandpa's liking for camping, walking in the country, his shared language with domestic animals and small children, his curiosity about the names of birds and plants. Dad's father, John Campbell, had been one of ten children, and Dad himself was the youngest of eight – in themselves eyebrow-raising statistics in the poorer areas of the city, suggestive of the Roman Catholic Church. And indeed we discovered later from census returns that the first Campbell relation of record, Charles, a "blacksmith's labourer", had arrived from County Armagh sometime during the period between 1835 and 1855, the year in which he was married near Glasgow to Helen Connahan, a "scourer" from Donegal. They were united in Paisley, "according to the rites and ceremonies of the Roman Catholic Church". Both gave their ages as twenty. Helen signed the 1855 form with an X, "her mark".

Their son, the first in a succession of John Campbells, found work in the shipyards. Dad reminisced about the sound of riveters thudding through the streets around the great shipyards on the Clyde – Fairfields of Govan, where his father had worked, Dennys of Dumbarton which could claim the phrase "steam-driven", John Brown's, Blythswood, Connell and Yarrow. At places near the river you could hardly hear yourself speak when passing by. In George Blake's novel *The Shipbuilders* (1935), the main character Leslie Pagan recalls how "up and down the river the bows of vessels unlaunched towered over the tenement buildings of the workers" and how "the clangour of metal upon metal filled the valley from Old Kilpatrick up to Govan". Dad talked of it sometimes as ancestral lore.

My paternal grandfather, the third John of record, married Emily, née McColl, in the Roman Catholic Church in Kinning Park. She was, however, a Protestant and the last of the Irish Campbells crossed over to the Church of Scotland before Dad was born. It was not a particularly religious household and I suspect that the conversion was undertaken out of social convenience, or perhaps for reasons of education. During our childhoods, he never mentioned the crossover, even once – Mum wouldn't have liked it – only crying out, in the course of a joke, "Campbells of Donegal!" When at the age of about six or seven I asked, "Dad, who were our ancestors?" he paused for thought before replying, "We come from a very distinguished family. We're related to Adam and Eve."

II

Apart from the awfulness of school lessons and the occasional bust-up at home, I wasn't having too bad a time. I was fair and open-faced, no matter how earnestly I tried to affect a tough exterior, and attracted the attention of girls. I had adventurous pals. I liked a fight now and then. It was mostly a version of the boxing-match workout recommended for centuries by teachers and superior officers to absorb adolescent energy, but in my case outside the ring. One Saturday evening, after a lager-and-lime session in a Buchanan Street pub (sixteen-year-olds had no trouble getting served back then), my drinking companion and I walked up one of the alleys that connect the main thoroughfares in the centre of town and had an exhilarating three-minute scrap, before heading downhill to Central Station to catch the 10.10 pm Blue Train back to King's Park, where we parted as the best of pals. The parents of friends seemed to think I was bright, in a way that my own parents did not, blinded by the smoke rising from the scorched wasteland I left behind in almost every classroom. My knowledge of progressive popular music was becoming as wide-ranging as my knowledge of Scottish football had been at an earlier age. I could reel off Rangers teams through the ages, and can do so now – Niven, Shearer, Caldow; McCall, McKinnon, Baxter; Scott, McMillan, Miller, Brand and Wilson – and could give you most of their club histories and places of birth into the bargain. The problem was school. I hated it. In return, it produced ample evidence – the evidence of the report card – that it could barely tolerate me.

Here are the figures from the last report card to be issued, May 1966: French 29 per cent; History 22 per cent; Maths 12 per cent; Geography 8 per cent. These are the ones I remember. In English I passed capably and in Art hovered around the midway mark, as usual. The science subjects I would drop on moving out of third year. The threat of a repeat had been avoided last time, but only just. Instead, I was shunted downstream to float among the Cs, where I sat next to Bruce in whatever subjects we shared. We used our jotters to exchange a concoction of *MAD* jokes and drawings and, from my side – a new thing – poems.

There could be no question of exhibiting these exam results at Kingshill Drive. The summer holidays were coming up: two months of open air, the feel of clean jeans on loose limbs, the annual trip to the Highlands and Portmahomack, to stay on the nearby farm at Rockfield where Mum had done her joyful service in the Women's Land Army during the war.

These once-enchanted holidays were starting to overlap with new-generation adventures, arriving too soon and too quickly and in too great a profusion to fit my parents' understanding: going on the road to Edinburgh, for example, with Bruce, to seek the sight, perhaps even the company, of beatniks; reckless bicycle rides on busy roads to places as far away as Saltcoats; the mingled scents and touch of neck and hair and flimsy nylon raincoat in a dingy tenement close; drawing more meaning, more intensely, from music than ever.

It was the nearest I would come to the freedom I had known in my blissful pre-Croftfoot Primary life, before the Fall. The expulsion from Eden arrived with the bitter fruit of knowledge: that school attendance and study (so-called) was a fact of life, destined to endure into the distant era of double figures – the ages of ten, eleven, twelve – carrying on through the teens: a daily, purgatorial stretch of classroom confinement. Dad explained to me that school would be followed by university, where studies would become even harder. I couldn't make sense of it. After all, I hadn't asked to bite the apple.

As those exam results came in, I was about to turn fifteen. Bob Dylan had replaced the Rolling Stones as my cultural amulet. The sounds of the American anti-war protest movement were now heard across the world, expressed in folk music with intriguing lyrics, and the vibrations were felt even at King's Park Secondary: "Oh deep in my heart, I do believe, that we shall overcome some day . . ." How beautiful it sounded – more beautiful, perhaps, than anything I had heard up until then – in the Joan Baez vibrato. The music took up residence in the body. "Last night there were four Marys, Tonight there'll be

Jean, with fellow students, at her Diploma Show, Glasgow School of Art, 1968. Phyllis would have her show the year after. *Courtesy of the Carey family.*

but three . . ." The sounds now came into our home in the form of LPs in interesting covers with long essays on the back, which my sisters bought or borrowed from their with-it – how Dad enjoyed using that expression – art school friends.

Everything about Dylan's songs attracted me from first hearing: the yearning in the voice, the melodies, the protest against racial injustice in some, the seductive American vernacular of others, the jokes in something called a "talking blues", direct addresses to the president of the United States, place names right, left and centre – "I'm going ba-a-a-ack . . . to Co-lo-ra-do" – dazzling imagery through it all. Unlike poetry that existed only on the page, the kind that Ducky Donald strove to interest us in, Dylan's poetry was transmitted to memory automatically, by melody and rhythm. I consoled myself on the road up to school in the morning by singing my way through one or two of his songs, just as literary folk of an earlier generation might have inwardly recited "Ode to a Nightingale" or a Shakespeare sonnet.

The key note was freedom, freedom. "How many years can some people exist", before freedom's embrace will welcome them? It didn't matter that Dylan had in mind whole subjugated peoples – an understanding gradually dawning. For now, the question applied to me.

During an English period, while Mr Donald promised delights in store between the covers of Great Expectations as he handed out class readers, I copied into my school jotter the words of an anti-war poem I had written after our weekend in Edinburgh, when I had met a little beatnik fellow with long dark hair from Castlemilk: John Cochrane, known as Coakie. He and I had ended up hitch-hiking home to Glasgow in the back of an open truck, while Bruce returned by bus. It left me with a new feeling – it went very deep – of "something I want to do".

Coakie was a member of the Young Communist League and wrote ban-the-bomb poetry. I didn't join the YCL, as he encouraged me to do – "A dustman's goanie make the same money as a doacter" – but I picked up on the poetry.

At the back of my school English jotter, the one with the fateful identity written in block letters on the front, the identity which had betrayed me at St Andrew's Square – "Jim Campbell, 42 Kingshill Drive" – I began writing lines on big subjects borrowed from the new, meaningful music that was suddenly all around, on the radio, on 7-inch singles, at parties. Freedom. Travel. Peace. War. It had evolved from Frankie Vaughan singing, "Honey Bunny Baby" to "We Shall Overcome" in just a few years.

One of my anti-war poems opened with the lines, "Death creeps slowly o'er the hill, / God's armies mass before the kill". With a bit of time, I might have ironed out that irregular beat. At the end, as a sort of coda, I appended the final stanza of Dylan's magisterial "Masters of War", a song addressed to cowardly politicians who shelter in offices behind desks while blood spreads and stains the field of battle.

Dylan had taken the melody for "Masters of War" from the English folk song "Nottamun Town", in the way that he appropriated many traditional tunes for modern purposes, and now I was borrowing Dylan's lyrics and folding them into my own protest poem. I tore the portmanteau work from the jotter and, without revealing the source of the final lines, passed it to Bruce, who read it as Ducky Donald ingenuously declaimed the opening words of Pip's narrative, in hope of hooking our attention.

We lingered together in the corridor during the brief interval before our next period. He liked the first part, my part, Bruce told me, but he mocked the ending, which I had pinched from Dylan. As we headed down the stairs to the first floor and Mr

Howard's Maths class, he spoke aloud the words of the song, until then unfamiliar to him, before landing on a laugh. "'Stand over . . .' What?" Then he came on with the strong Scottish voice, as he sometimes did: "Till ah ken ye're deid? Come off it, Campbell!"

Bruce loved the Beatles, as he had loved our *MAD* comics and the James Bond novels. His elder brother had got the Beatles album *Rubber Soul* for Christmas in 1965, and I listened to it in the New Year while lying on the shaggy cream rug before the electric fire in their TV-sitcom house in Toryglen. I was growing out of the comics but had not grown into the novels, and never would. On Coakie's recommendation, I was trying to read Wordsworth – in the park, while doggin' off – without much understanding but conscious that the words transmitted some odd feeling, nevertheless. It took you away for a few moments, and when you returned something had altered, as the light was altered by a cloud melting.

In class, Mr Boyd the long-nosed History teacher – Beaky Boyd – asked each of us what he or she would like to do when the moment came to step out of whatever college we had chosen for our further education and go forth into the world. We had played this game in primary school in a composition, "What I want to be when I grow up". The boy sitting next to me, Andrew Miller, son of a postman, wrote that he wanted to be prime minister. I said I wanted to be a lollipop man. My inspiration was the white-coated figure at the top of our crescent, who saw us safely across the busy road each morning on the way to school with his red-and-white "children crossing" lollipop.

Now, when Mr Boyd's question came round, I told the class I wanted to be a tramp. The teacher, no doubt expecting something of the sort from the disruptive boy, "the twins' younger brother", showed his exasperation and his scorn. He had never heard of Jack Kerouac and neither had I, but there was something in the air that only I was capable of picking up – something screened from Mr Boyd and the rest of the class – a new kind of hip vagabondage. Dylan and Joan Baez were spinning a web of song lines all round the world and I was ready to follow the threads.

All my life the blues has come and gone.
I'm only getting started, it's time for movin' on,
Honey, you won't see me here by dawn.

It was a new language, expressing a new spirit of adventure, and if it shunted old Beaky Boyd aside . . . well, he was just a History teacher anyway, a man of the past.

I was acting the smart alec, trying to deflect attention from my paltriness in the academic department, and he could see this but didn't know what to do about it. If there were an opportunity for a retrospective apology, I would send one to him without hesitation. But there was some truth in the ambition that I myself could not have made articulate, and in a few years' time I would set out to fulfil it.

Dylan brought his voice, his hairstyle, his shades, his cunning – the message was in the hairstyle and the cunning as much as in the lyrics – to the Glasgow Odeon in May 1966 on the famous tour with the Hawks, and I went to see him. The concert took the form of a sublime first-half solo acoustic performance, followed by a plugged-in electric set with the Hawks, the Band in all but name. People called out from the stalls, "Give us the real Bob Dylan", as Robbie Robertson and the Hawks kicked up an unprecedented racket in folkie ears. In the middle of one

The twins, Phyllis and Jean, Christmas, 1953, in our living room at Castlemilk Crescent, Croftfoot.

song, Dylan extended a hand to silence the musicians behind him. "Bob couldn't make it tonight", he said, addressing the hecklers in the near rows. "I'm here in his place. My name's Donovan."

The crowd laughed and clapped, even though they still felt that the man in Cuban heels with the Fender Telecaster wasn't the real Bob Dylan. To others, he satisfied all present needs, with a smidgen of our native Donovan thrown in. Joan Baez, also part-Scottish, by ancestry and by art, was more to my sisters' taste, and I liked her, too. How could anyone not like her? "I'm having a good time tonight," we heard her say on the album *Joan Baez in Concert*, "and if nobody objects I'm going to take off my shoes." The whole family sat round the small black-and-white television in the living room, to watch a two-part concert on the BBC, one of the two channels available.

The face itself is a good enough reason for watching it now. Joan Baez's magnificent voice, by which, she said, she was simply possessed, is often spoken of; but her face is almost equally captivating. As she leans towards the microphone between songs, testing her pitch, the sound takes control of her features. Her heart becomes visible. The world would be a different place without the faces of that era: the face of Baez itself is a work of genius. So is Dylan's – a face that will change twenty times in twenty separate photographs, taken over a period of five or six years. It goes without saying that the 1960s would have been different without the music of the Rolling Stones, but we can also say it would have been different without Mick Jagger's face.

Jean was in the second year of study at Glasgow School of Art now – Phyllis had followed a year later – and brought home records by Bert Jansch and Davey Graham: new songs, new ways of singing, scintillating twists of scarcely credible virtuosity on a six-string guitar. It was music for youthful intellectuals, and it spoke directly and forcefully to me. Something was stirring in that old A stream inclination, without me knowing much about it.

III

Here is the story the report card told, as it approached 42 Kingshill Drive, shuddering nervously in my canvas haversack, one late afternoon in May, 1966: French 49 per cent; History

42; Maths 42 – Dad would never have believed anything higher
– Geography probably a miserable 38 per cent, but what else
could I say? The single-digit results were easiest to forge, and
therefore welcome in that respect. In English and Art I had
passed without distinction. I didn't find it necessary to tell myself
not to get carried away in making the latest improvements. I
wasn't doing this to gain approval: that would have fitted my
haphazard conception of dishonesty. I simply didn't want there
to be a scene. It was to no one's advantage.

The card walked up the garden path, entered by the front
door, never locked in daytime when Mum was at home, and
presented itself to Dad when he returned from work by the
"Blue Train", from Glasgow Central to King's Park station, at
5.40 pm, as he did almost invariably. Meanwhile I stood to the
side in mute apprehensiveness.

There was a fuss, but not too much of one. I had to give
myself a shake, pull up my socks, get stuck in. I said I would –
of course I would – convincing no one, certainly not me. Then
I went upstairs to play the Davey Graham album *Folk, Blues and
Beyond*, which Jean or Phyllis had borrowed from some suitably
with-it fellow art student. The sleeve notes, which I read with
a degree of attentiveness never squandered on classroom
lessons, mentioned Big Bill Broonzy, Reverend Gary Davis and
Blind Willie Johnson – the constructions themselves rich with
suggestion and the promise of other worlds, other place names
– beyond Colorado and states hymned by Dylan – other folk
and other colours, other ways of seeing things and being in life.

I was already addicted to the sweet taste of Ray Charles
singing "Take These Chains From My Heart" and "I Can't Stop
Loving You", and I played the 45 rpm singles – again borrowed
from friends by Jean and Phyllis – over and over. They had

bargaining power, those twin sisters: looks, talent, common sense, all-round feminine good nature. They could have got away with a lot, but had no need to try. The lot came to them. Life liked them, as it liked our mother, who had passed on these qualities to her daughters.

The next day I went back up the hill to school ("How many roads must a man . . .") with the signed report card and returned it to the teacher, as directed. By now it was getting to be an old trick, and I was a jaded conjuror, blasé about his magic. The ink eraser was set aside. My ingenious performance no longer required the presence of a rubber assistant. The card entered the historical archive at King's Park Secondary in its fictional state – not good, not even *not bad*, but not kept-in-at-night awful – never to be retrieved.

Or that's what I assumed would happen. One day near the end of term, in a French class – "The past historic is formed by taking the root of the present indicative . . . Bruce, tell us when to use the past historic . . ." – the deputy headmaster Mr Crawford entered and spoke to the lovely Miss Christie in low tones. She always wore a black, flowing academic gown over a blouse and skirt, setting off her blonde hair which she pinned up. She had only to shrug off that gown at the end of the teaching day to appear to be undressing in front of us. The way she walked into the room at the start of a lesson when we were all seated, pointer in hand. The way she looked at you with a young woman's maternal fondness – no matter what – that I was capable of comprehending only later, in memory. Children of her own lay in the future; in the meantime, she had us. She had lately married, but was still Miss Christie.

When someone higher up came through the door and interrupted a lesson, everyone in the class assumed it must be about me, and it was. Summoned from my refuge at the back of the room – French was actually something I was working up an interest in – I traipsed along the corridor behind Mr Crawford, followed him sheepishly down the stairs to his office at playground level and sat on a chair, as instructed, while he tucked himself in comfortably behind his desk.

Ah, yes, now. How were we getting on?

Not bad, thanks.

People said I had a nice speaking voice. Deep down, much deeper than the words the voice itself could call on, I knew that, despite everything, it projected a better self, a me that one day I would become familiar with. Some of the boys and girls at the new school since it had moved from King's Park up to Simshill (though it remained King's Park Secondary) wouldn't feel that. They were different from my sisters and me. Their coarse, untrainable voices were, in many cases, their nature and their future.

How were things at home?

Shrug. Grunt. Gaze at the wall. "OK."

A pause. A look, half-concerned, obviously false, not even intended to convince. It was all stagey. He was leading up to something and I thought I knew what it was.

And the evenings – what did I do in the evenings? Played football, mostly. Better not to mention girls and "getting somewhere" – not far – and the odd harmless fight to work off energy and stealing apples from gardens after dark in the autumn, and Bounty bars and Cadbury's Flakes from corner shops in daylight. Bruce and I sometimes went to see what he had been told, by his brother or by Big George, were risqué films, including *Yesterday, Today and Tomorrow* with Sophia Loren. At the end, Bruce promised, she removes her bra during the striptease she is performing in a bedroom for Marcello

Mastroianni. I can recall our excited approach on the top deck of a bus to the Toledo cinema in Clarkston Road, the odorous, faded blue-velvet seats on which we sat throughout two hours of Italian romantic comedy dubbed into English, only to discover during the crucial scene, a few minutes from the end, that she has an attack of Catholic conscience and keeps it on.

So mainly football, yeah. That was about it. I hadn't made it into the school team, though I had been a goal-scoring inside-left in the last year at primary – Ralph Brand's position at Ibrox – and had fancied myself at the secondary school trials. Instead, I was playing for the Boys' Brigade on Saturday mornings, for which "everyone gets a game", as someone who was selected for the school First XI was tactless enough to tell me. That had been a great disappointment. The old King's Park was smaller, the pupils more aspirational in their sums and sentences. I would definitely have been selected there. Here, the boys from rougher areas kept me out. They were always the best at sports like football. The teacher in charge of the teams, Mr Howard, had promised me a second trial – "You look like more of a player than some of them", he had said with kindly world-weariness – but it had never come about.

"What about homework?" Mr Crawford asked, coming to the point. He was still doing the genial act, though now with a dollop of obligatory sternness. "Do you spend much time on that?"

A bit. Not as much as I should, probably.

A look of mock surprise. His tone changed again, becoming avuncular. He couldn't fool me and he was barely trying to.

"How are the lessons going?"

"Uh . . . Not so good . . ."

"What about the exams just past? How did you get on in the exams?"

"Not very well, if I'm honest."

I had to be honest, obviously. It was a great inconvenience, but the other thing – dishonesty, which had served me well until now – had run out.

"Maths, for example." Mr Crawford was himself a Maths teacher, though I had never been in his class. "How did you do in Maths?"

". . . Not very well . . . I think . . . twelve per cent."

"Twelve!"

He was taking it all the way. Enjoying it? Not really. Maybe he thought it was easier on me to go through this pantomime. He slid open the drawer of his desk and withdrew a repulsive-looking thing, my report card. "It says here forty-two per cent." Our eyes met for a second. "How about Geography?"

"Only eight."

"*Eight per cent!*" He extended his arm across the desk with the pamphlet-shaped report card open at the latest exams, Spring term, 1966. "What does it say there?"

It said thirty-eight per cent. My modesty in making the changes was surely some kind of accomplishment in itself, but not enough of one to win him over. He went through the others, then flicked back to previous tables of exam figures, where the grubby evidence of the ink rubber – not such a miracle worker, after all – suggested historical tampering.

Mr Crawford didn't rant and rave. He wanted to show as much patience as was available to him. They were decent people, the teachers at King's Park Secondary, and they wanted their pupils to be good and decent, too. "I see and aim for better things." That was what we were all there for, with a few vicious Castlemilk exceptions. We were in it together. It was just that, in my case, the togetherness had fallen apart. Other than being belted earnestly from time to time by Mr Forgie, which hurt, and reluctantly by a few others such as Ducky Donald and Beaky Boyd, which didn't, I can recall little unkindness from teachers. It was we who were unkind to them. Lies and insolence and ignorance: that's what they got in return for aiming for better things.

"Butter wouldn't melt in your mouth, Jim," Miss Christie had said with a kindly smile on presenting me with one of the card-framed portrait photographs we all sat for. Her good nature wanted to like me, and I would have liked being liked by her. Other teachers liked me, too, when I put myself up for affection, which wasn't often. But something had stood in the way of my being liked, and of my learning, and there didn't seem to be any way of removing the obstacle other than by removing myself from the school.

My twin sisters wanted their troublesome wee brother to prosper, but there was an element in their solidarity with one another and their with-it, pretty friends, their twin-ness in the face of the world and the immediate society surrounding our family, all linked to their small but real and forward-looking successes, that cast me into an intimate solitariness. It was mine, in the way that little else was, besides the music and the jeans and the elusive fragrance of some Toryglen infatuation in a glistening raincoat. I had no choice – I wasn't even aware of the possibility of "choice", acting by instinct alone – but to extricate myself from the predicament on my own terms. It sounds trite to say the "existential predicament", but that's what it was. I could *choose* something else, but first I had to identify the nature of the choice, to recognize that there was a choice. Pulling my socks up wasn't going to do it.

Mr Crawford let me know that he was not going to punish me. The case was beyond the reach of routine school punishment. He would have to write to my father, which even he seemed to realize was far worse from my point of view than a few strokes of the silly old belt. Then we would see what could be done, before the summer holidays came along. The most likely outcome would be to repeat third year, this time with little room for negotiation. I was immature. Time would take care of it. Academic performance would improve along with everything else, if we gave it time. After I had repeated third year, I would be set fair for O Grades at the end of fourth.

"You're good at some things," he said sympathetically. "What happened?"

Everyone knew I was good at English, though they also said that if I tried harder and paid attention, I could be much better. "Careless" was a word often used. Miss Christie, with permissive fondness, called me a dreamer, and it's true I preferred the classroom window beyond which lay mountains and seas and the lonesome road down which a man must walk many times, to the blackboard with its ugly words like "imperfect" and "subjunctive".

"You used to do quite well at Latin," Mr Crawford said, flicking back to marks he could tell at a glance were authentic. I could count and do long division. The Arithmetic side of Maths wasn't the problem; it was Algebra, the cryptogrammatic language of the Devil, together with the confounding theorems of Geometry, that made my head spin and took malign possession of my will. I had learned my multiplication tables at primary school and would never forget them, as pupils at neighbouring Catholic schools were not allowed to forget their catechisms and classical scholars their Virgil. "What happened?" Nobody knew.

I left his office. This was no time for dreaming. I had to pull up my socks and give myself a shake. There was a job to be done: the letter that Mr Crawford was about to write and send to my father would have to be intercepted before it dropped through the letterbox at 42 Kingshill Drive.

4

THE LAND GIRL AND THE PETTY OFFICER: AN INTERLUDE

I

The war demanded service from both the school janitor's daughter from Moss Side Road and the range fitter's son from Quentin Street, as they emerged from their teens. He was called up for the Navy in late 1942, posted first to Plymouth, then to Invergordon in the Scottish Highlands and later Ceylon, in readiness for the battle on the Eastern Front. She went into the Land Army, the "replacement agricultural force" from which women stepped willingly into the fields to stand in for men on military duty. Seeking a Highland position, so as to be not far removed from his Navy call-up, she was taken on at Rockfield Farm in Easter Ross, near the seaside village of Portmahomack – always spoken of among familiars as "the Port".

It was Mum's great good luck to be billeted with the shepherd and his wife at Rockfield. To her and the young man courting her, they were Mr and Mrs Young, and remained so when the newly married couple went back up north for family summer holidays, three years out of four, for two decades and more after the war had ended. To the twins and me, and later Julie, they were always Uncle Willie and Aunt Mary. Out of hearing, Dad called him the Big Man.

Originally from Cromarty in the Black Isle, south of Portmahomack, Willie Young was a Highland shepherd in a manner unchanged by the passing of centuries. The world he and Aunt Mary inhabited was a different world to the one we lived in, preferable in many ways. It was a folkloric home from home, where the green fields, the dry-stone dykes, the sand and the sea came up to the door, just as schools and shops, cars and buses, busy roads and lollipop men to help you cross them were at ours. You spent the entire day under the sky, half of it on the shore, all of it in the gladness of imagination. When Uncle Willie and his mysteriously authoritative dogs, Fly and Glen, shepherded the baaa-ing flock to market, from Rockfield Farm to the burgh of Tain, twelve miles by farm track and tarmac road, it was no less fascinating an adventure than a Chaucerian pilgrimage would have seemed, had I happened to witness one on the way to the sea.

Each time I made the journey from the shepherd's cottage to the Port on my own, aged nine, ten, twelve, Aunt Mary would say, "Just go down to the road, Jim. You'll get a lift." Sure enough, the first approaching vehicle would pull up alongside the fair-haired boy, and the driver would scoot him to Portmahomack in exchange for two miles' worth of jetty-fishing and rockpool-dabbling conversation. No raised hand or thumb was needed. The drivers always seemed to know that we were lodged with Mrs Young. Sometimes they even knew my name.

On the first day of the holiday, Dad and I would go together to the jetty at the Port, but not before making an excursion to the all-purpose Co-operative on the front to buy a net, a hook and a line. On the wet sands we would use my spade and pail to dig for lugworms. The line needed a weight, however – what Dad called "a sinker" – to take the baited hook to the depths where fishes lurked.

Once, as we came out of the shop, Dad spotted a scrap merchant's horse and cart on the main street of the Port. Horses were not so far from having been regular farm workers.

As I admired this one, Dad quickened his step to catch up with the driver.

"Hello there, Jimmy!"

The carter tugged the reins to bring the horse to a halt.

"Have you got a wee bit of lead for a sinker for the boy's fishing line?"

The Highlander was happy to oblige. Then he shuffled the reins and muttered something to his four-legged companion.

"Thanks a lot, Jimmy!" Dad shouted after them.

He fixed the weight to the line and we headed to the sandbanks, where orphaned ancient tarry anchors bit massively into the sands.

"How did you know that man's name was Jimmy?"

A pause. A gaze over placid waters.

"I met him in the Navy during the war."

In the evenings, if we happened to be in the Port and not at the farm, Mum would ask one of the wise fishermen loitering near the harbour to read the sky and foretell tomorrow's weather. "I doot it'll be fine, Ina," he would say, rubbing his hands together and smiling warmly. These fishermen returned from the Dornoch Firth with herring and mackerel by the box and bucketful, to be shared widely among villagers and visitors like us. Sometimes a silent salmon would make the journey back to Glasgow in Dad's golf bag.

The closest neighbours to us at Rockfield Farm were chickens. Two horses stood loyally in the field, Prince and Silver Eye, the latter named for his left-side blindness. Milk from the cow, cream from the milk, butter from the churn, oatcakes and crowdie, honey from the comb, peas from the pod, berries from the thorn, eggs from the henhouse, and on special days a chicken on the table. Laughin' tatties were floury potatoes whose skin split on the cool dinner plate when removed from the pan, letting the steam rise up. The front porch at the cottage was peopled by giants' boots, tweed jackets, waterproofs matt and glossy at the same time, varied hats, shepherds' crooks worn smooth by shepherd's grip, curiosities such as a lobster creel and conch shells through which you could listen to the sea. Like that sound, "creel" was a word that came into play only on holiday, and precious for that alone. The same went for items of new knowledge. I learned for example that, as companions, sheepdogs could never be compromised.

The Youngs had a daughter, Ishbel, born in the late 1920s, a teenager in wartime, who became my mother's lifelong friend. Their two younger sons were Malcolm and Derek, and the infant Malcolm served as a stand-in for my mother until her own son came along.

The Land Girl's work was not unpleasant. "I spent the day today planting potatoes and sewing peas", Mum wrote in a letter to her Navy sweetheart. Throughout the remainder of her long life, she felt blessed by this posting, and as the war drew to a close thought of taking a job and staying up North, hoping to lure her husband-to-be into agreement. She was popular with the local people, as she was everywhere she went. When Mum and Dad celebrated their Golden Wedding in Portmahomack in 1996, the folk I encountered in the seaside street still asked after her by her maiden name, Ina Beveridge. One former farm worker from Rockfield mistook me for my father. "By Jove, but you're lookin' well, Harry!" At the party after the anniversary dinner, as at many parties before and later, she played the piano in the bar at the Castle Hotel, while Dad grasped the microphone with life-and-soul assurance and sang "Bye-bye Blackbird".

My mother had taken piano lessons in Shawlands, but her most remarkable talent was her ability to play by ear. She could play practically any song a party-goer wished to sing – "Give me a key . . . just start . . ." – and never declined to do so. As a girl at home next to the school, she used to listen to the latest pop songs on the wireless in the evenings. "Then I would go through to the room with the piano and pick out the melody," she told me. We were sitting on a bench at Newport, looking towards Dundee and the Tay Railway Bridge which spans the Firth of Tay. She had just entered her nineties and had recently given up playing the piano in the residential home in which she now lived, named after St Serf, the mentor of Glasgow's patron, St Mungo. "Once you had the tune, it was easy enough to fit it together with the harmony."

A written record of Mum and Dad's service came to light unexpectedly at about that time: a small leather suitcase packed to bursting point with letters exchanged during wartime. When he was stationed at Invergordon, they wrote to each other practically every day, and went on doing so when his ship sailed for the Far East, and later when he was again at Plymouth, awaiting demob. For over three years, news, messages, declarations, recollections – sometimes twice daily – created a continuous back and forth between a primitive Highland cottage, where drinking water had to be pumped from the well in the yard, and Royal Navy ships in Invergordon, then Devon, then Ceylon. "This is my second letter to you tonight," she wrote in one, "as I am playing at a dance in Nigg. It is in the Norwegian refugee camp."

"I received no less than three letters from you today," he wrote back from SS Empire Spearhead in Plymouth, "and I feel good. I could have made an announcement on the BBC."

Above: The shepherd, Willie Young, and his wife Mary (centre), at Rockfield Farm, Easter Ross, 1949. Mum is to the left, with the twins in front. The two boys are the Youngs' sons. At right, their daughter Ishbel, Mum's lifelong friend, with her baby son. *Below*: Mum at Rockfield during the war.

Delays in delivery would be compensated by the arrival of older letters that had been bobbing on the perilous seas for weeks. "I don't want you to be annoyed with yourself because you miss one day of writing," she told him as she sat down to convey the news from the Scottish Highlands. The letters, most of them carefully replaced in their envelopes, many with oriental stamps at top right, number about a thousand. Almost every one begins, "My Dearest Darling . . .", followed by a promise of everlasting love, an expression of impatience for the war to be over, the explicit longing for the climax of marriage and the beginning of family life in Glasgow. At one point, he predicts three boys and a girl. Instead, they got twin daughters, one boy and, ten years later when Mum was nearly forty, a surprise third girl.

It was a love affair dependent not only on the post – and the piquant feelings of separation it helped to soothe – but on a bicycle. The road between Invergordon and Portmahomack to the north was a rural road, about twenty miles long, and my father relied on two wheels to pursue his courtship, cycling from the ship up to Rockfield Farm, or perhaps for a rendezvous in Tain – "Outside the Post Office at 4" – whenever he wanted to see the janitor's daughter, now the shepherd's ward. Not forgetting the Highland weather. This was written on November 29, 1943:

I had quite a pleasant run back on Saturday, apart from the fact that I got drenched. However after the rain had soaked through to my skin and I got used to it, I felt quite comfortable. I was fairly soaked by the time I got here. The rain started when I was about a mile away from your place, it started as a drizzle and gradually got worse till I got to Fearn where it really did rain. By the time I reached InverG. you would have thought I had been for a swim in the Dornoch Firth.

He wasn't to be put off, however. In another letter, he reported:

I had a lovely run home on Saturday and never felt the time drag at all. It got a lot lighter later on and I had no difficulty in finding my way. The bike will soon be able to do the road riderless so if it ever comes up that way without me, just send it back by rail.

It wasn't long before rumours of her musical ability circulated through the scattered burghs and villages of Easter Ross, and she began to receive invitations to play at dances for farm workers, servicemen on leave, local women and other Land Girls. "I am going to be very busy next week, Darling. I am playing every night except Tuesday night at dances . . . We won't be very late Monday and Thursday as they will stop at 12."

There are many mentions of a call out of the blue to the girl from Glasgow to provide entertainment. A messenger arrives by bicycle at the shepherd's cottage at Rockfield Farm on a Saturday afternoon, to ask if Ina Beveridge can stand in for an absent pianist that night – in Fearn, where the nearest railway station was, or Balintore, just down the coast from the Port but not half as pretty, or perhaps in Portmahomack itself, where the dances were held in the Carnegie Hall, opened in 1902 by Mrs Andrew Carnegie. (Twenty years after the end of the war, I would be there when Mum was playing, dancing with girls named Cathie Ross and Margaret Duff, and trying out the chat-up line, "My mother's in the band".) In her letters to Plymouth or Ceylon, she doubtless thought it more tactful to leave out other attributes of the "smashing players" she sat down with night after night, but those of the twenty-two-year-old at the piano – self-assured, humorous, lacking airs and graces – would not have gone unremarked by the boys on leave.

Their penmanship is good, the grammar and spelling more or less faultless – Harry's punctuation occasionally stumbles – their command of the formalities of correspondence easygoing. In the Navy, he tried to learn touch-typing, and crumbling exercise books show that he engaged in a correspondence course in German – motivated, I suspect, by his love of music more than by a wish to communicate with the enemy. He was proud of his own musical taste, which drew him to the stern Romantics: Beethoven, Mendelssohn, Tchaikovsky. Mozart was just too much in the Classical mode to please him. Haydn squeezed in. He thrilled to the drama of the Beethoven symphonies and piano concertos, in particular.

There is no doubting the sincerity of his love, nor her loyalty, but in his letters I often catch a note that makes me cringe, mostly for her, a little for him, and just a tiny bit for the boy whose existence lay seven years in the future, but who would hear it frequently in the awkward age to come. It strikes with a heavy sound in a letter written from Glasgow to Easter Ross on March 13, 1944, at the beginning of her dance-band career, in which he invokes his own efforts to play the piano:

How did you fare? No doubt you felt pretty strange at first, however as time goes on you will acquire more confidence, and it will at least be a hobby for you. Too bad you haven't a piano to practice on. Maybe if you speak to the lady next door she'll let you have the use of hers. I'll send you up a few Beethoven sonatas just to impress her. As long as you don't try to play them you'll be alright. I don't think there's any chance of you doing that anyway. It's a band pianist you are, not a soloist. After the war we'll both go to a really good teacher and learn from the beginning again, the competitive spirit will make us keen and although I say it myself, I think I'll win, as my style (what there is of it) hasn't been polluted with boogie-woogie and repetitional bumping, call it jazz if you like.

He wasn't inclined to be severe all the time. Ten days later, now based in the south of England, he succumbed to the charms of "repetitional" music and the associations it held:

Are you still bumping out that Rhythm with the Fearn band? Do you still play "I'm thinking tonight of my blue eyes" and the other regulars which, on hearing, I immediately think of Fearn. I was listening to the radio today and all the tunes put me in mind of you. It's funny how music or popular tunes do that more than anything else. They played that tune "Put your arms around me honey" and it just put me in mind of our very first night together in Portmahomack, you were singing it as we walked down the road, and we were both very happy.

He was present at the evacuation from Dunkirk. In a letter dated June 8, 1944, two days after the assault on Normandy began, he described "a run over to France on Tuesday morning" where he saw "everything that was going on". The Tuesday referred to was D-Day. The mission was to monitor early developments at Gold Beach, on the south-western edge of the Cotentin. But the view of Operation Overlord from on board SS *Empire Spearhead* that morning was evidently a restricted one. "Things were just starting there, there really wasn't much to see, as the enemy put up very little resistance to our sea forces." He might well have been conscious of the censor looking over his shoulder. "Our shipping losses were very slight, the biggest relief was the absence of the Luftwaffe."

She lost three cousins in the war, but compared to many people, including friends, they had a relatively uneventful campaign. When his ship was directed to the Far East (with no advance warning, according to procedure), the enemy was boredom. "Of the 8 weeks I have been on this ship, I could have been on leave 7 of them, as I haven't done a day's work the whole time."

They were married in Glasgow, in May 1946, but still he had to return to Plymouth to await demob. The wedding photographs show a good-looking young man in his petty officer's uniform and a pretty girl in a veiled mini top hat with a lovely smile. They found a tenement flat in Dennistoun, and the twins were born in August 1947.

"I have no idea what a good secure job is going to be after the war", he had written in April 1944. The grandeur of the Clyde shipyards that had made a legend of Glasgow in the years leading up to and after the First World War was already fading. In any case, Ina was not set on being a range fitter's wife. Soon my father had a job as a clerk in the London, Midland and Scottish Railway, the start of a career that lasted the rest of his working life. After the LMSR was integrated into British Rail in 1948, he stepped up the career ladder one rung at a time, eventually attaining a position of seniority in what became the Scottish Region, and later in the Western Region in the South of England.

Mum and Dad on their wedding day, Glasgow, May 1946.

II

Within three years of being married, they were able to move into a ground-floor cottage house in Castlemilk Crescent, Croftfoot, with tidy gardens fore and aft, as the ex-petty officer was apt to say. I was born in the front room, their bedroom, at dawn on June 5, 1951.

Few people in the crescent had cars and other drivers had no reason to pass through, unless to visit. It was a perfect arena for children's play. At different times of the day and on different days of the week, this or that "man" would come round the crescent, proclaiming his wares in sonorous tones: even when the words themselves were incomprehensible, the sound of the voice identified the arrival. There was the lemonade man, to whom we returned empty screwtop bottles from the week before, for a penny off the latest purchase; the roll man – morning and evening – whose powdered products cost three farthings each, five fresh rolls totalling threepence three farthings; the fish man, whose haddock and cod were economical purchases, compared to meat. If we had fish on a Friday, Mum would say, "People will think we're Catholics." Which, in some distant, secreted gene in the family body, we were.

A less regular visitor was the knife man, with his fierce and shining machine for sharpening kitchen implements. The rag man, often accompanied by a ragged woman, collected old clothes, to be sold at Paddy's Market, near Glasgow Cross. The first Sikh I ever saw was standing at our front door with an open suitcase full of useful things such as dusters – dusting was Dad's regular task – and dishwashing brushes and towels. This was the twins' job, one washing, the other drying.

My chore was to "clear the table" after the family had finished their tea, a more or less endurable event that lasted from about six o'clock till half-past. I liked to dart in from whatever post-school activity I had been pursuing, then shoot out again as soon as possible. Football, rounders, improvised children's games of every sort took place at the "recs", our word for the immense recreation grounds, two minutes' sprint from the living room with its dining-room table now hastily cleared. These glorious grounds were covered by four football pitches, where our school matches and later Boys' Brigade games were played, in organized leagues, come rain, come wind, come frost and ice, to an assembly of parents, local boys and girls whose turn in this or some other sport had just been or was yet to come, and assorted idlers.

The recs hosted a gymkhana, with colourful and proudly costumed riders and handsome horses, and had a pavilion with changing rooms and a gymnasium which was furnished with good equipment. On late Saturday afternoons, as rumours of the professional football results reached us through the grapevine – occasionally the shocking news: "Rangers got beat" – we were free to roam around the gym, clambering on to the vaulting horse and trying to lift 50 lb weights. The wide spaces rang to the happy voices of hairy men stripping off, showering and getting dressed – grown-up men, it seemed to us, though only a few would have been out of their teens.

The recs (always singular) was a stone's throw from the high-up platform of Croftfoot railway station, from which Dad would watch games while waiting for a train. He had his first sight from the Central Station-bound platform of Jean's boyfriend Millar Hay, a stylish and soon to be locally famous player. The last time I passed the space where the recs had been, the pitches and pavilion had disappeared and the ground had been given up to a housing project with an absurd pastoral title.

Nine years and eleven months after me, Julie was born in the same room at 45 Castlemilk Crescent, at a similar time of the day. In the most tender awakening I ever had from Dad, he touched my shoulder and said, "Come on through. You've got a wee sister." How it had happened I really wasn't sure, but there she was, in a tiny cot, an hour or two old. There was Mum sitting up in bed and smiling. And there was the midwife, also happy, clearing up and preparing to leave.

5

THE APPRENTICE: WASHIE'S

I

At 7.30 in the morning of Monday, October 3, 1966, I boarded a number 13 bus at the stop on Aikenhead Road, a few minutes' walk from our front door. The bus rolled past Hampden Park stadium, nosing into the lightening day via Govanhill and the Gorbals, setting me down with others at Glasgow Cross, the entrance to the district known as Townhead, never spoken of by any familiar or resident as anything other than Toonheid.

To me, until now, it was a foreign country, known only as the base camp of the fearful sounding gang called the Calton Tongs, arch-rivals of the teenage Gorbals tribe, the Young Young Cumbie. Tongs ya bass. YYC ya bass.

From the Cross, a five-minute walk up the High Street led to Ingram Street, opposite the site of the Old College, the city's first university and the fourth-oldest in the English-speaking world. Far to the west along Ingram Street, towards George Square, was Stirling's Library, and less than halfway down, at a sharp juncture, Albion Street, the location over time of various Scottish newspapers. Each of those institutions, in different ways, would come to have a shaping influence on my life, but at the time I lived in ignorance of their existence.

At the corner of Ingram Street and Shuttle Street stood a formidable grey, three-storey warehouse with an angled balustrade fringing the top. The surrounding streets housed the Glasgow Fruit Market, where Dad had pushed a barrow as a school-leaver before the war. Mum's instinctive, forward-looking respectability discouraged discussion of it, as it did of the Roman Catholicism deep, but satisfyingly distant, in his background. Now here I was, back on native territory. By 8 o'clock in the morning the gutters were clogged with cabbage leaves, grubby green sprouts, crushed apples, squelched oranges and bruised banana skin.

The entrance to the printing factory was through the close at No. 48 and up one flight to the first floor. There, at eight precisely, I coincided with Mary McIlwham emerging from the cludgie on the stair, already reeking of smoke and gin. Or perhaps it was what Glasgow drinkers at the lower end called "the wine", a sweet sherry such as Lanliq – Lang's Liqueur – Four Crown or Eldorado, relished without exception for price over taste. Mary would have known the new boy was due to start that morning. She smiled in a guileless way that I was to grow familiar with, and spoke a few words of kindly greeting as she continued towards the shop floor in an elegant feminine step, with me at the rear. She had grey hair pulled back in a bun and a face blushed and lined with "the wine".

It was the first day of my apprenticeship at Washington Irvine's, printers, paper rulers, bookbinders and stationers. Four months earlier, I had turned fifteen. On the days after my interview with Mr Crawford, I had contrived to meet the postman as he came towards the house in the morning. With a shifty hello, I would ask if he had "anything for Campbell". He would hand me a bill or a postcard or other things that I could tell by the postmarks had come from somewhere other than the school. I had a paper round at a local newsagent and during those dangerous days I timed its completion to coincide with the postman making his regular approach. After several turns of mooching about with no result between 8.15 and 8.30,

I dared to hope that Mr Crawford had decided to let it go.

One morning, a week or more after the report-card meeting, I arrived back from delivering the papers to find my father still at home. This was unusual – I never knew him to stay off work even because of illness – but the reason was immediately apparent. Mr Crawford's letter lay open on the table. My mother stood in the background, a handkerchief pressed to her face. My father picked me up, threw me on to the settee, whacked me across the side of the head with the back of his hand – the favoured side – and continued with what I suppose has to be called a beating, though I don't remember that it hurt at all. Mere blows seldom did.

It was decreed that I would be kept in for a month. I would copy out two pages of my school history book each day, which I would then read aloud to him when he got back from the office

Washington Irvine, printers and stationers, occupied the first and second floors of this building, at the heart of the normally bustling Fruit Market. The factory entrance was through the close visible to the right of the Morris Minor.

in the evening. I protested: "But Dad, it's the summer holidays," gifting him one of his good lines: "Holidays? Holidays are for boys who've been working. You've been on holiday *all year*."

At the end of August (the cruel sentence was soon commuted, thanks to the intervention of Grandpa), I had returned to school to face the humiliating prospect of repeating third year. There could be no starker evidence of my lack of academic aptitude. My contemporaries, beginning fourth year, were taking the first steps on the path leading to O Grades, the Scottish equivalent of O Levels, the following spring. I wouldn't have stood a chance. Repeat appeared to be the only option.

There was, however, another option: leave.

One day after school in early September, my mother raised the subject tentatively. Our next-door neighbour, Mr Wells, a stationer, was the client of a small printing firm in Ingram Street. He had mentioned to Mum that the company had a vacancy for an apprentice paper ruler, and she had discussed it with Dad.

It was only a suggestion, she said . . . we just thought you might be happier . . . you know, school and all . . . since you don't seem to be really suited . . . maybe this is . . .

Her modest dreams for my future had turned against her with almost daily displays of blatant mockery. Neither discipline nor indulgence had worked. Mr Crawford's letter was the final confirmation. One of her hopes was that her son might become a dentist. A chartered surveyor was another profession she spoke of with admiration, though I had no idea what either "chartered" or "surveyor" referred to. My father had offered to get me a start behind a desk in the railways, just as he himself had launched a successful career there twenty years earlier. The lure of "ten pounds a week" was set before me.

He was a thinking man who had never had the opportunity to refine and shape his intelligence with the quality essential to its development: curiosity. He would have loved to go to "the university", as he always phrased it – there could only be one – caressing the words as he spoke them. Such a move was economically out of the question for any member of a family like his in the 1930s, and anyway history stepped in: the Royal Navy had given him his education. He had trained as a medical orderly on board ship in the Far East, and devoured works on the long voyages by Dickens, Dostoevsky and Hugo. One of the great reading experiences of his life was *Les Misérables*, which he pronounced "Lez Mizer-*a*-bulls". Another was *A Tale of Two Cities*. My father was one of only two people I've ever met who referred to "the Brothers Singer", Isaac Bashevis and his less well-known sibling Israel Joshua; the other person being Clive Sinclair, the author of a book on the two writers. For my sisters' benefit, he looked hard into Rembrandt and van Gogh, visited the Tate and the National Gallery when in London, but his abiding passion was the music of Beethoven. It must have spoken to him of other worlds than the stone-tenement world in which he was brought up, other expressions of emotion, in ways that the names of Big Bill Broonzy and Blind Boy Fuller – the names as much as the music – were beginning to suggest different realities to me.

Now that the benefits of learning had been extended by a victorious society to embrace all deserving younger citizens, he imagined that he might enjoy by proxy the days of study and comradeship amid the quadrangles at the university that he had once longed for, through me. Both twins were established at Glasgow School of Art – the first in the entire extended family to make the leap into higher education. Their talent had shone through early, and Dad had encouraged them, after some initial resistance, up to the happy moment of their acceptance. They wore their paint-smeared artists' smocks at every chance, facing down the light protests voiced by Mum at the dinner table. Her vain hope had been that the two girls would go to the Dough School in the West End, properly called the College of Domestic Science.

I was to be next. If not a surveyor or a dentist, then maybe a teacher. No one had foreseen a humble trade, an apprenticeship projected to occupy the next six years, a square brown wage packet handed over on a Friday at 3 pm (the timing being a safety measure, allowing the pubs to close for the afternoon), a dilapidated factory sunk in the mouldy Fruit Market, its entrance next to our wide-open "pen" where vans backed in for the unloading of paper and card. Batches were carried up to the second floor in the hoist – another new noun – to be cut to manageable size and trimmed by Gilbert, the cutter (yet another), on his manually operated guillotine. Two fingers on his left hand were shorter than the others.

Maybe it would be a solution of a sort to the outer disturbances my inner turbulence had caused, and seemed likely to go on causing. At the completion of my training I would be a certified journeyman, a master paper ruler, with a job for life.

I accepted the proposal without hesitation. There was a final interview at school with Mr Crawford, who in his time had doubtless taken leave of boys more troubled than this one. "So you're going where the big money is!" he said – the printing trade had that reputation – before I walked out of the school gates on to Fetlar Drive for the last time.

The big money Mr Crawford was referring to belonged to the world of newspaper printing. It had nothing to do with the sort of jobbing work undertaken by Washington Irvine. The firm received its own orders from regular clients, and in addition undertook tasks contracted out from famous Glasgow companies such as McCormick's and Collins the publishers. Both were situated within walking distance of Ingram Street, and in my first year at Washie's I did part-time duty as a messenger boy, delivering and collecting parcels to and from various addresses in town, something I was always pleased to be asked to do. Now and then I was given a few pennies for bus fares, which of course I kept, walking quickly – sometimes not so quickly – there and back. A common mission was to be dispatched with a sturdy plastic container through the old Townhead streets – their inhabitants existing not so much in a different place from the people of King's Park, as in a different century – to the slaughterhouse and Meat Market near the Gallowgate, where Dad's maternal grandparents had lived and were married – in the flat which they shared, apparently, at 543 Gallowgate – on May 7, 1875. There I had to ask for "a quart" (never two pints) of ox gall.

I enjoyed the adventure of meeting muscular workers in bloodied aprons and wellington boots, dodging the lorries manoeuvring into place at the entrance to disgorge their bellowing cargoes, glimpsing the bespectacled men dressed in incongruous suits and ties doing the accounts in glass-fronted offices, neat secretaries by their sides, seemingly oblivious to the echoing shouts and the clatter and grind of overhead trolleys from which hung rows of massive carcasses. The slaughterhouse was made the setting for Archie Hind's novel *The Dear Green Place*, published in that year, 1966, one of only a few works of its time to embrace the noise and air and colour of Glasgow. But I knew nothing of that yet. Later, I would come to admire Hind's novel. "In the middle of the pass, barrows were being pushed up and down as the labourers collected the offal: tripes, livers, hearts, lungs, heads" – and somewhere in among it my quart of ox gall.

The job to which I had committed my future was putting lines on paper. The foul-smelling gall was added in tablespoonfuls to large porcelain bowls containing the inks that created the lines, to keep them fast. Starting pay for a first-year apprentice was £4 12s 6d a week, rising in increments of between £100 and £150 per annum, to settle at around £16 per week for a journeyman, about the same wage as might be earned at the time by a first-level schoolteacher. "And with overtime," people on the shop floor were always quick to add, "you can make a lot more . . ."

There were opportunities on Tuesday and Thursday evenings, 5.30 to 7.30, and on Saturday mornings, from 8 am till midday, all paid at the rate of time and a half. If you clocked in more than five minutes after eight in the morning, your pay would be docked a quarter of an hour, in my case amounting to about ninepence. There were two weeks' holiday in the summer – the Fair Fortnight, starting mid-July, during which the factory closed its doors – and a further holiday to be taken during the months of January or February, the "winter week". Membership of the union SOGAT (Society of Graphical and Allied Trades), which had negotiated these benefits, was obligatory. I was invited to join the menodge. This meant contributing two shillings (10 pence) a week to a general fund, with nine others – there was more than one menodge in operation on the shop floor – resulting in a sum which would be paid out to each member in turn. In this way, I would be poorer by two shillings for nine weeks in a row, but a rich man – a whole pound was mine – on the tenth.

The factory floor was dominated by three paper-ruling machines, one of which I would in time be given charge of. Two of them were neat modern apparatuses, known as disc machines, or just "the discs", both operated by the journeyman; the third was a quaint old edifice made largely out of wood, on which I was to learn my trade. This was a Shaw Pen Ruling Machine.

In the first stage of every job, the Shaw was operated manually, using a crank handle to cause a sheet of paper to advance slowly over the moleskin canvas, allowing necessary adjustments to be made to the spacing and balance of the pens, and to the density of the lines they were about to draw. When everything was set up and ready to go, a green button was pressed to power the machine by electricity, heralded by a low grumble. Paper was introduced by a feeder, always a woman or girl, dressed in a nylon overall. Mary McIlwham was the most experienced paper feeder on the floor. The first model of the Shaw Pen Ruling Machine was produced in Huddersfield in 1890, and development continued until the early 1930s. At a guess, mine was made somewhere in between.

It looked like a small four-poster bed, with a solid wooden frame. The slowly rolling blanket carried the paper through to the delivery box at the end opposite to the feeder. An upright frame supported threads, which went round on their own smaller rollers, keeping the paper firmly in position on the blanket. As the large sheets of crown passed along – more than 1,000 an hour at the top rate – the brass pens which had been slotted into crosswise wooden carriages rose and fell according to a regulated scheme. It was the paper ruler's job to fit the pens into the carriages and to slot cams into the timing wheel which caused the carriages to lift when one sheet of paper was ruled, then to come down on to the next sheet at the proper moment, leaving lines of a desired colour and pattern – the basic being the universally familiar page of horizontally lined writing paper.

It was the ruler's job, too, to spread flannels neatly across the tops of the carriages above the bracket which secured the pens in place, and to ensure that the flannels were refreshed by regular applications of ink to flow into the pens – but not so regular that the downward flow would cause the pens to flood. The standard colour of ink was "feint"; there were also shades of blue, red and green.

Each job came with its own ruling specifications. Some were quite complex, requiring a perfectly timed drop of vertically running single-line pens on to hitherto ruled horizontal double-line bars, with perhaps a thick single line or two underneath.

A Shaw Pen Ruling Machine, similar to the one on which I served my apprenticeship at Washie's in the late 1960s. This one was probably made round about 1930.

This might be for the pages of what would be cut, folded with a flat "bone", and then bound on the second floor at Washie's into an account book or ledger. For some patterns, the paper was fed into the machine two or three times, front and back. The lines on one side ought to correspond perfectly with those on the other, and the "show-through" should be minimal.

The ink was contained in a bowl near the ruler's right hand and added to the flannels on the carriages by means of a small brush. If the ink dried up, through the ruler's negligence, the lines became scratchy. Too sudden a reapplication of ink would vary the density of the lines and cause too much show-through. Achieving a uniform density was among the paper ruler's principal tasks. At the end of a run, the paper was emptied from the wooden holder at the machine's rear end, counted into quires of twenty-five sheets and stacked, each sheet ready to be folded and cut according to the appropriate size: folio, quarto, octavo.

This was the labour that filled each of my working days, once I had acquired a basic mastery of the machine.

Long before then, when my first pay packet arrived, I was surprised to discover that nine shillings (45 pence) had been deducted in advance by the Inland Revenue, leaving £4 3s 6d. Union dues meant a further reduction. My mother took £3 for my keep – a concept apparently inseparable from my new status as a working man. Out of what was left, I was expected to pay my own bus fares from King's Park to Glasgow Cross and back again, leaving less than a pound as spending money after a forty-hour week, not much more than I had been earning on my morning paper round. Sometimes I managed to skip my fare on the bus, or else I walked home from work in order to save a few pence.

II

The owners of the firm were two brothers, David Irvine and Washington Irvine, known to the workforce as Mr David and Mr Washie. It was said that they didn't get on well. The third director, Mr David's son Alister, acted as the main liaison between management and workers. Just over thirty at the time of my arrival in Ingram Street, he was addressed by us as Mr Alister.

My journeyman and immediate boss was John Pollock, a thin-faced, dirty-minded man who made it known to everyone that he could never bring himself to work with a Catholic. It was not a policy held to by the management – there were several Catholics among the sixty-strong staff, but John Pollock didn't like to mix with them, and wouldn't have taken me on if I'd been a left-footer, a Fenian, a Pape, an RC, a Tim Malloy, a Mick or a Dan. Rangers fans from the Bridgeton area, who included John Pollock, were Blue Noses or Billy Boys, and before we became acquainted in person, John would certainly have made inquiries as to the name of the school I had attended. The likes of Saint Bonaventure's or Saint Aloysius in the reply would have made my employment in the paper-ruling department at Washie's impossible. John found it painful even to enunciate the names of certain central Glasgow streets, such as Saint Vincent Street. They reminded him too forcefully of the sickening accoutrements of the Roman Catholic Church.

Just as important as John Pollock to my early training at Washie's was Jeanette McGowan, the principal feeder after Mary. She wore an elegant, fitted, yellow nylon overall with white pinstripes and turned-up white collar – I seldom saw her in anything else – and the resident expression on her face throughout the course of a day was in equal parts humorous, sexy, intelligent and hard. She was a type common in Glasgow and its satellite towns – Jeanette lived in Shotts, about fifteen miles away by bus – both feminine and inviolable. Not even John Pollock, who bullied Mary McIlwham mercilessly and teased his fifteen-year-old apprentice with innuendo barely understood, would have spoken out of turn to Jeanette. She took me in hand in a way that made me feel I could rely on her.

I was teased by one and all for speaking "polite" and regarded with mild suspicion by some for emerging from a bought house in King's Park, with sisters in higher education and a general background more commonly associated with the middle classes and management, a pairing that would have charmed my mother. But any sardonic, over-the-shoulder remarks from Jeanette – her eyes closing languidly, then opening halfway to gauge the reaction – were meant kindly, unless my behaviour didn't merit kindness, in which case she addressed it directly. She was twenty-one at the time of our meeting, and the dynamic was elder sister to younger brother, one I was quite accustomed to. Jeanette was effectively second-in-command on the floor. She was engaged to Michael Heaney, who worked in lithography and – his name told me before John Pollock went out of his way to do so – was a Catholic.

Other feeders were nice to be around, too. Jesse, for example, aged fifteen, gauche, good-humoured and with the gift of being totally natural. Nancy was older, pleasantly plump, and married to a "man" – the only word she or the other women ever used for their own or anyone's husband – she always spoke of warmly. She and Jesse reached almost daily for a word I had never heard until now: badness. "That's pure *badness*", they would say of some speech or action of mine or someone else. It could be either trivial or truly wicked.

When a round-faced, red-haired fifteen-year-old also called Nancy joined the team, the first became Big Nancy while the new girl was Wee Nancy, even though she was already taller than Big Nancy. Wee Nancy didn't have to wait long before she became the target of several of the boys from the printing and stationery departments on the second floor, though Big Nancy tried to protect her from dubious predators. Pregnancy outside of marriage was the greatest personal catastrophe and deepest social shame that could befall any of these girls. But the romantic kidology and horseplay in the air throughout the day was welcome, softening the harshness of the regime: 8 am till 12.30 pm, and 1.30 till 5 pm. On overtime nights, add two hours. The reams of paper in their waxed brown wrapping were stored in the basement, stacked in great, head-high piles with corridors in between, to create an underground maze, a likely place for smooching or, as we said, winchin'. Once Mr Alister caught me at it with yet another Nancy, and sent us both upstairs, after a dressing down, to get back to work.

Even so, you snatched at consolation where you spotted it. If the union, SOGAT, bargained with management to guarantee our holidays and annual pay increases, it had little influence on working conditions at 48 Ingram Street. When it rained heavily, as it often did, the floor around our feet was covered in water. A complaint about cold in winter – John Pollock and Mary McIlwham wore fingerless gloves – was answered by Mr David with the suggestion to turn on more lights and profit from the electric heat generated by the bulbs. It was forbidden to make or receive telephone calls during working hours – there was one black Bakelite telephone with a silver dial on the windowsill not far from John's disc machines – except in dire emergencies. Each morning my mother would prepare my "piece", which, if it contained bacon or sausage, perhaps topped by a well-fried egg, could be heated in its greaseproof paper on one of the radiators that was fitted under the Shaw to help the ink dry. After five minutes the mildly toasted white bread would be warm and deliciously saturated with butter and bacon fat.

III

One day, about a year after I began working at Washington Irvine's, I looked into the face of a guitar for the first time. It belonged to Áine Carey, a folk singer who would go on to record an LP – a rare thing in those days – of Scottish folk songs, as part of the Gleanna Four. Áine (pronounced as Anne) was an art school friend of one of the twins, Jean. The vision remains: burnished orange-red maple top; elegant neck with mother-of-pearl inlay and crosswise silver frets; bronze strings stretched along the neck from ivory bridge to gleaming brass keys. The prospect was erotic.

For the family group, Áine played Bert Jansch's famous instrumental "Angie" (adapted from Davey Graham's original "Anji"), with its thudding descending bass, while the index and middle fingers gave the sparkling suggestion of a melody on the treble strings. Jean bought Bert Jansch's first LP – just *Bert Jansch*, already the object of widespread wonder – and I was allowed to listen to it.

According to the sleeve notes, Bert, born in Glasgow, was "raised 'in the field' in Edinburgh". What on earth did that mean? At the time of making these miraculous recordings, at the age of twenty-one, he didn't own a guitar. How was this possible?

Not long after I had fallen under the spell, first of the instrument and then the album, Jean offered to teach me the

Áine Carey, at about the time she came to the house in King's Park and played "Angie". Here she holds a Spanish guitar, not the burnished steel string I fell in love with. *Courtesy of the Carey family.*

rudiments of guitar playing, which she herself had learned from Áine Carey. My first chord – everyone's first chord – was a C at the first position. The G chord was also playable, though forcing the joints of index, middle and little fingers to do the work was a mighty task. Nothing on the fret board was comfortable for those untrained digits. For the F chord, the index finger of the left hand had to hold down the first and second strings at the first fret at the same time, a next to impossible feat. My tender fingertips ached. But with practice, Jean promised, it will come.

She told me that finger-picking was the thing to do with the right hand, more sophisticated than strumming, and gave me a basic 4/4 pattern that Áine had taught her: thumb for the bass note . . . now the ring, middle and index fingers – one at a time – on each of the treble strings . . . Same thing now on G7 . . . no, try again . . . now on the F . . . OK, it'll come. Now back to – that's it – C!

Equipped with just those three chords to play, one was initiated into a rare fellowship. Stir an easy E7 into that progression – "I'm going up the country, through the sleet and snow" – and it opened up the prospect of a whole new life.

Scottish, Irish and English traditional folk songs told beguiling stories, occasionally cruel, but the Mississippi country blues led the singer down the road to a luminous underworld, even if that singer was sixteen years old and living in a respectable suburb on the Southside of Glasgow. Early Rolling Stones and Beatles records had pointed the way, but it was the real thing only for me from now on. The country blues, which borrowed fragments of the ancient traditions, was the living, continually changing folk music of the present day. These black and blue hobo troubadours still walked Big Bill's highway and rode Robert Johnson's railroad blinds, hanging on for rides from state to state beneath the carriage to the sound of a lonesome whistle. White people met them, talked to them, listened to them, took down their stories and wrote books about them.

By means of the magic carpet of music, the blue mood of the old South – of cotton-picking and "plantation", of "trouble in mind", a mind that reached back to slavery – could be felt in the room I shared with our little sister Julie in Kingshill Drive. The first African American people I encountered lived in places like Greenwood, Mississippi, in the 1920s, 30s and 40s. It would not be accurate to say that I met them only on the page or on disc; they lived in the strings and frets and bridge and tuning keys of my guitar, too; they lived in the sounds that emerged from it, however inadequately I might have attempted the songs.

The feeling I got from those meetings was vivid and transformative. It entered into me then like a form of religious instruction, or a program of military discipline, and has never gone away. I bought a record on which Big Bill Broonzy not only played and sang but talked to the Chicago journalist Studs Terkel, his fingers running up and down the neck of his guitar with golden touch as he spoke. I found Big Bill's speaking voice, full of honeyed light and shadow, almost as thrilling to listen to as his singing.

"Bill, tell me about the blues. What *is* the blues?"

"Well, the blues really came from the way people *live*, and the *way* . . . some of them . . . the way they're treated . . . and from the *places* where they live and the *work* they do."

We had our native singers, who were just as exciting. Jean borrowed records from fellow students: *Midnight Man* and *Hat* by Davey Graham, the Incredible String Band's self-titled first album, *London Conversation* by John Martyn. Both he and the Incredible duo, Robin Williamson and Mike Heron, were Scots, like Bert Jansch (Davey Graham had a Scottish father, so we were told) and even Donovan, whose early years were spent in Glasgow. John Martyn belonged to us more than most, because he, like Mum, was a former pupil at Shawlands Academy. Grandpa, the janitor, must have known him. His real name was Iain McGeachy and he had lived in a smart tenement building at the top of Tantallon Road, past which we walked every time we went to visit Grandma and Grandpa at the house attached to the school.

All communicated thrillingly in this new musical language – a blend of old-world and modernist folk, just as the songs that Big Bill learned as a teenager ("reels" he called them in the interview, not "blues") were a blend of British and Irish folksong and Southern woe, bound together by African rhythm. All were magically talented. John Martyn's first album was recorded when he was seventeen and released just after his eighteenth birthday. On it he played "Cocaine Blues (Traditional, arr. Martyn)", its clean notes woven tight with seductive expertise, cushioning his still boyish voice. The photograph on the sleeve showed him sitting outdoors, barefoot, cradling a guitar. Somehow or other, he had been born with that guitar in his arms, the way certain footballers were born with a ball at their feet. Even so, it was possible to attempt "Cocaine Blues" in a primitive version in the living room at Kingshill Drive.

Keep doing it, Jean would say, as no doubt Áine had said to her. It'll come.

IV

One day, while acting as the feeder for my Shaw Pen Ruling Machine, which I had long since mastered – I was scheduled to move on to the discs in my fourth year of training – Jeanette surprised me by saying she had told John Pollock that I wouldn't see my apprenticeship through to its full term, and that he had agreed with her.

"How not?"

"I just said to him. I told him. I said he's too clever f'rit." Jeanette let her eyelids close, in that familiar way, eyebrows arching as they did so.

It was as if someone had set off a controlled explosion on a chosen site, in order to clear away unwanted detritus, before a new work of building could begin. It wasn't that no one had ever told me I was "clever", now that I was free of school and had dumped "If you had 20 per cent more brains you'd be an idiot" behind; but Jeanette was at the present centre of my world. If people are shaped by how other people see them, then I was, day to day, being moulded into other forms.

My circle of friends was widening, and some people on its outer reaches had had a sort of education. Some passing pal had said I was a "philosopher" and I took it as a compliment, though I wasn't sure what it meant. Jean gave me William Golding's novel *Lord of the Flies* to read. I enjoyed the tale of civilized schoolboys stranded on an island, being sucked down towards an innate savagery. But the important thing about this first mature reading experience was my understanding that a story can be about something other than what the story appears to be: there could exist another story hovering above the realistic events recounted on the surface. Story No. 1 might be "an allegory" – an interesting new concept, which applied to the stories told in songs as well – of story No. 2. The second story – the story that wasn't really there, or not visibly – could turn out to be the more important one. Incidents that are described could be "symbolic" – another new thing – of events that are not. It was up to the reader be an active participant. Reader and book were in a relationship.

This was an aesthetic revelation every bit as momentous as hearing Áine Carey play "Angie" in our living room. Jean's suggestion was that *Lord of the Flies* was an allegory of Christ's agony on the cross. I failed to see it that way. But here was another aesthetic revelation: we could disagree.

For a while after that, I regarded every novel and poem I read and every play I saw in the theatre – when at last I began attending the theatre – as operating on a level above the visible story. Of even the most realistic work (*The Importance of Being Earnest* or Brendan Behan's *Borstal Boy*, both of which I saw at the great Citizens' Theatre in the Gorbals), I would ask myself: but what does it symbolize? What's the real story? In later years, I found this habit hard to kick.

At Mum's urging, I enrolled in a night class at Langside College and studied for the O Grade English exam, which I passed. I introduced some of my friends to the songs of Bert Jansch and the Incredible String Band. Without intending to, I began to see my intimate circle divided into those who were capable of connecting with Big Bill Broonzy's protest song "White, Brown and Black", with the psychedelic sounds of the Incredibles' *5000 Spirits or the Layers of the Onion,* and those who were not, for all they might have tried. This comprehension or lack of it separated me from boys and girls who up until then had been my good friends.

A button had been pushed inside my head and from now on I responded to a call at some hitherto undetected frequency. My feelings after reading Golding's novel projected me into another atmosphere, made by art. As I counted out chords and finger-picking arpeggios over the weekend, in the bedroom I shared with Julie, I was counting myself not only into new melodies but far-reaching myths:

I'll sing you this October song,
Oh, there is no song before it.
The words and tune are none of my own,
For my joys and sorrows bore it.

Robin Williamson, whose song this is, also sang: "Birds fly out behind the sun, / And with them I'll be leaving". Why "behind" the sun? Because he was bound for another hemisphere. He spoke of "fallen leaves that jewel the ground"; of meeting a man "whose name was Time / He said 'I must be going'".

It was bewitching. It cast an inescapable spell. The language sounded familiar, as if it had long lain in wait, in expectation of my hearing it. But at 8 o'clock on a dark October Monday morning, I had to leave those weekend fancies behind – not to hitch-hike to Morocco, where it was rumoured Robin had gone immediately after singing with a blend of weirdness and lyricism on the Incredible String Band's first album, playing guitar, fiddle and penny whistle, too – but to return to Glasgow Cross on the No. 13 bus and walk up the High Street to Washie's.

I had "October Song" to console me, and I sang it to myself as I turned into the close at No. 48, having braved the early-morning West of Scotland autumn weather, meeting red-faced, smiling Mary emerging from the cludgie on the stair, nodding a good morning to John, putting on my stiff grey flannel overall and preparing to give my hands up to ox gall and ink stains all over again. I liked Jeanette – and Big Nancy and Wee Nancy and trusting Jesse – but Jeanette had looked into the Ingram Street future and had failed to see me there.

6

THE SCOTIA BAR

I

I had been at Washie's for two and a half years when my mother made an announcement: Dad had been offered a high-up job in the Western Region of British Rail. It would mean Mum, Dad, Julie and me leaving Glasgow, to live in the south-east of England. He would have his office at Paddington Station, but the likely outcome would be to seek a house in a green outer suburb or somewhere further afield. Mum didn't want to live in London.

After some searching, a pleasant house was found in Booker, a leafy outpost of High Wycombe in Buckinghamshire, no more than a hundred yards from a wood, from which large hedgehogs came up at night to munch the garden plants. A traditional neighbourhood pub, The Squirrel, was a few minutes' walk away. Dad took up the role of Stores Controller for the Western Region. Every morning, Monday to Friday, he got on the train at High Wycombe Station and made the thirty-minute journey to Marylebone. From there it was a short walk to his office.

In the spring of 1969, Jean and Phyllis, still at Glasgow School of Art, were on the brink of leaving home anyway. Julie, turning eight and a pupil at King's Park Primary, would go to a new school "down south" – a phrase now heard often in the living room. As usual, a question mark hung over me.

On hearing the news, John Pollock suggested that the union might find a way to insinuate me into an English firm, in the town or its environs, where my apprenticeship could be completed, enabling me in due course to enter the world as a journeyman. "You don't want to lose your trade." It was SOGAT's duty to fix it. What were we paying our weekly union dues for, after all? Surely not just an extra light bulb burning through the cold weather on the first floor at Ingram Street.

But I saw the change in my parents' lives – they were in their mid-forties at the time – as an opportunity to change my own. At home, I was sparing with the advice and assurances John had put out. I might even have hinted that such a move would be difficult to bring about – which I believe it would have been. There was unlikely to be a sheaf of paper-ruling firms in High Wycombe willing to adopt an unsettled apprentice in his third year, without interview or trustworthy reference.

The decision was made that I would rent a bedsit in the West End of Glasgow – people of the post-war generation still called it "digs" – and continue to manage my Shaw machine at Washington Irvine's.

I was nearly eighteen, the age at which many people left home, in most cases to study, and I was entitled to my own choice. It must have made my parents, in particular my mother, unhappy and relieved at the same time. I would visit them down south. Things were gradually improving between us, and when I walked out of Kingshill Drive and all its strife, most of it caused by me, setting up in a place by myself in the West End, they would get better still.

I found a spacious room on the top floor of a massive tenement in Saltoun Street, facing Ruthven Street, at the entrance to which was Byres Road. Next to me were other bohemian bedsit dwellers, all of whom were welcoming and helpful. I had a guitar, a record player, albums by Robert Johnson, Bert Jansch and Lightnin' Hopkins. It was the first room of my own I had ever occupied. I had cast myself adrift from one society and had washed up safely on the shores of another.

II

I am happy to have spent the years I did working at Washington Irvine's. It was a kind of growing up. Planetary navigation is required to get from the dark side of fifteen to the brighter surfaces of eighteen, nineteen. The people I met in Ingram Street helped speed my evolution into a different sort of animal from the one that had lashed out dumbly against restraints on all sides at King's Park, causing so much whispered kitchen discussion and sleeplessness in my parents' bedroom, next to the one I shared with Julie.

What was the problem? It wasn't that particular school – though my mother was right to worry about bad company, in the shift from the smaller, local senior secondary to the socially comprehensive institution in Simshill – or the teachers. It was my reaction to being obliged to go to school in the first place. Only once I was free of it, and able to travel according to my own compass, did I begin to get over the sense of living under occupation.

The West End was yet another territory, with its student population and liberal customs. I fitted in right away, but I wouldn't want to have got there free of charge – that is to say, without having made the hazardous journey through Glasgow Cross, High Street, Shuttle Street, the hoist and the dank, worn steps up to the first floor at No.48 Ingram Street, from there to the Meat Market and beyond. Without paying my dues: literally, union dues. My mother and father had hoped that their children would be spared the bad air of Townhead, Calton and the Gorbals. It was the old Glasgow, a place with old-town diseases and hungers, ill-fitting hand-me-downs and deprivation of even hand-me-downs, a place that had been consigned to the fading pages of a history book while it still existed. The atmosphere that Mum and Dad breathed now was fragrant with fitted carpets, central heating, sliding doors, "all-electric", a family car, a separate dining room and good crockery and cutlery, for occasions when relatives came to visit.

Mum and Dad were familiar with the smells of the old city, however, as were, more so, their own parents: its poverty and filth, the single-end flat, the jawbox – a large kitchen sink, in which everything could be scrubbed, including manky infants – the jeely piece flung from the tenement window. They knew it all, even the barefoot weans glimpsed in the distance in black-and-white photographs, innocent fringes dependent on and fated to be victim of the low-level criminality of their parents. It was a life that came with its corresponding old-world thrills: pay-day drunkenness, loose love and Saturday-night singsongs in cider-only pubs. The folk I worked among at Washie's were more akin to the type of people Mum and Dad themselves had grown up with than those we lived next door to in Kingshill Drive. They were people Mum and Dad wished to steer me away from. My choice of company – a choice I didn't have to make – was a return to older territories, an instinctive seeking-out of West of Scotland first-nation peoples.

The free mixing of young men and women at Washie's, most of them older than me, the suggestive chat of the boys and the witty backchat of the girls, led by Jeanette, was civilizing. The stratum of working-class Glasgow from which they emerged, with very few exceptions, was decent and law-abiding. Dear, decrepit Mary, alternately giggling at John's hearty jokes and girning at his heartless chastisement, belonged to a different class, but her good nature, her fags, her secreted miniature bottle for a mid-morning slug in the cludgie, enabled endurance. John told me that she prostituted herself at weekends to get money for drink. He made jokes in her hearing on Monday mornings about her leaving her knickers up a close in the Gallowgate. Mary tittered in embarrassment and said, "Oh John", with an isn't-he-awful look, as she adjusted herself with professional poise and prepared to feed the large crown sheets into one of the disc machines.

Mary's Saturday night pub was the Saracen's Head in the Gallowgate – the Sarry Heid – rumoured to be the oldest in Glasgow. It was licensed to sell only cider and "wine", meaning cheap sherry of the Eldorado variety. The Sarry made its own wine: White Tornado, sold by the gill. The liquid was clear or, as Mary and others said, "white". The pub sign showed a swarthy, turbaned man. People said that Samuel Johnson had once lodged there, whoever he was.

I was introduced to alcohol in the Gallowgate by the firm's bright young stationer, Ian McCalister. Some lunchtimes, Ian took me to drink a pint of cider at the Sarry Heid or a lager and lime at the Red House in Ingram Street or a pint of McEwan's heavy at the Old College Bar up the hill behind Washie's on the High Street. John looked disapproving when he heard about our midday trips to the Sarry – he was moderate in his drink – and advised me to avoid the place after dark. Maybe on a Saturday night with the fire of White Tornado in her pitiful belly, Mary was a different sort of person, but as far as I could see she had no badness in her.

That old Glasgow was disappearing, acre by acre. Districts like Townhead, neighbouring Dennistoun, the Gorbals and surrounding areas on the south side of the Clyde – Tradeston, Hutchesontown, Kinning Park, and by the end of the 1970s our King's Park neighbour Govanhill – were being bulldozed. In the haze of tumbling bricks and mortar, people saw phantoms of their lives pass before them. The resulting mushroom clouds dissolved, leaving swathes of desolate wasteland. These outer changes caused inner bewilderment – the ground was literally disappearing beneath people's feet. The shattered walls of the houses exposed fitments, surprised shadows on the walls, as in a public display of dirty underwear. They stood in the street and looked up at what had been their living rooms, fireplaces ripped out like bad teeth, severed piping in plastered relief, flame-like patterned wallpaper stubbornly clinging on to shredded memories. It turned out that a house, until last year, last summer, last month, last week, the embodiment of security and shelter, was just an assemblage of rotten brick and stained mortar. Anything that remained would disintegrate or be bulldozed tomorrow or the next day. The words "oor close", suggestive of an entire plan of existence, embodying courtship, coupling, procreation, child-raising, daily nourishment and weekend intoxication, sickness and health, were laid off, the lived life swept away in the swat of a wrecker's ball in the space of a miserable midweek Gorbals afternoon. What's "the Gorbals" anyway, if it has just been demolished? So where am I? And if I don't know where I am, then who am I? Folk took to saying that the Luftwaffe, which had bombed outlying areas of the city during the war, didn't do half as good a job.

When these neighbourhoods went, their binding spirits, which make people quarrel and occasionally injure to the same degree to which they act on the instinct to shelter and protect, went with them. Tenement flats housing several families, a curtained-off bed at one end of the living room and the jawbox at the other, would exist only in recollection. No. 48 Ingram Street is no exception. The stairs leading up to the cludgie, with the Fire Station across the road and the leftover products of early-morning business at the Fruit Market littered all around, has ceased to be a built place, designed for life and work, and has been spirited into memory. Without my immersion in factory life at Washie's, among Jeanette and John and all the Nancys, they wouldn't belong in my memory at all. That old Glasgow is now a parallel world, and an invisible one. Thanks to my paper-ruler's apprenticeship, albeit broken, I had a last-minute chance to live in it.

The times were changing in other ways, and I was an early herald of the shift in mood at Ingram Street. One day, Mr David, dressed in full-length management beige overall as always (the male workers on the factory floor wore grey; the women's nylon overalls were mostly blue, Jeanette being a colourful exception), hirpled down the interior staircase – he walked with a bad limp – and handed me half a crown. I was surprised by his approach, as he had seldom spoken to me before.

"Take this," he said in his cloudy, withheld voice, pressing the coin into my palm and peering at me through filmy spectacles with his one good eye, "and get a haircut."

With a mixture of bafflement, defiance and politeness – instinctive reactions, in that order – I declined.

It became a talking-point. "What did he *say*?" The younger girl feeders were impressed. Big Nancy shook her head: it could only lead to trouble. Jeanette raised her eyebrows, folded her arms across her chest and fixed me with an expression blending loyalty and severity that said: *I saw it coming*. John's thin lips – thinner now than ever – maintained their silence. He knew what was coming anyway. Mary took it as an opportunity to make her way to the cludgie, patting the side pockets of her overall as she went, making sure of fags and flask.

III

In the evenings, after completing my overtime shift, happy in the knowledge of extra cash at time-and-a-half to come in the following week's wage packet, I cut down Candleriggs to Argyle Street, then turned left at Stockwell Street and walked towards the Clyde. The Scotia Bar was the centre of gravity of the Glasgow folk scene. Dublin was on top – the Merseyside of the folk-music revival – with the cosmopolitan magnet of London not far behind. In joint third place were Glasgow and Edinburgh. There were folk clubs scattered all around Glasgow, and the standard was high. Hopefuls in the audience – "floor singers" – could come up and try out a couple of numbers, with the possibility of being asked to return for a paid engagement.

The Scotia Bar was one continuous folk club. From Thursday evening, when some people received their wages, through Fridays, Saturday lunchtimes and on into Saturday night, the sounds of fiddles, penny whistles, squeeze-boxes, pipes, guitars and quavering human voices filled the smoky corner rooms, each of them a cell in a living folk tradition. Billy Connolly was often seen there, already a local star. Soon he would bring Gerry Rafferty with him. But at the centre of all Scotia action was a bearded bear called Mick Broderick, leader of the Whistlebinkies.

Standing tall and broad in the back room, his apparently self-replenishing pint glass never far away, he held an 18-inch diameter bodhran (usually pronounced b'-*ran*) with his left hand at chest height, while he drummed a routine with the right on the goatskin surface, using a twin-ended "tipper". Mick could sing with just his bodhran as accompaniment, or else keep time for other musicians. His first group, the Jacobites, included Billy Connolly, an elementary but capable banjo player, and Tam Harvey, a fine plectrum guitarist. When Billy and Tam paired off to form the Humblebums, Big Mick, as he was known, gathered a more traditional set around him, with fiddle, pipes and concertina. The pipes were not Scottish bagpipes – seldom an accoutrement to any folk ensemble – but Northumbrian pipes, emitting a milder sound. They were attached to the waist by a belt, the sound powered by the player squeezing a bag under one arm while fingering a lowdown melody on the chanter.

Big Mick Broderick, leader of the Whistlebinkies and king of the Scotia.

My modest guitar playing dared make only the most furtive of appearances at the Scotia. But you could watch, listen, occasionally ask. "Show me again what you did there . . ." The better players were generous, as the higher-ups had been kind to them: a folk tradition in itself. The same songs were pulled out with different titles. "Fennario", "Pretty Peggy-o", "The Bonny Lass o' Fyvie-o" – all the same song with varying words and contested origins. An Appalachian ballad with a lamentable civil war history – "If ever I return, Pretty Peggy-o, / If ever I return, all your cities I will burn" – or the tale of an Aberdeenshire soldier and his lass? The answer is it is both. Guitars were tuned this way and that to produce different modalities. Someone showed me how to pick Bert Jansch's classic "Strolling down the Highway", a British Beat Generation blues. Even the canonical "Angie", with its thumping descending bass, yielded to repeated persuasion.

Accomplished players blew in from Edinburgh to the east, or from down south or across the Irish Sea. These fiddlers and squeeze-box players seemed to move with enviable ease from one ensemble to another, halting only to place an order at the bar on the way, as if they were members of an elect and this battery of vibrating single syllables and silvery phrases and long melodious paragraphs was their native language. How did they come to be on first-name terms with such a wide array of whistle tunes and battle songs and love laments with memorable poetry?

> O the winter it has passed
> And the summer's come at last,
> The small birds they are singing in the trees.
> Their little hearts are glad,
> O but mine is very sad
> For my true love is far away from me.

The dead centre of the Glasgow folk scene. You could watch, listen, learn . . .

There were modern folksongs, too, often making strident political gestures – commemorating a strike, a sit-in, a march, a Clydeside disruption. Big Mick, a committed socialist, always seemed to be on his way to a protest somewhere, beret on his head, or was marching under a slogan-bearing banner from one historic site of oppression to another.

Some of the modern songs were the work of Matt McGinn, whose appearance at the Scotia was likely to cause a stir, or one of the Hamishes – Hamish Imlach, the most famous person on the Glasgow scene until Billy Connolly took over, or Hamish Henderson, based in Edinburgh at the School of Scottish Studies and more academic in his aims than most of the crowd. A few members of the core brigade were students; others worked at humble jobs; yet others strove to find a way of living by music and song.

The mundane folk style of Matt McGinn and Hamish Imlach did not attract me, strong performers though they were. It lived side by side at the Scotia with the exciting new "folk baroque", characterized by virtuoso guitar playing and a blue mood. Robin and Clive, as some fortunate people referred to them – Clive Palmer being the third member of the Incredible String Band for its first and most folksy record, though it was still gloriously avant-garde – had been at the Scotia before my time. Their very names, like certain place names, held out promises of pleasure and wonder. Was it possible, just maybe, to sing Robin's "October Song" at the Scotia on a quiet night and not be laughed at? Clive's "Empty Pocket Blues" was a join-in favourite and virtually foolproof, even with a fool at the helm of my Harmony Sovereign steel string.

There were Saturday night parties after closing time (10 pm), fuelled by beer and singalong music, to which a runt could sneak in under the door. An address would be mentioned, some hangover-ensuring cans bought, and off we would go along Howard Street. Or else we would head towards George Square and the Glasgow Folk Centre housed in a tenement building in nearby Montrose Street, run by Drew Moyes. I saw the Humblebums there several times. Billy Connolly was comedian, banjo player, guitarist and West of Scotland chronicler, all at once. He took the current pop hit "Everyone's Gone to the Moon" and turned it into "Why Don't They Come Back to Dunoon?", a comic defence of the declining Firth of Clyde resort. Tam Harvey filled in with clever phrasing on a cutaway Fender acoustic. He had long blond hair, parted on the side, and a handlebar moustache, Wild Bill Hickock-style. In my memory, he is always trying not to laugh at Billy's deadpan patter.

The stage cleared, the laughter and applause died down, and John Martyn came on, curly-haired and barefoot, a creature from a different part of the forest, though he and Billy had grown up in Glasgow within a few miles of one another. There was a touch of adolescent narcissism about his manner, and the more traditionally minded members of the audience were impatient with his over-excited self-presentation. Some of them disliked progressive folk music altogether. But when John Martyn played "Seven Black Roses", a virtuoso tune of his own devising which involved moving the capo up the fretboard midstream, passing from one section of the tune to the next without stopping, raising the key by a full tone or semi-tone while maintaining the melody, increasing the headlong pace as he went, even the sceptics had to clap in wonder.

Drew Moyes's hero was Doc Watson, the blind country singer from North Carolina, one of the great bluegrass guitar pickers of the era. His music proved, as if proof were needed, that the quilt of country music was sewn using patches of the blues, that the blues borrowed from country, which was made of Scottish, English and Irish folk. To elaborate the pattern further, there was nineteenth-century music hall and minstrelsy and "reels", to use Big Bill Broonzy's word. In the early part of his musical life, Big Bill told Studs Terkel on the record I played over and over at Saltoun Street, he hadn't known that he was playing "the blues". This music drew us all into a delicious melting pot.

It was said that Drew had been willing to pawn his Gibson in order to pay for Doc Watson's flight from the Carolinas to Glasgow, though I don't think Doc Watson ever came. Davey Graham, however, travelled from Notting Hill to the Folk Centre and on a Saturday night the small top-floor room in the Montrose Street tenement was packed with expectant cognoscenti. Davey clambered on to the stage, smartly dressed in black-and-white concert attire, eyes opaque, staring deep into his own self's numerous tribulations and exaltations. The lights went down, a hush descended, and he proceeded to chant and moan for forty-five minutes: "Nnnnawwawww, nnnnnaaaaaaahh-awwwo-o-o-o, nnnnnawwwwawwwwiio-o, a-a-a-a-aahhhhh, nnnnhhhhwww", running up and down mock-oriental scales all the while.

The Folk Centre crowd were unimpressed, not to say angry. Drew Moyes might have had to return some admission money, which had been increased for the occasion, to pay for Davey's fee and expenses. The evening took on a legendary status at the Scotia. Davey's veins shimmered satisfyingly with heroin, and the inward harmonies sounded sublime to his soul, which was pathetically unharmonious in everyday life when deprived of the narcotic; but what he sang was simply rubbish to the ears of the Folk Centre faithful. Nevertheless, I was sorry I missed him.

Every now and then, a group would set off for London in a packed van, barrelling down the A74 on to the A6, over Shap Fell, through the night, in search of work or a music gig. A single train ticket cost £6 – not far short of a week's wages for me at Washie's by that time. Or there would be an expedition to the Highlands, to pass a weekend in Glencoe among climbers and noisy students – anyone who seemed more posh than us was called a "student" – at the Clachaig Inn. I read the sign on the door: "No Hawkers or Campbells", which seemed to everyone a terrific joke. There was usually a tent to sleep in or, in winter, a caravan. At bedtime (there were no beds), we filled thick glass lemonade or screwtop beer bottles with boiled water to warm our feet. Once, I removed the bottle in the middle of the night when it had cooled, and in the morning found it frozen solid next to my head.

The Scotia had its resident poet, Freddie Anderson, an Irishman from County Monaghan, who sold his poems in broadsheets and pamphlets, placing the coins he received immediately on the bar for liquid exchange. We thought of diminutive, bearded Freddie as an elderly and odd chap, though he was friendly to all, but I realize now that his age at the time was around forty. His subject matter was socialist in intent. In his play, *Krassivy*, about the Scottish communist John MacLean, Freddie took the role of Lenin to whom he bore a shrivelled resemblance.

People at the Scotia seemed more knowledgeable about politics and more engaged with all manner of social affairs than I could possibly be. I didn't even know the name of the Prime Minister. My politics were intensely personal: they involved a lengthy domestic struggle, an industrial dispute in nineteenth-century working conditions, a property grab in the West End of Glasgow, and the price of bread and beer. Liberation came in the form of a wisp of a beatnik chick with a bewitching nonchalance, long black hair and heavy eye-makeup. Everyone knew her as Wee Jeannie. The nonchalance, it didn't take long to discover, was only a style.

There were other poets, with more romantic subject matter than Freddie, and a little later I would present myself as one of them. I also played for the Scotia football team on nearby Glasgow Green, and on a Saturday afternoon, in between lunchtime and evening sessions at the pub, scored a goal while Wee Jeannie looked coolly on from beneath her fringe. There were other girls at the Scotia: careful girls and careless girls, nice and not so nice girls – one I remember acted as a honey trap for punters, who would follow her up a close where they were beaten and robbed by her accomplices – girls who couldn't be persuaded and girls who couldn't persuade me.

And there were nice guys and not so nice guys. One of the latter asked one day: "You've got your own pad. Can we use it to fix up?" Before I could reply – probably in the affirmative – one of the nice guys stepped in. This was Coakie, whom I had first met in Edinburgh with Bruce some four years earlier, and who had introduced me not to heroin but to ban-the-bomb poetry and the perfect society envisaged by the Young Communist League. We had shared a brief friendship after our pioneering hitch-hiking trip home to Glasgow in the back of an open lorry. Until that moment I hadn't known, even since I had begun to see him again at the Scotia, that he was doing hard drugs. Now he scolded the one who had tried to enlist me, by association, into the junkie fellowship. "Shut yer mooth. Ye cannae ask the boy t'dae that."

IV

No one from Washie's ever accompanied me to the Scotia after work. They were separate worlds. I was being drawn from one, and pulled towards the other. Jeanette was right when she predicted that I wouldn't see it through to the end. It was in the summer of 1969 that I started going down that long lonesome road, nearly three years into my apprenticeship. A persistent cough and tightness in the chest led to a trip to the doctor's surgery in Hyndland, where I came across Billy Connolly sitting shyly in the waiting room. The doctor gave me two weeks off work, which led to another two and then another. I had not achieved the level of seniority that would entitle me to paid leave, so I applied for sickness benefit at the dole office – the burroo – the first of many encounters with one or other of those places.

After a month or two I was finding a way to live with my bronchitis, while becoming accustomed to a new style of life, perhaps the style I had always been aiming for: not idle – I never wanted that – but as master of my own time. The guitar was one part of my occupation, travel another – hitch-hiking to London with Wee Jeannie at my side, finding a day's work here or there; then to Dublin in the same way. In the July Fair Fortnight holiday, before my sick leave began, Jeannie and I had hitched up to Portmahomack, the great Campbell family holiday destination, and spread our tent out in a field, with the clear and thrilling sound of the North Sea in our night-time ears. We heated meals on a Primus stove and lay together in a sleeping bag on the ground, each dependent on the other's teenage softness for comfort.

There were firsts: we watched the first moon landing on July 20, 1969 – that is, we watched the moon as the astronauts were said to be landing, while we sauntered along the front at the Port, in sight of the massive tarry anchors and the jetty where Dad had once upon a time taken me fishing for flounders; it was my first visit to the Port without my parents and sisters; Jeannie and I made love for the first time in the tent in Inverness on the way home.

Taking sick leave was a way of prolonging this idyll. Life was more meaningful than it had ever been, with new discoveries at every flick of the calendar. I was getting used to being a state-sponsored pioneer. And who would dare to say I wasn't paying my own way? Hadn't I paid tax, as none of my student acquaintances had – starting at nine shillings a week (45 pence) and increasing – since October 3, 1966?

One day I went to the doctor's surgery to pick up my benefit note and saw a strange face behind the desk. Not the kindly, biddable female doctor, as usual, but a man I had never set eyes on before, bearded, bespectacled, brisk. What's the trouble here then? OK, let's have a listen to you. Pull your shirt up . . . Right . . . breathe in . . . now out . . . Right then . . . OK, shirt down. Everything sounds fine to me – *a little smirk* – you'll be glad to hear. Dressing a bit more warmly might help. Your present note runs out at the end of next week, and you can start back at work the following Monday.

Sitting down, head bent over the desk, silently scornful of my discomfiture.

"Tell me again the name and address of the place. Irvine or Irving, like the author?"

Other people I knew were being prescribed drugs by their GP: Mandies and black bombers. Yet others were said to receive forged prescriptions for methadone and even heroin. I didn't ask for anything like that. I wanted the doctor to prescribe Freedom. So far she would – women were usually on my side – and now he wouldn't.

I let Mr Alister know that I would be coming back to work, after some ten weeks away, ten weeks' worth of even longer hair than Mr David had been willing to tolerate, ten of the best weeks of my so-called adult life, a return to the primary-school holidays of the earliest years, which had been crowned by untethered adventures at the shepherd's cottage on Rockfield Farm and on the harbour and shore at the Port.

Mr Alister appeared unimpressed when I outlined the respiratory ailment and what my (original) doctor had told me about it, that it was likely to be the result of prolonged exposure to damp. My top-floor flat in Saltoun Street was watertight; at Washie's, rainwater sloshed around our feet when the skies opened. Upstairs on the second floor, under the roof, above the three-fingered cutter's head, there were tarpaulins in some places and broad brown swathes in others, as if someone had swept them on to the ceiling with a broom dipped in damp. In winter you could trace your breath indoors, while standing next to the moleskin blanket and cloth-covered pen carriages on the Shaw Pen Ruling Machine.

It was a pleasure to see Jesse and both Big and Wee Nancy again, to deflect Jeanette's sardonic remarks, as before, but a distance had already opened between us. I had left the back-to-front alphabet of the upstairs compositors' benches, to spell out a different life. I had found my present tense. No matter how brief my departure had been, it must have seemed to them pre-ordained: they knew from my way of speaking polite and from the sight of my father, who had turned up at the factory in his impressive hat and raincoat more than once, that I was only tarrying at this ancient contraption, in another century, with the smell of ox gall in the air. Sooner or later I would book my time-travel and go.

There was a dim whispering around Jeanette now, always involving Big Nancy, and it wasn't long before I discovered that it concerned the rupture of Jeanette's engagement to Michael Heaney. John closed his thin lips to it and turned his narrow, grey-overalled back. Mixed marriages were destined to go wrong. Even John could see that Michael had no badness in him, but a pape was still a pape.

Mary was more of a genial simpleton than ever, walking in her elegant step to the cludgie with greater regularity, but John's lips grew yet thinner as he understood that his apprentice was on his way out.

The tightness and wheezing in my chest came back a few days after my return to work. Jeannie sent me to the surgery again, where to my relief I found the woman doctor, who willingly signed another sick note. It couldn't go on. I told Mr

Alister that I would have to quit Washie's and renounce my paper ruler's apprenticeship. His response was just the same: the ailment I complained of had nothing to do with the damp which was visible on the ceilings and the floors of 48 Ingram Street.

I saw John Pollock only once after I had left Washington Irvine's. He was walking at a rapid pace down Buchanan Street in the direction of Central Station, as if in pursuit of some Catholic misspirit, or else in flight from a demon that was sucking nourishment from his insides at every step. He was too preoccupied to take notice of me.

One day in 1982, close to George Square, not far from Ingram Street, I saw Mary McIlwham at the centre of a company of convivial winos. She was half-dancing and asking selected passers-by for money, while the bottle passed from hand to hand – Lanliq or Four Crown – then from mouth to hand and back again. When it came my turn to stump up a few coins, I made a remark about Washie's, but Mary didn't catch it. She had voyaged too deeply into the land of Lanliq to recognize anyone from outside, including me. A dozen years had passed since my departure. In the battle raging in Mary's life between wine and Washie's, even in my day, there could only be one winner. A song started up and another joke caused waves of joviality as I turned away.

7

LIFE IN THE UNDERGROUND

I

My dad's university had been the Navy. Mine was the Scotia Bar. Tutors included a new friend, Jimmy Dunn, who arrived in my life trailing a legend behind him: he had hitch-hiked to Morocco and back, had eaten maajun with djellaba-draped nomads on the fringe of the Sahara – the hotter it gets, the heavier the clothes they wear, Jimmy said – and returned with tales of camels blocking the road, goats in trees, snake charmers enchanting the market square and prostrate donkeys hypnotized by storytellers.

Jimmy had long fair hair, a soft, pointed beard, and laughter lines darting from his eyes. He bore a passing resemblance to Robin Williamson, as much a style icon for us as Elvis Presley had been for a previous generation. Around his neck were strung odd beads and amulets bartered for on his travels. Others did the same, but Jimmy paced the track with an original gait. Only a year or two older than me, he was the first in a sequence of friends from whom I would absorb all the "learning" I could.

It wasn't street learning. It certainly wasn't academic, though Jimmy, who had left school at the same age as me, similarly unqualified, was knowledgeable about a surprising range of things. It was the kind of intimate education in which the teacher is unaware that the pupil is under his spell. After those mid-teen years of being closed off, I was suddenly open. The switch in direction was as rapid as a change of scenery in the theatre. The narrative development was classic and the outcome was the happy one. Here was the landlocked student. Over there, the instructive navigator. For me, there was homework aplenty. I was already in the elementary music class, trying to gain knowledge from elders such as the great West End guitar player Alan Tall. And now something else, a harbinger of benign climate change on planet Me: reading.

Jimmy gave me a library copy of *Of Mice and Men* and I read it over the course of an afternoon in my bedsit at Saltoun Street. After that, he passed on *Cannery Row*, *Sweet Thursday* and *Tortilla Flat*, fondly outlining the personalities I would find in Steinbeck's pages, and setting me off on an affair with American literature that has endured to the present day. Jimmy said that Mack and the boys in Cannery Row were bums, a bit like us. Anyone at the Scotia could have made that remark. What set Jimmy apart was that his favourite character in the novel wasn't a bum at all: it was Doc, the scientist and owner of Western Biological Laboratories. Jimmy saw himself in Doc, who reflected his own interests.

Doc's speciality was marine life; Jimmy's was the secret society of the Highland gateway woods near his home in Balloch, not far from Loch Lomond. As we walked there on different days, he identified bird calls and named wild flowers; he collected owl pellets and took them home, to his mother's affected disgust, to anatomize the feathery, bony, vomited contents. I was learning new words all the time, and that day I added "regurgitate" to the lexicon. He used advanced geographical terms to try to explain tides and winds, chronology and latitude, tropics and hemispheres. On other occasions I went to his parents' house in Balloch, which was connected by rail to Glasgow Queen Street, and we would hitch-hike up to Luss on the banks of the loch, passing the night in sleeping bags on the sandy shore.

Jimmy had a sister, Lorraine, younger than him but still too advanced for me – in maturity more than in years – who nevertheless accepted me. I was drawn to these big sister relationships. They confirmed me in a role which felt familiar: the younger brother. Lorraine was studying English and French at Glasgow University. It was a revelation – I was open to revelations – that her close friend Kate Reader had such a thing as a "favourite writer": Graham Greene. Since I was also open to influences, there was every chance that he might become my favourite writer, too.

Kate collected photographs of T. S. Eliot – another strange but alluring habit – and gave me a Faber paperback copy of his *Selected Poems*, which I still have. Its pages were full of mysteries, of a stimulating kind. She lived a little way outside Glasgow, in Eaglesham, and sometimes stayed over in my bedsit, sleeping next to me like another sister. On more than one occasion, the three of us, Kate, Lorraine and me, slept in my single bed – those two at the top, me at the foot – giggling our way into a sound sleep. Kate took away my T-shirts and jumpers to wash – one favourite green sweater, she let me know, had to be done twice over – and gave me firm instructions how to make my way to the nearest public baths. The three of us hitch-hiked up to Portmahomack during the Easter holidays – Kate and Lorraine, as "the twins", going ahead, me following on behind – and stayed in a tent by the North Sea, as Jeannie and I had done before.

On arrival, I learned that Uncle Willie had died. Although he lived at Rockfield Farm, two or three miles away, not in the Port itself, the place felt empty without him. He had told me he never took a holiday and as a child I had thought that logical. Why would he, living here, where he was on holiday all the time? I walked up the farm track to the shepherd's cottage to visit Aunt Mary, now blind. She put a hand against my cheek and felt my long hair. "Oh, you've got a beard, Jim!" There were tears as she recalled how I used to sit on his knee and go with him at dawn across the fields with Fly and Glen to tend the sheep. "He was a good man, Jim."

Eventually, I left to return to the Port.

Just go down to the road, Jim. You'll get a lift.

On this occasion, though, I didn't. My long hair and strange clothes had drawn a barrier between modern me and the reliable old Port customs. When the fishermen in the bar of the Castle Hotel were reminded that I was Ina Beveridge's boy, the faces brightened again.

Back in Glasgow, we occupied "The Room" of Jean Cocteau's novel *Les Enfants terribles*, sometimes staying up all night and sleeping until five in the afternoon. Cocteau: "The Room prolonged its rites into the small hours. This made for late awakenings." Elizabeth was the sister of Paul in the Room of Cocteau's novel, and Lorraine and Kate were the sisters of Jim in the mini-Room we created in the West End. It was the first stirring of a feeling that one could live in literature – not exclusively but in a parallel fashion; be bodily in a flat somewhere off Byres Road, yet inhabit another realm – not Paris itself, but the Paris of the story – in imagination. It was a prelude to, training for, the travels I was about to embark on.

Reading to oneself and out loud to others, talking about the ideas discovered there, could become a way of life. Sartre's plays, Camus's novels, Cocteau all over, as well as Eliot and Greene, were as much the currency of Kate and Lorraine's conversation as the lyrics of Neil Young and Jefferson Airplane made up that of others. In that life, I reckoned, I could glimpse a small space for me. Just a corner: but it was a corner of The Room.

If the ideas of these great writers were half-understood, at best, no matter. There were a lot of things I didn't understand. Had I been familiar with it at the time, I would have identified with the comment made by Robert Graves to Ava Gardner. According to the actress, she said, "You know, Robert, I really don't understand poetry." To which Graves replied: "My darling, you're not supposed to understand it, you're supposed to enjoy it."

It was a new language. It had to be learned, and I was in the act of learning it. Those who were fluent in the tongue were charmed at the efforts made by the outsider – *l'étranger* – to communicate. I had evidently not grown up in my family as a "literary type". In fact, I had been a shocking failure at everything concerning the life of the mind. I had had another life. But if the life of The Room could be transposed on to that one, without doing fatal damage to it, then I might find a way to live with myself, as myself.

Jimmy told me that before going to sleep at night he liked to read a little, and when he woke up in the morning, he read a little bit more, while still in bed. That way he got through a book in about a week.

I did as Jimmy did, and read every one of Steinbeck's novels – even the turgid tale of labour activism, *In Dubious Battle* – as well as his travel book, *Travels with Charley*, the companion being a dog. At Kate's urging, I plunged into D. H. Lawrence's novellas, then started on Graham Greene. Lorraine gave me *L'Etranger*, which I read in translation as *The Outsider*. She explained that it was Meursault's indifference to his mother's death that condemned him in the eyes of "society" – a concept that was quick currency in our conversations. From Camus to Cocteau is a giant step, yet they remain neighbours on my bookshelf, having entered my life in adjacent weeks and made similarly deep impressions.

From Stirling's Library in Royal Exchange Square – just down the road from Washie's – I borrowed books about the blues, in which rural singers talked about the music and about their lives: *Conversations with the Blues* by Paul Oliver and *The Country Blues* by Sam Charters. This opening up of cultural canals – to Greene's Africa, to Camus's Algeria, to Cocteau's Paris, to Big Bill's Mississippi Delta – was the most important event of my teenage life to date. It was enriching, and the cultural capital – counted in units of imaginative freedom – could only increase. Cultural wealth is a rare thing among investments: it is foolproof. It never decreases in value and it never lets you down.

II

I had officially left Washie's in September, 1969, three years into the six-year apprenticeship. I was still drawing sickness benefit, more or less commensurate with what my pay had been – in other words, very little. In one of our many pursuits of money, usually with the thought in mind of "going away", Jimmy and I fell in with a group of London-based freaks, of a seemingly superior tone to the native species. They were party to an aesthetic scam: mass-produced works of art, in acrylic or pastel, were taken round the houses in the middle-class suburbs of Glasgow and its environs. We posed as artists and the artworks posed as originals, by "members of our group".

It was a fiasco, as these things always were. (One evening, the door of a house on which I knocked was opened by Mr Washie, Washington Irvine himself.) But the young English men and women we met, while failing miserably to raise any money worth counting, were better educated than we were, more hip to the latest fashion in awareness, to the newest way to "be here now", or so it seemed to us at the time.

I had moved to yet another pad, at 3 Thornwood Avenue, off Dumbarton Road, well west of the university district, and an associate of the English gang came to stay for a couple of weeks. He remained in the room when I went to Glencoe with Jimmy Dunn – as I remained in the caravan while Jimmy attached his crampons and climbed a mountain – and was waiting there when I got back. We grilled sausages and deep-fried chipped potatoes and heated baked beans. I was puzzled by the amount of time he spent sleeping. Only later did I understand what was wrong: he was a druggie, with an uppers and downers habit. One minute he was bouncing around on black bombers, the next he was dead to the world on Mandrax. He had hidden the fact, and I was too naive to notice. At the time, I knew nothing about it.

Before this realization dawned, he proposed an exchange which appealed to me: I could go and live for some weeks in his apartment in London; meanwhile, he would continue to sleep in my room in Partick. While I was gone, he would pay my rent, £3 a week, delivered in person to the Pakistani landlord who lived a few streets away. As for the London place – no need. It was all taken care of.

I agreed enthusiastically.

It was no small event to go to London for a few weeks. People looked at you with new interest. So it was that Kate and Lorraine, Jimmy and others, assembled at the bus station one evening in early October to wish me luck, after a few rounds of drinks at the Scotia (my guest remained asleep in Thornwood

Avenue). The bus left from the station at the top of Buchanan Street at 10 pm and rolled through the short Scottish night into the long English early morning, arriving at Victoria Coach Station at 8 am. In my pocket, the address: 11 Queensway, right next to the Tube station and close to Notting Hill, dead centre of the counterculture. I don't remember receiving a single instruction about what to do once inside the flat – heating, bedding, towels, gadgets, gas and electricity – but I could sort all that out by myself. There was only one thing I needed to know: fetch the key from the neighbour at No. 9. No name, no gender, no nationality, just "the neighbour".

After a cup of milky tea with some charcoaled toast in a café at Victoria railway station, I went down to the Tube platform, to make my way to Queensway. I had been in London recently with Wee Jeannie. We had worked for a few days moving stock from one boutique to another, near Carnaby Street, so I didn't feel altogether like a country bumpkin from the north. Afterwards, we had sat in the pub at the corner of Carnaby and Marlborough Streets, watching the people passing by in an extravagant ballet of frill and flower and flair, listening to the symphony of otherworldly accents – English, mostly – conducted in what seemed a chorus of alien assurance. On the wall of an underpass at Piccadilly Circus I saw the spray-painted graffito: "Clapton is God".

That was some months earlier. Now I emerged from the elevator at Queensway station on to the street itself, a boulevard running north from Bayswater Road to Westbourne Grove, happy to feel the wash of another adventure making its way through me like a dye, its hue only heightened by my apprehension about the key. The first thing I saw, on the left, was a large plate with "No. 1 Queensway". A good start.

But there was nothing in sequence with the figures 9 or 11. At street level, the buildings were mostly shops and, as is often the case, the numbers were missing. I walked down Queensway, then back up. The numbers lacked the plain logic of a Glasgow street, which would go: 19, 17, 15 – skipping the unlucky 13 – landing safely at 11. Next door to that would be No. 9. Inside would be "the key".

But there was no door with a No. 11 plate screwed on to it. Nor was there any No. 9, behind which lived a helpful neighbour, pleased to receive news of our mutual acquaintance, fast asleep in Glasgow. In fact, there weren't even any likely-looking residential buildings. The only possible one was a six- or seven-storey modern apartment block, starting at first-floor level above the shops, which unfolded all the way down Queensway to Princess Court at the next corner. It was called Queen's Court, and the metal box to the side, with a battery of unfamiliar buzzers, told me that it contained flats numbered from 1 to 30. When a man of genial appearance emerged from the double doors, I asked what number of Queensway was Queen's Court.

"This is 15."

Together we looked to right and left. Logically, it should be two doors up, in the direction of the station entrance. But that was a baker's shop, helpfully open on Sunday morning. I inquired inside.

"*This* is No. 11."

"Eleven Queensway?"

The baker looked at me: just a bumpkin, after all. In a movie, he would have drawled, "What do you think, Fifth Avenue?" But we weren't in a movie, or not one that had any kind of comprehensible plot. Even the cast – the neighbour at No. 9 – had failed to turn up.

The helpful extra of a moment ago had likewise disappeared. Outside, I went back and forth, towards the Tube station in one direction and Princess Court in the other, at the next corner down, towards Westbourne Grove, trying to figure out an answer to the numerological problem.

Eventually, I returned to stand before the entrance to the block. It surely held the clue. And it was up to me to pose the question in such a way as to elicit the answer. Systems of house sequencing often presented riddles which revealed their solutions with sudden clarity. When another resident exited, I held the door, deflected her questioning expression with a polite smile, and entered. Up in the lift to the second floor, directed by a sign. The lift opened on to a row of doors. Let's see: 7 . . . 7A . . . 8 . . . 8A . . . 9! My new home, 11, was evidently on the next floor up.

I knocked on the door of No. 9. There was no response. After another knock and a wait of a few moments, a woman's head appeared round the edge of the door. It sized me up, a foreigner, with a stranger's regard. I smiled and tried to explain the situation. I mentioned my sleepy friend's name.

"*Eh?*"I couldn't see more than some tangled hair and a dressing-gowned shoulder. It was Sunday morning. She had never heard of him.

And the flat at No. 11? – keeping up the smile – nice boy – from Scotland – not some outlaw region, after all – pointing in the direction of the upper floor – was it occupied?

"*Eh?*"

"Do you know if someone lives there?"

She hadn't a clue. She didn't care. Her husband would be home soon. Goodbye.

No. 11, on the third floor, was not unoccupied in expectation of my arrival. In it lived an elderly man, also not English –

English people were foreign enough for me – but slightly more forthcoming. At least he was willing to reveal his full person in the doorway. It took a moment for him to grasp the nature of the problem. This wasn't 11 Queensway, he said. This was Queen's Court, No. 15. Eleven was just the number of the flat in the block. Queen's *Court*. Not 11 Queensway. Queen's Court. This was just his flat, with *that* number, in *this* block of flats. Not *way – court*. It wasn't 11 Queensway.

Where was 11 Queensway, then? A shrug, from foreigner to foreigner. He took a step out of the door into the corridor and looked at the floor, as if we might see the missing house there. To the left? Downstairs? Outside? No. I had looked everywhere. "There's a baker's shop there." This appeared to be news to him. My friend's name meant nothing. Should I try the door at No. 10? A hand gesture. As far as he was concerned the conversation was at an end. "Not this. This is not 11 Queensway."

I walked down the stairs and emerged into the street. After more searching, I had to conclude that the flat at No. 11 Queensway was a phantom. Had my friend – he was no longer my friend, obviously – chosen the number because he knew it belonged to a shop? It was 10.30 am on a Sunday in October. I had no return ticket and little money. I had had the intention of making my way in the capital, one way or another. What to do now?

There was a girl in Notting Hill, a member of the same group of English freaks that Jimmy and I had fallen in with, in the phoney artworks affair. She, too, had found that there wasn't any money to be made from the ridiculous scam, and had returned to London. It was she who had put into my head the idea of coming to stay for a while. Over a late-night drink (for me) and joint (for everybody else), to the sound of some far-out rock on the record player. So in a way she was expecting me.

I had been meaning to pay her a visit anyway, when I arrived, but it was going to be sooner than intended. She might not have anticipated the arrival of a new flatmate, but now there didn't seem much else I could do.

III

It wasn't far to Portobello Road. With the help of a few passers-by, I found my way to Powis Square and located a house number – one that actually existed. No one telephoned in those days. Her name was Allie. She opened the door to my ringing, with a cry of – what? pleasure? despair? – and listened to my tale.

"But it's obvious what to do. You must stay here!" Nice woman that she was, she managed to appear delighted to see me and welcomed me in. There was only one bed, a mattress on the floor, but that didn't appear to be a problem. I was used to sharing beds in Glasgow flats with Kate and other girls who were not my girlfriend. People sat around in rough circles drinking beer or tea or coffee, cracking jokes and singing songs, then crashed out. There weren't that many beds, so you took a cushioned surface wherever you found it, and sometimes the pillow next to you supported a friendly head, sometimes female, as often as not partly or fully clothed.

The famous market at Portobello Road was nearby, and Allie and I went there to look for a job for me. But although Allie knew lots of stallholders and much joshing conversation was made with curly-haired cockney men and warm-cheeked women in a multiplicity of scarves, I had no success in finding work.

In the evenings, and often in daytime as well, a procession of friends would arrive at Allie's place, hanging around for hours, smoking dope, drinking herbal teas, discussing macrobiotic diets and the horrors of straight ways of living. To each one, Allie told my story, and all looked on me with condescension and pity. What was he doing in London? "He's looking for a job," Allie answered.

People said – addressing Allie, mostly – that they liked my accent. "Scotland, yeah." Another drag on the joint. The word "beautiful" came into play. There would be some anecdote of driving in a rickety van to the Highlands where Gino from Camden or Lucy from Dorset had bought a beautiful cottage on a croft. Did I ever do crofting? No. I knew about share-cropping in the Deep South and picking cotton in the Mississippi Delta, but I had scarcely even heard of crofting. Did I wear a kilt? "Beautiful, man." I began to feel like a tartan doll. It was not the life of The Room.

One unforgettable event occurred when someone mentioned Davey Graham. He lived close by, apparently. *Davey Graham* – the very syllables had thrilling potential. I could hardly believe it. That would make it all worthwhile. If only I could pass Davey Graham in the street in Notting Hill, and return to tell the tale, my journey would be justified, my presence at the Scotia transformed, for however brief a period, from black-and-white to full colour. Allie pointed to one of her friends who had his arm crooked in anticipation of the circulating joint, and said that he knew Davey Graham well. The way they said "Davey Graham", in a certain tone, tailing off in the direction of the final sound, pronounced "Groy-im", made me feel that their respect did not match mine.

Still, here was someone who knew Davey Graham. "Really?"

A mouth opened. "Davey Graham owes me five bob." The mouth accepted the joint and sucked in a lungful.

Another voice: "Davey Graham's a fucking hopeless junkie." Dope was cool, but junk was not. Junk borrowed money and

Davey Graham, "midnight man", the source of the great 1960s flowering of folk and blues guitar technique. *Courtesy of Brian Shuel/Getty Images.*

didn't pay it back. Junk let everybody down. My mention of him as the greatest guitar-playing genius alive – his seniority placed him above even Bert Jansch – got a shrug or a yeah or a used-to-be.

A few days after my arrival, Allie said she had to go and visit Joy Farren to deliver a parcel. Did I want to come? Of course I did. I was eager to meet the denizens of this new planet. "I don't know if Mick will be there."

I had heard of Mick Farren, rock star bizarre (later one of the many editors of *International Times*, and later still a prolific novelist). He led an iconoclastic group called the Deviants. At music festivals, Mick Farren gathered together a band of free-music subversives, the White Panthers. They were more political than most of those on the freak scene, trailing an aura of violence. People reached for the word "heavy", as they did with junkies. It wasn't my thing, but the White Panthers had been known to protest against admission charges at music festivals, and tear down the fences so that those without tickets could enter free of charge. This I would be quite happy to take advantage of the following year at the Isle of Wight, while leaving the gross act of subversion to someone else – to Mick Farren, in fact.

The proto-punk sound of the Deviants was not to my taste at all – "I take some pills and go to bed / I might get lucky and wind up dead" – but they had a reputation nevertheless. They were famous Underground people, or at least he was. It was for this that I had entered this new ecosystem, to seek out remedies and serums, study obscure documents and codes of communication known only through rumour in the remote north.

The promise of the key to a flat that didn't exist might just have been a rite of passage, one that would lead through a non-existent door to a back-to-front "knowledge". Here I was, after all, barely arrived, and already I was keeping watch for Davey Graham on the street. Maybe I could save up and pay off his five-bob debt? And now I was about to meet a rock star with mammoth shades and afro-style hair. That Queensway flat – perhaps it was a good thing? My fortunes had turned. This would make it three tales to tell when I returned to Glasgow: first the phantom, then Davey (another phantom, since I hadn't seen him yet), and now a visit to Mick Farren's pad.

Allie and I walked over to Colville Road, just a few hundred yards from her place in Powis Square. Joy admitted us at the first-floor, then returned to her chair in a large living room, like a high-up member of the reigning royal family of Notting Hill, which, in fact, she was. She was wrapped from head to toe in a dress of black crinoline that caught the light and sharpened the splendid effect, with high collar and an ivory pin brooch at the neck such as your grandmother might have chosen. She was wearing little round granny glasses, too, the ironic fashion of the time. She couldn't have been more than twenty-five.

The Farrens had covered the walls of the high-ceilinged room with silk and cotton hangings. A four-part oriental folding screen stood in one corner, creating a mini-room within the larger one, with teasing vintage slips tossed purposefully over the top. There was a mirror with an elaborate frame positioned at a tilt on the floor, and a handsome wooden fireplace. Even though she was married to a monster – a marvellous monster, Mick – Joy remained a gracious figure. Her style was natural and pleasing. For half an hour or so, I enjoyed her not unfriendly talk, and through it all held to the thought that the event might climax with a glimpse of the deviant star.

"The new album's arrived!" Joy announced to Allie. Her conversation, like that of most people I had met so far, bypassed me, but on this occasion I didn't feel offended, as I had with the anti-Davey Graham lot. Mick would know Davey, surely. Inwardly, I overheard myself talking to him about the eclectic assemblage of tracks on Davey's great debut, *The Guitar Player*. He might invite me to come back to Colville Road to play a couple of Bert Jansch numbers.

Joy went to a pile on the floor that I had noticed from the corner of my eye but hadn't taken the measure of, and picked up an empty record sleeve. It was called simply *The Deviants 3*. On the cover was a lipsticked nun – a model, obviously – sucking an ice-lolly with a lascivious gleam in her eye. The title of the opening track was "Billy the Monster", which sounded just right. I could probably get to like the Deviants, even while ignoring their music. Photographs of Mick on the mantelpiece showed a man with Hendrix hair but a style of cockney stallholder menace in the face – I knew it was only a style and although it repelled me I was prepared at that moment to tolerate it – that Hendrix didn't have. He was wearing outrageous spectacles, a scowl, and of course flamboyant clothes.

Allie drew Joy's attention towards me for a moment and said: "He's a musician, too. His hero's Davey Graham."

"Davey owes Mick ten bob," Joy said.

After about an hour, we left, without seeing Mick.

Mick Farren of the Deviants and Joy, "high-up member of the reigning family of Notting Hill".

I stayed on at the Powis Square flat for another two weeks. As October looked towards November and bright autumn skies clouded over in preparation for winter, it became clear that Allie had had enough of me. I was broke. I had no desire to be her tartan-doll lover, as perhaps she had thought I would be. During my stay, she often expressed her horror of "straights", and although I didn't count myself as one I might have been seen that way after a fortnight's exposure under the glare of the far-out heads of Notting Hill. I had a Mum and Dad in High Wycombe. I had nice elder sisters now working as art teachers, and a little sister for whom I felt a deep protective love. Julie's own loves were ponies, children's television presenters with names like Wendy, and a boyish pop star called David something.

Where did all this fit into the deviant world that Mick and Joy and Allie were shaping? Not only had I not struggled free of the intolerable occident (another new word), emerging into the transcendental zones of India or Morocco, as several of Allie's friends had done, I had never even crossed the English Channel. I liked pubs and I bought my round. I venerated Davey Graham, but when it came my turn to bite into the maajun cake, I refused. Maybe I was a straight, too?

I moved out and went to stay at Blackheath where my sister Phyllis was living in a commune run on strict principles of equality and redistribution. Everyone's pay packet went into the pot and spending money was dispensed to each according to their needs. Under pressure from the communards to find a job, I started washing dishes in a café on Lewisham Road, at the foot of Blackheath Rise. The Turkish Cypriot manager wondered why the Scottish boy was in London and asked a question which pleased me as much as any compliment: "Police looking for you?" He paid me £9 a week, cash.

The words Mao and Maoist were spoken at the commune, which was mainly made up of Oxford and Cambridge graduates. There was a social-work element to it, too. They looked after drug addicts, ex-prisoners, malcontents of various kinds. Possessions belonging to the commune dwellers, such as cameras, were sometimes stolen from bedrooms – almost expected to be stolen, as no locks were permitted on the doors – and sold on the street or in rotten pubs for money to buy drugs. I attached myself to one of the less complicated figures, and he offered to give me a tattoo on my left wrist – an authentic prison tattoo, as I've happily told people ever since. No one could mistake me for a straight.

He had learned the art of tattooing while serving time in a borstal in Kent. First, sketch the desired pattern with a pen on the arm or other body part where it's wanted – the forehead was a favourite in the borstal, he told me – then take a decent-sized needle. Wrap thread around, close to the point, to create a tiny ball. Dip the threaded tip into a jar of Indian ink and jab hard into the skin of the tattooee, leaving a single black dot on the flesh. Repeat as necessary, until the pattern is complete.

In my case, it was some kind of fertility symbol or perhaps a letter from an ancient alphabet, a hieroglyph borrowed from the back sleeve of an Incredible String Band LP, or somewhere like that. I've never been quite sure. After several dozen painful stabs, we were done. Amazingly, I never suffered an infection or any other ill-effect. In mid-December, I returned to Glasgow with this and my various tales, souvenirs of a trip to London during the chilly autumn of love. Sharon Tate and four others had been murdered by members of the Charles Manson cult in August, three months before.

Word had got around that my flat-share friend had woken up, broken into the gas meter, taken all the money he could find, then departed with that and a few of my meagre possessions – *Blonde on Blonde, The 5000 Spirits or the Layers of the Onion* – leaving the door ajar. Some pals from the Scotia went to Thornwood Avenue and tidied up. The police were summoned by the landlord and one evening after I was settled back in, two plain-clothes men arrived from Partick police station.

My lack of guilt must have spoken for itself and I never heard from them again, but the landlord had understandably had enough of my tenancy and before long I was on the move once more, this time to a pleasant, central room, with a nice address: 1001 Sauchiehall Street. It was here, without making the connection to *Arabian Nights*, that Jimmy and I would drop acid at midnight and spend the early morning hours in the enchanted groves of Kelvinside Park.

There was a party to celebrate New Year at a house outside Glasgow at which Big Mick Broderick and other members of the Scotia crowd roared, laughed, hugged, kissed – as the bells tolled – drank and drank and drank, then sang and sang. Good morning, 1970. It was no longer the 1960s.

PART TWO

THE LAND OF AWAY

8

ISTANBUL AND SPETSAI

I

Only a twist of fate brought me to Greece, where I had never intended to be. My compass pointed in the other direction, towards the East. I was on my way to India – so I told everyone in Glasgow. My friend Dudley and I talked endlessly about travel, referred to as "going away". This one was "away" in Spain, where things were as cheap as you dared to imagine; that one in Morocco, a more feasible destination than the subcontinent, exotic none the less, where the world would represent itself beguilingly back to front. Everyone wanted to be going away to India, which had a mythical status in our imaginations and in our conversations. We knew little of the reality, drawing half-nourishment from crumbs scraped from black-jacketed Penguin Classics of the *Bhagavad Gita* and the *Upanishads*. Those few who managed it returned gently bearded, adorned with amulets, jangling with bracelets, encrusted with parables and riddles, telling tales of holy cows in the street and unholy bathers in the Ganges. They kept us spellbound in our bedsits, as joss sticks smothered the northern chill and familiar West of Scotland rain pelted the windows.

Most people Dudley and I knew lived in a single room or a shared flat, where they draped oriental hangings on the wall and positioned fat cushions on the floor. People could go for months without sitting on a chair. Bricks and planks were modelled into bookcases, housing Timothy Leary, Richard Alpert (*Be Here Now*), Richard Brautigan, Jeff Nuttall, anything by Khalil Gibran –

The Prophet was essential – the poems of Yevtushenko. No author was likely to outnumber Hermann Hesse: *Steppenwolf, Demian, Narcissus and Goldmund, Siddhartha* and, of course, *Journey to the East*. Perennially smiling people encountered in these rooms introduced new words to the language, such as *futon, kilim, chillum, soya*. Brown rice mixed together with vegetables *sautéd* – another one – with soya sauce, was stated with wistful certainty to satisfy most dietary requirements. Various sorts of brown bread were served, as foreign to our parents as green tea or Lebanese red. The word "uncool" was heard often, usually in reference to dress, bad temper, alcohol, meat and people over twenty-five.

Just the act of saying that I was going away – "To India?" . . . "To India . . . yeah . . ." – gave me pleasure, as if it were somehow a credit to me. At last, I would step up into that vagabond elite, the Kings of Away, who roamed the East. I might not yet have reached the place itself, where an inner initiation would automatically occur – a vacuuming of industrial Glasgow unmindfulness – but I had stated my intention. The quest was begun. News circulated: Jim's going to India. Far out.

I sought the advice of some well-known hippie elders, and everyone assured me it was possible. "Go via Germany, then through Austria. The Alps. *Man!* Yugoslavia could be a wee bit of a problem . . . Big Tam got his hair cut off at the border – of all people! . . . but after that you'll be in Bulgaria. It's straight on for Istanbul. Simple enough."

More simple than one dared to imagine. "Stay in Istanbul for at least a week. There's lots of hostels for heads. Then take a bus through Iran and Afghanistan. Bonn voy adge." The thought of the journey produced a kind of fear which I succeeded in repressing, but which remained like a dormant ailment. I wasn't going on a journey so much as taking a test.

I travelled without a rucksack; just a shoulder bag, which contained a sweater, an extra T-shirt, a copy of *Cain's Book* by Alexander Trocchi and another paperback or two. I had a towel, a toothbrush and a pair of sandshoes, elsewhere known as plimsolls. I remember with fondness a crew-neck sweater knitted out of green wool. Each morning, on whatever patch of grass I rose, I would roll up the sleeping bag, secure it at each end with a rope, then loop the rope from one side to the other to make a strap and sling it across my shoulder with the bag. Somewhere I might find a cup of coffee or tea. Hot water for face and hands was a luxury. In public lavatories I washed my plentiful hair with soap. From time to time I even washed the T-shirt. Then I did what I did best, my proper skill, my living: I stuck out my thumb.

So: starting from the ferry port at Ostend, first drink a Belgian beer – shockingly expensive, with a sharp, lemony foreign flavour and a vexing inch of lather on top – then find a place to crash. In the morning, buy some bread, cheese and ham. Next, seek out the right autoroute through Belgium, nudging past the Netherlands – though I found myself to my surprise one pleasant evening stranded in the border town of Arnheim – carrying on through Germany.

These were all good countries for hitch-hikers, and Germany was the best. Just keep travelling due south. After "east", "south" was the second most desirable direction. North and west you turned your back on. On my feet, the sandshoes or a pair of leather sandals of oriental design, with a hard coil for the big toe, a herald of India, bought in one of the incense-heavy head shops in Glasgow's university district. As a guide, a map of the most elementary kind (later I developed an obsession with maps and walking shoes). Most of the time, I depended on road signs: Cologne . . . Karlsruhe . . . Stuttgart . . . Salzburg . . . Zagreb . . . Sofia . . . Sometimes I overshot an *Ausfahrt* and had the driver to set me down at the next one, so as to hitch or walk back a few miles to pick up the proper connection. Whatever happened, I would find the way. Just go down to the road.

Occasionally, on this journey or another, a driver would ask: "Where are you going to sleep tonight?" and I would reply, "By the side of the road", and he would invite me to dine and to sleep at his home. By these acts of mostly disinterested kindness, on different journeys, I became more cosmopolitan. For three or four nights, I slept in a luxurious double bed at the home of a middle-aged couple at in the French foothills of the Pyrenees. Our consolation was mutual. Their son and daughter had recently left home and they were happy to pamper a Scottish boy who, for all his past delinquency, was ever-attentive to the ordinary courtesies instilled at home. In the daytime, I took the daughter's bicycle and explored high-hedged country roads.

Near Bologna, an American motorcyclist picked me up and positioned me on the pillion of his exciting machine, my arms around his waist, both of us unhelmeted. In the evening, after he had settled me in a small spare room with a single bed, he made a telephone call and then announced that we were going out to dinner at the home of an American friend, married to an Italian, "who looks rather well".

She was delightful and pleased to see this roadside straggler, but her beauty did not strike me as the sort that was generally advertised in advance. She served a pasta dish with an oil, garlic, tomato and anchovy sauce which I have tried unsuccessfully to emulate in the decades since. Then – just when I thought the meal was over – chicken drumsticks in their warm and crispy aromatic skin. Salad. Cheese. Dessert. Coffee. Nothing in the fabled East could be more exotic than this to a Glaswegian Southsider. I realized only when my American friend and I had parted the next day, after another thrilling bike ride to a convenient hitching place, that he had said of his compatriot's wife that she "cooks rather well".

When I was travelling through Germany with a girlfriend the year before, a muscular young man in a suave car brought the pair of us back to his flat in the centre of Dortmund. He told us he was a footballer, working his way up through the ranks at the local team, Borussia Dortmund. That was interesting. Otherwise, he was not, but we were pleased to be sitting under a safe roof in comfortable armchairs, sipping the famous German beer and nibbling slices of fatty sausage. Were we married? No, we were not. He smiled. Not to worry. There were two spare bedrooms. In the middle of the night his hold on his strict moral code slipped and he tried to climb in with Linda, something she told me when we were out and free and on the road again.

It was one of only a few occasions on which the offer of hospitality, or just of a lift from one town to the next, came with unstated sexual complication. I could usually get the signal and take steps to avoid it. My fearlessness was a twin to my naivety. It wasn't deep in the bone but it was useful. Therefore everything was possible and everything, in the end, was easy. I had no ambitions of the other kind: study, career, marriage, property, money. They existed in another land of away, a lower-case country, in the direction opposite to the one I was taking: west not East.

I reached Istanbul in an off-duty tourist coach, driven through Bulgaria by a crew of Turks. They already had a young Englishwoman and her obnoxious blond South African boyfriend as passengers. His contemptuous remarks about peasants working in the fields, as we zipped by, embarrassed her. The Turks took a dislike to me – perhaps because I didn't join in the backslapping and pidgin-English jokery – and as we approached Istanbul the portly South African gave me to understand that while he and his girlfriend were being guided by the hosts to a hotel, I was expected to get down as soon as we were inside the city boundaries. I was glad to be rid of them. I felt sorry for the girl, who seemed uncomfortable among the flashing-eyed Turks and the over-ebullient blond man.

Istanbul struck me straightaway as belonging in different zones of time and space from any other city I had been in. So this was the East. In tiny booths along the road leading to the centre, craftsmen of every imaginable kind – the micro kind – worked into the evening: cobblers tapping on their lasts, tailors stitching and sewing, barbers shaving, scribes attentive to dictation, watchmakers, metalworkers, heads looking up as I passed. Young men held hands in the street. A couple, two couples, three, surrounded me smilingly, as if greeting a sudden arrival from an outer atmosphere. At corners, elderly musicians with faces charting ancient topographies played on curvaceous instruments. Once, I took a borrowed guitar to accompany one of them. There was a crowd and everyone applauded when the young European with the long hair and the old turbaned Turk reached the end, but I blush now to think how it must have sounded.

"Stay in Istanbul for a week or so," the sage adventurers of Glasgow had advised. "Then take a bus to Tehran. It's amazingly cheap." At the hostel near the Blue Mosque at which I found a bed, I made inquiries about schedules and fares. Amazingly cheap turned out to be quite a lot – things always cost more than the estimates you heard in advance. I could manage, but it would leave me little money with which to carry on through Iran and Afghanistan to the mythic destination.

Take another bus when you arrive in Tehran, they had said, to get to the border. What kind of bus? Starting from where? Which border, anyway? There was no such thing as preparation for a journey of this kind. No one I knew ever opened a guide book or looked at a detailed map. It was travel by grapevine, by rumour, by good tip (or bad tip), finally by faith. I never considered the need for visas which, when required – information received from other hitchers only as I got close to passport control – could be obtained at the frontier. There was only *the road* and the instinct to get *there*, wherever there happened to be. It was Away.

I had recently read a story in the newspaper of two hitch-hikers disappearing in Afghanistan. My shallow-rooted fearlessness shuddered protestingly. The dormant ailment stirred. I would be completely broke by the time I got to India. I tried not to think about it – not thinking about things came naturally – and told myself that something would turn up.

And so something did, though not in the form expected.

II

One afternoon in Istanbul, at an orange-juice street stall, a middle-aged man in a short-sleeved shirt approached. He had the beak of a raptor and had eyed a long-haired young morsel. He was German. He said he was a lorry driver and he looked like one. "You are going to Tehran?" Yes. How did he know? "Because I made a guess. I see you with your friends in a café last evening. And I recognize the hair."

He put on a friendly look, but it failed to mask a shadow I can bring to mind even now. "If you want, I can take you to Tehran. I often help the young people." Hearing himself use the word "help" obliged him to smile. "I make the journey each two-week and I like the company. We are able, we can, to leave tomorrow."

This was captivating. The sound of it blotted out other sounds I ought to have paid attention to. A truck was preferable to a bus, any time. Faster, smoother, less crowded, more like hitching.

"You will have to pay me a little, but it will be less than the bus."

Pay? He named a sum, which he made me understand he wanted in advance.

Just then, I felt the fear again, but I banished it, to prevent other fears clustering round. Fear or fearlessness was a choice. Now was the moment: India or not? Do I commit myself in union to the person I claimed I wanted to be, a mariner of Away? Could I blend being and performance to create a single entity, emerging as "me"?

There could only be one answer. Already, at the orange-juice stall on that thronged but still half-Western street, on the near side of the Bosporus, I saw myself writing letters from an oriental café, curry smells on the heated air. I had heard that a café owner in Kabul or Delhi would pay a European to sit in the window, in order to attract other hip young folk. Imagine being paid just to be the person I was, or was becoming. "Dear (somebody-or-other), Yes, I've arrived in Delhi. It's something else, man. The food is far out . . . you can eat for just . . . the people are great . . . there's music tonight in a . . . did I tell you I played in the street in Istanbul? . . ." The script was being written even as I stood there facing my German.

People looked closely at us as they walked to and from the orange-juice stall. One man tried to engage us in a friendly manner – in Turkey people think it natural to talk to strangers – but the German kept his guard. Slightly hunched in his short sleeves, grey hair slicked back, grey face again unsmiling. I was a naïf, but my animal instincts sent messages urging me to attend to the vibration. The word "Tehran" exercised a pull in the other direction, the one to which I had pledged allegiance.

Yes, I said.

"You are going to need money in Iran. I can change for you on black market" – he pronounced it "on *black* market". Wasn't his main concern for my well-being, after all? We were travelling companions now. "The difference in value is –" he made a broadening gesture with two hands. "I get you good exchange." A shadow smile, a sage wink, a softening tone. "Don't worry."

The naïf went to the hostel to fetch his pitiful purse, then came back to the orange-juice stall to rejoin the driver, waiting patiently. Wasn't that a good sign? He took the money, then led me to an underground car park. Tomorrow – this was serious – nine. "Nine o' clock?" His head nodded once as his finger pointed to the concrete floor on which we stood. "You know where to come."

The next morning, I returned to the car park he had led me to – the precise spot – after taking custody of my banknotes. He stationed his truck there overnight, he said. I waited under the concrete structure, grey like him, for more than an hour. I had said farewell to my friends of the past ten days at the travellers' hostel, and accepted their blessings in English, American – that lonely guy I'd had a long conversation with about *The Dharma Bums* – Dutch and probably German as well. Now I had no choice but to go back, admit that I had been had, and hope my bed wasn't already taken. Angry? Not really. Humiliated and bewildered. And relieved. I kept that part secret.

I could now add a new performance to my repertoire: the one in which I told the tale of how I was prevented from reaching the East. No one could say it was only the fear that had kept me back. Who would travel these dangerous roads with just a few pounds in his threadbare pocket? I had instead been initiated into another caste, lower than that to which the high priests of Away belonged, but not without honour: the travellers who had been Ripped Off. "Did you hear about Jim? . . . Turkey? . . . Poor guy."

I hung around Istanbul a bit longer. I felt strangely free now. The back alleys seemed to be lit all the way along by one continuous sizzling grill, and I ate there with a young man from a town reassuringly close to my parents' home in High Wycombe. In the streets near Agia Sofia I met a French freak called Pierre whom I knew from Glasgow – encounters like these were surprisingly common occurrences in the Land of Away. Pierre was a close ally of Dudley's: extravagant, untrustworthy, explicitly attached to drugs and the petty crime they brought with them. We exchanged news and he offered consolation, but we didn't waste time on each other.

Then I was safely seated on a bus at last: but in the unmystical direction, back to the European frontier, a jolting four-hour journey from Istanbul to the border town of Ipsala. I stood for the first time in sight of the light blue and white, horizontally striped flag and an overhead sign saying "HELLAS", with the crescent moon and twinkling star of Turkey already behind me. A customs officer on the Greek side rummaged through my little bag without conviction and motioned me forward with a backward switch of the head. My naivety was my shield, as much as my passport. Soon I was in a VW campervan with a bunch of genial Americans heading south to Athens.

III

The prospect of returning to Scotland after just two or three weeks away, when friends had seen me off on a voyage expected to last six months or more, was too shameful to contemplate. But what to do? The money I had kept back from the con man would see me through another fortnight, not far beyond. In Athens, you could sleep in a hostel for the equivalent of about fifty pence a night, and I loved the tavernas, which were a riot of Mediterranean light and smells and shouts and clattering cutlery. But the most inexpensive bed or meal was still expensive to me.

One afternoon I was crossing Syntagma Square when a fellow at an outdoor café table signalled from about thirty yards away for me to come over.

A cup of coffee, a cigarette, a sign. "Girl wanted, to work on island with horses." He was a confident type, older than me – even people my own age seemed older to my eyes – heavily bearded, recognizably American.

He squinted behind the glasses. "You're from Scotland, right? . . . Glaz-gow?" He pronounced the second syllable to rhyme with "cow".

What did I say? Had he heard me chattering and exchanging stories with fellow travellers in a café on the same square the night before, as the thief in Istanbul had claimed to do?

"Your name's Jim Campbell?" It was posed as a question but stated with certainty.

Jerry Robock and his travelling companion Richard had spent the night on the floor of my bedsit in the West End a year before. Dudley and I had met them one evening as we roamed Kelvingrove Park. Now, when I was seated at the table in a café on Syntagma Square, we calculated that the anniversary of that encounter must be practically to the day.

Jerry had told us then that he intended to make his way to Israel. Richard wanted to set up a poetry magazine, publishing work not only in English but in German, in which he was fluent. For the time being, they were both students, which in America seemed to mean living a flexible, free life, with plenty of time to work as a guard on a ski slope in Oregon, or somewhere geographically indeterminate, earning the kind of money we never even talked about. They seldom hitch-hiked, but travelled on student rail passes – another mystery. They clutched copies of *Europe on $10 a Day*, which was meant to suggest a tight budget but was about five times what I permitted myself. Americans were different from us: bigger, with more assurance, more good humour, more information on how things operated, more know-how. We shared a language; that was all. We were more fluent in their dialect – learned from Dustin Hoffman, Bob Dylan, William Burroughs – than they could possibly be in ours. We liked and admired them – likeability was one of their main features – but as much as we understood their ways and habits, they were ignorant of ours.

In the park, Jerry had looked at Dudley. "And you two? Also studying?" Dudley answered yes. "At the university of life." It was uttered so spontaneously and earnestly that the travellers didn't think to laugh. The conversation went on amiably, with some mutually amusing linguistic interventions. Not Edin-*burg*: Edinburgh. Not *Lok* Lomond: loch.

"Where are you going to sleep tonight?" I asked. They looked at one another, then at us.

"In the park." Jerry gave what was already his familiar shrug. "It's not against the law?"

I sensed that it was likely to rain later. I also felt an unburdensome obligation to invite them to crash at my place. It was the etiquette of the day. They would have invited me. At any rate, they would now invite the next unsheltered body they encountered. One small brick in the construction of the new world.

We walked towards my latest pad, a red sandstone tenement building high up on Wilton Street, near the Botanical Gardens, where first of all Dudley and I introduced them to the Scottish-oriental music that was our speciality – he as percussionist, me on my DADDAD-tuned Harmony steel string. A kind of Caledonian raga. Then Dudley left to go home – he lived with his parents – while the rest of us settled down to sleep: me in my bed, my two new friends in their sleeping bags on the floor. In the morning, I offered them muesli and some herbal concoction to drink before they left for Queen Street Station, still practising how to say *Loch* Lomond. They were nice guys. I didn't think much more about them.

And so it turned out that in Athens, twelve months later, Jerry was able to place his own new-world brick on top of mine, stabilizing it. I recounted the sad story of the theft in Istanbul. He listened impassively, then, without seeming to consider it at all, said, "You want to take this job?" He indicated the sign.

"But it says 'Girl wanted'."

"Don't worry about that. We'll find a girl."

"I've never been on a horse."

The no-problem shrug. The squint. The half-smile. "We'll teach you."

For the next two and a half months, I became a horseman on Spetsai, an island grouped with others in the Saronic Gulf – Aegina, Poros, Hydra – about five hours by boat in those days from Piraeus. We did find "a girl" that afternoon, a pleasant young American, but she didn't take to the set-up and within a week had decided it wasn't for her. She was an experienced rider, however, and she offered me a couple of lessons. I mounted. I sat up straight. I held on. And throughout a summer's trotting, cantering and galloping, I never fell off.

I thought then, and I have thought often since, of my German lorry driver (if he ever did such a thing as drive a lorry), of how much I owe him, and of how his actions must have punished him – I was certainly not the first of his petty victims. Recently I read, in a novel by Françoise Sagan, words given to a character who has been sacked unjustly from his job and reacts without bitterness. "I have never lost anything from what I have given. It is what you steal from others that costs you dearly." (*Un peu de soleil dans l'eau froide*)

IV

We were employed by a local man, Takis Pareskevas: overfed, superficial, curt and arrogant in his dealings with the visitors from whom he made his living. He owned apartments on the island, which he rented to tourists, several sailing boats and speed boats, tennis courts I heard about but never saw, and the horses, of which we were the masters, Jerry and I. It was Takis who opened the discotheques on the island in idyllic places, where before there had only been tavernas; and Takis who closed down the old kafenia and put up neon signs saying "Bar". There is a Takis on every Greek island or resort to which foreigners are drawn, slowly spoiling the things the seekers claim to come in search of, and he is usually native born.

We were given a house in which to live, high up on the hill above the port, with a half-acre yard and five horses: Caesar and Romeo were Jerry's favourites. I chose Zorba to be mine, possibly because of Nikos Kazantzakis's novel, which was on sale at the harbourside kiosks in the chunky Faber paperback and was being passed around in dog-eared form. The others were Oliver and the endearing chestnut Rufus, with a touch of the mule.

Spetsai is a small island, oval-shaped, about 7 km long at its greatest stretch. Private cars were forbidden. It has a port town (Dapia) and no other villages. Up above the port there is a pine forest, through which one walks to reach the opposite shore on the island's south coast, stumbling over tortoises (American friends called them "turtles"). Aghia Anargyri is now a tourist spot, but then it was a more or less deserted cove, with just a whitewashed chapel, some frayed straw sunshades, and a makeshift café for refreshments, if desired by riders.

Leading the little posse out of Spetsai port, one passed the imposing English school, built in 1927, where, Jerry told me, the "leaders of the Greece of the future are educated". I learned its name later: the Anargyrios and Korgialenios School, modelled, so they said, on Eton.

Takis did not pay us any wages, as such. He presumed that the two-storey house on the hill, in full view of the Aegean and with a glimpse of neighbouring Hydra, was the best part of our reward. From each circling of the island with a tourist group, we were granted a small commission. For a full tour of four people on horseback, for example, the fee might be 350 drachmas. To Takis, who seemed scarcely ever to shift from his seat in the office by the port, went 300; to us, the remainder. We were sometimes three- or four-strong up at "the ranch", as Jerry liked to call it, but the commission stayed the same and was shared among the company. I had looked forward to the opportunity to earn some money. No matter how hard I worked, however, I remained in the same parlous state throughout my stay.

The house on the hill was splendid in its way. It lacked basic plumbing and electricity but we had lamps with canisters, and candles in reserve. On a gas-powered cooking ring, large stew pots simmered. None of the rooms had much furniture, though there was a proper bed in the living room, in which I slept, Jerry in the hammock hitched to the ceiling beams not far from me. Others kipped down wherever they could, sometimes outdoors. Dawn broke through the unshuttered window to the buzz of persistent flies. I might wake to find a body beside me

The house on the hill on Spetsai, "a glorious shell". The stepladder used to access the upper floor is seen at left. *Courtesy of Jerry Robock.*

that hadn't been there when I had lain down the night before. There was no interior staircase: the upper floor was reached by an unsteady wooden ladder perched against the wall outside, leading to a gaping window. No glass in any of the windows and no flushing toilet. The house was a shell, a glorious shell, overlooking the cerulean sea studded with ships and vague humps in the distance, islands large and small, inhabited or abandoned.

Each morning at about nine, we led the horses to the hay that was stored in an outbuilding, brushed them down, one after the other, then waxed the bridles and saddles. More than once I found a tick in my armpit, fattening itself on my blood. One of our gang at the time of the first discovery was brought up on a farm in the north of England and he knew straight away what to do: first sponge the armpit with vinegar, then pull out the capsule with tweezers. On the ground, the tick would dissolve in a red splotch: a blood brother.

Before leaving Glasgow, I had begun writing a novel and had brought the notes with me. In a café or in the sociable hostel in Istanbul, I continued with it, and now, in the more tranquil interior of the hilltop house, I covered a page or two every other day. It wasn't a novel in the ordinary sense, rather a series of experimental philosophical reflections. My lessons in The Room with Kate and Lorraine, or at the Scotia, or by the midnight shore of Loch Lomond on the way to Glencoe with Lorraine's brother Jimmy, had given me an education and a vocation.

The writings had not yet gained a title. There was, at this stage, no main character or anything of that sort, just a first-person truth-teller whose enigmatic parables were mixed together with naturalistic incident, some of it now based on life at the ranch. There was "the hangman" and there was "the deserter". Just as my imagination wished to draw my feet to the nebulous Land of Away, so my pen was guided by the gravitational pull of epigram and paradox.

The model for the work was *Cain's Book*. Alexander Trocchi's best-known novel – though it was only barely a novel – was originally published in New York in 1959. When a friend in Glasgow gave it to me to read, I was electrified. Even the title had something extra, some glow, that the titles of other books did not possess. "Cain's Book": the book left out of the Bible. The book of the Pariah dog, the un-Chosen. Trocchi lived on the extreme margin of society, and would have liked to go farther out than that. For me, the book itself became a kind of Bible, something to believe in, to adhere to and act by. Other books were measured against it, and found lacking.

– What the hell am I doing here?
At certain moments I find myself looking on my whole life as leading up to the present moment, the present being all I have to affirm. It's somehow undignified to speak of the past or to think about the future. I don't seriously occupy myself with the question in the "here-and-now," lying on my bunk and, under the influence of heroin, inviolable . . . One is no longer grotesquely involved in the becoming. One simply is.

The author's hollow-cheeked face stared at you from beneath bushy brows on the cover of John Calder's Jupiter Books edition: an inverted prophet, a Glasgow hard man protesting against social constraints not of his making; wise, tough, *against*. It was the seduction I was ready for.

V

On Spetsai, we had several clients who came regularly to ride their favourite horses, including two Greek girls of about fifteen or sixteen. One, very pretty and already well groomed, always chose Romeo, perhaps because he flattered her self-image. The other, Lia, was not so pretty in the simple sense but full of humour and wit, with freckles and a thatch of straw-coloured hair. We liked them both and treated both well. Lia had the eagerness of a girl from an adventure story. I wrote her into one of the more realistic sections of the book.

"Tell me something happy," I said, "and then something sad." It was almost midnight. We clambered down the rocky path, touching our way with our feet, not wishing to walk too hurriedly or to leave one another's company but bound to fit her mother's deadline for return. It was her last night on the island, thus the permission to visit the farmhouse for dinner and the extended time limit.

She sighed heavily. "I won't tell you about my parents – they are divorced, you see – that's much too complicated." Silence. "Well, there was a boy –"

"Ah," I said, lightly mocking.

"Yes, I know," she replied quietly, "there is always 'a boy'. Anyhow there was this boy – a Greek boy – I met him on another island. I wanted to make love to him but he wouldn't. He said I was too young and that we must wait."

We broke out of the maze of streets on to the seafront. Despite the lateness of the hour people were dining on balconies which overlook the sea. I watched the moonlight spin across the water.

Lia always wanted Caesar, the most wilful horse in the stable. Riding fast excited her, she told me in the earnest tone she adopted for almost everything she spoke about. Normally, the girls' parents paid us at the end of the week, or else the riders brought the cash themselves for each tour, but when they had passed their pocket-money limit and came up the hill to the ranch together with hopeful expressions on their golden faces, Jerry let them get up for free if business was slow. He was the boss around the farm, and an easy-going one.

At about seven o'clock each evening, we went down to Takis's office with the takings for the day. While we stood by his desk, he remained seated, counting the money and checking it carefully against the bookings. Then he would hand over our small commission. He didn't interfere with our lives otherwise, only repeating two things: "Don't touch Greek girls" and "Don't forget to feed the horses."

Jerry used the word "lecherous" about him, the first time I had heard it. There were many words and phrases I was hearing or reading for the first time, some of them in *Cain's Book*. Its diction was more exciting to me than its tender descriptions of drug-induced states. "The present being all I have to affirm." I could never have written a sentence like that, simple as it was. Or selected "inviolable" in the way that Trocchi did. A partial list from my increasing vocabulary might go: *propitious*, *adventitious*, *impracticable* (not impractical), *in abeyance*, *innate*, *perspicacious* . . . Sometimes I would write them down – *distaff*, *gimcrack*, *erstwhile* – checking in a dictionary when I found one, or else asking Jerry.

If we had arrived on horseback in Dapia straight from the final tour of the day, we would get back in the saddle after our duties with Takis were fulfilled, then ride uphill to the ranch in the gentling heat to feed the horses, drawing glances and greetings from locals and visitors. We were "a sight", and we enjoyed being figures in a romance of our own making. With the horses unsaddled and fed, we would sit on the plank-and-brick bench outside the door in the remaining light, trading tales of home or Away. Later in the evening, we might all walk downhill, through town and past the English school to the strip of beach where tavernas perched on stilts, around the ankles of which sea water lapped sweetly. It was easy to spend the meagre commission from a day's work, in view of moussaka, fasolakia – the green beans in tomato sauce that I particularly liked – kalamari, and one orange tin jug after another of retsina, ordered by kilo or half-kilo, rather than by litre. As a result, in spite of all my efforts, I was no less broke than before.

When the end of August arrived, the holidaymakers thinned out and business slowed down. Our groups of friends moved on to other islands or began to talk about going back to college in the States, where it seemed they mostly studied subjects to do with sociology, business or film, seldom sat exams, and were already planning more time off to pursue adventures that were bound to be costly. Where did they get the money? Jerry shrugged. "They get loans. Their parents help them. They can get jobs and save." It was as much a foreign language to me as the language heard in the kitchen of the taverna when we went inside to relish the evening dishes before giving our order.

One day, Jerry announced his intention to leave. His friend Barbara had arrived by aeroplane from New York. She wanted to see some sites of antiquity, which Jerry named but which I hardly recognized. There was another American girl at the ranch – not my girl friend, nor a worker, just someone grateful for a roof above her head – who also wanted to leave. Who was going to do the work? What would happen with the horses? What was

I going to do? I had been away from Scotland for so long that any nagging remnants of homesickness had evaporated. I had no definite desires. Anything positive would have demanded a budget. I would be what I always was, a mast leaning with the wind. Just as mild breezes had carried me safely from coast to heavenly coast, an ill wind like this one left me grounded.

We were having this conversation on the brick-and-plank bench outside the front door of the house. Jerry squinted behind his tinted glasses in the afternoon sunlight. His black hair was drawn back in a pony tail and he had kept his bushy beard all summer. He was only a year or two older than me, but seemed at times to belong to a different generation. In between our first encounter in Glasgow and the unexpected reunion in Syntagma Square, he had fulfilled his stated ambition of going to Israel, which he talked about with subdued pleasure in his characteristic, even tone.

Me on Zorba, leading a pair of riders into town after a tour of the island. *Courtesy of Jerry Robock.*

Heading back to the ranch on Spetsai, with Carl (left), and Oliver, Romeo, Caesar and Zorba. *Courtesy of Jerry Robock.*

"You could go to Kibbutz Mishmarot for the rest of the season and live there . . . work there. It's not autumn yet, but soon they'll want people to help bring in the avocado harvest. They won't pay you anything, or not much, but you can live for free. Get all your food and a place to sleep. Interesting experience. Why not?"

Why? Because Israel is separated from Europe by the Mediterranean. I made that or some other petulant comment. "It's difficult to hitch-hike across the sea."

Jerry said nothing more about it. One of the horses needed a new shoe and we took him down to the port to be shod by a man in a Stetson hat and leather boots with decorative stitching, into which he tucked his trousers. We knew him as Black Bart. While Bart hammered in the nails, Jerry cupped the upright hoof in both hands, his back pressed against the horse's rear haunch, as if he had been doing this kind of thing all his life.

Jerry helping Black Bart, the local blacksmith. *Courtesy of Jerry Robock.*

The next morning, after we had brushed down Caesar, Zorba and the others, Jerry told me he had been thinking about my situation and was going to suggest something to help me get off the island and make my way to Israel.

"Quite a few people haven't settled their accounts for some days", he said. "That Greek girl, for example, Lia's friend, who rides Romeo, you know the one . . ." Of course I did: her beautiful face and bobbed hair consoled me during lonely nights at the shell. *Don't touch Greek girls.* ". . . her parents owe us", Jerry was saying, ". . . probably a decent sum. Then there's this one and that one. Friday's going to be a busy day, with several rides, starting early. Barbara wants us to split at the weekend – but I haven't said anything about it yet to Takis."

He looked at me for a moment fixedly in the silence before going on. "Saturday evening, we can ask a fisherman to take us in his boat to the other side." From the harbour in Spetsai to the mainland coast of Sparta was a short distance. "Then we can all hitch up to Athens the next morning. We travel in pairs and meet there. You can buy a ticket for Tel Aviv from one of the travel agencies."

I had been in every country in Europe and had placed a sandalled foot in Asia, but had never passed through the doorway of a travel agency.

"Don't worry about the price. You'll have enough."

At the end of the week, we collected the outstanding money. I remember the look of surprise on the Romeo girl's face when I told her that Takis wanted to bring the accounts up to date. Could she ask her father about it and let me have it by five? Her name has disappeared from my memory but not the puzzlement that shaded her features, before they lightened beautifully again and she said, "Of course" with the soft Greek "f" and "s" which added to her charm. My charm that day was of a different kind. I knew it but kept the knowledge hidden from myself, or tried to.

On Saturday evening, as the sun bedded down beyond the Peloponnese, we packed our bags – a task that took about ten minutes in my case – said goodbye to Romeo, Zorba, Oliver, Caesar and Rufus, and went to an apartment being rented (from Takis, of course) by some friends we had met at the harbour café. Jerry had arranged the evening voyage out with a local fisherman, who was naturally unaware of the nature of our scheme. We left a note behind at the house for Takis. "Don't forget to feed the horses." Someone suggested adding, "Don't touch Greek girls", but that would have been going too far. Jerry might have scribbled some kind of philosophical justification for our action.

It was already dark. At the smaller of the two jetties that defined the harbour, we climbed aboard the fishing boat, settling down as the leather-faced captain gave the engine cord a sharp tug. Half an hour later, we disembarked on the mainland, near a village called Kostas. After Jerry had settled up and we had thanked him individually, the fisherman made a 180 degree turn and bobbed back to Spetsai.

In my pocket there was enough money for a ticket to Tel Aviv; in my head, the excitement of a new adventure about to begin; in my breast, an unwelcome grumbling. Takis had exploited us, no doubt about it, and the money represented only a kind of tail-end grab-back of what we had earned and passed to him over many weeks. But we had accepted the job on the terms he offered, frankly and explicitly. Coarse as he was, he had never shown us any deliberate unkindness. Underneath the hilarity that rang around our evening table at the taverna on the Spartan coast flowed an uneasy current.

The next day, we set off for Athens, hitch-hiking in pairs. Once in the city, the young woman from LA who had been my travelling partner said goodbye. I had made a plan to rendezvous with Jerry and Barbara at the same café in Syntagma Square where I had met Jerry by accident almost three months before. "There would be a nice symmetry in that," Jerry had said. (I jotted down the word "symmetry".) At the travel agency, he talked to the woman at the counter in his worldly way and reserved a place for me on a flight to Tel Aviv that same evening – my first time in the air. Then he gave me what was left of the money, not a large sum. Maybe he even added a few bills from his own fold.

"You live for free on the kibbutz," he said. "After that . . . something will turn up."

He outlined directions on how to find the bus station in the centre of Tel Aviv, told me which number of bus to take to Kibbutz Mishmarot, where to get off, to walk about a mile down the little road to the kibbutz and to ask for a woman called Tirza.

"She'll know my name. Give her my regards."

After saying goodbye to him and Barbara, I walked towards a park where I could sit and read while waiting for the bus to take me to the airport. The plane was scheduled to arrive in Tel Aviv in the early hours of the morning. When I turned again to give a last wave of the hand, Jerry and Barbara had vanished. A Greek policeman who had appeared at the corner paid me no heed.

9

KIBBUTZ PHILOSOPHY

I

The flight from Athens began its descent to Tel Aviv at just after three in the morning on September 4, 1972, my first trip at 33,000 feet. When all the passengers had disembarked and filed through passport control, I wandered out of Arrivals into a field, together with a French girl I had met on board. We slept together, soundly and chastely, in a single sleeping bag, without attracting the attention of police or military, until woken by the overhead roar of morning flights.

We parted at the bus station in the centre of the city. Jerry's instructions were to seek a bus going to Haifa, which would drop me within walking distance of Kibbutz Mishmarot. Get off. Just go down to the road. Once there, ask for Tirza.

When the driver let me down, I obeyed a sign with the name of the kibbutz in both Hebrew and English and an arrow pointing towards a slight incline away from the main road. After half a mile, the parched red ground gave way to moist, green terrain, freshened by sprinklers. There were no guards in view as I approached the settlement, no protective fence, only a semi-circular row of neat houses and an assortment of farm and family vehicles. People were moving about in the distance. I asked a woman who regarded me quizzically about Tirza.

"I am Tirza," she said. I told her I had arrived overnight from Athens. The name Jerry Robock was mentioned. An unsmiling nod. I said I had come to work on the kibbutz.

Tirza's interested look changed into something I now

suppose to have been restrained incredulity. New arrivals were required to apply through the agency in Tel Aviv, she said, which would assign them to kibbutzim that had registered requests for foreign workers. This one had not applied for any. Her English was practically faultless. "You can't just come out here."

A flesh-and-blood refutation of that statement stood before her.

"But now you're here." The magic word "Jerry" had charmed her, after all. I was accepted for volunteer duties, with the advice, somewhat sternly administered, that tomorrow I should find a job.

On the way to the volunteer quarters, Tirza stopped to speak to a tall, fair-haired Canadian, whom she asked to take me in hand. My fugitive status was outlined and she left me in his care. Where was I from? Where had I been? Was Scotland beautiful? Was I going back to school? The usual questions, no less congenial for that. I was assigned a bunk in a concrete row of two-bed rooms, shown the communal lavatories and showers, told where to find a towel and bedding, and given other bits of friendly advice.

My roommate was a stocky Italian who spouted jets of operatic melody at the end of every other sentence. The first Israeli food I tasted was a grape from a huge bunch he extended, of a richness unsuspected in the West of Scotland. The helpful Canadian, Gordon, pointed out the kibbutz office, told me to go there in the afternoon, say that Tirza had accepted me, and that I would like a job. I would be given cigarette coupons. If I didn't smoke, take them anyway and do an exchange with someone else for beer or candy coupons.

"If you're looking for an alibi this afternoon, you can help me dig this trench. Show willing and all that." He shrugged.

"It's a job."

An unpaid job. A tiny financial recompense was dispensed at the end of each week. My two months and more of service on Kibbutz Mishmarot gave me sun, some expertise, such as driving a tractor and managing irrigation systems, bed and bread – but next to nothing of the other sort of bread. For visits to Jerusalem and Tel Aviv over the next ten weeks, I had to rely on coupon exchange and the good will of fellow volunteers, chiefly Dennis, a yellow cab driver from Flushing, New York, with the spirit of the city ripe in every friendly fake snarl and funky joke and gesture. Like me, he had no studies to return to at the end of September, and he planned to remain in Israel as long as he could. Eventually, he married a girl from the kibbutz and became a member.

Kibbutz Mishmarot was relatively small, with about eighty full-time inhabitants. Most were second or third-generation Israelis, with some recent arrivals from Russia and South America. There were a few American members, and a group of black Moroccan Jews who lived a separate life and moved to the beat of another metronome.

Among the twenty or so volunteers were Olivier from just north of Paris, and Peter, a rock-music dropout from east London, the only Englishman. Most were North Americans. A sharp-talking woman from Chicago was called Blair. There was an angular Dutch girl and a couple from Argentina. Gordon was Scottish on his paternal grandfather's side, he said, which accounted for his Celtic features and fair hair, but felt fully Jewish. I was one of only two gentiles on the kibbutz, a detail never mentioned in my presence. Yet we were in Israel, sure enough. The bloody interlude of the Munich Olympics brought us together round a transistor radio during my first few days in the country. Eleven Israeli athletes were taken hostage and murdered by a group of Palestinian militants known as the Black September Organization. The atrocity bound the volunteers together, creating a bond between them (the Americans, especially) and the Israelis.

Among the kibbutzniks were many army veterans, women included, some of whom had been active in the Six-Day War in 1967. They had an aura, as if lit from a different angle. At intervals on the road stretching all the way from Tel Aviv to Haifa, male and female soldiers waited for lifts.

Maybe I could hitch-hike to Tel Aviv?

"Don't even think about it."

"Unless you're in uniform."

"Don't worry."

"Buses are cheap."

People always said that.

II

About three years before leaving Glasgow, I had seen Fleetwood Mac playing at Green's Playhouse in Glasgow, a roomy cinema in the centre of the city that doubled as a concert hall. They were known as Peter Green's Fleetwood Mac at the time, after the founder. They were the leading proponents of the white electric blues, and Peter Green was one of the three recognized kings of the genre. Some connoisseurs elected him to the highest seat, ahead of Eric Clapton and Jeff Beck. "Clapton is God" said the graffiti, which is rather crude; Peter was "the Green God", which made some kind of pleasant sense.

I preferred the unamplified music that had formed the backing track to my post-King's Park Secondary life: country blues. My heroes were the black troubadours of the Mississippi Delta of the 1920s and 30s – I had only recently learned what "Delta" stood for – and the young virtuoso British folk-blues players. The supremacy of Bert Jansch remained, a youthful indoctrination. Neil Young had called him the Jimi Hendrix of the acoustic guitar. Not to me. Hendrix as the Bert Jansch of the electric, perhaps.

Even so, Peter Green was a star, and the concert at the Playhouse on Renfield Street stayed in my mind. I can still conjure up fragments of the spectacle: the lighting, the deep-lying pulse of the electrified blues, the yearning in the dark-hued voice of Green the singer. At the close, after an encore – maybe "Black Magic Woman", the rousing favourite kept till last – the black-haired, bearded Green embraced the second lead guitarist, Danny Kirwan, his opposite in looks, fair and soft-skinned. "My blues brother!" Green looked joyous. "You are the best audience *in the world!*" We were thrilled.

I had been on the kibbutz for about a month when Dennis approached me after lunch one day in the kitchen, where I was doing the washing-up for a hundred diners. He was in a state of excitement, as he often was, sometimes over something as trivial as receiving a packet of razor blades through the mail from his mother in Florida. This time, the current was so vivid it seemed it might lift him off the floor. A new girl had arrived. "A fox, Jimmy." Dennis rubbed his hands in uncontainable delight. "A FOX!" I remember the word because it was the first time I had heard it used like that.

Later in the afternoon, I caught sight of her from a distance: long black hair, beautiful in the beau-monde manner, dressed in a stylish skirt, top and heels. Just the thing for our little company, I said to myself. Then, as usual, I took my guitar and began to play my open-tuning Scottish-oriental raga, which could last for half an hour or more. Evenings were long on the kibbutz. A single television set served all, in a bleak community viewing room to which I never wished to go, even when the film being shown was in English. There was one gramophone, locked away and requiring permission to listen to the scratchy old discs in faded paper sleeves that were stored with it. There was no such thing as a café or bar. I had bought this light and wiry guitar in Athens for the equivalent of a few pounds. It had given us some entertainment up at the ranch on Spetsai during the summer, and now it amused me – if not all my fellow kibbutzniks – into the autumn.

In the middle of the night, after I saw the fox for the first and only time, I was awakened by a grand commotion. When the sun rose, she was already gone.

"What was that all about?" I asked Dennis on the tractor, as we bumped along towards the avocado fields.

"Who knows? Something to do with Peter, I think."

On first arriving, a short time after me, Peter had sat apart from the rest of the volunteers in the *heder ochel*, the dining room. He wasn't part of our doorstep congregations in the evenings, when we talked about the atrocity in Munich, the chances of Nixon's re-election in November, trips to Amsterdam or Florence or Rhodes that people had made before coming here. The lousy youth hostels. The great trains. Meat-eaters vs vegetarians. I read all the books that were lying around, and people were starting to use me as a library. Peter was clean-shaven with medium-length black curly hair and a long, sad face. For days on end, he might talk to no one, except Dennis, who found a way to talk to everyone. Dennis reported back, calling Peter a secretive type. "Kinda private."

Nevertheless, the kibbutz was a limited space, without much to do during the looming free hours after work, and soon Peter turned up to one of our groupings. Little by little, he grew more sociable. If you lasted long enough on the kibbutz, you could, when somebody left, take possession of one of the small cabins that stood on what we called Desolation Row, overlooking a line of eucalyptus trees. I had moved into one about a fortnight after arriving, and when the cabin next to it became vacant, Peter took up residence. They were good places, those cabins, and Peter was a good neighbour.

In the evenings, I would play my raga outside my door, as usual, and soon Peter took to accompanying me on a pair of Moroccan drums. We became an "act".

There was sadness all around him, even in his sense of humour. He had not expected or wanted to see the fox, who had followed him here from some other country. He told me that he hoped to meet a maternal woman on the kibbutz, "with big hips for child bearing", which was an unusual thing for someone to say.

One evening as we prepared for a party, Peter unfolded a new T-shirt. "We might meet our future wives tonight," he said in his east London voice – "moight" and "woives". The seven o'clock October air was sweet and caressing. Peter stood before the door of his cabin with a broad smile, showing off the crisp garment. No, not that particular night.

He had a sharpness of wit, and a strong intelligence without the interference of intellectualism. He never read books, never talked on the subjects of art or music, or about global politics, as the rest of us did in our evening parliaments. He expressed solidarity with the Palestinians, which took some volunteers aback, especially the Americans. He could be sardonic, if not unkind. One afternoon when we were in the shower, after our

Dennis, left, and fellow volunteers at Kibbutz Mishmarot, with the cabins of Desolation Row behind.

return from the fields, I sang a song in French. At the end Peter said, in a dry tone, "Very *good*, Jim." He had picked up on my showing off and didn't hesitate to let me know.

One lunchtime, a rumour circulated in the *heder ochel*. It was Dennis, naturally, who spoke the first word. Could it be possible? We were aware that Peter Green was the invisible man of rock and roll. The case was well known. "He was working as a grave digger," I said, a detail I had picked up from one of the music magazines at a time between the Green's Playhouse concert and the present. "After that? Who knows?" How to discover the truth? We could of course just ask, but no one wanted to be tactless.

It was me who came up with a way of finding out. I recalled another magazine article, which reported that Peter Green of Fleetwood Mac had a small, handmade tattoo on his forearm, in the form of a cross. The fact stuck in my mind because of the similar tattoo on my left wrist, imprinted by the ex-borstal boy in my sister's Blackheath commune in 1969. I told Dennis about it, and said I would probably be able to confirm by breakfast.

So, next morning, we drove out to the avocado fields as usual, three or four kilometres from the cabins. On the way, if you were lucky, you caught the metallic blue of a kingfisher as it flashed over the surface of a canal, or you might grip an orange from a tree without needing to brake. We stepped down from the tractor and set about the task of reorganizing the irrigation pipes, unlocking the fifteen-foot-long aluminium sections, then moving them, piece by piece, to lie between adjacent rows of trees. There, they would be locked back together again. This was done every day or every other day. When the moment came to twist the tap and turn on the water, it was a joy to walk through an avenue of rainbow spray as the sun came up. By 7 am, it was already hot.

Right, Pete. Sleeves up. Let's get on with it.

And there it was: a small cross on the forearm.

Later in the day, while we were taking a walk around the kibbutz in the settling dusk, I put the question to him, and he replied simply, "Yeah." The rock industry had sickened him, he said. After distributing his money among various causes, including a charity for Biafran war orphans, saving only £80 for himself, he had given away his guitars to friends. He kept one: a favourite Fender Stratocaster, which was at his parents' home in Bethnal Green. He didn't want to receive royalties from his songs, some of which had been enormous hits: "Black Magic Woman", "Save Your Love for Me", "Albatross", "Man of the World". One member of the group, Jeremy Spencer, had simply walked out one day and disappeared – into a religious commune in Los Angeles, or into the jungle, or on to the moon. "Not surprising," Peter said.

His blues brother, Danny Kirwan, would later leave the group and be seen living as an addict on the London streets.

We had made a circuit of the kibbutz fringe and now were walking back in the direction of Desolation Row.

"Want to play a little bit?"

"Why not?"

"On the guitar?"

"No, thanks. I prefer to leave that to you." That dry tone, with an ironic twist. "I'm learning to play the drums."

Peter Green's electric guitar playing is admired by connoisseurs for its tone and feeling more than for speed or noise. Dazzling flurries of notes on the upper reaches of a Strat or a 1959 Les Paul were not his style. When his sound was lovingly characterized as "out-of-phase", Peter replied he didn't know what out-of-phase meant. "Bit messy", he was known to say when invited to comment on a treasured passage of his own playing.

He was generally tactful enough not to make comments on my droning DADDAD raga routine, for which he provided percussion, but one afternoon he let fall an unkind remark in front of a kibbutz visitor who was himself a decent guitarist. It stung, needless to say, and the sting persisted. Later, though, I read in a music magazine an interview with Christine McVie, of a subsequent Fleetwood Mac incarnation. "He was definitely in charge. He turned to Mick Fleetwood after a gig one night and said: 'I've got more swing in my left bollock than you do.'" If you must be the target of Peter Green's sharp tongue, it soothes the pain to know you're not the only one.

The sojourn ended with promises and an exchange of addresses After I left, I heard from Dennis that Peter had gone south to Eilat with Blair. Like me, he had no place of his own in Britain, so we swapped the numbers of our parents' homes.

Peter Green when he was lead guitarist of Fleetwood Mac. In 1972 on Kibbutz Mishmarot, where he and I were next-door neighbours on Desolation Row, he was clean-shaven.

When I called there one day from a telephone box in London, his mother said, "Peter is in Bermuda." Perhaps he had accepted some of those "Albatross" royalties, after all. It was the only time I tried to get in touch with him. We had re-entered our former lives.

On the kibbutz, after I had broken the news of the tattoo, Dennis was thrilled. "I remember I saw them at a concert in New York. It was great, man! They were fan-tas-tic. At the end, you know what he said? 'You are the best audience *in the world*'."

III

When November arrived, people told me, the cold would begin to bite. Someone demonstrated the working of a tiny paraffin heater, which was supposed to keep my cabin warm. Only a handful of volunteers would be left. The harvests would be in. But who knows, my heating engineer said, "You might find something interesting to do." Once again, as on Spetsai at the end of August, I began to see myself as a left-behinder.

The problem – the only problem, really – was the Mediterranean. Once transported to Athens, I could make the journey by thumb to Ostend or Calais without much difficulty. It took five days. When the last car dropped me on the northern fringe of Belgium or France, I would find a way to get over the Channel. There, you could ask the solitary driver of a truck or car to take you as a non-paying passenger. From Dover, it was a day and a half's thumbing to reach Glasgow. When leaving in May, I had given up my bedsit in Wilton Street, where Jerry and Richard had crashed on the floor, but I didn't consider that to be a problem either. The Med was the problem. It required a boat. The boat demanded a ticket. The ticket wanted money.

I wrote to my father. He and I were not on good terms, largely because of my disinclination to study or look at regular employment. I had quit my six-year apprenticeship at Washington Irvine's three years in, and ever since I had been doing what I had always wanted to do, what all my friends were doing, what it seemed everyone ought to be doing – my own thing. Someone in Glasgow owed me money, I told Dad. It wasn't a lie. Not much money, but almost enough to get me on to a boat and over the sea to Piraeus. If Dad would advance me the sum . . .

It took about a week for a letter from Kibbutz Mishmarot to reach High Wycombe, and another week – assuming the recipient answered right away – for the reply to arrive. The mail for volunteers was distributed every lunchtime in front of Desolation Row. People waited in a group in anticipation of hearing their name called and being handed a letter, and sometimes it was my name. One morning an envelope was extended with my father's handsome handwriting on the front. I opened it carefully. There was no money. He used the occasion instead to deliver a lecture and remind me of "the family motto: No reward without effort." It was the first I had heard of a family motto.

I wrote to one of my sisters. She sent a pound sterling. I wrote to a girl I had been seeing in Glasgow before setting out for Turkey and then taking up with Jerry and the horses. I thought we had an on-again, off-again relationship, which had suited me fine. I thought it suited her, too. She took the opportunity to tell me it didn't, but she included another pound. I had about one-tenth of what I needed.

Dennis suggested looking for a job in Tel Aviv. He gave me a copy of the local English-language newspaper. I scrutinized the lists and found a likely one: "American Pizzeria. Help wanted. Dizengoff Street. Telephone . . ." I rang from the coin-operated kibbutz public telephone and – just like that – had a job.

"Can you be here Thursday at ten?" the voice asked.

It meant temporarily quitting the kibbutz, where by then I was in a position of some responsibility in the avocado fields, working with Dennis or Peter. My cabin on Desolation Row, overlooking the eucalyptus trees – their brittle leaves emitted an exotic perfume when crushed – was homely. I had books and a ruled pad for writing, on which I tried to add some recent Greek experience to the novel: the smell of horse and hay, the reassuring smack of leather, sun and sand, fun and flight.

In the long kibbutz evenings, I read or wrote or sat outside thrumming my open-tuning Scottish-oriental rag, with the former lead guitarist of John Mayall's Bluesbreakers beside me providing percussive accompaniment on Moroccan drums. (Peter had been Eric Clapton's replacement in the Bluesbreakers before forming Fleetwood Mac.) Now that I had to leave it, it seemed like just the life.

I packed a few things and caught the bus from the top of the road into Tel Aviv. The buses were always busy with soldiers who seemed to be treated by everyone as sons or brothers, Arabs excepted. As usual, there were uniformed figures along the road, hitch-hiking east and west. They never had to wait long. Sometimes a bus driver would stop for a pair of them, pushing back the fare. Female soldiers also got around by hitch-hiking. It was one big family, in every shade of skin and kink of hair and rhythmic gait imaginable; a once-in-a-millennium sense of belonging in a land that had been returned by providence and politics.

The words of an elderly kibbutznik who walked me round the limits of Mishmarot one afternoon never left me: when he came here from Russia, before the Second World War and the foundation of the State of Israel, it was "stone, dry, desert". We passed through orange groves and skirted the avocado fields. "The land was thirsty. Now look." I was touched by his pride. I didn't think a lot about the Arab passengers on the buses, who were themselves Israeli citizens. They didn't look defiant or benighted. They cultivated an atmosphere of neutrality.

The first thing to do in Tel Aviv was find a place to live. The choice was limited. I chose a space in a hostel, ten or twelve beds to a room. The next morning, I went to Dizengoff to meet the owner of American Pizzeria, my new boss. He was called Jim, like me, an open-faced American with a big smile. He repeated what he had said on the phone, that the pay was three Israeli pounds per hour, about 30 pence, the equivalent in today's spending power of – let's be generous – roughly £3. (The Israeli currency changed from pounds to shekels in 1980.) I had known that before I arrived, but the meagreness had failed to impress itself on me. On the first day, I worked ten hours. I had to pay for my bed, naturally, and for something other than pizza to eat after work. It was still hot in the Middle Eastern October, and I was not in any case inclined to stay indoors in the evenings. It was easy to spend a day's wages before midnight.

In a bar near the hostel, I met a young Englishman who I was pleased to learn was a student of English Literature. Despite my lack of formal education, my Scottish autodidactic instinct had served me reasonably well. There was a Hip Bibliography: Hermann Hesse, of course, Camus and Cocteau, Sartre, Beckett, the Black Mountain poets (not the Beats), Dostoevsky before Tolstoy, the odd Penguin Classic from Ancient Greece or India tossed in for wisdom's sake. In my full callowness I was by now well versed in it. Kate, Lorraine and others at Glasgow University had studied French and philosophy, and I adopted their opinions second hand and made simple use of them. I was able to make a pretty decent attempt at literary conversation while the saucers piled high.

One evening my new friend and I sat up late talking about Sartre, still the hero of the time. In the intervals, he listened to my story. Stranded in Israel, eh? A touch of drama to enliven the rendezvous. Let's have two more beers. He was sympathetic, yet blasé – "Cheers" – it needn't be a problem, all hang-ups were of your own devising. "You need to *act*", he said. "*Do* something. Don't hesitate."

I liked the sound of that. It made me feel at home, among the existentialists of Glasgow's West End. *Act*. Do something. "But what?"

Be authentic. Commit yourself. Don't be a victim of bad faith. Become engaged. He might have used the French pronunciation, as I certainly would have. There were philosophical solutions galore. "Choose freedom."

Together, we cooked up a plan – I remember the evening as if I were watching a film – shuffling the variations to increase the exactness of the execution. When it was too late to go further, we shook hands and arranged to get together again the following evening.

In the morning, I learned that I had been promoted. I hadn't been there long, but Jim said: "We are going to turn you into a pizza maker!" He gave me a humiliating paper hat, under which I had to tuck my hair. "You need to wear this." Jim also told me that I would be in receipt of a raise: from now on, I would be earning four Israeli pounds per hour (about 40 pence). When I told my English friend in the bar that evening, wondering if we should call off the plan, he raised his glass above his head and laughed. "You have to act. It is simply not possible to *live* otherwise."

The next day I approached Jim. "There's something I'd like to talk to you about in confidence, if you don't mind."

That big American smile. Jim had told me he was from California, which had associations with Joni Mitchell, Laurel Canyon, various writings with Big Sur in the title.

"Sure, Jim. Wait for me outside and I'll join you in a minute."

We seated ourselves on a bench on the boulevard, in front of American Pizzeria. It was a beautiful sunny day, like all the days. In Glasgow, it would be rainy and windy, people would be turning up their coat collars and raising fatalistic eyebrows as they passed each other on the street. Glasgow was another family. From inside the restaurant, the aroma of baking dough reached us on the bench. We specialized in thin crust, the house secret. Lunchtime rush hour was our best time.

"What's on your mind, Jim?"

"There's a little problem."

Suddenly, he was looking straight at me. "If I can help you, I will. You can be assured of that."

I explained that I was staying in a kind of a hallway – a dump, frankly, with nine other people, snoring, coughing, coming in late, getting up at all hours. "It's not exactly comfortable. So much noise. And kind of dirty." Jim offered a sympathetic nod. "I have the chance of a room – another dump, actually" – we laughed – "but at least a place of my own." I told Jim I was writing a novel in my free time.

"Really?" He looked interested. "What's it about?"

"It's kind of an existentialist thing. The landlady . . . she's asking for a deposit."

Jim was looking pensive, but not about my book. After a moment, he asked, "How much?"

My café-intellectual friend and I had calculated that it would cost 150 Israeli pounds to buy a ticket from Haifa to Piraeus. Then it would be necessary to live for five days while hitch-hiking to Ostend or Calais. I knew I could hop across the Channel for free, but there would be another twelve or fifteen hours on the road before reaching Glasgow. I had no concerns about surviving once I was there.

"She wants 300 pounds."

How long a pause? How searching a look from his eyes into mine? How sincere a gaze in return?

"I'm going to speak to my partner, Jim. But I can tell you that I like this plan. It's so difficult to find workers like you, who work hard and are willing to stick around in Tel Aviv. You're not a student?" Just for a moment, he seemed put out. "You're not going to disappear back to school in a month or something?"

Not at all. I was "free", in a sense that Jim was incapable of understanding.

"Let me speak to Jeff. We like you. I'll speak to Jeff and give you an answer this afternoon." His firm, friendly hand made a warm impression on my back. "Right, let's get to work. Pardner!"

The next day, a Friday, Jim brought 300 Israeli pounds in an envelope, for which I thanked him. I worked until five, then went back to the hostel, picked up my bag and checked out. At six, I was at the bus station, now familiar, and took my seat on a bus, surrounded by Israeli citizens of every kind. I patted my bag to assure myself of the security of the envelope. The bus would take me to Kibbutz Mishmarot.

All through the journey I looked out of the window at the soldiers, the women with children, the labourers who had finished a day's toil and were returning home to spend the evening with families. I was not in their world, nor in any world that felt real. I was a character in a film, made on a low budget – a budget of 300 Israeli pounds.

I stepped down as before at the stop nearest the kibbutz and walked along the sloping path leading from the main road to the entrance, where I had arrived full of anticipation about my new life two months earlier.

At first I thought I was alone, but soon realized I had company. For the entire length of the route, a small, scruffy dog followed me, barking constantly. I had walked up and down this path many times, but had never seen or heard that dog before. I never saw it again, and it must have died over forty years ago, but I have never forgotten it. It is by such characters that one's own character is formed.

Finally, I made it to the kibbutz, the philosophy of dogs still sounding in my ears, and entered my cabin for the first time in almost two weeks. Familiar things welcomed me: the guitar, the books (including *Being and Nothingness*, left behind by a previous occupant), the comfortable little bed by the small window, the smell of crushed eucalyptus leaves when you stepped outside. There was some kind of outdoor theatrical event going on that evening. Sitting on the grass in front of the stage, I recounted my adventure to Peter.

"Right," he said, and fixed me with the same look that I had seen on the face of Jim outside the pizzeria when I made my request. Peter, who had escaped a life of unwanted celebrity, had given away thousands, maybe millions, to poor people throughout the world. I was poor, too, but not like them. "You'll be free to leave now."

"I needed to do something. To act."

I had been looking forward to showing off a bit to Dennis, to setting off his vibrancy. We had spoken before of a ruse whereby one could pose as a victim of theft, claiming that one's Traveller's Cheques had been stolen, then cashing them quickly. Or cashing them first, before reporting the "theft". I forget which. I had never had Travellers' Cheques. American Express was apparently under obligation to reimburse the amount stolen.

But Dennis failed to congratulate me. He looked at his feet.

"Jimmy." Then his eyes creased and he peered at me with a fierce-friendly gaze. "Jimmy, you can't go round Europe rippin' people off. You gonna find yourself in prison, man." He raised a hand to shield his eyes from a kibbutz spotlight behind my head. I still see the hand and the squint. He had his own philosophy. "You ever heard of karma?"

The next day, Shabbat, I put the banknotes in an envelope. On the front I wrote the address of American Pizzeria, Dizengoff Street, keeping back a little for the work I had done, as I explained to Jim in my covering letter. Honesty had not yet taken full possession of me and I made some flimsy excuse for my peculiar action. It seemed better not to mention existentialism.

The following morning, I returned to the avocado fields where the sun was welcoming and reassuring. We worked for two hours before climbing on to the tractor and heading back through the orange and banana groves for breakfast at nine. Then we set out for the fields again, shouting excitedly at the magic glimpse of the kingfisher along the way. I have never been so brown. My hair was yellow. When I told Peter about returning the money, he looked at me with the same expression. "You did the right thing."

I never discussed it with the dog.

*

A footnote: It was Dennis who gave me the money to help me leave Kibbutz Mishmarot and return to Europe. One day in the avocado fields, he put a stop to my complaining. "OK, Jimmy, I'll give you the money to get over to Greece. At least I'll get some fucking peace that way."

We went together to a shipping office in Haifa where he paid for an overnight voyage to Piraeus. Dennis then cashed a traveller's cheque and handed me twenty dollars.

On my first trip to New York, in 1981, I carried his telephone number with me, hoping to catch him by surprise and hand him the money. But there was no reply. In the White Horse Tavern in Greenwich Village, I had a drink with Jerry Robock, but he couldn't tell me where Dennis was. I made occasional efforts to locate him after that, and thought about him often.

Arriving in New York, I could see that Dennis had introduced me to the city in advance, in his voice, his jokes and gestures.

When the internet era arrived, I discovered that he had remained at Mishmarot, marrying a kibbutz girl, as he had hoped to do, but was no longer there. I still hoped to return the money – partly as a token souvenir of old times' sake. A clue came from someone who had been a Mishmarot volunteer after my time, overlapping with Dennis. She said he was living in Florida.

I tracked down the address – it mentioned "prior: Flushing, NY" – and sent a letter by mail, recalling our mornings in the avocado fields, Desolation Row, Peter Green and the loan waiting to be repaid, but received no reply.

10

TROCCHI'S PAD

I

I arrived back in Glasgow from Israel in November 1972 with the pages of my *Cain's Book* pastiche stowed in the bag, so far untitled.

> The Hangman is mocking me again . . . My head is lowered to the ground. I know I can rise and walk away, but only when the Hangman's smile is removed will I be able to stare into his eyes. That is the condition of my release. To leave now, while he still laughs, I would have to rearrange my terms. And that I refuse to do.

The editor of *Glasgow University Magazine*, known as *GUM*, heard through mutual friends that I had this and other writings, and we arranged to meet. By the age of twenty-one, Jack Haggerty had a developed taste and a sense of literary style far in advance of his contemporaries. While others tricked themselves out in Goulimine beads and amulets and embroidered tunics, Jack preferred to dress in a sober suit, sometimes with that truly exotic accessory, a tie. Everyone grew their hair long and parted it in the middle, while Jack's was usually tidy and properly cut.

Each Friday, he bought a new novel in hardback from John Smith's Bookshop in Saint Vincent Street, frequently by an unfashionable author, perhaps an English provincial such as Stanley Middleton, while the rest of us surfed over the Hip Bibliography, trusting in paperbacks, bought, bartered or borrowed. Other people mentioned pocketing the occasional volume from Smith's, sometimes justifying it as a species of revenge against "the system", which seemed to mean whatever was convenient to make it mean at the time. These acts of simple dishonesty fell under my judgement of *mauvaise foi*, translated in *Being and Nothingness* as "self-deception". Between them, Dennis and Jean-Paul Sartre had persuaded me that no act of dishonesty, however minor, could remain unexamined.

Jack read with attention to nuance and detail. Why this word and not another? Why "essential to" and not "integral to"? Short sentences create one mood; long, unbroken paragraphs something different. Adjectives and, particularly, adverbs – here Jack might invoke Graham Greene, his ultimate arbiter – should be handled with care. The backbone of every sentence is the verb, which must be made as strong as possible.

For a brief period, like most of those in our circle – I was an exception – Jack was a student at the university, but after a year he quit his courses in order to pursue a career as a journalist on a local newspaper. Nevertheless, he continued to act as editor of the university magazine. No one needed to know that he was no longer a student. Those who did know didn't seem to care. He was divided into two: Dr Jack and Mr Haggerty. During the day, he worked as a reporter in Clydebank, near Glasgow, a town that had gone into decline with the shipbuilding industry it had existed to serve. The opening of a new hospital, a school's annual sports day, a grandmother who gave chase to a thief while wielding her frying pan; Jack was there, notebook in hand. By night, he returned to the pubs and cafés and student bedsits in Byres Road, in the university district, and assumed the role of literary editor. His parents lived in a modest council flat on a housing estate on the western outskirts of Glasgow, and Jack continued to stay there, unlike most people we knew, who rented a bedsit or shared a head pad (not a "hippie flat") with others.

He had grand plans for the student journal. Jack was a devoted reader of the *New Statesman*, *Encounter*, the *TLS*. He would put on an amiably sceptical expression when *International Times* or *Rolling Stone* was mentioned. If someone was going to be in London, Jack would ask to be brought back *Esquire* – "*Esquire* magazine", he would say – or *Harper's*, with specific instructions as to where it could be bought on Charing Cross Road. When we arranged to meet in a café or one of the restaurants he liked to frequent, I might arrive to find him already at the table, pencil in hand, marking some well-turned phrase in a review, or underlining a word that was new to him. He would later slip those words into conversation. *Epicene*, he muttered once; Brando was epicene. Someone's literary comments were *sophomoric*. The criticism was administered gently. *Diaphanous* – referring to the light blue blouse on the pretty girl at the party. A decorous unbuttoning gesture. "Wouldn't it be marvellous to be the one . . . ?"

Physically, he could be seen walking through Glasgow or leaning on the bar in a pub with me at 6 o'clock, beginning a conversation that would last until after closing time. In his imagination, we were in New York, where he occupied the skin of Norman Mailer or Gore Vidal, writers who held the place in his esteem that rock musicians did in that of others. It was he who introduced me to the name of James Baldwin, a man who would come to figure importantly in my life; and to books by Truman Capote, F. Scott Fitzgerald and others. To judge solely by his first-name conversation – "and you remember what Truman replied when Norman said . . ." – you might have thought they were intimate friends. Neither of us had been to

America. Jack had never travelled outside Britain, except to go to Dublin for a wedding.

He was capable of quoting long passages of prose, verbatim, as others could reel off poetry, and he recounted anecdotes about modern writers as if he had heard them from someone who was there when the action took place. *He* was there, in every sense – in every sense but the real one – and *there* was a good place to be with Jack. To grant Vidal or Mailer a continuous speaking part in his imagination was to lend a glow to the dank West End of Glasgow night as 1972 crossed over into 1973: a glow of words, the right words in the right order, one of Jack's maxims.

All the while, he was keeping up with English provincial authors, who offered a more naturalistic reflection of his own experience, and whom he esteemed equally. Baldwin occupied no greater a place in his pantheon than Stan Barstow. Styron was not a grander figure than David Storey. Mailer was a prince, but there was an honourable place at the Court of King Jack for humble Stanley Middleton.

Jack read a sheaf of my stories – I held back my *Cain's Book* meanderings which, now that I was removed from sun and sea and sky, seemed to have lost course – and printed one of them in *GUM*, with an illustration. I began to assume the role of assistant editor. We had the right to use a small room in a university building on Gilmorehill, but Jack preferred to do most of the magazine business from a little café-restaurant called the Grosvenor, next to Hillhead Subway station in the dead centre of Byres Road.

He ate there most evenings, the only person of my acquaintance who never hesitated to dine out, and who knew how to conduct himself when he did so. My introduction to the look and taste of spaghetti carbonara, even the sound of the words, took place in the Grosvenor Café. The sumptuous plate was followed by Black Forest gateau and then "un espresso" – splendours suggestive of the other world from which I had lately returned, the one beyond dark-at-4 pm, drookit Glasgow.

All the waitresses smiled on him, and he always left tips. Jack was a figment of Jack's imagination, with the leading role in a movie called *Jack*, directed not by Jack himself but by his brother. George Haggerty really was in that glamorous American world, though in his case it was Hollywood, where he was learning to be a film director. The cinema – or, to be more precise, the writing of realist drama for television: The Wednesday Play, Play of the Month, Armchair Theatre; David Mercer, Dennis Potter, Jeremy Sandford – featured among Jack's own furtive ambitions, and he talked often of the short film George was on

Jack Haggerty (right) with Gerald Mangan (centre) and others in Dublin, 1971. *Courtesy of Gerald Mangan.*

the point of completing with the actor Stacy Keach. Jack was disappointed to learn I hadn't heard of Keach. It was released in 1975 as *Hamburger Hamlet*. No one I knew had ever met George.

One evening, Jack summoned me to his office – that is to say, the café next to the station. He finished off his carbonara, lit a Gitane and hooked an arm over the back of his chair. He said that the editor of *Cosmopolitan* had once gathered all the staff together in the boardroom and announced that he wanted them to come up with feature ideas for a new magazine which the company was about to launch. Brilliant suggestions poured in, whereupon the boss revealed that there was no new magazine. So, he wanted to know, why had those ideas not been put forward for *Cosmopolitan*?

After that, Jack began to speak about his latest plans for *GUM*. First and most important, we had to find a new design and a new title. GUM? Bubble gum? There was a huge department store in Moscow called GUM. Did we want to be identified with that? What would Norman say if asked to write for a magazine with a name like *GUM*? Never mind the news about student associations, charity drives and so forth, which we also ought to get rid of.

For a title we settled on the *Moving Review*. I was the one who came up with the name, though it wasn't entirely original. There was an underground magazine run by Jeff Nuttall in the north of England called *the moving times*. Alexander Trocchi was associated with it, and William Burroughs was a contributor. I had never seen a copy, only knew that it was vaguely "underground" and the name had stuck in my mind. Jack thought about it for a few seconds, then murmured: "I like it . . . yes, I like it, my friend." At these moments, you were expected to feel proud, and you did.

There was an assistant editor called Brian Hannan, a student – so much the better – who was an energetic contributor to the magazine and the Grosvenor café meetings. He had another idea for the title. I forget what it was. I didn't have much in common with Brian, and he felt that I had usurped the place in Jack's kitchen cabinet that he had occupied himself. With good reason. Brian wore large black-framed spectacles and had a 1950s hair style. Not retro – that wasn't a concept in fashion yet – but straight (to say "square" was square). He was the link to the university. Jack chose my title anyway, and Brian was made to feel that he was part of the old regime.

Jack had the idea of placing at the centre of the *Moving Review* interviews with celebrated writers, in this way satisfying his desire for big names. He would telephone somebody out of the blue – John Braine, for example, or Alan Sillitoe, two of his Angry Young Men idols – and would hold them in conversation for an hour. He had the knack of keeping up a pertinent line of questioning, at the same time sounding intimate, without being intrusive. The writers must have been flattered by his familiarity with their work, by his curiosity, his strange air of worldliness despite being so young. Some kind of future rendezvous would be provisionally agreed.

One Saturday afternoon, as we were coming out of a café of the superior kind in Buchanan Street, where I had chosen the cheapest thing on the menu and Jack the most expensive, he crooked his arm and looked at his wristwatch. "Oh dear. Three o'clock. I was supposed to be meeting Alan Sillitoe in London . . ."

"Today!?"

"Right now . . . at his house in Ladbroke something." It was the first time he had mentioned it.

Jack wanted those good ideas. In the café next to the Subway station I proposed an article on the subject of Trocchi. Why wasn't he talked about in the pubs and lecture theatres, or written about on the literary pages of the heavy Sundays or in *Encounter*? The novel was in a dire condition in Britain – it was a cliché even then to say that the novel was dead, a cliché steadfastly resisted by Jack – yet *Cain's Book*, a masterpiece, a *mastercrime*, was never mentioned. *And* he was Scottish. So much of contemporary Scottish writing was "stale porridge", Trocchi had once pronounced at an event in Edinburgh, at which Hugh MacDiarmid and others were present. "Of what is interesting in Scottish literature of the past twenty years, I myself have written it all."

In their ignorance, journalists, critics, the reading public, dismissed this majestic declaration. In my ignorance, I embraced it.

Jack rubbed a hand across his chin without at first giving a response. He had heard of Trocchi only from me, had never read his infamous book, which was not his kind of thing. *Cain's Book* was a minority taste – "a cult", and I was the most enthusiastic cultist of all. I knew few others.

Not only did Trocchi live outside society; he lived outside the law. He was a drug addict. He had devoted his life to the habit, in a literary fashion, in the tradition of Baudelaire and Cocteau. Opium was not necessarily a prison. On the contrary, with heroin in his veins he was free – super-free. "I would recommend that heroin be placed with lucid literature pertaining to use on the counters of all chemists (to think that a man should be allowed a gun and not a drug!) and sold openly to anyone over twenty-one."

Cain's Book revelled in the kind of literary tricks that excited me. For example, the anti-hero, Joe Necchi – Trocchi himself, in every pertinent particular – is in the middle of writing a novel, and the title of the novel is *Cain's Book*. One evening, after having shot up heroin in a New York pad with some derelict cronies, he reads aloud a passage from the work-in-progress by firelight. But the section in question does not exist elsewhere in *Cain's Book* – that is to say, in the novel you are holding in your hand. The reader has the teasing thought that there is another book of the same title, existing in an alternative zone – a hidden book, of which we are granted only a glimpse: a pair of hooves beneath the hem of the curtain. It was as if an actor in a film had halted the projector and stepped out of the screen to stand before the spectator. A film by Cocteau, the great modernist conjuror, in my eyes, from the fantasy country of France before and after the war. Trocchi was from Glasgow, not a fantasy land at all; it was the land in which I had first read his book.

Trocchi described with precision and some beauty the effects of narcotic drugs. I didn't feel the desire to emulate the author or his character. I was, rather, intoxicated by the effects of this writing, a species of magic, even when I could not fully understand it, as any form of magic remains at best partly understood. I carried *Cain's Book* with me to the pubs of Glasgow, the souks of Turkey, the ports of Greece . . . and preached its gospel like a downy, adolescent priest.

II

Finally, the editor showed his approval. But not a literary essay, *please*. He preferred the big projects. "Why not an interview? Do it long. We'll rediscover him."

I wouldn't have known how to go about finding the man whose face I had gazed at so often on the cover of the John Calder paperback. How to start, even?

Jack had no such hesitation. The next day he called the publisher in London and asked for the author's telephone number, explaining what it was we hoped to do. With his mysterious power of authority, he got straight through to Calder himself – like us, like Trocchi, a Scot, which might have helped – all done from the telephone box on the street outside our "office". Calder gave him the number and promised to send a copy of Trocchi's latest publication, *Man at Leisure*, a collection of poems. Jack then rang Trocchi and they talked for a quarter of an hour, as Jack pressed coins into the slot.

The great man was flattered by the proposal. He was himself a former student of Glasgow University, news which surprised and pleased Jack. He would welcome the reporter from *GUM* (we hadn't changed the title yet) whom Jack recommended, and asked that he – me – call to make arrangements.

How did Jack learn to do all this – to ring publishers and request review copies and telephone numbers with complete confidence? He had grown up in a typical Glasgow working-class family, attended the local school and still lived with his parents. He had met few people of literary accomplishment and probably only one or two who had actually written a book.

"If he invites me to shoot up heroin with him," I asked, "then what?" Jack didn't hesitate. "You must accept. Go ahead. It'll look great in the piece."

I took the night train to London – the cheapest – and arrived at Trocchi's place one wintry Sunday at noon, as per arrangement. He lived in a top-floor apartment at 4 Observatory Gardens, between Notting Hill Gate and High Street Kensington, in those days still a dowdy district, with his wife and two young sons. I can picture myself from outside my body, as if in yet another film, ringing the doorbell – the clench on the heart, the halt on the voice. Trocchi proved himself to be not just a tough face on the cover of a Calder Jupiter Book by responding on the intercom, the first of its kind I had ever encountered.

"Ah. It's you." The door opened with a metallic click and I began climbing the stairs to his apartment. He was waiting on the landing at the top floor, looking down at the figure below, a man of enormous frame in a black T-shirt, with a protruding stomach and a nose like the inverted horn of a rhino – a nose so large it was impossible not to focus on it. He smiled when he saw the long-haired emissary from his home town. I wrote: "One is immediately struck by his sallow complexion and the scars on his arms which are white like snow."

As I approached the landing where he stood, he said: "I was just about to give myself a fix. Can you wait?"

I had walked through the mirror, like an actor in a film by Cocteau, and entered into the pages of *Cain's Book*.

III

My girlfriend of the time, Pamela, was with me when I pressed that first intercom buzzer. Trocchi invited us to sit down in the living room and served tea together with muffins hot from the oven, which he recommended with a bafflingly un-outlaw-like enthusiasm. "Danish, I think they are." We met his wife Lyn, seated on the sofa behind dark glasses, though it was murky December, and two boys, one of whom obeyed a gentle command to lower the volume on the television. It all seemed disquietingly normal. He had the decorators in, and suggested that I return the next day, when he would be better organized and we would have more time in which to do "this thing", our interview. "Do it properly," he said.

I loved the sound of it. His voice was still strongly Scottish, and I was already planning to re-read *Cain's Book* through the filter of our native accent. In the meantime, he gave me a copy of *Helen and Desire*, the most mainstream of his six erotic novels written in Paris in the 1950s and published by the Olympia Press, and an American journal with an essay about him by the Black Mountain poet Edward Dorn. I suppose he hoped it might lend some seriousness to the article I was proposing to write.

The next day I returned alone and we settled ourselves – on the floor, of course – in his wide attic studio. There were books everywhere, as well as loose-leaf binders, a typewriter, letters unfolded from their nearby envelopes. A "comfortable shambles", I called it in the article.

"Like are you just going to fire questions at me?" His sentences were dependent on that word "like", the peculiar Scottishness of which has been overlooked. He apologized for the mess. "That's one thing about drugs, like they certainly make you disorganized."

The subject was not slow to arise. In *Cain's Book*, and in anything about him I laid my hands on to read, which wasn't much, Trocchi played the evangelist in promoting the salvational effects of heroin. It was one of his gimmicks, like asking you to wait while he gave himself a fix, a part of his grand outlaw persona. Drugs removed him from the mundane despond. Though I didn't want to share in it, the drug-taking nevertheless had an outsider aspect, and any hint of outsiderism was sure to appeal to me. Jack was more pragmatic and mature. Before I left Glasgow, he had insisted that I read to Trocchi a few lines from an article by Cyril Connolly which had recently appeared in the *Sunday Times*.

A striking observation is the anti-intellectual climate that prevails in the networks. All who have known someone addicted to drugs . . . will have remarked on the increasing indifference to reality, whether to the time of day . . . or reading, or any of the pleasures and passions, food, drink, love, sex, places of art or the acquisition of knowledge, which make life worth living, friendship a joy or conversation a pleasure.

As soon as I read this aloud, I knew that it described better the context in which I aspired to live than the scenes of junkies hungrily seeking an uptown fix in *Cain's Book*, or in anything written by Burroughs or one of the other underground authors being passed around. I didn't even smoke dope. Yet I continued with my romance, for I enjoyed it. It was exactly that: a romance, a literary fantasy. It consoled me and provided a temporary rescue from my state of under-development. It occupied the place in my imagination that the works of Tolkien did in that of others. They didn't seriously think they were going to enter Middle Earth and meet the wizard Gandalf, but the fantasy consoled them.

Trocchi treated Connolly's eloquent objection seriously. In my 4,000 word profile which appeared in *GUM* several weeks later, in February 1973 – probably the longest piece about Trocchi to have been published to date – I wrote: "Trocchi looked at me a little sadly. 'What is one going to say about that?'" He answered with reference to some great literary figures of the past. Here is what he said, transcribed from the recording I made of the interview on a borrowed tape machine the size of a small suitcase:

I suppose up to a point it's true. But it's referring to a particular group of people who, whether they used drugs or not, would not be involved in this or that intellectual pursuit, would not be interested in reading. I think it's true that many people who use drugs do use them as armour against experience but I don't think that could have been said about Coleridge, for example, or de Quincey, who if nothing else were intellectuals.

He didn't wish to suggest that it was necessary for everyone, or anyone, to turn on to heroin. From the tape again: "I think that for me at a certain time it was necessary to take up this attitude and go far out – but it's something that can either enrich your experience or destroy you. It can destroy you very easily if you give way to all the social fictions about it. People tend to become what society believes they are."

What undermined and ultimately ridiculed the outsider stance was the difficulty of obtaining the drugs he wanted, and the penalties attached to doing so. One of the reasons Trocchi had returned to Britain from the United States was to be eligible for the prescription of narcotics on the National Health. In short, the great outlaw became more dependent than most others on the rules established by the society he wanted his readers and literary peers to think he was plotting to overthrow. Who ever heard of a state-subsidized outlaw? He had walked into a trap outlined in a passage in *Cain's Book* which had always delighted me:

For centuries we in the West have been dominated by the Aristotelian impulse to classify. It is no doubt because conventional classifications became part of the prevailing economic structure that all real revolt is hastily fixed like a bright butterfly on a classificatory pin; the anti-play, *Godot*, being from one point of view unanswerable, is with all speed acclaimed "best play of the year"; anti-literature is rendered innocuous by granting it a place in conventional histories of literature.

While I was thrilled at having laid eyes on my hero, Pamela, when she saw him that first day and sat on the sofa sipping tea beside dark-eyed Lyn, said she could "smell evil about his person". I was too much in awe for any such perception, but it chimed with the opening poem in *Man at Leisure*, which had arrived from Calder just in time for me to read it on the journey to London: "Where to begin / which sin / under what sun . . . ?"

Where to begin with sin? And where to end? It is well established now, though I was ignorant of it then, that Lyn had been forced into prostitution in the US by Trocchi, in order to raise money for drugs. She was a junkie herself, and died not long after our encounter in Observatory Gardens. Another of his gimmicks was to say things like, "I've no objection, if I myself am incapable for one reason or another, to finding some young bull for my wife . . ." I didn't put that into the piece.

It was the flipside of the charm, though charm there still was. And there was another sort of charm for me in hearing the names of Robert Creeley, R. D. Laing, William Burroughs and others, let fall elegantly, without name-dropping clumsiness. Norman Mailer had referred to Trocchi as "the most brilliant man I've met". Creeley had written a gnomic preface to a 1967 reissue of one of his pornographic novels. "In *Thongs*, as in other novels he has written in this genre, Trocchi defines the *isolation* of persons in sexual rapport . . ."

image of profligate associated with the man. When I mentioned that an arts lab should be opening in this city shortly, he was pleased but sceptical. He said it was pitiful that the final say on sexual licence for such establishments rested more or less in the power of a few councillors. It is this attitude which has awarded his books their unfortunate reputation.

The three main distributors in this country will not handle *Cain's Book*, though they still sells and is shortly being made into a film from which he will profit. And at the time of that book's original publication in Britain it was banned and burned in Sheffield.

Lady Chatterley, Ulysses, Henry Miller, Cain. It is no secret that we are afraid over what we cannot assert ourselves; scared of the unrecognisable, or of what becomes uncomfortably familiar. *Cain* is honest and true and burned.

'I always felt it was strange that the butcher Abel should be preferred to the agriculturist Cain.
Abel waxed fat and rich breeding sheep for the slaughter while Cain tilled ...
And soon Abel had vast herds and air-conditioned slaughterhouses and meat package plants, and there was a blight on Cain's crop. And that was called SIN
And Abel saw his elder brother and he was thin and with a starved look and held the spade to no purpose in his hand
And Abel approached his brother, saying,
Why don't you give up and come and work for me? I could use a good man in the slaughterhouse.
And Cain slew him.'

And so Cain was cast out. And Trocchi is cast out. And Cain wore a mark that he be protected against random homicide and he was the first city builder and he inaugurated the first civilised life.

Through his book (with respect to literature), through his habit (with respect to consciousness), through the political sigma project (with respect to a civilised society) and through himself Trocchi, wearing the mark, protected by himself and his ways against indiscriminate judgement attempts to erect, assert himself, attempts to inaugurate something of which he, the man and his ideas are the primogenitor.

His contemporaries have always eyed him nervously. In 1962 at the International Writers' Conference, organised by John Calder in Edinburgh, Scottish writers formed the mainstay of the crew with McDiarmid in power. He brushed roughly up against Trocchi and Burroughs, writing them off as nothing more than a couple of drug fiends. 'I've nothing against the man,' Trocchi says now with an apologetic grin, thinking back to the event. 'I mean, he is sane, in a relative fashion, isn't he?' But he started attacking us, babbling on about matters he knows nothing about, and all that brigade were drunk out of their skulls with their drug while Burroughs and I were quite *compos mentus*.'

Trocchi became involved in a debate with McDiarmid and said that all Scottish writing over the last 20 years, his own sport, was a lot of 'stale porridge', and that only he had written a book which was living and would remain alive. *I am a cosmonaut of inner space*.

In *Cain's Book*, he states his view more placidly. I told her that the great urgency for literature was that it should once and for all accomplish its dying, that it wasn't that writing shouldn't be written, but that a man should annihilate prescriptions of all past form in his own soul, refuse to consider what he wrote in terms of literature, judge it solely in terms of his living.'

It was around this time when Trocchi landed in England from America that he began to channel his energies away from direct artistic out-put into some-

thing which had occupied his thought since the Paris days, but in a far less serious manner than he now began to involve himself with it: project sigma.

The whole chapter of underground vicissitudes of that time — the sixties — is related and discussed at some length in Jeff Nuttal's *Bomb Culture*. It will suffice here to sketch in a few background relevances. To put it roughly, the Underground was just coming 'over', ie it was communicating itself, involving more than only the directly self-consciously involved. Tom McGrath launched *International Times*; beat-writing, having learned to walk with Kerouac, was starting to run with Ginsberg and Burroughs and for many — impressed by its exuberance and lack of pedantic pretensions — was running a deal faster than the slow-moving straight movement. The poetry reading at the Royal Albert Hall was a congregation, a success and proved to be a landmark. R D Laing, the psychiatrist, was involved with David Cooper and Esterson, in the Philadelphia Foundation. anti-psychiatry. Laing was telling us that LSD is where it's at, and Alpert was finding out that it wasn't.

But for all of those people, and others, rebels; sigma became a cause. Their centre was sigma and Trocchi was the central force.

Trying to define sigma is like trying to define zen. The proof is not apparent. The physicality is not in evidence. Only the actuality exists.

'For myself, I think it is not so much a question of choosing to exist as of discovering oneself in and of the "invisible insurrection" by virtue of one's practical posture. The (R)evolt is taking place at the level of symbols; there is no question of our ever meeting the forces head-on in a war on their terms. But it is happening. If you are aware of it, you are *ipso facto* involved. ‡

The fundamental ideal of sigma is to make intelligence self-conscious, to channel the new amounts of leisure time which are already on us and must inevitably grow in the future, into routes more creative, more self-conscious than civilisation has previously instanced. Ostensibly, sigma (the word represents in mathematics any number between nothing and infinity) is an elitist theory using culture as the means of an insurrection — an insurrection of minds; more than anything else it is

simply a new way of looking at things, a common viewpoint which would eventually involve everyone to a higher level of intelligence, but which must begin with the few conscious) — 'Only those who are able to comprehend those conditions and exploit them are responsible for their own biographies. It is to those we address ourselves' though they choose themselves, are not elected. ‡

Trocchi is humble without objection 'That may sound a little far-fetched. But it's all we can hope for. For men to learn to live with one another, to manipulate their energies toward something more creative, something other than ideas of how to destroy each other.'

The small group at the outset in the early sixties included R D Laing, David Cooper, William Burroughs, Ginsberg, Leary, Alpert, Tom McGrath, Jeff Nuttal and Trocchi himself whose part in the fundamental problem of communicating sigma was probably the largest. He had essays by himself and the others run off on Gestetner sheets and sold at cost price, and tried hard to set something concrete, something deliberate moving around sigma. Now he still has the ideas, the hopes, if not

A page from *Glasgow University Magazine* (*GUM*), February 1972, with my profile of Alexander Trocchi: a first extended appearance in print.

I carried the cassette tape home to Glasgow, a touching blend of callowness and diligence. In my Wilton Street room, which I had regained after returning from Israel, I wrote a report of the adventure in longhand and gave it to Jack, who printed it in *GUM*, without benefit of editing.

Among the other material I brought back from this first literary expedition was a short article in typescript by Burroughs, "M.O.B.", which in the Burroughs lexicon stood for "My Own Business". I had asked Trocchi for a piece of writing of his own for *GUM*, and he regretted not being able to offer something. But he held out "M.O.B." with one of his confidential smiles and said, "Why not publish this?" It consisted of three pages, in Gestetner duplicator form. "Just phone up Bill and say I suggested it."

He wrote down Burroughs's Mayfair telephone number: 01 839 5259. When I returned to Glasgow I dialled it, Jack-style, and sure enough Burroughs picked up the phone, listened to my stammered explanation and answered my polite inquiries.

Answered in his fashion, that is. To everything I said, Burroughs replied, *"Shu-ah!"*, in an elasticated drawl. Or *"Yea-ah!"*

So, that's OK then?

"Yea-ah."

Permission given?

"Shu-ah!"

William Burroughs could from then on be listed among the contributors to *Glasgow University Magazine*. Money wasn't mentioned (there was no such thing anyway). He became expansive only when I asked for his address, to which would be sent a copy when the piece appeared later in the year: "8 Dook Street Saint James", and put down the phone.

11

HITCH-HIKER'S PERSONALITY TEST

I

The state of original desire in the Land of Away was Morocco. Therefore, I had one more journey to undertake: through northern Europe to Sicily, over the Gulf of Tunis, then by land across North Africa, and down through the labyrinthine Moroccan roads to Marrakesh. It was a route of some 7,000 miles, though I would not have been able to tell anyone that then. A journey without maps. I decided to go when *GUM/Moving Review* was on lengthy sabbatical during the summer holidays.

My starting point was a squatters' community in North London. On an April Sunday evening in 1973, I emerged into light rain at Tufnell Park Tube station, looked around to take my bearings – this was as much a foreign turf as any I had trod so far – turned right along Junction Road and arrived at No.9 Poynings Road, almost midway between Tufnell Park and the Archway roundabout. The terrace houses, classic early-twentieth-century two-up, two-down, were earmarked for demolition and several had been abandoned to the elements. The most forceful elements here were young people in search of a place to live at a next-to-nothing price. Four or five of the houses in the upward sloping, acutely curving street – standing at the foot of it, you could not see past No. 7 – had been taken over by a mixed assembly of Londoners, Irish, a number of Scottish guys whom I didn't know before and two Scottish sisters, former school friends of Dudley's, whom I did and who had offered me the introduction.

No one seemed to be expecting me; no one seemed surprised to see me. As with others who had come before, I was accepted, like a pilgrim at the gates of a mountaintop monastery, on the incontrovertible fact of having arrived. In a first-floor front room, I was assigned a mattress. Bathroom and lavatory were pointed out. In what would have been called the refectory on the mountaintop, food was heated in a casserole and scooped on to a plate. There was one American and some coming-and-going Europeans. Everyone was welcome, so long as the vibe was OK. It didn't have to be a good vibe: what mattered was that it wasn't a heavy one. "Heavy", like "uncool", could stand for a whole suit of negative characteristics, responses and consequences. But even that might be accepted on compassionate grounds. They were tolerant, the people of the Order of the Squatters: aspirant misfits and aspirant mystics, druggies and aspirant ex-druggies, drop-outs and, in one or two cases, aspirant drop-ins, secretly grateful for the unannounced arrival of a parental rescue squad.

During the week, I would begin looking for a job, with the end in view of advancing to Tunis in June.

II

My *Cain's Book*-style writings took on a new dimension in the upstairs front room at No. 9, becoming more naturalistic and introducing a named first-person narrator, Luke. I scribbled on a foolscap pad while reclining on the mattress on the floor, back propped against the wall. In the pages I have retained, I find the occasional marginal note to self: "May 10th 1973: It is important that I begin to write systematically as soon as living circumstances permit, otherwise I will find myself lost in a tangle of ideas & sketches." Even in these little literary instructions, however – at once standing apart from the fiction, yet destined to be incorporated into it – I hear the voice of Trocchi.

Included in the story was a French freak I called Henri – "French freaks are rare, but French freaks are always the worst" is among the book's maxims – based on Dudley's friend Pierre, who was semi-resident at Poynings Road. I had often seen him with Dudley in Glasgow. They made journeys from south to north and back again in Pierre's illicit Austin van. Dudley told me that Pierre had taught him how to siphon petrol from other vehicles (before the days of secure petrol caps).

I disapproved. Dennis's lesson on the kibbutz – "You ever heard of karma?" – and the sour taste left by the petty theft itself were among my meditations at the squatters' monastery. The aura surrounding Pierre was alluring but not the one for Dudley, and by association didn't feel right for me. It was Pierre I had met in the street in Istanbul a year earlier, after being robbed by the German lorry driver. He was dark and spindly in appearance, electric in gesture and reaction, long-fingered and neon-lit, a kind of Jimi Hendrix without the genius, and he died similarly young.

Otherwise, I got on with everybody. I was on a more even keel than most, perhaps because I did not seek guidance in drugs, or not habitually, and drugs were a way of life at Poynings Road. Mandrax, hash, grass, acid, and various pharmaceutical concoctions that could be bought over the counter at the chemist's without a doctor's prescription. There were no junkies among the regular inhabitants of the street. But some came from neighbouring squats to sit at the kitchen table in one or other of the houses – Nos 9, 7 and 4 were the main ones –

Scribbling something or other, in a caravan.

waiting on junk time, passing through junk space, speaking in junk speak, smiling mild junk smile, thieving junk goods. There was always someone willing to greet them with a pot of tea and a joint. People managed to sit around all morning, or, if they had managed to skip the morning by remaining asleep, all afternoon and evening, too. It was a form of junk meditation practised by some of the monks in this hospitable community.

Living in an adjacent room at No. 9 was a young Irishman called Gerry, basically decent, like so many, but the pawn shop on Junction Road housed not only every last personal object that Gerry suspected of having monetary value, but his soul as well. It was Gerry who said one day, apropos of I don't know what, "You're the most together person in this street." I mention it only to make clear that it isn't my intention to characterize myself as a near-miss, as someone forced into a choice between survival and perishing in this arena. I was there, but as a chiel taking notes. By now, the novel had a title: "Spread Eagle". I gave some of the characters the names of actual people from the street. This passage is based on a real event:

> Gerry and I had dropped some medicinal high of which an amount comes one's way every now and then but with this the only buzz was a sore head and if we were laughing in the kitchen it was because of the brotherhood that develops between two beings in moments of adventure the more ill-advised the adventure the greater the bond. Gerry stood up to walk towards the sink but he only got as far as the oven and he fell against it like he had been shot, with an excruciatingly painful countenance like he was being castrated and his fists clenched and teeth set together, his eyes rolling twitching all over and sliding down the front of the oven – Oh man he's OD'd Henri said – Gerry was on the floor now still twitching and having turned white green and now going blue and the four people who were in the room looking helpless and me and Henri worried because we had taken the same stuff without having any notion of the effects and me seeing my face in Gerry's face on the floor and going oh fuck I wish I hadn't and Gerry coughing and grunting . . .

In the story he died. The real Gerry rose again a few moments later and survived to make another visit to the pawn shop. In both fiction and life, the narrator suffered nothing worse than a sore head.

Several people in the street worked, and I was one of them. Work was not difficult to find and was untrammelled by bureaucracy. At eight in the morning, following the advice of a Poynings villager, I turned up at a builders' yard close to Tufnell Park Tube station, and asked the age-old question: "Need any men?" The foreman looked me over and posed his own inquiry in return: "Can you start right away?" That's why I'm here. "OK, go with him. He's another the same as you. *Jock!* Take this lad to the house in Prince of Wales and tell Bernie to get him mixing cement and on to the paving . . . At the *back* not the fucking front." And I was hired, no further questions asked, a blistering shovel affixed to my tender grip, cash to come on a Friday afternoon without the mediation of the taxman.

The job led me to Kentish Town, Primrose Hill and other North London sites, and brought in more money in a week than I had earned at various places of toil in Glasgow in a month. I was thin and flexible and relatively fit, but after my first day of mixing cement, digging trenches and clambering up scaffolding, moving from left to right in Spiderman choreography, I returned to the house at Poynings Road and tumbled on to my mattress, a ball of pain. The sinews loosened quickly, though, and before long I was more flexible than ever.

The other Jock was an ex-convict, a red-haired, slight man with a mild nature and the marks of a broken life scrawled all over. He might as well have been covered in knots and crosses. An air of surrender clung to him. Of his conversation I remember mainly the hard labour of making time pass in a Pentonville cell. "Countin' thae bricks . . . Oh Goad, ah don' waant t' be doin that *ever again*, naw, naw. "

Simple, harmless Jock was one of my teachers, though he would never have guessed it. He, too, led by example, poor man: shovel in hand, forsaken eyes never tested by love.

III

When my purse had filled up with about £100 – more money than I had ever had in my life – I made plans to be off. Go down to the road. Form the signature salute: right hand out (left, when in Britain), thumb raised. Head up, features open. Climb in with a grateful smile, careful to extend polite thanks when stepping down.

The direct route to Marrakesh would have led straight to the south of France, over the Pyrenees, with a stop at the peculiar Principality of Andorra, fathoming south through Franco-ite Spain to the port of Algeciras. There, the ferryman accepted tribute to spirit the traveller across water to Tangier, from this world to the other, the staging post at which one entered the much-desired zone of Difference.

In the hitch-hiker's personality test, however, France emerged with a low score and an unfriendly reputation; Spain, a fascist, fearful country, did even worse. People swapped stories of standing by the side of the road under the sun for six hours, waiting in vain for a lift. I knew that wait, and that sun. The delay was maddening, both for itself and for the fact that it permitted no deviation. You had to comply. Take a break – to read, to eat, to pee, to look around the nearby streets – and every car that whizzes by has the mark of being the one that could have plucked you out of this plight.

So I travelled via Germany, the most efficient hitching country. That way, I could cross from Northern to Southern Europe via the Alps, arriving in the unexpectedly snowy upper reaches of Italy. When I touched the outer tip of Europe, my magic thumb-travel would once again be interrupted by water: again the Mediterranean, though now the stretch separating

Sicily from the Gulf of Tunis.

From Palermo, a ferry left for Tunis. From Tunis, a road ran along the Barbary Coast, through Constantine and Algiers, on into Morocco. I longed to be within the walls of Marrakesh, to see with my own eyes what had lit up my imagination when, in my chilly flat in Partick on a grey Glasgow Saturday after returning from the lunchtime session at the Scotia, Jimmy Dunn described scenes in the marketplace: storytellers with donkeys beside them on the ground, sly merchants unfolding soft cloths to reveal Goulimine beads and amber amulets, camels blocking the road. People had mentioned the town of Essaouira, to the west of Marrakesh. You could stay there cheaply, they said; few words were more likely to seduce me than that one.

On an autostrada slip road somewhere north of Rome, a lorry stopped and the driver asked, "Dove?" When I shouted up, "Palermo!" he said "Bene", and I got in. I stayed with him for two days. In a roadside restaurant filled with other long-haul drivers, he treated me to a meal of spaghetti with an unforgettable tomato sauce, followed by plump sardines bearing the stripes of the grill, and white bread with hard crust that softened under the cinder-flecked oil. We drank proper wine – not "the wine" in the Glasgow sense, nor the resinous yellow wine of Spetsai – something that had happened only a few times before in my life. There was a paper table cloth, which retained dark red rings left by the carafe, as I myself would have liked to retain them. I had seldom sheltered under such an agreeable web, spun by weather, food and drink, and companionship. I spoke just a scattering of Italian and he had little English. At night he slept in the cab, while I unrolled my sleeping bag next to the mammoth front wheel. He took me across the Strait of Messina in his cab and let me down monosyllabically on the other side, in Sicily.

The Tirrenia ferries left Palermo for Tunis only twice a week, something I didn't learn until arriving at the port and approaching the ticket office. I would have to bed down in Palermo for a few nights, which I did in the local campsite, sleeping on the ground in the open air, using a sweater on top of my sandshoes as a pillow.

Eventually, the ship cast off for a voyage scheduled to take ten hours.

On the quayside, as we waited to load, I had spotted a trio of Americans of about my own age, in a yellow VW campervan. Once aboard, I fell into conversation with one of them, Jeff, a dark-haired, squarely built footballer type, with a New World innocence not suggested by his rugged appearance. Jeff introduced me to his two travelling companions, the owner of the van, Russ, and his girl, Annette, and suddenly we were a convenient foursome on the open sea.

They planned to drive from Tunis, through Constantine and Algiers, all the way to Morocco. First, however, there were visas to be obtained for their American passports. The prospect made them nervous. "They'll speak English, won't they?"

"In North Africa the second language is French."

Russ and co. didn't know anything of that. They had barely a *oui* or a *non* among the three of them.

"And you?"

Yes, I did. By then, I had studied French for a Scottish Higher certificate and had passed with a decent grade, moving beyond the low horizon of the final report card at King's Park Secondary (adjusted to make a modest 49 per cent). From time to time, when we were wandering in Kelvingrove Park, Dudley would say, "Let's talk in French for a while", and we would play a game that involved approaching people in the street and asking for directions. If they didn't understand our elegantly phrased question ("Sauriez-vous me dire, madame . . ."), we would continue, seeking the way to "Sochi-aal Street" in broken English. "Ah, you mean Sauchiehall Street?" "Soo kee aal! Ben, oui!" I had enough to get the four of us served at café tables; enough, maybe, to talk to somebody in the Consulate about visas; enough to seek directions once we were on the road; possibly even enough to get us through an awkward situation at passport control.

That was one good reason for taking me on. Another, perhaps the main reason, was that Russ and Annette were fed up with Jeff, and he with them. It wasn't long before Jeff told me so himself. They slept in the campervan at night, while he lay outside, calm or storm. He and I quickly struck up a rapport, however, and I began to understand his irritation with the other two. Still, we were all going to be travelling companions, and it was best that we get along.

In order to obtain the visas, we had to spend a few days in Tunis. A place was found near the sea where we could park the van. On a visit to the neighbouring coastal town of Sidi Bou Said, I inquired of a crepe-skinned, turbaned man squatting on his haunches outside a café where I could buy a stamp "pour l'Israël". I had a letter for Dennis, who was still on Kibbutz Mishmarot. The Arab snapped into an instant rage and struck my shins hard with his cane without rising to his feet.

At some stage I learned that Russ and Annette, once in Morocco, planned to travel into the Atlas Mountains in order to purchase a large quantity of hashish. They said they were going to smuggle it out of the country into Spain, then sell it in Europe. The scheme had been born in the US before they left. They had it all worked out. They knew where to go in the mountains to buy the hash, and even had the name of a seller, presumably passed on by some other dealer.

Cannabis was illegal in Morocco, as in Europe, but personal use was widely tolerated. People smoked openly in cafés and other public spaces. Sandal-clad travellers came from all over to indulge their habit freely. The markets in the city squares sold wooden pipes with ceramic bowls and earthenware chillums of the sort favoured by cannabis connoisseurs. I had seen those connoisseurs in Glasgow and Poynings Road. Just to say "chillum" in a familiar way placed the user on a higher step.

It was equally well known that peddling drugs, or possession of a large amount, was not permitted in the country. The act of smuggling from Morocco into Spain was likely to be punishable by a long term of imprisonment. I felt about it the way my father felt about gambling and burglary: there must be easier ways of making a living.

Russ and Annette filled me in on the details of the scheme as we prepared for the journey across the Barbary Coast, projected to last several days. They planned to package the hashish in metal tins – labelled "poire" or "prune" – then to re-weld the tins. It was not a new trick. It was one that an old sniffer dog might have learned long ago. Why they told me about this reckless idea I don't know. Perhaps they hoped deep down that I would talk them out of it, or perhaps it was to seek temporary relief from the tension it generated inside them, and among the four of us, which was evident throughout our time together. Its effects were frequently directed towards Jeff.

Russ and Annette smoked dope every day. In a small public park in Sidi Bou Said – just a patch of parched yellow with a bob of scrub here and there – I accepted the joint, although my experience with Gerry, Pierre and the over-the-counter medicinal high at Poynings Road ought to have warned me off once and for all. I had told Russ I didn't smoke, but he insisted this was different: pure grass; there wasn't any tobacco in the joint, a gold-standard guarantee to certain potheads.

I inhaled and when it came round again I inhaled once more. I realized I was about to have one of my familiar sessions: of feeling that the natural world had been drained of all energy and capability, that the earth was grey and dead and that we were automatons moving through airless space.

All through the long Algerian days, Russ drew periodically from a joint as he sat at the wheel of the VW. He smoked in the morning and he smoked at night. The campervan had a mattress in the back, on which Russ and Annette stretched out when the day's driving was done. Jeff and I were usually content under the stars, but one night, at a stopping place on the coast between Algiers and Tipassa, it poured with rain so heavily that Jeff slid open the door of the van at 5 am and asked to be allowed to shelter inside. They said no. Our sleeping bags were dripping wet and we had no choice but to get up and stand under a tree, watching the rain batter the roof of the van, and the sea, hoping it would relent.

When it did, we went for a drying-out walk along the sand. The temperature rose quickly as it became light and we shook off our moisture. On the beach we came across an Arab fisherman who had just made a catch. A few words of French were exchanged – his was almost as pebble-mouthed as mine – and he invited us to share breakfast in his cabin. The freshly fried fish and hot black coffee, prepared over a fire built at the sandy threshold to the shack, eaten and drunk in sight and sound of the sea with the African sun coming up, cheered us so much that the downpour that had splashed us awake at dawn now seemed a blessing. On our return we enthused about it to the couple in the van, who responded by scolding Jeff again for having woken them up.

It wasn't our only experience of Arab hospitality in Algeria, but Russ and Annette were disinclined to be aroused by the esoteric world. What were they travelling for? Like other Americans I met on the road – the exceptions to the rule – they appeared surprised to discover that life wasn't arranged the way it was in Chicago and Washington DC, that *Time* magazine wasn't on sale in the kiosks under the arcades in Algiers, so reminiscent of Paris, that their Scottish travelling companion wasn't familiar with the nefarious manoeuvrings of their President and his outlaw band, that Coca-Cola was unavailable in the backwater café-cum-restaurant we would head to for an evening bite. To get to one of those rural places, Russ and I walked across a vast, empty patch of earth that was cracked like crazy paving, familiar from photographs I had seen in the pages of Jimmy Dunn's *National Geographic*, a sight I now found thrilling. Once inside, Russ asked in English for a hamburger and Coke, to the bafflement of the *patron*. Their only news was American news, their only history recent American history, their expectations domestic ones.

Somewhere along the 1,200-mile coastal route to Morocco, Russ and Annette smoked the last of the hashish they had brought with them over the border into Algeria. They discarded all traces of drug detritus, and the van was clean as it rolled into Zouj Bghal, the westernmost frontier post between the two countries. Darkness had fallen by the time we got there and ours was the only non-official vehicle in the compound. Somebody took a deep breath and said, "Here we go-oh". My companions showed the approaching officials their US passports with the newly issued visas.

They were freshly stamped and correct, but it wasn't enough for the impassive men in the military-style uniforms and peaked caps. Russ was asked to turn off the ignition and we were invited to step down and enter the office. The Americans were taken into a side room where they were strip-searched. For some reason, the British passport-holder was left alone. I picture myself – it might be one of those false screenshot memories but I'm sticking to it – leaning on the desk in the North African evening, chatting to the uniformed officers at the front counter ("Pas beaucoup du monde ce soir, hein?") while the others were subjected to a humiliating routine behind closed doors. Annette, too, by a pair of pretty female officers. The van was searched, as was the luggage, but in a haphazard way. No drugs were found, in their pockets, their bags or their innards. Even a small amount retained out of carelessness could have landed the lot of us in prison.

After an unexplained further hour's delay, we passed through. Not far from the border town of Oujda, we found a place to park and stretch out: Russ and Annette on the mattress inside the van, as usual, Jeff and me on the ground by the wheels.

In the morning – it was Morocco. As they let me down at the city wall, we shook hands and made promises and exchanged thanks: me for the longest lift I had ever had; they for the rudimentary but useful French. Jeff and I made a no-arrangement arrangement to meet in Marrakesh, which we kept.

A memory, in my relief at being free of the yellow VW campervan that I had first spotted on the quayside at Palermo a week before: that there were suddenly African men all around, distinct in gaze, gait and shape from the black people I had seen in London; and that the ankle-length djellabas and piled headscarves of the women on this side of the border were more colourful than they had been in Algeria.

I was *here*, like Jimmy Dunn before me, like Robin Williamson before him. Soon I would have my own tales to tell, of small sturdy glasses stuffed with mint leaves, of stepping out like a mad dog in the midday sun, of visits to an oasis, a word with biblical resonance. And indeed this oasis was surrounded by men and boys, goats and camels, out of *The Children's Illustrated Bible*. The bearded elders squatted on a mat in their thick-weave djellabas and turbans, sketching incomprehensible diagrams in the dust with a stick. That incomprehensibility made perfect sense to me. It was just what I had come for.

IV

Throughout my journeys in Morocco, south, west and finally north towards Tangier, I slept outdoors: on a sandy ridge by the side of the road, or in an unoccupied building – construction sites were particularly convenient, if I happened to be near one. From time to time, I granted myself the luxury of a night in a pension, with the intention of taking a shower, but at the level of accommodation I could afford I ran the risk of coming out the next day grubbier and more bug-infested than when I went in.

I got lifts without much trouble, and saw the Moroccan social spectrum from the passenger seat: one ride on a potholed road between two desolate small towns in the back of a pick-up at the wordless invitation of an illiterate goatherd; another in a Mercedes, across a good stretch of duel carriageway with a French- and English-speaking charmer dressed in Polo shirt and sharp slacks. From him, I learned about Polisario and a recent uprising springing from the Atlas mountains against King Hussain, and about the underground prisons in the desert housing prisoners with no name, no number. There were policemen at road junctions, stopping drivers, confiscating documents and probably vehicles, too, smiling at bribes. But visitors from the north, half-clothed and unsheltered though we might be, went largely unmolested. We were a species of royalty, respected for our wealth. Drop-outs in our own lands, we were welcome drop-ins here.

Somewhere towards the south, as I was starting my voyage back to Marrakesh from Essaouira, a man picked me up in the evening on a stretch of semi-desert road, with no other living thing in view but goats on the hillside. Here and there you would see them grazing the leaves in the branches of a tree. We drove a little way with few words exchanged. Then he stopped the car. With a questioning expression, he formed a circle with the thumb and index finger of his left hand, while making a poking movement with the middle finger of his right. My French, and my sign language, were up to a polite no thanks. I no longer had a lift.

It would soon be dark and there was nothing for it but to continue walking or to hope to be rescued by another driver. The roads were practically empty, but eventually I came in sight of a cluster of flat roofs and angled walls, all at about the same height, all tinted dirty white or grey. Children stopped their kicking games and stared. Women stopped their sweeping and stared. Men passing by twisted their necks to stare.

After reaching into my purse for a beer and slab of indeterminate meat at a roadside lean-to café, to be consumed under the unrelenting gaze of the proprietor and his small son, I left and lay down on a dusty bank by the roadside on the outskirts of the village. I was in my sleeping bag, using my shoes for a pillow as usual, with pullover on top; comfortable enough. Let the cars roll through the night – I was in for a good sleep. Tomorrow, back to Marrakesh. Then Rabat. On to Tangier, Algeciras, Europe.

As it turned out, the cars were not the enemy. Before I could fall asleep, I heard a scratching next to my ear . . . then silence. Again a scratching . . . What is it? *Scratching* . . . silence . . . *scratching*. Could it be that scorpions live here? A noise at the other ear this time . . . at my feet . . . everywhere. I began to believe they were in my sleeping bag. When I stood up, the noise stopped. When I lay down, it started again. Could it be rats? Would I prefer a rat to a scorpion? I was briefly the hero of Maupassant's novella *Le Horla*, who goes mad from hallucinations of intruders. Eventually the scratching stopped and I fell asleep. If I dreamt, I dreamt of a soft bed raised safely off the floor in a secure bedroom.

It was because of my night with the rat or the scorpion that I responded to an invitation some days later in the course of my journey towards Tangier. After seven weeks in North Africa, more than half of it spent in Morocco, I was on my way. No map was needed for getting from Africa to Glasgow. Just a rudimentary homing instinct: keep heading north to Rabat, the capital, skipping Casablanca on the way; follow a string of small towns up the west coast to reach Tangier. It was a distance of some 400 miles to the border post, three, at most four days' travel, allowing for poor roads, short lifts and a bit of sub-tourist loitering. Then I would be in Algeciras, back in the continent of pavements, streetlamps, sloping roofs and people who dressed lightly under the sun rather than piling on extra layers.

I had reached the outskirts of Rabat. The medina, where I had spent the afternoon looking round in desultory fashion, was conveniently to the north of the city, and as the sun sank swiftly I marched through a dusty suburb in hope of getting a lift to take me within reach of Kenitra, the next town of any size. The long-form hitch-hiker is always prey to temptation: that last lift of the day, the lure of a few more miles. If not that, then settling on a place to stay for the night, before resorting to some roadside café with scattered tables made from oil drums for a supper of chicken in soupy orange sauce and a glass of mint tea. Next day, under the sun, more cars, more curious or silent drivers; another hundred miles closer to Europe.

A small, swarthy man dressed in a beige bus driver's uniform fell into step alongside as I made my way through Rabat's final outpost. It was a stretch of road dotted on both sides with filling stations, open-front shops selling car tyres, wheels, slack jump leads and exhausted batteries to attach them to, entire engines, radio fronts without radio backs, dislocated television screens and cathode tubes, screws incompatible with neighbouring screwdrivers, eternally tangled wires, goods of mangled metal waiting to be put to unimaginable use. These shops were all over Morocco.

"Take-i-reasi," he said. "Take-i-reasi. Où allez-vous?"

Take-i-reasi was practically the limit of his English. He must have seen the scorpions in my head. I told him in French that I was heading for Tangier.

"Pas ce soir!"

No, not tonight – there was still about 150 miles to go – "but I'll keep on for now, until I find a place to sleep".

"Américain?"

It was the eternal question. If not that, "Deutsch?"

"Scottish." It was the obligatory reply. "Ecosse." The name of the country meant nothing to him.

"Bretagne," I said. "England. Angleterre. Pas anglais, moi, mais . . . c'est d'à côté."

"Cous-cous." He made an eating gesture with fingers and thumb. "You like. Cous-cous. Vous. Faim." They were not questions.

Through smiles and gestures and bursts of repeated phrases, I let the image flirt with my hunger. I would be keen to eat from a plate of cous-cous in a Moroccan home, with a Moroccan family. A pleasant picture formed in my head. He invited me to follow him, and my stomach gave permission to do so.

The bus driver lived in a modest house fifty yards or so from the road, one of a row, painted blue on the bottom half, with whitewashed upper. I was always struck by the lack of even boundaries between the foot of a house and the sidewalk – you couldn't call it a pavement, for there were no defined pavements in poor areas; no concrete or slate, only hard earth, rock, or mud.

Inside, I found not a bus driver's wife but two girls of about thirteen or fourteen, surprised by the apparition from the Different world. They began to giggle, and continued giggling all through my stay, except when asleep. I could scarcely see what they looked like, because they were not allowed to be in the room with me or even to be seen with heads uncovered, but they embarked on a continuous procession of tiptoeing out of the kitchen or one of the side rooms in order to steal glimpses of the stranger.

While the driver and I collaborated on a duet of franglais and hand signals in the small living room, the girls set about preparing the cous-cous. If one had to pass from the kitchen, which was through an arch to the left of the living room where we were, to a room on the right, a colourful killim would be ostentatiously stretched and finger-pinned across the open space by the other, so that the first could dart, faux-furtively, from there to there. The accomplishment of these missions was concluded by intense bursts of hilarity.

When the food was ready, the driver and I ate together where we were, while the girls remained in the kitchen. There was no table. We sat on the floor. The cous-cous filled a white enamel basin of the type my mother once washed small clothes in. We used our fingers. There was meat and gravy and soft flat bread to scoop it up with. I patted my tummy in appreciation.

When it was all done, the driver produced some hashish and offered to make a pipe. After my dead-world experience in Sidi Bou Said, I had renounced even the social obligation of smoking. A few weeks before, at an oasis outside Marrakesh, in tribute to Davey Graham, I had accepted maajun – the sweet, sticky cake baked with hash, after which he had named one of his orientalist tunes – leading to the same old result. My excuse was that it was in honour of a hero. Davey's shimmering "Maajun" I could tolerate, but not the thing itself.

"Is it possible that I could have a drink of something or other?" I asked my host. "Du vin, par exemple?" Ever since my magnificent dinner with the Italian lorry driver in the roadside restaurant north of Sicily two months earlier, I had grown fond of sun-and-south-suggesting red wine and its effects, so different from the weather-resistant heaviness of draught ale. In the cafés of Marrakesh, it had been easy and cheap to order a glass.

Not so easy now, though. He looked at me for a moment. Possible? Yes. First, though, he would have to telephone a friend. A man who knew how to acquire wine. We would go to meet him in the medina. "Dans le médina?" He assured me it was not that far from where we were sitting. "In Rabat?" I thought it was all a bit elaborate. All I wanted was a glass, two at the most. I wouldn't have mentioned wine had he not asked me first about the hashish. But another adventure, and why not? Things were going well. The cosy room. The giggling girls. The feeling of hot food in the neglected belly. The Moroccan night. The prospect of a bed, a bed, a bed.

A bed where, by the way? Which bed? Before I could take that train of thought further, he said, "Et bien?" I said, "OK." My host repeated "OK", with a conspiratorial smile as he got to his feet. He had changed out of his bus driver's uniform, and was dressed in a white, ankle-length garb.

"OK" and "et bien" were not all that were needed to get us started on the quest for a glass of wine. First, he told me, it was necessary that we take a shower.

The evening was turning out to be full of surprises. No wife. Happy girls. An offer of hash from a bus driver. A secret rendezvous in the medina of the Moroccan capital. I enjoyed making the imaginary link with the film *Casablanca*. Now a shower. And only then the wine! Who knew that the inkling for a glass could lead one into such a labyrinth? But why not? In any case, I hadn't had a shower since leaving the *riad* in Marrakesh.

The next surprise was that the shower was not to take place at home, since there was evidently no bathroom in the house. Instead, we walked through the neighbourhood towards a public bathhouse. On payment of a small fee, we entered a steamy room full of cubicles with wooden three-quarter-length doors of a sort familiar from the Calder Street swimming baths in Glasgow, where I had gone during the school holidays with Jean and Phyllis. Each cubicle housed an individual shower. I made my way towards one with an open door. Inside, I pushed it closed – there was no latch – and undressed. In a flash my naked host was in with me. It was a small room, now rather full, and we were squeezed tightly together.

The bus driver prepared to soap his guest, but with only a little persuasion he found his own shower room, and all was well. When we reconvened in the waiting area, he seemed not at all put out by my insistence on taking a shower in private. We were clean, there was no denying it. And now . . . some wine?

We left the public baths and took a bus towards the medina, which was more or less deserted, though it was not yet nine o'clock. At a crossroads free of traffic, from which one could see shadowy colonnades and flat roofs in all directions – as if we had to be watchful for the police – we kept the rendezvous with our dealer.

As I was introduced to a dark-skinned Arab with a thin moustache, I had the uncomfortable sensation of being presented in an unaccustomed role, a guest of honour. In among the Arabic gutturals I heard the shuffling of words like "Deutsch" and "Américain", percolating down to "Anglais" – inaccurate, but this was no time for pedantry. There were nods and smiles. The messenger produced from within the depth of his djellaba a bottle of some sort, of which I was granted a glimpse before it was once again folded into safety.

How does that seem? "Ça va?" I could only shrug my shoulders. I knew nothing. Even if I knew something, I had seen next to nothing. "Oui, ça va." At least it was red.

From that moment on, it was an embarrassing assignation. The black-marketeer named a large sum, in Moroccan dinar – let's say the equivalent of ten pounds at the time, a hundred pounds or more in today's money. I was used to living on under a pound a day.

Excuse me, monsieur, but it's simply not possible.

Immediately, he reduced the price by half. But it was still far too much. I never enjoyed this kind of bargaining anyway, which was expected of the Westerner in Morocco and placed the native vendor in the role of con man. The wine seller came down again, but – I am afraid it's impossible. His good humour, such as it was, drained away, and he got angry with us for having wasted his time. What had he been led to expect by the driver? A meeting with "an Englishman", probably, with all that it implied. Poor chap – he had found only poor me instead. He turned and walked away without a farewell. The driver and I made our way out of the medina back to the house. I would have to live without a glass of wine that evening.

Inside, the little flat-roofed house was tidied up, dimly lit and quiet. The two girls were asleep already, or pretending to be asleep, and we were soon to follow. In the living room, the driver gestured towards the seat-cum-bed against which I had rested my back while we consumed the delicious cous-cous and meat.

So kind! Yet again. "Et vous?"

He pointed to the floor. There was a rug – we were standing on it – and beneath the rug, red tiles.

During the night, my host decided that the tiled floor was too severe to sleep on, and he tried to join me – clean as I was – in the bed. His own bed, after all. But no. For this night only, it was mine. As with the shower cabin, we would have found it cramped for two.

I would have liked to say, "You are like a scorpion, my host." But all I said was: "No, monsieur, but if you want we can change places."

He returned to his hardness on the floor.

Morning came and I swished my feet over the edge of the bed on to the cool, now vacant tiles. From the depth of their headscarves, the lovely girls served coffee and flat bread left over from last night's feast, with fig jam. Flavours: the crusty *batbout* in the palm; a sweet black syrup; a girl's shy smile saved up all through the night – impressions that endure through five decades. I felt – or imagined I felt – their aching to be free.

The bus driver appeared, dressed again in his beige uniform, ready for work. I thanked them all and went down to the road in search of a lift to Tangier.

12

THE MAGUS

I

On my return from Morocco, the Glasgow autumn already frowning, I took my seat at Jack's side in the Grosvenor Café in Byres Road once again and tried to come up with ideas for *GUM/Moving Review*. It was September 1973. The magazine had suspended publication over the long summer holiday. Jack continued working as a reporter in Clydebank, while Brian Hannan developed his interest in the new British cinema.

Jack and Brian appeared to me mainstream in their tastes, whereas to me the mainstream was a diversion. I cherished the identity of the dropout. At Langside College on the Southside, where I began to study for Highers and A levels in preparation for applying to university, I established my identity as the traveller who had just come home from Away. I had walked among the minarets of Marrakesh and seen the goats in the trees. I had tasted maajun. I had stood with a foot on either side of the Bosporus and plucked stringed instruments with turbaned minstrels. I had taken tea with modern British literature's most famous junkie. He had offered me a Danish pastry instead of a fix.

A book I read between classes was Jeff Nuttall's Bomb Culture. I was hungry for any news about Trocchi, and he and Nuttall had come together in the early 1960s, plotting to overthrow the oppressive system and change society. Co-conspirators included the alternative psychiatrists R. D. Laing and David Cooper, the Fluxus artist John Latham, the sound poet Bob Cobbing, and our own Tom McGrath, who was then the editor of *Peace News*. The satanic majesty hovering above them all was Trocchi.

The name of the master plan was project sigma (subversively lower-case), otherwise known as the Invisible Insurrection of a Million Minds. Trocchi declared it a *coup du monde*, distinct from a *coup d'état*. The invisible insurrection would result in "spontaneous universities" shooting up like consciousness-raising mushrooms across the nation, and in power passing to the elect, which would in time include everyone. The semi-criminal drug addict Trocchi – a wanted man in the United States for providing narcotic drugs to a minor – would assume temporary leadership. After the fulfilment of project sigma, the leader's role would dissolve.

William Burroughs was among those who had made written offerings to the sigma portfolio. In fact, his "M.O.B.", which Trocchi had given me in typewritten Gestetner form, and which we were about to publish in *GUM/Moving Review*, was his contribution to the project: one junkie supporting another down the road to perfectibility.

"Let's get this clear," Nuttall reported Trocchi telling him one afternoon in a pub near Marble Arch. "What this is all about is the rejection of *everything* outside that door." Nuttall had misgivings about Trocchi and about the rest of the plan. Was he himself a dropout with the inclination to drop in? He wrote amusingly of his predicament, as he made his way to a weekend convention of project sigma at a country house rented for the purpose, in Oxfordshire, in 1964. "At Reading I missed the bus so started out on the Oxford Road. An old man gave me a lift; courteous, kindly, at peace with himself, he seemed the embodiment of all that was good about the way of life we were out to destroy."

Jack travelled to London to interview Edna O'Brien, "who guards the privacy of her London exile like gold dust", he wrote. His long article for the next issue of the *Moving Review* – Burroughs's "M.O.B" was on the inside-front page – was widely admired among the 1,000-strong readership of the magazine.

"I don't do many interviews these days," she said. "I find my time rather, um, precious. You must just have caught me in the right mood. The proper vibrations, eh? I don't like being interviewed by the professionals from Fleet Street. They know all the things they're going to ask before they come." She thought a moment. "Glasgow University, now is that the one where you have that man as your, what is it?"

She was referring to Jimmy Reid, who led the Upper Clyde Shipbuilders' work-in in 1972. The word she groped for was rector. Jack returned from the visit to her house in Chelsea with his pen full of fine phrases ready to be transposed to print, about her "loose-curled, gold-red hair", her neck "almost as long as one of those erotic Modigliani models". Her eyes, he wrote, "look to be green, but she winks and says ah, just put down grey like your own, love".

My own first contribution on returning from North Africa was a piece about press coverage of the October 1973 Arab-Israeli war, sometimes known as the Yom Kippur War. Jack suggested I was well-placed to write a commentary, and the bold-face intro reflected his newspaperly instincts: "Why has the British press been lying on an Israeli slant since the fourth break-out of the Middle East war? Jim Campbell, who has travelled extensively both in Israel and in Arab lands, argues for a more balanced sympathy in current newspaper coverage."

If I was an expert on anything, it was hitch-hiking, travel, Away – I could lead you from Piraeus to the bar of the Horse Shoe, through Yugoslavia and over the Alps, in five or six hard-earth nights, plimsoll-shod and lacking a compass. Still, I was keen to write, keen to learn to write. Jack and I discussed the matter while leaning on the bar at the Horse Shoe.

"How *do* you learn to write?"

Jack: "By writing."

"Any other way?"

"By reading."

I launched the piece with some remarks made by Bertrand Russell three years earlier – "What Israel is doing today cannot be condoned, and to invoke the horrors of the past to justify those of the present is gross hypocrisy" – and combined them with historical facts filleted from a pile of books in the Mitchell Library. In the *Guardian*, the *Express*, *Telegraph* and other papers, I found little or no sympathy for the Palestinian cause. The word itself was seldom used at the time, giving way to "Arab". I bound my new-found knowledge together with impressions left by life on Kibbutz Mishmarot. It was untutored, no doubt a little glib, but not dishonest. It was, like the Trocchi piece, the result of hard work. I was finding out that that was a literary virtue in itself. Discrimination and restraint were guided by it; talent was futile without it.

It was dishonest, on the other hand, to have allowed Jack's flattering intro to my Arab-Israeli piece to go through, and I blushed when I saw it in print. But blushing teaches lessons, too.

At Langside, I would take classes that would lead towards exams that would lead in turn, I hoped, to university. There would be no report cards and no ink rubber, no disapproving father staring at the crudely improved marks, no Mr Crawford to find me out and no desperate salvation in the shape of a rickety printing factory in the old Fruit Market. The Glasgow Corporation bursary was modest but sufficient for part of a year. The exams to come would not be hideous traps into which I was certain to fall, but stepping stones to higher learning. "I see and aim for better things", the old King's Park Secondary motto come home to roost.

An application to a range of universities had to be made halfway through the academic year – a term it was now a pleasure to hear myself say. My first choice was Glasgow, so that I could stay in close contact with Jack, Jimmy Dunn, Kate Reader and others in a growing circle of literary and artistic friends in and around the university itself. After all, I still had some claims on an office there, with Jack, as co-editor of the *Moving Review*. All under vaguely false pretences. I'd had a happy time with vagueness. It had given me a decent run for my money. Now I wanted something more definite. After Glasgow, I put down Edinburgh University and after Edinburgh, Reading.

On the application form, I set out the courses I would be following at Langside: A levels in English and Sociology; Highers in Art, French, which I already had but wanted to re-sit to gain a better grade, and something called Modern Studies – politics, current affairs – which was advertised as an easy option. In response, each university applied to would say either No – the answer I quickly received from Glasgow and Reading – or Yes. That came from Edinburgh, on condition of specified minimum grades.

My parents were pleased at the idea, and I was developing a faculty that permitted me to be happy to see them pleased. The centre of gravity was shifting. Instead of Gilmorehill, just a few minutes' walk from my flat, I was bound for the east coast. In the autumn of 1974, when I got there, I would have turned twenty-three. Another motto: "No reward without effort", in the name of which the father had forsaken the son and left him to wander among the Children of Israel. When I did come back, thanks to a Samaritan from Flushing, New York, he greeted me warmly: "The return of the Prodigal! We'll kill the fatted mince."

II

I had read John Fowles's novel *The French Lieutenant's Woman* before arriving on Spetsai. The story was set in the year 1867 in the seaside resort of Lyme Regis, a century before its composition in a farmhouse where Fowles lived, just outside. I knew nothing about the Dorset town in reality, only the dressed-up Victorian version at the centre of the novel. The discovery, from magazine clippings I consulted – again in Glasgow's Mitchell Library – that Fowles himself now lived there, gave a shine to his fictional representation. As Trocchi was present in the New York City he described in the so-called novel *Cain's Book* – like his double Joe Necchi, he worked on a scow amid the commercial river traffic on the Hudson river – so Fowles the erudite puppeteer was an actor in his own nineteenth-century staging in Dorset.

I was bewitched by the illusion of the writer emerging from the writing – stepping out from the page to shake hands with the reader. It was the same thrill that I had felt with Cocteau and his mirror: choose to walk into the world of art; then choose to walk out again. Why separate the two? You could live an ordinary life in Byres Road and, at the same time, an extraordinary one in the pages of *Les Enfants terribles* or *Cain's Book* or *The French Lieutenant's Woman*.

The most famous feature of Lyme Regis is its long, curved harbour wall, the Cobb, which plays a role in Jane Austen's *Persuasion*: ". . . the principal street almost hurrying into the water, the walk to the Cobb, skirting round the pleasant little bay . . ." In *Persuasion*, Louisa Musgrove loses her footing and falls down the stone steps at the side of the Cobb. *The French Lieutenant's Woman* takes the reader to the Cobb on its opening page, "a long claw of old grey wall that flexes itself against the sea". The enigmatic figure of Sarah Woodruff is standing "at the seawardmost end", staring out across the waves, "like a living memorial to the drowned".

Before I had left Glasgow in the June of 1972, with the intention of travelling to the Far East, a regular in the Three in One on Woodlands Road, the pub that Jack and I favoured in the university area, had let fall a surprising verdict: Well, *The French Lieutenant's Woman*'s good, she said. But *The Magus* . . . That's incredible. *The Magus* was the big one.

Apparently there was something I didn't know that I ought to have known. *The Magus* was his best book. "Remember?" our friend in the pub went on. "The house of the Magus, Maurice Conchis – *conscious* – and all that . . ." I kept quiet. It was a poor show to be a Fowles propagandist and not to have read or even to have heard of *The Magus*.

During the time off from my labours over the pizza ovens on Dizengoff Street, I had looked for the big novel in the second-hand bookshops of Tel Aviv, which were well stocked with English and American paperbacks. I found a copy, and when I returned to the kibbutz after my existential adventure involving the 300 Israeli pounds, I began to read it outside my cabin on Desolation Row.

About eighty pages into the story of Nicholas Urfe and his visits to the house of the Magus, I had an unusual experience, one that the creator of a fictionalized location perhaps does not intend to provoke in his readers, but which he surely ought to welcome.

> I came to the ridge again. The sea was a pearly turquoise, the far mountains ash-blue in the windless heat. I could see the shimmering green crown of pine trees around Bourani. It was about noon when I came through the trees out on to the shingle of the beach with the chapel. It was deserted . . . A long way south a plump caique thudded past towing a line of six little lamp-boats, like a mallard with ducklings. Its bow-wave made a dark miraging ripple on the creamy blue surface of the sea, and that was all that remained of civilization . . .

As I continued turning the pages, the island on which the Magus dwells began to assume the shape of the island where I had lived and which I had recently left, Spetsai. The Phraxos of the novel is small, with a single town, no cars and a pine forest through which one must pass in order to reach the beaches and caves of the south-west. I had walked through that pine corridor, decorated with smells of oregano, thyme and other olfactory delights yet undiscovered in Glasgow, as well as the previously unknown sound of cicadas. As Fowles's narrator, Nicholas, puts it, "they racketed in a ragged chorus, never quite finding a common beat". And "huge hornets, midges, bees, bots, and ten thousand other anonymous insects".

The Lord Byron School of the novel, where Nicholas is a teacher, was unmistakeably the imposing Anargyrios and Korgialenios School, which Jerry had pointed out from the saddle. It is the place where, the author tells us – as Jerry had

The Anargyrios and Korgialenios School, Spetsai, lightly disguised as the Lord Byron School in John Fowles's novel *The Magus*.

told me – the future rulers of Greece receive their education. It didn't look like any school I had known in Scotland: a white-and-ochre cube, three or four stories high, with pilasters framing the grand entrance. If Jerry had said it was an army barracks, I would have believed him. Only later did I discover that Takis, owner of Romeo, Zorba and the other horses – our patron, our exploiter, our victim – was one of its products. He would have been thirty-three or thirty-four when we worked for him on Spetsai. It is possible that he had been coaxed into his fluent, acquisitive English some twenty years earlier by the author of *The Magus*.

Six years after publication of the novel, the island in the story would have been recognizable to any attentive reader wandering over Spetsai itself. It was impossible not to see it. But unless they had been there and possessed some sense of curiosity about Spetsai's wilder parts, readers of The Magus would have been unaware that Phraxos was modelled on a specific place. Fowles had never made the information public. Spetsai was a popular destination in 1972, but not yet the overstuffed tourist resort it would become. There was no airport; the boat journey from Athens took five hours (the rapid Flying Dolphin had yet to surface); beyond the port, there are no villages and no antiquities to speak of; the military junta of the Colonels was still in power.

The events that take place at Maurice Conchis's villa Bourani – the elaborate, staged masques of which the sole spectator is Nicholas, the Fowles character in all but name – are fantastical but, like Phraxos itself, the house is not a complete invention. To judge by the cartographical references provided by Nicholas in the novel, Bourani is the imaginary counterpart of a real house called Villa Yiasemí, situated in the area between the bay of Aghia Anargyri, past which I trotted every other day with a posse of happy riders, and another beach at Aghia Paraskevi, or Holy Friday bay. Sometimes we stopped for drinks beneath one of the tattered thatched umbrellas. If I close my eyes and rummage through my memory, spreading my legs over the saddle again, I can convince myself that I see the whitewashed chapel at Aghia Paraskevi, visible from the seaside track and frequently mentioned in the novel.

Villa Yiasemí (jasmine) was owned by a member of a well-established local family, Ioannis Botassis. In a journal entry dated November 30, 1952, Fowles described an accidental meeting with Botassis after a swim in the bay. He had encountered the house's owner on the sands, "bald but for a wisp, in shorts and a green shirt, brown-faced, freckled, with pleasant, amiable eyes". Fowles was invited to come for coffee after he had shaken himself free of the captivating sea. It was during the course of this visit to Villa Yiasemí that the seed of *The Magus* was planted.

In the fictional realm, the beauty of the site is heightened by a concoction of magic, menace and eroticism. On first seeing Conchis at the villa with the mysterious sign nailed to a pine tree, "Salle d'attente", Nicholas regards him as "this man who had come to 'my' desert island".

I knew how he felt. In a back-to-front way, Fowles had come to mine.

III

"Why not John Fowles?" I said one evening when Jack was presiding over a Big Ideas meeting at the Grosvenor. "The most interesting English writer of our day." I felt confident in my approval of writers I liked, as I was assured in my disdain of those I had never read. Any mention of Sillitoe or Storey would draw a look of arrogant ennui, though I later came to admire both, and many of the writers associated with them. At the time, I was too provincial to appreciate their advanced approach to provincialism.

Jack liked my suggestion and I went out into the street with the lightness that comes of having a commission to fulfil. Fowles was rumoured to be reclusive but, an old hand now, I obtained his address from the publisher without any trouble and wrote a letter requesting an interview. His reply came quickly. "Fine, but I live a hell of a way from Glasgow, as you perhaps didn't realize when you wrote. Best wishes . . . John Fowles."

I realized it perfectly well. I had accompanied Nicholas Urfe, the hero of *The Magus*, to Conchis's house on the other side of the ridge on Phraxos in more than the usual imaginative sense.

I wanted to share with someone the revelation that I had spent ten weeks in 1972 living in a fictional place, and who better to share it with than the author himself, the architect of "The Godgame", the novel's working title? That I wasn't a *Magus* crank who had travelled on purpose to Spetsai after falling under the book's spell, but had had an independent life there in the house up on the hill, with Jerry and the horses, made my discovery more piquant, more "weird".

A quick, nervous phone call from our student offices and it was arranged. Fowles suggested a date: December 8, 1973.

IV

After an overnight stop with my parents in High Wycombe, I stepped down from the train that Saturday morning at Axminster station, the nearest to his home, as instructed. But where was his home? I was without any information about transport – I realized only then – or even whether there was such a thing as a bus to shuttle me from Axminster to the domain of the Lyme Regis Magus. How big a town was Lyme Regis, and how would I find him? I had the name, Belmont House, but it could have been anywhere.

There was a public telephone on the platform and from there I dialled the Belmont number, which fortunately I had brought with me. Fowles sounded intimidatingly grumpy. He didn't drive, he said . . . but . . . (a muffled off-receiver exchange) . . . his wife would come to pick me up.

Elizabeth Fowles was tall and warm and friendly. I can see now that she was accustomed to compensating with kindness. "Are you a Hardy fan?" she asked as she switched us down the rolling, wintry, rural roads. I wasn't. I hadn't read much Hardy. I hadn't even clicked that we were in "Hardy Country", as she called it. I could talk to her about William Burroughs, Alexander Trocchi, Jean Cocteau, Hermann Hesse, John Fowles. I had read *The Magus*, and I had accepted the invitation to inhabit its imaginary land. Half a million others had read it too but, unlike them, I had tramped the real-life terrain of which the story was a reflection: that shaded and scented and sea-washed place where the Mediterranean was "most itself". I was, like Nicholas Urfe, like Conchis, like Fowles himself – Elizabeth, too – a resident of Phraxos, the conceptual isle. I had come to Lyme Regis to claim my citizenship.

Having heard the crunch of gravel in the courtyard as Elizabeth parked the car, Fowles appeared at the door of Belmont House to welcome us. "Big, bearded and burly", I jotted down later. "He transferred his cigarette to his lips and his Scotch from right hand to left in order to greet me."

Throughout the day, Elizabeth treated me with benign patience, as she would have a peculiar nephew; only much later did I learn that it was an instinct in search of an object. "She has so many steady, earthy, commonsense qualities beneath the waywardness", Fowles wrote in his journal in 1953. "A gangling, elegant creature." I sensed her maternal warmth straight away, without having to explain it to myself . What might she have seen? A slim boy with long blond hair in a military jacket and funny-coloured trousers, half-starved, in need of a bath, probably, socially unformed but striving to be polite.

Belmont House, two storeys high, washed in shaded pink, has the shape of a double cube. Built in 1777 as "maritime villa", it sits at the top of the hill on the main road leading into Lyme. At the back is a large, sloping garden, with a view of the Cobb. Fowles bought the place in 1968, moving from an isolated farmhouse, Underhill, not far away. He started *The French Lieutenant's Woman* at Underhill and finished it off here,

Belmont House, Lyme Regis. Fowles opened the door – "big, bearded and burly".

in the room above the lobby in which I was now standing. He loved Belmont, but had loved even more the solitary existence of Underhill Farm. They had to leave, he explained, because landslips on the cliffside on which the house was perched had made staying impossible. Elizabeth, I discovered, hated the loneliness of her life in both places.

As we ate lunch in the spacious kitchen and I blethered on profusely, any residual nervousness now released, he made attempts to be chatty and cheerful, but it wasn't his proper mode. When he saw the tape recorder, he said, "Oh, you use one of those things, do you?" (For a long time afterwards, I made it a point of principle not to.) When my Scottish two-pin plug failed to fit his English three-pin socket, he scowled and impatience filled the air. Elizabeth stepped in and we drove together half a mile to an electrical goods shop on Lyme's Broad Street, sloping down to the sea ("the principal street almost hurrying into the water", as Jane Austen wrote), where she bought an adaptor. I would happily have spent the afternoon being shepherded round the town and on to the Cobb by her.

By the time we sat down before the fire in the living room in order to "get down to business", as Fowles put it, he had recovered his mood, and he spoke generously to his young interlocutor. "Some critics have said *The Magus* did not achieve what it set out to do." Did I really say that? What critics? Why did I pay attention to them instead of relying on my sense of gratitude and wonder? "No argument from me," Fowles replied disarmingly. At my prodding, he expanded: "You must remember it was a first novel and I tried to say too much."

Fowles had begun writing *The Magus* in the 1950s, several years before completing *The Collector* (1963), his publishing debut but not his first novel. After the success of that book, in Britain and the US (a film by William Wyler was released in 1965, starring Terence Stamp and Samantha Eggar), he resumed work on what was at different times called "The Godgame" and "The Magos".

"It was written by a young man," he said into my tape recorder, "who really didn't have very much experience of life, but who had a tremendous love of narrative. It says so many things and nothing really is concluded. One thing that worries me about it now is that it's not terribly well written. One day I hope to rewrite it." Three years later, he did so.

He talked about his deep sense of Englishness. If anything, he felt part Greek and part French, but English all over – "not British".

"You are as much a stranger to me as any American."

Creative-writing courses were not yet a feature of university

John Fowles in Lyme Regis, circa 1973. *Courtesy of Sarah Fowles.*

English faculties. Fowles would have hated them. He spoke disparagingly anyway of "the whole academic set-up" as a "grave block" to the writer. "If there's one gang of people I'd like to see thrown into the sea it's the professors of English Literature."

He had a belief that "capitalism must outgrow itself", but was not drawn to the idea of a "violent overthrow" of the system. "Because there's a massively powerful fascist element in Britain, and a potential disaster could occur." This is one of the ideas behind the action of *The Collector*. The central character Clegg's feeling that he has the right to suppress the freedom of another, Miranda, grows out of his lack of understanding, and eventually hatred, of art and culture. It was one of Fowles's obsessions: the menace posed to society by philistinism, in which he discerned a nascent fascism. He went on to say that *The Aristos*, his carnet of personal philosophy, was "the sort of book a French writer would publish naturally". His editor had advised against it, "but you have to take the iron fist with publishers occasionally. I wouldn't want this American situation where your publishing editor dominates your life."

The information that I had just returned from Greece, where I was staying on Spetsai – "it's the same, isn't it? . . . it's Phraxos" – surprised him. He allowed a moment's pause in the middle of one of his diatribes against the ruination of Greece, as if his power of speech had unaccustomedly stumbled. Then he said, "Good Lord", and called for Elizabeth.

He had never returned to the island that the world knew as Spetsai, but which we – the elite assembly of Conchis, Elizabeth, Fowles himself and now me – called Phraxos. He did not wish to visit Greece while the Colonels remained in power. Their influence was only slightly more oppressive than that other tyranny, tourism, which had overtaken Spetsai and many other Greek islands. Like others who loved Greece in the 1950s – Patrick Leigh Fermor, for one – he abominated the curse of progress. I knew little about the Colonels, who had not prevented me from discovering the pines and the tortoises, the "pearly turquoise" of the sea, the tavernas, the retsina and fasolakia, Romeo and Zorba. I was oppressed, rather, by the tyranny of rain and cold and wind, under which we spent our lives in the north.

The remainder of that long afternoon passed awkwardly. The next train for London, the last of the day, did not depart from Axminster until a quarter to seven. I should have offered to take a walk by myself through the streets of Lyme Regis, but I might have wandered too far and then missed it. One or other of them could have volunteered to escort me down to the Cobb, if only to make the time pass more quickly for the relief of all, but no. Fowles gave me a tour of the house, which included his collection of nineteenth-century erotica. He mentioned a

French tale of a black slave girl, dating from the early years of that century, which he would "one day like to translate into English". I asked him to repeat the title. "You won't have heard of it." He brought out *Ourika* by Claire de Duras (1826) in a limited edition four years after our meeting.

At some stage, unable to put up any longer with questions about which records he listened to and if he had a favourite pub – Miles Davis's *In a Silent Way* was one answer to the first question; to the second it was the Masons Arms in nearby Branscombe – Fowles disappeared upstairs to his study, leaving me alone with Elizabeth in the big kitchen. She cooked a cheese omelette, so delicious I've never forgotten it, fortifying me for the journey back to High Wycombe.

At just after six o'clock, we all three climbed into the car and headed for Axminster. Although he had chosen to live in out-of-the-way places, Fowles told me he would be "a menace behind the wheel". He had eyes only for wildflowers by the roadside, a butterfly or a bird darting overhead. He gave me a copy of his latest book, a collection of poems, published in the US. It has a cobalt blue cover, an echo of the sea surrounding Phraxos, with just *Poems* and the author's name.

As I stepped on to the train, Elizabeth asked me to be sure to send them a copy of the article when it appeared.

V

Not long after I returned from Dorset, it became clear that our magazine was headed for trouble. The Students' Representative Council had withdrawn its funding, not unreasonably, since the publication was no longer called *Glasgow University Magazine*, or *GUM*, but the *Moving Review*.

Looking back at the issues we produced, I find a report by Brian Hannan on the film director Lindsay Anderson, "returning to work in his old stamping ground, the theatre" (*The Farm* by David Storey opened at the Royal Court in the spring of 1973); an interview with Stephane Grappelli ("*GUM* went along to meet the grand old man of swing"); a discussion of football violence in Glasgow. There was Jack's Edna O'Brien piece, and an interview with George Melly – again by Brian, a better writer than I had the decency to acknowledge at the time – my commentary on the Yom Kippur War, and a good deal besides. But there was hardly anything about local activities or student organizations. The very idea of acknowledging Freshers' Week or events of that sort would have embarrassed us. Of the principal figures involved in the magazine's production, only one, Brian, was studying at the university. The *Moving Review* had already moved itself in spirit out of Gilmorehill. Now it was going nowhere.

My Fowles piece, towards which I had been making notes since he and Elizabeth saw me off, clutching the signed copy of *Poems* to my breast, remained in limbo. It was to be another two years before I transcribed the tape in question-answer form and submitted it to an academic quarterly at the University of Wisconsin, which accepted it for publication.

I dutifully sent the typescript to Lyme Regis for approval, as required by the journal ("Mr Fowles has seen and approved the text"). It came back with inky emendations on every page, and a letter. "I wish you could have given me more warning, as I feel it badly needs editing. I should hate to see it printed in its present verbatim form. I've done what I can to make it a little more coherent." For the first time, I felt offended by his characteristic bad temper, and huffily omitted to take on all the suggested changes – something I would never have done later without good reason.

Publication in the handsome Autumn 1976 number of *Contemporary Literature* went ahead. It was book-size, floppy and desirable, on good paper, with a scarlet cover. "An Interview with John Fowles" had top billing. I added a brief introduction:

> We conducted the interview before the fire on a winter's day after lunch. Mr Fowles frowned when he saw the tape recorder. He speaks in an English public-school voice, which he punctuates with such gap-fillers as "you know", "I mean" and "sort of", quite often leaving his sentences incomplete and dangling in the air between the two speakers. He answered with impatience one minute and with friendly warmth the next, but in the end his confidence – "I don't need people, really" – is not difficult to believe.

*

A footnote: In 2006, the second volume of Fowles's *Journals* was published, covering the years 1966 to 1990, and I was asked to review it for the *New York Times Book Review*. I recalled his brief note to me, dated November 9, 1973: "Fine, but I live a hell of a way from Glasgow." Might he have made some record of our meeting? Unsurprisingly, I consulted the index in the book to see if there was any reference to it; equally unsurprisingly, I found none.

The entry for October 31, 1973, however – nine days before his reply to me was written – revealed that Fowles had just declined an offer to give the Clark Lectures at Cambridge University. In addition, he had received "a profile request from the *Sunday Times*. Also refused." The suggestion from a student magazine in Glasgow must have arrived a day or two later, and to this he acquiesced, giving up most of a Saturday to answer questions posed by a raw youth from a foreign country. It's hard to dislike that.

★

A second footnote: In 2015, forty-two years after Fowles had sat before the fire speaking into my mammoth cassette recorder, I received an invitation, in my capacity as a columnist on the *Times Literary Supplement*, to spend a night at Belmont. The house had been bought by the Landmark Trust from Fowles's widow, his second wife, Sarah, and after extensive renovation was to be launched as an up-market bed and breakfast. "We are about to open Belmont", the message read,

> which is John Fowles's former home in Lyme Regis. It is
> a beautiful place and he wrote much of his work there
> including *Daniel Martin* and *The Ebony Tower*. *The French
> Lieutenant's Woman* was completed and published while
> he lived there and the writing room has a view over
> the Cobb. I wondered if you could cover the launch of
> Belmont in a considered way, including its history and
> Fowles's time there. We might even be able to organize
> a night for you there, to absorb the setting.

I was tempted, and in response set out a little of my Fowles history. "The house will be rather different to when you visited it before," came the reply. "However of course some of John Fowles's books are there (the ones we could recover from auction), some have his annotations. His writing room is still there etc. Décor-wise it will be very different to last time."

I contacted Sarah Fowles (Elizabeth had died in 1990), who told me she was not pleased by the changes the Landmark Trust had made. "They have pulled down all he and Elizabeth lived in, ditto with me," she said. "They have cut down all his trees, planted by him. The garden I have been told is desecrated." She felt that Belmont had been turned into a "vulgar villa", reminiscent of "a millionaires' row-style of house you might find in certain avenues in North London. It's not John Fowles's house, because they have pulled down all the part we lived in."

In the end, I was unable to arrange a convenient time with the Trust to stay overnight in Belmont, where I had heard the gravel crunch under Elizabeth's braking wheels in December 1973, and where I beheld the bearded and burly Magus of the south coast at the door a moment later. I didn't really want to go anyway, as a pawn in a publicity stunt. Belmont was being promoted as a house haunted by Fowles, in which things were to be explained to would-be pilgrims in a mundane way. Better to settle for the spirit in memory.

13

"HOW LONG . . . HAS THAT TRAIN BEEN GONE"

I

Edinburgh University welcomed me for my first lecture on Monday, October 7, 1974. I was accepted in spite of paltry qualifications – age might have been taken into consideration – and gratitude has never faltered. On my arrival there I had the feeling of sheltering under a benign climate. My wish was to study for a four-year MA (Hons) in English Language and Literature, specializing in American Literature. The general Bachelor of Arts (BA) degree entailed three years of basic study in English, Philosophy, History of Art and other subjects of the student's choosing. I was advised to enter as a BA candidate and to seek to switch to an MA, with the chosen specialization, after two years. That way I would avoid outright rejection on the grounds of insufficient qualifications, or because "the course you inquired about is full". It was predicted – correctly, it turned out – that some places booked in advance by MA candidates would be vacated after two years, either by a change of mind or through exam failure.

With Colin Nicholson and Faith Pullin in charge, I therefore began my study of American Literature in the autumn term, 1976. It was, really, a two-year course in reading books and talking about them with people who knew more than you did. We studied William Faulkner, John Dos Passos, Ernest Hemingway and other writers of the 1920s, 30s and 40s, not forgetting the nineteenth-century greats. Nicholson and Pullin also placed a stress on the literature of our own time. This was America, after all: a vastness still in the process of being discovered.

A feature of the course was the separation of literary work according to school or ethnic group. It was unusual in the mid-1970s in having a section on Native American novelists – N. Scott Momaday and Thomas Berger (author of the novel *Little Big Man*) were two – and in giving serious attention to African American writers. We read the one novel by Ralph Ellison, *Invisible Man*, as well as his essays, a novel and autobiography by Richard Wright, a play by Amiri Baraka (LeRoi Jones), two novels by the little-known William Melvin Kelley, which we all liked (*A Different Drummer* and *Dem*), and a book of short stories by black women: Paule Marshall, Gwendolyn Brooks, Alice Walker and others. The contemporary emphasis gave our studies an up-to-the-minute feel, a sense of personal involvement with the author through the work. This turned out to be more than usually the case for me with one writer, in particular.

II

My father's job at British Rail in London had taken a turn into what he felt was a dead end, and my parents moved from High Wycombe back to Scotland in 1975, buying a house in the Perthshire village of Braco. They were also worried that Julie was not being tested sufficiently at her school in Buckinghamshire. The twelve-year-old Glasgow girl had merged with a Home Counties double. Now she would change back again.

For my father, it was convenient for the golf courses at Gleneagles. For my mother, there was the subconscious attraction of its closeness to the village of Blackford, where she had lived as a child in the 1920s while her father worked as an all-purpose builder on the construction of the Gleneagles Hotel.

One Sunday evening, after Dad had seen me off on the train at Dunblane on the journey back to Edinburgh, I opened a book that was on the slate for discussion in the coming week. It was gratifyingly slim. The dedication itself was stylish:

> *for* James
> James
> Luc James

It consisted of a brief introductory text – "My Dungeon Shook: Letter to my nephew on the one-hundredth anniversary of the Emancipation" – followed by a longer piece; together, they amounted to under 100 pages. I had thought I was beginning a short novel but once settled in the carriage realized I was reading a personal testament. The opening declaration of the extended essay hit forcibly:

> I underwent, during the summer that I became fourteen,
> a prolonged religious crisis. I use the word "religious" in
> the common, and arbitrary, sense, meaning that I then
> discovered God, His saints and angels, and His blazing Hell.

The cover of the Penguin edition of *The Fire Next Time* showed James Baldwin dressed in a sheepskin coat holding an infant black boy whom readers ever since have assumed to be his nephew. In fact, the child is an orphaned youngster whom Baldwin had encountered on the day the photograph was taken (by Steve Schapiro) in 1963, while on a reporting trip in Durham, North

Carolina. The boy's eyes wander away from the camera, as the photogenic author in profile gazes pensively downwards.

Not only did the essay at the heart of *The Fire Next Time* have a gripping opening, it came with an arresting title: "Down at the Cross: Letter from a region in my mind". These titles were all drawn from the words of Negro spirituals, in the scriptural shorthand of which the author had been immersed as a young man. Before reaching the end of the first paragraph, he has set his fourteenth birthday in an alarming context:

> What I saw around me that summer in Harlem was what I had always seen; nothing had changed. But now, without any warning, the whores and pimps and racketeers on the Avenue had become a personal menace. It had not occurred to me that I could become one of them, but now I realized that we had been produced by the same circumstances.

Unusual in many ways, Baldwin struck me as being unique in this: he held all his experience at the ready, both personal and ancestral, in a continuous and dramatic present. It was always at the front of his head, prepared for persuasive argument or for heated rhetoric, the one frequently following the other. The task of digesting this experience, making sense of it, or trying to, was a perpetual engagement. It meant understanding, or, as he might have said, "decoding", the actions of white people, since – as he strove to make readers see – his existence as a mid-century American Negro was at the mercy of their moves, whims, strengths and fallibilities. And his desire for change was directed at white people, too, often in a tone of sympathy. "Any real change involves the breakup of the world as one has known it, the loss of all that gave one an identity, the end of safety."

It was thrilling to be brought face to face with a contemporary
writer at the front line of a modern existential conflict. Baldwin
was an eloquent, patient, even tender guide. With the deftest
of touches, he made social and historical "circumstances"
mirror the circumstance of his own life. A line of Scripture, a
snapshot of a school classroom, a parental lecture, a humiliating
encounter with warm, budding girls so recently familiar from
Bible lessons – these and other phenomena are brought into
play in the first few paragraphs of *The Fire Next Time*. The words
skimmed across the ocean that autumn Sunday evening to give

the reader on the Dunblane–Linlithgow–Edinburgh train, four decades removed from the 1930s setting, a high-resolution picture of an unusually alert and sensitive Harlem boy.

From that slim volume I moved to others: novels, collections of essays and short stories. Quite soon I had read them all. Those that were hard to find, I sought in the library. Just the mention of a piece that did not reveal itself between the covers of a book – *Notes of a Native Son* (1955) and *Nobody Knows My Name* (1961) were the two main collections besides *The Fire Next Time* – was enough to set me on a quest. I studied every magazine article about him I could lay hands on.

There were book-length essays, too. One morning, I went to buy the newspaper at the newsagent across the street from my flat in Forrest Road and was amazed to see on the revolving bookstand a copy of *The Devil Finds Work*, Baldwin's disregarded book on blacks in the American cinema. I had ordered it some weeks earlier in the National Library of Scotland, where I had sat at a desk among scholars and browsers and read it fleetingly. The discovery in McColl's lightened my day, my week. I read *The Devil Finds Work* again, and then again. The rhetoric rumbling through its pages was committed to memory and recited to indulgent colleagues. "The grapes of wrath are stored in the cotton fields and migrant shacks and ghettoes of this nation . . . and in the eyes and hearts and perceptions of the wretched everywhere, and in the ruined earth of Vietnam, and in the old men, seeing visions, and in the young men, dreaming dreams . . ."

These light Corgi paperbacks fitted neatly into the pocket of a corduroy jacket and entered Edinburgh pubs, settling themselves at a table or on a barstool, desiring to be opened one more time. I would select something from the bookshelf, then set off alone on a Friday evening after the last lecture, intending to visit three or four different pubs, to read an essay in each, finding a fish supper in the interval. This way, I entertained myself. I was having a conversation with Baldwin himself. An essay by him was a storehouse of eloquence and charm, a lesson on style and dynamics – how to manage tact and presentation – a lecture on morality: "Notes of a Native Son", "Equal in Paris", "The Black Boy Looks at the White Boy" (about his bittersweet friendship with Norman Mailer), "Alas, Poor Richard" (a triple-decker on his mentor-turned-adversary, Richard Wright). There was pleasure in revisiting slighter essays – "Notes for a Hypothetical Novel", "East River, Downtown" – in the hope of imbibing again some neglected perception. "Hatred, which could destroy so much, never failed to destroy the man who hated, and this was an immutable law." What kind of personal ordeal bestowed the authority that allowed one to declare, at the age of about thirty, "this was an immutable law"? One day a friend from university entered my flat and, seeing a familiar book on the table, said, with an affectionate laugh in her voice, "Oh, Jim, you're not reading *The Fire Next Time again!*"

The Devil Finds Work had been practically ignored by the British press at the time of its original publication in 1976. Regarded in the mid-1960s as a whirlwind, Baldwin was now viewed – with relief by some, perhaps – as a storm played out. Just an extreme weather event. The mood of the civil rights movement in the US had changed and its public face had hardened. The outstretched hand of James Baldwin was rebuffed by the clenched fist of Eldridge Cleaver; the Harlem boy's toothy grin was overshadowed by Stokely Carmichael's frown in dark glasses. It happened as early as 1966, when the Black Panthers began to occupy the limelight in the civil rights arena that had once belonged to him. Baldwin opened his arms to greet his younger brothers, but they didn't even share the same body language. Cleaver wrote menacingly about the "faggot" at the back of the room. Their militant posturing was miles removed from his natural stance, yet he strove to see things from their point of view. People began to ask: what *is* Baldwin's stance? As the years passed, the question became increasingly hard to answer. He was here (non-violence); he was there (militancy); suddenly he was nowhere to be seen.

Little by little, I uncovered facts about his present existence and the reasons behind the perception of him as a yesterday man. He had spent most of his adult life abroad, sometimes in Turkey but mainly in France. ("I was born in New York, but have lived only in pockets of it. In Paris, I lived in all parts of the city.") Settled since 1971 in the bijou Provençal village of Saint-Paul de Vence, surrounded by a camp of mainly non-literary friends and hangers-on, reading the newspapers at a day's remove, he could hardly fail to be out of touch with trends in America.

This happens to people tricked by time in all walks of life: the music changes, leaving them dancing the same old steps, looking mildly foolish. As a public intellectual, a worse fate had befallen Baldwin: he was boring his audience.

Leaving McColl's in Forrest Road with my neat black-and-red paperback of *The Devil Finds Work*, I had no cause to be occupied with these questions. "For I have seen the devil, by day and by night, and have seen him in you and in me . . ." At the end of a university seminar, a passing member of the faculty overheard me enthuse to Colin Nicholson about an earlier but equally neglected book, *No Name in the Street*. He regarded me with polite curiosity. "Is he still around?"

The question irritated me. I replied that he certainly was. Before long, I would be trying to have him around here.

The university had rewarded me handsomely, not only in respect of studies. In my early weeks as a student, in a Philosophy tutorial, I fell in love, a first experience of sublime passion. Her name was Diana, she was from another country – England – and the relationship fitted itself as a parallel to our education. Before the climax of final exams and degree, however, she decided she wanted to leave the university, to leave Edinburgh, to return to London to seek work in the theatre, to leave me. We continued to be friends, but the great event was over.

I felt lonely, and particularly lonely at weekends. In order to outflank time, I invented ways to generate excitement. One Saturday morning, on the spur of the moment, I set off for Glasgow to watch Rangers vs Celtic in a League Cup Final at Hampden Park, expecting to buy a ticket at the ground – and did so, finding myself as a half-hearted Rangers supporter in a section of the Hampden stand reserved for wholehearted Celtic fans. I didn't hide my allegiance, and the surrounding spectators were open about theirs. When Rangers scored, I cheered. When Celtic did, I applauded. A whisky bottle was passed along the row of seats from hand to hand, with a small glass. I can't remember who won the match, but I have never forgotten the people who surrounded me. Ever since, when asked the question that inevitably comes a Glaswegian's way on the subject of football, I provoke bafflement by replying that I support Rangers *and* Celtic. It was only later that the facts of our family background came to light.

Sometimes I phoned my mother on a Saturday morning and said, "I was thinking of coming through . . ." Dad would pick me up at Dunblane. There would be drinks at six. A roasted pheasant on the table at eight. One of my sisters might arrive. The next morning, while Mum made her way to Ardoch Parish Church, where she would soon become the organist, Dad and I walked in the Highland foothills near Gleneagles. They were understanding about Diana, about whom Dad had said, "She's a looker, all right. The mystery is what she sees in you."

One morning I arose with a different idea of how to fill the yawning weekend hours: I would write a letter to James Baldwin.

This I did, at some length, trying to express in mature terms what his writing had meant to me. I rounded it off with an invitation: would he consider coming to Edinburgh, to talk to the students at the university? If so, we would be thrilled to have him. Sometime in May would be best.

I folded my letter into an envelope. Then I telephoned Diana in London. I had learned the previous year that a man she knew, a film-maker called Michael Raeburn, was a friend of Baldwin. They seemed to be part of a jet set that existed for me only in fiction and in the pages of magazines: meetings in London, in Paris, on the Côte d'Azur. Michael was trying to raise money to make a film of Baldwin's second novel, *Giovanni's Room*, and they were writing a script together. I had met Michael at Diana's attic in Belsize Park, where I now went to visit, as she sometimes came to Edinburgh to stay with me.

I told her what I had done and asked if she thought Michael would be willing to pass on Baldwin's address. He obliged, and soon my fan letter (I would never have thought of it like that) was on its way to the south of France.

Did I expect to receive a reply? I think I probably did. It duly arrived one day in March, on a Saturday morning, suitably enough. There was stylish handwriting on the front, and the name and address in the top left corner: Baldwin, 06570 Saint-Paul, France. The brief message inside was not written by Baldwin himself.

Dear Sir,
Mister Baldwin would prefer to speak to the students of the University of Edinburgh in April when he is on his way to California. The date would be between the 15th and the 20th of April.

It was signed: "Yours truly, Bernard Hassell".

What was supposed to happen now? The reader may well ask, for I hadn't a clue. James Baldwin was coming, and I was to be his host. I would go to the pub as I had before: the Café Royal near Princes Street or the Bailie at Stockbridge, where I had dipped into his books and imagined myself in his company. But now *I would be in his company*. We would talk about *The Fire Next Time* and *Another Country* – not just in my Friday-night fantasy, but in reality. I had the letter from Saint-Paul de Vence. It said so.

I went to see Faith Pullin. With her assistance and that of Colin Nicholson, we could easily find somewhere for him to speak. There were plenty of guest speakers at Edinburgh, but usually they were academics or local authors. Sometimes a prominent politician was invited. I have no idea if they were paid, but if they came from the south of France, on the way to California – never mind if they were world-famous or not – they expected to have somewhere comfortable to sleep, wash and dress, to be fed and otherwise refreshed, to be ferried from the airport when they arrived and back again when it came time to leave. To be put on an aeroplane and have the fare paid. No doubt to have all these things arranged in advance. *By me?* I had only been in the air once in my life, on the furtive flight from Athens to Tel Aviv.

Faith was enthusiastic, but she had few more ideas of how to go about hosting the great writer than I had. She suggested applying to the cultural wing of the American Consulate in Edinburgh. Perhaps they had a fund for events such as this? I did so, and received the written equivalent of a shrug. We talked to one or two people in the English department about it, but got scant interest in return, and no money. We did a brief accounting, and I jotted the results on the back of an envelope – the envelope in which the acceptance of the speaking engagement had arrived:

£20 students
£30 NAASP
£30 Eng
£25 Faculty

I wrote "understand not normal" and "course running B" – prompts suggested by Faith to persuade "other orgs" to help finance our project.

One hundred and five pounds: that is the sum we hoped to find in order to bring "B" to Edinburgh in 1978. The "£20 students" I assume was meant to be the proceeds of a whip round. The organization sheltering behind NAASP has escaped from memory. In the event, we raised none of it.

April was approaching ("The date would be between the 15th and the 20th of April"). If James Baldwin wanted to come to Edinburgh, I wasn't about to be the one to tell him not to. I consulted Michael Raeburn, who didn't seem unduly worried. "He might just appear out of nowhere and sleep on your floor.

That's the kind of thing he does."

This was encouraging. It would have suited me fine. All the other stuff that didn't concern me – money, principally – I could assume, for a satisfying moment or two, did not concern him either. We would sort it all out once he got here.

April 15 came and went, without a ring of the telephone to say that he was on his way, or a knock on the door to announce that he was already with us, happy to bed down on my floor.

News arrived in the form of a Post Office telegram. I was at home when it dropped through the letterbox. It bore the date "18 Apr 78".

Nice/TF/STPAUL 25 18 1505
MONSIEUR JAMES CAMPBELL 22 FORREST ROAD
EDINBURGH / 1
UNABLE TO MAKE THE DATES SET FORTH IN YOUR
LETTER PLEASE CONTACT ME FOR LATER DATE
JAMES BALDWIN STPAULDEVENCE (93) 328 790

I was disappointed, though also relieved. I was touched by his considerateness, and by the suggestion of a "later date". It would give me more time to make the preparations, though I still had little idea of what they were. For now, there was the challenge of a telephone call to the South of France.

I made it one early evening, on the spur of the moment, as I passed a red telephone box near Tollcross. With a pile of coins at the ready, I dialled the number. A distant voice answered – a gruff, trochaic "Hey-lo" that would soon become familiar. This was followed by a voice that said, "May I speak to James Baldwin, please?" The words seemed to have been spoken by a person standing next to me.

He came on the line and I heard that low-slung, honey-and-brandy tone for the first time. I told him how much I had admired his most recent book, *The Devil Finds Work*. He acknowledged this with "You are very kind", a stock response which he imbued with a natural elegance. He was sorry not to have made it to Edinburgh. Something had turned up and he wasn't going to California, after all. As for the later date: "I thought I could come to Edinburgh in August, and speak to the students then."

That suited me fine, I said, but unfortunately it was a month when most of the students would be on holiday. Ah, then – here he used a phrase that was new to me – "It's a dead letter."

I understood what it meant. I was prepared to let it go. We wound up the call with polite formalities, and I left the telephone box.

IV

With the start of summer, something else turned up. At the conclusion of four years of study – in the library, in the lecture theatres of the David Hume Tower and in the eighteenth-century terrace of Buccleuch Place, I passed my degree exams and applied for a job. It wasn't much of a job, in respect of the money to be earned (hardly any), but in terms of the scope it offered for literary exploration, for a different reading of "trouble and travel" – experience, in a word – it was the best I could have wished for.

The editorship of the *New Edinburgh Review* (*NER*) had become vacant. The quarterly magazine was published by Edinburgh University Student Publications Board (EUSPB) but it was not a student magazine in any recognizable shape. Under the EUSPB constitution, the editorship had to be advertised every two years. The sitting editor was free to reapply, in hope of being re-elected. Those were the rules.

I had already been a member of the Publications Board – Gordon Brown was its dominant presence, with the air of prime minister-in-waiting even then – and I had been writing regularly for its weekly broadsheet, *Student*. I applied for the post of editor of the *NER*, for which I would be interviewed by people who were, in some cases, my friends. The same went for certain other candidates, including the current editor, Owen Dudley Edwards, a lecturer in the History department.

By then I had added to my portfolio by writing some pieces for the *New Statesman* and publishing a number of poems in magazines, including the *Scottish Review*, edited from Glasgow by Maurice Lindsay. In its pages, my lines appeared alongside those of George Mackay Brown, Norman MacCaig, Iain Crichton Smith and other Scottish poets to whose work Diana, the colonial girl from Kenya and Surrey, had introduced me. I wrote about Norman Mailer and Hermann Hesse for the *New Statesman*, about Andy Warhol for *Student*, and reviewed art exhibitions in the city. I tried to craft a prose style in which I would hear my own voice. The hardest thing of all in writing is to sound like yourself. Eventually, I reached an understanding that the kind of writing I liked kept its feet on the ground. It was a Scottish style: commonsensical, sceptical, impatient of cant, alert to the value of subterranean humour.

Somewhere amid these developing cadences I felt the air of a place where I might live. I wasn't reckless enough to refer to this possible future as a career, but I began to think I could mould my life to fit the contours of my sentences, if only my resolution were strong enough – to make a living by my pen, in short. A skimpy living, of course. But what else was I going to do?

I was not casual in my application for the editorship. On a Friday afternoon, I sat before the interviewing panel with sensible things to say about the direction I foresaw the *New Edinburgh Review* taking, about the people I intended to ask to write for it – all the poets mentioned above became regular contributors – and about what I saw as the weakness of its present state. It was not wide-ranging enough. There were too many single-theme issues. The articles – many by academics from the university – were monotonous and overlong.

Before the day was out, a member of the interviewing panel came to the door at 22 Forrest Road to tell me the job was mine.

V

My editorship was still in its early stages when a book arrived in the office: *The Making of Jazz: A Comprehensive History* by James Lincoln Collier. It didn't take long to decide what had to be done. I wrote another letter to Saint-Paul de Vence, tucked it into Collier's book, and put the parcel in the post. His writings contained many allusions to jazz, I pointed out to Baldwin (I felt entitled to write as if I knew what I was talking about), but he had never written a separate essay on the subject. "It occurred to me that you might welcome the chance to do so."

It took three months, by which time I had given up, but one day I went into the office to find my own letter on top of the in-tray. It had been returned to me with a message underneath, in large writing in black ink: "Would love to arrange to do a long piece: but cannot do it within the dead-line. Am not free before the end of May."

No "please contact me" this time. It was taken for granted that I would – weren't we old pals by now? – and, once I had worked up the courage, I did.

One rarely got straight through to Baldwin on the telephone. The call was usually answered by a secretary or a guest or a brother. They sometimes sounded gruff, but once I gave my name I was handed over. And the welcoming words were always warm and delivered in the same melodious tone: "Hey, baby, how are you?"

I said I was thrilled to learn that he would write about jazz for our magazine.

"I'd love to do that, baby. Can you send me the book?"

I pointed out that I already had. Baldwin said he must have lost it. Not to worry: I would have another delivered direct from the publishers. We agreed a date in July. I told him to write as long a piece as he wanted.

There was one other matter, which I thought best to settle now.

"This magazine . . . it doesn't have much money . . ."

There was a pause at his end. Then he came back with one of those imperishable remarks that leave themselves engraved on memory, like Bruce Dryden's insistence to my father at the police station in St Andrew's Square that "Jim didn't steal anything".

Baldwin said: "Who mentioned money?"

I had consulted the higher-ups at EUSPB and it was agreed that we could stretch to £80.

"Eighty pounds? . . ." Another of his eloquent pauses. "That's OK."

I put down the receiver with a feeling of elation. James Baldwin. Writing for the first time about jazz. Commissioned by me. Who mentioned money?

In the first few months of my editorship, I combined *New Edinburgh Review* duties with a summer job that I had held the year before and had enjoyed, as a driver for Edinburgh Council Department of Social Work. The garage, a vast hangar filled with cars, vans, single- and double-decker buses, was situated near the foot of Leith Walk, but daily duties took me all over the city and beyond. Sometimes I would park a van or small bus outside EUSPB's Buccleuch Street office, then dart inside to pick up the mail and send out suggestions for essays and reviews, or requests for stories and poems, to writers I admired. We published articles by Angus Calder (on African fiction), Douglas Dunn (on Hugh MacDiarmid), Allan Massie (on the resurrected James Kennaway), Tom Nairn (on the 1979 referendum on Scottish independence), the playwright E. A. Whitehead on Brecht, Rick Cluchey on producing *Waiting for Godot* in San Quentin prison, stories and poems by Ron Butlin, Edwin Morgan, Naomi Mitchison – a frequent contributor, and the only one born in the nineteenth century – and others.

My stated intention at the interview had been to blend a Scottish perspective with an outlook on the wider world. George Mackay Brown was generous with short stories, Iain Crichton Smith with poems typed in a mangle of red and black ribbon, on crumpled scraps of paper torn from other scraps, but always worth printing. Norman MacCaig sent poems with a covering note: "If they seem worthwhile, print them. If not, put them in the bin." I persuaded James Kelman to return to publishing after he had given up for some years in disgust and desperation. His story "Keep Moving & No Questions" was printed in the Winter 1979 issue, together with an article – at the opposite end of the Scottish intellectual spectrum – by David Daiches on Thomas Carlyle.

For the internationalist, there was an amusing account by Henry Miller of meeting his mother in heaven (Miller died on the day after the issue was published; I later found out, to my disappointment, that the piece had been published before) and a foreword to a new edition of *The Collector* by John Fowles. In London, I visited Trocchi at Observatory Gardens and heard from his own lips the admission – expressed with a great and weary "Ach!" – that his heroin addiction was "a drag". We went together to an afternoon drinking club, where Alex took delight in baffling the waiter by crying out, "A hauf an' a hauf, Jimmeh!" But I had no luck in extracting something publishable for the magazine.

Instead, I reprinted the short Burroughs article, "M.O.B.", that Trocchi had given me a few years previously, which had originally appeared in *GUM/Moving Review*. The *NER* contributors' budget being exhausted by then, I sent Burroughs my personal cheque for ten pounds. He forwarded it to his literary agent, who returned it to Buccleuch Place with an unamused note and demand for a larger sum. Pat Kavanagh was also Douglas Dunn's agent, and I asked Douglas what to do. "Drag your feet", he said.

On July 24 – the arranged deadline for the jazz piece – I entered the office to find another telegram.

I FEAR YOU HAVE AN ESSAY I CANNOT DO
JUSTICE IN THE LENGTH PROPOSED HAVE BEEN
TRYING TO CALL YOU PLEASE CALL ME
JAMES BALDWIN IN STPAULDEVENCE (93) 328 790

Once again, I felt the elation, once again I picked up the telephone, and once again I heard a watchdog at the other end: "Who's calling?" Baldwin then came on with, "Hey, baby, how are you?"

I was fine. How was he? More to the point, how was the piece?

"You've given me something very important to think about. Something about my *life*." He was in earnest mode. He needed more space – was that OK? Of course it was. And more time.

"Call me Friday."

I did, taking a break from social-work driving duties to do so. He said, "I'm working on it, baby, I'm working on it. Call me Monday." And when I called him, he said, "I'm working on it, baby. Call me Thursday." I called him on every day of the week that he suggested. The introductory voices softened.

"Oh, Mr *Campbell*! How are *you*? Jimmy's expecting your call. He's in the shower – oh, *here* he comes. He must have heard the ring tone."

July slipped into August. Our cover designer, Jim Hutcheson, came up with a nice scheme: a photograph of the star writer below the upper-case headline: "JAMES BALDWIN ON JAZZ". It looked great. All we needed was a piece to go with it. "I fear you have an essay." Was I about to be midwife to the new *Fire Next Time*?

"I'm working on it, baby, I'm working on it. But it's *very hot* down here." There was also his fifty-fifth birthday party in August to consider.

"Keep working on it," I said. "We've got the cover printed, with your photograph on the front. It looks terrific."

The electric jolt at the other end was transmitted all the way up through France, under the Channel to England and over

Hadrian's Wall to Edinburgh.

"*I'm on the cover, man?*"

Well, of course he was.

"Oh baby."

One of those pauses.

"I'd better get to *work*."

He did, and the piece arrived, with, as so often, a wonderful title: "Of the Sorrow Songs: The cross of redemption". It wasn't the sequel to *The Fire Next Time*, nor was it as long as I had been led to expect. At the top was a date: 29 July, 1979. It began: "I will let the date stand: but it is a false date. My typewriter has been silent since the 6th of July, and the piece of paper I placed in the typewriter on that day has been blank until this hour." The false date was left because it was the birthday of his "baby sister" Paula (the youngest of eight siblings). The style was improvisational, occasionally shaky, but the tone was unmistakeably his:

> The music called *jazz* came into existence as an exceedingly laconic description of black circumstances: and, as a way, by describing these circumstances, of overcoming them. It was necessary that the description be laconic: the iron necessity being that the description not be overheard . . . not be "de-coded". It has not been de-coded, by the way, any more than the talking drum has been de-coded . . .
>
> I am attacking, of course, the basis of the language – or, perhaps, the *intention* of the language – in which history is written – am speaking as the son of the Preacher-Man. This is exactly how the music called *jazz* began, and out of the same necessity: not only

to redeem a history unwritten and despised, but to checkmate the European notion of the world.

It appeared in the Autumn 1979 issue of the *New Edinburgh Review*. Baldwin was pleased. The author of *The Making of Jazz*, James Lincoln Collier, replied from New York at length, in mainstream terms, at the opposite reach from Baldwin's black-and-blue tone. "This music belongs on the auction block . . ." The cheque for £80 was sent to Saint-Paul de Vence. I doubt that it was ever cashed.

On the telephone afterwards, he said: "You know . . . I'd like to meet you one day."

I stammered a suitable reply.

"Because – *you* – are the most *persistent* – *person* – I have *ever* – KNOWN!" Followed by a great gale of laughter. He invited me to visit him in Saint-Paul, "if you happen to be down this way".

I was probably not the most persistent person he had ever known. I simply thought that a writer, when he said he would deliver a piece, went ahead and did so. Nevertheless, I resolved to be "down this way" before long.

VII

It took over a year, but on a Thursday afternoon in July 1981, I entered a Post Office in the Champ-de-Mars area of Paris, where I was having a spring and summer sojourn, and asked to be put through to the number in Saint-Paul de Vence. I closed the collapsible door of the booth behind me and waited for a response to the piercing tone. I had been lucky, in previous communications, always to find Baldwin in France, for he was often on the road, in the US or elsewhere. It was his fate to be restless. His latest books had received lukewarm receptions. "Is he still around?"

And I was lucky again. The customary gruff answering voice passed the receiver to the honey-and-brandy one. "A little tight," Baldwin replied, in answer to my polite inquiry, "a little tight. But that's OK." I said I was in Paris and was wondering if I might come down to Saint-Paul, as he had suggested.

Baldwin barely hesitated. "I'd love that, baby."

I said I was thinking of the following Tuesday, which happened to be Bastille Day. There was space for a mental check. "Toosday? . . . Tha'd be fine."

"Should I call you before I leave?"

"Only if you have *time* . . . only if you have time."

He made it sound like a gospel refrain. I left the Post Office knowing that I wouldn't have time. I had my invitation: why set myself up for a cancellation?

Early on the Tuesday morning, I boarded a train at Gare de Lyon, ready for the nine-hour journey to Nice. I remember what I ate in the restaurant car – *petit salé aux lentilles* – the miniature carafe of wine I drank, whom I talked to, that I sat on the left-hand side of the carriage, facing forward, how north announced its change to south by way of the façades of provincial railway stations.

In Nice, I entered a café and requested a *jeton* from the barman.

For the first time in our by now extended telephone acquaintance, Baldwin himself picked up the receiver. He told me to take a taxi to Saint-Paul de Vence. "Do you have any money?" he asked with kindly urgency; I later learned that he was accustomed to people turning up with none. He said he would meet me at the Café de la Place in the central square.

It was a public holiday and the village was lively. Men played *pétanque* in the early evening sun on the sandy flat before a bank of café tables. I positioned myself at one of them and kept watch. Before long, a neat black man, not tall, wearing large sunglasses, appeared at the far corner of the square. As he paused to look around, I approached and extended my hand. Baldwin pushed the shades on to his forehead.

"Are you him?"

We crossed the square to his usual place, the Colombe d'Or, where he returned the greetings of staff and regulars with easy grace. We arranged ourselves at a snug table opposite the bar and had fifteen precious minutes to ourselves before the barman summoned him to the telephone. It was Bernard Hassell – pronounced Ber-*nard* Hass-*ell* – calling from the house. When he came back to the table, Baldwin explained that he had recently completed a piece for *Playboy* about the Atlanta child killings, then under investigation, and Bernard wanted to tell him that the editor had phoned from Chicago to say he liked it. The news put him in a happy mood. "They liked the piece!" he repeated, more than once, with a widening smile. The omens were good.

Half an hour later, Bernard joined us: a lithe, alert New Yorker in a white jump suit, zipped to just above the navel, with a sceptical but not unpleasant expression on his face when setting eyes on me. An amiable black American woman with tumbling locks came into the company, and when we walked downhill to the Baldwin residence, a quarter of a mile from the village, she accompanied us. Bernard insisted on carrying my bag, on top of which rested a Harris Tweed double-breasted jacket I had brought with me, in case I needed to appear smart.

"Where – are – *you* – going, with a tweed *coat!*" the woman asked. It was about 30 degrees. At the house, it seemed we were having an impromptu party. There were more drinks and Bernard began making preparations for dinner. Fireworks sounded from the village and spangled the sky. The woman departed, leaving laughter behind and talk of "Yves and Simone", who had a house in the village. Baldwin asked about Scotland, of which he displayed an almost complete ignorance. "It's joined to England, right? Not like Ireland." I offered some details of the centuries-long troubled relationship with the dominant neighbour, and Baldwin said something that took me aback: "So it's a bit like being a nigger?"

Nevertheless, he now had a literary connection to the country. Bernard told me that he had enjoyed writing for the *New Edinburgh Review*, and had agreed to do so because he was touched by my original letter, the one containing the invitation to address the students at the university.

I stayed at the house on Route de la Colle for six days – "Where we goin' to put this chile?" Bernard had asked, before going ahead and making up a bed in the spare room – during which there were dinners and all-afternoon lunches (Baldwin usually rose around noon) and late-night talks over the daily bottle of Johnnie Walker Black Label. Baldwin told me that he owned the portion of the L-shaped house in which he lived. The other part still belonged to his former landlady, Mlle Faure, an elderly local woman from an old Saint-Paul family – she was the author of a small book about the village – with whom he was on affectionate terms. He planned to purchase the remainder in due course.

The land attached to the house covered about three acres. It ran wild in places but the garden areas were pleasantly cultivated. Bernard was responsible for the arrangement of trellises and paths and rockeries, and there was also a young Algerian who went around singing Arabic songs softly in a low voice as he worked.

The village was popular with café society and celebrities. Dirk Bogarde had a place nearby. Simone Signoret and Yves Montand were regular guests at the house. Baldwin mentioned casually that Georges Braque had once had his studio where we were sitting now, but this proved hard to verify. The local Fondation Maeght contained works and architectural designs by Braque, Miró, Chagall and Giacometti. Baldwin seemed vague about it; his attention was consumed by his predicament. "The very time I thought I was lost, My dungeon shook and my chains fell off" . . . day after day.

"Are you James or Jim or Jimmy?"

I said I was usually Jim, but didn't object to any.

Baldwin gripped my wrist and said with a sudden intensity that I came to recognize as characteristic: "I will call you *Jamie*."

I had brought the current *TLS* from Paris (easy to find there) and I fished it out. The lead article mentioned *Uncle Tom's Cabin* and Baldwin's 1949 essay "Everybody's Protest Novel". It included a phrase I was happy to pass on: "Flaubert would have understood Baldwin better" (that's to say, better than the author of the book under review). He pushed the paper back in my direction and, leaning with his elbows on the outdoor table, said, with typical good humour, "Oh well . . . I'm up for grabs again!"

He loved to talk, but not to answer the telephone, and in a bit of role-reversal I found myself lifting the receiver in the living room when Bernard was absent – Baldwin's bedroom and study, "the torture chamber", was at a level below – and asking, "Who's calling?" in as gruff a voice as I could manage.

There was a certain tension between the two. Baldwin thought – or at least was encouraged by his brother David to

James Baldwin and me, on the terrace outside "the torture chamber" at Baldwin's house in Saint-Paul de Vence, July 1984. On this occasion I was there to interview him for *The Times* on his sixtieth birthday. *Courtesy of Fanny Dubes.*

believe – that he was being taken advantage of by Bernard, who was supposed to perform secretarial work. If he didn't do as much as expected, it was partly Baldwin's fault, for he was in the habit of hiring friends to do what would have been better left to professionals. Once when I mentioned something about the arrangement with Bernard – in a favourable light – he looked away and mumbled, "That's something else I've got to get sorted out." On another occasion there was a female friend of Jimmy's (we were on first-name terms now) from 1940s Paris days staying at Saint-Paul, who did not get on well with Bernard. To me, he referred to her with a chuckle as "Jimmy's girlfriend", which I, thinking it was amusing, thoughtlessly passed on. Jimmy was not pleased. "He said that, did he?"

Bernard stuck to his post. When, some years later, I asked about him during a meeting with Baldwin in London, he replied, "He's indestructible", with mirth in the voice but not in the sentiment. (Bernard was not indestructible; he died of complications from AIDS in France in 1992.)

But Bernard was fun. "The Côte d'Azur is back in business!" he would exclaim at the sound of a telephone call or the appearance of an unexpected guest. He used to stand on the balcony of the gatehouse, where he had his quarters, and sing operatic airs. It was he who told me to stay on when I offered to make myself scarce. Perhaps, unwittingly, I relieved the pressure. The evening before my departure, there was a party at the house of an American expatriate near Nice, to which we drove in the chauffeured Mercedes Bernard called on in these situations. On entering, Bernard had his hand grasped by a well-known English thriller writer. "James Baldwin! I'm so pleased to meet you." The grip was disengaged. "I'm Bernard Hassell. That's James Baldwin. This is Jamie Campbell."

Stylish as always, Jimmy took the now awkward hand and offered, with almost imperceptible irony, "Enchanté".

There were conversations lasting most of the day and half the night but I took few notes. When once or twice I sat on a wall near the Colombe d'Or to jot a few things down, I felt as if I were betraying the occasion. When I said so many years later to a friend, Darryl Pinckney, he replied: "You did the right thing. You didn't take notes: you hung out."

The following remarks are derived from what I scribbled into a notebook in 1981.

Norman Mailer: "Norman has absolutely no sense of humour." Later: "The problem with Mailer and Hemingway is the problem of homoeroticism."
Gore Vidal: "A ridiculous man."
Naked Lunch: "It's not a book; it's a convulsion." Later: "Bill

Bernard Hassell, Baldwin's secretary, stands lithe and alert, "a sceptical but not unpleasant expression on his face", with Baldwin at Saint-Paul de Vence. *Courtesy of Carlos Freire.*

would take people and get them strung out and then leave them there . . . And you can't do that."

Trocchi (in anger): "I hate him. And if you see him, tell him that from me."

Allen Ginsberg (shaking his head affectionately): "He's a beautiful man."

In Cold Blood: "I sent Truman a telegram: It's a dead end. Congratulations, baby."

"England is on fire!" (There were riots at the time in several cities.) With a perceptible sense of having been neglected: "If you'll forgive me for reminding you: I told you so."

Mrs Thatcher: "I would like to coat her in chocolate and turn her into an éclair" (bit mysterious, this one).

Ralph Ellison: "He doesn't like me." Does he like him? "I'm glad he's there." *Invisible Man* was the winner of the National Book Award in 1953, which he believed to be the reason *Go Tell It on the Mountain* did not win in the following year.

Marlon Brando: "We were never lovers. We no doubt should have been lovers . . ." He said the same thing about Bernard.

Scott Fitzgerald: "The most overrated writer of all time – apart from *The Great Gatsby* and a few of the short stories."

Between the two bards of east coast suburban life, Cheever and Updike, he chose Cheever. "There was something there I could relate to. We now know what it was." Laughter. (Cheever's homosexuality had recently come to light.)

On "The Death of the Beat Generation", the name given to a party in New York arranged by his friend Robert Cordier: "I wasn't sure that it had ever been born, but if it had been I was sure it should be dispatched with a minimum of fuss."

"You cannot *learn* how to touch a woman unless you *know* how to touch a man." (This came on the first evening, after

I had rebuffed his advances.)

"In Italy, people are not afraid to touch – one – another."

"People fear love more than they fear death. *Think about it!*"

"Be true to the clown in yourself."

I said that in November I was planning to visit America for the first time. After New York and Philadelphia, I wanted to go south to New Orleans.

"Be careful."

Was I likely to be in danger?

Jimmy's eyes widened. "I'm just a nigger." His sense of drama, and his timing, were exquisite. "You're a traitor."

The now taboo word was not used sparingly at Route de la Colle. Bernard would come out with "This nigger don't know which way his ass is up", or "The trouble with these niggers is . . ." At the Saturday night party in Nice, there was an African American woman with heavily pancaked face and dyed and straightened hair. She seemed mild and pleasant to me, but the next morning Bernard referred to "that lady with the brown face", which brought a knowing chuckle from Jimmy. I was, in their eyes, an innocent, someone who had never been to America, not really a "white" person at all, in the sense in which they used the term. At one point while we were sitting on the terrace outside his work room, Jimmy went off on a riff about white people this and white people that. Seeing the unease on my face, he placed a hand on my knee, and modulated his tone. "I'm not talking about you, baby. I'm talking about the people who think they are white." As with many things Baldwin said, the meaning of this seemingly cryptic remark became clear later.

In the event, I was mugged on that trip, held up at one in the morning on East 12th Street, New York, by a boy and girl who were not far advanced in their teens. The girl poked the barrel of a small gun in my face, withdrew it and poked again. They took a wad of dollars from my pocket and ran off. I told Baldwin about it at our next rendezvous, and he regarded me sadly. "Were they black?"

During that first week and on future visits, as well as during meetings in London and elsewhere, Baldwin assigned me a role in his company: "one of my editors". It was said with a twinkle in the eye when he introduced me to people. It pardoned me for having barged in, in the first place, and cleared me of any suspicion – on my own part as well as that of others – that I belonged among the hangers-on.

I see now, though I was too young to see then, that I could have taken this role more seriously, that I could have accepted it as a responsibility. He needed editing, and he wanted it. He had relied on his brother David to assure him that *No Name in the Street* was ready for publication in 1972, when really it is a sequence of notes in search of an arrangement. In the central place of Saint-Paul and in the Colombe d'Or, he was regarded as a celebrity catch, a segment of local lore – Yves and Simone, phlegmatic Bogarde, Matisse settling his bills at the Colombe with a drawing, Jeemy *le noir Américain* – but he lacked everyday contact with literary people, ordinary conversation, agreement and disagreement. There were old friends aplenty, with new ones arriving on the doorstep, among whom might stand a fugitive lover – "Are you him?" – but there was no one with the critical resolve to say: This is too shrill, Jimmy; this is off the point; you are being repetitious.

That editor would have found much to do. Baldwin talked to me about a trio of works in the pipeline. One was a novel, "No Papers for Muhammad" – the melodious gardener, an illegal immigrant, was behind it. He was also working on a play, "The Welcome Table" – the one and only work to which he gave a Saint-Paul setting – and a "triple biography" which took the working title "Remember This House". Its subjects were the three great stalwarts of the civil rights era, Medgar Evers, Malcolm X and Martin Luther King, all assassinated between 1963 and 1968: a first, second, then a third and almost fatal blow to the heart of the man sitting opposite me at the table on the terrace – what some chroniclers have seen as "the welcome table" itself – in the garden at sunny Saint-Paul de Vence.

He gave me poems to read in typescript and hinted strongly that they were available for publication, "in magazines like yours". Two I remember were "Staggerlee Wonders" and "Christmas Carol". The second pursued a longstanding theme: the conversion of Saul to Paul: "how bright is the light / of the unchained night". There was nothing more basic in Baldwin's personal theology: confession, followed by conversion, leading to delivery from what he had elsewhere called "the sin that cannot be forgiven", slavery, which held Americans in bondage, black and white, as he had written in his *NER* essay, "until this hour".

That boyish eagerness when he asked the next day: "Did you get a chance to read the poems?" At the outdoor table we discussed them, and I said something about poetry allowing his voice to be "released from discourse". Jimmy repeated this pensively more than once, as it was his habit to do, staring at his interlocutor in the meantime. "Released from discourse . . . Released . . . from . . . discourse."

I've told myself since that I should have taken "Staggerlee Wonders" – now quite a well-known late Baldwin piece – for the *New Edinburgh Review*, even though I didn't feel enthusiastic about its addresses to "Duke Wayne" and "towering Ronald Reagan" and "the Great Man's Lady", as well as its scattered references to China, Russia and Patty Hearst. My test was to ask if I would have accepted it if it had arrived in the mail with an unfamiliar name attached. I was turning down decent work by local writers all the time, for lack of space to print it. Could I justify accepting something I didn't care for, just because the author was famous? (Relating this story to a young Baldwin scholar much later, I heard myself say, "It was by James Baldwin, for chrissake!")

One afternoon, after the usual long lunch, he indicated to me and to the housekeeper Valérie that he was about to go down below to the "the torture chamber" and "la machine à écrire" – making typing motions with his fingers before the adoring Valérie's eyes – in order to work on the "Medgar, Malcolm and Martin book".

I excused myself by saying I would go up to the village to read and have a beer, to fill the hot, vacant hours while he worked. Jimmy immediately changed his mind and said he would come with me. It was after five, a beautiful July evening in Provence, just before the hour when the landscape changes to offer the idler a deeper understanding of Impressionist light. On the quarter-mile walk uphill to the Café de la Place, he began softly to sing a blues.

"How long . . . how long . . . has that evening . . . train
    been gone.
How long . . . how long . . . baby, how long."

It is one of my most precious memories, but I knew even then it was not the way to go about writing the new novel and the triple biography. In the eight years that elapsed between drafting a letter to his agent in which he set out his initial thoughts for what he called "the Martin–Malcolm–Medgar book" and his death in 1987, he produced a sheaf of about thirty pages. "Since Martin's death . . . something has altered in me," he wrote in his account of the tumultuous period, *No Name in the Street*. "Something has gone away."

And yet, something positive and volatile remained. Something that one sensed could be "grasped in handfuls, tapped for electricity, bottled, used for blasting, set fire to", as Patrick Leigh Fermor wrote, not about a solitary, small man in a temporary setting, but an eternal geographical region, the Mani, in the southern Peloponnese.

I departed on the Sunday at midday, with careful directions from Bernard as to which train to take to Marseille, where I wished to spend a few nights, and how to find a hotel once I got there. I had been in the presence of a force that could be used for blasting, tapped for electricity, for all its altering and cutting-down. It happened each time I was in Baldwin's company, and I began to look forward to it as much as to anything else: the moment of stealing away with the electric beat still pulsing inside.

14

LEWES PRISON

I

It was one of those seemingly inconsequential events, almost a non-event, that by the end of the afternoon on which it happened has changed your life, in that the rest of your life can be seen in retrospect as depending on it.

I can date it precisely, even pinpoint the time, as I can with certain other events: April 8, 1980. I was on one of my regular, brief visits to London. Under my direction, the *New Edinburgh Review* had produced several issues, with a new one in preparation. I had persuaded James Baldwin to contribute to the magazine but had yet to make the expedition to Saint-Paul de Vence. Here I was at five minutes to 1 on the Tuesday after Easter, walking eastwards from Holborn Tube station in the direction of the curious little turning into Lincoln's Inn Fields called Great Turnstile. It had an appealing Old London ring when I saw it given as the address on the editorial page of the *New Statesman*.

By this time, I liked to think of myself as an almost familiar face on the third floor at Great Turnstile, where the arts and book reviews were discussed, commissioned, edited, proofed and made ready for the printers. I had first gone there a year before, to see Julian Barnes – deputy literary editor under Martin Amis, but by that stage in more or less sole charge – and to deliver my review of a biography of Hermann Hesse by hand. When Julian left to take up an equivalent post at the *Sunday Times*, I had applied for his job and had been interviewed as one of a shortlist of three. The other candidates were Paul Binding and Craig Raine. "You were second," Julian told me later. "Craig" – the front runner – "was just too mad." It went to Paul, who began work at Great Turnstile under David Caute, the new literary editor. How grand they seemed, those job titles, when spoken aloud in Edinburgh.

I continued to write for the books pages. And now I was swerving through the lunchtime crowd on Holborn, on my way to keep an appointment with Paul Binding. It was press day. He would be busy but not too busy to see a contributor. I had telephoned to say I was in London and we had made arrangements to have lunch. I would enter by the small door in the alley, always open, make my way upstairs without impediment, to be greeted by one of the secretaries, Gillian or Angela, or by Paul or even David Caute. I met Christopher Hitchens there for the first time, and overheard him ask Caute, "Who's running the paper next week?" before suggesting that he "telex" his article from Cyprus. To have such questions in one's mouth as part of one's daily bread. To be integrated into such important matters. "Who's running the paper?"

On a different afternoon, I entered the room to find Salman Rushdie leaning against the table that was always covered in newly arrived books, spines upwards. "Perhaps you know?" he said, without introduction. "We've been trying to remember the first name of Raskolnikov in *Crime and Punishment*." To my regret, I did not know.

Now I was back again. As I came within fifty yards of the narrow entry, a figure emerged from it and stood at the traffic lights in an almost frozen state of agitation, waiting to cross Holborn. It was Paul. As I was arriving at the office, three minutes before the appointed time, he was leaving it. Had

I boarded the train at Tottenham Court Road after the one I did board, I would have missed him. Had Paul left the office a minute earlier or had the green man lit up thirty seconds before he did, I would have missed him that way, too.

I approached and said, "Paul?" leaving a baffled question mark inside the syllable.

His agitation all at once became visible. He was on his way to the *Times Literary Supplement*'s offices on Gray's Inn Road, just a few minutes' walk away (more like fifteen), to read and correct the proof of his article on Isaac Bashevis Singer for the issue due out at the end of the week. Angela had instructions to relay his apology and ask me to wait. "I'm so glad to have caught you," he said. Would I perhaps walk with him?

The green man gave his permission and we made our way into Red Lion Street. This was a new adventure. I could just about put aside my queasy recognition that I had been on the point of being stranded for an hour upstairs at Great Turnstile between two politely embarrassed secretaries. When we walked into the open-plan office of the *TLS* in the building it shared with *The Times*, the *Sunday Times* and the other supplements, we were greeted by Blake Morrison, the fiction and poetry editor, who was overseeing Paul's review. Blake, a Yorkshireman, was slight in build and reserved in manner but immediately friendly. He knew of the *NER* and had read the symposium "On Reviewing" that we had run the year before. He said: "Maybe you could do something for us?" and invited me to pore over the books shelved irregularly by his desk while he returned his attention to Paul.

I picked out three that appealed to me straight away: a collection of essays by Robert Creeley, with the likable title *Was That a Real Poem* (the hidden subtitle being "or did you make it up yourself?"), an assortment of interviews with Creeley's

Black Mountain associate Edward Dorn, and a non-fiction book by the Beat poet Gary Snyder, which reflected his interest in Native American traditions.

"Maybe you could link them all together," Blake said.

I could. And without much delay, once back in Edinburgh, I did.

As we were leaving the office, Blake introduced me to the paper's editor, John Gross. He, too, was reserved in that already recognizable way of English intellectuals but, like Blake, in a not disagreeable way. It was a body language I was becoming accustomed to – tight smile, folded arms, questions asked in order to avoid giving answers – as I was growing used to other curious English habits.

"I see Blake's given you some books," John Gross said, in his gentle fashion. Under the headline "Musing from the Mountain", my Creeley-Dorn-Snyder piece appeared in the TLS of May 30, 1980, the first of many reviews and articles to appear in the paper.

Just under two years later, John left the TLS to take up a position as a commissioning editor at Weidenfeld & Nicolson. One day in Edinburgh in early 1982, I opened an envelope to find a letter typed on Weidenfeld headed notepaper, with his neat signature at the foot. In a few brief sentences, he set out his reason for getting in touch. Was I thinking of writing a book? If so, could we discuss it?

I had never received an invitation like this before, but I knew when to keep my head. As luck would have it, I did have a book in mind. It had already been rejected, as a proposal, by Collins. I wanted to make a tour of Scotland, by bus, by train, by thumb, and to write about the places I saw, the people I talked to, folding my evolving literary experience into the narrative as I went. Edwin Muir had done something like it fifty years earlier and had written *Scottish Journey*, a book I admired.

I wrote back. Perhaps encouraged by the recognition that I was ready, John said he liked the idea. We met and talked about it some more, and Weidenfeld offered a contract: *Invisible Country: A Journey through Scotland*, with an advance of £2,000, payable in three instalments.

The book was published in April 1984, by which time John Gross had left Weidenfeld and taken up a different literary job. Another John, a genial man called John Curtis, an old hand, took over his authors – they were few, but I was one – and he invited me to suggest a follow-up.

"Something keeps saying to me, 'Ireland'," this John said, thinking, as publishers do, that a form of continuity is desirable in an author's work. It didn't take me long to understand that I wasn't up to that. I considered a return journey across the Barbary Coast, in backwards motion, from Morocco to Tunisia, starting at Tangier, pausing for recollection at the border post near Oujda, dawdling under the Francophone arcades of Algiers, investigating Constantine while drawing old Istanbul breath in readiness for an expedition to the country's vast desert interior. Rolling forward in the VW camper, Jeff, Russ, Annette and I had skipped it all, preoccupied with drugs (them), with getting *there* (me), mistaking a real land for the Land of Away, contenting ourselves with a flat exterior. Now I had changed, the times had changed, writing about remote regions was in vogue. But I soon admitted to myself that I wasn't up to that either.

There was a third notion, and this one stayed with me. In terms of physical movement, it was the opposite of a travel book. It was a journey of a different kind, to a different sort of interior.

II

On a drab morning in November 1984, I stepped down from the train at the station in a pretty Sussex town, crossed the railway bridge, turned left and took the steep road uphill. I was on my way to work at Her Majesty's Prison Lewes. It was my first day and they were expecting me.

After much manoeuvring, repeated requests and meetings with prison governors and Home Office officials, I had received permission to enter a prison in order to write a book. Thanks to the governor-in-chief at HMP Lewes, it was this prison. Denis Brown's acceptance of my proposal had had to be ratified by the same Home Office official in London who had done his best to put me off the project altogether. In the end, though, he went along with Mr Brown's welcome, and now, at 9.30 am, under a grey sky, I was hammering on the door of a high security English prison, asking to be let in. A peculiar kind of freedom.

The idea was to write a book with "the atmosphere of a novel", as I had put it to John Curtis. Non-fiction making use of the strategies of fiction was in fashion in the early 1980s: Ryszard Kapuściński did it; Bruce Chatwin did it. My hope was to do it, too. The intention was to mix freely with prisoners, to fathom the "inner life" of the prison. I would have preferred to write about a Scottish prison, but my request to the relevant department north of the border was rejected out of hand. When we met in a pub near Victoria Station in London, the press officer at the Prison Department of the Home Office – a Scotsman, as it happens – tried to rule it out, too. On practical grounds, he said. It would be necessary to have a member of staff assigned to me at all times, to ensure my personal safety.

There simply weren't the numbers. The workforce was already stretched. Open-and-shut case. It was nice meeting you.

I was disappointed but I wouldn't have wanted a prison officer on my tail anyway. An official shadow would restrict my movements and thoughts, and make candid conversation with inmates impossible.

I kept at it, and someone with experience of the Prison Department gave me useful advice: you are going about it back to front. The thing to do first, he said, was to find a prison governor willing to take you in. Then return to the Home Office with a ready-made plan in want of a rubber stamp. The Governor of HMP Lewes was recommended as a relatively liberal sort. I wrote to him and he replied with the invitation to come down – in a homely phrase that still makes me smile – "to spend the afternoon and evening with us".

I did, and found Mr Brown as likeable and open-minded as his phrasing suggested. Eventually, the necessary permissions were obtained. Even that afternoon-and-evening reconnaissance visit had required Home Office approval, but in retrospect my acceptance into HMP Lewes, a Category B prison – high-security, though not the highest – seems astonishingly free of bureaucratic impediment. I was going to be in a place where people are confined for large parts of the day, with four gates to be unlocked and passed through before the incomer reaches the core. Once there, however, no one tried to prevent me wandering from place to place on C Wing. It housed 150 long-term prisoners, roughly a third of them lifers.

Within the confines of the Benthamite panopticon – in theory, ever-observed – I went from kitchen to classroom, gym to chapel, library to laundry. In the evening, during the recreation period, between 6 and 9 pm, I often returned to the main gate after a light supper in a pub or at the house I had rented in town, sauntering on to the wing, where prisoners watched television and played games. If invited – I often was – I made up a foursome at table tennis or billiards with three cons; or I went into a cell to sit on the edge of a stark bed, waiting for a cup of tea.

Mr Brown issued a pass which enabled me to turn up whenever I wanted, to enter through the twin flat-topped towers that flank the main gate – exchanging a friendly greeting with the officers on duty – and step into the yard.

All this took place before there was such a thing as the writer-in-residence at British prisons. The poet Ken Smith came under that rubric later, and wrote a book about HMP Wormwood Scrubs, published in 1989. I was in residence, and had hopes of calling myself a writer – but "writer-in-residence" had no

HMP Lewes, main entrance. Day after day, for six months, four gates were unlocked to allow me to reach my cell.

currency as a phrase in this context. To those who asked, I liked to call myself a reporter in a forbidden zone. I thought of it as a second travel book, in which the traveller was confined to a walled city.

Just over a year earlier, I had started a part-time job as an assistant editor at the *TLS*. My duties took me there on Mondays and Tuesdays, leaving the rest of the week free. So I began to divide my time: two days of sub-editing and proof-reading at the *TLS*; three or four at Lewes prison, sometimes spilling over to Sunday as well. I attended services in the prison chapel. On Christmas Day, I was invited to call out the numbers for the pre-turkey bingo. A prisoner took me on an impromptu tour of the laundry, as the purser on a steam ship might offer to show a passenger the engine room. Before long, I began to look forward to my march uphill in the direction of the well-made building, solidly installed in the 1850s, to a day of exchanges with people whose company was in some cases stimulating, in others indifferent, seldom uninteresting and only rarely hostile.

I was assigned an office: a cell, in fact, which until my arrival had served as a barber's shop. A chair was provided, and a small table – the only furniture in this stark little oblong with bars on the high-up window– on which I placed my tape recorder and notepad. Nothing was taped without the speaker's consent. After a week or so, I was used to friendly cracks of the "Back again? You must like it here" variety. On Christmas Day, I came through the main gate to find a Scottish prisoner clearing snow from the yard with a shovel.

"What are you doin' here? It's different for us. We get paid for it."

When I left the prison on that first day in November, I bought a newspaper, went into a pub and drank a pint of the local Harvey's Best Bitter at the bar. Half an hour later, I was on my way to the train. Seated in the carriage, I was able to choose between writing up my notes or reading the paper or a novel by John Cheever: *Falconer*, based on his period as writer-in-residence in Sing Sing, New York. Looking from the window at the scatterings of the town illuminated in the darkness, I thought of my new acquaintances and the multifarious forms of confinement they were about to introduce me to.

Gate Fever was published in the spring of 1986. It had a mostly warm reception, including two reviews – one in print, the other on the radio – from Britain's most famous ex-prisoner, Jimmy Boyle. Memory tells me that the least favourable notice was in the *TLS*. I remember complaining that Laurie Taylor had treated the book as sociology, something I had been desperate to avoid. I had suggested to the editor of the *TLS* that he ask the crime novelist Patricia Highsmith to review it, a favourite writer of mine and a regular reviewer for the paper. It was not done for authors to choose their own critics, however, and the idea was ignored. Looking back, I see that Laurie Taylor remarked that the author "fearlessly records the actual nature of inmate life in the cells", which is what I wanted to do. Memory, as I've been finding out lately, can act like a trickster.

During the six months of passing in and out of Lewes prison – sitting in my barber-shop office, perched on the edge of a bunk on C Wing, praying in the chapel, visiting some wretched solitary soul in "the block", where prisoners were sent for punishment – my mind would occasionally wander to the six hours spent with Bruce in the police cell in St Andrew's Square in Glasgow, twenty years earlier. Now I was on the other side of the lock. The key had turned in the opposite direction for me. In the basement at Boots, I had tried to fool the police officers with

James Baldwin at the Edinburgh Book Festival, in conversation with me before a live audience, August 1985. We had quit the bar of the Roxburghe Hotel at five o'clock that same morning. Baldwin charmed and thrilled the audience nonetheless. *Courtesy of Fanny Dubes.*

one of the most inept presentations of an alternative identity they had surely ever experienced: the hapless James Gunning. But in the end, thanks in part to the integrity of Bruce Dryden – and thanks to all the other people involved in that miserable drama, in particular my parents and sisters, not forgetting the exasperated schoolteachers at King's Park and even the St Andrew's Square policemen – I had forged another identity, an alternative to the delinquent schoolboy I had seemed to be then: some sort of existential entity I could claim was "me".

A few months before *Gate Fever* was due to be published, James Baldwin and I had sat at tables in the large tent in Charlotte Square at the 1985 Edinburgh Book Festival. Our mid-morning interview before a large audience had ended. Now he was half-hidden behind pillars of books, pen in hand. A queue formed and people came forward with copies of *Go Tell It on the Mountain*, *Another Country* and other books. Jimmy greeted each in turn with some kind words, a twinkle in the eye, and his miraculous, healing grin.

Suddenly, the reader in front of him was my father. He and Mum had travelled through from Braco to be present. Dad thrust forward a paperback copy of *The Fire Next Time*.

"I'm pleased to meet you, Mr Baldwin. I enjoyed your talk very much."

Jimmy gave him his full-attention stare.

Dad nodded in the direction of the other figure sheltering behind the table. "That's my son."

Jimmy looked at me, looked back at him. Then he took the book, which I have before me now, and wrote: "For Harry Campbell: God bless."

ACKNOWLEDGEMENTS

Morris Dickstein, Lindsay Duguid, Jennie Feldman, Douglas Field, Diana Maxwell, Maren Meinhardt, Robert Messenger, Quentin Miller, Marjorie Perloff and Faith Pullin read parts of this work while it was in progress. My sisters Jean, Phyllis and Julie did so, too. Craig Raine of *Areté* in Oxford and Alan Taylor of the *Scottish Review of Books* in Edinburgh published portions of it, in different form. My cousin Norma Young helpfully supplied family documents. Jerry Robock and Dudley Cole recognized themselves in the portraits found here. Jerry went in search of old pictures from our Spetsai days. Martin Smith and Jo Evans were on hand to scan them and others. My thanks go to Robin Williamson for gracious permission to quote lines from "October Song". For current information about Robin and Bina W. Williamson, see their website www.pigswhiskermusic. co.uk. I am grateful to all.

The telling of this story goes back to the one-to-one French lessons I began with Viviane Blanchard in 2011, continuing to the present day. In tackling the mechanics of the French language, we talked, listened to one another and read aloud. And from time to time I presented Viviane with a short memoir. I would read a little episode from my past, paragraph by paragraph, and she would patiently correct it. At one stage, these tales emerged weekly or fortnightly. Short memoirs became longer. There was something unexpected in reading about oneself in a foreign language. I found that my use of the first person singular was different from my use of it in English. The tone of the writing was new and I was free to write things – and say things, since they were read aloud – that I wouldn't have written or said in my native tongue.

Later, I translated some of the pieces into English, partly for the amusement of my sister Phyllis, partly for my own. I tried at first not to take advantage of the greater fluency of my own language, and to keep something of that new tone. The narrative of *Just Go Down to the Road* has undergone many developments since then, but there are still traces of its origins beneath the surface.

It was my friend and former editor at the *TLS* Peter Stothard who, several years ago, first urged me to write a memoir. Warm thanks are due to Judy Moir for her sensitive copy-editing and structural suggestions, and to Neville Moir, Alison Rae and others at Polygon.

I am indebted most of all, and in every way, to Vera Chalidze.

A NOTE ON THE AUTHOR

James Campbell was born in Glasgow. His books include *Invisible Country: A Journey Through Scotland*, *This Is the Beat Generation*, and a collection of essays, *Syncopations*. He is a former editor of the *New Edinburgh Review*, and was for many years an editor and columnist at the *Times Literary Supplement*.

PENGUIN BOOKS

THE ANGLE OF INCIDENCE

Alex Benzie was born in Glasgow in 1961. After studying English literature at Glasgow University he worked for the Glasgow District Council, and then went into community journalism. His first novel, *The Year's Midnight*, was published by Viking and Penguin to huge acclaim.

THE ANGLE OF INCIDENCE

ALEX BENZIE

PENGUIN BOOKS

PENGUIN BOOKS

Published by the Penguin Group
Penguin Books Ltd, 27 Wrights Lane, London w8 5tz, England
Penguin Putnam Inc., 375 Hudson Street, New York, New York 10014, USA
Penguin Books Australia Ltd, Ringwood, Victoria, Australia
Penguin Books Canada Ltd, 10 Alcorn Avenue, Toronto, Ontario, Canada m4v 3b2
Penguin Books (NZ) Ltd, Private Bag 102902, NSMC, Auckland, New Zealand

Penguin Books Ltd, Registered Offices: Harmondsworth, Middlesex, England

First published by Viking 1999
Published in Penguin Books 2000
10 9 8 7 6 5 4 3 2 1

Set in Linotype Sabon
Printed in England by Clays Ltd, St Ives plc

For Anna, sempre

One

Cameron was five years of age when he saw his mother and father in the act of generation, and for years afterwards, even in his years of reflection, he could never remember exactly what had driven him out of his room. It could have been because he needed someone to reach up, beyond his small child's hope of a reach, into the kitchen cabinet for a glass tumbler, and then to pour him water from the bickering tap the council couldn't be bothered fixing. That would have been a good reason for going into his parents' bedroom at two o'clock in the morning, at least good enough for his age, but he never remembered being thirsty, and so wondered if that was why, especially as he remembered padding on the hard floor, which would suggest that he had been trying to keep quiet. One thing he did recall; through the membrane of the wall, vibrating like an eardrum with every sound, passing secrets from one side to the other like neighbours gossiping across a fence, he was certain that he heard the sound of struggle. He thought it might be wrestling, exertion to achieve a dominant position over another; while again there was a sense of harmony, just occasionally, exertion to a purpose in common, as if two were on either end of a great mass, this way, that, this way again. At other times he thought he was listening to a conversation, an argument from which the words had been stripped, naked blades colliding, dashed one against the other, open and unsheathed; another listening and there was a theme, a duet without a voice, laced, braided with the delicacy of cotton twine. Perhaps, and this was a later thought once again, his thirst was nothing more than the horse his curiosity rode across the hall, a drought of convenience caused by the will to investigate, taking him with good reason to the room next door to his own, to open it, because this was his house as well, where he was safe, enclosed.

An absurd hat of a shade guided the metallic light paid out by the crystal bulb, and Cameron remembered that the shade had been a present from an aunt and uncle, the only reason it was given room in the house at all, where only his parents need ever see it. It was made of beige synthetic fabric tautened around the wire ghost of a bell-shaped frame, with the bulb as its clapper, ending in a tasselled skirt as a flourish, and it made the light in the room as soft and as supple as bronze cloth, so that his mother and father were held in its penumbra, the sheets thrown away from them as if they were now readied for their permanent display. The door was partly opened before the hinges yelled like an arpeggio whelped from an ill-tuned violin, and the first thing to happen was that Francis half turned his posture, as if caught in the totalitarian sight of God Himself, a clean and revealing nimbus which revealed flaws in his fallible china skin; his hand scurried for cover, to take a grip of the trailing sheets, and the look that Cameron saw on his father was that of a man fallen from grace, staring in the eye all innocence, all cleanliness and purity incarnated in his son, who for that moment may as well have been God. The second thing to happen was that his mother, Catherine O'Hara, began such a laugh, so raucous and serrated, as you might imagine to yourself was the sound of a blade turning earth, it had the forgiveness, the promise, the very smell of opened ground, the laugh possessed her and animated her like a spirit on its own so that she found herself giggling and twisting beyond her ability to control, and leaving Cameron standing in the doorway in a fine confusion. It was always like this whenever he caught them in something like a kiss, a caress without thinking; Francis springing to one side as if seen indulging a weakness in his fibre, Catherine laughing her head off as much at her husband's ludicrous shame as at her son's precocious curiosity, and Cameron remembered where he had heard that laugh before, at Calderpark Zoo one afternoon where they had stood and watched apes in their cages, look Cameron, look at that one, he's peeling a banana, look! and so he was, unzipping the rind from around the erect white pulp and discarding it on the floor of the cage to splay like a child's daubed sunshine in a painting, and there was her dancing, kinetic laugh as it tucked in, staring at her, not knowing, wanting to understand, what about itself was so funny.

Catherine O'Hara would not give Francis the freedom of movement he needed to find the sheet under his fingers, but instead seized him tightly in her arms, and gripped him with her legs and thighs about the waist, locking him inside her as if they were complementary halves of a single clasp without whose joining the world would fly apart. She had him so firmly held that even his eyes were drawn towards the north of her staring, attracting his full attention as if by natural right, and when she was certain that she saw nothing in his eyes but her own picture, surrounded by the iris like a portrait in a locket, she held his head still between the palms of her hands and spoke to him in a voice which shook with urgency,

I won't have him thinking this is wrong, Francis. Let him stay if he wants. Remember what we agreed.

For that while, she dominated the will of Francis, not by the brutal exercise of naked power, but by allowing him into the veins of wisdom that glittered in the depths of her, long seams of compressed and deposited knowledge, bitter experience. Still inside her, he relaxed a little, causing her to release him now that he no longer squirmed, and leaned over to her ear,

I hope ye're sure,

ashamed that his professed beliefs should prove to be so brittle in the face of it. Still impaled by Francis, Cameron's mother turned her head to one side and raised it from the pillow so that she was nearly at the level of her son's eyes on the tall dais of the bed, and she coughed, readying herself to speak. Cameron had his hands joined behind his back, clasped together so that it seemed as if he were shading a prayer from the sight of his parents, and wriggling like a worm on a pin, stuck through by the silver uncertainty of the moment, because it looked to him as if his father had managed to wrestle his mother to submission, he thought of brawling in the street and

3

wondered if this was how his parents conducted their fights; but Catherine saw all of his uncertainties as clearly as if he had sent them out to be heard, and she said to him,

We aren't wrestling, Cameron, not like you see on the telly. D'you understand, Cameron? We aren't fighting.

She made him nod understanding before she went on,

I know you can hear us through the walls, but listen to me; nothing you hear is hurting us. It's like, you know when you have an itch on your arm or your leg, and you scratch it and it goes away, and it feels good and you go, ah! you know what I mean? Well, that's what it's like, it's not painful at all, it's very nice. Your dad's on top of me just now, but I can go on top of him, you see, he isn't holding me down or anything, I'm allowing him, see?

Catherine O'Hara kept her eyes on her son, softening them so that she might take the sting out of the confusing sight, and then, at the end of the explanation, inclined her head, which caused him to nod, received, understood; smiled at him, an invitation he always replied to; and then she kicked Francis's flanks as if she had spurs in her heels, giddy up, just to show that she had an equality of control over what was happening, and Cameron stayed exactly where he was, because no one had told him he could go yet.

Catherine O'Hara had walked past the cinema at the end of Sauchie-hall Street, near the rim of Charing Cross, with its slender marquee projecting out and over the paving, and there she had seen young boys in short trousers bobbing under the sight of the woman in the pay booth, dashing as quietly as they could up the stairs. The cinema showed a full day's programme of erotic movies, and the boys were entering in the afternoon, when they should have been at school; Catherine O'Hara imagined her Cameron as one of them in later years, tempted into prurience like Pinocchio to the island, smoking in the back row while watching a pageant of violence and suffering and learning through the example of company how to enjoy the sight of what he was watching. One night, before she and Francis had been married, she had whispered into the dark, no child of mine'll ever learn about this from a bloody priest, twisted brutes so they are, not at all, Francis, not-a-bloody-tall, and of course Francis agreed with

4

her, because he really did agree with her, there's a time comin, he said, when priests, aye, ministers as well, willny matter a damn to the likes ey you and me, meaning young and hopeful people with their eyes on the stars and their movements, and they believed, not just that night but every night, that love might just tip it, enough love in the balance would cause it to tilt away from venality and bitterness, they were children standing, hand in hand, before the star at the top of a Christmas tree, wishing hard. That was why you said things to yourself, considered Francis, things like the world must be safe for children, like ignorance and repression are evil, you say them because to do so is to throw switches in your heart and if nothing lights up then you call it hypocrisy and people think that the panel is just there for display; and so when he remembered that night when he had said to her, no boy r girl ey oors'll be tellt onythn but the truth, I swear tay God, Kate, he remembered also that she laughed and said, don't swear on what you don't pray to, didn't you think of that? pulling him closer so he could smell that her perfume was slowly decaying, losing the sweetness so that she was dusted in cinnamon like a pastry, her perspiration washing away the scent of rosewater, and Francis laughed with her because he felt a different person when he was laughing with her, he could laugh at his mannequin self, the stupidities it committed, without recognizing it as being his mirror self, and this felt like a great comfort to him.

Francis tried to forget, for the sake of a promise he had made to the woman under him, that there was anyone else in the room with them. The best way he found to maintain his hydraulic readiness was to imagine that he was being watched by his father; at first imagining him at the window like a spectator against the pane of an aquarium, then placing old Thomas in the doorway, powerless to move from the sight of his son's bare arse flaying away, the damned insolence of it, kiss it da cause one day I'll confound ye, and ye'll no be there to see that neether, erasing Cameron from the doorway as if he had been drawn on the air in pastel chalks, sketching Thomas there instead, and even hearing his own old man say, stoap that right the noo, ya bam ye, wee pup that yu'r, gaunny stope that wi yir faither here, whit a disgrace tay the faimly y'ur.

*

5

Catherine O'Hara felt the shock of her husband's anger through her body, a pulse and a repeated detonation of pleasure, again, again, and made sure by absorbing it with the tension in her legs, bracing herself against his haunches, that her watching son could not see in their movements the violence she felt. It was as much a surprise to herself as it evidently was to Francis that she was able to go through with this promise, and so she discharged her duty to it as meticulously as she was able, making sure that the only lessons her son would learn from this was that there was nothing to be afraid or ashamed of, and this was how she would conduct his broader education, starving him of nothing, listening, talking to him in a way that her own father never did. To this day she remembered her taciturn father over the water, and how he claimed everyone's friendship after a nip of the whisky, everyone's but that of his daughter, his son, his wife; nobody a stranger to owl Colum O'Hara, except for his family. She used to prod him with questions time and time again, questions sharpened to a point and which irritated him like a rash, da, why is the sky blue? da, why are there stars? da, what are mountains and rivers and waterfalls? pricking him one after the other, but nothing moved his sad inert flesh, God knows, wee one, because God made it, now stop giving me bother and away and play in peace. Or else it was, a man works hard so he doesn't have to answer stupid questions like that, Colum O'Hara never understood why his daughter needed to know things like why the sky was blue because there it was, as blue as you like from the day you draw your first breath until the day you let out your last, a foolish question to ask on account of a thing that would never change.

Oh, and what a devout man was old Colum O'Hara, known for a churchgoer the length and breadth of the county, a good man, though how the two had become confused and blended, the going to church and the goodness, was a mystery to young Kate, walking through the wreckage of one of his tempers, holding her mother and saying, don't give yourself any blame, mammy, and then there was Michael her brother who took the worst of it, for some reason none of them could imagine, unwarranted rage at the pretender, who knew? Catherine O'Hara remembered the evening that she stood up to him, finally, roaring at him, so this is how a good churchgoin man behaves, is it, da? and it was nearly one question too many, but then the old fox surprised them all, please Kate, not you of all payple, he came close to her and laid his filthy open hand, the hand he had raised to his wife not a moment before, on her cheek, she recoiled as if the very sweat from it were as mordant as vitriol; I believe in God, sure I do, Katie, but sometimes I swear I don't know how He makes us the way we are, and he was caressing her cheek with a slight and affectionate touch, enough to pass a malignant lightning of a charge through her; I wish ye wouldn't cry, darlin Katie, I don't mean ye harm, I'll never mean ye harm.

What Catherine O'Hara sacrificed to maintain the equilibrium of this collection of strangers in a box; to keep the balance true, to spare others. When Colum O'Hara burst into her room and found that his daughter was sharing more than just a bed with her brother, he cried her for all the names he could think of, he pulled them from the deepest pit, the most stagnant well he could imagine, the sound of them alone reeked and fouled his hands, but she said back, No more than you do yourself, y'owl drunkard, I'm fed up protecting this family from you, now you'll take a belt to me because it's not the old bull himself I'm servicing, isn't that the truth now? She said it as loud as it sent her mother fleeing from the house, screaming enough to loosen the bite of the bracings in the roof, and her father was too busy chasing after his wife to give her a thrashing, but Michael said to her, you'd best leave as soon as you're able, Kate, he'll never forgive you for that, and promised to make sure, now that he was getting older himself, that their mother would be safe from the old man.

Only Michael and her mother were invited to the wedding over the water, and when Michael said that the old boy was at home, and that his heart was breaking, she said lightly, lessons are never easy in the learning, Michael. He had a camera attached to his hand by a short lanyard, a Kodak, and he danced around the procession and the ceremony and the cutting of the cake at the reception afterwards, he had a cone flash which blared out a cool stroke of light for the indoors and which gouged out a black shadow behind every object in its road, miles and miles of film, and for the whole day Kate made sure she had her broadest brightest grin on her face, for the sake of later

7

eyes, and for a laugh she said to him, my God, Michael, any more photographs and you'd be able to see the wedding at the Odeon. That night, as she slept with Francis as his wife, remembering Michael's tender and releasing kiss before he took to his room, Catherine O'Hara found that two things came to mind. The first, strangely, was that the O'Haras had never owned a camera before in their lives. The second was that she would not be the mother of a child who stayed in ignorance, of anything, because knowledge was power, was choice, and she would give this child choices, as far as she was able.

Cameron watched with interest as his father surged and retreated, surged and retreated like the tide against the shore of his mother. He saw what looked like pain on both the faces of his mother and his father, each of their faces broke time and again to be recast in new moulds, and all of them expressing this singular pain which he had to tell himself was in fact nice for them, remembering what his mother had told him, seeing that their eyes were slivered to near closing, that their breaths were quickening and telling of the exertion, every sound he had heard through the flimsy wall now explained. He began to think of them as a paired engine, because he had seen engines from many years ago on the television, locomotives which seemed to share the same drive as he was seeing before him, the same hot and forced breath, for every action an equal and opposed reaction, faster they went and picking up speed, the old bed underneath them could hardly tolerate it and reared and kicked like a pony while the springs developed a rhythm under them, they were falling to the centre, driving, Cameron could almost feel, almost see an exultant power gathering around them like a static charge and they were crying out as if for release from torment; then one last cry, a push and a final drive to spill over the lip into that release, and there they were, collapsed and empty as cloth bags, almost nothing left but skins and slack exhausted pulp. Cameron wondered what he was expected to do in the settling quietness, as Francis lay flat on top of his wife, as Kate stroked the hair about his ears, petting him as if he were a kitten, as if she had just drawn a thorn from his paw, smiling towards her son, not forgetting him, making sure that he knew he had seen nothing to be afraid of, saying to him,

8

That's how babies are made, Cameron. That's how you were made.

She spoke to him for a long time, and generously answered all the questions that burst from his mouth while Francis went to the kitchen to make them all a cup of tea. She impressed upon him that this was not a thing he should presume upon anyone, that it was a matter for consent and agreement and desire coming together, and she made certain that he understood this, asking him to repeat it back to her, and then to frame it in his own words so that she might correct him if he appeared to have absorbed the wrong lesson from her; but he was word-perfect. Finally she said to tell no one of what he had been allowed to see, even engaging his child's delight in being part of a conspiracy, especially not to be told to his grandmother, because none of them would ever hear the end of it, and she made him inscribe a cross on the exact centre of his chest with the point of his index finger over his striped pyjama top, and that was it sealed with his life, while Francis drew a splutter of hot tea from his mug, looking to the Persian pattern of the carpet and sitting on the edge of the bed with his back to his wife and his son, excluded from them, excluding them.

Cameron was sent to his bed with a kiss from his mother and a goodnight from his father. He dreamed of giants fighting, wrestling for supremacy, the size of gods but without faces, without features, in an arena of sand and fused rock, with only himself as a spectator. He sensed immense powers in them both, but there was no lashing out, no brutality, nothing like a blow or a punch, and he wakened up before he could tell which if either of them had won the contest.

Two

On the day Francis came home from the hospital, Catherine had the house prepared for his arrival; everything proper and dusted and laundered, pure in the sunlight that came slanting from outside. Everything ornamental was right and balanced exactly on the mantel, a photograph here of their wedding from her brother's Kodak, a carriage clock at the fulcrum of the arrangement, a photograph there of her seated coddling the baby, with Francis leaning over the back of the chair, his arm like a roof over his wife and child, you could see the pride in him, disbelief if you caught it in the appropriate light. There was the smell of aerosol polish about the place, a bright reflective smell which gave her a catch in her throat, and this chased her to the windows, lifting their sashes to let the fresh summer air in to cleanse out the room, all the rooms; in a minute or two there was a new scent to the house, floral and expansive, sweet and braided so she couldn't draw a single thread out of it and say, this is peony and this is tulip, and it would have drawn a smile from her if she hadn't remembered the gravity of the day, the reason for her being so busy. It put her in mind of a particular thing she'd considered all day while she had been working; she went to their room, to the teak wardrobe bargained for in an antique shop in town, and before she used its prim brass key to open it, she let the flat of her hand trace the grain of it, the furl and blaze of the veneer, a warmth almost of flesh against her, the remnant of the sunlight it had absorbed through the window. The key turned in the lock, the door opened with a squeal and a deluge of lavender and gentian she used to sweeten the fibres; she wondered why today of all days she was unusually sensitive to the way things smelled, gathering the strands to her like yarn in a ball, aware of the least vapour.

She found the dress four deep on the right-hand rail, but she saw the shoulders of it the moment she opened the door, brighter than any of her other dresses. She'd grown to dislike it recently, I look like a girl's doll in it, she complained about a year ago, when the illness was still a secret Francis harboured inside him, but, rubbish Kate, he said, it makes ye look lik a summer queen, trust me, as he sealed her up in it with a stroke of the zip, and she had to concede to him there was a certain flounce to it, a way you carried it, or it carried you, one of the two, she was never too sure whether she was worn by it, shaped to its preference. She brought it out of the wardrobe, easing the hanger's question-mark hook from the rail, separating it from all the day-to-day coats and blouses and skirts, empty skins rippling in the draught; closed the door over and locked it, held the dress up to the clean light of the bedroom window.

The dress shone like the silk its artificial fabric was meant to imitate, and in that moment she thought she could see what he did in the cut of it, tapering from the bands made to lie over the shoulders like epaulettes to the waist, flaring from there to the shins; sky blue, patterned with roses, thornless stems. In this light it fired through like stained glass, and perhaps, she thought, it wasn't too excessive after all for a day like this, when she wanted to be as much a home to him as the house itself, familiar as the chair against his back, it wasn't too much to ask of her, though her gentle Francis would never think of asking; perhaps that was why she was so ready to please him, because he'd never demanded, about the only man she'd ever known like that. For her day's tasks she'd been wearing a roll-neck jumper of mixed wool and acrylic, nylon slacks, good enough for inside and work, her overalls, but not for a home-coming; she laid the dress out on the bed, still widened on the shoulders of the hanger, and quickly changed, thinking how smooth these new fabrics were when she compared them to the memory of the old linens and cottons her mammy over the water put on her, washed the old way, dried still stiff with soap in raging winds. She called Cameron through to finish the last few inches of the zip, felt him as a smaller presence behind her than she was used to, reaching, stretching to lift the tab secure. She turned to look at him, opened out her arms and struck the pose of a model she'd seen in a women's magazine, hands resting on hips, her torso pressed forward, one leg crooked against the other; smiled as much as she was able.

There, Cameron. D'you think your dad'll love me for ever, all done up like this?

She had never seen a face like it on a child of his age before, unnaturally solemn, carved of a piece like a mourning mask. Not for the first time, Catherine wondered if maybe she should have taken him with her on her visits to the Royal, hoped that her talk with him the night before would be enough. Seemingly not; because Cameron said,

Can I go through to my room and play with my motor cars?

Catherine came back to herself, with the need to draw the sting from what she was asking of Cameron, of herself. She shook her head, slowly to make it seem as if she'd given his request a reasonable consideration, reached out to sort his hair, shaping it along the parting.

No, Cameron. We'll both be waiting for him when he comes.

Cameron put out his underlip thoughtfully, dropped his eyes to regard the carpet, looked up at her again.

Can I bring my ambulance through to play with while we're waiting?

Catherine smiled; just like a wean to test the limits of the fence around him.

As long as you put it away when your dad gets here.

That seemed to satisfy him; he nodded, scampered away and out of the room to fetch it, his feet clumsy on the carpet. Catherine wondered to herself if there was anything she would ever refuse him, in these few weeks when the family would be together again. It was just as her look was straying about the room, as if there was something she'd forgotten, that she saw the jewelled bottle among all her other fragrances and palettes of make-up on the dressing-table, that perfume he liked, the paints she used to signal to Francis in a way she hoped Cameron wouldn't understand, intentions made scarlet on the canvas of her face; there she went next, settling herself on the stool in front of the triptych mirror, pressing the skirt against her so the fabric wouldn't bunch and crease. The light was timid on this side of the house in the afternoon, but there was enough to see by; she made up her promising face, rouge on her cheeks over a pale foundation, her mouth reddened by lipstick, and last of all there was the perfume in its bottle, the liquid climbing the sides from the way she'd jittered the dressing-table with her concentration on effect, from how she'd leaned on it. It didn't look much, like well-watered whisky in colour, and she picked it up to look at it before she applied it; she'd worn it for years, one more enticement, but there was once when he was in her room, he'd said it made her smell nice, she pressed him on it, he was good with compliments but only when he was prompted, nice, what d'you mean nice? tell me how come nice? and he said, like one ey they pastries ye get, ye know, cinnamon, and she laughed and threw the sheets over them both, as long as you're never tempted by anything else in the baker's shop, and then his face went all stiff and serious on her, I'm no tempted by anybdy else, Kate, honest, and she made herself as solemn as Cameron had been a moment ago, a mirror to him almost across the pillow, keep it that way, Francis, only then he saw the mockery through her eyes, she loved teasing him for his innocence, his inexperience.

Catherine held the bottle away from herself, pinched the bulb between her thumb and forefinger in three pulses; the atomizer sent out the vapour in long cool plumes, and she turned her head to let it strike all over her face, the pillar of her neck, the shaped valley as the dress fell from her shoulders. She caught the scent drifting on the air; and then too late wondered if it would be good for Francis in his condition, if the sharpness of it would cause him irritation, a fine thing it'd be if the very day he came to his family was also the day he wished he'd stayed in the hospital.

By the time she was finished, she had all the make-up paints and the bottle of fragrance placed exactly where she had found them, so she had only the evidence of the mirror to tell her that she had ever used them at all. The liquid danced in the bottle again, roused easily by the least wee tremor; went still after a while of agitation. Catherine decided that there was her lesson to be learned; shook her head to cause the flailing of her black hair, rested for a calm moment on the stool, thought as best she could of nothing, and then stood up. She slipped her bare feet into her flat shoes of black suede, and then left the room, marking it behind her with the fragrance like a cat leaving its trace.

Cameron was sitting in her seat by the fire when she arrived in the living-room, the one with its back turned to the tele set as if she'd fallen out with it, which in a way she had, that globe with all its blather and its nonsense. He was running his toy ambulance along the curved arm of the chair, from the end turned on itself like a scroll down the slope to where it joined the body, making a motor sound far in his throat and letting the vibration rise into his nose. At any other time she'd have thought him clever for the way he observed the gear changes, the Doppler swelling and tapering of the engine note, but she said,

Could you not do that into yourself, Cameron? This isn't a good time for it,

and he nodded slowly, went silent so she could only hear the plastic wheels scraping against the wood like a mouse at the skirting-board, which she tolerated sooner than have him unnaturally quiet for a child. She went to the window, and there leaned against the folding table in front of it, compressed to make room with its leaves fallen; her hands raised creases on the white linen cloth she had over it, there in case of visitors like Danny and Agnes, less frequently her mother-in-law who couldn't resist coming to find fault with her housekeeping, spiteful old biddy she was, always trailing a finger over all the surfaces and coming away with some or other thing on the end of it, dust only she could see scattered by the tip of her thumb, as if Catherine would be shoddy with the dusting when she'd a house to herself, it was an insult just to think of it.

She was leaning with her arms spread apart, hands flattened on the cloth, and she cast about the street, waiting, a thing she hated to do for the way it made you weak and powerless. There wasn't much to be seen outside; children playing kick-a-ball in the width of the road, just, using the kerbs as touchlines; she looked over her shoulder at Cameron, engrossed in the short journey of his model ambulance, and wondered if being solitary was in his nature, if there weren't times when he heard the cries and the bawling and didn't feel them as magnetism to his charged curiosity, what it would be like to join in their playing.

To see better out of the window, Catherine parted the net; the fabric was rough against her fingertips, but the delicacy of it brought to her a vivid memory of another touch, many years ago. She placed her hands on the table again; the linen was warmed by the sun, and she remembered being given the cloth as a wedding present from some relative of Francis's, she didn't remember who or what measure of in-law it might be; and then the memory printed on the tips of her fingers came to her like the sudden expanding of a picture on the tele set. She was thinking of the morning of her wedding; and she was thinking of the dress in its box, newly arrived from the hire shop at the house of Francis's mother, where she had spent her night apart from him, not her own superstition, but theirs, and so she respected it, she tried so hard to get on that old woman's good side, if she had one. Catherine remembered herself as distantly as if she'd been a wee girl at the time, the way you distort size in all your thoughts of the past; roads becoming longer, rooms turning into giant chambers, caverns eked out of hiding-places. What a lassie she'd been, knowing she was despised by the woman of the house, thinking she heard the crazed old voice declaring slut when it wasn't, preparing herself by thinking how the next day would release her from all of it, more than just the old biddy's spite; nothing there but the light ticking of a cheap old clock, steps to take her to the day after. The old missis wouldn't even make dinner for them that night, putting on her dowdy coat to go to the chip shop, I canny be bothered waitin hand and foot on onybdy comin here disruptin this hoose, and that was her dinner, clothed in old newspaper, rank with vinegar, turned out on to a plate, fish like the sole of your old boot, chips thick and flaccid with grease; she thought of her mother and Michael, staying with Francis over at Agnes's and Danny's, longed to spend the night with them. She bore them all, the silences, avoidances, grudged cups of tea; carried them like a punishment with the thought of tomorrow to strengthen her, when the old missis wouldn't have them in her reach, and so she sipped her tea out of a plain enamel mug, nothing special for the slut who'd be wed in a registry office sooner than have the proper chapel service, right heathen so it was.

Catherine was shown to the other bedroom, the one Francis and Danny had slept in when they were younger, before they left home, in fact where Francis had slept up until yesterday; the old missis reached around the threshold to close the switch, the least she would do for a guest, said, noo's yir chance tay sleep in his bed, fr a cheynge, since he'd hardly seen it after meeting Catherine. Catherine turned and smiled, almost pleased to be stirring her, denying nothing. She made a point of asking which of the beds, placed at right angles to each other, was Francis's; delighted in the look on the old missis's face as she indicated the one with the scraped wooden headboard against the wall beside the window, the eyes were dull and venomous, curdled as she turned to leave for her own bedroom, closing the door. Catherine undressed quickly in the light of the dying bulb, breathed the smell of the room, proudly clean, and saw as she took her nightdress out of the overnight bag the curious pallid squares on the walls, tiny pricks at the corners of ghostly pale vacancies where the wallpaper was as fresh and colourful as it had been when it was unrolled; around the two beds, and some of those mosaics of absence were triangular in shape, especially on Danny's side of the room, those mystified her, though she knew they'd been made by pictures of some kind, fixed to the wall by drawing-pins. Once she had the nightdress on, drifting and modelling itself against her, she knelt on top of the cotton bedspread and sketched the silhouettes with the point of her finger; thought were any of them film stars, were they just stripped from the walls yesterday the whole gallery of them, wondered at the depth of imagination in him, in both the brothers. She went to put out the light, drew aside the sheets and folded herself up in them, and then, just like a wee lassie, it made her smile now to remember it, she gathered the white linen blanket nearest her skin and tried to detect his scent from it, sniffing the hem of the blanket; she forgave herself for being young, now she did anyway, though it hadn't been that many years ago, but he smelled like freedom to her, from over the water, from her father, like the first breath she'd taken of the air of the sea when she boarded the ferry, maybe she'd do the same now, she wouldn't swear to it she wouldn't.

The morning after, she had a breakfast of toast and tea, more of the black bitter stuff milk could hardly lighten, and then she had a bath in the absurd wee cup of a tub in the bathroom, the walls ripe with sepia damp, the paper unfurling from the rim of the bath to the ceiling and exposing spores and rotted plaster underneath; my boay'd fix it, the old missis had said sullenly, if he hudny ey been busy lately, and Catherine smiled again, the day itself was her proof against the old woman. There was an old bathtowel, frayed and with a hole in it, on a wooden rail secured beside the wash-hand basin; Catherine padded herself dry with it, then wore it like a sarong to return to the bedroom to brush the length of her hair out and straight, she had a toilet bag cluttered with everything she'd need for the day. Her hair took an age to dry, and while she was waiting she bent down to reach under the bed, to slip out the thin box of pastel blue card delivered the day before, placed it on top of the bed's covers and sat beside it, and all she did until she was certain her hair was dried to the ends was look at it, you'd've thought to see her she was afraid to even touch it, charged like a battery. Soon enough, Catherine was properly dry, and she delved into her overnight bag for her liberty bodice, the shell with her shape ready to step into; and when she was finally inside it, becoming used to its pinch and constriction, she went to the box and raised the lid, taking a long breath and closing her eyes as if it was her Christmas.

The exposed tissue paper was layered like millefeuille, and when she reached to touch it, there was the faintest spark and crackle against the tips of her fingers, and a breath of fragrance from it that she couldn't identify, rose petals perhaps. She was careful enough not to tear the paper as she folded it back and back, opening it out like a flower until there was no more of the bloom and there was only her dress, her dress for today, to be seen, folded without creases, and that was when she touched it for the first time since the wedding shop, when Danny and Agnes had gone with her, the touch which revealed the delicacy of the weave, white organza. She lifted it reverently out of the box by the ribbons of the shoulders, took a step back and pressed it against herself, standing on the ends of her toes to raise the lace trim above the worn carpet; there wasn't a mirror in the room, a man's room right enough, no place for vanity, and she just had her memory of how it had looked in the shop to guide her, of how Agnes had breathed and said, yon's awffy gorgeous, Kate, ye look a million dollars in it, Danny had smiled like his brother, winked archly, aye, Kate, marry me and leave that bum alane, and Agnes made to slap him in the face, all in play, eyes tay the side, you, ye've a wife tay support, and he looked all innocent and said, aw aye, so I huv.

Just as she was straining to fix the pearl beads through the eyes of thread in the hem at the level of her shoulder-blades, with her arms seized ungracefully behind her, she saw the old missis standing at the threshold to the room, watching her. Catherine felt the pearl in the fingers of one hand, the cotton thong in the other; but she'd already failed to connect them in a number of passes, and it made her angry to think the old missis had been amusing herself for a while. The old missis came fully into the room, planted herself in front of Catherine and looked up at her, age drawing her down to a child's height; for a moment Catherine fixed on the eyes of the old woman, and it was as if all the years she'd on her fell away, she was a wee lassie not in the way that Catherine felt, buoyant and excited, but cold and malicious, she'd pluck the wings from a fly you'd think and feed it to the spider in her web. Catherine let go of the pearl and the thong, not wanting the sour old bitch, forgive her for thinking it, to take any more pleasure from her awkwardness. The old missis kept up her glowering until Catherine wanted to demand, what is it you're after? leave me in peace to do up the dress. Catherine felt herself measured by the old woman, opened her mouth to ask was there anything she wanted; the old missis shook her head, and said, ye widny ask for my help, ye'd be here a' efternin if ye'd tay day it yirsel, and then she said, turn roon, and Catherine obeyed, raising her hair to allow the old missis in. The elderly hands were rough against her back, drawing the fastenings together and mating them quickly and efficiently, tugging hard enough to make Catherine fear for her balance, pulling at her like the brush working the knots out of her hair. At last she felt the dry hands come away from her back, sweeping briskly against the ribbons of silk, and then the old missis said, turn roon, again, and again Catherine obeyed, hating that she was responding to the crack of the switch. The touch of the old missis wasn't a tender one, as Catherine let her hair fall the hands were all about her, but at last they were both at peace, each facing the other, and the old missis said, aye, yon'd be a fine dress for ony wummn; and there was something like jealousy in her eyes, Catherine saw, which made her stop and look at her properly, like Michael used to pick up this and that whenever they went walking in the country. The old missis was in her own nightgown, lemon-coloured and decorated like Catherine's dress with trims of white lace, as if she was the bride of sleep, married to her nights of loneliness when exhaustion seduced her. For the first time Catherine heard the spilling of water from the slightly ajar door of the bathroom; thought of what the old woman was forever saying, if my Thomas had been here, and then the thought jumped across the gap between them, she said, if my Thomas had been here, he'd'a been awffy proud ey his son jist noo. She turned and shuffled away out of the room in her fleeced slippers, not waiting to hear Catherine's thanks for her generosity; her man was like the ghosts of the pictures on the bedroom walls but she could still carry his messages with certainty, and she wasn't going to be thanked for that service. Catherine wished the old man had been here, for Francis as well as herself; she'd seen the photographs on the mantel, the family on seaside holidays, standing by some or other monument she couldn't recognize, not a single one of them with the old woman in the frame. They were the only windows she looked out of these days, Francis had told her, bleak and monochrome and poisoned by damp; but Catherine was in no mood just now to give her pity, not after the way she'd been treated the last day, and reached into the box for her veil, and the train which fastened to the back of her dress.

Cameron said,

Is that the ambulance? Does it look like this one?

He was standing beside her at the table, with his toy ambulance in the palm of his hand like a small pet. She heard the dull motor sound from outside, began to waken, saw the vehicle, identical to the one Cameron held, slowing down above the hedges and coming to a halt on the border of the pavement, as if Cameron had picked it out of his hand and placed it there. She said,

That's your dad come back, Cameron. Be a good boy and put the ambulance away in your room.

Cameron closed his fist around the toy, looked down again at the carpet, then raised his head to look at her; she was surprised to see how grown-up he looked.

Is he any different?

Catherine went down on her haunches to talk to him at his own height; tried not to sound as if she was pleading with him, that'd just stir his worries, unsettle him.

He's still your dad, Cameron. He's had a difficult operation. He looks a wee bit different, like I told you, but he needs us to help him. Now away and put the ambulance back.

She said it gently, like a suggestion. Cameron nodded, then turned and held the ambulance in the air as if it was running on a road, sang me maw, me maw, me maw, in imitation of a siren, until he was out of the door. Catherine stood to her full height, pressed her hands down the front of her dress, from bodice to skirt, ironing flat the creases she imagined were there; when she bent a little to look, it was immaculate. She took a breath of air, now stinking with petrol exhaust; and then she was away, dancing on her toes towards the front door, using the geometric pattern of meshed diamonds on the hall carpet as Cameron did himself, as stepping-stones to guide her.

The first thing Catherine saw when she opened the front door on the landing was the glass panel in her opposite neighbour's door; the glass was frosted, dappled in a pattern that reminded her of fish in a fishmonger's tray, nose to tail, as if they'd been crafted to sit together in death neatly, the rounding of the belly accommodating the arc of the one below, but only when they were placed in opposition to each other; that kind of fit. There was a movement behind the pane, the shape of a face broken by the pattern, assembled imperfectly so that Catherine couldn't make out the features, although there was a crown of silver about the head, she could guess which of the two pensioners it was. There was the smell of frying onions about the close, and a heavy smell wound round it of grease and meat which seemed to wrap itself fast about her, snaking from upstairs. Catherine heard the ambulance doors shutting outside the oblong portal to the close, the driver's door from the sound of it, and this made her go to the portal, to the three steps leading to the front garden path, she took them at a run and hurried along the concrete paving to the slight lip on to the pavement against which the ambulance was parked.

It looked exactly like Cameron's model; a strange grin of a radiator, a high forehead drifting back against the square hull, white like a surgeon's coat; too bright, she thought, to be a hearse. It had disgorged two men, one of them came round on Catherine's side of the ambulance, said,

Ur you Frankie's missis?

He was taller than her, and quite broad, used to lifting and carrying, but she looked at the ends of his arms and saw that his fingers were all sticks and spindles, more like the surgeon's at the hospital, the one she'd argued with for hours that Francis should come home. He had a thick face; not thick stupid, but in proportion with the rest of him, except the hands, big-boned, so big in the skull with it, cushioned by plenty of flesh, and he smiled delicately; he knew the value of a smile at the right time, the right warmth to make it, he was good and professional about it. Catherine stood on the pavement, held herself about her waist as he went round to the back of the ambulance. She felt a quickening in her belly, surely it wasn't nerves, she'd seen him every day for all the weeks he'd been in the Royal; she knew there were eyes against her, felt them as the touch of moths' wings, and she turned to see Cameron standing at the portal, peering from behind the jamb of it, he was like this on Christmas morning, wanting to see his presents under the tree before he'd approach them as if they'd grow legs and hurry away from him. The ambulance man was at the back now, and she turned to him, said,

I call him Francis,

trying not to sound too precious about it; he braced himself against the chrome door handles, allowed himself a wee laugh.

Gien him his Sunday name, eh? Aye, very good, well, dinny you mind, missis, we've seen him tay the hoaspitl, Goad knows we're gonny see him safe this wee bit.

Catherine frowned; remembered their faces.

You were the ones who came to take him.

Aye missis, the very same,

he said, pulled on the handles to throw the latches with a force that rang through the hull, widened the doors; Catherine smelled the antiseptic released by the opening, as if the ambulance had held the breath of hospital air all the way along the road. The other man leapt on to the board while the one who'd opened the doors reached in to grapple with something hidden from Catherine; she heard what sounded to her like a file drawn across wood, watched while the two men adjusted themselves to manage a lift, each preparing to balance the weight, and then the ambulance man she'd spoken to said,

Right, ur we ready, Frankie? Wan two three and hup!

Catherine didn't see him properly until the wheelchair was settled on the tarmac, when the thick ambulance man went to the back of the chair. She thought she'd've been happier, more relieved to see him, but there was so little of him left in the chair, he was as light as kindling, held together by string, and she wondered why she'd argued to have him back, whether it'd been for his own sake or just to get the better of Dr Haldane, him with his far distant eyes and the way he had of treating you like one of a dozen letters he'd received in the post, madam, what could you possibly do at home we couldn't do better for him here? and that only because she'd followed him down the corridor and made him answer her, because by God she was going to trail him into his office and ask for a cup of tea if he wouldn't. Only when she saw him, parked on the kerb just like the ambulance, she had doubts into herself, but she made herself believe she was happy, and it was all she could do to stop herself from running to hold him, afraid in case she broke the sticks he had instead of bones.

Another thing was, it was easy to see him in his bed at the hospital, she'd known he was sick and you expect to see people broken by illness whenever you go along the corridors with their bold lighting, their echoes, the smell of medicine and antiseptic. But in the sunlight, it was as if the look of him had changed; he was more geology than flesh, the eyes glimmering in their sockets, cheeks overhanging and the matter gouged away underneath them as if by the slow erosions that shaped cliffs, and she could hardly bear him smiling at her, because then she couldn't tell the difference between him and death, there wasn't a grain's thickness between them. It took effort to reply with a smile of her own as the ambulance man turned the chair and wheeled him over the rise in the kerb; he was wearing the clothes he'd had on the day he was admitted, a white shirt draped over him as if it was on a clothes-horse for an airing, dull blue corduroys with the belt girdled around him like a child's hoop, as ill-fitting now as his skin. The wind took the spare material like sails, inflating him for a while, and Catherine saw how little there was of him inside them now; she'd only seen him above the chest in the ward.

She looked up at the other ambulance man, who was pulling from the back of the vehicle a scarred cylinder of oxygen with a breathing mask attached by a rubber umbilicus; beyond him she saw to the other shore of the street. There were two women standing halfway along the garden path, arms folded, talking to each other in lowered voices, dressed for the house in pinafores and stained old woollen skirts in earthen colours; on their heads each of them wore a scarf tied under the chin, concealing a bristle of hair curlers, and on their feet each wore a pair of slippers, red cooled down by dust. Every so often, one of them would flick her head towards Catherine's side of the street, go back to talking, then the other, and sometimes both together for an indiscreet moment. It wasn't just them; Catherine rounded the side of the ambulance, and saw a string of curiosity trailed along the paths and the mouths of the closes, ones twos and threes, saw windows up that hadn't been opened in their lives with the curtains licking the lips of the casements in the louring façade. Catherine drew cross-hairs on the two standing in the opposite path, but spoke loud enough to be heard the length of the chain,

My husband has cancer of the lung and he's going to die; there's the latest news now, all right? Have you seen your fill of us yet, or would you like the time of the next bulletin?

The two opposite were shamed into their homes, hooded by the shadow in the close, they had the decency to slump their heads on the way, caught at it. Catherine looked along the street, saw the links of the chain gradually fall away. Catherine turned to walk back to the pavement, just as there was a voice from high above, calling out from the façade like the voice of the stone itself, weathered like it, an old woman's,

23

Away and fuck yirsel, ya Fenian bitch, who fucken cares?

Catherine lashed around, and there were other eyes strafing the windows, looking out for a movement. Whoever it was would pay for that later, when the weans would have her running her arthritic legs off answering the door to nobody, or to chalk marks on the landing, proddie dog. Catherine felt little sympathy for her, when she knew what most of the folk in the estate were; but she said aloud,

You don't know what I am, you with your gutter manners, using language like that with children about. I hope what's happened to my husband doesn't happen to you, cause then you'll be sorry for that, even sorrier than you are just now.

She caught her hair with her fingers, persuading it away from her face to fall over her shoulders, and again she turned to walk to the pavement, by the side of the ambulance, to the man standing by the chair; she had raised her head, had gone rigid, as tall as a queen in a picture book. The ambulance man looked over his shoulder at her; his face was distorted, as if he'd passed an open stank, and he shook his head.

Never you mind, missis, ye've yir man back; she's jist a drunken auld prune wi nae decency in her.

Catherine smiled, nodded thank you. She stood beside the chair, looked down at Francis, at what was left after the illness; felt stronger, strong enough to bend down and kiss him on his empty cheek, and she said close to his ear,

You're with me now, I'll take care of you,

and she was even strong enough to bear that smile she'd feared, the skull's grin before his time to die.

The garden path, the border of hedges disciplined by wooden fences on either side, was so narrow that they had to make something of a parade of it; the ambulance man pushing the chair at the front against the bias of one sticking wheel and avoiding the partings between the stones, Catherine behind him, her paces short on the concrete, the other ambulance man behind her, carrying the oxygen cylinder and the mask in one hand. Catherine looked around the shoulder of the ambulance man, he had such a broad back she couldn't have hoped to look over him; Cameron was still at the mouth of their close, half there and half behind the jamb, too big for the opening to swallow in one. It was the look on his face that worried her; as if he was being forced to meet a stranger, a plausible man with sweets in a paper poke, staring into the excavated eyes, and then he looked away, afraid, Catherine thought, she could hardly blame him for it, though she resolved to have a talk with him later, reminding him who the Guy Fawkes dummy in the chair was, what was owed to him.

They had Francis over the three steps leading up to where Cameron was standing without much difficulty. The ambulance man reversed the chair and looked to his mate for help, but Catherine said to the slender man,

Don't bother yourself, I'll do it,

and bent to seize the chair where the front wheels were fixed to the frame, just below the plates which swivelled down to become footrests; the ambulance man walked backwards up two steps, and then gave a count again, wan two three and hup! Catherine braced her legs against the ground, preparing herself for the weight of it, but there wasn't much more than the chair itself, as if Francis had air in his bones for marrow, as light as the chrome piping and cloth that cradled him. They placed the chair on the landing tenderly, Catherine letting herself be guided by the ambulance man so as not to put Francis down with a shock. Cameron had gone to stand at the threshold of the house; and as Catherine smiled at him, she thought he seemed dull and withdrawn, separated from them by a pane that would make the ends of his fingers white and bloodless if he pressed too hard against it. Beyond the light from outside, the mouth and the close were cool and uniformly grey; but Catherine thought Cameron's face was the colour of stone, his eyes stark and looking only at the chair, not at his father. He turned away, allowing them to resume the parade through the narrow hall and to the living-room, and Catherine wondered at his silence, what it meant.

Once in the living-room, the ambulance men arranged the chair close to where Catherine indicated, Francis's usual coming-home seat by the fire; each of them took a side and raised him out of the wheelchair's canvas, bearing him to his feet. In the enclosed room and without any distracting sounds, Catherine could hear Francis begging for each breath, and the weight that gave no trouble to the two ambulance men was like a burden of rock to him, his legs shuddered under the strain of it as he pulled himself, was pulled upright. The men walked him to his seat, taking care not to wind their legs around his, and the taller of them, the one who'd wheeled in the chair, said,

Shall we dance, Frankie? At's the way, gie's a hand here, at's the gemme,

until they were all in the right position, taking him down and settling him on the cushion; the wooden frame cracked as usual when any demands were made on it, but only a little, Catherine noticed, one small complaint and that was it. The men made certain he was comfortable the way they'd left him.

Ur ye all right, Frankie?

asked the broad one; the other was thin. Catherine looked at him properly for the first time since he'd arrived, with a sensitive air about him, and nothing much to say, his partner poured out enough words for both of them, but he was looking on as if the sight affected him too deeply for the need to express. Francis nodded; said thanks to the broad one, nodded towards the thin one. Something inside him turned over, sent him into hacks and spasms, you could hear the fluid in him, and he reached into his shirt pocket for a handkerchief to spit the curds into. It reminded Catherine of the time when this cough of his, he'd had it for long enough and said it was nothing, came up marbled through with blood, she made a proper nag of herself for days on end, you'll come with me to the doctor if you won't go yourself, she wasn't having any talk of what about my wages, damn your wages, Francis, tomorrow and that's all I'll hear of it.

At last the ambulance men had to leave, and the broad one gripped Francis's arm and said,

You take care ey yirsel, Frankie, ma friend, ye're wi yer ain folk noo, and that's the best place fr ye.

He reached down to the wheelchair, collapsed it into a single profile of folded cloth and piping. The thin one picked up the oxygen cylinder from where he'd left it, behind the fireside chair, and quickly showed Catherine how to use it, the twist of the stopcock, suggested she place it beside the chair or beside their bed at night; she nodded, surprised to hear the sound of him talking, a voice pitched as high as her own, like birdsong. She looked over her shoulder at Cameron, standing in the far corner of the room; he was looking at the cylinder as the thin man placed it beside the ceramic of the fireplace, standing it on end and passing the mask into Francis's hands. There was a final warning from the oxygen man, not to stand the cylinder close to the open fire, and to touch it often to see if it was getting warm; there was an explanation which she didn't take in, something about pressure and heat, and then, ye dinny waant yir hoose blawin up, and she shook her head, and smiled.

She saw them out to the front door; the broad one stopped there, blocking her from opening it, and dropped the folded chair gently on the carpet. He reached into his pocket, and came out with an object Catherine didn't look at, not at first. Quietly, so as not to be heard in the living-room, he said,

I'm tay gie ye this as well. Jist, ye'll no waant the wean tay see this.

Catherine looked down into the palm of his hand, the strange delicate hold he had. There was a syringe, blunt-ended, the plunger fully pressed home; beside it, needles in a plastic wrap. Catherine frowned when she saw them; there seemed to be a mist, she saw what was in his hand through it, but it could have been any shape, a bag of sweets, a glass bottle, anything innocent. She saw he was expecting her to take them, and her hands went out ahead of her thinking, she gathered them into her palm, the glass of the syringe cool against the swell of her thumb, the needles jostling in their cocoon. There was something else; from the same pocket he took a small glass ampoule, held that out for her to see, and he breathed in and began to speak.

He'll be in a lot ey pain jist afore, ye know whit I'm sayn. This's fr tay help him oot ey it.

She took the ampoule out of his hand, into the other one, like weights in opposite pans of a balance. She stared at the contents of each in turn; she felt as if she had been tapped, run clear of any grief. She said,

When will I start?

The ambulance man shrugged.

He's in pain the noo, missis. When he complains about it, that's yir best time fr it.

Before he left, he pointed out to her the calibrations in red on the syringe, told her where it should be filled to relieve Francis of pain, showed her how to squeeze the forearm to make a vein stand out.

No that ye'll huv difficulty in findin wan soon enough,

he said, regretting it the moment he said it; but she wanted to know more, and so he advised her in a rush; boil your needles before you use them, use a fresh one every time, never use the same one again, don't jag it in like it's a dart and practise with an orange with the syringe full of water, don't forget to boil the syringe after use and before using it again. This time when she nodded, it was because she was understanding everything he said, retaining it all as clearly as if she was writing it down point for point; at last he said,

That's yir lot, missis, will ye mind it a'?

Catherine gave a final nod, for emphasis.

Gie a ring tay the hoaspitl if ye frget ony o' it. And mind this.

The broad man leaned over her, placed his finger on one of the higher calibrations.

This's whit ye cry yir lethal dose. Huv ye goat that?

He looked at her, sustained it for a while, as if there was some further communication in the stare Catherine couldn't penetrate for now. She nodded; he stood back, bent to pick up the wheelchair, straightened with it under his arm. Catherine thanked them for all their help, which seemed to embarrass them both, it was what they were paid for after all, and then they were away, the thin one opening the door while she had her hands full, closing it behind him.

Catherine held the syringe and the needles, the ampoule, for a moment. She felt them as an intolerable weight, heavier than anything she had carried for a long time, unless it was her baggage on the ferry over, the weight of all the rest of her days. At last she took possession of herself; looked to her left, to the bathroom door at the end of the jut in the hallway. She went into the bathroom, to the medicine cabinet above the sink, the mirrored doors dividing her face in two; opened one of them with the hand containing the ampoule, since that was the one with more freedom in it. Beside a package of cotton wool and a jar of Vaseline she put the syringe and the needles, on the shelf above she put the ampoule, between a bottle of liniment and a jar of aspirins; closed over the door, left them there, to be forgotten for just now.

Catherine looked at her face, cut in two by the mirror of the cabinet; stronger than she might ever have hoped for, there wasn't a crack in it. She took a breath, an indulgence when she thought of Francis in the living-room, and then prepared herself to introduce Cameron to his father.

Catherine saw Francis from the back first of all; the brown hair following the curve of his ear, the sudden angles of his face, all the more precipitous now; he turned at the howl of the door hinges, slowly, smiled so as not to show his teeth, the lips painted across the skull. She saw Cameron standing in the corner of the room, his arms across his chest; it made him look grown-up, she thought, but his eyes were fixed on the carpet, the patterns of fallen leaves and the autumn colours of bronze and gold and red. She knew he was afraid of the stranger in his father's chair; saw that as she came deeper into the room Francis was continuing his smile while his eyes changed the meaning of it, forgiving his boy, he'd seen a mirror that morning, that was what he appeared to be saying with it, but it wouldn't do for her, not after what she'd said to the wee one the night before. Then there was the way he breathed, perhaps that; heaving his chest just to get a good wind in him, releasing it as if through organ pipes, it was an effort for him to do a thing you never considered until it was taken from you. Those together she could understand frightening a child, but she was determined, she had played Francis's coming home in her head long before today and this wasn't how she'd seen it acted, and so she went to the corner of the room and stood beside Cameron, seeing the hair she'd parted with a comb that morning from above.

Look, Cameron, she said, your dad's home. Come over and say hello to him.

She took his shoulders in her hands, prised him out of the corner gently; remembered her father's old horse over the water, how it resisted whenever she tried to coax it out of its stable, the hooves gouging into the earth like shovels. She felt him tight against her, his push back against hers forward as she steered him to the chair; he went anyway, stopped when she tugged on his shoulders, stood quietly enough, though all the time she felt him shaking as if he'd be off his mark without her holding him. She knew he was staring down at the carpet where the legs of his dad's chair were rooted; suddenly she felt so frustrated she almost thought about straightening out his head for him, grasping it so there was only one thing in all the room to look at, but she waited until he lifted his head for himself, and at last he was seeing through the skin of his own eyes, as intimate as touch.

Francis could barely raise himself in his seat. He drew another breath, his eyes bright under the eaves of his brow, almost willing his son to keep looking no matter what. At last he had enough air to speak with, said,

Some diet they pit me on, eh, wee man?

Cameron squirmed free of Catherine's hands on his shoulders and broke from the room as if the devil was after him. It was likely the gaunt and deathly look of his dad, minding on her own shock when he'd been let down from the ambulance, different from seeing him in a sickbed. Maybe it had been the voice from his mouth without the strength to carry. She turned to see him scamper out of the door; heard his feet heavy against the carpet, faster than when he'd gone to fetch his ambulance; heard the door to his room closing, she'd have laughed at how quietly under any other circumstances, obeying her even now, only bad-mannered children slam doors, Cameron.

Francis was looking at her when she turned back; he shook his head, slowly, took one of his breaths, shaped the words inside him before he spoke.

I know, Kate, I'm a bloody sight.

Catherine hadn't an argument in her. She stood like a failure beside his chair; the brass frame of her wedding picture fired in the light from the window, though she didn't look directly at it.

I don't get dressed up like this, she said, for any old sight.

Francis held up his hand to excuse himself; more coughing possessed him, far down in his chest, ended when he took the handkerchief from his shirt pocket, spitting into it behind the concealment of his hands. Catherine bent down, as he folded the handkerchief and put it into his pocket again, stared at him.

He shouldn't've done that. I told him you weren't well.

Ye're no well when ye've a cold, Kate.

I'll go and talk to him,

she said, and laid a hand on Francis's shoulder, feeling the bone under his loose shirt.

Cameron was lying face down on his bed when she went into his room; the light was muted, and on the floor Catherine could see the city Cameron had made for himself out of the boxes his model cars came in, tower blocks fastened with paper glue, suburban houses with sloped cardboard roofs, all fixed on to pavements of stiff paper so they wouldn't topple. His ambulance was parked next to a house settled in front of the window, and she wondered if he'd been playing at his dad's arrival before she'd come in, or if that was where he'd put it when she told him. She went over to the bed, sat herself down on it, made a well he rolled towards; she began combing his hair with her fingers, thought she was stroking him like a cat, for reassurance, for whose she didn't know. He didn't appear to be crying. She made butter and honey of her voice, low and persuasive.

He's your dad, Cameron. I told you he was different. What's the matter?

She waited for him to tell her, even if she did know what was coming. He was rigid under her hands, wire and string wound tight. The first time he spoke it was absorbed by the bedding, as if he was afraid to lift his head in case there would be the dying man in her place, all sticks and straw. She asked him to say it again; he turned his head, looked up as best he could from prone, said,

Why does he look like that?

Everything was a question with him these days, mum why this, mum why that; it kept her reading books from the library just to be able to answer him, so she wouldn't treat him and his inquisitiveness the way her father dismissed her, with an excuse like God knows. She told him it was because of the illness his father had, that was what it did to you, made you thin like a scarecrow and stole the breath away from you, and gave you pain worse than the toothache because it was inside you all the time and couldn't be taken out with a pair of pliers, would get worse before (here she chose to soften it a wee bit) the end. Cameron listened attentively, as attentively as when she'd told him what she and Francis were doing that night a long time ago; she stroked the hair away to follow the rounds of his ears all the while, read his eyes to see if he was understanding, he was nodding, stirring the blankets, raising a wake. When she was finished, he said,

I can't help it, mum, I'm scared to look at him,

and Catherine scattered the hair she'd spent so long ordering into contours, smiled and said,

What's wrong, Cameron? Are you a crow or something, you're so easy scared by your dad getting thinner?

She was at least glad of his smile; now she would have to pretend that her own smile was meant, when she was wondering if she wouldn't be better just filling Francis with the contents of a full syringe, just to put an end to everyone's suffering.

She'd always thought it strange that when you lay with someone, anyone, you lost the scale of things, they suddenly became as big as the world in darkness, drew you like gravity, held you fast to them. Even as he was now, it was as if he made her turn on her side in the bed to have a look at him, more like worn stone than he had been in the daylight, she imagined she'd rub her skin to tatters on him. A while ago, he'd taken the air from the cylinder she'd stationed by his side of the bed after the light was off; the mask over his face, leaving only the eyes to be seen, the dreamer's eyes his mother seemed to think were a family flaw, only now they appeared to Catherine to have been drugged by the purity of the oxygen, more than his single sack of a lung could take. There'd been the business of undressing him for bed, opening his shirt and seeing the long cicatrice of surgery, when she'd thought that the material he'd been made of was flesh after all; a hooked wound in him, with the points of suturing on either side of it, where he'd been opened and his sternum broken to lay exposed the cancerous lung, and she wished just then she'd been there like a mother to ease the moment of violation as he went to sleep.

She thought of their wedding night as she heard the breath come and go from him; the way he'd been when everyone was gone from the hotel, after Michael had given her his kiss and she'd made her way to their room. He was there already, Francis, and he was standing just in front of the mirror above the wash-hand basin, oblique to her, not knowing whether to face the door or the image of himself as he was today; the suit tight about him, a thick wedge of a tie knot driven through the trunk of his neck, his hands as useless as wet leaves in front of him. His voice was thin and low, and he said, Whit've we jist done, Kate? but she wasn't having any of that, not regret if that's what it was; she was still in her wedding dress, except for the train which she'd drifted over the room's only chair some hours before when they'd first arrived, and so she stepped out of her shoes, with long pins for heels and shining like mother-of-pearl, left them at the junction of the skirting and the door, and approached Francis on her stockinged soles across a carpet as rich as grass underfoot, saying, evenly, we've made ourselves respectable, Francis, that's what we've done. The dress made crests before her with each of her steps as she rounded the bed, and when she stood in front of him she took both of his hands in hers and tugged him down to kiss him briefly on the lips; his rigid back melted, as if she'd shamed him into it. She released his hands, and then turned her back to him deliberately, dropping her head so that her black hair rose like a curtain on the pearl fastenings of the dress; when the wait went on she said, well, Francis, have you forgotten so soon, or d'you think these things come with instructions? She felt his laugh against her hair, stirring it, aye, very funny, Kate, but it was said lightly, and he gathered her hair into two parted sheaves the better to see what he was doing, and soon enough it was done, almost to the rhythm of her breath, what a time to think of that now; he was shaking as if there was a chill in the room, and it was a thing she felt too, as if they'd never done this before, as if there was a surprise at the end of it. When she was free of the dress, she stepped aside from it and cast it over the back of the armchair, and then turned to see that Francis was down to his woollen semmit and was ready to throw his suit beside her wedding skin; the look of him made her laugh, my God, Francis, you're like Alf Tupper the tough of the track in that thing! and he laughed with her, he was always doing that, laughing against himself and sometimes she wanted him to fight for his dignity, but not this time, because he did look comical on a night like this, you could tell his mammy dressed him. They were in bed once she'd taken off her nylons, had persuaded him to undo the catches on the back of her shell of a liberty bodice; her first night wearing his surname, she could almost forget she was her father's daughter, she was no one's but her own, which brought her to thinking of the camera, and the rest of it.

Catherine made a strange request of Danny and Agnes, when she and Francis were staying at their place after the honeymoon while the council found them a place; would they mind if she made a bonfire in their back garden, near to the shed, and Danny said aye, all right, mind ye don't set fire tay my shed while ye're at it. At the heart she placed a cotton dress that looked far too big for the wee girl who'd wear a pattern like it, swirling with flowers like her mammy's; worn on the boat over, lived in for weeks after her landing, falling on the structure of twigs with a flounce and making a decorative marquee over the liberty bodice Francis had unclasped from around her on their wedding night, shaped by the bones like an insect's skeleton, Michael told her long ago that flies wore their bones on the outside. Daniel and Francis stood and watched her from the doorway to the kitchen, and Daniel said something she didn't hear, there was a laugh which could have been either of them, as she placed a firelighter briquette on top of the pile, collapsing the tent in the middle. The match caught; she protected the squirming flame in her hands, bent down and touched it to the firelighter, to the sticks and fabric, dropped the match on to the fire. The wedding dress had gone back to the shop long ago, or else it might have been here as well, but it seemed right to Catherine that it should go to transform someone else. She watched as the fire took the clothes she'd worn over the water; she watched longer than the brothers' patience could hold, she didn't care if they thought she was mad, she watched the stem of black smoke drift into still air and root itself above her; watched until there was nothing left of her past but black snow and the charred ribs of the bodice, and that was all she was waiting for, glimmering shapes defining the last of the scraps, and if that was madness then she didn't care, she'd made sense to herself at least, and damn the one who wouldn't understand her.

There were moments when Francis's breathing stopped, and Catherine sat up in the bed and listened for the next one; it always

34

followed, no matter how long the interval, and she lay back not knowing whether to be relieved or to wish he would stop altogether, so that she'd never have to go into the bathroom cabinet.

Three

Daniel knew nothing of his brother's admission to hospital on the day he heard the barking of the rag and bone van's horn across the street; it was a Tuesday, early closing at the electrical shop, and he was back with Agnes and had time on his hands by the yard, with no tele to watch but the mesh of the test card, and only the sound of Agnes preparing the evening's dinner to distract him. He had read the Evening Citizen from headline to sports, was looking sullenly at it folded on the coffee table in front of him while he stretched his legs from the sofa to the teak veneer surface, a thing he wouldn't dare do if Agnes wasn't busy. There was a cup of tea resting in its saucer beside his crossed and settled feet, as much of it as he could be bothered to drink; he hadn't been to the library that week, and so he didn't even have a fresh book to read, and he was just thinking about going for a walk when the horn went repeatedly, taking him to his feet and over to the window. He knew what it was the first he saw of it, and he cried out,

Heh, Agnes, err's the rag and bone bloke, have we anythn fr him?

As it worked out, they did; old blankets worn to tatters from before Daniel got his job, shirts of his with the collars and cuffs frayed, blouses of hers with accidental tears on the sleeves, all prepared neatly in order of size. She smelled of onions when she came through, she was drawing the tears from the corners of her eyes to the backs of her hands as she led him to the airing cupboard, nodded for him to pick them up because she was saturated in the juice and didn't want to transfer it to the cloth. Daniel laughed at her fussing.

It disny smell ey roses in the back ey his van, I'll tell ye that,

and she went away, muttering something about keeping up standards and being proud of your house with a shiver to her voice that made Daniel wonder for just a moment if it was just the onions doing it; her house slippers slapped across the linoleum in the kitchen, and she was sniffing as if she'd the cold. Daniel went to the front door in his socks with the bundle, stopped to put his feet into his brogues, and then left down the garden path to where the van was parked hard against the pavement.

The rag and bone man was standing beside the cavern of the open bay, the doubled doors thrown apart to show off the wares inside. He had the same smell of must and neglect about him as the discarded clothes and bric-à-brac rioting in the square space; his own clothing seemed repaired time and again, patched here and stitched there with incompatible designs, checks and stripes, tartans and polka dots, so that Daniel wondered if there was anything of the original fabric in his coat and breeks, and it gave him the benign appearance of a clown, apart from his face and skin being cured by years of outside living.

Right y'are, sir, the wee man said, let's see whit ye've goat fr me.

Daniel spilled the cloth into the back of the van, and the wee man turned to examine it; he was a hard bargainer in spite of the way he looked, always rubbed the fabric between thumb and forefinger before quoting a price, and he'd have you there for hours in an argument over coppers. It was while the wee man went into his scrutiny that Daniel saw the other relics and cast-offs, electric lamps and a chair with the shin of one leg broken, an occasional table, a printed photograph of a rural scene dirtied by the gloom, an old telephone with a tulip cup for a mouthpiece, a folding bed with the mattress split and disgorging stuffing through the wound; and on top of the headboard he saw the elderly Kolster Brand wireless set, with its cable spooled around the body of it.

He got it for a price that took into account the cloth he'd poured into the van, one bob and it was his. The wee man pointed out the two-pin plug wired into the end of the cable, at least he had that much honesty about him, but said,

Ye'll be able tay wire it up tay a three-pin nae bother,

delving into the van and wading among the ocean of clothing to reach the wireless, returning with the weight of it, passing it on to Daniel before shaking his feet free of the wrappings he'd gathered. Daniel held the wireless in one arm while he searched his pocket for a shilling coin, found it, held it out for the wee man as he descended to the street.

I know, he said, I work in an electrical shoap.

The wee man took off his cloth cap, smoothed back the sprigs of hair at the front of his scalp before accepting the coin from Daniel, turning it over in his palm with his fingers and then securing it in his pocket.

If ye'll no mind me askin, he said, whit wid ye waant an auld jalopy like this fr when ye'll be able tay buy a new yin in yer shoap for a discoont?

The weight of it dragged Daniel's arms down to full extent.

For wan bob, he said, and nae questions asked,

and then spun around with his find and marched to the garden gate, imagining the face on the wee man, pleased enough to mystify him.

Daniel took the wireless into the house, heard Agnes busy at something in the kitchen; he hadn't felt this ridiculously excited over anything in a long time. He took it in with him to show her, but she had her back to him, working over the sink, she didn't even hear him stumping across the lino. There was a pound of mince on the table glistening in unfurled brown paper, and there were vegetables waiting to be cut alongside a wooden chopping board, in order, one carrot, a half turnip on its flat side, the onion already done because she liked to get it out of the way first; she was nothing if not methodical. He could hear a blade whispering through a potato, water raining from her bare arms into the sink; it wasn't right she should be working while he was feeling light and childish, and so he settled the old KB on to the Formica of the table, behind her meticulous arrangement. It made a dull contact that drove through the tapered legs, and that claimed her attention, caused her to turn round. She had a small paring knife in one hand, a half-bare potato in the other with a spring of clean peel coiling down from it, and her eyes went first to him, there with a daft grin splitting his face, then to the wireless as big as a doll's house on the table. She made a click in the back of her throat without meaning to, shook her head slowly, took a long breath.

I hope you goat that fr free.

Daniel felt as if he was plugged into a socket himself, alive and charged with enthusiasm; he tried to make it jump the gap between them.

Look at it, Agnes. Jist look at it.

Agnes wasn't having any of it; she'd long insulated herself from him and his obsessions.

We've goat a perfectly good wireless set jist noo.

She was about to turn back to her peeling when Daniel reached out his hand, captured her arm gently to keep her there; she let out a long sigh.

Danny, it's an auld wireless. Whit else am I supposed tay see?

Daniel wondered if he had what she called that look on him; the one he always wore whenever he was telling her something he presumed she didn't know, shining his eyes on her like there was a light source at the back of them focused by mirrors, she said he was like a doctor examining you with one of those funnel lights on the end of a stalk. Agnes didn't go for being tested, judged like that. She waited for him to put on his dry teacher's voice, broke her gaze away to look at the kitchen's pale white wall, the freckles of damp; when she turned she was wearing a shallow frown, protection against him, always full of opinion, her Danny, full of himself, she wasn't going to open herself to him like a tumbler, wasn't going to let him pour his notions into her when she had her own he wouldn't hear. Daniel let the frown go; she never listened to him anyway.

It's no jist an auld wireless, Agnes. It's tryin tay be furniture, like a table or a chair or somethn. Look at it.

Agnes squinted at the dejected old thing, wondering what he was meaning about a wireless being furniture, because it was a wireless and that was all there was to it; a wooden box filled with all the voices in the world fankled up inside like yarn, the edges of it gentle and rounded with a window at a slant like a skylight on top which she thought lit up when the set was on, inscribed with names like Third, Light, Home Service, names she'd heard her mother talking about. There was a golden mesh set into a circular frame at the front, and on either side near the base of the cube there were two fluted dials, one for tuning and one for volume; the wood of the thing was dark and lacquered as coffee and you couldn't find any seams in it with your eyes, other than a panel fixed at the back with heavy screws, simple board punched with holes as if the box contained a creature needing air to breathe. It was a wireless, as plain as the eye could see, and it didn't matter, he'd still gone out with blankets and come back with this old dusty thing and less money than before, and she told him, gripping the knife and holding it with the point out at him,

See if there wis a wee boay aboot here, there'd be two weans in the hoose, and there widny be the money tay throw away lik that.

She went over to the sink again, and he didn't stop her this time. Her back was like a wall against him; he heard a splash, the peel falling away, and then she began another potato. Daniel felt as if his feet were turning to granite, anchoring him to the ground after his playfulness went. He lifted the Kolster Brand from the table, left by the kitchen door; Agnes's staring from the window above the sink was like a pressure against his back all the while he took the radio down to the shed. He placed the wireless on the untidy grass as he unclipped the padlock, and once he was inside, only then did he feel safe from her judgement, with the door closed over behind him.

That was the thing about Daniel's shed; it was wired up to drain the power from the house, because there wasn't a room inside spare that would allow him to work the way he liked. He liked silence, and he got that in the shed aside from the weekends, which he felt he owed to Agnes anyway, and he liked solitude, or more like the idea of a place he could go devoted to his own concerns, and Agnes wasn't very understanding of that. It's a marriage, Danny, she said, a bee ell oh oh dee why marriage, ye know, two people, wan hoose, happy ever efter, that kin ey thing, but Daniel was down on that from the start, aye, very good, Agnes, and ye'll cook and sew and press my trousers for me, and then whit? and she didn't have an answer for that. She told herself at least it wasn't the pub, she could have married a drinker instead of a dreamer and been feared for the time he came home demanding food kept warm and dried to scabs on the plate; but she couldn't understand why her husband would choose loneliness, it was demeaning and he couldn't see it, and she couldn't explain, she couldn't make the words in her mouth because they were slack and raw in her head.

All she could do was watch. She watched him splice cable to the house's supply in the mains cupboard, spool it out of the kitchen door from a heavy cardboard reel, along the garden through what she called the jungle; saw him through the kitchen window threading it into the wee hut with the council's choice of deep green paint rising in boils and flaking to expose the dull pine boards. She watched him build another house for himself, give it light and an electric fire, take it planks for shelving and even bring in an electric kettle bought from his work, and on the day he was finished he took her inside to let her see what he'd been working on. She could tell from the way he carried himself he was proud of it, like a wean who'd finished a model ship, and he stood to one side to let her pass. When they were both inside, she knew he was sweeping his eyes against her time and again, waiting for her to say anything about it.

She smelled fresh-cut pine dancing around an odour of damp and earth, the beginnings of rot in the old timber. There was a work surface at chair height about three walls, and three layers of shelves above cut apart by the window; the edges of the new wood were frayed and unfinished, straight precipices with no attempt to round them, just there for utility. At the end of the workbench nearest the door she saw his kettle standing beside a plain tin teapot, a stubby cylinder with a small pouted lip, and an enamel mug with a chip off the rim in the shape of a crescent. The kettle's flex trailed down to the first of the sockets he'd wired up; the white cable then clambered like ivy to the ceiling, fixed in place by rounded staples, and wound in a spiral around a low rafter beam and dropped to hold a hundred-watt bulb suspended above them; more branches were propagated about the walls, one for the portable electric fire nudged against the wall, you'd think they'd all grown from seeds the way they divided and wouldn't stop until the shed was thick with them. Daniel took his seat by the side window, one of their chairs borrowed from the kitchen, turned to look at her, and there was a smile on him that infuriated Agnes.

Aye, nice enough, she said. D'ye waant me tay stitch ye a wee sampler for the wall? Hame sweet hame, somethn like that?

The next thing, she was back in the house, not even remembering having slammed two doors on her way, the door to Danny's wee obsession nest, the kitchen door; the kettle was whistling enough to split your ears, but she couldn't remember when she'd put it on, before or after leaving the house with Danny. It had all happened in the shed, the ignition of her temper, obliterating her thoughts in a hot white flare; so proud of himself in the wee house he'd made to be away from her, look at mammy's wee handyman. When she got back in the first thing she saw was the open door to the mains cupboard, the insulated cable, a thick white vein transfusing the electric blood from his real home; she was so mad she nearly made a fist around it, tore it out by the roots, but she'd enough reason in her not to risk it, no matter how tempted she felt. By the time her anger had settled, she was aware of being in the living-room, on the sofa, and she was crying into the paper handkerchief she always had secreted in the sleeve of her cardigan; she hated the mask she was making of it when she didn't know why she was crying, nothing as strong as hate, resentment maybe, a sense of being abandoned.

She heard the latch to the kitchen door shrieking, a thing she'd been on at Danny to fix for weeks while he was busy at that damned shed. There was a percussion of metal, one rattling off the other; the kettle lost its breath, began to tune down the scale into nothing, and then she heard footsteps, Daniel and his brogues hammering the lino. She looked into the corner of the room, beside the bay window; the tele was laughing demurely, and she saw darkness coming over a room like hers in the picture, seemed to remember a comedy on when Daniel came to prise her out of her seat and now it was finishing with names rising past the roof of the tele and babbling signature music. A teaspoon rang inside china; his shoes were softened against the hall carpet; Agnes gathered herself together, skinning the house slippers from her feet, drawing her knees tight against her chest and shoring up her legs by pressing her feet on the rim of the sofa, but it was so slippy, her stocking soles on the leatherette, she couldn't sustain the acute angle of her knees for long before she'd to adjust it all again, scrabbling like a mouse, wee and ridiculous.

Daniel came in with two cups of tea trailing ribbons of steam behind him; looked at her on the sofa from the doorway, said nothing. He went to the coffee table, put one tea in front of her, one in front of where he intended to sit; the pretend leather squealed like a pig against his corduroys when he sat down, his weight displacing her towards him, which she resisted by leaning away. Daniel leaned over to pick up his tea, took a drink of it; noted the handkerchief stained with damp and crushed in her hand. The thought of tea he'd borrowed from her. At last, over the driving theme of a current affairs programme starting on the tele, he said,

Talk tay me, Agnes; I'm hopeless at readn minds.

Her arms were fastened about her legs, latched like the spring of a jack-in-the-box. He couldn't see her face for her risen shoulders.

Damn you for dayn this tay me,

she said, without expression; you wouldn't've known she'd been crying from listening to her. Daniel kept it gentle, spoke softly:

Dayn whit tay ye?

She raised her head, looked above her shoulder, towards him.

Oor hoose isny good enough fr ye, ye've tay make wan fr yirsel.

Now Daniel knew what her thoughts were, knew what to say to her. He reached an arm around her, felt her go tense under the skin; he pulled against her, gently, gently, and all of a sudden she began to cry again and all the angles and edges she'd presented to him fell apart, she pitched to the side and fitted into him like a puzzle and the lot spilled out of her, he had his shed, he was leaving her alone for that work of his, but he'd be in the shed, as near as you could throw a stone at it from the house and break a window, what was wrong with her, and he said, nothing, which was true when he said it. She smelled of perfume and talcum, beautiful and pampered, her hair was pulled back in the fashion, bound by an enamelled clip; she'd never wanted to be one of those old biddies, dumpy women in pinnies and clothes dyed in all the colours of muddy paths and rotten leaves, she spoke to Danny about them with acid in her voice. She made the house cushioned and graceful for herself and her husband; bought all the newest fabrics that looked like silk and cloth of gold, carpets thick under the feet like wool, but you knew the difference whenever you touched anything conductive, or even Agnes herself, and he had to explain it to her, it was the carpet and the kind of forces that charged the clouds which made lightning between them, but she never believed him.

Daniel told her that his shed wasn't home, for all that it had light and heat and the means to make tea, but it was the place he needed to pursue his interests, because that was how they'd make their money, it was all to come but only if he was given the time to learn.

Y'understand me, Agnes? he said. It's no tay take me away fae you. It's fr you and the weans we're gonny have someday.

Daniel felt her swelling in his arms with all his talk of weans and tomorrow; she raised herself to look at him, eyes wide.

Weans soon?

she said, smiling like a wean herself.

Soon's we've the money, aye,

said Daniel, and he meant that when he said it and all.

So he was in the shed when the phone call came, and a while had gone by since his promise, and still no money, no weans, just evenings to himself, learning. Agnes complained often, she'd set her compass by Kate and Frankie, married after them and now with Cameron growing and well into his schooling; they always came up when her patience ran thin and the time of the month played her like a screaming guitar, that was how Daniel saw it, you could draw the date in your calendar when Agnes would be sitting on the sofa embracing her legs and scowling at him after a long evening in the cold of the shed. He knew it was coming, it was like the charge he got from the carpet, felt the crackling about him, the hairs on his arms standing like grass, he could almost see her filled with blue light, filaments of it tearing away from her; and he always said something to start her sooner than have her building it up for days, he knew well enough how a capacitor worked. Ye'll no have weans, but ye've pea eye ess essed away enough money tay feed and clothe twins, never mind jist the wan; whit is it ye're dayn in that shed, wi a' they funny things ye're comin in wi; I'm just the hoosekeeper, that's no why I married ye; every month it was played again, the way she played her records on the Dansette, obsessively until the songs eroded channels into your

44

head and you couldn't rid yourself of them. It was like that with her arguing, and all he could do was give her the same answers; aye we'll have weans, cause it's all learnin, Agnes; I'm dayn whit's best for us, Agnes; that's no why I married you eether, Agnes, mebbe ye jist need a joab or somethin.

Not that there was no love between them; she never argued when Daniel insisted on wearing what she called that bee ell oh oh dee why sausage skin, apart from the first time, she still went to the chapel and confession and that, and Daniel said, it's my sin, Agnes, no yours, but she thought it was just words, there were still intentions and God saw those as clearly as if your head was glass to Him. She always said they should never forget how weans were made, though, eventually deciding that God could take it up with Danny when the time came, that time after death he didn't believe in; weekends were theirs, Friday till Sunday evening, and the shed stood vacant for the duration, and Agnes was forever asking him, I've goat ye tay mysel, haven't I, Danny? ye're no thinkin aboot, and he told her no, he wasn't, which was true then.

The old wireless was landed on a Tuesday, so there was Danny doing his work in the bee ell ohoh dee why shed, and when he came to think of it later he was doing to the Kolster Brand what the surgeons would to their Frankie the day after. He had the back off it, and he was looking at a city in a shell like something out of an old sci-fi film, except the components had a thick pelt of dust reaped by the attractive force they generated; cat's whisker, domed valves, a thing like a multi-storey block with the face torn from it. He knew what he'd been guiding Agnes to like a blind woman the moment he'd seen it; the cabinet trying to blend in a house of graceful antiques, a chest filled with the treasures of modernity but an object in itself, one to polish until the wood shone with its own light like a dark pearl. This was the kind of thing his electronics magazines taught him, there was something to be learned from the inside, this was how he would make his money in a world where voices were spun into the air and now pictures too, people felt lonely without these things and that was what Agnes couldn't understand, not until her own tele shrunk to a point and refused to bloom into a picture, and then he'd show her soon enough.

45

The vitals were nearly all out of the wireless when Agnes came to the shed at about half past nine; damn near had the door off its hinges with all her rattling on it, a continuing beat as if she was trying to waken him out of deep sleep, and Daniel looked up with a shock from the component he was turning end over end in his hand. She said,

It's Kate on the phone fr ye, Danny,

after she finished her knocking, and even her voice was clenched like a fist, driven through the planks. His first thought was that she must know what Kate wanted him for, because there was something in her manner, something grave in the message she was carrying. He went to the door, opened it; Agnes looked away the moment he faced her. She had her arms doubled across her chest, the fringes of her red cardigan seized in her hands, and not just against the cold. She stepped to one side to let him out. Daniel snapped off the switches to the electric fire and the overhead light before he left; she waited until he'd passed her before following him to the house two steps behind him, he could hear her carpet slippers rousing the lengthy grass like a light wind. She went with him as far as the kitchen, and he turned on his way to the living-room to see her going to the stove to fetch the kettle.

The phone was unhooked, the receiver resting on its side with the cable festooned over the edge of the table. Daniel sat at the extreme end of the sofa, beside where the table was placed, reached over the sofa's arm to pick up the receiver, said hullo into it as a question; Kate came back with his name as a question too. It sounded as if she was in a chapel, somewhere that gave resonance to voices, and he was surprised, Kate in a holy house, he wouldn't have thought it. She wasn't in a chapel; she told him she was in the Royal, and that it wasn't her but Francis. Daniel sat upright in his seat, asked the first obvious question, and she said, evenly, it was cancer of the lung, and apologized for not being able to call him earlier. Daniel heard the words, but it was like hearing the name of someone you knew at school and not being able to retrieve a face; Francis in hospital, Francis with a serious illness, it wasn't right, he didn't want to make a picture of it. She spoke about an operation, having to open him up, like he was a purse or something, take out the diseased lung; her voice lost the echo, sounded intimately in his ear but stripped ragged by the distance and the instrumentation, and he said,

Is the wee man there with ye?

She said, he's with me, and Daniel could hear her fraying strand by strand, but still holding. Determination came over him, with the first understanding of the news, and he said boldly that he was going to the hospital, even stood up from his seat with difficulty, the intention hardening, clear and precise; but Kate was sharp with him, she said,

Stay where y'are, Danny, they won't let you in, visiting hours are over.

Daniel never responded well to being told; he looked down at the teak veneer of the coffee table, saw the light bulb overhead reflected in it, the image shattered by the weave of the grain. He wished he had Kate in front of him now, to let her see what he was like.

They're no over fr me.

Kate spoke above him, printing her words on his.

They're even over for me, Danny. Don't you dare go upsetting him. Not now.

She let her silence pile on top of him; slowly he bent under it, felt his legs taking him back into his seat. He asked her if she'd told their ma yet; Kate said no, and she wouldn't tell her until the result of the operation was known, which seemed right to Daniel, the last thing Francis'd want would be her and her rosary strings and her blessed objects, readying him for his death. She said the operation would be tomorrow, quickly because it was an emergency; and from the way she spoke about the surgeon in charge Danny guessed she didn't much care for him, and he smiled as much as he was able for under the circumstances, just like Kate to rub against someone casting their authority about the place. Just then the pips went, hacking the call short; Daniel asked her to ring when it was all right to visit, and she said she'd do that, and squeezed in how sorry she was to have to tell him like this before the line was cut. Daniel held the phone away from himself, for how long he didn't know, until the purr of the dialling tone went on and on, and he hung up the receiver at last.

Agnes came in with two floral cups of tea, gave one to Danny as he sat slumped forward in the sofa, his head supported by his arms,

arms supported by his legs; the first he knew of it was when she held the cup, his cup, in his field of vision, so that he couldn't ignore it. She'd seen him like that often enough, everything went transparent in front of him whenever it was less important than the world in his head, and if you weren't in his bowl of thoughts then you weren't anywhere. Daniel had been thinking of him and Frankie when they were both weans; him walking on the rim of the bunker surrounding the midden, in the back garden, Frankie calling to him, get doon offy there, ya eejit ye, ye'll fall! and then Danny's legs tangling, the dustbin on the inside of the bunker rearing up to swallow him, the stinking mess from somebody's kitchen slathering his good clothes, fragments of eggshell, sodden rags. Frankie hoisting him out of the bin, whit did I tell ye? their ma clouting them both when they got home, Danny for being so stupid, Frankie for being so stupid as to let him. Then there was the cup in front of his eyes, there was substance and immediacy to it, that was the funny thing, she just held it there for as long as it took him to notice it, and he traced her arm all the way back to her face, serious and concerned for him. She was prepared to stand like that until he took the tea from her; which he did, at last, Agnes's medicine, her answer to everything, she'd even got him relying on it whenever she needed calming. She sat down beside him, began to drink her own tea; she was looking at the shimmer on its surface, and Daniel shook his head stiffly, looked sideways at her.

Gonny read the leaves fr Frankie when ye're done?

He was being cruel for the sake of it, and knew it; she continued to stare, her eyes almost crossed by how close it was.

I'm no in the mood, Danny, ye can frget it.

He tried to break the string of her gaze just by looking at her.

No in the mood fr whit?

You'd think she was standing on the shore of a loch, tranquillized by the scenery, when it was just that bloody cup fascinating her.

Whit are ye no in the mood fr, I'm askin ye?

She looked at him abruptly, held the cup a little away from her lips.

I'm no in the mood fr whit you're lookin for. Ye think I'm some kin ey eejit.

48

Daniel put down his tea, brought his arms over his knees and laced his hands together, pressing the palms against each other.

I don't. How day I think ye're an eejit?

Ye must think I'm an eejit no tay see whit ye're efter.

I don't even know whit I'm efter mysel.

Aye ye day. First it was gonny be the tea leaves. Then it was gonny be I'm turnin tay the horoscopes in the paper, and then ye were gonny gie me a hard time for thinkin aboot prayin fr Francis when it's no up tay me or God. Or am I wrang, and ye wereny efter an argument?

Daniel fell back in his seat, the leatherette creaking with him. He rested his joined hands on his belly, and looked at Agnes to the front and side of him. The red cardigan was taut across her back, and the nape of her neck was above the collar, and he thought about stroking her there, but she'd say he was treating her like a pet when she was like this. The room smelled of the freshener she sprayed into it whenever she'd finished the dusting, a chemist's dream of violets. He breathed it in, and thought of Frankie, and the operation; and the tight ball of frustration in the pit of his stomach which wouldn't open out until he'd seen his brother.

I widny stoap ye prayin fr Frankie, Agnes,

he said, suddenly feeling the punch of his heart against his chest.

It was a few days before Daniel got to see him; Agnes tried to persuade her man to go to the hospital at least looking decent, by which she meant dressed in a respectable suit and with his hair shortened, but he'd been telling her for some time the fashion was for longer hair and less fuss over your appearance, and he'd been letting a thin beard sprout for a week or two, and that was another thing she thought he could change, but he just laughed at her. He wore an anorak against the cold and the possibility of rain, and his usual corduroys, and when she complained at the door before they left he said, he's my brother, Agnes, he knows whit a scruff I am, but it wasn't a sign of respect in her eyes, and she was silent for most of the bus journey, except to tell him the time and to say they'd be late for visiting hours.

In the event, they weren't; Frankie's bed was directly opposite the doors to the ward, and when Daniel saw his brother, he thought he looked elderly and fatigued, more like his father. He was wired into an oscilloscope monitor with the sound turned down, the display showing a cold green line bristling with heartbeats, and a cord of clear plastic was rooted into the vein of his forearm, feeding him milky liquid from a pouch hanging on a thin metal frame. Daniel's feet slowed to see his brother like that; thought of his arrangement of wiring back in the house, the tap from the mains. Agnes went to the single chair placed beside the bed, positioned her handbag so it didn't slip while she lifted the chair to sit at right angles to her brother-in-law. She settled herself uncomfortably into the scoop, opened the handbag, brought out a brown paper bag and rested it on Francis's lap, carefully, as if it might bruise him.

Oranges fr ye, she said. They're lovely and fresh.

Daniel tightened; for all the good they'd do. There was a get-well card in the sideboard at home, they'd even signed it before Kate made her phone call. He was scrutinizing Frankie for some kind of lead, to see if there was mourning in him yet, understanding, anything. He was smiling, but there was no guidance in it; could've been sedatives or Frankie shrouding himself in acceptance, or even the bridge he walked over and feared to look down, you just didn't know, so Daniel said nothing. The smell of antiseptics and waste clotted in his head; he minded on Frankie as a wean, cared for by their mother in their bedroom, the fevers he sweated through, the viruses he caught. Frankie reached down the bed to where the brown paper lay on him, his hand crawling by degrees like a spider until he fastened on it, drew the bag to the side and pulled it up, looked inside; the labour of it made him breathe hard, he'd hardly any to spare for talking.

So it is, he said, thanks very much.

He didn't look as if he had the strength to tear the peel. Agnes was about to reach into the bag to fetch one, said,

D'ye waant wan jist noo?

but Frankie shook his head, a slight movement from side to side, barely causing the creases in the pillow to shift.

No thanks, he said, I'm jist efter, bein fed.

Agnes took the bag from him, put it on the bedside table, the white Formica surface.

Aye, she said, quite right, Francis, here they're for later.

She was awkward, not right; Daniel wondered if it was the chair, or something else. He couldn't find the right place for his hands; in his pockets, clasped behind him; in the end he crossed them in front of himself, holding one wrist in the other hand, hoping he didn't look too much like a mourner at a funeral.

How're ye feelin?

Agnes's head came round suddenly, sharply, the way she'd looked at him earlier when the doctor had used words like secondary tumour and lymph nodes, and Daniel had asked him to say it all again so he could fathom it; ignorant article, she'd called him when the doctor went from hearing. Frankie was smiling, though, his face carved in two by it.

I'm a wee bit, short ey breath, he said. I've had a lung oot.

Daniel smiled, too; they knew how to be ironic with each other, even if Agnes didn't understand. He said,

That bloody cough ey yours. Whit did ye think, it was the measles or somethin?

Frankie went on smiling, despite Agnes's reaching out to put her hand flat over his.

I thought, it was a, bloody cough. It was a, a bloody cough. I'd a pey packet, tay bring hame, wi me.

Daniel felt his hand tighten about his wrist. There was another, long-ago argument opening before him. He'd said to Agnes on the bus over; she'd thought it was the last thing Francis was wanting to hear now, but he was determined, and Francis had started it by talking about his work. He was taking a breath of the sterile air to reply when Agnes stood up, sending the chair shrieking back. She leaned down and kissed Frankie on the forehead, straightened and looked furiously over her shoulder at Daniel.

I'll come back fr this wan later, she said to Francis. Take care ey yirsel. I'll see ye next visitin time.

On her way past Daniel she said,

It's no bad enough yir brother's had a lung oot, but you waant the heart oot him as well.

She said it quietly, as far as Daniel and no further, swung her bag so the breeze of it hit him in the face; left by the ward doors, her heels crisp against the wine-coloured linoleum. Daniel went to the empty seat, pulled it closer to the bed, sat forward against its tendency to make him slouch. He thought how little Frankie looked like their father, too thin for it, though that might be the wasting of his illness; Frankie had always been thin, but muscle thin, not like this, not like a sapling. You might have seen Frankie if you'd peeled the fat away from the old man, if you'd stopped the old man eating the rim of fat from a chop or spooning the grease from a plate of mince; maybe seen himself, too. This close to Frankie, you could almost smell the decay off him; and Daniel couldn't gather his anger together when he saw his brother held upright by the pillows behind him. He said,

I meant, how're ye feelin in yirsel?

Frankie looked overwhelmed by the question for a moment; gave it some thought for a while. His eyes were half closed, seemed weak and diluted.

I couldny tell ye, Danny. There's Kate and the, wee man tay, think aboot. There's mysel. I canny think too much.

A cough swelled in him, and Daniel heard the fluid shifting inside; Frankie brought it up in spasms, reached for a waxed paper cup on the bedside table, too far away for one effort. Daniel got it for him and put it into his hands, and he folded himself up to raise the container to his mouth, deposited the spit inside as secretly as he could; Daniel took the cup from him and put it back while Frankie rearranged himself against the pillows, falling back against them.

Ye seen oor ma yet?

said Daniel. Francis held in a laugh, more trouble than it was worth.

No yet. Do us a favour, will ye?

He seemed serious enough when Daniel said, aye, of course; but the smile came back.

Go roon tay oor ma's hoose, get a' the holy water, and rosaries and saints, ye can find, and do whit oor Kate did wi, her dresses, in your back garden.

Daniel smiled too; they'd always called their parents' bedroom the chapel, with all the figurines of saints and shrines there were on the tallboy, water bottled in Lourdes, portraits of the Virgin Mary and Jesus on the cross, all hers, even their father when he was alive came to call it the chapel after they revealed their name for it, he thought it was a rare joke. Daniel said to him,

Mind whit we used tae call their bedroom,

and Frankie said the name back instantly, and laughed with all the air in him until he went into spasm again and had to call for the waxed beaker to discharge what he'd brought up. When he was settled back on the pillows, there was the good taste of laughter in his mouth, but he said,

I'm no cheyngin my tune, jist cause ey this, Danny. It widny be right.

Daniel remembered his admiration for his brother whenever he said it; the way Frankie'd be hours away in the local library, you'd think his eyes'd be skinned raw by the friction of all the print he read. Even after Frankie had his job, the one he didn't want, the one his da got him, while Daniel was making a conspicuous waste of his schooling, Frankie was still in at the library and borrowing even when there weren't any examinations to pass; it meant that when the Sunday came that Frankie refused to go with them to the chapel, and their ma asked how no, he could come out with a name like Darwin, a name Daniel recognized from the cover of one of the books he'd seen loitering about the floor of their room, and his ma had to ask who this Darwin was and where he lived so she could go to his door and rattle some sense into the man. Daniel was in his Sunday clothes, watching this from the door to the hallway; his brother looked like a plaster saint, the way his face told of suffering, persecuted for his different faith, while his ma said, we're away tay midday mass, my boy, and if you're no at the six ey cloack mass this evenin, ye'll be lookin for another hoose tay stey in, she tried anger on him since he was far too old for a leathering. They came back from mass, and the time went on; Frankie was in his room like a monk or someone in holy orders, reading one of his borrowed books, Daniel couldn't remember the title of it, only that the cover was plain blue and sheathed in plastic, perhaps Francis's fingers were covering up the print. Daniel asked him as he lay on the bed, book propped on his belly, one hand supporting his head, whit wid ye day if oor ma threw ye oot? she was talkin aboot it oan the wey up the road fae the chapel, and Francis closed over the book so it bit his finger at the right place, said, then I'd go oot, whit else wid there be for it? Danny'd always thought, like the rest of the world, like their ma and even their da, that Francis was quiet, wouldn't say boo to a goose, that kind of thing; but there was steel braided into him that afternoon, you could see from the way he was, like a martyr prepared for the consequences of his will, and he said to his brother, if I went tay chapel, there widny be any meanin tay it, I widny be there cause I believed, I'd be there cause I was forced inty it. I widny say prayers cause I doubt there's anyone listenin. I might as well be in my room readin. If oor ma needs me jist tay stand there, well and good; but I'd be takin part, and that's me bein a liar tay mysel as well as her, and she's bein a liar as well if she knows I'm there and no believin. D'ye understand?

Daniel shook his head now, as he'd done then; now it was affection, but then he'd been confused, just three years behind his brother, old enough to receive the words, young enough that what Frankie meant evaded him. Now his understanding was made of different stuff; perhaps he had begun to think like his brother to extend his ma and da's disappointment in him, but now it was sewn into him, moved when he did, jumped when he jumped; if it had ever been an affectation, like a suit of clothes, now it was his skin, you couldn't part it from him and say it was still Danny.

There was a sound from behind Daniel, which made him turn suddenly; an old woman, dressed in a dark green coat speckled with grey and wearing a turban hat in the same shade of green, and the sound was her crying into a paper handkerchief, trying to smother it in the folds. She was seated three beds down from Daniel, and she was looking up and around herself in shame, while three nurses came to erect a screen around her, pulling the frames on screeching castors.

Same as me, said Francis. No the same cancer, same result I mean.

Daniel had glimpsed the old man in his bed; you could hardly tell him from the cloth, too weak even to sit like Frankie. He turned back quickly, even the brief look had seemed intrusive, not right. Frankie smiled again.

It'll jist be like the lights gaun oot, wee man, he said. No a thing, tay worry yirsel aboot.

Daniel nodded.

Ye're no gaunny let oor ma turn yer heid then?

He might have laughed now, but he kept it in.

When did oor ma ever, day that?

Daniel wore a lopsided expression just then, bright and cheeky, like when they were growing up.

Aye, it was jist oor da. He swayed ye, good and proper. He's pit ye in here, n a' ye hud tay day wis take yon bursary. It's his bloody joab in the foondry landed ye in here, a' thon burnin in the air. Whit wis it he says? A son wilny turn doon his faither whn he's gied the chance tay work alangside the auld man? Cash in yir haun, no degrees in the hereafter? He's stitched you up jist lik the bloody surgeon, n ye're gonny foally him intay the grave.

Francis pulled his brow down, warning his brother.

No here. No this time, wee man.

He stared at Daniel as evenly as if at a mirror, knowing the flaws in the image, where the picture would crack. Daniel dropped his head; if the argument had been won, then here was Frankie's admission, and he felt dirty for having drawn it out of him. An electric alarm sounded, and a sister of formidable size came in and wedged open the ward doors, stood up and looked at her pendant watch on her lapel. The doors were open, and the sister looked as if all the patience and pity had been crushed out of her; but Francis said that was just for the visitors, she was kindly to invalids and would likely give the old woman behind the partitions a few more minutes once the ward nurses told her what had happened. Daniel stood up, replaced the seat at the corner of the bed, said,

If oor ma comes roon and sterts gien ye bother, phone us and I'll talk tay her.

Francis nodded, said,

Tell Agnes I was askin fr her. Tell her, we're kin, you and me, we're allowed, tay have arguments.

On the way through the corridors, Daniel realized he was afraid of his mother and her granite-certain faith, what she might do to influence Francis, what she might say, now of all times. The sound of everyone's feet came to him, clipped and multiplied, he was in the middle of the other visitors, and he looked at them, from one head to another in front of him, in their pairs, singly, all silenced like him by what they knew. Some had brought Bibles and rosaries with them, comfort to the dying; none of them spoke to anyone else, not wanting to hear, and Daniel understood why. At the end of the corridor, he saw Agnes standing, leaning her back against the smooth wall, and wondered how he could explain that was how things were in his family.

Daniel would never know how Kate managed to persuade the doctors to let Frankie out of their hands; maybe a grieving wife was harder to deal with than someone like him you could set the polis on. However she'd done it, Frankie would die in his own house, and Daniel was there by his side when the day came, when his brother lost recognition of who was in front of him, when he said things you'd spend the rest of your life trying to understand, sense and nonsense all stirred in a pot, regrets and intentions and stuff you wouldn't have thought he had in him. He spoke to his mother, although she wasn't there, had refused to come unless there was a priest to give her son his last rites, the way his father had died; ma, he said, ye haveny seen whit I've seen, then ye'd know why no, but it was broken into bits, as much as he could deliver in one short breath, and Daniel, kneeling by the side of the bed, held himself closer to his brother's lips to hear him better. He spoke to his father, as if drawing nearer to him; why'd ye no leave me be, fuck ye da, fuck ye, and Daniel found himself going cold to his roots, Frankie had never sworn like that in his life, as if with the last of his heat he was melting and running, his whole substance, even the thoughts he'd contained, words he'd heard from others. Daniel remembered an old English teacher of his, hardly old when you came to think about it, a bookish young woman with a Kelvinside voice, and she was forever saying in despair whenever one of her pupils let her down, sometimes deliberately so as not to appear too snobby, oh that this too too solid flesh should melt; he remembered it now, because that was Frankie.

Kate was in the front room with Agnes, and every so often you'd hear Agnes in the hallway on her way to the kitchen to brew up more of her strong tea; Daniel wondered why Kate wasn't in the room with him, and with Cameron, who'd been kneeling on the opposite side of the bed from Daniel all the time. Both of them seemed as calm as if they'd been injected themselves with the morphine she'd used to smooth over Frankie's passage; it was more disturbing to Daniel to see it in the wee man, you'd think he hadn't realized his father's life was closing over like a book, or didn't even care. Maybe it was living alongside the smell of rot every day, seeing his father worsen when you'd think it would only go so far; Daniel wondered if perhaps they'd come to wish him dead, Cameron and his ma both, just for the release.

By the time it was late afternoon, Francis wasn't talking to anyone, dead or living. Daniel had been holding Francis's hand through his delirium, anchoring him to their world; but now it seemed he was fastened on to something loose and disjointed, and cold to the touch, and so he let go, leaned over the blankets, keeping his hands apart in case it was thought he was praying. His corduroys were pressing their ribs against his knees, hurting him a wee bit, but he wouldn't shift position, a wee twinge next to his brother's pain. There was a silence in the room, they were insulated by the breadth of the house from the sound of cars passing; a sacred kind of silence, for all that there were none of the fetishes about the room the brothers had been used to when they were growing up, and Daniel listened to Francis's breathing, quick and erratic followed by slow and barely audible, the scraping at the back of the throat that made the air sharp and splintered like needles of glass. Daniel closed his eyes to hear the rhythm better, but maybe also to keep Cameron out of his sight; the hissing was jagged and uneven, there was a breath and then a pause, two short breaths then one long, another pause that made you think his throat had sealed and then a long grateful intake, and at last Daniel became aware that he was timing his own breath with his brother's, in and out, in in in then long out, matching him like a shadow.

He was wondering what Cameron thought of him, sharing the end like that, when there were three even beats on the front door, which opened his eyes for him. He stood up without pressing on the bed, went into the corridor, saw a figure in mosaic in the dappled glass square of the front door, and said over his shoulder,

I'll get it,

to reach as far as the living-room, thinking it was a strange thing for anyone to be visiting at a time like this, hoping it wasn't who he feared.

57

The day was grim and cold, and it came in with the opening of the door, intruding like the worst kind of neighbour, filling the hall with its presence. It wasn't who Daniel had feared on the other side of the threshold; it was a man he didn't recognize, as tall as Daniel himself, wearing the garments of a priest and with a black hat to crown them. He stood with his hands crossed in front of him, supporting a brown leather Gladstone bag in the joining of them. Between the black hat and the white collar there was a face round and swollen like the moon, but red and fleshy, full of blood, with vibrant capillaries redder still tattooed on the skin. Those, and the lines gathered about his eyes and the paunch of his cheeks, the effects of ageing, had been as good as a disguise for Daniel; he had the eyes themselves as a clue, the way of fixing you through like you were a thing to be displayed, lancing eyes which had never changed or weathered.

Daniel said, Father Gallagher, as politely as he could, seeing as he'd come so far. Father Gallagher stood patiently, not presuming to come in until invited. Or perhaps, like a proper theatrical, he was just standing there so that Daniel couldn't fail to register the gravity of his attendance; Father Gallagher, who'd come to Daniel and Francis's school once a week to give them doctrinal instruction as he put it, urinal instruction as some unholy wee snips had it. He'd asked them from the pages of the small red catechism one day, who made you? and when it was Daniel's turn to answer he said, the hosiery shop made me, father, it says it on the label ey my jumper. After the laughing subsided and the echoes rounded off, there came the priest's voice like warmed-over honey, and he smiled and said, very clever, Daniel, God likes a joke as much as the next fellow, after all did he not make joking and laughing as well as a pitiable wee article such as yourself, now I'll give you my wee joke, and so Daniel had two weeks in which to write out the whole of the catechism in two fresh school jotters, and since it was before Daniel learned insubordination he did it, only to see the work torn in half by the priest's hands, as white as the paper he'd written on, and thrown in with the litter. He was a terrible thing to see at the altar for his leisurely masses, spoken high and clear into the chapel's iron webbing of rafters, he played long variations on the theme of his reading in the unending sermons, and if he sensed the least hurry in the congregation's reply to the liturgy, or any expression of communal will to be out quicker and into the street, then he'd call a halt and make them say every syllable, observe all the commas, give three beats for each full stop before the beginning of a new sentence. Daniel's ma thought he was an awful holy man; it was even rumoured he bled from stigmata opening like screaming mouths on Good Fridays, sealing up again on Easter Mondays as suddenly as they appeared. It was doubting Francis who said blasphemy against it to their ma, a wee while before he stopped going to masses, I could have a stigma mysel, he said, and a wee rub wi alcohol, and their ma smacked him about the ear for his doubts, it's a sign ey a man chosen by God, noo wheesht you wi that talk and eat yer dinner in peace, but the brothers smiled at each other across the table, knowing what the other was thinking. They'd heard the story going around at school, from a couple of children who'd said they'd gone to the priest's house separated from the chapel by hedging, meaning at first to ring the doorbell and hide in the shadow of a sycamore tree, deciding to be more daring still and peer in at the old boy's window like visitors at a zoo. They said they'd seen him on Good Friday evening with a bottle of altar wine, draining it from the neck like you'd see any old town centre destitute do, tilting it back for a right good swallow, crying out in a soured perversion of his altar voice, get thee behind me, Satan, you master of harlots! and then bringing the heel of the bottle down against the mantelpiece, animating the fire in the grate with the last spits of wine; and then, man oh man ye shouldey seen it, with the broken stub of the bottle, one of the pinnacles of green glass, he began to gouge at the palm of his hand, changing grip to scar them both, before the other priests came into the room to stop him. That was the story Daniel and Francis had heard, and Francis believed it because he knew Johnnie Boyle, the rat-faced leader of the mischief raid, hadn't the imagination to come up with a story like it if he hadn't seen it, and besides, Francis had to tell Johnnie what a harlot was, which made the wee troublemaker laugh even more richly to think of it, mebbe he's been peyn for hoors a' these years.

Father Gallagher held the Gladstone bag tighter, drawing out the veins on the backs of his hands. No matter the stories Daniel had heard, no matter that the priest was of an even height with Daniel; it still seemed as if the chill wrapping around them emanated from Father Gallagher himself. The old man's voice was still warm and honeyed as he said,

I'm here at your mother's request, Daniel. You'll know why.

Daniel brought his arms across his chest.

We're no lookin for guests the day, Father. Oor ma widny come hersel, and we're sorry. Jist the family, nae others.

I'm not here as a guest. I'm here to enact a mother's wishes for her son. Are you refusing her that, Daniel?

There was the lilt of reason in Father Gallagher's voice. Daniel's arms tightened, as if to protect a softness in him.

I'm no refusin her. Francis didny waant it. D'ye no think his wishes come intay it?

Oh, very clever, Daniel, he said. Now the devil's got you making his points for him.

Ye canny believe in the devil if ye don't believe in God.

Father Gallagher took a step forward; a confident step, the beginning of the journey he knew Daniel would allow him to complete eventually.

That's when he has most power over you, Daniel. He's the prince of lies. What greater lie than the notion he doesn't exist? How better to lull your reason to sleep like a baby in his arms?

Daniel stood back a step.

My brother's dyin, Father Gallagher. If ye don't mind.

What will it mean if you're both wrong, Daniel? Your brother will die without his last chance to be accepted back into the faith he was born with. Are you pleased enough to bear the responsibility for sending his immortal soul to hell? Let him make his peace with God, Daniel, if he wishes.

He's no talkin, Father. He's past that.

Father Gallagher searched Daniel for any sign of untruth; finding none, his demeanour changed, pitying, but just as determined. He raised the Gladstone bag level to his chest, patted it with his free hand.

He can still be helped. I have in here everything I need to perform the sacrament of extreme unction, in accordance with your mother's wishes, and surely that can't do any harm if as you say neither of you believes?

Daniel opened his mouth, aware he'd be speaking for his brother, but no sound came. The priest leaned forward, the bag, his head, over the threshold.

For your mother's sake, Daniel.

If the living-room door hadn't opened just then with a crash, Daniel didn't know what he might have done for their mother's sake; opened the door wider to let him by, closed it in his face; so much was in his head, Francis declaring he'd die with integrity, his mother pleading with him over the phone to let the rites be observed, whit aboot whit comes efter, Danny, I waant us a' thegither, I couldny be at peace if I didny think that; a feather of a doubt in either pan could have tipped him one way or the other. But he hadn't the chance to think once Kate was away, trailing her words behind her like the speech banner unfurling from the mouth of a medieval cartoon figure inscribed in all the hot bloody colours of outrage.

What're you like, you owl vulture you? You're like one of those pests from a van, trying to sell a box of soap powder!

Daniel looked at Catherine tearing towards him, trying to glimpse over Daniel's shoulder the cause of all the commotion; she put an arm across Daniel's chest the moment she arrived at the doorway, shuffling them like cards so that she was to the front of the deck like a queen to his jack, staring at the priest, daring him to draw his trumps or aces. Daniel found the first thing worth smiling at all day in the face of Father Gallagher, clearly not used to dealing with this heat of anger and certainly not from a woman. His eyes were blunted and uncertain; but you had to admire the nerve of him for keeping his voice even.

If you were any wife to that man in there, you'd see to it your mother-in-law's wishes were carried out, and he died in the full dignity of the faith he was baptized in.

Even from behind, Daniel could see the cords stand out in her neck; Francis had known what to do about her furies, you didn't challenge her like that, you crawled into a wee shelter of silence until they'd passed over, and then spoke kindly to her hours afterwards when the rage was gone.

A faith that makes saints out of liars, she said, and honest men out of rogues. No thank you, Father whoever you are,

and he said Gallagher back to her, but it got caught and lost in the spin.

I don't care if you're the archangel Gabriel and all the heavenly host, my husband doesn't want the kind of dignity you have to give him, he told that to his mother when he was in hospital and I'm telling it to you now, so take your bag away from my front door to your own and don't be upsetting the house today of all days. Go on, get away with you!

The entire close sang with it, repeating it like a taunt, get away with you, get away with you, until it seemed as if everyone in the close had opened their doors to chant at the priest, get away with you. Daniel saw behind the glass of the door opposite a silver head, the one Kate said hadn't the courage to come out and make her curiosity known, in fragments like broken biscuits. Father Gallagher let his bag plumb his arm down by his side; he said, sadly,

Then I'm sure he'll be looking forward to your company in hell, and I hope he forgives you.

Kate closed the door on him with restraint, making certain it was properly shut over before letting the tongue slip home into the latch. Daniel watched as Kate shivered in the cold the priest had allowed in with his visit; began now to smooth down the pleats of her skirt, a black one she'd put on, out of reflex perhaps, Daniel didn't know her well enough to say. Both of them turned away from the door at the same time; the doors to both the living-room and the bedroom were open, making shallow slants of daylight, and Agnes was there at the living-room and Cameron at the other door, both looking perplexed in different ways. Agnes was the first to express it.

It widny've done any herm, she said. It's jist words.

Kate went to the bedroom door to stand beside Cameron; her white blouse inflated with light around her.

It's not just words, she said. It's meanings.

Agnes looked to Daniel for support, explanation, anything; he shrugged, said,

Frankie never waanted it. He said so.

Cameron looked up at his mother, who had settled an arm around his shoulders. There was a frown from him, making his face look busy.

Was the man trying to get in?

Daniel had never known a day pass when the wee man wasn't asking questions. Kate answered him as levelly as she could; Daniel wondered if she'd been ready for the priest's intervention, had expected it.

Yes, but your dad didn't want him in the house, so we didn't let him in.

She looked up at Agnes, anticipating a reply, an argument, opposition. Daniel couldn't look at his wife, not when it wasn't her decision to make; instead went to the bedroom door and opened it wider to allow himself to pass Kate and Cameron, let them have their disagreement away from him. He went back to his devotional place by the side of the bed, knelt down and leaned on the blankets, arranging his arms in the ruts he'd left in the linen before the knock at the door. Daniel looked at his brother's face, tilted back on the pillow; the eyes, not quite closed as if fighting against the tiredness overcoming him; heard the breath swelling and diminishing in Frankie's throat, and knew it was near the time to call Kate and the wee one in for the death, as she'd requested, for if Cameron had been shown honestly how life began, then she was just as determined that he'd see honestly how it ended.

Four

Catherine knew she hadn't been herself lately; it culminated in the evening she literally beat the fuck out of her son.

She sat, no, found herself sitting, in the chair Francis was always used to sitting in whenever he returned home from his work at the foundry. She thought of how the poker looked when she took it out of the coals after riddling them in the grate, the tip blooded red by the heat, how it cooled to black in a minute, that was how she was just now. She held out her hands, still tingling from hitting the bare flesh of Cameron's calves above his short socks and below the cuffs of his short pants; looked at the tips of her fingers, you'd think there'd be a flame around them, she should have been alight from the violence in her, and just then she heard Cameron crying in his bedroom, and she hid both of her hands by folding them under her, bringing her arms over her breasts, she couldn't even stand to look at them. They were the hands of a cruel witch of a woman, grafted on to the stumps of her wrists, and she couldn't have stopped them whenever she heard that venom word drop from Cameron's mouth even if she had tried; the holy rage had taken them, and for that time, Catherine couldn't say how long, she was more purely her father's daughter than her gentle mother's, cleansing her son of whatever had possessed him, whatever had made that word gather inside him, the hated, hateful word her father uttered when he spent his drunken furies on the house, its objects, her mother. It was as if she had been charged at that moment with the task of drawing the seed of owl Colum O'Hara from her son, before the roots of it clenched around his child's heart.

It was only after a time of being wrapped in her misery that Catherine realized there was stamping above her, footfalls against the ceiling, the prizefighters squaring up for another bout and calling each other for everything, the words sharp and perfectly audible, slut whore cunt, prick arsehole bastard. Catherine heard them twice, through the ceiling, clean and clear through the open window, Francis always laughed at her, my god, Kate, ye're a country girl right enough. She looked up at the light and the shade trembling, and she wondered if she was to blame for touching off the argument, it was a guilty thought, beyond reason; but she'd felt beyond reason for some months now, beyond reach of Daniel's comforting blather, that was jist Francis, Kate, he widny listen to a word anyone said.

She found herself wondering, despite herself, if there were devils that used you for their vehicles to do what they couldn't accomplish themselves. That was always her father's excuse when he awakened with his tongue as dry as linen while her mother and Michael swept fragments into tin shovels, the promises Catherine called them, because he was forever coming back with some ornament of glass or china whose value lay in its fragility, how easily it could be dashed to pieces, sure and this is ten times more valuable than that owl thing that got broke, as if it had fallen from the mantel all by itself, and it was always the first thing to fall in his next rage, he hooked whatever it was from the wooden mantel, a plate with a country scene in pastel on the dish never meant to be eaten from, a whole menagerie of crystal had been slaughtered that way, deer and lions and tigers; and then he would waken to the chiming, he would say mildly, aye, there's no stopping the devil when he's in ye, and no one would bother to look at him, to condemn, because his memory was long, and shone most brightly when he was bright with the drink.

He'd sent a present along with her mother and Michael when they came to the wedding; a vase made of Waterford crystal, with a faceted onion bulb for a bottom, a faceted tulip cup for a mouth; it teased the colours out of the sunlight along the bevels, gave her a rainbow across her hand, and she'd thought about dashing it to the ground along with the rest of his promises. It was in a drawer now in her room; her room, the words came bleakly into her head; in its box, never opened from that day to this. Since the birth of the wee one, she'd long thought Cameron might like it as a toy, and he might break it in his slippery child's fingers, saving her the bother, the wee one was fond of fragile things, things that glittered and threw nets of light on the walls.

She heard the crying through the two open doors, to the living-room, to his bedroom; intolerable suffering sounds. She stood up, and quietly went to her bedroom, to the chest of drawers opposite the bed. In the top drawer, underneath a lasagne of folded clothes, underskirts and stockings and bras, she found the box; plain yellowed card, the folds of the lid bent back into triangles, and she lifted it out and with one hand closed the drawer. The box had more weight than she remembered, a dead mass, dull and meaningless; she kept it closed all the way to Cameron's room, held delicately in both her hands, and stepped around the open doorway as if she knew he'd be sleeping, her bare feet light and tentative, not knowing what to expect now that Cameron seemed to have stopped crying. The last time she'd come through here like this; she reined back the thought before it fled away with her, and peered inside.

The room was different to when she'd last come in to comfort him. His cardboard city was under the arched legs of the tallboy for safety, hidden under a dull wooden sky the daylight had to work to penetrate. There was an accident of toy cars under the window, whether because he'd been playing at accidents or because there was where they'd fallen she couldn't tell. Beside them was his soldier doll, on its back and throttled by the sling of its own rifle, a casualty of Cameron's boredom. His wee toy magnifying glass was beside the soldier and close to the bed, warping the carpet in its sight, and on the other side his learning picture-books from the school library, space flight she read from the spine, a hundred and one experiments you can do in the home; sure and he'd a good wee head on him, and she was modest enough to think it was his father's.

The other thing that was different was Cameron himself, not prone this time, but upright and sitting with his back to the headboard, and he was hugging his legs tight against his chest, his feet raising creases in the blankets. He still had his shoes on, but Catherine decided to let it pass, it would be better that way. It was his eyes that concerned her; raw about the rims, not surprising after he'd been crying, but you'd think they were burning like that to emphasize the cold, unforgiving look that radiated out of them, accusing her. She remembered the look well herself; he never resembled her more than just then, when she seemed to be staring into a mirror of time and seeing herself as she glowered at her father, the mornings after his drunken furies; the look reached into her, raised all the dirt and sediment, made the weight in her hands seem shabby and duplicitous. There was a sound from above, Cassius Clay and Joe Louis at it again, stamping on the ceiling like bulls, but she couldn't tell if it was a fight beginning or still the prelude to one; how she could judge them, today of all days, she'd never know, there was no end to the shame she felt.

She approached the bed with her gift, hoped he could tell from the softening of her carriage she wasn't angry at him any longer; she tried smiling, but it wouldn't hold up properly, and he shrank from her as if her skin had split and a new creature had thrown it aside, something new and monstrous from one of his picture-books. She came closer, sat down on the bed and angled herself towards him; the fabric of the blankets was soft against her leg. She held out the box awkwardly between them, holding it in the air for what seemed like a long time; Cameron's arms were still binding him together, and he looked sideways at her in confusion.

Wee present for you, Cameron.

Now here she was giving promises; this one she resolved would stay intact. Cameron unwrapped himself, reached out to take the box with both hands; his arms fell with the weight of it, as unexpected to him as it had been to her. He straightened out his legs and took the box on to his lap, lifted the lid on it sullenly, rationing his forgiveness. There was tissue inside, reminding Catherine of her wedding dress; but tissue of a different kind, rough and dragging. He parted it carefully, making certain not to tear it, until the vase was revealed; Catherine saw a look on him she only ever saw on Christmases, his eyes widening, gathering in the shape of the object; and sure enough, as she'd thought, he took it from the box and turned it about in his hands. He held it up to the window, spun it around; threads of prismatic light were cast about his face, vividly coloured,

67

and Catherine forgot the argument above, which this time seemed to be ending with him stumping along the corridor, you could trace him from the progress of his feet on the identical topography of the flat upstairs, slamming closed the door with a force that caused the walls and the floor to shake around them. The house went quiet, with only a whisper of cars from the other side of the building; it seemed right, to let Cameron better contemplate the facets in the vase, and he tilted it so he was looking at her through the mouth of the vase. He seemed to have brightened, came to kneel facing her so he could see her through the glass without twisting himself; Catherine felt a huge relief pass through her to see it. His eye was engorged to bursting with this new way of seeing, but divided too around the facets, and Catherine wondered how he was seeing her in the kaleidoscope. She said,

Here, let me look,

and he gave it to her, still solemn while she put it to her eye as he'd done; the image of him was clear in the centre, the flattened end of the base, but the bulb's facets were alive with the spectrum, took light and visions from all about the room. Michael had told her this was how insects saw around them, with eyes made out of entire honeycombs of smaller eyes. The vase was cold in her hands, warming a little with the touch, and it was like ice against her face; she handed it back to Cameron like a trophy, and he took it, placed it on his lap, looked down at it as he poked a finger into the mouth of it. It seemed to be the right time now he was distracted; she asked,

What made you say that, Cameron?

He took a while to tell her; it was a boy at school, of course, who'd been giving him trouble for weeks and months, and tried to make him say it, say it, catching his head in a grip, ye think ye're better'n us, ya snobby wee bastard, fucken say fuck or I'll kick yir fucken arse for ye! This had been happening for a while, after school, in the playground, until that day, when the boy Cameron wouldn't name came over to him with a poke of sweets and his mates on loyalty strings, offering a candy ball which Cameron took suspiciously at first. His mates said, whit're ye dayn? gie the wee snob a fucken doin, but the boy turned to them and said, I'll make friends wi who I like, and I've decided tay make friends wi Snobby here, so fucken shut it.

The candy ball was turning sticky in Cameron's fingers when the boy said, ye no gonny eat it? and Cameron put it in his mouth and felt it melt like slow ice, sweet and delicious; just then the boy asked, whit dis yir da work at, Snobby? Cameron tried to say, my dad's dead, but the candy ball was like a cork in his mouth, and the boy said, speak up, Snobby, I canny hear ye; Cameron rolled it like a boulder with the point of his tongue to the side of his mouth, but now the words were indistinct, and the boy said, his heid? whit aboot yir da's heid? and his mates were laughing like clowns at the state of Cameron. At last he made a pouch like a hamster's in his cheek, rolled the candy ball into that; he'd always thought candy ball wasn't a good name for it, he explained to Catherine, because it wasn't round at all, more like a pyramid, brown as a chestnut, and he said this to make her understand that the edges had cut into the flesh as he held it there, he was very precise about the detail of it. Finally the words got past, my dad's dead, and by this time the mates were spinning around and tugging on each other's coats and laughing out of control; but the boy held up his hand and said, heh yous, fucken shut it, Snobby's lost his da, how'd yous like it. To hear Cameron tell it, the anonymous boy had been protecting him, but Catherine was alight with anger, and she wondered if he should play more with other children; he seemed blind to their cruelties.

The boy chose to walk home with Cameron, held out the crushed paper poke and let him take more sweets. His mates went their own way, and so he and Cameron talked; he said he was sorry to hear about Cameron's father, and Cameron thought it was good of him to say so. He asked Cameron why he didn't like football like the rest of them; Cameron said it was because he couldn't play it, and besides his mother told him it wasn't football they were playing on the park, not in this town anyway; there were faiths colliding, wee battles fought when the causes were best forgotten, and apart from that, he wasn't interested in the game, and that was all there was to it. That was when the boy said, Is it yir ma wilny let ye say bad words? and Cameron told him yes, and so the boy took Cameron closer and let him into a wee secret; she'll no have tellt ye this, but, and then he said it was all right if you said it in a special way that grown-ups didn't mind, and he spent the rest of the walk home teaching Cameron to say it after him, reciting it like a poem so he'd know when and how to use it.

Catherine sat back, suddenly understanding; she made sure to tell Cameron, to emphasize to him, that no it wasn't all right to use it in any way, because it was just dirt and filth in your mouth no matter how you said it. Cameron looked to his new toy, away from her, stirred the air inside the vase with the point of his finger and said,

Why's it bad? What does it mean?

Catherine had shown her son what men and women do in the bedroom without a thought or a care; now she knew how others must feel when they had to explain it to their children. She asked him to remember what he'd seen a couple of years ago in her room, with her and his father; he nodded, he remembered, and she said,

Well, it's a rude word that means what we were doing that night. You're not to say it because it's only bad people who say it.

Meaning her father; fockin this and fockin that, never when he was sober and right in the head, only to gash her mother when he was drunk, using it like a razor. She couldn't tell Cameron how much it'd cut her to hear it from his mouth; now she was raging against this anonymous wee gutter boy for making her hurt her son like that. Cameron was still puzzled; but he nodded anyway, and she said he was a good boy, and then stroked his hair until she pulled a smile out of him, and left him to make their dinner.

She only had to heat it, she'd spent the afternoon cooking the mutton and the vegetables to make it ready for him coming home. She stood in the kitchen, watching the steam lift from the pot on the cooker's hotplate, thinking of Cameron coming into the house when she'd asked him, would you like your dinner just now? and he'd said to her, in the formula he'd been coached to say, she now knew, I don't give a fuck. She wished Cameron would break the confidence of the playground and tell her the name of the wee tormentor; she had her father's rage kindling her, and this time she was minded to give it to the one who deserved it, and not her son who'd just been following orders.

There were times in the evenings when Catherine would look over at her son, sitting in Francis's chair, and she'd look for signs of Francis in him. There was the forehead, shallower than her own, that was Francis's doing, and she'd smile at that; his nose, longer than hers, with tunnels like inverted commas opposed to each other, and that seemed to be his father's gift as well; the eyes were hazel, and could have belonged to either of them, but he had his father's look of distance about him, like the windows of a toyshop, as if he was collecting everything he saw, wrapping it in linen, to be opened someday. She thought the mouth was hers, quite full lips he had on him, and it was all composed in a heart-shaped face which seemed to be hers as well. It seemed strange to her, that all the ingredients of herself and Francis could be shaken in a bottle and here they were, seated quietly in front of her, and you could see what she had added and what was Francis's. There were times she was glad of it, searched in his face for what there was of Francis, but there were times too when those features seemed to have been put there to laugh at her, like the times when Cameron would catch her staring at him, would stare back at her, and it would be too much like Francis looking at her; she'd say, something the matter, Cameron? and she could barely keep the challenge out of her voice, and he'd ask her, why d'you keep looking at me? As much as Catherine had promised he'd never go without an answer, it was the one thing she couldn't tell him; and then there was the day she realized the mouth he had on him had been her father's as well, that dirty mouth swollen with bile and sweet with promises, and she began to wonder what had come to him, if this was cheek she was hearing instead of an innocent question.

Oh, she'd cook and clean for him right enough, because there were still threads of Francis in him, there was dinner on the table whenever he came home from school, less elaborate now that she was relying on the parish; but she was on the alert for all the wiles of her father, and seeing wee hints and evasions from him. The time went on; she'd bark at him, for the love of pete, Cameron, can you not go out to play once in a while? because he'd just be sitting there watching the tele, and it was as if Francis had left him behind as a keepsake, a wee ornament she might have picked up and thrown against the wall in a moment of bitterness and then spent the rest of her life fixing together. Cameron said, I don't like playing outside, everybody just plays football, I don't like football, and then he was just being obdurate, another gleam of her father in him, and she'd say, fine, just sit there like a wee ornament, and he'd be silent for the rest of the evening until it was time to go to bed, afraid even to let out a breath in case she'd notice him again.

This was Catherine's new routine.

First, there'd be her wakening by the alarm clock, the clapper drring against the dome bells until she reached out to the bedside table to trip the lever and shut it up. The alarm left echoes behind in the air, dents in the peace you could almost see; her head was still thick with dreams swirling down the stank of another day, and she had to spend at least five minutes sitting against her angled pillow before she felt ready to be up on her legs. She dressed in house clothes, nothing bright or coloured, because there was no reason for it; oatmeal sweater of pure new wool, black Bri-nylon slacks with stirrups that looped around her bare feet, and that was her ready. A quick look in the mirror of the dresser; combing her hair through once with her fingers to work out the obvious knots and tangles; that was enough to be going on with.

Next, she went through to Cameron's room, straight to the curtains, holding them by the fringes and spreading her arms to part them. Cameron always turned away from the window whenever she did that, hearing the curtains whispering on the rods, but she had to sound bright, come on, lazy, on your feet, time for up, and you'd have to say he was always good with waking, as much as he hated it; on his feet right enough, taking himself to the bathroom where she'd hear the water spilling into the sink, the toothbrush ranging about his mouth, his delicate wee spitting.

While he was doing that, she was making him breakfast; whatever she thought he might fancy for the day, hot porridge if it was cold out, toast with melting butter and a cup of tea, a whole orange because that was his vitamins. She had the radio on to fill the house with music and incentive, and sometimes there was a song she knew which she might sing to him while he was eating in Francis's chair, it seemed a waste to have the leaf of the table up when there was only two of them. While he was eating breakfast, she was making his lunch for him in the kitchen; two pieces and whatever came to hand from the cupboard, mostly thin cloths of gammon she'd buy from the butcher's wrapped in wet greaseproof paper, one to a piece of bread and the excess trimmed and put inside the sandwich. When she finished, she put the pieces in a spare paper bag, maybe the one the gammon had come in, and then took the lunch into the living-room and handed it to Cameron; his satchel was propped beside the chair, and he'd put the bag into a special strapped pocket in the front of the satchel, and then he was ready to leave. She walked him as far as the front door, told him to watch for cars on the road and not to talk to strange grown-ups on the way, and that was it, a kiss from her and he'd be away without a look back, and she closed the door over, hoping he'd be safe.

Then the silence would settle about the house; and it was what she did with the silence; cleaned the house, dusted, set everything right, because she had a home to keep, she wasn't going to let that disintegrate around her. She did it harshly, bringing out the light in all the surfaces, almost punishing them for being as solid as they were, until she was tired of it; and then there was one day after she'd sent Cameron off to school when she couldn't start herself, she stood by the door and listened to the jangling music, and she just couldn't be bothered.

Everywhere Catherine had ever been, there was a mirror she remembered. There was one at her home, her home over the water, a simple square of reflecting glass in a plain frame. As the years took it, a blight spread on the silver, a tarnish that transferred itself to your face like a birthmark. The stain eventually claimed the whole of it until you looked like your own grandmother's daguerreotype down from the attic, all in sepia. Owl Colum O'Hara was always going to replace it, but it was never broken, so there was no need. She thought of it as the diseased mirror, as if she'd catch a plague from the sight of the old man every day when his face was as rough as sandpaper, his eyes wan and bleary; passing it to them all when their images touched the silver, giving all of them his jaundice. That was the first, the one she could recall her face in when she was a girl, hung above the kitchen hearth for his convenience, between the baptism pictures her Uncle Finn had taken of herself and Michael.

73

She showed the mirror the marks he'd left, the troughs dug into her by his dirty nails when he wasn't caring he'd torn her open, the bruises that sprawled across her face like his plague on the glass. She wondered if the girl in the mirror felt the pains she did.

The next of her mirrors was the one in the work she got not long after she was over the water, in the graceful employ of Mrs Kilsyth. It seemed ridiculous to be wearing a maid's uniform just to be cleaning up after the old duchess, but she saw herself in it whenever she looked in the good mirror in her room, which was also the kitchen. It was jewelled and beautiful; oval like an eye, with scallops for bevelling that gave your face the aura of a rainbow if you strayed to the edge of it. One of her tasks was to keep the glass as clean as to give you back a pure image, clear and unblemished; she did it as much for herself as for the old biddy with her wants and demands, because it was the first time she'd seen herself without the dirt on her. Mrs Kilsyth wanted her tea just then, her dinner at such a time, put to bed by ten and no later; Catherine said, and what did your last servant die of, ma'am? but the duchess liked a bit of insubordination, friction to generate warmth, and she smiled under her white hair and said, of disobedience, young Miss O'Hara, now I will have my nightdress ironed and laid out for me for quarter to ten prompt. How she could have airs like that when the bed was in the room she lived in all day; Catherine understood that this was her on the last of the family money, hoarded for centuries, now bled away by something the mistress never spoke of, gambling, a redirected will, not for Catherine to know. Catherine's bed was in a recess in the kitchen, and when the old lady was asleep it gave her the chance to play in front of that mirror with the make-up she'd bought from her walk down Sauchiehall Street. She was learning, because even with the first of her wages and new clothes she felt small and unsophisticated, there was something about the women who walked the streets in the evening, with their men or in groups for belonging, they didn't know how miraculous they looked to someone like her. She tipped all her materials on the mahogany kitchen table, too grand to be in a house like this; compacts shut like mussel shells, lipsticks describing the spectrum of red from wine to barely pinker than her own flesh, tubes of wet kohl, liquid foundation of many skin tones from dark to pale, a fat bottle of cleansing milk to wipe away failed experiments.

The mirror saw her first face; she'd wanted it to look like one woman she'd seen going into Pettigrew's, tall and huddled into a fur coat as rich as sin; she'd seemed tanned and healthy, but the closer you went to her, Catherine was drawn to her, you saw the powder in grains on her face, gathered like warts, and Catherine wanted a better face than hers. The result was dark sure enough, with great scythes of rouge under her cheekbones, the bow of her mouth raw and bloody, but there was her hair to ruin it, as black as the woman's, certainly, but wilder once it was out of the hold of the grips, not sculpted or rolling as the woman's had been, tails and filaments here and there. She tried again, something pale this time, and it ended up as white as bone, with dolly-red cheeks and her lips bloodless and frostbitten; she made herself laugh, she'd turned herself into a clown. Thank heavens she was alone in the room, otherwise Mrs Kilsyth might've thought a corpse had got up on its hind legs to haunt her.

Over the weeks, she became better with the practice. She went down the street, to tea rooms when she was called upon to fetch the occasional message for Mrs Kilsyth, to clothes shops on her time off; she plucked faces like fruit, remembered them all in detail, used the memories as models for herself. She became good enough to be able to pick a face to match with her new wardrobe from a growing collection; dark and like a gipsy, light and floating, all she needed was a look outside the third-floor window to check the weather and then a look into herself, how she was feeling, and there she had a face for it. They would've put her mammy and her da in their graves early, those faces of hers, other women's; even at the wedding, when she'd chosen a pale look for herself like a page nothing had ever been written on, she felt her mother's staring at her, there was still art to it and not wholly approved of.

Her next mirror was the one at home, the one on the dressing-table. She'd chosen it for those panels, how you could angle them to collect the light from the window, frame yourself three times over, do the job properly with yourself seen from all sides, the way you'd be seen by others. Cameron hadn't come along until some while into the marriage, and she and Francis still had their wee occasions, going to the dancing or the pictures; Daniel on one of his visits said for a joke,

75

ye're merried, the perr ey ye, it's no natural dayn a' that stuff noo, but she loved the dressing up, the preparation, you had to show you were still trying. The night they went to the Locarno, when she made her decision; I'm going to show my thanks to you, Francis, her chin resting on his shoulder while they spun with the mirror ball overhead, in a blizzard of lights. Is this a reward r somethn, he said, us here lik we're still winchin? maist men and their wives settle doon efter they're merried. The music warming her the way she imagined the drink did her father; wait till I get you home, Francis, you'll see thanks then.

She couldn't remember how soon after Francis's death this ritual started, what was in her head the first morning she looked at herself in the mirror and decided she needed the transformation. She'd switched off the radio, the blether she couldn't listen to once she'd sent Cameron away, once it had done its work of filling the house with the sounds of life. Maybe her fingers had touched the compacts and the lipsticks, and there was a memory in them of the faces she'd gathered, the occasions she'd used them for, maybe those memories had possessed her hands, just to show her what she'd been like on those nights she'd been out with her husband. Whenever she was finished, there was an awful time when she would look at the face she'd constructed for herself, tilt it this way and that, and there'd be a line under her chin where she imagined you could grasp it like a false face, a mask for Halloween, lift it of a piece up and over her brow, flex it and crush it like paper, throw it in the tin-can bin next to the dresser.

She loved the beginnings of her faces; hated their endings, when there was no reason for them and she had to clean them off. She undertook it like any labour, reluctantly, with cleansing milk and pads torn from a bale of cotton wool; hated the cool greasy slide of the pad over her skin, the bleeding and melting and the tracks in her, because when it was done and she was glistening with the milk, there she was with her own face back, the one she was hiding under all the paint, and it was time for her to be thinking about making Cameron's dinner.

Sometimes she felt as if Francis had braided himself into the fraying ends of her; they'd repaired, strengthened each other. She began to feel frayed again; fastened to nothing and in fear of everything around her; strange licks of shadow in the corners, the edges of knives, night pressing like cloth against the windows. She'd only ever been afraid of her father before, his thirst as well as his rage, and she took to wondering how much of him there was in her, and how much of him she'd infected Cameron with; perhaps she was afraid of how she used these ancestral tempers, this inheritance of hers, of Cameron's.

Catherine began to look at her son's face for the possibilities in it. She imagined him grown, with that mouth of her father's sucking on the tit of the bottle; how it made her owl man look like he'd been caught in a sneer. There was one night, about a week after he'd said fuck, when the wee one was playing with his motor cars and she thought she saw it. He was steering his cars, one in each hand, around the carpet in front of the fireplace, just at her feet, and there seemed to be a chase, the cars weaving about each other, his arms crossing then widening apart. He was imitating the scream of the tyres and the crying of brakes. Catherine wondered where he was getting his wee drama from; a detective show on the tele, something like that. The chase ended in a collision, head on; a kiss of chrome-painted radiators which Catherine heard as a click before Cameron made the sound, an explosive release of air drawn across his throat, and it was the way his mouth went that troubled her, pressed shut except for a hole he made at the edge of his lips, like a hole you'd drain the drink through. At first she smiled, because he was playing, he was a child playing, you couldn't help but smile at it; but it was when he looked up, not smiling in reply. There was joy in him, joy in destruction or at least the thought of destruction, an innocence she'd've seen in the owl man when he was sweeping his arm across the mantelshelf and broke another of his promises, you wouldn't think it but he watched everything tumble as if one day it would all drift up and lodge on the ceiling and he'd be there to see it; that kind of child's experimental will, now she came to think about it, and she was thinking maybe he'd never have been like this if it hadn't been nipped in the bud when he was young enough to learn a lesson.

The next thing she knew, she'd hunted him into a corner of the room, the other corner from the tele set, come here you, don't you ever look at me like that again! There wasn't any more fear in her; knowledge, just, that she was right in her punishing, she hardened herself to administer it, a punishment as much for herself as for the wee one. He fell to the floor; cunning wee article, he was on his side and his arms were braced over his head, a structure solid as rafters to protect himself, but there his legs were poking out the cuffs of his short trousers. She had to genuflect to reach him, all tangled as he was the way the doctor had told her he'd be inside her while he was waiting for his birth.

Catherine felt so calm after the operation, not like the last time; a poison had been drawn from him, simple as that. The prints of her hands were hot and red on his legs; she'd tried to crack open the shell of his arms about his head to strike properly at his face, but he wouldn't release, so she'd had to hit what she could. The heat was dying now; she rested back on her heels, gathered her hair together because it had lashed around her eyes while she'd been punishing him; drew it through her fingers and let it spill behind her. She became aware of a terrible pain on the sole of her bare foot; looked over her shoulder and saw on the floor one of Cameron's overturned cars, she must have stood on it, the marks were there in her, a red oblong, four dents like hyphens at the corners. The breath came back to her slowly, and she said,

It isn't nice to be destructive, Cameron. You're not to do it.

Cameron still wouldn't come out from the shelter of his arms and legs.

I was only playing.

You never played at destroying things before. What's in you these days?

Cameron brought his arms down from his head, pulled them tight against his body. He was heaving powerfully, as if to be sick. His eyes were closed, tightly, but they were wet.

You wouldn't've, done that, if my dad'd been here.

Catherine stood up abruptly, as if she hadn't heard. She brushed down her slacks from knee to shin, even though she'd hoovered the carpet only that day. Cameron was still on the floor, afraid to move, still crying, his whole body surging with it. She had a bag of reasons why it had been necessary, and she thought he should know them;

but the longer she looked at them herself, the more like lies they became.

There was a news programme on the tele; the reader's voice was steady and efficient, telling of a famine in Africa. A picture came on the screen of a boy with the legs of a heron, but the swollen belly of a glutton; Catherine could never understand how they could look so sated and yet be starving at the same time, until Francis had explained one night it was called kwashiorkor, it happened to malnourished children. The boy had insects exploring his face, and no strength in him to ward them away; he was kicking among dust, carrying his empty pregnancy with him as he walked here and there. Catherine stood watching until the end of the report, when a tall man came to the foreground with a microphone in his hand and declared that aid efforts were being hampered by a war, said his name, the channel he was reporting for, the name of the country he was in. She wondered if he gave them any food; the light shirt he had on was certainly tight enough around him.

When she became aware of the room again, she saw that Cameron was gone from the floor. She went out of the living-room and into the hall; it was dark, but there was a pin of light cast from under the door to his room, which was switched off as she waited. Catherine felt suddenly tired, exhausted by her own passions. She went back to her seat in front of the fire; there was another report on the news, but she couldn't listen to it. She wondered if she'd ever come to live within herself as vividly again as she had when Francis was alive; but now here she was, with only Cameron as a keepsake, and her will that he should be more like his father, not hers.

When the dithering bell of the alarm clock went off the next day, Catherine became aware she'd been interrupted in the middle of a dream; lashed out to her side, stilled the clock, and then settled back against her pillow.

She remembered the smell of baking; she'd been in the kitchen, and Francis was there as well, standing by the white Formica worktop alongside the sink. She was standing in the doorway, so she could see what Francis had in front of him on the worktop; a perfect loaf of white bread, the crust black on top, sitting on the wooden cutting board. She'd never made bread for him, but her mammy had done it many a time, loaves born from the oven black like that and shaped like wee cottages, rounded roofs, straight under the eaves. Without a word, Francis went to the drawer under the sink, pulled it open until it stuck; she remembered a promise he'd made, weeks before he was diagnosed, he'd get around to fixing it when he'd the time. He reached in and took out a long serrated bread knife, the blade narrow, rounded rather than pointed at the end; held it up for her to see, reflecting a slice of herself back to her. Francis closed the drawer, took the knife over to the loaf, began to saw at the crust; and just then Catherine felt a pressure against her, across her chest, driving her against the jamb of the doorway, she was fastened to it, couldn't move. She only felt the pain when Francis tore through the crust, carving into the white of it; the gash breathing out a pale steam, like the mist on your breath on a cold day, the smell of baking now all around the room with the opening of the loaf, beautiful and homely. It was the pain of being carved through like the bread, but she clutched at the place she felt it and came away without blood or any sign of violation; she took in a breath to cry out, Francis, please stop, but the air had become hot around her, and there was nothing for her to do but wait until he'd cut the slice from the loaf. She wondered if this was the pain of being under the knife, of being cut open like bread, the isolation of the hospital, that he was sharing with her; but he didn't know he was causing her suffering, simply bent over the loaf and stroked the knife through it until the thick ender fell away, severed.

That was as much as she could remember; but there'd been another before then, or maybe after then, she couldn't put anything in order these days, let alone her own head. She was small again, under the kitchen table, a triangle of linen hiding her. She saw legs clad in filthy trousers, the feet shod in boots slathered in mud. A broom handle kept metronome time against the floorboards, tap tap tap. Come out of there, ye fockin scamps, come out for yer thrashin, ye know what'll happen if ye don't. Breathing beside her, and Michael's face a mirror of hers in their shelter.

Catherine pulled back the bedsheets, went to the window to pull aside the curtains. The day outside was grey and dreary, not raining but the light was the colour of ash, dirty and clinging to the pebble-dash walls, the gravel path in front of the drying green, the field beyond strung around with wire fencing enclosing the industrial estate, all of it seemingly coated in dust. She dressed herself quickly in her make-do morning clothes, plain oatmeal jumper, black slacks, what she'd worn last night really, and prepared to go into Cameron's room to waken him.

He wasn't there. He was in the living-room, dressed already in his school clothes, eating a sandwich he'd made himself, too much meat inside it, drinking from a tumbler filled with diluting orange. She said,

Did you not want me to do that, Cameron?

He was seated in his father's chair; the hearth was gawping at her, black and unlit, and she felt like a thoughtless mother. He looked down at the plate as he rested his sandwich on it, shook his head.

She went to the kitchen to make a pot of tea for him, sandwiches for the playground; but while she was filling the kettle, she heard the front door click gently shut, and when she went back through to the living-room, Cameron was gone. The plate was on the floor, with crumbs scattered on the china, a half of a sandwich with a bite removed; the glass stood beside it, a little orange syrup left at the bottom. She sat down on her chair, put her head in her hands, feeling the weight of it all of a sudden, and knew where the blame for this morning lay.

She bought all the groceries she could afford at the shops just beyond Cameron's school. They were contained in a bunker of a building hardly taller than the rooms in her house, divided evenly in quarters among a butcher's, a grocer's, a greengrocer's and a tobacconist's confectioner's newsagent's what-have-you shop. Each of them had a metal rafter set into the façade from which louvred rolls of steel could be drawn down at closing time, five-thirty, six or seven for the what-have-you shop. If you went past the building at night, when the shutters were locked securely in place, you'd think they were fortifying themselves against a siege, and there were names sprayed in black paint on the brick sides and the steel blinds; Davie A—, Andy B—, Kenny C—, along with strange fankled letters joined in a seal, m y t in capital letters, the valley of the m forming the battens of the y, the cross of the t struck through the y's upright. Catherine thought it looked like one of the television aerials you saw fixed to chimneys. The seal was the mark of a gang, that much Catherine did know, but she'd never seen them wandering the streets, even though she knew the shutters were there as a defence against them. The little guttersnipe who'd planted the seed of her father's filthy tongue in Cameron would likely be one of them, she thought, or it'd likely be his only ambition he had if he wasn't already; she'd warned Cameron to avoid him like a mad dog, and she could only hope he was heeding her. She looked at the school on the way past it, a net of glass around the grey sky, she wondered where inside it Cameron was, and hoped he was safe; thinking to herself, maybe he was safer there than at home, the way she was these days.

She approached the butcher's shop first; two old women were standing like pillars by the jambs of the glass door. The one facing her as she came into the shade looked at her over the other's shoulder, from gathered hair to the black leather shoes she'd put on to give pride to her walk; Catherine returned the look, from tied cotton headscarf the colour of dog mess, down the shapeless coat of grey flocked wool to the old boots of dull brown leather creased like your palm from too much flexing. When Catherine divided them to push open the door to the butcher's, the one she'd been facing said, cheeky wee tart, just as the smell of dead flesh, lard, drained blood came to meet her. She went in and bought what she needed for the weekend coming; on her way out, she said,

Your manners are disgraceful, you spiteful owl besom.

Catherine kept her eyes firmly to the front once she'd passed them, wouldn't look behind her. She heard the old boots clapping on the paving, the screech of the voice.

Disrespectful wee slut! Huv ye nae respect for yir elders? Did ye no hear that, manners fae a painted Jezebel lik yon, I'll no be spoken tay like that!

Catherine just uttered a laugh like a butcher's hook that twisted into the old wife's carcass and dragged her to the door of the grocer's where she stood glowering outside until Catherine had bought what she needed, and then left as Catherine went to the door, pulling sour cheese and the game smell of cooked meats with her, and she was nowhere to be seen by the time Catherine emerged into the cold.

Catherine didn't think anything of the seated figure on the steps when she turned into the path towards the close, until she went nearer. She had all her messages in an expanding net bag, heavy to carry; but she'd been calmed by the journey and its reminder of the mechanical pleasure of walking. She'd hardly been out of the house for any other purpose since the funeral, and it was good the cold of the air, the heels on her shoes causing a pull on her calves; there were days she wondered what power kept her in existence, she couldn't sense the physicality in herself, the draw of muscles, the flow of blood. She'd been trying to remember when she'd last got out of the house to test herself in the world, not just for the shopping, when she came to the path, saw the girl on the steps, smoking a cigarette which was long enough just to have been newly lit. She dressed young, like a schoolgirl, a truant dodging a particularly dismal class, and she was bowed over her legs, resting her arms on her knees; looked sullenly up at Catherine as if she'd been the teacher sent to fetch her back. There was a deeper blackness in the close that fell over her like a cloak, which was why Catherine didn't see the bruise on her face until she went nearer; not long given to her, by the way it appeared beetroot red around her eye, extending to her cheek and the line of her jaw, no blood though. Either she'd been crying or it was fluid seeping from her nearly closed eye; and when she saw that Catherine had slowed to look more closely, she turned her head away, ashamed of her injury. Catherine wondered if she was suffering confusion after the punishment she'd taken; but the girl took a suck at her cigarette, said,

Did ye pey the man at the front for a fucken ticket? It's wan and six for a good look.

She seemed alert enough; Catherine stopped by the front step, unable to climb past without finding out if she was all right. It wasn't curiosity, not the curiosity she was being accused of, at any rate.

Are you the girl that lives upstairs?

The girl raised a hand, a shutter drawn across her face.

Whit fucken business is it ey yours?

It was said quietly, but it was savage enough, enough to make Catherine ask herself what she thought she was doing, what help she imagined she'd be able to offer. Her father's face came into her head suddenly, teeth bared like a dog's.

I hear you and your man dancing sometimes.

The end of the cigarette fired, smoke came streaming into the wind, was thrown over her like a shawl. There was a tremor along her arm as her hand became less steady by the side of her face.

Whit's that mean, dancin?

I mean, dancing but no music playing.

The girl forced air through her nose, drew it all back, dropped the partition of her hand to wipe it away.

Fuck aff, ya big hoor. Leave us alane.

Catherine shook her head, dragged her hair back over her shoulder.

I was called the same thing by a woman six times your age at the shops. Well, nearly the same thing. Is it just my day for meeting folk with no manners, or is it something about me?

The girl looked up sharply; you could see the blood was beginning to darken already, swelling the eyelid, fattening the cheek.

Mebbe it's yir claes, missis. Mebbe it's a' the war peynt ye've on. Like fucken Sittin Bull.

Catherine laughed. The girl stared viciously at her.

Whit's so funny?

Because my husband and me, we used to call you Cassius Clay and Joe Louis.

The girl looked away from Catherine, not even bothering to disguise her injuries any longer.

Aye, ye're a fucken comedian right enough, missis. Away on tay a steyge n tell it.

Catherine put down her bag, resting it against the step. She sat down beside the girl, making sure her just-in-case raincoat was billowed out behind her so she settled on it, sooner than have her blue dress ruined in the dust; turned her head to look at the girl from the same height. The girl was wearing a pair of black high-heeled shoes like her own; Catherine held out her leg so that their shoes touched at the side, to compare them; the girl spun her head around, looked down to where Catherine was looking.

At least we shop in the same place, said Catherine, see that? You have good taste in clothes.

Aye, said the girl, that r the same rotten taste.

The girl had copper hair drawn back over her scalp, with filaments combed forward in a fringe. She pulled her leg back, separating herself from Catherine; made dirty by the miserable day, like all the buildings, like Catherine herself. Her cigarette was burnt down to the filter; she took a final drag on it, then dropped it under her foot, the same one Catherine had used for comparison, and crushed the stub vehemently. Her packet of cigarettes and a box of matches rested on the lap of her skirt; she picked it up, pushed out the drawer and took another fag out of it, put the filter between her lips, on the side that wasn't rising like dough. Without looking at Catherine, she held the packet out to her; Catherine raised a hand,

No thank you, she said, I don't.

The girl slid the packet closed, put it back on her lap.

Might ey fucken known ye widny.

She took a match from the box, stroked it along the glass paper away from herself; there was the rotten stink of sulphur, the flame springing uncertainly to life and wriggling like a fish. She made a windbreak out of her free hand, fired the end of the cigarette; once it had caught she threw the match away from herself, down the path, where the breeze snuffed it before it landed on the concrete paving. This close to her, Catherine could smell the smoke off her clothes, as thick as if it was herself burning. Catherine said,

My father was drunk when he beat me. He was drunk most nights.

The girl let the smoke from her fag wander in her mouth before she breathed it out; the wind changed direction, tugged the waste along the path, thinned it out, dispersed it.

Dis yir man no gie ye a baytin?

He died recently. But I wouldn't've married him if I thought he would.

Soarry. Didny know.

Catherine shrugged, to show there was no need for being sorry. The girl milked the cigarette again, tried to blow the smoke away from Catherine.

Ye widny merry ony man if ye thoat he'd gie ye a baytn. Flooers

85

afore and fucken Cassius Clay efter. Yir ma widny've married yir da if she'd known, wid she?

Catherine couldn't remember blaming her mother for her bad judging of a man, for allowing herself to be so easy fooled. She wondered if her mammy had ever blamed herself, if she'd confessed her sin of stupidity to Father Byrne.

Is it just when he drinks?

The girl held her arm over her stomach, and Catherine wondered if he'd hit her there.

Whn he drinks. Whn he's fuckt aff wi his life. Whn he's fuckt aff wi me. Whn he's fuckt aff we've nae money tay day nothn. No every day, I'm sayn. Noo and then, jist, no jist efter he's been drinkin.

Catherine thought, at least her da had only been like that with the whisky, the frustration towering in him until they were all too small to be noticed. She was biting down on her annoyance with the girl using her father's word as easily as God bless you, but she was allowing for circumstances.

Have you somewhere to go?

The girl plunged a hand into her hair, smoothed it back, ploughing it with her fingers.

Naewhere he couldny catch up wi me.

She turned to look at Catherine, threatening to smile, except her face was going rigid with the swelling.

I'm no so bad wi make-up mysel, she said. Christ knows I've hud the practice.

They exchanged names; she was Bernadette, and Catherine thought it was an innocent name, a name for a wee girl and you'd never think she'd grow up with it; she had a quality Catherine remembered in herself from years ago, the capacity to be surprised by the world. Catherine said,

Have you seen The Song of Bernadette?

Bernadette shook her head.

Whit is it?

It's a film about a girl who becomes a saint because she saw the Virgin Mary in a grotto. It's supposed to have happened in France, place called Lourdes. People go there to get healed if they've an illness.

Bernadette fixed her good eye on Catherine.

86

You're no a virgin, but. You've goat a wean.

Catherine smiled for both of them.

I never said I was the Virgin Mary.

Bernadette leaned close to Catherine's ear, as if afraid the wind would trail her words away like the smoke her fag was spinning.

Waant tay hear a secret? she said. I'm no wan neether. Jist that wan ey us canny have weans.

She leaned back so that Catherine could survey her as one woman to another. Her good eye was open wide; the other one was open as far as the limits of the swollen lids would allow. Catherine had to make an effort not to stare at the bad eye, darkening to a plum colour, seeping clear juice. Maybe she was trying to shock Catherine with how open she was being about it; but there was no challenge in her, she was as sullen as she'd been at the beginning. Bernadette's free hand was at the back of her head, spooling her hair around her finger like a length of copper wire. She was holding the link open to Catherine, inviting her to fasten to it, and Catherine wondered if this was the right time for a suggestion; she pressed her hands together in front of her, said,

I left home because of my father. You just have to be determined, Bernadette. I just packed a bag and went somewhere he couldn't touch me.

Bernadette changed like the wind in the close.

Ye left yir da, she said, no yir man.

I'd've left my man, if he'd hit me even once.

Bernadette pressed her hand flat against the top step, twisted herself so the leverage drew her to her feet, balanced awkwardly on her high heels.

Aye, ye're sayn that noo, efter he's deid. Whit's up, hen, ye jealous cause I've goat a fucken man?

Catherine pushed herself upright off the step to bring them level, said no, it wasn't true; but Bernadette was murderous by now, and she pointed the ember of the fag towards Catherine, so close she could feel the heat of it against her skin.

Ya fucken bitch, she raged, ye're jist no waantn tay be the only wan auld and no wi a man.

She spun on the point of her heel and rattled into the close, to the stairs, went up cautiously, leaving smoke behind her. Catherine quickly reached down to take up her net bag, called on her to wait, but there was a chiming of keys, a latch thrown, and then a scream, ya fucken bitch, tearing through the close, the door shutting with an explosion that Catherine felt under the soles of her shoes, like a gas main going off in the distance.

All the rest of the afternoon, Catherine heard Bernadette stumping from room to room above her. It could've been thoughtlessness, or it could've been spite, now she knew Catherine could track the arguments above her by the feet. There was only one good thing about her meeting with Bernadette, and that was that Catherine was now thinking of the advice she'd given, how you should always run from a beating, and she felt like a hypocrite after the night before, after Cameron had left her in silence. Catherine undressed herself in her room, and then set about her face with the cleansing milk, knowing she'd soon have to start on Cameron's dinner; by the time she was her morning self again, she knew what she'd have to do to make it less of a performance she'd given outside, remembering what Francis had said about saying a thing and meaning it, and the next place she went was to the table in the front room, the telephone, to give Agnes a ring.

Cameron was still silent and circumspect around her after he came home from school, even when she approached to kiss him on the forehead; he shrank away from her, and this convinced her more that what she'd arranged for him was right. She'd made a favourite dinner of his, one of her stews costing her the last of the money in the house, as an apology to him, but it was worth it to see him shine for a moment when he caught the smell of it on the air.

Across the unfolded dinner table, she watched the wee one digging at his plate, and wondered if he could ever become inured to her tempers the way she had to her father's. She was crushed in a fist of misery, but she smiled over at him when he looked up to show her he was enjoying it, hoped he was forgiving her; thought, he never would again once she'd told him what all this sweetening was for. All kinds of things had turned around in her head after she'd made the call to Agnes; why she'd never been so hard on him with Francis there, not even when he came in on them when they were in bed together; she'd thought, he was wee and curious, had heard hurting sounds and wanted to know what they were about. She saw all the gentleness in Cameron that he'd learned from his father, enough to oppose what she hated most in her own blood, the quietness, how he could look as if he'd been caught in a maze in his own head, all the things she'd loved in his father because they were so unlike her. But she was beginning to lose Francis's shape, and there were only clues left that he'd ever been there at all; the depression in his chair, the width of the bed she no longer needed for herself, and she could hardly imagine him any more except as he was incarnated in Cameron, the wee one polluted by her flesh and her failings, and she saw more clearly than before how she was punishing herself for surviving in Cameron as well, and it was hardly Cameron's fault she was drifting.

She promised herself to go up and see Bernadette during a quiet afternoon, to make apologies for her meddling; for trying to take the mote out of her eye.

After they were finished the stew, Catherine made two cups of tea and loaded a plate with chocolate biscuits; more sweetening, she thought guiltily, brought them through, sat opposite him while he ate and drank; three biscuits he had before he said he'd had enough. He wanted her to eat the rest, but there was a sourness on her tongue, and nothing would cleanse it away. She remembered her mammy slaughtering chickens for the pot; a swift turn of the wrists and the neck would hang like rope, the head drawing it down like a plumb-line, and the chicken was still fluttering as if it needed to be told of its own death. She said quickly,

I was on the phone to your Uncle Danny and Aunt Agnes today. How'd you like to stay for a while at their place?

She put all kinds of adventure into the sound of it; trips to the zoo, picnics, days by the sea. There was a frown on him, an equals sign ruled across his forehead.

Where would I go to school?

You can go to a school near your aunt and uncle. You'll be well away from that boy that made you say the bad word. There'll be lots of new children to meet.

Her mammy had always sounded optimistic, talking about silver linings even as she was sweeping up the glitter of her father's messes, until Kate was old enough, when she was the one steering the broom. She heard the same tone in her own voice just then, wondered if Cameron was believing her; she'd never believed her mammy. Cameron's arms were tight against his sides and lodged against the cushions, locking him into the seat.

I'll take you to their place on Sunday night. There's a few days to go yet.

He looked at her like a dog with a temperamental master, was he to be fed next, petted, hit, sent away, he could never be sure.

Can I take my toys with me?

She said of course he could, all the toys he wanted, and they'd always be here if he'd forgotten any. The fire was burning down to a rim of gold over the ash, she noticed, and a look in the scuttle told her she'd have to be going to the bunker outside soon to fetch some more in.

Why am I going away?

She went over beside his chair, knelt so she was at a level with him; tried to answer him as fully as she did the night he walked in on her and Francis. She told him that grown-ups needed time by themselves for a while after the death of someone they loved very dearly, and that sometimes this could be hardest for others they loved just as much; made sure he'd understood that he wasn't being abandoned, that he was the one she loved now. She didn't tell him about her fears; how she wanted to tear his grandfather out of him by the roots; how she was afraid of the blood in her, how afraid she was for him, that she might rage out of control and hurt him. She heard it in herself while her mouth made the shapes of other words. The effort of separating the truths made her weary by the end of it; she leaned back on her heels, remembering the last time she'd leaned this close to him, wondering if he was trusting her now. He said,

My teacher gave us homework to do.

The satchel was leaning against the seat; he picked it up and unclipped its leather mouth. He put an arithmetic book on the table, beside it his school jotter, beside that his pencil, sharpened to a point; then he opened all the books and began to copy answers into the jotter, the pencil scraping against the paper.

Catherine's cup of tea was cold, and she put it on the end of the mantelpiece. She thought, Francis would've known she was right, but as she sat down in her chair, she realized that she'd no clear picture of Francis to call on, as she sat across the width of the hearth from where he'd been accustomed to sitting. She was thinking she'd have to pay a visit to the cemetery to recover the memory of him; and she made a promise to herself, that she'd do it soon, and it wouldn't be one of her father's promises of glass broken after a fall off the mantel; she might even bring Cameron with her, so they could remember him together, although it could wait until he'd settled in with Agnes and Daniel, a while, maybe.

Five

Catherine first saw Gianfranco through the window of his café. She'd gone on one of her walks to the shops, and before she'd known it she was far away, with no mind to go back home. The house had folded around her for weeks after Cameron left; the television was gone, taken back after she couldn't afford the rental, and the truth was she didn't miss it, except for its pretence of company, voices around her. On the day she went as far as Garibaldi's Café, she dressed for the biddies at the shops in case they were there again, made herself into what they thought of her; dressed the way she'd've done for Francis if they'd been going to the dancing, all for the sake of a cube of all she could afford of cheese and a few thin slices of cold meat, and bread of course.

Maybe she'd walked to find them, those old women in their dowdies, to be an offence to their sight; maybe it was escape, because for weeks she'd heard feet about the house, not from upstairs but definitely on the floors. For a while she thought it might be Cameron's pattering on the carpets, she'd be ready to find him coming through the door to the living-room and she'd make a great mothering fuss and prepare his tea for him; then she'd remember, put on the radio and listen to nonsense, a trickle of songs she could hardly bear. She had nothing in to eat; that prised her out of the house, the walls were just a shell around her, the barest protection. She dressed in front of the mirror, something special and confectionery, wine-coloured pretend silk with a plunge to it. She made her face up, one she'd copied from memory again, a woman she'd seen when she and Francis had been out dancing before Cameron's birth, before his conception even; skin smoothed by powder, rouged, she thought, fresh like the skin of a waxed fruit.

In the event, she'd no reason for wearing an outfit or a face like that, no sign of the old dears, she was a wee bit disappointed because she could've done with a fight to clean herself of the muck in her head; there, she thought, was why her feet wouldn't stop at the bunker of shops, carried her further.

She didn't know why she stopped at the café, what there was about it; cloud above her, the sun locked out as if it'd forgotten its keys, and two big slabs of light laid over the paving from the polished windows, it seemed cheerful, she went there like a moth to peer in the glass. She couldn't see herself in it, there was that much brightness beyond, but she saw a wean at the counter, and there was a tall man behind it, sculpting a globe of white ice-cream with a tool for the purpose, thumbing a trigger which released the ball into the wafer cone he held in the other hand. The boy was Cameron's age, was looking at the ice-cream as if it was the Host; the man tilted towards the boy over the counter, spoke to him, Catherine couldn't hear the words, but in response to what the boy said back the man reached under the counter and came up with a white plastic bottle capped with a red plastic funnel. The man upended the bottle with a theatrical gesture, you'd think he was conducting an orchestra the way he made a performance out of it, and drizzled thick red syrup the colour of one of Catherine's lipsticks generously over the dome of the ice-cream. She thought the boy must've been well mannered to be getting so much. He reached over the counter to hand the ice to the boy, who took it in one hand and gave over his change with the other; the man counted it by sight, turned to the till by the window and banked the money, and it was this movement that brought Catherine's eyes to the sign sellotaped to the pane in front of her. The sign was written in blue biro ink on plain white paper, but there was a border of asterisks around it, uniform in size and made by a fastidious hand, evenly spaced from each other, from the edge of the paper. Inside the box of stars was a notice in tilted block capitals: WANTED, ASSISTANT FOR DAY AND OCCASIONAL NIGHT

WORK IN BUSY CAFÉ, GOOD RATES PAID, MUST BE
PLEASANT AND HARD-WORKING, APPLY WITHIN.
Catherine found herself liking the look of the hand that had written
the letters, strong enough to impress on the paper. She wondered if
it was the man who was waving to the wean as he left the shop
dipping the point of his tongue into the glaze of syrup and the ice
beneath. He went to the far corner of the counter, ran water into a
steel basin, washed his hands clean for the next customer. She squinted
beyond the counter, to the seats and the narrow tables; pensioners
in the main, with papers and their cups of tea, quiet and placid-looking
like cattle out to grass. She thought it might've been the atmosphere
of the shop itself that was keeping them tranquil; it seemed peaceful
from the outside, and she felt a thirst about her all of a sudden, a
thirst she hadn't felt since she'd seen through the window, and she
wondered if it was only a thirst for tea that was drawing her inside.

Catherine went to one of the vacant tables, pulled out a cane chair
and sat on it, pulling her net shopping bag alongside her on the floor,
where it collapsed shapelessly against a chair leg. She was the youngest
person in the shop; it made her uncomfortable at first, like being in
a church not of your own faith, but she tilted her head up with a
pretended confidence, she'd be defiant about it at least. There was a
menu leaning against plastic sauce cruets shaped like ripe tomatoes,
red for ketchup and brown for brown sauce; glass pawns of salt and
pepper shakers, a bowl of white sugar. She lifted the menu, looked
at it; typed on white card, blemished by spills the colour of tea, bent
about the rim and dog-eared at the corners. It announced all kinds
of things she'd've expected in any café in town, fish and chips, sausage
and pie and egg and chips, buttered rolls filled with cold meats, bacon,
lorne sausage; but there was a doubled line separating all of it from
the specials, made by pressing the equals key from edge to edge of
the card. She'd no sooner read the word SPECIALS than she became
aware of warm garlic on the air, as if the aroma had sprung from
the words on the card, tagliatelle carbonara, spaghetti bolognese,
lasagne, penne in hot tomato sauce; she didn't recognize most of the
names of the dishes, but it was as if her tongue had always known
them. She ran a finger down the menu to the drinks at the bottom
under another doubled line; saw tea, coffee, more things she didn't

recognize, then cola and Irn-Bru, ice-cream floats with lemonade; it wasn't a cold-drink day, so she decided on tea, and put the menu flat on the table to show the man at the counter that she'd chosen. She spent a little time looking around herself, and from where she was seated, just in front of the half partition, she saw two old men in the corners, reading their newspapers. One of them had his opened and raised like a modesty screen so you could only see his fingers holding on to the edges; his arms must've been as wide apart as a fisherman describing his catch. Occasionally the hand nearest his cup of tea would let go and the paper would fall away from him, which seemed to make him nervous enough to sip quickly from the cup and then replace it, grasping the lowered end of the paper. Catherine watched him while his face was exposed; he was racked by tics about the eyes, fearful of discovery. The other preferred to read his paper in columns, folding it along the ruled lines and keeping a finger through the lug of his cup until it was time to find another strap of news, pleating it along to exclude other distracting items; his journey through the paper was a rearrangement of geometry, turning a creased page, making new folds, finding new priorities. She thought him obsessive just to look at him; neat in his dress, in a suit she thought he might even have been given for demob, polished as black and reflective as his boots, even the lenses of his spectacles were mirrors when he turned and the glint came to them of the fluorescent strip lights above.

The man from the counter was alongside her before she'd had the chance to turn and pretend she hadn't been that curious. He had a notebook in one hand and a pencil in the other, but he didn't seem to be hurried, or hurrying her. She liked the pattern of creases overwhelming his eyes, not yet folded or sunken, promising a jovial appearance in old age. He raised the needle of the pencil to wet it with the tip of his tongue, said,

I no see you here before, I need to write what you want here. What you want? Cappuccino, espresso, coffee? You want a special? Good fresh pasta dishes all the way from Italy, brought to town by the best cook in Tuscany? You want tea, a hot meal? I ready to write, you tell me you want.

He said it like a seduction, warmth and a genuine will to please. He was bent over the table the way she'd had to defer to Mrs Kilsyth in her time of service, but he wasn't just bent over by the lever of profit, or to catch sight of the purse in her bag, to see how fat it was. She said,

A cup of tea, please.

The man looked up from the pages of his notebook to her as if crushed by a thoughtless remark. Still courteous, he copied down the order, but he said,

Tea only. My Rosa, she will not be happy. She cook her specials over, you call it, hot stove, beautiful meals of home, every day we make dinner of them for ourselves, I take to her paper with tea, roll and this, fish and chip, I see her face, I know she is not happy.

Catherine tilted her head in sympathy, even offered him a smile in compensation, but she was having none of it.

Maybe another day.

The man separated his arms, breathed in slowly through his nose so the air whispered as he harvested it; he was like a man on a pier drawing in the purity of the sea, even closing his eyes in appreciation. It filled him like a sack until he was twice the bulk, and when he released the breath, he pulled his arms in front of him ready for writing once again, drugged by the fragrance, opening his eyes and staring at Catherine.

The beautiful aroma, he said, it no make you hungry, no make you think good food, no?

There was no doubt it did, but she had little money in her purse for the most expensive items on the menu. She was about to say so when a woman two tables in front of her, sitting with a paperback romance and a cup on its saucer, leaned forward against her table and said,

This you tryn tay sell yon foreign muck tay somedy else, Gianfranco?

The woman had black horn-rimmed spectacles with nearly oval lenses; from behind them she winked at Catherine and made a grimace of amusement, stirring the pot herself, pleased with the vapours from it. The man, Gianfranco, half turned to her, letting his arms drop by his side as if in despair, wiped the palm of his pencil hand on his apron; he smiled, taking no offence, but he wasn't prepared to let her be for that cheek.

Foreign muck, you say, Isa; what you call fish and chip, eh, boil in oil? Or the mince, eh, boil in water? Is good food, you say to me?

Isa went earnest as she put the book to one side on the table top, open like a roof at her page, leaned further in her seat to speak directly to Catherine. She had brown liver spots on the backs of her hands, like spilled tea not cleaned up. She was a genial witch with moles like black studs on her face. Catherine had seen farming women like her with outdoor faces shaped by exposure. She made a pointer out of her hand, tapped her finger against the veneer of the table; her claws ticked like a clock against it.

Ye jist don't know whit they're pittn in yon food, poison mebbe. It's no lik food ye get in yir ain country, ye know whit's gaun intay yon.

Gianfranco shook his head with pity, looked towards Catherine, threw his arms into the air, stared towards the ceiling as if directly into the eyes of God.

I too know what go into your food, he said. I know you, Isa, you no eat here but you eat roll and this, fish and chip, where you poison by the food of my country, eh? No here, for sure.

Isa winked at Catherine when Gianfranco was turned away, gave a perfect even smile, too regular to be anything other than false. Catherine wondered why she was tormenting Gianfranco; said,

Food isn't poison, you either like it or you don't, that's all.

Gianfranco smiled like the sun coming out, turned to Isa and held his arms towards Catherine as if she was there on display as the exhibit of a reasonable woman for the world to see and measure itself against. Isa's smile fell a little, but she said with determination,

We wereny fed oan a' this muck I canny even say, n we turned oot fine.

Gianfranco's smile didn't diminish as he turned back to Catherine, saying over his shoulder,

My daughters eat the food you no eat, they turn out fine. Maybe you eat the muck, you turn out more fine, eh Isa? I go for lady's tea now, fore you chase away my customers, eh?

The smile lasted to the curtain of ribbons at the back end of the shop, and he walked high and proud until the ribbons lashed together and claimed him into the darkness of the passage to the kitchen. Isa picked up her book from the table, and before she returned to it, she raised the cup from her saucer and took a silent drink from the rim with cracked old lips, then said to Catherine,

Mind, he makes an awffy good tea, but. N a rerr roll n sausage.

Catherine wondered how she could tell one shop's from another's, but she smiled anyway, letting Isa chase the words across the page with her pallid old eyes.

By the time Catherine had finished the good tea Gianfranco had brought her, she'd made another of her decisions, because her feet were dull, aching from the walking she'd done on raised heels. She took her purse from her bag, twisted the brass clasp of two beads leaning into one another; the mouth opened wide as if aghast at the needless spending she'd committed. She put a thrupenny bit under the shade of her saucer for Gianfranco to collect afterwards, then took out the coins she'd need and went to the counter, the heels clicking smartly on the tiling. Gianfranco took the money, pleased with how she'd stood up for him and smiling like a father to her, went to the till and came back with a penny change, dropping it into her palm. He said,

I hope you come back, no? Try our specials? You eat poison, I give refund, is fair, eh?

I was wondering if I could talk to you about your sign in the window.

Gianfranco regarded her as if he didn't understand, then his eyebrows went through the roof of his head. He nodded slowly, then went to the trap in the counter and lifted it, waved her to the seat she'd just left.

I think you want another cup of tea, what you say, on the house, eh? Then we talk together.

On the morning she started work at the café, Gianfranco took Catherine through all the things she'd need to know immediately about serving behind the counter. He stood in front of her with his feet a little apart, his arms held behind him; he looked immaculate, from the hard shine of his boots to the white apron starched just enough so you'd think it was paper, the collar of his shirt pointed like scalpels. Above that came his face, not as severe as to give his tone too much authority; she didn't feel like she was a child with her teacher, nor even an employee with her employer, warmer than that. He was clean-shaven, almost ridiculously so, not a spine of growth or beard on him, and his warm dark eyes, the colour of melting chocolate, drew Catherine to him, held her as if you could see the words etched on the pupils before he spoke them. She was leaning against the trap leading out to the café's avenue of tables before it spilled into what Gianfranco called the piazza, where the ironing-board-wide tables pointed from their fixtures in the wall towards each other. Catherine looked over her shoulder before Gianfranco began his training proper; the partition running behind her, closing the counter around her, didn't mate with the partition extending from the wall opposite, gave her a sight of the tables diagonally opposite her, towards the far wall of the piazza. She thought it might've been a house before, with a dado rail separating terracotta tiling from a wallpaper textured with fleurs-de-lys and glazed like earthenware pottery, and there were long mirrors in wooden frames carved with oak leaves, with frosted borders for bevels. She wasn't certain, because this would've been an odd shape for a room, but she resolved to ask Gianfranco about it later.

He waited for her to bring her eyes to the front, until she was giving him her complete attention. There was a bit of theatre about his manner and movements; he liked to be heard. Catherine pushed herself off the trap and stood upright, feet self-consciously together, and she put her hands behind her too, so he wouldn't see her fingers writhing like worms in apprehension. He began the lesson.

Now I take you through the café like I see her, you understand the meaning of her with me. You ready?

Catherine gave him a quick nod, the way Cameron used to whenever his father was explaining things to him, to let him know he was understanding. Gianfranco smiled, teeth like too many passengers crowded into a bus.

Bene. Good. I tell you now, I think of my café in three, like the trinity, the Holy Trinity; I no have Father, Son, Holy Ghost; I have back, middle, here, the front. The back is the kitchen, I call Inferno. You know why I call Inferno?

Catherine shook her head, and Gianfranco took up the motion, shaking his head to the same time as her.

I no think so. Inferno is you call it hell, you hear of Dante, no? La Divina Commedia? No? Inferno is hell, folk punish for their sins by God, pride, envy, lust, they are punish like for what they do wrong in life after they die, you see? Rosa and me, we are condemn for what we do not know to go to cooker, go to fish fry, go to chip fry, wash the dish, cut the chip, all this, all that, and it is as hot as Inferno when, you know, when you busy, like the world want eat.

Catherine had seen the open doorway in the far wall of the piazza when she'd arrived, with a curtain of red ribbons tasting the currents of delicious air which were the breath of Inferno; darkness beyond the curtain, slices of light along the passage. She nodded; she was trying not to laugh at Gianfranco's earnest, tortured face as he described the hell of the work. Next he brought his arm out to indicate the piazza, the table in front of the counter, said,

The middle, here you see, I call Purgatory. We serve, you call it, lost souls, they come for our heat, read the paper, we are all they have, their children go from them, they have only time, you know? They our best customers, we respect them for how long they live and know things, you understand? Bene. Good. No just old we serve; weans, you call it, they like the gelato, the ice-cream, raspberry sauce on it and all things; couples, they go maybe to cinema, come here before, like sweet things together, you know they like, eh? We give all folk respect, weans, they are what is to come, and couples, they make what is to come, you know?

She looked around Gianfranco's Purgatory, then at him; his face gone mischievous as if his last thought had stayed with him too long, and she smiled to catch him with it like a boy with horse chestnuts hidden behind his back. He didn't seem the least bit concerned, went on,

Here, where you are now, I call Paradise. Here, from here, come the sweetness in my café.

It wasn't hard to see where the sweetness was coming from; boilings and candies on shelves, in glass jars like pills in an old pharmacy rising to the ceiling; chocolate bars on a shallow tilted arrangement to the front of the counter; two metal lids like the kind you saw on dustbins covering a pair of churns holding clouds of feathery ice-cream, mist spilling over the rims when Gianfranco doffed their hats to show her what was inside.

But this, he said, it make this Paradise, I think,

and he turned her around to show her the industrial bulk of the Gaggia thundering away to itself in the corner against the partition. She'd seen her mother slaughtering chickens for the pot, the cords of intestines uncoiling on to the table, springs held clasped in the cavities she exposed; like that, chrome guts spun into monstrous shapes, pipes here and pipes there, and chrome silver around the cylinder, crushing your reflection like a fairground mirror. He showed her how to work it to make the coffee he called cappuccino; he had a can of Lavazza from which he spooned a mound of dark grains into a small pan with more handle than basin, packed the coffee in level with the belly of the spoon. He showed her what he called the altar, a recess in the body of the machine with pipes and outlets on its ceiling, showed her the place where the pan was locked with a twist of the handle, flanges on the rim of the pan marrying with gaps in a steel circle. He pointed out the switches and then took a white ceramic jug filled with water and poured it into a hopper above the pan he'd just made secure; told her the difference between espresso and ordinary coffee, like what you call it, atom bomb and grenade, little cup with much power, bigger cup not so much power, you know? Catherine nodded through his teaching; it was most of it straightforward, though she felt more like a mechanic than a waitress when he encouraged her to take the pan for herself, unlock it from the altar and then return it just as he'd shown her, like this? she said, and bene, he replied, good. She felt the heat of the cylinder against her skin, and then she understood, it was a small boiler, like the one in her cupboard at home only without the jacket of glass fibre and canvas, more like an overfed kettle. He gave her a cup from a pillar of them by the side of the Gaggia, made to fit one inside the other, nodded that she should put it on the drainage mesh on the floor of the altar under the pan, pointed to the lever switch. She reached for it as if she was expecting it to reject her with heat; it was warm to the tips of her fingers, nothing more, and it snapped when she closed it. She was aware of Gianfranco staring at her, and she knew without turning to look he was smiling at the timid way she approached the machine.

It cleared its throat at her, retching and hawking the liquid into the cup. Gianfranco's laughter at the look on her face was as warm as the coffee, but it made her feel all the worse for being such a wean about it.

The smell of hot coffee from a thing like a gasworks, it was a bit of a miracle, and Catherine covered her fear of it by watching the coffee drooling from the hole in the pan into the cup, the steam tangling around the apparatus. Someday she'd learn not to come to it like a child to fire in the grate, but that would take a while. Gianfranco said,

You see? You make your first cappuccino, easy like pie. The next, easy, eh?

Last of all he showed her how you took the milk at the end of the jug and held it on to the rosette at the tip of a long spout above the altar to scald it to froth, pouring it on top of the cappuccino; gave her a shaker of powdered chocolate and told her to shower it over the foam. When she was finished, he took the cup from the altar and held it in front of her, like a wee sacrament.

Like soufflé, eh? he said. Drink, and I open the café, you see why I call this Paradise.

He raised the trap, went around the counter to the front door, where he turned the sign from closed to open on its hook. Catherine sipped the cappuccino; sweetened by the milk but with the coffee's bitterness; the foam with its chocolate dust light as web, surprising at the end. It wasn't anything like the ditchwater she'd drunk in any of the oily cafés she'd been in when she first came here; it was a true pleasure, pressed from the angry machine like juice, and she found herself enjoying the taste.

After the door was unlocked and Gianfranco had returned the keys to his trouser pocket, he went over to the open trap and closed the counter around her. He smiled,

You grow moustache, Catherine?

She felt the foam crackling above her lip, wiped it away with the point of her tongue. She'd forgotten what it was like to work for someone after so long of being wedded to the home as well as to Francis. Gianfranco couldn't've been less like Mrs Kilsyth, which was no bad thing, and it was a good start she'd had with him. She was still cautious, though, even after such a beginning, or maybe because of it; she could hardly point to a single thing in her life that hadn't been ruined, and if there was one thing she'd learned it was that no one or nothing ever disappointed you to begin with.

They employed her because Beatrice, Gianfranco said it bay a treechi, and Francesca couldn't be as much of a help to them as before, on account of their schooling, and Gianfranco had to carve time out of his work to pick them up from their convent schools at different parts of town. They did their homework whenever they arrived home, and when they were done with that and dinner, usually eating what was left of Rosa's uneaten specials, they were allowed to help at the counter, taking orders, bringing meals to the customers. Each of the two girls had deadly eyes, Rosa's and not their father's; in their working pinnies they were like dolls modelled on Rosa, except that Beatrice was the dumpling of the two, heavier made, so was more like Rosa than her sister was. Rosa coddled her more than her elder sister; sometimes Catherine would be coming into the Inferno with an order from a table, ready to spike it on the board next to the entrance, and see Rosa feeding ripe sauces to Beatrice from the end of the wooden spoon, Beatrice eating like a wean, saying what Catherine didn't know, liking it obviously; Rosa had little English, knew please and thank you and little else, and Beatrice knew her mother's tongue at least as well as it was another birth tongue for her. Maybe, Catherine thought, it was to do with the difference in ages between the girls; Francesca was in the big school a couple of years now, knew how to poke a stick at her wee sister and make her wriggle in front of strangers, but Beatrice looked the more indulged, though you wouldn't say excessively so.

After Gianfranco had introduced them to the new counter assistant, the two had a good look up and down at her, until they were satisfied. Next they examined her uniform, the same as theirs only bigger; Catherine wanted them so much to trust her. From the first evening she met them, it was plain they had very different temperaments; Beatrice was more cautious and analytical, Catherine was a stranger to her until she'd proven herself, and especially whenever she went near Beatrice's toy, the Gaggia. I'll do that, Kate, said Beatrice when a young couple came in for a cappuccino; she dragged the library step used for reaching the topmost of the sweet jars over to the Gaggia, and when Catherine said, mind yourself, Beatrice, it's burny, she turned on her and stared as if what a curious article this adult was, and then she went serious while she unlocked the cappuccino pan, filled it with coffee, locked it again, poured water into the hopper, threw the switch, scalded the milk, topped the cappuccino with it and sprinkled it with chocolate. She raised the cup to let Catherine see, then handed it over to her so she could take it to the woman in the corner, and started on the second cup; Catherine smiled to one side of her mouth, and said, all right, Beatrice, I'm new here, remember, and she was warm after that acknowledgement, if not completely trusting.

It was through Francesca that she first came to know Beatrice; the older girl loved to make her wee sister red as the end of a match, but she spoke to Catherine as boldly as one woman to another. She preferred the first school she'd been to, she said to Catherine, because there'd been boys there, and she brushed the air with her lashes as she said it. Catherine watched the way she played with the fringes of her pinny, rubbing the nylon between thumb and forefinger as if it was silk; she seemed brilliantly aware of textures and surfaces, arranged herself about them as if to be photographed. Catherine remembered her days of that kind of confidence, she'd never felt it in the bone, but she'd worn it with her clothing, her faces; this one's confidence was like the blood in her, never a matter of doubt. Whenever she spoke about boys, Catherine heard a tired breath behind her; Beatrice, fed up of hearing about boys from her sister, let out occasional impatient hisses like a punctured ball, and you could see it was irritating Francesca, there she was giving all the wisdom she had wrapped up in bows and Beatrice was throwing it to one side without even glancing at the label on the box. Finally the older girl stood upright and cruelty came to her face, she said, tell Kate about that boy you want to kiss in your class in school, what's his name again? Brian Donnelly is it? Catherine had never seen the like before; Beatrice leapt off the library steps and scurried over to the older girl, making one hand into a fist and swinging it around straight as a hammer, dunting her sister on the shoulder once, twice, three times. Francesca leapt back, but she wasn't defending herself, she was laughing at what she'd provoked, and at last the wee one turned to Catherine and said, don't you listen to her, Kate, I don't want to kiss anybody, I hate boys. She spun back to her sister, said with vehemence, anyway, you're the one that's boy daft, all those pictures on the wall, you'd like to kiss them and you've never even met them. Francesca said, what do you know, I like their music, I don't want to kiss them, and Catherine smiled at how the wee one had made her sister lose her poise, fold up as awkwardly as a deckchair, all juts and bends in the wrong places. At last Beatrice turned back to Catherine, she thinks everyone's daft on boys like herself, Kate, and then she gave a wee smile, and after that Catherine was trusted; Catherine let her run the Gaggia machine until it was time for her bed, about nine o'clock, and it was a few weeks before Beatrice told her about the boy she liked, Brian Donnelly, when Francesca was busy at a table, trusting her the more for not hurrying it out of her, or humiliating her like Francesca.

Francesca could never stand the Gaggia, bright satanic thing in the corner, squatted there like a creature contented with its place; she could operate it well enough, but she never trusted it; Catherine could tell from the way she twisted her face around whenever it made its spitting and farting. Her preference was for the ice-cream in its churn, she could make it obedient where Beatrice could make nothing but a slavering white mess whenever she was called upon to help with it. Francesca made cones with the scoop, coddling a ball of the ice-cream into the socket of the wafer. She made what Catherine learned to call an oyster, filling a scalloped half-shell of wafer with a pearl of ice-cream and then closing another half shell over it. She made wafers with another tool that reminded Catherine of a brickie's hod, with shallow steel walls that shut around the oblong wafer; there was a spatula you took the ice-cream out of the churn with, the stuff was the texture of butter and you smeared it into the hod on top of the wafer, levelled it with the walls and then placed another wafer on top to make a sandwich, and then you pulled a trigger to open the trap around it after you'd finished. Francesca was the best of them at that.

One day when the girls were away at their schooling, Gianfranco told Catherine what he thought each of them would do when they became older. Francesca, he said, I see her with gelato, I think she good with her hands, she will make things. Beatrice, I show her how you do with machine, she know after, she do it no help, I think she work by brain, you say, eh? Catherine smiled, told him about her son for the first time, how Cameron used to play with his model rockets, of his cardboard city of boxes, and she'd wondered like Gianfranco what dreams and ambitions were collecting in his head for later. Gianfranco's brows raised, and he said, you no say you have a boy, Catherine, you bring him, I give him ice-cream, he meet my girls, eh? but Catherine said, he's staying with his aunt and uncle for a while, Gianfranco, but if he can make it, certainly. He went solemn, then shrugged and said, I ask no more, Catherine, you no tell, you no here for me to, what you say, to pry.

Catherine would've preferred Gianfranco's harshest judgement to his understanding just then, but he didn't have it in him; judgement was for God, he said, not man, but she'd wished he could've assumed God's burden there and then, punished her for her weakness with his condemnation. She promised herself to take Cameron to the café for one of Gianfranco's excessive knickerbocker glories, one day when she'd the money, and promised herself it wouldn't go the way of her other avowal, to go to the cemetery to visit Francis's grave, another promise that had as yet gone unfulfilled.

Gianfranco gave her that great beam of a smile of his when she said she'd use her Sunday off to visit Cameron; he approved of families and closeness, lamented the death of his mother almost daily to her, mama she say this, mama she say that, until Catherine thought she knew his mother better than she did his wife. He seemed to be trying to encourage her to tell more of her family by telling her more of his own, like turning over the first card in a game of snap, the game would make no sense if she didn't follow suit, though of course he'd never what you call it pry, but she could be subtle herself if need be. She wondered if he knew she'd use her day off for just that, if this was another opening he was providing for her, but she thought it was a lonely woman like herself who'd think others could be that intricate in their deceptions, and she prepared for her Sunday by considering how best to approach it.

On the day, she made breakfast for herself, planks of bacon, a bright egg fried in the bacon grease, toast, a cup of tea. She burst the blister of the yolk the way she'd always done since she was a girl with the tines of the fork before eating it; watching the gold swelling from her injury. She'd made these Sunday breakfasts for Francis and Cameron, how you made the day different from any other in the week when it hadn't any other significance for you, and yet she couldn't help but think of Sunday as a day apart. Francis always suggested they use the day by going to the park opposite Cameron's school, or the zoo, or the Botanic Gardens, so Cameron could see creation without the intervention of God, and the wee one was filled with questions, like a trick beaker of milk that never emptied. There were many of the places closed for the Sunday, though, closed by the kind of folk who'd call the day the Sabbath; many a plan had to be changed for that reason, but there was enough nature around them, in the field out the back of the house, down the road from the estate if you walked far enough and it hadn't been engulfed by development. Catherine never knew any of the answers to Cameron's questions, unless it was an answer she'd been told by Michael; it was almost as if he was asking for two, on her behalf as well, and Francis was swollen with his book knowledge, with museums as his cathedrals, his places of worship. They'd be walking in the park and he'd say, see, wee man, seeds're made by ither flooers, lik we made you, ye know? Remember? There's a male n a female wan, the male wan makes pollen tay blaw in the wind, n the female wan catches it n makes seeds; that's whit ye ca' fertilizin. Or if they were in the zoo, he'd be severe if the wee one laughed at the monkeys capering around in their cages, because it was like laughing at yourself, and he'd tell the story of how they came to be us. Catherine couldn't see it herself at first; they were beasts with the promising intelligence of weans in their eyes, and surely their resemblance to men could only be coincidental; but Francis told her of skeletons they'd found across the world of creatures that stood like men and women but with heads neither human nor beast. Cameron listened with his eyes as wide as the monkeys', utter belief in his father shining in them, so that it was only for Catherine that he had to spell it out. If there wisny a Goad, he said, then there wisny Adam r Eve, n if there wisny Adam r Eve, whit wis there? If ye cut oot a Goad, a' ye're left wi is the bones, they're yir right story, no Adam r Eve r yir Genesis. He was the one who changed her sight of creation; the books came out of the library as much for her as for the wee one, with their pictures of thick-featured animals bowed over with the weight of their bestiality, altering form and adopting a more dignified carriage along the progression of years until they were as light on their feet and as upright as dancers. The more she read of it, the more it made sense to her; you needed to crush God in your hand before this kind of revelation came, because if you didn't you were thinking like a carpenter who saw tables and door lintels and wardrobes and thought of craftsmen, not trees with the roots fankled in the ground, or raw wood. Francis was the one who rinsed the last of God out of her, something that might've silted up into a dense kind of belief in years to come, and the knowledge he gave her was meaningful to her, and she'd had experience of the animal that hid under the clothes of these upright men; it was an explanation for her father, and now, more guiltily she was thinking with Francis gone, for herself as well, as her father's daughter.

Catherine finished her breakfast, washed the dish and the cutlery at the sink, went through to her bedroom. She made a demure face for herself in the mirror, memorized from a woman on her way to church, pale, not looking for attention, a powdered complexion like set honey. She took the dress from the wardrobe she'd worn on the day Francis came back from hospital, wondered if Cameron would recognize it. She arched herself to grasp the tab of the zip behind her, pulled to seal herself in, remembering Cameron had done that for her last time it'd been worn; gave her hair a last brush, tugging on the length of it until the quills of the brush went smoothly through. When she was finished, she turned this way and that to examine the final effect; she was ready, no more reason for her to wait in the house any longer, so she gathered up a handbag of pretend black leather, dropped her purse inside, closed it and went into the wardrobe to find a proper coat for a cold day early in winter.

*

On the bus journey to Agnes and Daniel's, Catherine stared out of the window with her bag on her lap, her hands laced over it; as much as she hated the smoke, she always sat in the upper deck for the view out, at the front if there was a free seat for her, which there was today, with not many folk travelling on the Sunday. She was feeling stronger and more capable already; her thoughts of Francis were keepsakes you wrapped in cloth and stored in the attic, and she could open these thoughts safely now. He'd never approve of a thought like this, of course, but she could almost feel his approval behind her, knowing she was going to see Cameron. He was with her on the journey, which she saw through the front window, looking down on the pedestrians tramping the quiet streets. Buildings flitted past, tall on either side of her; constructed from sandstone, they seemed to have been carved out of black rock. Francis had told her the natural colour of the stones was blond, like compressed gold dust, and he showed her when they found that a black scab had fallen away from one of the buildings on their walk, rubbing the clean wound and coming away with his hands powdered in gold. They were walking along Sauchiehall Street the evening he mentioned it; she'd said the buildings were as black as you could walk into them at night; she was being fanciful, they were just newly courting and her head was stirred with all kinds of daft notions. He surprised her when he told her this wasn't their right colour; it was because of the broth of effluent from the old factories; glue and chemical works, places where sulphuric acid was made and distilled, places for making soap and soda ash, roasting kilns for malt, foundries of course; he smiled at that last one. Decades of steeping in grime had blacked the town's face for it, and he remembered his granda telling him of the days when you'd need a scarf not just against the cold but the thick swaddling that made the sun gutter like a candle flame. She said, it hasn't been like that since I've been here, and Francis nodded, aye well, this wis years ago, no much indistry lik that noo, and you'd almost think he missed the idea of being in the stew of filth, the way he said it.

The town centre was making her think too much of Francis, and she shook her head to scatter her thoughts. She was trying to look forward to visiting Agnes and Danny, and of course Cameron after all that time away from him; but she felt altered by her time alone in the house, making fires for herself. She was grateful for the new routine of the café, the first time in ages she could remember a difference in the passing days; but the girls talking about their school and their homework reminded her of Cameron, and she'd wonder if he was doing his homework, if he was growing used to his new situation, if he was a bother to them. Daniel told her on the phone the wee man was no bother; he'd said that when she'd first called to suggest it, it's nae boather, Cath, he's my nephew, n you're my sister cause ey Frankie. He was always asking if she needed money, and she always rejected it, even when he said, we're a' famly, Kate, nae boather, nothing bothered him; she wouldn't have him thinking she was trawling around for charity, not even if it would've been welcome. She comforted herself to think that at least, with Agnes ready and desperate for children, at least Cameron would be in a home that was ready for him, and not the disfigured house she had to offer.

The bus cleared the town centre, went on to Great Western Road, past the terraced houses on their shallow embankments, shredded through the elm branches. She saw a woman on the long string of pavement with a pram, a great trolley of a thing supporting a crib. The woman was young, dressed for the cold in a woollen coat of subdued purple; Catherine thought she was older at first from the way she carried herself. She'd stopped to unfasten the clear plastic screen protecting her baby from the wind; Catherine remembered her old pram, almost exactly like it, now folded flat in the hall cupboard, she'd promised it to Agnes if the day ever came when it was needed. The woman reached into the crib, having opened the screen halfway across, rummaged inside and pulled out the baby as if it was the last thing she expected to find; the baby appeared to be crying, was a girl, Catherine thought, if the rose pink of the woollens she was wearing was anything to go by.

Another thing came back to her, the hospital, after the wee one's birth; Francis sitting beside her, waiting for their son to arrive, Cameron wearing a bracelet of string with his surname spelled out in plastic beads. His exhausted wee face was framed by the cloth drawn around him, and the nurse was crooning like a dove into the parcel. He was heavier than she'd've thought, but the nurse said, nae heavier than whn he wis inside ye, surely? and reminded her she'd just been through a birth, the least pressure on her belly would feel like a boulder. Francis leaned over the bed from his seat, and she caught herself trying to see the mould of his features in the baby; nothing, but she was certain he'd develop his resemblances in time. His face seemed swollen, fat with sleep. She was peaceful after he'd been driven out of her; her first look at him was a discovery, he was flesh, he had shape in her arms. She was amazed the nurse was still speaking to her after the way she'd been before; they'd told her she was being difficult when she asked how the operation would proceed; she said, bloody right I am, I'm the one having the baby and I'm not doing it for your convenience, she wouldn't be intimidated by them, not when they were spectators. Francis looked up from the baby for a moment when she told him and said, bloody hell, Kate, they're jist tryn tay help, anyway he's oot noo, n ye're fine yirsel, and he combed her hair with his fingers. She'd've laughed at him if she'd had the air for it; the frightened look on him as he held the parcel for himself, but she only understood once he'd gone that it was a fear of what might change between them now there'd be feeding to wake up for and cleaning and all the care it'd cry out for, and she was thinking she'd have to work on him to make him understand it was their baby, not hers, cutting away at him until she'd revealed the shape of a father underneath.

The woman and her baby were tossed aside by the bus as it drove past, discarded before Catherine could see what she was offering the baby for comfort. The last thing Catherine saw from the height of the bus was the woman's hair, fixed tight over her scalp by a scaffolding of grips and clasps, loosened by the wind the bus breasted before it.

Agnes answered the door to her, and Cameron was with her, standing just behind. Catherine said hello to Agnes, and Agnes stood to one side as if she was a door herself between Catherine and her son; she was as nervous as a foster mother, and the blood made her giddy to see him in the clothes he'd brought from home, grey v-necked jumper, black short trousers, black shoes his father taught him to polish until they shone like wet tar. She didn't recognize the tie around his neck, plain and black, and she thought it must've been a purchase of

Agnes's; she was thinking he'd been dressed awful formally for meeting his mother, and wondered if that had been deliberate, to show him at his best. She dropped to her knees to collect him in her arms; he went as soft as cloth, more as if he was allowing her the privilege of intimacy. She separated herself from him, and then went into her handbag, took from it a brown paper package which she put into his hands, saying,

Your mother's brought you a present; I hope you like it.

Her eyes weren't quite level with his; he was taller than she was when she fell back on her haunches, and it seemed as if he'd grown, even in the time he'd been in Agnes's and Daniel's keeping. She heard herself say, your mother; as if she'd needed the reminder herself; as if he'd needed it too. He looked down at the package, the paper unfurling at the neck of the bag; he was smiling, but it was almost as if he'd been taught that by Agnes; he looked to his aunt behind him, throwing her shadow over him to keep him warm.

Thank yir ma fr the present, Cameron.

Catherine looked over Cameron's shoulder; there was little warmth in Agnes's smile. She was wearing an indigo jumper, tight pressed against the structure of her brassière, the cones lifting her breasts; a black skirt, pleated into vanes and just covering her knees; her legs were bare, dappled red from sitting before the electric fire. She had her hair in a new style, clipped straight across the forehead, curving to knife points on either side of her chin. Catherine looked back to Cameron, who was still looking at the package as if uncertain of what to do with it; he said thank you in a clear voice, and then began to open the paper, peering inside the bag. At last he reached inside, took out the cardboard box, examined the illustration on each of its faces. Catherine hadn't known what kind of model car to buy him; it'd felt curious, not knowing her own son's preferences. In the end she thought he enjoyed using emergency vehicles in his wee dramas, so she'd bought a police car, a Black Maria with chessboard squares painted on the bonnet and a lamp of blue plastic on the roof, which she was honest enough to tell him was just for show, and didn't flash on and off like it did on a real car. He pulled on the flap at the side of the box, tilted it a little to ease the model out of its garage; there were also two policeman figures, sealed in plastic, one directing traffic, the other posed heroically, arm outstretched and pointing with a tiny splint of a finger, his whistle held to his mouth. Catherine waited for him to become excited by his present, but he just stood there. She said,

You could make another house out of the box, couldn't you? Add another storey to one of your buildings,

because the town of boxes had gone with him, along with his cars and the books he read most often; and the vase, of course, to remind him. He said,

I demolished it.

Catherine frowned.

That's a shame. When did you do that?

I don't know. Not long after I came here. I wasn't playing with it much, so I had a big disaster. Everyone was killed.

Maybe there wouldn't've been so many folk killed if you'd the police to help you.

They'd've been killed too. It was a big meteor from space.

Agnes put her hands on the wee one's shoulders, causing him to look up at her.

It's a lovely present, pet, she said. Yir ma's thinkin aboot ye, see? I tellt ye she'd come wi somethin nice fr ye.

Catherine stood up, clipping shut her bag.

You can tell me all about your new school, if you like.

Agnes had dinner cooking in the kitchen, and tea to make for them, so she left them to it. Catherine put her hand on Cameron's shoulder to steer him through to the living-room, but he walked a little forward, leaving her hand empty. He made a fist around the model car, and when she sat him on the leatherette sofa beside her, he put it inside its box along with the figures, and put it on the coffee table, never touching it the whole time she spoke to him.

It was like pulling at a ball of string talking to him; nothing was offered to her she didn't have to pick at, and then it was cut off, leaving her with more to unravel. He embraced himself around his waist, pivoted back and forth in the seat, causing a squeal of friction against the leatherette, as if he wanted away from her, frustrated by the blood they had in common. She told him all about her job in the café, and about Gianfranco and his daughters; she had a feeling he'd get on well with Beatrice, and he was probably too young to take Francesca's interest. She promised she'd treat him to a knickerbocker glory, and that Gianfranco had said he'd make one specially for him, but when he turned to look at her, it was as if he could see the bribe in her hand, too obvious for him, and she wondered if he'd ever come back to her the same as he'd left.

Agnes came into the room to offer a second cup of tea. She made certain Catherine knew her son had been as good as gold, and Catherine did the polite thing, smiled and said she was pleased to hear it, thinking Agnes had grown in different ways herself, the mother hen out of the coop now, her sense of possession strengthened. Cameron looked bashfully down at his feet. The television was playing in the corner, a Sunday programme of hymns and worship. Catherine knew there'd been arguments between Agnes and Daniel about what was to be done about Cameron's spiritual education, him having come from a devoutly disbelieving house to one split down the middle on the matter; Catherine had settled it herself by declaring it wouldn't be Francis's wish to have his son inside a chapel unless he'd done the thinking for himself, arriving at his own decision after years of proper consideration, which ended the discussion. Agnes was still the only one in the house to dress for the journey along the road to Saint Bonaventure's with its chalet roof and its carvings of the Passion over the lintel. Catherine wondered if she'd maddened Agnes into good motherhood with this decision; she was certainly fluttering around as if she'd something to prove to her sister-in-law, worrying over dinner almost as soon as she'd left it in the oven, pulling the smell of it into the living-room behind her. She'd even made a cake, swollen with glacé cherries. It went heavily down with the cup of tea and plunged like a weight through Catherine, reminding her of her mother's cooking, more substantial than elegant. Catherine picked a second wedge from the cake dish.

Are you getting cake like this every day, Cameron? I wouldn't want to come home, if I were you.

She smiled at Agnes before nipping a cherry in half with her teeth.

Aye well, I think it's nicer made at hame thn buyn it fae a shoap, ye make it the wey ye waant it, d'ye no?

She sat on the other side of Cameron, encouraging him to lift a wean-sized wedge from the cake dish. She asked about Catherine's new job, was it getting her out of the house, was she enjoying it; Catherine said she was, told her the same as she'd told Cameron, about Gianfranco, Rosa in the kitchen, the daughters.

That's good, Kate, mebbe bein aroon anither famly'll make ye feel better. It's no good fr ye tay be in yon hoose by yirsel.

Oh, of course it does. You'll know yourself, when you and Daniel start a family of your own. I miss Cameron not being at home. It's awful big, the house now, awful quiet.

She leaned towards him, but he leaned from her as if repelled by the like pole of blood in her. Agnes ate a corner of her own slice of cake; with its density, it let down few crumbs on to the side plate she held under her chin for politeness.

Well, ye wid miss him, I'm sure. We were jist sayn the ither day, Danny n me, whit's Kate dayn, noo she's there hersel? Danny says, she's no huvn parties there, that's fr sure, she'd'uv invitet us if that was the case.

Well, said Catherine, I think it's better that Cameron stays here for the time being. He knows things are different when you're grieving. You know that, don't you, Cameron?

This time she wouldn't allow him to turn aside and avoid her. Cameron looked towards his lap finally, where his hands were resting, and nodded at last. Catherine stared levelly at Agnes, and in her look was a reminder to the wean's aunt, never forget whose blood he is. She ate a corner of the cake, let it roam around her mouth for a while.

You know, Agnes, this is a really good cake. A few less eggs and it'd be wonderful.

Daniel came through for his dinner from the shed, and immediately gave Agnes a telling for not sending Kate and Cameron through the moment she'd arrived. Agnes looked sourly at him, but for Kate's benefit she made a joke of it.

I canny win, d'ye know that? I get a bawlin fr interruptn him, n noo I'm gettn a bawlin fr no interruptn. I give up.

She left Catherine with Cameron and Daniel to see how the dinner was getting on. The change in Cameron when Daniel came into the room was immediate; he brightened as his uncle settled down on the sofa beside him, disarrayed his hair that his aunt had spent all day parting, and Cameron laughed, a thing she hadn't seen since long before his father died. Daniel promised Cameron he could come out to the shed later to see what he'd been doing all afternoon; saw the toy police car on the coffee table, leaned over to pick it up, turned the box end over end the way Cameron had himself earlier.

Did yir ma bring that fr ye? See whit I wis tellin ye, wee man? Ye're no far fae her thoats, even when she's no jist wi ye.

The look Daniel gave her was like Francis forgiving her; she had to make herself tight so she wouldn't cry to see the same eyes in Daniel as in her son. Cameron opened the box to let him see the motor, and the policemen too, and with the fuss Daniel made over it, Cameron came to think of it as a special present, even ran it once or twice across the coffee table before Daniel suggested he should take it through to his room to play on the carpet. Cameron ran away, his feet lighter on the stairs up to the room, and Daniel laughed and shook his head.

Two month, he said, n I still canny interest him in a gemme ey fitba'. Gie him a toay motor n he's a happy wee man.

Catherine looked to the tele screen; a historical drama, men in frock-coats, women draped around with more fabric than they needed. Daniel leaned over to the coffee table, traced the scar of the hard plastic tyres of Cameron's police car over the varnish, smiled at Catherine.

The chairs at home have marks like that on the arms, she said. He thinks I haven't noticed.

Daniel laughed, then went solemn.

Ye know ye cn keep him here as lang as ye waant, Kate. Nae boather.

Catherine said she wouldn't impose any longer than need be, but Daniel was clear about it; it wasn't just for her sake, he was mindful of his responsibilities to family. She thanked him; he shrugged, it was nothing, settled into the sofa, arranged his legs in front of him like a trestle. Her bag sat on the floor beside her; she reached for it, opened the clasp and found her purse. She took a five pound note from it and held it in the air between them, closing the purse and dropping it in the bag with one hand. Daniel looked at the money, then at her, and he'd a face on him that said, it must be a joke, but she could drag him down with her own solemnity. He said,

Naw naw, Kate, nane ey us eats a fiver's worth, no in a week.

For the electricity he burns, then. Whatever else you never had to pay for before.

Ye'd think he wisny welcome r somethn.

Catherine folded the note in half, held it along the crease in between her first and second fingers.

I'm telling you, Daniel, if you don't take this off me, Agnes'll be cleaning a shelf somewhere in this house and she'll wonder what it's doing stuck to her duster. Or she'll never notice, and it'll be on the floor and away up the Hoover along with the spiders.

Daniel tried to stare her out, but she'd had years of getting the better of eyes just like his, and he knew there was no use in arguing with her. She knew it felt like buying a stake in her own child, but it was important to her that she pay for him, if only to remind her that there was a responsibility to him that would cost her, and that made Daniel surrender. She leaned over the table and put the note in front of him, waited for him to pick it up, but he didn't, just nodded, and then changed it to an affectionate shaking of his head and a wry look at her.

Frankie said he widny dare staun in yir road if ye were at a jumble sale.

Even buy him a wee present with it, and make sure you tell him it was from his mother.

She spent Christmas with Agnes and Daniel; Cameron was still acting the stranger towards her even as he tore open the wrapping from her presents; a gift set of miniature cars, meant to be carried in the transport vehicle nested at the centre of the box; a space-flight book, bright with illustrations of how rockets were powered and of men in their puffed-out spacesuits; a selection box of different chocolates, most of them favourites of his. He thanked her without prompting from his aunt, but he was quiet for the rest of the evening, reading from his book, running the cars along the carpet, and she wondered if it was because of the same reason as herself, the first Christmas without his da. He still wouldn't tell her how school was; and Agnes made her flicker with resentment, the way she was carrying on as if she'd begun to mistake him for her own flesh, whit a studious thoatful wee boay he is, she said, as if she'd given him that. Even Daniel noticed, enough to keep reminding his wife of her place when the wee one's right mother was there with him, aye, he said, brains fae his faither, beauty fae his mither, and then he gave Agnes one of those mind-your-place looks, a bolt from his eyes to quiet her.

By the time Hogmanay came, Catherine was wondering if she'd forfeited her son, if she'd ever see him back in the house. She was left by herself, sitting in her front room, listening to the year's end, without even a tele for one of the celebration programmes to make her feel at least as if she was part of the festival. There was a party going on in the house over her head which overwhelmed the noises she'd expect to hear on a quiet evening, the fire murmuring under its breath, the wind stroking the window panes, her own heartbeat. Bernadette and her man had their mates round for the bells, and there was music screaming from a Dansette, and the walls shook so you could feel the pulse in them, like when you touched your wrist. In the hours after the pubs closed, the street was lively with folk coming upstairs; singing their way into the close with power given to their voices by the old hatreds in the words of their songs, ancestral hatreds Catherine thought she'd more of a right to than they had at their remove; she gathered herself tighter in her chair as more and more of them arrived. Soon there were enough folk to leave the spoor of their hammering feet behind them on the ceiling, and it was like all the fights Bernadette and her man had ever had all going on at once. She was an eavesdropper in her own house; she couldn't go into any room without hearing something, goat enough BOOZE in the fucken place; fucken bells, man, goat tay be ready fr the fucken BELLS. The row was worse in the kitchen, and it was loudest in the bathroom, conducted by surfaces that reflected sound as well as light, you'd think they were shouting down at her, the voices raw and direct.

A while later, the Dansette had its tongue abruptly cut out for it, and a voice familiar to Catherine from the arguments cried out, fucken SHUT IT yous; Catherine wondered what was happening until she looked at the clock on the mantel, the hands ready to join at the head of the dial. Catherine thought, she'd never seen Bernadette's man, couldn't tell him from a thousand like him. She remembered they'd gone to Agnes's and Daniel's last year, her and Francis and Cameron; Agnes made a fuss of her nephew, gave him the treasured end of cake, and had blackcurrant cordial made ready for him; Catherine thought madly it was like she'd known of Francis's illness before any of them, was laying her preparations even then. She'd told herself that tonight of all nights she wouldn't remember, but it was difficult not to compare last year, when she still had a husband and a son, to this, with bedlam above her, and her own bedlam of memories, and the house vacant around her.

A grave and ceremonial voice came from above, like an actor's or a minister's. It said, in these troubled times, as we stand on the threshold of another New Year, we recall the words of the immortal bard Robert Burns as he wrote, for a' that and a' that, a man's a man for a' that, and many men the warld ower wid brithers be for a' that; and now please raise your glasses as we say farewell to the old year and welcome in the new. The Westminster chimes sounded, and with the first chime the calm ended and everyone went riotous and battered their feet against the ceiling, and the music resumed on the Dansette, and Catherine never thought she'd ever be so grateful for not being able to hear herself think.

Catherine couldn't hear the first few notes of the phone for all the creeling guitars and chanting; it was only when she heard that the rhythm of the bell was different to that of the music. She stood up and went to the folded table by the window, reached out her hand to pick up the receiver. She felt the electricity of the bell through the tips of her fingers, conducted through the black casing, but she couldn't seem to close her hand around it. She let the ringing go until it died of exhaustion, and when she couldn't feel it birling any more, she let go of it and went through to the kitchen to make herself a cup of tea, to relax her, almost relieved not to have to talk to anyone.

She felt calmer for not lifting the phone when it insisted on her twice more. After the third call, she was beginning to feel cold, and she looked towards the fire, realized she'd let it burn down to almost nothing. She put out her hand to the scuttle and took out the first brick of coal her hand fitted around, cast it into the hearth; it shattered the cairn of ash into grey fragments that broke open to reveal the fire they'd been hiding like a secret, causing angelic sparks to rise with the smoke up the flue. Absently, she began to rub her fingers across the palm on her hand; the black coal dust had bedded itself in her fingerprints, making them slippery but in a dry way, and without thinking, she picked up her cup from its saucer without using the lug, and then after she put the cup back down, she noticed the black spirit of her touch remaining on the china.

That was herself, she thought; only the soiling she inflicted on everything had been made visible, the darkness she spread.

By the time the doorbell went some half-hour later, she'd left her prints around the hearth like a child, and on the wallpaper around the mantel. She'd knelt down before it as if it'd been an altar, the only thing she'd ever truly worshipped, the home she'd surrendered herself to after her marriage, and deliberately left the curse of her touch around it to make her own fault visible to the eye. She walked her hand over the paper, looked at each of the black starfish she'd left behind her, fading as the dust rubbed away; she felt purer for leaving evidence behind her, as if her guilt in the destruction of her home would be there for all to see. It seemed appropriate to soil the hearthside like that, because that was where the family had gathered every evening; she could've equally dirtied the tablecloth, where they'd eaten every night, or the bedclothes, on the bed where Cameron had been conceived and where he'd caught them. The paper she remembered because it was the first improvement she and Francis made to the house when they first moved in; she'd chosen it because the roses were stencilled roughly on the paper, and it seemed more like craft and less like the kind of fat romantic blossoms old folk would prefer. It was the first thing they'd done to make the house more theirs and less the council's; they were like children playing at being responsible when they came round to putting it on the walls, pelting each other with paste and laughing their heads off. Maybe that was why she'd blackened it with her hands; it reminded her too much of a happiness she'd never quite believed she deserved, and the stain was on her hands like her own irrational thought that she'd been the cause of Francis's infection, she'd been the one fouling the nest from the very start, and Agnes had been quick enough to see that, knew she'd be taking delivery of the most precious possession of her marriage from the day Catherine and Francis met.

Catherine had a whole year's tiredness to gather like a stowaway's belongings into a cloth, and she thought she could sleep through even the riot upstairs. She still had enough presence of mind to go to the bathroom first to wash the remains of the dust from her hands, and while she was watching the black water seep down the drain, she heard pounding on the ceiling, laughter. They'd turned off the Dansette a while ago, but they were still making as much noise singing, rebel songs with their cockerel's strut, a thick morass of drunken sentiment. There was a dragging and heavy steps, like the carrying of a body, and then she heard it enter the bathroom with her, water flowing in harmony with the water she was holding her hands under, and there were voices overlapping, c'moan man, this'll waken ye, nice bit ey waater in the kipper, 'ats the gemme, canny see the fucken New Year in in a fucken state lik that, and she smiled to think of the baptism above her.

She was in the bedroom when the doorbell went, beginning to undress with her jumper up and over her head, turned inside out, the arms trailing from the ends of her hands. She thought at first it might be Bernadette come to invite her to the brawl; the last place she wanted to be with Bernadette's man drifting around the room like escaped gas waiting for a light, and besides she'd be weary with refusing the drink they'd throw at her, thinking they were doing her a favour, and they'd turn on her for setting aside their hospitality. Quickly she pulled her towelling dressing-gown from its hook on the back of the door, wrapped it around herself and fastened the tape belt around her waist in the hope that she'd be protected from invitation.

The last thing she'd expected was for her mother-in-law to be standing at the door at an hour like this; it was like Father Gallagher at the death all over again, unwelcome visitors at inappropriate times. She was dressed in the outfit she always wore for family gatherings, big olive-coloured woollen coat with freckles of gold and burgundy through it, the dowdy skirt lapping around a pair of flat boots with their fur collars turned down over her ankles. She had on a pair of grey woollen gloves, and she was holding out a hand in which was a lump of coal as a first-footing gift, a deference to custom rather than meant with any sincerity. She displayed her vanity with an extravagant turban hat of wound burgundy silk, with a cockade of preserved heather and the blade of a capercaillie feather arcing from the source of the pin. She was looking at Catherine like always, summing her up as a poor choice of wife for her son. She spoke wearily over the sound of the party from upstairs, which was now beginning to sound maudlin and aggressive at one and the same time, her voice scoring through the racket.

Nae wunner ye couldny hear the phone, she said. Daniel rang ye three times. Him n Agnes were awffy worried.

Him and Agnes were worried; not her. The cold made Catherine pull the gown tighter around herself, and once that was done, she folded her arms over her breasts.

No need for worry. I was just going to bed.

The coal was still held up steadily between them, and she was just as steady with her eyes through the lenses of her oval spectacles.

Took us a good oor n a haulf tay find a taxi, this tim ey night efter the bells.

She'd never come that close to pleading again. Catherine stood to one side of the door, allowing her mother-in-law to drag past her the smoky air from all the flues in the street, a light violet smell of air freshener Catherine knew to be Agnes's favourite, and a faint animal odour of incontinence, not strong but definitely there. She manoeuvred herself out of her coat, managing it one-handed and not even dirtying the lining with coal dust, holding the coat out to be taken, exchanging the coal for this favour. Catherine took the coat from her and hung it in the bedroom, on the hook from which she'd taken the dressing-gown.

She told her mother-in-law to find herself a seat in the living-room, and then went into the kitchen to make tea, as much to escape her as for any other reason. Catherine and her mother-in-law hadn't been in the same room since the funeral, not even at Christmas, when she'd said she'd be over the next day to give Cameron his present, reminding Daniel that Christmas had never been much celebrated in this part of the world until lately, folk still went to work part shifts as if they were a nation of Bob Cratchits working for a nation of Ebenezer Scrooges. Catherine remembered the last words spoken to her by the old woman, after the casket was lowered into the grave. Her mother-in-law had worn holy black for the occasion, stood there at the head of the opening assuming the place of the priest, ordained for the day; she had a black prayer-book in her hands given to her by Father Gallagher, and she read out the words through a black net cast from the prow of her hat which captured her eyes like fish while she said, ashes to ashes, dust to dust. Daniel put a hand on Catherine's forearm before she could go and rip the book away from her mother-in-law, said, lee her, Kate, no the day; she'd even brought holy water in the plastic effigy of the Virgin Mary the brothers always had such a laugh about, screwing the crown from off the head of the queen of heaven and sprinkling a few drops over the blind facet of the coffin. She wouldn't even cry openly, as if she wanted her quiet dignity to be compared like a monument against her daughter-in-law's fretful display. The last words she'd said to Catherine were, disrespectful bitch, ye widny even bury him in his faith, at least doing her the courtesy of saying it under her breath for only Catherine to hear. Catherine had her own tribute of a rose to throw on to the casket, and she hadn't the fight left in her to argue with the old besom then, but she was in a rare mood for it now.

She brought the cup of tea through to the living-room, gave it into her mother-in-law's lap; she was seated in the chair she was used to herself, holding her hands out flat to the dying fire, collecting a warmth from it that Catherine wasn't giving her. The coal was on the rim of the hearth, on the side she expected Catherine to sit at. Upstairs, the Dansette began again, a record from a group Francesca had pictures of on her bedroom wall. Her mother-in-law arranged the cup on the nap of her skirt, drank a sip, fell back satisfied into the cushions, though she was making a face at the noise from above.

Ill-bred folk, she said; I'm surprised ye were thinkin ey sleepin through thon to-do.

Catherine took her seat, the seat expected of her, shrugged.

It's a young couple,

she said. The mother-in-law lifted her eyes to the ceiling, like Gianfranco calling for strength from above and a deliverance from adversity.

Young folk nooadays, she said. They'll no care aboot nothn.

Young folk've always been annoying their elders.

Mebbe young folk lik yirsel, she said, r theym upstair. If ye didny day whit yir elders tellt ye in my day, they'd rattle yir ears fr ye. N fine well ye knew ye deserved it.

The empty gloves curled around the rim of the fireplace; her bare hands, resting on the saucer, clutched around the ear of the cup, were hard and leathery.

What if your elders were wrong?

Yir elders knew whit wis right fr ye.

Catherine had a thing or two to say about that, but not to a sour old creature like her, who could twist truth until Catherine would've been the seducer, and not her father the lecher. She caught the old woman looking over the mantel, at the photographs of the wedding, her and him with the unchristened baby; she seemed to be about to speak when another dunt made the entire room quail; more steps, more laughing, Bernadette's man again with his megaphone voice, tellt ye no tay huv ony mare fucken DRINK, man. The mother-in-law looked up again, not for guidance this time, just as far as the ceiling; breathed abruptly and then trapped it in her mouth. She shook her head again, then spoke into the fire,

No gonny complain? No call the polis nor nothn?

They'd only make noise and trouble for me for weeks after.

Cheynged days. There's nae peace in the world ony mare. Nae wunner there's wars.

She wasn't noticing Catherine's open yawning, or the fact she was only speaking when she was spoken to, which from what Francis had told her should've made her the ideal daughter-in-law for the old wifie. She tried looking for common flesh between the mother-in-law and Francis, Daniel, Cameron, but there was too much rigidity in the old face, lines drawn when she was too young to change them, paunched out by age. Finally Catherine had had enough of politeness, said,

You can go back and tell Agnes and Daniel I'm fine. Really. I don't need watching.

The missis shook her head, sadly, with a kind of missionary look in her eyes, soft and ungiving at the same time.

It's a damned shame, she said. Yir faith wid'uv been a great comfrt tay ye at a time lik this. Whit made ye gie it up? There's no a thing makes ony sense wi nae faith.

Faith in what, exactly?

In the wan that made ye. I thoat wherr you came fae, everywan hud their faith.

The faith was beaten out of me, she said, by one who made me.

Yir da?

Why'd you say that?

Menfolk aye find it easier to doot than women. Mebbe they canny stomach the notion there's wan higher'n theirsels.

Catherine laughed in surprise that she might agree with the mother-in-law.

My da was as faithful as you are. It was the drink made him believe he was God. I lost my faith through example.

Through example?

Yes, through the example of a fine God-fearing man. I was more afraid of him than I ever was of God.

The mother-in-law shook her head in pity. She put her teacup down on to the rim of the hearth, and that brought her eyes level for the first time with the prints around the fireplace; she looked at Catherine's clean hands in wonder, stared at them while she spoke.

The wee one's lookin awffy well these days.

Catherine saw her fascination with the prints.

Redecoration, she explained. To suit my mood. What were you saying?

Agnes's takin awffy good care ey him. Buyn him claes, feedn him. D'you think she does it better than me?

I think, she said, Agnes knows mare aboot ither things than clothn n feedn a wean. Lik whit's best fr him, ither ways.

Catherine sat waiting, until the mother-in-law, unsettled by her silence and the signs of her mutilating her own house, shifted uncomfortably for the first time since arriving.

Fr the love ey Goad, tell me ye know whit I'm sayn tay ye.

Catherine shook her head. The mother-in-law took in a wavering breath.

She hus her faith, I mean. You n Francis hud yir faith, afore ye baith turned fae it. It's no good fr a wean no tay stert wi it. Cause ey you, they've sent him tay a Protestant school, n he's in trouble cause he willny go tay the assembly in the mornin.

Catherine shrugged.

That's how we want him brought up.

The mother-in-law rose in her seat.

Ye day whit's best fr yir wean, Kate. Ye dinny gie a wean whit it waants itsel.

You don't know the half of what I've done for his good.

Aye, but I know whit you've done ill tay him.

Catherine leapt out of the seat. She knew the mother-in-law could simply be blaming her for emptying the wee one of spirituality, but her own guilt drove her out of her seat as she wondered if her punishing hands had given her away. When she recovered herself, she was standing in the corner of the room by the door, her back against the right angle; she was holding herself with her arm across her, her other hand pressed against her mouth, the knuckle of her thumb between her lips, and she was worrying at it with her teeth. She stared at her mother-in-law as if to fathom what she'd been meaning, but she thought, this was how Cameron had felt to be hunted into the corner, to have a fist raised to him.

I won't be spoken to like that in my own house.

Ye'll respect whit ye're tellt by yir elders, madam. Ye've pit my son in hell, n ye'll day the same wi yir ain if ye dinny lee Agnes tay day whit's best fr him.

Catherine straightened, put her arms by her sides.

I'll have him back, so I will. I hope everyone concerned understands that.

The old besom drilled her eyes through Catherine.

Leave him tay a wummn that'll no day ill tay him. Fr Goad's sake, n my deid boay's sake as well. I'll away noo n tell Agnes n Daniel no tay worry.

She spent the next hour with her mother-in-law until the cab blared its horn outside, not saying a word to her, and fetched her coat quickly from the bedroom, seeing her to the door, not replying when the old besom wished her a happy New Year. When the door was closed, she leaned her back against it and then went to the living-room. She saw the coal resting on the hearthside; picked it up, hurled it into the fire, as much to see the reminder of the old besom's visit incinerated as to get the use of it. She sat down just as another record started upstairs, and the dancing to it began with the last few survivors of the party putting out enough noise to shake the ceiling; but her own thoughts were louder still, and the first of them was that the old besom had known she wouldn't wish ill on her own son, and she should be thinking of his welfare before her own. The way she was just now, mad enough to leave her prints on the wall, she couldn't guarantee that the punishing wouldn't start again if he were to come back to her, and that meant that the old besom was right, if not for the reasons she'd stated. Her next thought was, I've lost my son, and there was no consolation for that, not even the consolation of his safety, and she began to cry on this morning of new beginnings, which for her meant a life without Cameron until her grief burned down and she'd be no danger to her son.

When she came back after the New Year, Gianfranco noticed the difference in her; distracted so that the simple tasks of the shop seemed beyond her at times, but the most noticeable of the clues was the fact she was wearing no make-up, her hair was free around her shoulders. He said to her, you no well, Catherine, eh? you sicken, I send you home right away, the old devil stand at the gates of Paradise today, tomorrow, long as you need, but she told him, no, it was nothing time off would help or cure, she'd sooner be away from the house than listen to it echo around her, and he shrugged hugely and said, as you wish, but be careful, cappuccino machine hot, ice-cream cold, so many ways to hurt if your mind no straight like die, eh?

Gianfranco never realized that the one place she never wanted to return to was home; she heard the word, but it was bare like the house itself, a cathedral she went into every night and she was thinking she'd the wrong keys. It was always bitter cold when she went into the living-room. This was Catherine's most recent routine; she'd be waking up these mornings, and the bed was as big as a field around her. She still walked along the hall to get the wee one up and out of his bed, and then she'd remember it was herself needing to get up. Sometimes she'd remember before she opened the door to his room; worse still, there'd be mornings she'd forget until the door was opened, and she'd feel her heart go like an alarm and wonder for a moment if he'd run away, or if he'd been stolen from her; and then she'd mind he was in another bed, stolen away in a manner of speaking, and then there was just herself to get ready. If she'd time, she'd wash her hair, and give herself a lick of water at the sink, and then go through to make herself some toast and a cup of tea; she never bothered with the radio these days, couldn't bear the motivating chatter and the overjoyed music that seemed to be for folk without a care in the world, and which consequently wasn't for her. The last place she went was the bedroom, to take her day's outfit from the wardrobe, and now and again she went to the mirror, and sat in front of it. Her make-up bottles and palettes were built like a suburb on the dresser, but it wasn't that she couldn't decide on a face. She remembered her mammy saying it was the business of the undertaker to make the dead fit for being seen by the living; they rouged dead flesh, put a pretend kind of blood under the skin, and sometimes it was the greatest flattery the man or woman had ever had, dead or alive, folk would say the corpse never looked in better health and they'd be half joking and half meaning it. That was what she'd be thinking as she looked at herself in the mirror; there was little sense in pampering the dead in their mausoleums, and there was just as little sense in making herself up when she only ever went between here and work anyway, and there was nobody to make up for.

She knew Gianfranco was concerned for her even before he said a word; but the last thing she needed was another father, honey in sobriety and vinegar in drunkenness, even if she'd never seen the like in Gianfranco. She did her work as conscientiously as she could, and when it was quiet, she leaned on the counter, waiting for the appearance of a miracle in any form. That was what she'd been reduced to by despair, Francis would've hated to think she was dependent on other powers to help her, but she'd earned Francis's hatred by allowing their son to be taken from her, so that the miraculous was all that was left to her; any miracle, no matter how mean or shabby, no matter how it was dressed, would've been welcome to her.

Six

The waitress looked hell of a distracted to Peter while she was waiting on him to tell her his order; she'd a smile on her the way some women wore a brooch, the more fake and obvious the cluster of glass was the more they wanted to show it off. She made an easel of her hand to rest her notepad on; she'd the pencil hovering above ready for the word, and Peter looked at the menu for something to eat as well as the cappuccino he'd promised himself ever since he'd caught the smell of it from outside. He was glad to be seated after being out in the cold for so long; he'd made himself at home by hanging his duffel coat over the arched back of the chair next to his, and putting his bag on the lap of the seat, not like the old biddy with her button nose in a paperback three tables away and opposite him, if she compressed herself any more in her seat she'd'␣ve punctured herself. The waitress, God bless her, wasn't hurrying him up with his choosing, which was fine by Peter, he quite liked her standing there in attendance; she was striking enough with her black hair plaited behind her and tied with a narrow red band. There'd been an abandoned old Irishman in the town centre once who'd lifted his scrubby old head and sung in a gentle lilt The Black Velvet Band; Peter was remembering the words he'd been singing, oh her eyes they shone like diamonds, and he was just thinking that while she was speaking, her with her voice and all. She called him sir, what can I get you, sir? would you like some time to have a proper look at the menu, sir? and it all made Peter feel he wasn't fitting right into the shape of the place, which was a pity, because he was thinking it was a fine place to be, with its warm terracotta tiling the like of which he'd never seen in any other café in the town, and the frosted glass panes beside the tables that softened you like pastels, giving you a grainy presence; he didn't need sir to make him self-conscious.

I've niver been a teacher, miss, nae need tay call us sir.

She became aware of him. She smiled, apologetically, waited for his choice. She'd the smell of old perfume dried into her clothing, though how you could tell with all the other aromas about; garlic, he noticed, beautiful food just calling on him; he was feeling hungry, and fuck it if it was pricey, he'd the money from his latest sale fat in his wallet, he was like the weans with shillings in their pockets calling in for a ball of ice-cream in a poky hat, having a chocolate flake and raspberry syrup on it, why the fuck not? His finger picked out the paragraph of the menu titled Specialities, this'd be his dinner, and he asked for a las agney, or however you said it; the girl wrote it on to the pad and raised her eyebrows while she was writing, ended up the order with the cappuccino, said,

I'll just go to the kitchen to order your lasagne, then come back and get you your cappuccino.

Las ah nia, that was how it was said. He looked to her feet while she was turning to split the curtain at the far end of the café; black leather shoes with low heels and circular buckles there for ornament, and she walked as if she'd been used to dancing at some time in her life, her feet didn't clip the tiling the way his had, what with the metal segs nailed into his boots, she was lighter than that and still mindful, you'd think, of a time when she walked a floor as if it'd been carpeted with feathers. While she was away, he fetched out his book from the duffel bag and cracked it open at the first page of sketches, of the boys and Elvis playing football; the dancing movements in it, described with a few lines, good enough for a sketch but not for a painting, too mobile. He turned past those exercises, to the page with Elvis, and just as he was studying the picture of the big man, he heard a conversation from the kitchen, the girl's voice first,

There you are, Gianfranco, a bite at last,

and then a heavier voice, spiced like the smell of the kitchen itself, You play joke with me, Catherine, no? Let me see, with own eyes, and then Peter lost it among rapid Italian between the second speaker and another woman who sounded as excited as if her birthday'd arrived. The pattering between them continued while the waitress came out to the counter, and when she turned towards the coffee factory nudged up against the corner she was smiling, and she looked over at Peter and kept the smile on him as if he'd been the cause of it. Peter replied by turning up the ends of his mouth, but that made her aware of it, and when she opened the big drum of coffee she was back to normal, her eyes they shone like diamonds, cold and polished, and Peter went back to studying his work thinking the life had been crushed out of those eyes of hers lately, and wondering what would be the cause of it.

The waitress, Catherine, brought the cappuccino, and he amused her by deliberately cultivating a moustache of the milk froth over his top lip, licking it away with the point of his tongue. It kept her close, close enough to see the picture of Elvis in his book, and suddenly she recoiled a little, as if the taste of shite had come into her mouth. Peter turned the book towards her to let her see it better.

I saw him playn fitba in the fields ey thon big industrial estate, he said. I waantit his picture.

Catherine shook her head, slowly, but her full attention was on the page; she was examining it closely, and she looked pitying, like he'd wasted his talent.

I was always afraid, she said, my son would fall among thieves like him.

Immediately Peter looked for the ring on her wedding finger, thinking it wasn't like him to lose details like that, but the wedding band was on the finger opposite, which led him to think divorce, separation, something that'd make her want to keep the value of it.

My son lives with my brother-in-law and his wife now, she said. My husband died of lung cancer months ago.

The way she stepped back; as if she'd surprised herself by explaining it so easily to a stranger. Peter thought this was why everything about her seemed past; the old fragrance, the step of the dancer turned into a walk, the eyes left to crystallize out of the solution of a life, like she was waiting to curdle with age, like the old woman with her back to the window who was looking at them speaking from time to time as if she didn't approve of it. Peter couldn't think of what to say, except,

I'm sorry tay hear that,

which didn't seem good enough, under the circumstances. She nodded to accept his condolence, then became more animated, kid-on cheerful, said,

So why on earth do a picture of the likes of him? You must be stuck for people to draw.

I could day portraits ey folk wi money wi the best ey them, he said. Jist, I sooner widny.

She closed over the book, read his name from the label on the cloth cover, opened it again.

No wonder I've not heard of you, Mister Caulder.

Peter laughed.

Yon's jist as bad as sir. Ye've no heard ey me cause the galleries're lookin tay sell landscapes wi deer in them for folk that canny afford the Monarch ey the Glen, or abstracts wi peynt splashed a' ower them for folk that think they're sophisticatet. If it wisny for Jonathan MacHenery n his wee gallery, the only wey I'd hing in this toun is if I kilt somebdy.

Is this the kind of thing you paint?

He drank some of the cappuccino; better than the burnt-caramel-tasting shite he made at home for the want of choice.

Punters, aye. No folk that exploit ither folk for gain, I could day that for a wee bit ey ready cash any day ey the week. Folk ye'll no see in yir galleries.

Folk like this.

She gave the book over to him; he put it down flat on the table. The change in her from when she was talking about her son and her husband was almost frightening.

Cn ye no see, folk lik Elvis make their ain rules cause naebdy gies a damn for them. They'd no be lik thon if they were housed decent, or gied proper learnin. They're made lik thon tay keep the price ey labour doon, lik valves in a telly set.

Is that what you call him? I've seen him about with a crowd of

133

other boys, and a few girls, round the industrial estate. I'm told they fight with the gang from the next scheme.

I wis tellt as well. He goat they scars in a fight.

And so would my Cameron, if he ever joined them. Forgive me, but I don't think he's deserving of a portrait.

Peter hadn't known her long enough to antagonize her, but he wouldn't leave it to go by him.

There's generals n admirals hingin in the gallery killin by the hunnert thoosand. Folk see fit tay day their portraits.

She twisted her mouth around, shrugged faintly.

I see what you mean, but they're none of them heroes.

Mebbe that's the point,

said Peter, and she could see the strength of that, and nodded.

When the lasagne came to the table, it arrived with as much ceremony as a birthday cake. Catherine's face split into a smile as she looked to her left, and Peter had to turn in his seat to get her view of it; the man who owned the café, Gianfranco, was holing the plate at chest height, and he had a solemn look about him, as if he was bestowing a sacrament. He wore a white shirt, and over it an apron painted with fats and oils on the canvas; he wore pinstriped black trousers that plunged from the lap of the apron to the shoes with their fine polish, so that he looked as if he was half of the kitchen and half of the counting house, like a centaur whose love of food was carried on the legs of commerce. Behind him, there was a woman in a red dress, her arms bare and dappled from the heat of the stove, her hair gathered and curled on her head; she was grinning a mouthful of gold at the customer who'd asked for one of her special dishes, and when he asked Catherine about it later, day they no sell a scrap ey food in the place? she told him not often except for rolls and bacon, rolls and sausage, that kind of thing, which explained the palaver. The woman's apron was better used than her husband's, and Peter thought Gianfranco must be the roll and bacon chief, the one who made all the easy stuff you could throw on a griddle to prepare; the nap of her apron was an abstract in itself, dabs of red juices and the green dyes from Peter didn't know what, and he bet it'd been clean on that day. Catherine withdrew to her counter to make room for the procession; Gianfranco stood in Catherine's place, and the woman stood beside him, her mouth still glittering like a jeweller's shop window, her eyes warm and appreciative. Peter moved his book to make room for the plate, and Gianfranco put it before him like the pretty dish to set before the king, deposited a knife and fork in their right places and a cloth napkin beside folded into a triangle, and then stood upright, casting a glance towards the old woman in the corner who gathered up all the creases in her face to make a frown, and you could tell he was triumphant as if he'd won the war after the loss of so many battles.

My wife, he said, has no good English, you know, but she say to thank you for you choose, eh?

Peter'd never had this treatment anywhere; when he went to drink coffee in the usual kinds of places after a day's work, it was dirty water slopped into a clear glass cup, and a plate of chips fried solid, a bowl of peas and vinegar, nothing like this. He said,

Nae bother, man,

and sat back ready to begin, but Gianfranco hadn't finished his wee ceremony yet.

You say, no bother, but I tell you, roll bacon, roll sausage, you know there is food fit for His Holiness wasted in kitchen we eat for dinner night after night. Is, what you say, eh, a pleasure, is right word, no? a pleasure to serve food my wife cook with own hand, made with the plant you no get in shop here,

Herbs, Gianfranco,

called out Catherine while she was pouring cream into the ice-cream maker, and Gianfranco nodded,

Yes, herb we grow in the garden, sauce made from the best tomato in your country, cheese we bring from home, eh? your best beef, Aberdeen Angus.

Peter thought this wasn't surely for his benefit, not all this, but the wife was waiting, and Gianfranco took her hand and placed it on the crook of his arm, holding it there with a slight pressure, as if their toddler was achieving its first steps in the world. Gianfranco urged him,

Eat, enjoy, say you think is good, is bad.

It looked like strange food right enough to Peter; a fat oblong of he didn't know what, slathered in a sort of custard, and under that it was flexible sheets and then mince in red gravy repeated to the bottom. The smell of it, though; a powerful sour-foot smell of cheese, and he was beginning to regret it when he took his knife and fork in his hand, cut an angle from it and gathered it on the fork; he couldn't look at them as he conducted it to his mouth, in case it was a disappointment.

Peter ate three cuts from it before he looked up at Gianfranco, and then Rosa, both of them like anxious parents. He sat back into his chair, and then licked away at a smear of the cheese custard on the back of his fork.

That's bloody lovely, so it is,

and Gianfranco relayed the news to Rosa, who looked as if she could hardly restrain herself from gathering Peter in her arms and kissing him on the cheek. She danced lightly away to the kitchen, saying something over her shoulder to Gianfranco which he translated for her,

Rosa say sorry, she must look after stove, but she thank you again. I say, you first to eat speciality in long time, so I give half price; is fair, no?

He looked to the corner, to the old woman, who was in her turn looking at Peter as if he'd done something treacherous.

So one man no think is foreign rubbish. He go tell ten more. Maybe Rosa busy now, eh?

Gianfranco gave a big wean's grin to Peter as he turned to go back into the kitchen, trailing his garlic aroma behind him. Catherine was smiling from across the counter, and Peter replied to it again; this time, it stayed with her, all the while she was doing her odd jobs filling the ice-cream churn, polishing the cappuccino machine, threading a spool of paper through the till. He ate more of the lasagne, digging it down by the forkful, thinking, this was the life, and those cunts that called him Picasso at the Minister's Stoup to make him big enough to fit in a matchbox could kiss his arse at this moment right now. He'd even have enough money on him to buy the materials for a painting of Elvis, and maybe more he hadn't considered yet; and some left over to buy another of the specialities when he came back tomorrow to finish the details of the school he hadn't managed, without Elvis around. Speculate to accumulate; his stepfather'd said that until he'd been sick of it. Maybe this time the old boy was right, though; speculate to accumulate, make a sale and invest in fresh paintings, and Peter was eating this beautiful dinner, and glancing over to the waitress as she went about her business on the other side of the counter, and he was thinking tomorrow he'd be back for certain, after his day's work.

There were blokes, down the pub mostly, who said life was cushy for Peter Caulder and the two wastrels he had as mates. They said, aye, yon bastard Caulder, comes in here n says he knows whit it's like fr the workin man; huv ye no seen whit his hauns're like? White as snaw n smooth as paper, loard ey the fucken manor so he is. Sometimes they said it to his face when they became contermacious with the drink, a few pints swilling around in them, the argument in them fleeing out on a spring like a jack-in-the-box. They called him Picasso for a laugh, because Picasso was famous and he wasn't, and Picasso was rich and ditto; they called him that as well because Picasso Caulder, Peter Caulder, it rang like his own name, p and p. But Picasso Caulder was one of them, so he kept telling them, and he was ready with his answers when they gave him snash about the size of his bank account and what big galleries he could be seen hung in, aye, hung right enough, should be hung fr bein a lazy bampoat, they said. Peter told them straight every time it came up, look, ya contrary bastarts ye, I'm fae the same streets as yirsel, n I mean Picasso wis a good comrade, but he went saft wi the cash, n his heid wis in the clouds, he didny peynt fr the people lik I'm dayn, so gie it a rest, it's my round next. All very fine and dandy, his critics never avoided a pint if it was coming along the road with them, and they had to admit he was generous enough when he'd the money for it, though never to his face, but painting for the people? Painting was for toffs and if it was a choice between the gallery and a good game of football, it was ten nil in favour of the latter, and no need for extra time. Now there was art for you; a sweet wee pass through the middle, the ball flying into the goal and swelling the net, all the better if it was the Gers; there was the way to spend your Saturday, not walking around one of those useless cathedrals going to your mates, aye, good

137

colour oan that, aye, nice bit ey canvas there. Painting for the people? More money in painting and decorating; they tried calling him Dulux for a while, he had the hair for it, like the dog on the tele, the long woolly straggle on his napper, but he wouldn't rise to it since he didn't own a tele and didn't know what the fuck they were on about, so there was no fun in that, and they abandoned it.

There was once, when the three of them in the house decided they'd go for a pint together to the Minister's Stoup. Heidless didn't need much persuading, any more than a wean needed telling to reach for his mammy's pap, and Codie was in dire need of escape from his wee gaol, so they went in a posse. The occasion was that Peter had sold a painting of the inside of a foundry to a trades union office, or rather MacHenery had in his wee gallery on Peter's behalf, twenty-five pounds of it that Peter saw after MacHenery had taken his commission. It was wealth beyond the dreams of those barflies, and he made sure they knew it; took out a five pound note from his inside jacket pocket and held it up so everyone could see, including Tommy the owner, said,

Nae rest fr us till it's a' drunk, Toammy.

Tommy was wiping dry the glasses he'd just newly cleaned while he was standing behind the bar.

Well heh, big spender, spend some ey yir cash wi me, whit ye fr, you n the lads?

Daft question; pint for each of them, heavy for him and Codie, which Codie drank like he was sipping a cup of tea, not used to his drink, and Guinness for Heidless which he took over to his own wee table in the corner and threw over his neck like Irn-Bru, he hadn't a bean to his name and he was after his money's worth of Peter's charity. Cunt would be into his plank later on when they got back, no doubt, drink he brought when he'd the national assistance for it and hidden away in case of droughts, bottles of whisky, and eau-de-Cologne when he was desperate. Folk said you could tell when Heidless was broke when his breath smelled like a rose, but he smelled like an overflowed stank. Somebody had to ask what was the cause for celebration, and it was left up to Davie Spence, dapper wee Davie who'd his dinner with the wife and then changed for the evening into a weddings-and-funerals suit which shone like it'd been rubbed with pumice, leaving her to tend to the weans; not as many pints yet down the road he was going, which was out of his cabinet with the weans put to bed by the time he was home so he wouldn't have to listen to their craiking. Davie says,

So whit's wi the spondulicks the night, Picasso, my man? Ye haud up a wean oot tay buy sweeties r somethn?

but Peter knew he had the aces this time, said back, calm as you please,

Sold a fucken peyntn, ya big slave tay capital ye, so ye cn shove that in yir Woodbine n burn it tay fuck,

and everyone made big round mouths and said oooh, which Peter expected, you couldn't impress folk like these as easily unless you'd scored the Gers' winning goal in the cup final. The next thing Harry Burns started leaning against the bar towards Peter, opening that wrecked mouth of his, half the teeth shattered like he'd been hit square in the face by one of those demolition balls, and his words came out like the smoke he was breathing.

Whit I waant tay know, he says, whit I waant tay know is, how cn a man work hard a' his life jist tay make ends meet, feed the wife n weans n keep enough by tay huv a drink wi his chinas, n you swan in here wi a fiver ye've been gied fr a thing ye've made while we've been oot a' day brekkn oor backs tay pey national insurance fr the likes ey yirsel; is that no a dampt disgrace? How cn you dare come in here n tell us yon's lik work we're dayn?

Harry couldn't make t or s properly in his mouth, they came out ch and sh, and whenever he spoke his mouth folded like an envelope over the gap in his teeth, but it was what he said, not how he said it, that made folk at the bar nod, and say, aye Harry, ye've goat him noo, we're peyn him fr his wee hoabby, n the cash jist rains doon oan him; even Tommy behind the bar, on whom more of their cash rained down in a day than Peter would see in his whole working life, nodded at that. Peter was in too rare a mood to be unsettled by pub talk; but he wasn't going to let pure bile like that away so easily. He let them have their wee laugh, and once they were settled he said, gravely,

I've let you jokers away wi shite lik that fr a while noo, but I'm gettn a wee bit fed up wi it, so I'm gonny tell yez jist wance whit goes intay the work I day; aye, work, same as Davie drivin a bus, same as yirsel, Harry, at the shipyaird, no lang tay yir retirement noo, 'm I right? I'm gonny tell yez, n if ye still think it's a fucken skive efter I've tellt yez, then ye're welcome tay gie me yir worst, grouse season is open oan Picasso Caulder, nae boather. But if ye cheynge yir mind efter whit I'm sayn, n decide it's no work ye cn day yirsels, then shut the fuck up n don't gie us ony mare ey yir shite.

Harry Burns lifted the glass to his mouth, tilted it over, but he was hiding behind it, you could tell from the way he couldn't look straight at Peter, looked instead to the spills on the counter. Dapper Davie said,

Nae hairm, man, we're jist huvn a laugh wi ye. Nae offence, like.

See, said Peter, I don't mind a laugh noo n again. But youse guys seem tay think just cause I'm keepin my ain oors n no workn fr a boass n I'm no in a union, I'm no dayn proaper work. Ye're lik the fucken aristocracy, so yez ur, ye're jist a bunch ey fucken snoabs in yir ain wey. Right then; listen n ye might learn somethn. Nother pint, Toammy, n wan tay keep they worthless bams gaun while I lay it oan the line fr thm.

The thing was, Peter told them, you didn't just start with a wee box of wean's watercolours and a blank sheet of paper and then make something up, like they seemed to think you did. You had to have an idea of what you were after painting, like God and his let there be light, now there was an artist for you if you believed your good book, which personally Peter didn't. You could only begin with a good idea, which folk loosely called their inspiration, it wasn't delivered into a letterbox in the back of your head along with the morning post, and Peter's inspiration came from the way folk such as were round the bar the night lived, and worked, and went about their business. The gospel according to Picasso Caulder was that you used the paint, you didn't let the paint use you, or else you were on your way to meaningless abstraction, shapes and waves that meant fuck all to the likes of Dapper Davie and Harry, it was like saying, hooray for fucking paint, look at what paint can do. You went and saw the world, not the world of wealth that was looking for diversion and decoration in a painting, because that was just a different kind of abstract, bribery to turn a blind eye to the mess wealth left behind it; you went deeper into the mess, because there you found real courage, the courage of folk who couldn't afford to make you turn their way. He came up with a for instance; he was coming along the road to his house and he saw this old dear pulling a wicker shopping basket on trolley wheels behind her, walking it like a dog, and the sketchbook came out of his pocket and he just managed to intercept her before she turned into her house; he'd been thinking to himself, what an unbeatable spirit she had about her, with the sky thick like curds over her head and the cobbled street curdled under her as well, like faces staring blindly at each other and her caught in the argument between earth and sky; he knew that had to be a painting the moment he saw it, and that was what was important, showing folk that other painters ignored, that was what it was all about for him.

So you had your idea, whatever it might be, but you'd work to do before you could begin. You could be a lazy bastard, and buy the canvases ready stretched on the frames, or you could do a wee bit of carpentry and do them yourself, which he preferred because it was cheaper, and because he was with the work from the start, involved you might say. You had to have a wee bit of the weaver in you as well, to know your cloth; if it wasn't for the work of the weavers, Peter wouldn't have a profession; and you had to know what was right for the work, cotton would do at a pinch, but linen was best. Now came the carpentry, the making of the frame; again you could be an idler, and buy one ready-made, or you could cut four tenon joints at the corners of your bits of wood you'd bought from the sawmills, and make battens for the middle. Tap them all together, clothe it half around with the linen, pull tight mind or else your canvas'll slide with age like your granny's dugs and make the paint split across for the want of a wee bit of care in the here and now, tap in nails to fix the cloth, and then hammer in wedges to each of the corners to expand the joints and make sure the canvas was tight.

A' that afore ye stert yir peyntn?

said Tommy while he was drawing a half gill from the optic for somebody who'd just come in. Peter and Codie had a wee laugh to themselves, if only,

Fuck no,

said Peter, and went on. Before you'd to lay a stroke of the brush on the canvas, it had to be primed;

Think aboot it, Toammy, whit happens if ye spill a pint ey beer oan that fine westcoat ey yours there?

Tommy brought the drink to the man who'd just arrived, no one they knew, and took the price of it from him in change.

I'm a' wet, n I'm no a happy man.

Whit aboot ile? Whit if ye spilt ile oan yirsel?

Tommy fetched a cloth from under the counter, wiped the beer pumps while he was talking, leaving them wet and no cleaner than before.

Ask my missis, said Tommy, she's aye oan at me efter I've fixed up the caur oan a Sunday, says she'll no get my claes back tay a colour.

All the men stared at Tommy; a car was well beyond their means. Peter nodded though, said it was the same with the bare linen; the oil in the paints soaking into the weave, and they never came out, rotting the cloth so that some time later the strands fell apart while the paints dried into coloured dust. To stop that, you had to paint the canvas with size, and here it was like cookery, dissolving grains of rabbit-skin glue in a pan of water nested inside another pan of water over a gentle flame on the gas stove, the idea being your first pan of water shouldn't boil or else the glue would thicken and be ruined. You brushed that on to your canvas and left it to dry a few days, and then the last thing was to give it a coat of gesso; Harry Burns asked if he was going to paint on the bloody thing or set light to it, and he said,

Gesso, ya eejit, no Esso,

white lead in linseed oil, which you had to cook up for yourself as well, two coats of that, more days waiting for it to dry,

n efter a' that, said Peter, ye're ready. Ye cn stert peyntn.

Harry Burns was slumped over the counter in that exhausted kind of way, as if he'd been through the work himself.

Whit a cairry oan, he said, jist tay pit a lick ey peynt oan a wee bit cloath. Gonny day us a' a favour, Picasso? Buy yirsel a fucken Kodak, n gie us a' peace.

*

So right enough, they had to carry Heidless back to the house when the evening was done, and severe damage was inflicted to Peter's fiver after all the Guinness he'd been soaking up. He was singing The Work of the Weavers every step of the way after he'd heard Peter mention it in the bar.

If it wisny fr the weavers, wherr wid ye be? Aye, wherr'd we a' be, Peter? N Codie, my big china, my china plate; why day we no go oot mare thegether? We're a unit, man, we're a team, we're a FUCKEN TEAM, so we ur,

and there was a speckling of lights following them all the way up the slope to home as folk ruffled their curtains to see what the row was all about, old folk in the main pleased to see it was passing them by and not up to visit.

Peter and Codie had kept their drinking within bounds, didn't want to be up the morning after with their heads not on right and their guts like sacks of manure; but that was the way Heidless preferred it, he didn't feel right until he was seeing the light from the window like a cut-throat razor paring the wallpaper, and he needed the whisky at his ten o'clock rising before he felt like coming out from that reeking den of his. Peter remembered staring into Heidless's eyes once, and thinking it was the kind of look you found in certain breeds of dog he was getting back; a near intelligent clarity, but a kind of a skin separating it from a full understanding of you, you from it, and you often made the mistake of imagining it was the same kind of intelligence as your own. Codie was always saying that the bastard was trouble, they should ditch him first chance they got, non-payment of rent or some excuse like disturbing the neighbours, which was true considering that Codie was in fact the bastard's only neighbour; but Peter was always sticking up for him, reminding Codie that their upbringing had been privileged in comparison to the big man's, and they should be forgiving of him. Easy for Peter to say, Codie thought, when he'd a room to himself, with a door that locked; Codie slept in the recess in the kitchen, with only the space under the bed for a cupboard as well as a wardrobe, and he didn't mind that, wouldn't even have minded the lack of privacy if he'd been living with someone more respecting of it. With Heidless around, he might as well have slept in Sauchiehall Street; the big man had made a habit of coming in at all hours and pulling the curtain from around the bed, no efter a wee chat, man? or, wid ye no like a wee whisky tay help ye sleep? and if Codie raised the objection that he hadn't needed any help with his sleep until ten seconds ago when Heidless threw on the floodlights and opened the curtain, the next thing Heidless would be roaring, think ye're too good fr me, ya fucken prick ye? no waant tay be wan ey the TEAM ony mare? and then stumble away, leaving Codie to mend his sleep as best he could.

That evening, Heidless was all for having a pish against the ground-floor wall of the close, until they told him he was three flights away from the bathroom; they strapped his arms between them and hoisted him up to the top, quietening him before he could start singing and the echoes wakened folk up. Once they were in, they pitched the big man into the bathroom and closed the door behind him; listened as he pished like a horse into the toilet pan. Codie gave Peter a look, not wanting to hear another word about what a shame the big man's dissolution was for such a man of talent; said aloud that he was away to his bed, and then Peter heard the lodging of the chair behind the door handle of the kitchen, a lock that worked sometimes and sometimes didn't for Codie.

Peter listened from his room, with the lock turned, as Heidless's feet dumped all the way to the far end room; and hoped that would be that, so he could waken rested for the big day tomorrow.

The big day was that Peter had decided to go on what Codie termed one of his safaris, when he went out and about looking for subjects. He liked to go on buses until the conductor said they'd reached the terminus, last stop, all ashore that's going ashore, and then walk around until something took his interest, and he'd open up the duffel bag he had slung over his shoulder, take out his wee sketchbook and his three pencils, an H, a B and a 6 B. If he needed to sharpen them, he had a craft knife in the bag as well, but it was better to do your sharpening at home, because if you took out a knife in the open folk thought you were some kind of a hooligan and gave you the big swerve, which wasn't at all what you were after. He'd been all over the town that way, though there were still some wee corners he hadn't reached; today he was going to one of them, to the south and to the east a bit. He'd done some planning for it, knew he was looking for an industrial estate with good big grounds, a road dividing the estate in two, and then the scheme he was after, a tear-drop on the map, swollen against the estate as if to drive development further back, narrow at the southern edge and tapering into countryside.

He packed his things away in the morning, could've died for a cup of Camp to rinse last night out of his mouth, but he wasn't wanting to disturb Codie, who might've been up and doing but it was only fair to give him his own room while he got himself together; he was hoping Heidless would be as considerate, but some hope that was, the big man barely looked after himself, let alone other folks' interests. He left quietly, went to the bus-stop at the end of the slope to catch his first bus into town, had a look up at the dark sky overhead; not good for drawing, but there were some days when you might as well have mixed your colours in an ashtray instead of a palette, and at least it was one of those even spreads of cloud the sun illuminated from behind, making the light a wee bit silvery and good enough to work with.

He caught the second bus in town, near the end of Sauchiehall Street, a number 51 with the radiator that looked like a snarling mouth, and the driver folded away and isolated in his wee cabin. The journey didn't take long, and when the bus stopped, the conductor walked up the aisle saying,

That's yir lot, ladies n gentlemen, I'm sure ye've yir hames tay go tay.

He was deposited on the road that bound the scheme together, heading around in one direction towards what appeared to be a prefabricated school building, and in the other towards the scheme proper, while the road dividing the industrial estate continued on like too much belt sticking out in a tongue from the buckle. The houses were tenements like anywhere else in the town, except for the parts nobody could afford to stay except doctors and lawyers and cunts in business; newer than round his bit, though, short wee bricks sealed with cement and pebble-dashed with quartz and tiny wee round stones like the kind you rescued off the beach when you were a wean. They all had open porches of the kind folk here called verandas, where old folk sat in the summer if the weather was nice, and where they'd put clothes-horses with all their just-washed laundry drooping over the rails so they could get some sun into the weave. The houses on the ground all had brief wee gardens with box hedges grown higher than you could see over, and some were lovely tended and had roses and poppies and hundreds of flowers Peter didn't have a name for, and some were just disastrous, the grass left to grow to seed, the borders thick with any vagrant weed looking for a bed; gardens were wasted on folk like that, Peter thought, it filled him with rage to think there were verandas two floors above with window-boxes and plants in clay pots beautiful-looking and cared for, and there were wasters below with the fucking garden and no intention of looking after it, it broke your heart, so it did. But it was winter now, you couldn't really tell from the way the frost was nipping the ground whose was the best garden out of any of them, so Peter thought he'd better start looking around for this subject of his before the light failed, round about three o'clock before it'd begin to get dark, and he hoisted his bag on to his shoulder and set out.

He went towards the industrial estate, because he was hearing children crying out to each other, gie's the ball, gie's the fucken ball, for fuck's sake, man, ye're dreamin, that's anither fucken goal fur him! ya fucken diddy ye! and one of them was being sent to the moon by the others for slack play by the sound of it. The estate was contained inside a wire and fence-post arrangement that looked like music script from the side, four lines of extruded steel wire stapled at regular heights to square-cut wooden staves, and now and again you'd see a melody of thrushes and crows playing along a fence; he could even hear the notes they were describing in his head, thanks to his stepfather's failed attempt to have some prim woman come to the house and teach him piano when he was younger. Why the blokes who ran the estate had even bothered with the wires was beyond him, unless it was to declare the intention of privacy without exercising their right to it as owners of the land; not only was there an entrance to the place halfway along the road, but there were no barbs on the wires, so the four weans playing kick-a-ball when they should've been at school couldn't've had the least bit difficulty in stretching them apart and climbing in. They were using saplings recently planted as goals, and the ball was running eccentrically over the rough grass;

Peter stopped and watched them for a while, until he realized one of them was taller than the others, better in control of himself, matching the dance of the ball and even now and again performing tricks with it, like now, kicking it up and over the heads of the smaller boys, hurdling them when they were sticking out their legs to trip him and then jinking so the fat wee goalkeeper threw himself to where the ghost of his motion had led him while the ball curved over his legs, a wee tap to send it home and no more.

Peter copied what he was seeing into the book as best he could; children at play, only they were at it as if they were playing for their lives. The big fella was humiliating them deliberately, using his bigger strength and reach and height, and the weans seemed to have forgotten about the ball, now the game was about flooring the cunt so they could steal the ball off him and score into the empty goal nearest to Peter; one against three, only if they'd played by the rules that one would've been enough to put up a big score against them. They were charging him from behind, making themselves into obstacles if they couldn't take the ball off him, but it was like training for the big fella, hardly calling the breath from him at all, while they were blasting out clouds of mist with all the exertion he was costing them. Peter watched for a while so he could see the character of each of them, choosing at first to render static details like the sprays of grass and the big fella's leather jacket which he'd folded and put down alongside one of the goalposts. There was the fat wee goalkeeper, probably chosen because he couldn't run much and because he blocked out more of the goal than any of them, although for most of the time he was spread out on his belly with his arms and legs at all points of the compass. The other two were in proper football strips, the green and white hoops on the shirts, and neither of them came up to the big fella's waist, it was like Gulliver playing fucking Lilliput United, and one of them was the sliding-tackle merchant, trying to chop the legs off the big fella, while the other one was trying to barge him off the ball, and you could hear him crying out, don't gie's yir shite, Elvis, it's fucken legal, it's in the fucken rules, man, look them up fr yirsel. Last of all, there was Elvis himself, in his white teeshirt and denims stained by the grass; Elvis, Peter was thinking, and he was nearly laughing aloud because it was so right for the big fella, big bow wave of black Brylcreemed hair cresting over his head, and the style of him, even how he moved on the ball, a wee jink of the hips and he could take your eyes one way while the ball went the other, that was how he kept scoring against them and that was the scene Peter eventually drew, Elvis riding a vicious tackle and putting the ball into the opposite corner of the goal from the dive of the keeper.

Peter might've been there until the light failed, if it hadn't been for Elvis allowing the wee team to score one past him, and the rules were if you let the ball go by you, you went and fetched it. The ball'd been booted so emphatically by the sliding-tackle merchant that it ran over to the fence, flattening the grass in its road and stopping in front of Peter, lodging between the bottom wire and the tarmacadam of the paving; Peter kicked it towards Elvis with the point of his toe, and as he came closer Peter saw the big fella was hard as concrete, except for two scars, one under each cheek, which looked softer than the rest of him; his hair had spilled forward over his brow, and he smoothed it back into place with the flat of his hand, wiping the oil away on to the nap of his denims before picking up the ball and nodding thanks towards Peter. The next thing, he saw Peter with the sketchbook and the pencil riding over it, and that stopped him; he came over, and it was as if the ball had made him elegant for a short time, his legs were apart at the thighs and he tramped the grass down with his feet side by side like a pretend cowboy at the flicks, and Peter was thinking, fuck.

Whit's the fucken score here, man? said Elvis. Whit're ye dayn wi that thing?

When Elvis looked up at Peter from the book, you could see there was something respectful about him: the hard face he'd on him crumbled and went all soft the way innocence was meant to turn you. The weans got impatient and ran all the way over, except for the fat keeper who tried a few dumpy steps and then trotted off behind them, coming in last; the sliding-tackle merchant was first to the fence, and he said,

Whit's gaun oan, Elvis, man? Keepin the fucken ba' tay yirsel? Heh, whit's this?

He went to snatch the book out of Elvis's hand, but Elvis pulled away from the wee lunge.

Your ma no teach you tay be cerrful wi ither folks' proaperty? Blok's drawn wur picture, look.

He held it up for them to see, wouldn't let them take it from him. The bargeman and the fat keeper arrived and stared, pointed at themselves in the drawing, looked at Peter when Elvis fingered him as the artist, and they were all jumping like monkeys for him to do a picture of them alone, but he took the pad from Elvis and said,

Sorry boays, another day mebbe, I've a wee proposition for Elvis here.

Elvis collected his jacket and followed Peter up the road like he was his uncle or something; could've been as well, Elvis didn't look that long out of school but he was as hard as a nut, seemed to be looking for someone to follow. That said, he'd asked for payment for the service he was to provide, no fool Elvis, and he knew just where to go to find it; took Peter into the heart of the scheme, to a single offy with a beleaguered-looking front of corrugated metal you could peel off and into the roof if you were feeling secure, only it never moved by the look of it. Elvis undid one of the zip fasteners in his jacket and took out some Navy Cut, offered one to Peter, took one himself when he was refused, lit it from a box of matches and threw the stick on to the chessboard concrete paving in front of the shop, and nodded towards the door for Peter to come in with him. The shop had olive-coloured lino and a wooden counter at waist height; notices that said NO SPITTING pinned on to the shelves where there were cans of food as well as the beers and bottles of cheap bevvy. The man behind the counter was more like an undertaker, and he'd a suit on as if he was saying, this is a respectable establishment and I'll have it treated that way, but the booze was reeking in it, and Peter wondered if the old man hadn't taken a sly sampling of his own stock, just to be getting along with. He said,

Hullo there, Elvis, whit're ye efter the day? Mare Navy Cut? Yir ma's groceries? Or it widny be a wee drap booze fr yirsel n yir mate there, wid it?

Elvis grinned, milked his fag for more smoke, stood a wee bit away from the counter.

Three cans ey Tennent's, Charlie, n yir man there's peyn.

Charlie raised his eyebrows, turned to the shelf, gathered the tins and put them on to the counter beside the till. He wrapped them like a present in the tissue paper kept for the purpose, drew out a band of sticking tape from one of those roller contraptions that made the adhesive screech when the tape was separated, stuck down the package so you could open it easily; Peter went into his corduroy pocket for the money, took out a ten bob note and laid it on the counter alongside the cans. Cunt gave Peter one of those looks, like he was showing off his money, and Peter was thinking to himself, aye, ya bastart ye, ye'll pit oan this voice when ye're at yir shoap, but ye'll likely be livin in Bishopbriggs aff the money fae it, and he wanted to tell him that was the last flush he'd be for a while, until he'd another painting bought and sold. Charlie rang it up on the till, and spoke to Elvis while he was doing it, asking him how he was managing now he was on the brew; Elvis said he didn't mind, only it was worth his apprenticeship just to sort out that slave-driving wee cunt that had it in for him, if ever there was a man asking to have his coupon stamped for him it was McBride, him and his fucking good experience, good experience if he hadn't to do the work. He ignored Peter as if he was smoke from Elvis's Navy Cut.

So they got away from Charlie, Charlie the right wee leech Peter had decided, and went towards the school, where Peter wanted Elvis to pose, a walk along a few streets of old folk and women pushing their prams. On the way, Peter asked him about that name of his, was that his right name or not, and Elvis cracked open his lips, he even had the sneer showing the tobacco stains on the teeth. He said it was after the way he dressed, of course, but it annoyed him a wee bit, because he'd been trying to copy the style of Marlon Brando, out of On the Waterfront, only folk thought of Elvis when they saw him, his right name was Patrick, Pat or Paddy.

But I'd sooner huv Elvis than fucken Paddy, he said, n I'd sooner huv Marlon Brando than eether ey them.

Once they were settled, and stood outside the gates of the prefab school, Peter let Elvis have one of his beers. From a different pocket than the one he'd taken his cigarettes out of, Elvis took out a tool for puncturing triangular holes in the tops of cans; he made two holes, one for drinking out of and one to let the liquid flow, and he offered one of the three cans to Peter, but Peter shook his head,

Ye're a' right, Elvis, said Peter, they're yir weyges, n it widny be right fr the boass tay be takin yir weyges aff ye.

In fact, he wanted the beer can in the picture, for effect as well as because Elvis wouldn't be dipping down to lift it from the ground when he was after a swallow. Next, he'd to fix Elvis in a pose he liked; he chose a place for him to stand where the geometries of the grid of windows appeared as regular as graph paper, and were dominated by the uprights of the iron fence girdling the playground; he took chalk from his duffel bag, which he left to stand on the tarmac beside him, and then went over to Elvis and drew the silhouette of his boots on the pavement.

Lik wan ey they polis films, int it? said Elvis. Ye know, cunt gets murdered n they draw oot the wey he wis lyin oan the grun.

Peter looked up at the big man while he was on his knees in front of him. The sky overhead was like cotton bales, still no rain threatened by the cloud, and it was queer, this angle he had; it was still bright enough for an optical illusion, the fence slicing Elvis like ham on a butcher's counter, and behind him the lights were on in the school, and you could see the heads of the weans by the window seats, distracted by the movement outside. When he looked into Elvis's face, Peter saw the two scars under the ledges of his cheekbones, one on either side, shaped like the hook of a question mark, and he'd been thinking about them on the way up the road. Now wasn't the time to ask, though; and Peter finished making the prints on the ground, pocketed the chalk and stood up, taking a few paces back to where his bag was resting, and then reached into it for his book and pencils.

Peter always made conversation with his subjects, because he knew how the boredom could get to some folk, especially the ones he paid in booze; they got the thirst in them, began to wish they hadn't agreed to do it, and you'd look down at your book and by the time you'd recorded a touch of shadow here and there and looked up again for a reference, they'd shifted just a telling fraction, and your shadow or your highlight or whatever you'd been working on wasn't there any more, and you had to aggravate them by asking them to move back to where they were so you could catch it again. Better to have them moving their lips instead of anything else, so Peter encouraged them to tell long stories so he could keep them spinning by going mm hm now and again, or nodding whenever he had to raise his head. He thought there was a story in Elvis's scars, so he asked about them; not that Elvis was shifting around, he wasn't bad as sitters went and the drink didn't make him too restless, if only Heidless could hold his drink as well, and he was asking things like, heh man, is the light no too dull fr drawn? and he was taking an interest in why Peter was using this pencil first and then another, maybe too close an interest, so Peter threw him a stick to fetch, asked him, I'm dayn yir face jist noo, Elvis, whit's the score wi they marks ye've oan ye? an oaperation or somethn? and Elvis laughed and said, aye, wi nane ey yon stuff they use tay pit ye oot fr an oor, and then he hooked the thumb of his free hand into the pocket of his denims, where it'd been at the start of the drawing, took in and held a breath, and began the story of how he'd acquired them.

There was the gable end of a house some distance away over Peter's shoulder. Elvis pointed to the red crest on it, MYT. This is oor scheme, he said, like him and his mates were the local garrison. He asked Peter if he'd seen the motorway on the far end of the scheme, the other side of the industrial estate, splitting the scheme from another one across the way. Peter said he knew about it from the map, but he'd never seen it. The cunts on the other side of the motorway called themselves the Mad Street Team; the right name for the place was MacDiarmid Street, but they shortened it to mad, they liked the sound of it, mad by name, mad by fucking nature. See, you respected your elders, you didn't make life hard for old folk, they were frail enough as things were; but the Mad Street cunts had their leader aff put into the gaol for burglary, receiving stolen goods, a list longer than your arm, so they'd a new, ambitious leader who thought he'd get in with the boys he'd ridden to secure the job by being bolder than the one before him. So the raids into the MYT's scheme started; they were thieving the pension books out of the handbags and pockets of the old folk on their way back from the post office, and then going back to their own scheme with the loot. The provocation began like that; it went on with burglary, a few assaults on folk coming out of the pub, and they were making the MYT look like charlies in their own bit, their territory you might say. That's whit they Mad Street cunts're like, though, said Elvis, dayn ower auld men n women, that's their fucken level, know whit I mean? So something had to be done, and it was, one evening when dark was falling. They planned it like Montgomery, knew where to broach the diamond-link fence so they wouldn't be seen, some half mile up the motorway, rubbed themselves into the shadows as they went towards where the Mad Street Team congregated, in the ruins of an old factory. The three incomplete walls sheltered the Mad Street bastards, and there was a fire inside, so they did a count before they attacked, surrounding them and then spilling over to give them their well-deserved doing.

Doin?

said Peter, to keep him talking.

Aye, man, a right doin. Fucken boatls, chibs, razors, craft knives, knuckledusters, man, the fucken works so it wis.

So ye goat they scars in the fight?

Naw, man, escapin efter it.

It was bad luck, mostly. The Mad Street Team should've been confused, tending to their wounded, in a right fucking daze after the hiding they took, but they were alert enough to see that Elvis, unlike the rest of his mates, had got caught in the web of the fence, his jacket pierced through by the barbed wire crowning it, and heard him struggling to free himself, unable to get any leverage to help. The ones that were able ran over to the fence, swarmed up the links, ten feet or so, and they weren't caring about the state of Elvis's jacket; tore him loose and let him fall the distance on to his side. He heard a pop like a cork coming out of a bottle, and then his arm was no use, like a dead one grafted on to him, except if it'd been dead it wouldn't've been so painful. He got to his feet by pressing on his good arm, but there wasn't any point in running, and he couldn't fight for himself properly, so he took the doing they gave him in return because there was nothing else for it, four of them on to him. They were getting tired of how easy it was when the leader aff had a new game for them to play with their toy, dancing him around the wilderness of shale in a tango and leading him by his dead arm while the others chanted, da ra ra rum dum, da ra ra RA RA, fucking him one in the balls with their knees on the beat, and then they were even tired of that after a while. The leader aff wasn't finished yet, though, and he told them to drop Elvis on to the ground; they landed him on his dislocated arm, causing the pain to hack at him when his whole weight settled on it, but he was determined he wasn't going to cry out like a wean, not for their satisfaction. The next thing, they were rolling him on to his back, and the leader aff sat astride his chest even though there wasn't any need to pin him; the daft thing was, Elvis was seeing the moon over the leader's shoulder, shining hard enough to plate the clouds around it, and then there was the leader by its side, his face just as ruined, he could feel the leader aff over him, pulling on him like the tide. The leader aff said, the patient's in worse shape than I thoat, nurse, he's gonny need major fucken surgery, razor please nurse, and that was when Elvis went as dead as his arm, though he felt the cold on his skin, and just a pressure on his cheek, nothing more than that.

It was like one of they westerns, the cavalry coming over the hill; the rest of the MYT hadn't done a proper head count until they got to the other bank of the motorway, when they realized they'd left one of their own in enemy territory. Probably the rush of cars had torn away with his yelling for help wrapped around the bumpers, but the main thing was they found him; the Mad Street bastards were good enough for punishing one of the MYT, but they weren't up to facing the whole crew, so they fled and left Elvis with two new mouths in his face. There'd've been murder that night if the MYT had caught up with any of the cunts, but it was their territory, they melted like snow and there wasn't a hope of finding them again.

Fucken Humpty Dumpty, man, Elvis said. Took the fucken hoaspitl tay pit us thegither again.

Naebdy ask how ye goat yir war wounds?

Aye, polis n fucken every cunt, man. Couldny day a fucken thing aboot it, but. We jist says, me n the rest ey them, hit n run, yir honour, messn aboot oan the motorwey, aye it wis a stupit thing tay day but we're jist minors, whit d'ye expect wi boays runnin aboot? Course, they knew different, but whit could they day when we jist stuck tay wur stories?

But Elvis wouldn't let it rest; once his ribs and his arm had healed up and the stitches were removed from his cheeks, oh man, I wis a fucken tiger oan the fucken prowl, believe it. He and his mates went in teams of two or three to check out the Mad Street crowd in their own roost, settled a few scores with the Indians before they went after the chief.

N then, man, they hud tay stitch him up like a quilt efter I'd done wi him.

It was cold out; Peter usually preferred to work with his coat off, just for the feeling of mobility it gave him, freedom of movement, but today he'd the duffel coat buttoned, and he'd to resist wearing his old granny gloves without the fingers to feel the blood in his hands. He was blending the tone of the 6 B pencil on the page to better represent the liquid quality of the shine on Elvis's jacket; he was using the end of a finger to achieve it, rubbing the blackness to make it softer where it followed the round of the torso.

Are they no gonny get yiz back for a' this, Elvis, man?

Elvis shrugged, looked down to see if his feet were still fixed in the silhouettes, returned his head to exactly where it'd been.

Naw, man. See, they'd like ye tay think they're mad, but ye've jist goat tay show them if they're mad, you're pure fucken mental.

Peter had the sketch finished on schedule, just before the bell rang to allow the weans out of their school, and as the darkness came down. Elvis hadn't thought he'd have to make like a statue for so long, and he was saying, if I'd ey known, man, I'd ey askt fr mare booze, but he was smiling when he said it, only a wee bit though because his field surgery had cut the strings of muscle which enabled him to smile; the scars were animated, turned into quotation marks around everything he said. Peter still had a bit of work to do on the background, the school behind him, but that was no reason to keep Elvis standing, he could just as easily do that tomorrow, so he thanked Elvis for his time and went into his pocket to give Elvis another couple of bob for being so cooperative; packet of cigarettes, cans of beer, whatever he fancied. Elvis was like a face carved on a totem pole, and he didn't show much in the way of gratitude, but he wouldn't let Peter away before he'd seen himself in the book, and when he gave it back to Peter, he said,

D'I hear you right, man; ye're gonny day yir drawn up as a peyntn?

Peter said yes he was, and put the book into his duffel bag along with the three pencils. It was a daft thing he did next, but he went into the bag and took out a craft knife, showed it to Elvis, who took it from him, extended the blade with a stroke of his thumb on the key, and then cut the air around him to ribbons, testing it like a wean with a new toy. He made sure the blade was in its housing before he gave it back to Peter, and there was admiration about the way he said,

Whit're you dayn wi wan ey thaim, man? You in yir ain gang?

Peter shook his head,

I sharpen my pencils wi it, Elvis. Ye cn day ither things wi it as well, see, part fae strippn the hide aff ey some poor cunt.

Elvis's eyes rolled like marbles in his head, like Peter'd just taken off his duffel coat to expose the robes of a priest, some kind of missionary.

I niver cut nae cunt that wisny askn fr it, man. Ye away jist noo?

Peter dropped the blade into his bag, pulled on the drawstring to close it, shouldered it.

Aye, I'm away. Is there a place near here that serves tea or coffee, mebbe a wee bite tay eat? I'm pure famished.

He was in bed, the night after he'd met Catherine, when the fight between Codie and Heidless began. His first thought when the crash wakened him up was that the polis had charged the door, and he was thinking it was all to do with his association with Elvis; that he'd been observed talking to a suspicious character, and that they were going to question him about how Elvis had come about his injuries; it was a thought out of a dream, and here was him drunk with sleep, driven out of his bed and into a pair of cords in case his own room door came down around him. He went for the light switch by the door, if he was going to be arrested as an accomplice he at least wanted to see the faces of the officers; it was like the A-bomb going off, the bulb flaring and withering his eyes, the room taking shape around him as he let the light seep in a little at a time through his lids; but there was nothing, except the din was further away than he'd thought it'd be, two doors distant at least and inside the house. Heidless and Codie were crying out again, and in his tiredness Peter was thinking to himself, I thought we'd got all that sorted. Peter was vacant with the sleep, thinking it was that fucking Heidless and his drink, he'd been sucking out of his planked bottles and he was brainless let alone headless after the alky claimed his reason. Peter left the room determined to lead the big man away from Codie and give him the telling he hadn't been able to earlier, hoping that Heidless was in a fit state to understand the row he'd be getting.

Peter's room was the only one lit in the house, and he walked the gilt spread in front of him from his door until it frayed halfway along the hall, when he had to reach into the open door of the kitchen to switch on the light there. He wasn't expecting to see a vicious bread knife in Heidless's hand, with its serrated edge ready to slice through Codie's chest, and Codie in a position of disadvantage, seizing the big man's wrists to keep the blade. Codie was being pressed down against the mattress by Heidless's weight; he was crying out,

Leave me be, ya fucken murderous bastart ye!

while all Heidless could manage was,

No wan ey the team, cunt ye, fucken take ye oot ey the fucken team!

The sudden light drove them apart; their eyes closed to protect them from the brightness, just like Peter's a minute before, and of the two Heidless seemed worse affected; the hand with the knife opened out and let the blade fall on the mattress while he tried to shade his eyes, but Codie kept a tight grip on the wrist, not knowing where the knife was, and both men were grinning with blindness. Peter took the opportunity to dart forward and pick the knife away from them, the king in this particular blind kingdom for now; said,

Right, yous two, I've goat the fucken knife, if yez waant tay day ony mare rough stuff there's jist foarks n butter knives in the drawers noo.

Codie opened his eyes, saw Heidless's hand was empty; rage flitted across his face, and he said under his breath,

Right, ya fucken mad bastart, I'll pit ye oot ey the fucken team, so I will.

Peter just watched as Codie worked on Heidless; he'd never seen Codie roused so much, but he gave the big man such a tanning you'd think he was after him for leather, and Peter allowed it after what he'd seen from the doorway. The worst of it was, the big man was so far gone with the drink he could hardly defend himself; Codie danced him around the open floor of the kitchen like Elvis being danced around by the Mad Street team, avoiding where his easel had been set up until the risk of Heidless falling into it was too great, and then he grasped the big man by the lapels and landed him in the hall. Peter was all for intervention at one point, when the blood from the big man's nose started up again, and he stepped forward and said,

Haud oan a minute, Codie, he's bleedn again, gie him a fucken rest fr Christ's sake,

but Codie was busy standing over the big man, moulding the mad bastard's face with his fists; he turned to Peter and said casually,

Aye, that right? Least it's comin oot ey a good hoanest sore face, no a fucken stab wound,

and then he went back to work.

Peter allowed it only as far as he thought the punishment was right, and the time to stop seemed to be when Heidless was beyond defending himself with his arms around his head. He went forward and pulled Codie away by the pyjama legs so he had to trot back with Peter, and Codie stood facing Peter while the big man wallowed around, feeling for the ground under him; both his eyes were fat and his lips swollen, his nose seeping with blood and snotter woven into the beard, he was a state and Peter argued that if an example was being made of the big man, then there it was, he'd likely never cross Codie again, he could be safely left in his den until the morning. Codie was having none of that, though; he was kissing the blood off his sore knuckles, said,

No fucken hope, man. He goes oot intay the street the night, alang wi the rest ey the dugs. Smell im, fr fuck's sake, Peter, niver mind the cunt's efter near stabbin us, aw Christ,

and it was true, the big man had evacuated himself, whether from fear of Codie or because the beating had stolen control of his bowels;

Peter recoiled from it, and even Codie took a couple of steps back, as much as he'd wanted to approach Heidless to resume the lesson. The least Peter could do for Heidless was to argue with Codie that he couldn't be put out until he'd found another place to live, and certainly not in the state he was in; but Codie was doubled over with his head between his legs and his hands braced against this knees, exhaustion taking him now, and in between breaths he said,

No, no the morra, no the day efter, next week r next fucken year; he takes his fucken hoose wi him, n he leaves this door fucken noo, d'ye hear me? right fucken noo, n then he cn shite oan the streets n pish himsel n make a fucken bog oot ey ony shoap doorway he cn cry hame.

Heidless was still on the floor near the front door, creeping like a wean; tried to haul himself towards the closed door of his room, stopped and leaned against the door, drew back from the tenderness of his bruises on the wood. Peter couldn't keep the two pictures in his head at the one time; Heidless leaning over Codie with that louring face on him, putting his weight into nailing Codie with the knife; Heidless now, beaten to the ground, beyond help or charity. He remembered Heidless from the days when he made sense; the art school, before they'd met Codie, when him and Peter would go to all the bars with only sawdust for a carpet. The big man knew how to talk then; he'd had a good brain in his head before the drink turned it rotten. They drank to the death of the ruling classes and the first day of the dictatorship of the proletariat; there were comrades organizing all around the town, and these comrades were heroes to them, seeing through all the wee tricks the bosses played to keep a fair wage out of the hands of those who created their wealth for them. Peter always minded on one time they were in the bar, and Heidless told Peter why it was all so unfair, this world of bosses and shite wages; know whit the biggest robbery ey a' time is, man? naw, 's no they fucken balloons n thon mail train, fucken monkey nuts, man, no worth fucken botherin. Biggest fucken robbery's the theft ey yir time, man, aye it is, aye it fucken is, tell ye why if ye'll gie a cunt the chance tay speak. The big man, big Karl, comrade Marx himsel, tells us cunts sell their labour tay the boasses, n it's the only bit ey the coast ey the proaduct they're makin the boasses cn pinch the pennies oan, 'm I right? aye I'm ur. Well, nay disrespect tay the big man, but that's shite, aye it is, man, aye it fucken is, gie us a fucken chance, man, gie the dialectic a chance tay develop, will ye? Right, shut it n listen. It's no jist yir labour they're buyin when a boass takes ye oan; it's yir fucken time n a', wid you no sooner be dayn ither things thn a shite joab fr shite weyges, aye ye wid, ye wid n a' ya lyin bastart ye, don't gie's this dignity ey fucken labour shite, whit fucken dignity is there in plankin bits intay a wireless set or fucken near gettn yirsel killed pittin a ship thegither? Aye, very fine if it's nationalized n we're takin the proafits, ye're workin fr yirsel then, but nay fucken good tay day it fr anither man's fucken comfort, eh? That's fucken stealin, so it is; they're stealin yir fucken time, these boasses, n there's nay coampensation in the world'll gie ye back yir life, 'm I no right? Peter didn't agree, though; called on the memory of his father, his real father, the pride he took in his work; how he'd always said that a rivet properly fixed was more than just work, it was a responsibility to the poor blokes who'd have to work and live on the ship, he was as much keeping them safe as he was earning his living, and that, Peter explained, was why folk needed to see the bonds between themselves and every other worker in the world, the loyalty owed to folk you'd never even met in your life and likely never would; the carelessly patched ship could kill by the hundreds, the badly made wireless could just electrocute someone, all of them your comrades relying on your honest good work. Heidless read his scriptures differently to Peter, however; the objects coined for profit were in themselves corrupt and were therefore undeserving of the worker's concern; and the two of them circled around the knot they'd tied between them, and at that time Heidless wouldn't let it interfere with his drinking, and so they chimed their pint glasses together and agreed to differ on it.

Peter saw his old comrade now after years of isolation, how he'd turned in on himself so the anger he'd put into his work that he wanted to force down the world's throat had risen to choke him, and he was saddened by it; but there was Codie and himself to think of, and there was only his own conscience left to appease.

Whit's the big man gonny day if we chuck im oot oan the street this very fucken instant?

Codie rubbed the points of his sore knuckles, started to walk towards Heidless's room.

Ever see the end ey Gone wi the Wind? Well, I'm fucken Rhett Butler.

Mind you, Rhett Butler didn't peel Tara from around Scarlett the way Codie did for Heidless while the big man littered the floor in front of his room, sleeping off the punishment. Codie took swimmer's breaths from outside before he entered the stinking hole of a place, and he was looking for anything the big man might be justified in coming back for if it turned up missing. There were clothes ankle deep on the floor, which Codie stuffed into a carrier bag, not even bothering which had been worn and which hadn't; there was the big man's gallery of watercolours over the bed, and Codie unhooked them one by one, and he was thinking that Heidless didn't have much to show for three years; nine pictures, and one on the easel alongside the bed, which Codie flattened and rested on the floor beside its owner.

Peter watched from the threshold of his room as Codie made a pile of tangled clothing, the watercolours dense with glass which was a thing neither Peter nor Codie needed with their works in oils, the easel with a work in progress fixed to it, more men in the boozer, which was Heidless's subject just as derelicts were Codie's. Peter thought it was only right they should try and cover the unfinished painting if they were going to be leaving it out on the street; Codie suggested they use his clothes for that, since paper would be no use if it began raining, and Peter agreed, and helped Codie with the shifts down the stairs. The last thing to shift was Heidless himself; but before they tried to lift him, Codie went into the kitchen, felt around underneath his bed until he found a pen and paper, and then sat at the kitchen table to write a message for Heidless for when he wakened up. It said: This is just to let you know why youve no home to go to, last night you tried to stab me in my bed with a bread knife, so now youl have to find a bed of your own as your no longer welcome to live here, signed, and on one side of the paper he made a signature, and gave the pen over to Peter, who was standing over him reading the contents. Peter didn't take the pen at first, but Codie wouldn't let it go or let it down on to the table, and at last Peter took it from him and signed on the other side away from Codie, muttering,

Hell ey an eviction notice tay haun tay ony poor cunt.

Codie took the pen from him when he'd finished, stood up with the chair clawing the linoleum behind him, folded the note in two with a severe nip of his finger and thumb to give the fold a sharp edge.

Hell ey a fucken wey tay get yirsel evicted, pullin a knife oan a blok.

Peter didn't even want to help Codie shift the big man down the stairs to rest beside his possessions, but one man couldn't've shifted him, so Peter took one of Heidless's arms around his shoulder, and they walked him down almost exactly as they'd walked him up the other night on the way back from the Stoup, with him strapped between them in a brotherly way. Codie held his head as far away as his neck would stretch to keep the reek from him, but Peter was watching in case their legs fankled together on the way down.

Eventually they got him down the stairs; Codie would've dropped him like a sack if it hadn't been for Peter lowering him to land softly beside all his things. His face was distorted by his beating; the tiles of his pictures were silver under the mercury lamps. Codie had to persuade Peter back up to the house with him; before they left, Codie took his message from out of his pocket, hooked his finger on the collar of Heidless's fisherman's jumper and put the message under it like the last rag of stuffing, and then he took Peter by the arm and guided him towards the close and up the stairs.

Before they went to their beds for the night, Codie shut the door of Heidless's old room on the rotten smell from inside, and locked the outside door with two turns of the mortise. He saw Peter standing by the threshold, went towards the kitchen, said,

Ye were tellin me ye've a wummn lined up, Peter. Least ye'll no be ashamed tay bring her hame this time.

Codie was about to turn away when Peter said his name, turning him back; he stared at Peter, waiting for him. Peter had his fists tightened, held by his side, and the look on him was as dark as the hallway between them.

Codie, we hud tay soart this, if the big man wis gonny be a danger tay us. See ye mind whose name's oan the fucken lease, right?

Codie shrugged, now the danger had been dealt with, like a leaking gas pipe or a bare electrical wire.

Nay boather, Peter, he said. If my stepfaither boat me a hoose, I'd huv my mates steyn wi me n a'. Mebbe I jist widny choose wan tay stey that wis aff his fucken heid, but mebbe that's jist me, eh?

Peter didn't know which made him more angry, that Codie wouldn't even mourn for the big man, or that the cheeky bastard had reminded him of the gift he'd had from Reginald, the gift of this house, which he'd only taken after his mother's pleading, and her call to the memory of his real father, he'd've wanted you to be secure, son, I know you'll never thank Reginald for it, but take it for me. He made her work for it, but not for too long; Reginald made sure he knew that he was only being granted the house as a favour to his mother, but he still demanded that she say his father's name to him in front of Reginald to earn Peter's trust, and he watched Reginald's face the whole time while his mother was composing herself and said in the snobby telephone voice she affected all the time these days, will you accept Reginald's gift for the sake of Thomas, your father? and Peter read the distaste from Reginald and said, aye, I'll take it fr his sake. It left him open to all kinds of slurs from them that didn't understand he needed a base from which to pursue his father's battle in art; class traitor, failing courage of convictions erected on sand, sell out, he'd heard them all, some meant in fun, some meant to scar his pretensions. But Peter knew he'd done the right thing; never asked for a penny in rent from Codie or Heidless, and as he said, every artist since the year dot had had their patrons; sooner it was in the name of his father, than that he'd have to set aside the battle his father had begun.

Codie went to bed, and Peter went after him, to his own room. He put out the light; didn't even take off the clothes he'd put on for going downstairs, just pulled the sheets over himself as he was. He closed his eyes once he was nested in the mattress, but he couldn't get to sleep for listening, Heidless howling in the dark the way he always did when he was agitated; but there was no sound, and Peter spun to face one wall and then the other, waiting to hear the cries from the abandoned wean in the street.

Seven

She was dressed for seducing the first time she went to Peter's house. She brought a small overnight bag with her to Gianfranco's so she could change in the staff toilet, and a make-up purse inside so that she could work on her face in the mirror above the cracked porcelain sink. The toilet was a wee booth of a place next to the stairs that took you to the family house over the shop; there were all kinds of smells in there, garlic from the kitchen, pine disinfectant, even the rot from outside where the waste went to be collected, all coming in through the pane of frosted glass Gianfranco always kept open for ventilation. There was hardly room for changing, but she managed; out of her waitress's clothing and into a black dress zipping up at the back, and the contortions she had to go into just to find the zip; she remembered Cameron fixing her into the dress the day Francis came back from the hospital, and then closed the lid on it guiltily. She had to bend down to see herself in the mirror to apply the make-up; put all of her bottles and palettes on the coast of the sink, in order, foundation, powder, eye-shadow, rouge, kohl, lipstick, fragrance, and set to work quickly, not having as much time as she'd been used to when she wasn't working. She padded the foundation on her face; put crescents of blue on her eyes, reddened her cheeks so she was blushing like a bride, exaggerated the blackness of her lashes, finished by spraying fragrance behind her ears, and then she collected everything up and put it back in the black purse, clasped it shut and returned it to the overnight bag. The last thing she had to do was to fetch out her stiletto heels and slip into them; and once that was done, she was high over the sink, and the mirror was reflecting her midriff. She thought of something before she bent to zip up the overnight bag; grasped the strap of her dress and brought the slack up to her nose; she was trying to catch the smell of the kitchen from it, because she always noticed how the grease and the smell of onions wove itself into the fabric of her work clothes, and it wouldn't do for tonight if she was going to be giving off the odour of one of Rosa's special dinners. Peter'd said it was a bit of a walk from the bus stop to where he lived, and she thought maybe the airing would wash it clean.

Francesca and Beatrice were in Paradise when she left the shop; they were both in their working pinafores, having each done their homework for the night. Catherine opened the woollen coat she'd put on against the cold, and put her hands to her hips, spinning like a model to give them a laugh; Beatrice had a disapproving mouth on her, tilted down at the ends, but her sister seemed to be admiring and jealous, wanting to be old enough to wear something like that. She said,

Is it that man who used to come into the café during the day you're going to meet? Are you going to the dancing?

The funny thing was, Catherine was thinking when she closed the door of the café behind her and stepped into the light it cast on the pavement before crossing into the dark, how she'd protected Francesca from knowing. She wondered if she'd've been the same with Cameron when he grew to be her age; it never seemed to matter to you when you'd a wean of your own whether it was the skin flayed off their knees after a bad fall, or worrying they'd commit the same stupidities you'd committed yourself, there was something in you that made you want to keep them away from hurt. She knew Francesca was frustrated her father had chosen a convent school for her education, maybe that was behind her boy madness; it was all statues and pictures when you went into a chapel, no way through the skin of seeming to the sacred heart, the mysteries they represented. Francesca'd allowed her up to her room once, played a recording of her favourite group on a Dansette, and Catherine'd thought it was a shrine she'd entered, pictures cut from newspapers on the wall, a scrapbook doubled in size and weight by all the articles she'd torn and folded. The record finished soon enough, but Francesca wouldn't sit on the end of her bed in silence, went over to the Dansette and lifted the arm, placed the stylus carefully on the groove conducting the arm towards the song; the music was worn threadbare, scored across by continual playing. She'd said to Catherine, perching on the end of the bed while Catherine stood looking at the same face repeated in a hundred different attitudes, I don't get to meet boys at the school, but I want someone like him to be my first boyfriend, and Catherine was thinking of herself, God love you, because it was all toys and collections just now, a game of pretend.

Catherine walked a little towards the stop where she'd catch the first of the buses she'd need to take. There was an elderly woman standing there already, with an old wicker pannier on her arm, and a flower-patterned dishcloth protecting the contents. Catherine thought of Little Red Riding Hood to see the basket, but the more she looked into it, her eyes growing accustomed to the sodium glare, the more she saw of it; the neck of a bottle piercing the cloth at the edge, and a liquid rising in the neck that the orange light made colourless. She looked up at the woman, who was wearing a headscarf that shone like silk, maybe was silk for all she knew; the old biddy had her own thoughts to hide, turned her head away from Catherine, but kept her eyes on her for a while, taking her judgement with her. It was as if the woman had heard her telling Francesca, yes, Fran, I'm going to the dancing; and she was thinking, she hadn't felt like this since the days she'd gone with her family to the confessional, when Father Byrne asked if you'd any sins to confess, and she'd wonder what her da'd said before her.

She had to walk up a slope to get to Peter's house, which wasn't easy in heels; and they hadn't got round to pouring tarmacadam on the road or the paving yet, and that meant having to keep her balance on the backs of cobbles rounded like lenses, and not catching the points of the stilettos in any of the fissures open between them. His part of town was strange to her, different to the scheme she lived in; there was a girdling of sandstone buildings around the foot of the hill, but on the slope there were smaller houses, grey like granite, the roofs dipping and peaking in waves, the slates lapping against the house at the top as if it was a modest wee baronial home secured behind the ramparts, a harbour fortress or something. Everything was made silver by mercury arc vapour lights at intervals, burning towards the head of the slope; she followed them, approaching the keep at the top, and when she stopped and looked up towards it, she wondered how she was meant to get inside; it seemed a terribly complicated wee place, huddling above the others, privileged somehow. It had faceted sides like a jewel, and light bulbs glimmering in the windows, and no way in that was obvious at a first glance. If it hadn't been for Peter's instructions, she'd've been taking the first door she saw, which Peter'd told her led into the old disused steamie in the basement the elderly folks in the building remembered doing their laundry in all together, but thanks to him she knew to go up the stairs laid into the wall on one of its jagged sides, walking through the strange wee dwarfed forest of clothes-pole trees rooted in the concrete to get to them. Once she was inside, there was a spiral staircase leading towards flat landings with doors set opposed to each other like men waiting to start an argument. There was lighting sprouting from stems on each of the landings, a single pearl bulb high on the wall, and she could see as she rose higher in the close that each of the household's doors were different, some glazed like her one at home with a panel of frosted glass so you could tell the shape of a visitor, and some of them blind, plain wood painted with dark stain, some lacquered dark and some of them left to show the grain, telling of the pride the householders took in how they presented themselves. The close smelled of butter and cooking, like her own, but she'd seen in the well at the bottom of the stairs stains of black piss against the dull green ceramic tiling, and she knew folk coming home from the pub sometimes weren't fussy about their toilets, wondered if it was anybody living here or not.

Peter's house was at the top of the stairs, inconveniently enough, which meant a long climb during which she heard the ticking of her heels coming back to her, draining into the deep stairwell like water spinning down a sink. She was using the banister to guide herself up, her hands made into claws around it, her fingers seized with nerves. At last she was standing in front of the right place; like every other house entrance in the close, it had two storm doors folded back into a recess, and a front door which was one of the blind sort, a single unlacquered, unornamented panel of wood, dusty in appearance, like it'd been newly cut for her visit. There was a simple letterbox of tarnished brass, and three names written in neat block capitals on a piece of desiccated paper taped to the wood, CAULDER, SKEL-MORE and PRENTICE, one under the other, with a biro line through the name Prentice; and there was a bell push set into the side of the outside door frame, a little above the lower hinges of the storm door. Catherine stood for a moment, then reached out to press the bell; from the other side of the door, she heard a dry rattling, an alarming noise rather than a noise like an alarm. The lock ground as the latch released the tongue, the door opened, and Peter stood smiling and ready to widen the door for her to let her in.

Welcome tay my humble abode,

he said, and stood aside politely for her.

His room was brief in all directions as if the stubs of leftover walls had been mated together, giving him somewhere with hardly more space than in a clothes press. The decor didn't seem to be quite him, either; oh, there were paintings on the walls, of course, floor to ceiling, a whole gallery with hardly a paper to be slid between the crowding of the frames, but the rest of it was hand-me-downs, furniture left by a previous tenant. Everything spoke of an elderly person's taste, probably a woman's; a Persian style of carpet not quite acquainting itself with the skirting and leaving a moat of floorboards around the room; a bed with a sunken mattress, depressed in the middle like a shallow bowl in which Catherine fancied she could trace the impressions of folk who'd died in it; a table near to the window on which he'd put his books in ziggurat order of size, huge picture art books at the bottom and works of fiction and paperbacks at the top; last, most obvious, the wardrobe as big as a standing stone against the wall nearest the window, on the flat top surface of which there were reams of papers risen almost to the ceiling. None of them looked like his choice; the house still belonged to someone else, and she wondered why he hadn't been minded to tear out the evidence of previous occupation, unless it was because he felt intimate towards the room, the warmth of old affections radiating from it. There were also the tools of his trade on the nap of the tablecloth; sable brushes of varying thicknesses and with the bristles cut into different shapes, some sharp as pins and others flat and chisel-headed; a palette of wood newly cleaned but with the memory of paint in its grain; a sealed jamjar that seemed to contain dirty water; implements she'd never seen before like small trowels with blades shaped like tear-drops or elongated diamonds; she picked them up to encourage him to explain them to her, but he maybe thought she wouldn't be that interested to hear.

He sat her down in a chair in front of the hearth; watched her put her handbag and the overnight bag beside her, said,

Anythn ey significance in the wee case?

He'd an ironic look about him; tight wee smile. He took the seat opposite her, and she looked into the hearth, saw there wasn't a proper fire there, only an electric fire with both bars switched on and the parabolic reflector aimed towards the room by a couple of books fixed under it as wedges to tilt it up.

D'you mean, is there anything significant about the case, or is there anything important inside it?

Peter sat back into the chair, and he laughed.

The Irish and their words, he said, yez're awffy fond ey words. Ye've goat me wondern whit I wis meanin noo.

Oh, she said, I think I can guess what you were meaning. It's got my work clothes in it. It's only polite to change when someone invites you somewhere, so I did that in the shop.

You're a' done up fur gaun tay the dancin, n my hoose's a' done up fur demolition. I'm ashamed ey my ain hoose.

Catherine was wondering if there'd be a day when she'd think of Peter the way she'd thought of Francis, in spite of the differences between the two men. She was worried that his way of seeing made him criticize things unkindly, and she was wondering how he was seeing her at the moment, like a girl dressing in her mammy's good clothes or like a confident woman. She could easily resent him for either observation, and she wouldn't be played like a fiddle by any man; that was what had taken her to Francis, he'd had knowledgeable but not knowing eyes, and she'd had the feeling about him that they were both feeling their way in darkness.

Don't be ashamed, she said. I'm sure you have your room exactly as you want it.

He let her look around while he was away making them coffee and seeing how dinner was getting on, which she thought was trusting of him; not that he was trusting his belongings to her, she thought at least he didn't think of her as a thief, but he seemed to be trusting to her judgement of him. She had a better chance to look at his paintings, and at the easel in the corner by the window, there she supposed for the daylight; it had the canvas of Elvis fixed to it, with his scars now represented in vivid blood colours. From there, she went on a tour of his gallery, starting at the wall over the mantel, and going clockwise around the room; the collection appeared to be deployed in themes, the fireplace wall was about portraits, and she assumed Elvis would hang there when he was done, near the top of the arrangement; the perpendicular wall, the space over the headboard of the bed, seemed to be concerned with industry, folk in the place they worked; and the longest wall projected towards the window was a mosaic of paintings of places were folk met and lived, housing schemes, children's playgrounds and the like. She was drawn to one painting above the bed; from a distance you'd think it was a volcano, but the closer she went to it she saw it was a foundry, with vast ladles on pivots pouring the incandescent broth of purified iron into mouldings, raising comets of spillage falling to the ground all about the figures who were stained with its raw, bleeding heat. She'd often wondered why Francis had stayed with that job, apart from the money coming into the house; he'd said, smiling, it gies ye a rerr heat in winter, it's lik workin wi stuff tapped aff fae the sun, and she realized she'd never seen him working, never spoken to him about what he did. Peter knew why, told her when he came in with their enamel mugs of coffee that a lot of the men wouldn't tell their wives because enough of their mates'd been hit by lashes of the liquid steel, and it didn't matter what protection you wore, the spit was hot enough to burn cloth or plastic and roast flesh once it was through. Catherine felt sick for a moment to imagine Francis there, and then it was as if she remembered why it didn't matter any more; drank a sip of her coffee to disguise the lapse, found it as dreadful as Peter had said it would be, and tried to keep her thoughts on why she was here, what she'd come for.

Another thing was, he seemed to have a morbid interest in the degradations of old age; how elderly folk either fought against or surrendered to their loss of dignity, their new dependence. It was just one work that caught her attention, but there were so many others that she wondered if Elvis had been a mistake. From a distance it seemed as if he'd spilled ash on the canvas, denser in some parts than others, but when she went closer she saw it resolving itself into differing tonalities, until finally it became an old lady walking her shopping trolley, against grey houses which could've been the ones downstairs, and a grey sky which was sluicing down with rain. The whole assembly needed some looking at before you could pick the detail from it, but she kept at it until she was feeling as if she'd intruded on the struggle of the wifie, you could tell she'd been in some sort of arthritic difficulty when she'd been drawn, and Catherine wondered how Peter had gathered the sketch when it'd been raining so hard, how he hadn't managed to soak the paper right through on a day like that. She asked him more about that one as well after he came through, and he told her of course old folk made an interesting subject; aside from the great fortune of experience and character inscribed on the faces of the old, he said he thought you could judge a society by how the elderly were treated; if they were abandoned to their own devices after their contribution to private wealth was over, or if they were provided for at a time when their health was liable to fail, and Catherine could tell he was angry about it. She said,

How d'you decide to make a drawing of someone? What makes you say, oh, I must draw this woman, or I must go into a foundry and do a painting of that?

Peter was swirling the mug around to disperse the coffee syrup at the bottom.

Ye never know fr sure. Ye jist see somethn, ye waant tay peynt it, like yon auld wumman, or Elvis. Or like, I've aye thought, whit's it like in a foondry? N I go alang n huv a word wi the foreman, n he says, aye, nae boather, jist set yirsel up away fae the furnace n day yir drawn, n if I'm lucky mebbe the work'll buy my peyntn aff me, n if I'm no mebbe somdy else'll buy it.

Once she'd seen most of the gallery, and said she'd enjoyed the look at it, he took her over to the easel in the corner beside the window, and showed her Elvis. He was painting it in oils, and it wasn't finished yet, but he didn't mind her looking at it. She could see the scars much better now, pinched together by stitching which she supposed must've been done at the hospital. She said,

Who'd want to buy it?

Peter clutched his breast as if he'd been shot, and told her he'd probably try Jonathan MacHenery's gallery in the town, where it'd likely hang beside his others, because MacHenery didn't much like his work either, although, as he was always saying to the artists he displayed, he could see the merit in it.

He made dinner for them, and she was polite about it; he joked that he never did abstract works until he went near a stove, and she could see what he meant. The macaroni was cooked until it was pulp, the sauce had strings of elastic molten cheese in a runny mess of butter and milk, seeded with little pearls of coagulated flour. She said to him she thought it was cleverness on his part to show her how desperate he was at cooking so she'd be forced to do it next time; those words, next time, never went away, and Peter said nothing, went on with his eating. When they were finished, Catherine said she'd wash the plates, and Peter resisted at first, but she was adamant about it, she wasn't going to come here and eat food he could ill afford and then not expect to make some contribution towards her lodging for the evening. Peter tried to argue her out of it, but he'd never come across a stubborn woman like her, and she doubled the plates together and settled the knives and forks on them, and perched the cups on top, said she wasn't going to put up with any of his nonsense, and then went through to the kitchen.

Maybe if Peter'd said these were also someone's living quarters as well as the kitchen, she'd've let him talk her out of it, but then, maybe it was Peter's way of introducing her to Codie. Or maybe he'd been so ashamed of the kitchen, he'd rather stay in his room than have to explain the mess to her. She didn't know which was more horrifying to her, the notion that anyone could live confined to a space not much bigger than the bed he slept in, or that anyone could live in squalor like this; dishes piled high on the table, worktops littered with crumbs and worms of bacon rind, and a cold rank soup of grease and the scrapings from pans steeping in the sink. The man in the corner, painting away without caring, turned his head so that his bowl-cut hair drifted around like a skirt, and over his shoulder he smiled, and then went back to his work while she approached the sink and the cooker. There were two enamel saucepans on the hob, one almost clean but with thin starchy water at the bottom, the other scabrous with the congealed cheese from the sauce, but there was a frying-pan at the back of the hob which was black and waxy with solid lard which she could tell had been used for more than just one cooking. The linoleum was pale and disfigured around the base of the stove, and there was a silhouette burned into the wallpaper behind it, around the shield at the back. She was just shaking her head and thinking, what a state for any kitchen to get into, when the man spoke to her without turning away from his painting.

It disny matter how many times I tell that c, em, how many times I tell him tay keep my room tidy, wan day later, wan day mind ye, it's back in this, f, em, this state. Tell ye whit, Peter wis cleanin this f, em, this place a' yisterday fr you comin here, n look at it noo. F, em, damn disgrace, so it is.

Catherine had to turn to see that he still had his back to her; he was eclipsing the subject of his own painting, but she could see dark, manky colours on the end of his brush, like camouflage. When she didn't reply, he turned at last; he had an appealing, friendly face, and he held the brush up at an angle, kept the palette against his chest, but tilted it down every so often as if the colours on it were shifting around its table, and he was trying to keep them under discipline.

See, I like my peynt thin, runny ye might say, lik egg yolk or jist cream. I like it yon wey, it's jist dreepin aff yir brush, n ye gie yir surface hunnerts ey coats ey it, nice n smooth. But I'm wastn hauf the f, em, hauf the peynt oan the flare, see, ye canny help it.

While he was talking, the pigment swelled like a berry on the sable, falling and bursting against the linoleum, which drew her towards the other drops planted there, in a perfect half-circle around him. He looked down, then back at her, shrugged, went on.

Thing is, I canny go tay my bed wi that mess oan the flare, I huv tay moap it up, see, that's jist me. But that c, em, that bugger canny be boathered cleanin up efter himsel, so eether I've tay day it, n I'm buggered if I'm gaunny clean it as fast as he cn mess it, r I've tay leave it, n nag oan at him tay day it, n he'll say aye, aye sure; well, Peter says aye sure, Heidless jist tellt us tay, well, niver mind whit he sayd, he jist sayd he wisny gonny day it, leave it at that, n it disny matter, cause he's no here onywey, jist as well, cause he wis a drunken bam. I tell ye, I've no hud the cheek tay ask a wumman back here fr two year noo; I widny dare.

She smiled, made a face of disgust at the cooker, the scabs of burnt food around the gas rosettes.

I'm afraid if I was living here, I wouldn't be putting up with this, but I told Peter I'd wash the dishes, more fool me.

Codie laughed.

Yon's a kettle joab, I'm afraid tay say. The hoat waater stoaps efter wan c, em, efter wan bugger's hud a bath.

Catherine found the kettle on the back of the hob, beside the frying-pan; it was a dumpy thing with a whistle spout and a wee beret of a lid it couldn't quite wear on the rim so it was tilted to seem rakish, and she filled it from the tap which was worse than her one in the kitchen at home. She let Codie guide her to the box of matches, on the canopy over the hob, lit the front right ring after taking the saucepan off it, bringing out the crown of blue flame, put the kettle on top of it. She'd a little time before she'd be able to clean the pans and the dishes, so she approached Codie to see more of what he was painting. He became aware of her over his shoulder, seemed not to mind; even stood a wee bit away from the canvas so she could see the work properly.

The paint was glossy where he was doing new work, and when she went closer she caught a similar draught of oil as she had from Peter's canvas of Elvis, only stronger with linseed from the thinner paint. It depicted an old man lying on the cobbles of what seemed to be an alleyway. He was definitely unconscious, more like sleeping than fainted, although there was a bottle sitting at his head wrapped in brown paper that was open around the neck like the collar of a lily. He was wrapped in newspaper like three pennyworth of chips to keep himself warm, and there was a thread of dark piss leading away from him on his side, wetting the paper and turning it grey. The subject of the painting didn't seem to be the most important thing about it; it was the detail, down to the fact you could almost read the headline and the story on the front of the newspaper, almost photographically complete in its observation. The wires of grey hair coiling from underneath the flat cap; the cracks in the brickwork behind him, the irregular laying of the cobbles he had for a mattress, everything was there, so unlike Peter's slapdash of collaborating lines and shapes. Codie said,

It's an auld man I came across wi my mammy when we were oot shoappn in the toun years ago noo. She wis dead ashamed ey me seein him, poor auld b, em, poor auld bugger. I've been meanin tay peynt him fur years, add him tay my collection.

He nudged her away from the canvas towards his own gallery, nailed to the three walls of the recess. There was only one theme to this gallery; destitution, men and women scattered throughout the town centre, some of them sleeping on the riverbank, some of them in alleyways, most of them in plain view, on the open streets. Each of them was executed in the same manner, like photographs, and it forced her to see the truth of abandonment in them, as if Catherine needed forcing after her own time on the streets, making the best comfort out of wet pavements and shelters before she was lucky enough to get her job. She even looked for herself, in the dress she'd burned later, with a carpet-bag for a pillow; cleaner than the others, because she'd discovered the toilets in railway stations were fine enough places to wash yourself, if you kept a few of the coppers you'd begged for to one side to pay for your entry, and she'd be a little better fed since she was using the rest of the money in bakeries and shops that sold cold meats. She wasn't there, which was a relief, but she was wondering how Codie could possibly stand next to these people with a sketchbook and not offer them help. Of course, she didn't say that, didn't know him well enough yet to antagonize him with criticism. Instead, she returned to his painting of the old man, said,

Who did you get to model for you? was he like the old man, or did you just imagine the rest?

Codie looked at her in a puzzled kind of way, his brows drawn low over his forehead.

Thon's him, he said. Thon's the auld blok.

Catherine said nothing, but she'd decided he must be as mad as the rest of them. The next thing, the kettle went off like a siren, and she realized the note had been climbing while she'd been wondering if anyone in this house was to be believed. She excused herself while she went to the sink to clean out the pots and the dishes, and it was a relief as well to have her back to him, especially as she'd the impression she was somehow lodged in the throat of his memory like a fishbone, and she thought she'd be wary of him from now on, or at least until she'd determined what kind of creature he was.

She told Peter she'd met Codie, which seemed to please him; told him she thought it was disgraceful, Codie having to live in that wee kitchen and especially with the mess it was in, but Peter said it was his choice, had been when they'd moved into the place because they'd had to give Heidless his room to pursue his habits, somewhere he could lock himself if he was howling with the drink and not disturb any of them if they were at their work, or even himself if he was tormented by the DTs, or any of his other illnesses caused by lack of drink. He saw the disapproval on Catherine's face, and it troubled him, he said,

Ye're no wan fr the drink yirsel, that it? I thoat that might be the case, ye look lik somedy who'd be feared ey the drink,

and then went back to what he was doing, examining the painting of Elvis he'd started. Catherine took her seat again, letting the heat from the bar fire warm her legs, crouching over in the chair so she could warm herself.

Are you not feared of the drink yourself?

Peter's head was served over the frame of the canvas, his legs tangled with the three legs of the easel, so that he looked like an amalgamated creature, bred out of wood and fabric.

I have a drink tay mysel fae time tay time. Whit's there tay be feared ey?

Becoming, I don't know.

He bent closer to the canvas, folding his head in under the frame like a bird hiding under its wing.

Lik wan ey they daft films, ye mean, wi a man turning intay a wolf? Drink shouldny day that tay ye. Ye huv mare ey a laugh wi yir mates if ye're a' a wee bit squiffy, know whit I mean?

What if you're drinking by yourself? What's the reason for it then?

Peter's head came over the canvas, and he looked at her for a long time, as if she was saying things he couldn't understand.

Then ye're no a happy man, he said, cause there's naebdy tay keep an eye oot fur ye, n ye're dayn it tay pit yirsel oot ey yir ain heid.

Maybe, said Catherine, you're doing it because you'd rather be the man you become when the drink's in you.

Peter frowned.

Is this me ye're talkin aboot? Ye've no even seen me drunk yit.

Codie was telling me about Heidless, and I was just thinking of him, she said. Well, not just Heidless. Was that why you called him Heidless?

Peter smiled, ducked back under the frame.

Cause he wis oot ey his heid maist ey the time, aye. No jist that, but. Codie sayd he widny pey ye the least bit heed, even when he's no miraculous.

Catherine laughed.

Miraculous?

Aye, miraculous. Full up wi the miracle ey the bevvy. Lik ye could beat the shite oot ey Cassius Clay, n walk hame usin the stars fr steppin-stanes, that feelin ye get when ye've been steeped in the alky fr days, know whit I'm sayn?

Catherine shook her head.

You must be a very well-mannered drunk, Peter Caulder, that's all I can say.

N don't you forget it. I'm no a bloody maniac wi the drink, lik some folk.

Talking about Codie reminded Catherine of the painting, and the old man in it; she began to question Peter about him, but he said,

If Codie says thon's the man he'd seen, that's who it is.

He explained to her by going to the wardrobe and opening it, making a dam of his hand to keep back the laundry threatening to flood the floor and reaching to the back. He found what he was looking for, pressed the surge of clothes firmly back in, closed over the door and locked it, and then sat opposite her. What he had in his hand was a wee snapshot camera, nowhere near as involved as the one Michael had been using at her wedding, a simple black box, with a rosette at the top for a flash cube, a window for framing your picture, a lens underneath. The maker's name was printed on to the bottom of the camera, and Peter covered the last two letters of it with his finger. He said,

Thon's the man Codie's seen, right enough, as sure as he's taken his picture wi this. He's goat whit ye cry a photographic memory, see.

She was beginning to understand; she was thinking, she'd be printed on him, and she wasn't sure she liked the notion of belonging to someone like that. Peter told her it was nothing to be afraid of.

He jist does peyntns ey auld men n women oan the streets, that's his interest, like, ye've no a thing tay worry aboot, lik ye're no gaunny be in a peyntn ey his unless ye hit the skids.

Catherine took the camera off him, put it to her eye and aimed it at him.

See how you like it,

she said.

Just when he was about to enter her, she pressed against his shoulders and pushed him back;

I thought I could, I'm sorry,

and he lifted himself away and lay beside her on the bowl of the mattress, on his side, leaving her to fall into the collapsed centre. She was grateful for it being dark so she couldn't turn and see him; if he was frustrated or disappointed or just angry at her. She heard him breathing abruptly to one side of her, and she wanted to reach out and find his head, stroke him until he was calm again and ready for sleep, but she didn't want the touch to remind him of her, of her rejection. The room was cold, and he quickly reached down and pulled the covers over them, saying bitterly,

We'll catch oor death lik this.

The blankets drifted over her, inflated with all the air he'd pulled in with them. He was still on his side, with the blankets gathered around him like a collar, letting his breath out carefully. He said, at last,

Why no, Cathy?

She couldn't say, it was because she'd been out for this kind of attention from the moment she arrived; since the evening before, in fact, when she'd come back to the empty house from Gianfranco's, and she'd a fire to build in the grate, and Peter's invitation to think about. She was on her knees before the hearth, lifting out coal from the scuttle and settling the black bricks inside it, and she'd thought, it wasn't a home any more, it was a lodging, pure and simple. She was even telling herself this aloud, just to hear a voice in the place, and she began to hurl the coal into the vacancy. She said, I know I shouldn't go to this man's place, Francis, but there's no one here to keep me, and it isn't as if I'm having an affair or anything, I never would do that to you. She felt better for telling the truth, began to play her trick, the one she'd taught to Cameron, rolling old newspapers into long cords and then tying them into knots and seeding them among the coal to start the kindling. She lit the papers, finally making the whole structure catch light, and she stood up from the work and looked at the palms of her hands, the coal dust on them, thought about her New Year when she'd marked the hearth, and then realized when she stepped away from the hearth that the remainder of the house was still as cold as charity as her da would've said, which told you what he thought about kindness. She said, aloud, if he's a kind man, I'll have him, I'm not staying in this place a minute longer than I have to, but the moment she said it was as if she'd committed blasphemy or something, broken a promise, and she said to herself, into herself, I'm sorry, Francis, you don't want to hear this.

Why not; because she was comforted enough just lying next to Peter, and she didn't need to offer payment for her board, no matter how good it might've been to have someone inside her. She reached out for him, drew him towards her, and he lay against her like a child, warming himself on her.

Because, she said, I'd rather wait, please understand.

She began to dream of the confessional over the water, and the infection of damp and moss on the walls and the smell of rot whenever you closed the door behind you; Father Byrne on the other side of the partition and not seeing much through the communicating mesh of wicker but the round shape of his face and the aura of his hair. It wasn't much like a dream, but it was like herself younger and remembering a particular visit, not long before she and Michael were found out and she ran away. She said, I have bad thoughts against my father, and she could hear Byrne shifting in his chair, bad thoughts? what kind of bad thoughts, speak up, girl, and it was like God's own voice, she thought everyone outside must hear him. She said, hatred, father, and heard the breath reversing into him; there was a while before he said, that isn't the right thing to feel for your father, my girl, doesn't it say in the holy book you must honour thy father and thy mother, now you'll say a rosary for that alone and then tell me what other sins you've committed in thought and deed. She couldn't understand why you punished thought and deed as if they were the same, sure and wasn't there the world between thinking of stealing the carving knife from the kitchen drawer and stopping the old man's heart in his chest and being moved to do it; but you'd think Byrne couldn't tell the difference, the way he treated them both alike. She remembered as well the smell of mint drifting through from his side of the partition, one of his weaknesses, he always said when he was feeling jovial, and thank God there was nowhere in the Scripture that named mint imperials as one of the vices or else he'd be sent to the fire when his time came. That was how she'd known it was him and not Father Delaney across the partition from her, but she was past caring how fearsome he was reputed to be, nor how much he was known to admire owl Colum O'Hara for the God-fearing he did in public, she thought it was time it was all known, so she began her confession again as if she'd just walked into the booth, bless me father for I have sinned, it is one week since my last confession, I accuse myself of no wrongs at all, and the one you'll have to ask about my sins'll be coming to you in a minute or two. There wasn't a sound from the other side of the partition until his chair creaked, and then she saw a single eye in the mesh, so he'd know her outside the seal of the confessional. He said, young woman, you're old enough to know by now you're a bridge to sin yourself for any man who'd cross you, and for your pride you'll say the rosary twice before you'll see daylight. Catherine drew her lower lip in and bit it hard; then I accuse myself of lying, sin of omission, isn't that what you call it?

for I don't know whose sin this is to be confessing, only I doubt it's mine, and if, if I'm a bridge to the sin I think you're talking about then it's the one who built me who steps out on me the most, and who's to say the penance for that? She hadn't known what would follow from it, only she'd been expecting the priest to ask her to tell him more, maybe even he'd want to see Colum O'Hara in the sacristy, demand to know what his daughter had meant; she hadn't thought he'd just let out a sigh that carried the mint on his breath across to her, there's many kinds of love God has brought into this world, my dear child, and all of them are precious, now you will say the rosary four times over, and you will not repeat these wicked accusations outside of this confessional if you value your immortal soul.

Why she should dream of this when she was in a stranger's bed; unless it was the time in her life when she felt the most powerless, next to all the times when she was in the kitchen and owl Colum O'Hara chased his wife and son away to their rooms so he could do the thing Father Byrne seemed to be saying was as precious as her mother's love for her, or Michael's. At least she hadn't compounded her mistakes by handing her company over so lightly to this man she hardly knew, and she was glad of that at least, that she hadn't been a traitor to Francis with the first man who'd shown her attention and kindness in many a long month.

Eight

She didn't have to work often for Gianfranco at the weekend, only when Francesca had a heavy load of weekend homework from the nuns, and couldn't do it; they were no respecters of a young girl's freedom, believed in giving much work to idle hands. He knew how much she hated weekends at the café; most of the folk that came in at the weekends drunk from the pub for their fish suppers were no bother, rowdy, but good-hearted, pulling blokes among their number up short if they were about to tell a story that was off colour. Let's no frget oorsels in front of a lady, said the ones who'd a better hold on their drunkenness to the ones who'd run the bit, and, awffy soarry, miss, they apologized, widny'uv spoken oot ey turn if I'd seen ye. Catherine just smiled and let it pass, although she wondered if they were as chivalrous of their wives after the key was turned and the door locked behind them. She went from Paradise to the kitchen to fetch their orders, used to it by now; the reek of malt from them breaking over her; hen and darlin from them, and there was even one bloke who sang, I'll take you home again Kathleen, every time he left with his parcel, having overheard her name called from the Inferno. She thought it was funny now, although she hadn't at first; she said to Gianfranco, thank you, how do I know he won't follow me home now? and Gianfranco wiped his hand over his face, and said, I so sorry, Catherine, I no think, I make good, yes?

Gianfranco made good by ordering a taxi for her if she was working late, and paying for it himself, which she thought was decent of him;

you no like drunk, you no meet drunk, is dark where you go through the industrial estate, no good for young woman. The road to the scheme divided the estate in two, but it wasn't at all well lit. The sodium lamps were meant to alternate from one side of the road to the other, the influence of the light overlapping like fish scales, but some vandals had torn the hatches from the lamp standards and severed the wires, making a bright island of the scheme in the distance separated from the coast of the main road. At least she felt safer inside the taxi; and it made Gianfranco feel like a virtuous boss, which meant every time he saw her he said, I no like some, Catherine, see, I no espect my girls to risk life for me, and she thanked him again and again until he was saturated in gratitude, and he could go to chapel proud of himself.

The evening of the break-in, she was seated in the back of the cab, thinking of the fire she'd make when she returned home all along the road while she was conducting a conversation with the driver. She was thinking of Peter as well, because his work round about here, his wee safari trip, had ended, and she hadn't seen him since waking up the morning after she'd been invited over, kissing him on the forehead before she left. It was late, but then he'd probably still be up, men alone were always less careful about the hours they kept; so she was thinking, she'd go back and make a fire for herself, and then draw the phone out and put it beside the hearth and then she'd call Peter, apologize for leaving before he'd wakened, ask him how he was, ask for a joke if he'd like to come to her place for a better dinner than he'd served to her.

The driver accepted his tip as always. She only saw the side of his face then, when she was handing over the fare and the light of the cab came on automatically. She always had to stop him from opening his door and coming around to open the door for her, saying, I can manage, and he said, right y'are, sweetheart, you huv a good sleep tay yirsel noo, jist cause I've tay work disny mean ither folk huv tay stey awake. Catherine closed the door firmly behind her, and while she was outside the close and heading towards the mouth of it, she began the lucky dip into her handbag to find her house keys, catching the ring securing them in her finger and pulling them like a catch of fish into the light of the close.

The length of time she stood in front of the door warmed up the keys in her hand, while she was thinking of all the reasons why the wood of the jamb around the Yale and the mortise locks would be broken. A fire while she was away; a mistake by the police coming to separate Bernadette and her man; by the time she'd thought why the door might be a little ajar, there was only one reason left, the one that frightened her the most, and the keys were hot enough in her palm to leave their mark, she was breathing mist out like a steam train, and she knew she couldn't just stand there any longer, not while her house was so open.

They'd peeled back the wallpaper so they could cut some mark of their passage into the plaster, names she'd never heard of, carved with some chisel-pointed instrument, in all likelihood the same one they'd used to break the locks. She thought of trying the kitchen first, but there was nothing important to her there, just crockery and cutlery and hardly anything but breakfast food since Gianfranco gave her dinner at the café. There was something broken like biscuit and ground into the hall carpet, sharp white crumbs she powdered underfoot, leading her towards the door to the living-room; she paused in front of it, and she'd the strangest thought just then; maybe she could have her fire after all, if they hadn't upset the scuttle or stolen the coal from it, she was angrier at the thought she mightn't have her fire than at the notion she'd been burgled.

When Catherine put on the light in her front room, she could see there was no shortage of material to burn around the place, paper off the walls, her furniture crippled by having their legs broken, chairs and sofa with their entrails of stuffing disgorged on to the floor. She burst something with her first step into the room after she'd switched on the light, an angle of ceramic tiling from the fireplace, bone white on one side, the colour of milky tea on the other, and she held on to it for luck almost, the way her mammy hoarded relics of saints. The next most obvious thing in the room was a construction of four squares of wood in decreasing order of size, which she recognized as being the leaves from the folding table at the window, and the doors of the sideboard; on top of it was her black phone, the cable still fixed into the wall, and beside the phone was a scrap torn from one of her kindling newspapers, on which was written in trembling block capitals,

NOW CAL THE POLIS
HA HA
MAD STREET RULES YA BAS.

She should've been raging, or crying that they'd desecrated the house, but she wasn't doing either. Instead she was looking at the table with its hinges gripping frayed ends of wood, the sideboard gaping empty with the drawers pulled out and wrecked against the wall. The only thing of value which had been in the sideboard was the dinner service given to her by her mother-in-law as a wedding present, and at first she thought it'd gone until she'd a better look around the living-room carpet and she wasn't that saddened to see the plates and bowls broken, couldn't think of a time when they'd been used except maybe at Christmas, when they'd had Agnes and Daniel over for a visit.

The next place she went was Cameron's old bedroom, and when she stood in the doorway, she saw that the tallboy he'd kept his model village under was tipped over so that it was leaning on the bed, and again the drawers had been taken out and splintered against the wall, and there were boot prints all over the bedding she'd kept tucked under the mattress in case he'd be staying over sometime. She was glad for the first time since he'd left that he was somewhere safe; if he'd still been here, and on his own when the break-in had happened; she might even have said a prayer of thanks, if she'd thought that way.

The last place she visited was her bedroom, and here the damage was if anything greater than anywhere else in the house. The first thing to hit her was the smell of ammonia and faeces; you went past closes with that kind of smell in some parts of the town, buildings fit for nothing but demolition where drunks made their toilet. They'd made a well out of all the clothes they'd pulled out of the wardrobe and the drawers of the dresser, in the middle of the room alongside the bed, added the bedclothes, pissed and laid down cords of shite in the centre of the well, but there was also a fragrance about the place of gardens and cinnamon, and she saw from where; the jewelled perfume bottle emptied into the air and then broken against the wall over the bed, the ragged paper discoloured by the wee splash of perfume left. This time, when they'd broken the drawers, they hadn't used the wall as an anvil to hammer them against, but the three mirrors of the dresser; there were long pins of glass still fixed by the clamps while the unsupported breakage had fallen on to the table surface. They'd found her jewellery as well, tested it with their heels to see if there was any value in it, and when they'd found it was all glass and cheap plate they'd stood on the lot, grinding it into the carpet.

Catherine sat on the bed her husband had died in, the guts torn out of it now, dismembered like the furniture in the living-room. The place had undergone its transformation in a very short time, from a home to a tomb to a dormitory to this, as if the historical processes which changed dwellings to matters of archaeological curiosity had occurred briefly, and the house was just waiting now for the land to close over it and seal the contents. She even started laughing at herself, for thinking anything might be beyond violation, her marriage, her son, her life over the water she'd made for herself away from the place where her violation had begun. She didn't even have God to blame this on; trust her not to think of leaving the lights on whenever she left the house, so she'd attract the kind of moths that were drawn to darkness. Francis had even told her, there was a way you lived in towns that was different from how you lived in the country, and it was all about not trusting too much, and here she'd been thinking all that meant was you locked your door and told no one your business.

Her head became full of the reek, and she stood up finally and went to the door, closed it over once she was in the hall. She went to the living-room, and picked up the phone from the wee altar they'd made for it, returned it to its place on the table. Instead of calling the police as they'd suggested, she dialled Peter's number; the carriage clock was smashed on the floor, the hands bent so you couldn't recognize a time of entry, but she was wearing a watch, saw from its face the time was after midnight and she wondered if anyone would be awake.

There was a click at the other end of the line, and Peter said hullo;

she thought he sounded tired, maybe she'd dragged him out of his bed to answer it.

Peter? she said. I wonder if I could ask you a favour?

She threw into the midden the clothes they'd soiled; one of them was the dress she'd worn for Francis on the day he came home. Peter was standing over her as she took the bundle of them wrapped in newspaper, the ones too stained to consider washing, and that made her task easier; he didn't know where the dresses and blouses came from, when they'd been worn, he was dispassionate about it, and she needed that just then. He was the one who'd found the pictures from the mantel. They were under the altar of boards the telephone had been placed on. The glass was almost crushed to a powder and this had made the photographs underneath worn and minutely scratched, like the kind of art he called pointillist, you could imagine tilting the frames and gathering the images in the bowl of a spoon, taking the rest of your life to pick them apart from the glass like grains of pepper, more than one lifetime to make another picture out of them. He said, whit'll I day wi these? because he knew they were important, you could see she was a bride in one of them, could see the wean in the other, but she said, put them on the sideboard, I'll decide later.

It was as much for the council she was tidying the place as herself; they'd claim the repairs from her if she didn't, and besides, Peter'd said to her, ye'll waant tay see whit tay keep and whit ye're best tay chuck. He hadn't seen the house until that morning; she'd arrived the night before with a suitcase containing the best of the clothes she could see at first glance, and while he was in the kitchen making her coffee, she said,

Everything, Peter, everything's for chucking, they turned the whole place into firewood.

Peter shook his head as he set the kettle on to boil.

Surely no the hale place?

but she leaned into the back of the chair and said,

Oh, one or two things, the tallboy, my wardrobe, but they peed and did their business on all my clothes, so what'll I put in it?

Codie had opened up the curtain around his bed for a while, reckoning on no sleep until the drinks were made and she was calmed

187

down; he shook his head and sighted to where his feet rose at the ends of the blanket,

Aw man, that's f, em, that's jist barbarians, they're needin their c, em, their heids kicked in for them,

which reminded Catherine of another thing. She turned to Peter.

I think your Elvis kicked their heads in once, this MacDiarmid Street crowd, they don't call themselves Mad Street as well, do they?

Peter leaned against the cooker, his hand gathering the warmth from the edge away from the burning hob.

Aye, I think they day.

She went into her coat pocket and unfolded the paper to show him the taunt.

Hell man, they're at it again.

Catherine wasn't letting him away with that.

Sure, Peter, she said, and your boy'll be doing the same to poor folk in the other scheme like a proper wee angel.

Peter handed the paper back to her, looked towards the kettle, shrugged, and there was silence out of him on that subject for the rest of the evening. Codie asked her what her plans were; she said, to move all her stuff out of the house, and find another she could live in without regret; and when he wondered aloud if the council would give a house to someone who'd as good as evicted herself, she said,

I'd sooner not go to an empty place if I can avoid it,

and both Peter and Codie understood that.

When Peter came to the house the day after with her, he was silent again, as if he'd never seen the like in his life. He was quite efficient about the cleaning, though; didn't tell her what should be done, and it occurred to her that maybe he knew her better than she thought, which was a bit of a comfort. He offered to tidy the living-room, and she didn't mind that. She went into the cupboard at the end of the hall, sunk in so the back of it touched against the wall of the kitchen, took out two brushes and hand shovels and kept one of each for herself, giving him the others.

Not the kind of brush you're used to, but you'll manage,

she said; he gripped it in one hand, the dustpan in the other. He said,

I canny believe ye're no hurt by this.

She wasn't in the mood.

There's work needing done, she said, and it won't get done on its own.

She didn't allow him into the bedroom, because it didn't seem right. She let herself look at the room for the last time, before attacking it with the brush. She had a pail for the manageable rubbish, the bits and pieces on the carpet, fragments of her perfume bottles, even the jewellery. She didn't give herself the chance to remember where she'd bought everything she was throwing out; nothing had cost her more than a few shillings anyway, and so she scraped them into the blade of the shovel, tipped them into the pail, heard them ringing against the tin. She dealt with the clothes next, reeking badly by now. She picked through them one by one, lifting up the dry corners and looking for clothes that hadn't been stained; she found the blouse and skirt she'd worn on the day they'd given a name to Cameron, the black dress she'd worn on the day of Francis's funeral; everything she'd ever worn seemed to have been doused, and she became determined she wasn't going to clean up their mess for them, and she stood up and left the room.

Catherine went back to the cupboard in the hall, and found the newspapers she kept for lighting the fire on the floor of it, lifted them all and brought them into the bedroom. She went into the kitchen, her feet pressing on a paving of lentils and dried soup vegetables and other things they'd emptied on to the floor in the hope of finding hidden valuables, and took a pair of rubber gloves and a roll of Sellotape from the corner in which they'd upended the contents of the worktop drawers. She felt cleaner with the gloves on her hands, sterile like a doctor; she was already beginning to think of it as an operation, surgery like they'd done to Francis, cutting out a tumour. Peter was calling through from the front room from time to time, whit'll I day wi this or that, and she instructed him, calling back, take it to the bins out the back, leave it on the sofa, just use your imagination, Peter, where'd'you think it should go? and she heard him stumping through the hall muttering, his master's bloody voice, and she smiled and thought he'd take some telling, this one, and she was wondering what it'd be like to stay for a while with mad folk; she was quite looking forward to it.

Catherine saw the dress while she was on her knees, pulling it over to the paper she'd laid on the floor. You couldn't miss how it shone, the bands to rest on the shoulders, how it went to a pinch at the waist, flaring like a bell, pleated around like a curtain. She lifted it by the bands, snapped it so it unfurled like a flag over the rest of the clothes; there was a big yellow stain on the lap of the skirt, drenched through to the other side. She knew it would wash, with enough care and plenty of time, but she felt beyond that now. She turned it so the wet skirt was draped over the bundle; wore the top against herself, holding its breast to her breast with the flat of her hand. She remembered waiting by the window in the front room, in this dress, watching for the ambulance. The perfume in the air, discharged by them last night, was as strong as if she was wearing it, and she could almost hear the wheels of Cameron's toy ambulance scurrying over the arm of the chair.

Catherine crushed the dress in her hands, because the bottle of fragrance was shattered and in the pail, and at any moment she'd ask Peter to help her lift the table and take it down to the midden, along with the stubs of its legs and the broken leaves. She put it first on the bed of paper and then hauled the rest of the cloth on top, in case she saw anything else that would bind her to other objects.

She carried the bundle under her arm and through to the front room to see why Peter had called her through; that was when he showed her the pictures, the frames buckled under the weight. Catherine passed the bundle into his arms and bent down to see what remained. They were like images fighting to become solid on a tele screen when interference comes to them, the glass fine as sugar, and she cleared it away with the edge of her hand; for a moment, she thought it wasn't as if there'd been any abrasion against the paper, but it was as if the images themselves had willed their own disappearing. It was that impression, not that they were trying to manifest themselves but that they were more likely bleaching themselves out of her thoughts, that made her undecided as to what should be done with them; she told him to leave them on the sideboard, and took the bundle back from Peter, told him to pick up the boards, they were going to the midden.

Peter leaned the boards against the bin, while Catherine lifted the lid of it with one hand. The bundle she had against her chest was soft, and she thought of something her mammy had said to her once when she'd been bought a new dress: I wish you health to wear it, strength to tear it, and money to buy a new one. She dropped the bundle into the gullet of the bin before the significance of any of the clothes stopped her, covered it with the lid, turned to him and said,

We've other things to get,

and led him back along the drying green, into the close, into the house, away from the wind.

They picked the last of the tiling and the dinner service from the living-room floor like shells from the beach, hoovered up the splinters, lifted the table out and put it beside the midden; Catherine led them out even though she'd her back turned on the direction they were going, and they got a laugh out of their clumsiness, how the stumps of the legs kicked against them,

The bloody thing's alive, said Peter, it knows we're chuckin it.

Stop moaning and put your back into it,

and Peter muttered to himself and took most of the weight on the stairs to the green, and that made her complain he was making it easy for her; he couldn't win that day.

It took them close to five hours, tidying in every room in the house. Catherine did the bathroom, where there was least damage, the medicine cabinet dragged off the wall and left with all the pills and bottles sprayed into the sink and over the floor and the mirrored doors were smashed beyond recovery, that was a job for a brush and shovel only. She joined Peter in the kitchen for the last of the work, putting everything back into their proper drawers, sweeping the dried food from the linoleum;

Ye've a load ey useless bloody stuff here,

he said, picking up a vegetable peeler as if he didn't recognize it, and Catherine took it from him.

It's only useless if you don't eat right,

she said, and then a notion came to her. She opened one of the cabinets under the sink, took out everything she could find there, cleaning fluids, scourers, bleaches, cloths; put them all on the worktop, and then turned to Peter. He looked at them, then at her, shook his head.

No the day, Catherine, have we no done whit we can here?

Catherine smiled at him as if, how foolish could he get.

Yes, here. But I'm not staying here tonight, am I?

Nine

Catherine wore a pair of his clean socks to the bathroom, not wanting her feet cold against the lino; they were threadbare like an old carpet at the toes, and she could see a hole waiting for a stitch to give way. He wasn't a tremendously practical man, at least not outside of his painting; he'd've been happy enough to wear his socks once his foot had burrowed through, and she was thinking he was a helpless man in many ways, like a wee boy waiting for his mammy to notice when it came time for the laundry. She could see her own foot through the net, a couple of sizes too small for the socks which billowed like a gas around the ends of her legs. She watched herself placing her feet on the floor; the traps to be avoided, floorboards that moaned when you trusted your weight to them, strings worked loose from the carpets; went to find her nightdress, cold enough for her to need it, and of course she might meet Codie on the way to the bathroom. She wondered if he knew yet, that they were living with a husband and wife's kind of knowing of each other, thought he must've been daft if he hadn't guessed, but it still wasn't a thing she'd like broadcast.

On her way to the bathroom, she caught the smell from the corner room which had lain empty and unvisited since Heidless was thrown out. It smelled like when you poked through forests, when she poked through forests with Michael, and he told her all the dead leaves fell and rotted into the earth, making food for the trees. She'd been on at Peter for weeks to do something about it; we're not leaving it as a shrine to your madman friend, Peter, she said, not while it could evict us like you evicted him, but Peter only covered his eyes with his hands and said, no while he's in the streets, Cathy, I waant tay be sure he's somewherr tay stey, and he wasn't moving on that; so far it hadn't been necessary, and she hoped it never would.

She closed the bathroom door on Heidless's influence; in her own house, there'd've been soap and perfumes to throw over it, but here there were only disinfectants, bleaches, carbolic. She hated this bathroom for the labour it was to clean; red marbled linoleum flaking at the skirting, the broad enamel bath with its bowed legs wearing through to the boards, a porcelain sink cracked in places and the dirt worn into it like the veins in blue cheese, a broad toilet pan with the cistern perched on two brackets fixed high in the wall by screws which were quietly rusting through. The two men had become used to rinsing out their brushes into the sink, or sometimes down the toilet pan; she'd come in now and again to find the oil paints they'd been using drifting on the lens of water caught in the throat of the pipe, and she'd left an ultimatum for them, either find somewhere else to empty their dirty turps, or don't slop it out but pour it in a continuous thread down the drainhole, making sure it didn't swell back up. They'd listened to her, so at least the sink was clean enough to wash at; a bath would've taken too long to run, and besides they'd just have complained later that she'd claimed the morning's hot water all to herself, which she'd sooner avoid.

She was busy cleaning down below, as her mammy called it, when she thought she hadn't had to clean herself for that reason in a long time. It made her think of Francis, their first time at Mrs Kilsyth's, when she was the old duchess's maid. Say what you like about the duchess, she'd had a good younger life, and the generosity not to begrudge any of her maids their taste of a young life as well. The duchess must've heard them laughing when they came in and straight to Catherine's kitchen quarters; as long as her young man was gone before breakfast, she didn't seem to bother, although she did make fun of her maid's yawning the whole day, am I to understand, young lady, she said, that your sleep last night was a troubled one? and when Catherine tried not to laugh and said, yes, Mrs Kilsyth, quite troubled, the duchess looked up at her from her wheelchair with a single white eyebrow raised and said, then I hope the cause of your troubles is presently far away, so that your mind may now be fixed on your duties; is this the case, Miss O'Hara? and Catherine promised her she would be every bit as punctual and ready to do the old lady's will whenever asked. Then, as now, she couldn't escape thoughts of how uncomfortable Francis had been; he'd been expecting a long courting, like his ma's and da's, and maybe a wait until a promise of marriage had been exchanged, but Catherine laughed and told him in the dark of the curtain pulled around the bed to exclude all light, I wouldn't buy a horse without putting a saddle on it first, would you? and she could only map his movements from the depressions he made on the bed and the touch of him, by which she knew he was leaning on his side, facing her. He said, You're an awffy forward kin ey woman, Kate O'Hara, nae noansnse, and she almost told him why, thought no, it wasn't his business yet; thought, later, when he unfolded his secrets, they could make a child's barter of them, a length of string for a glass marble.

She thought of last night, and all the others with Peter. He was more aggressive than Francis; meaning that Francis had learned her wants and pleasures, while Peter had his own pursuits, and if any pleasures came for her, then it was no bad thing, only he didn't know where to begin to look. He seemed to like nursing at her breast, and she found it all very well and relaxing, but there were times she thought it was as if he hadn't been weaned, her satisfaction was accidental to it. When he mounted her, it was done suddenly, opening her legs like gates, driving through; she had no means of stopping him, and occasionally he stayed with her until her climax, and that was fine, but mostly he just emptied himself inside her and turned on to his back, not seeming to care. She didn't mind; even Francis had been quick at first, and it'd taken all her patience to remind him he wasn't alone in the bed; Peter would be the same, she thought, it would just take time, and a degree of awareness of her.

She wore his socks back into the room after she was cleaned up, took them off and left them for him over the arm of his chair, reminding herself to suggest he should have them mended. She was feeling lively and awake, even if it was still dark out; went to the wardrobe and chose her blouse and skirt for the day, no different to any other, white nylon top, pleated black skirt with folds like vanes. The light being on wakened Peter, and he wormed around in bed as if it was the first torture of the morning, the brightness shining against his eyelids. He sat up in the bed after a while, in enough time to catch her as she buttoned her blouse from bottom to top; narrowing his eyelids to crush the excess light from the scene, the way you crush a cloth to make it damp; he smoothed back his hair from his face to his scalp, and he was smiling to watch her.

Ye're dayn it the wrang wey,

he said. Catherine did up the collar button, pulled on the fringe of the blouse to level the creases.

What'm I doing the wrong way?

Buttnin up yir shirt. Dayn it fae yir belly tay yir neck. 'S awffy weird, that.

Catherine stepped into her skirt.

I've always buttoned them that way, she said. It's not that weird.

'S an awffy heeland wey tay day it.

Heeland?

Peter's eyes were opening as he became used to the light.

Aye, heeland. Highland. Ye know, lik folks fae the highlands.

He said it in an exaggerated English accent, like a newsreader.

So they button their blouses from their bellies to their necks as well?

Naw, they day everythn weird, no jist how they buttn their claes.

Like what?

I d'know. I've niver met a heelander. My ma jist tellt us, if I did somethn the wrang wey, ye're dayn it lik a heelander, 's an awffy heeland wey tay day thon.

Not Irish?

Sorry?

Not an Irish way of doing things? Don't you say that here when you mean somebody's doing something all wrong?

I widny say that.

You mean you wouldn't say that, or folk wouldn't?

Aye well, some folk might, but I widny. Gie us peace, you.

He'd wakened up enough to see the wicked look she had on her. The last thing she'd to do was to slip her feet into her low court shoes, the ones with the circular buckles she'd on when he'd first met her. He spoke rapidly, had the look on him of a waiter who had to serve his notion up quickly, before it scalded his fingers.

Come wi me the day. I'm gaun away oan safari.

Catherine balanced herself on her flattened, unshod foot, resting a hand on the back of her chair, using the crook of her finger to pull on the shoe so she could settle inside it.

I have to work today. The weekend, maybe.

I don't work oot at weekends. C'moan. I've seen you at yir work. Ye cn call the boass man fae here.

What do I call and tell him?

Tell'm ye're no well. Simple as that.

Catherine put both feet on the ground, not quite ready yet for going out; still had her face to apply in the mirror hanging from the wardrobe door handle, and she said quickly,

Persuade me before I put my face on, and I'll think about it.

Gianfranco offered her the next day off if she still wasn't well enough to come in, and she thanked him, said she'd use it if it was necessary, cradled the handset feeling a wee bit bad about lying to him. Peter had chosen where they were to go by the time she went back to the room; he found it on a street atlas and showed her, to the south-east of the town centre, though she wouldn't've known from the way the town was broken up in the pages of the book. She watched as he equipped himself, putting everything into the duffel bag which usually rested in the bow of the window; a handful of pencils, a couple of sketchbooks like the one she'd seen him use in the café, a big pad he got down from the top of the wardrobe and which she hadn't seen before because of the crown of the frieze; that seemed to be it, and he throttled the neck of the bag with one good pull of the drawstring and swung it on to his back, straightening up and grinning like a wee boy off on an adventure.

Aff tay hunt fr game.

He preferred the top decks to the lower saloons, as the gold-lettered notices warning of the bus's capacity called them; lower saloon, he said, and upper saloon, laughing as if the formal sound of it was a good joke. On the two buses they had to take to their destination, he led Catherine up the spiral stairs both times; sat them in the front seats, the Cinerama seats, he said, so you could see the injuns attacking from the sides. She hadn't seen him in a mood like this since she'd met him; wondered if it was her being there, or if the prospect of work always made him like this. She was beginning to hate the upper saloon the longer she sat through the smoke, but Peter said he came up here for the banter, how folk talked to one another. He made her listen to the women, out for their day's shopping and things you could only buy in the town centre; some of them had their hair in curlers and headscarves to protect the whole structure, and Catherine had seen their like before in her old street, the hair was never unbound and they wore different headscarves every day. Those ones seemed to be the most talkative; everything from their men and cooking for them to the best cuts of fish, and there was one whose voice rose above the others, deep with tobacco, I like a rare-tasted bit ey cod mysel, but I hate kippers, mind, lik dampt yella pincushns so they ur, Wullie likes kippers but so I get thm fr the weekend fr his brekfst Sunday efter we've been tay the chapel. The next woman said she didn't like fish much, Sunday was their ham and eggs day, and Catherine turned to Peter, whispered,

Is this where you get your menus from?

Peter laughed, coddling his duffel bag on his lap.

I love hearn a' this stuff. Thon's real folk talkin.

He made her change channels, to another conversation happening behind her; elderly men, their working lives spent, settled into their gabardines and hiding their eyes under the brims of their flat caps as if the new world around them was too vivid for their dull sight to bear. One of them was talking about the tele as if it'd been invented yesterday; see they programmes? he said, load ey rubbish, there's folk swerrn oaths ye widny utter tay yir worst enemy, an wimmn gallivantn aboot in their underclaes, ach! ye widny credit the manure I've pit up wi efter my set wis installed by the rental folk. The other man's voice was gentler, more forgiving; aye, but it's compny, is it no? he said, n I waatch the news evry night, is it no a miracle ye cn see whit's happnin places ye've never seen in yir life? and, aye, said the first of the worthies, n places nae Christian man wid waant tay see neether, fightn n starven n runnin aboot lik savages, whit m I interestit in their boathers whn I've boathers ey my ain tay concairn me? Catherine started when she felt the hand on hers; Peter had put it there as a distraction, having seen her jaw tightening and her frown gathering like cloud.

Calm doon, he said. We're gettn aff soon.

She was in charge of his duffel bag so he could draw unencumbered, or at least not have to worry about where it was. He'd lost the lot once, he said, on a corpy bus taking him home; one lapse, and he was halfway up the road before realizing he was lighter about the shoulders than usual. The bloke in the corporation bus depot's lost property office had a rare laugh about it, aye, man, he said, there wisny much tay steal, so ye've goat it a' back intact, but Peter showed him a few pages out of one of the sketchbooks, nude studies from his life classes, and the office man's mouth opened like a fly trap, Jesus Christ man, nice work if ye cn get it, sure it is, c'mere n we'll swap places.

You've never shown me any of those,

said Catherine as Peter got out a sketchbook and the right pencil before giving the bag over to her.

Mebbe let ye see thm later,

he said, and began cueing up the scene ready for the first sketch.

It was the first time she'd ever thought of what he did as work; the wintry glaur in the sky capped the tenements, thick as quilting, but there was no heat in it, and a wind like pure ice vapour drew across their faces, leaking between skin and clothing. She had to fasten the collar of her coat around her neck, and regretted not thinking of wearing her slacks today; but Peter stood in place, holding the sketchbook tight so the wind wouldn't dog-ear the pages, and wearing black woollen gloves with half the fingers scissored off them so he could feel the pencil; a wonder he could, with his fingers bleached white and bloodless. He divided himself between the subject and the page, and his subject was the ground-floor window of a tenement, in which sat many different varieties of china dolls, some with gingham print dresses, some with severe Victorian school uniforms on them. She watched him assembling the lines; an oblong, which with a few strokes he made into a pane of glass in a frame complete with reflections, although he excluded the reflections of himself and Catherine from the sketch where she could see them both in the true window, peering over the picket fencing. Next, he drew the dolls on the sill; hair tight and spiralled under the bonnets, the heart-shaped faces from which deathly blue eyes stared, smiles moulded around exaggerated regular teeth. One of them had a rocking chair to herself in the centre of the display, and seemed to be the queen of them all; cared for through the years, her dress laundered until what had started out as navy blue had worn to the colour of tarnished copper. Some of them had been repaired, not all of them well, with scabs of glue around the joins of their injuries; the obviously later ones had been much better prepared and finished, the edges mated properly, the adhesive invisible. Catherine thought those ones looked the most harrowing, because you could imagine all kinds of reasons for why the dolls had been broken; torn out of a child's hands during a dreadful punishing, a domineering brother or sister treading on the fragile heads, even the child herself turning on an old favourite. One of them had been split from forehead to chin, exposing the white powder behind the skin of paint, and the crack ran diagonally across the socket for the eye, and there was a rim of darkness circling the restored bead, as if blindness was eating away at her. Catherine looked over Peter's shoulder, to the sketchbook. He seemed especially fascinated with that doll, for all the time he spent on it, tracking the pencil along the wound, giving it the proper look of a substance moulded from cohering dust, and she was just as fascinated by his work on the sketch, how he achieved his effects; but it was a mystery, hidden by the hand bearing the pencil, a few passes and then she was seeing the same cracked doll in his book, as if he'd folded the three dimensions of the doll into two, brought it to the page and then raised it into three dimensions again, draining the colour from it in the process. He sketched all the dolls like that, and when he'd finished, he put the pencil in the fold of the book and shut it, and handed it over to Catherine to stow in the bag. She did that for him, pulled the drawstring tight and then held the bag out to him; but he walked past her and on a few steps. She said,

Hoy, it's your bag.

He looked cheekily at her over his shoulder.

Evry artist's goat his assistant.

Catherine caught up with him, having none of his chancing. He let her raise his arm and thread it through the cord, and then settle the bag against his back.

Every other artist pays for an assistant. Where to now?

Wherr tay noo? he said. Tay wherre'er's maist interestn.

The sky was like plate steel that day as the sun asserted itself through the stifling cloud. There was no heat in it; but the wind turned light and feathery, until it was pure stroking your cheek, lifting the pages of Peter's book. Catherine followed him into closes and drying greens, other folks' property, which he walked through like an inspector, his shoulders thrown confidently back, eyes like the darkness in an empty barrel. She was thinking of the differences between him and Francis; both of them with those kinds of eyes, but Francis had looked under the surfaces where Peter was pleased enough with the arrangement and structures of things. Some of Peter's sketches were just bold, rapid outlines; he'd drop the bag and take out the book and copy what he saw, a geometrical trick played by fencing, a door someone had made personal in some way, the collapsed lung of an abandoned football by the side of the road; anything and everything, and she was minding on her brother, his treasures when he was a boy, grubbed out of the earth so he could examine them later under the eyeglass their mammy bought him for his birthday. Peter wasn't like that; he preferred crafted objects, like the dolls, the fence, footballs; they told more about our needs, he said, for companionship, security, attention, recreation; land was just paper or canvas, he said, but what we wrote on it or designed for it or abandoned to it, that was another matter, that was expression pure and simple. Catherine listened without understanding the half of it; thought, she was his paper as well, on which he was writing his manifesto, and she closed her covers on him and made a dialogue of it, just to remind him she wasn't so much like paper but more like stone, not just there to take his word as gospel.

Have you ever run a farm?

They were walking along a net of roads binding the estate; names were sprayed on the gable ends of the houses, black and red cords against the brick. Peter looked over at it curiously for a moment, decided it wasn't worth taking down, turned his head to the side to look at her, with a small crease of a frown on him.

Canny say I huv. Why, whit's the deal?

We didn't leave much on the land. Stuff to make the crops grow, maybe. But you couldn't trust it to give you crops back at the end of the year, the growing year, I'm talking about.

Peter was bumping her gently with his shoulder as they went side by side, nudging her away from the kerb; she didn't think he was doing it deliberately, but she moved in further, just in case.

Aye, that's farmin ye're meanin. I'm meanin a toun like this wan. Folks make hames fr theirsels. Concrete the grun a' ower. Make touns, ye know? These're wherr folk come thegither.

But, said Catherine, I couldn't tell you the name of anyone who lived around me in the old place. Bernadette upstairs, aye, but I still can't tell you her man's name, nor the old couple opposite.

Haud oan, said Peter, haud oan; ye're strayin, Cathy. Ur ye sayn folk wilny come thegither in touns?

If this'd been her with Francis, she'd've gone arm in arm with him along the road; but it didn't seem right with Peter.

I'm not saying any such thing. I'm saying, maybe there's a lot of folk in one place, but nobody knows anyone else.

The cord had slipped from Peter's shoulder; he jerked his arm to ride the cord more securely along.

Aye, but d'ye no see, Cath, that's whit makes it so important tay show folk they make these schemes come alive; it's no the bricks n mortar, it's theirsels. Thon auld wumman n her dolls; if they're no there, thon's jist anither windae.

Or man.

Soarry, whit?

Or it might be a man. Maybe it's a man collecting dolls. A young man, even.

Whit wid a young man be dayn, collectin dolls?

How do I know what a young man'd be doing collecting dolls? I don't even know what an old woman would be doing with them. It's just a bloody miracle they're still in the window. They can be quite valuable, you know.

Peter smiled towards her, archly. He licked the point of a finger and drew a mark on the air beside her, as if, one nil.

Jist cause you've hud a brek-in, he said, disny mean everybdy livin in the schemes is scum.

While they were walking, Peter got on to the subject of how he was brought up, just to demonstrate to her that you didn't have to be middle class, or heading that way, to treasure things like loyalty, or what was right and true. Catherine had never said anything of the sort, but she thought, he was more likely using the occasion to tell her more of himself, and that she was interested in. He told her how he'd been his father's last gift to his mother, a surprise after the old man was called back from leave; his ma used to read him his father's letters, even though he was too young to understand them, but he did know that his father's words in his mother's mouth were kindly, and she made a great ceremony of reading the letters with their black obscuring banners over giveaways the censor had deemed unsuitable for them to know. There was one letter she didn't read to him; more tidily sealed than usual, and this one had not been censored, it meant exactly what had been said, and she sat in the corner with it, crushed it like a handkerchief in her hand, and all the while her eyes were settled on the corner of the room, and she was singing to herself, smile though your heart is breaking. She never did tell the wee one what the letter contained, and never said why he no longer had a father like the other children.

Peter Caulder's mother was an extraordinary woman. She had the looks of a film star, and a dress sense to match; made her own to economize, stitched as if her life was in danger if she stopped work for a moment, more especially after she'd received the letter. She bought the paper every day, and left Peter in the house on his own for whole evenings at a time; and when she came home with two scrolls of paper and held them open one after the other to show him, a diploma in Pitman's Shorthand System and a diploma in touch-typing, she seemed to be expecting him to be celebrating with her, but he'd spent months listening to the radio and its dreich snobby voice for company three evenings a week, and he didn't understand she was holding not just paper you'd wipe your arse with but keys, who needs yir faither? who needs a faither? no you, son, there'll be money comin intay the hoose n we'll eat proaper. She wore gravy browning on her legs instead of stockings, and used an eye pencil to pretend a seam; would show it to Peter and say, there, 'm I straight, son? 'm I good enough tay eat, d'ye think? and giggled like a schoolgirl at a joke he never understood until later. She had a secretary's post in a law firm within a short while of achieving her diplomas; she walked proudly down the streets towards the tram stop, and folk said, thon's that big floozy wi her airs n graces, she'll no look the road ye're oan, watch this, then louder, hullo there, Missis Caulder, fine day, is it no? and when she ignored them they turned to their companions in scandal and said, there ye ur, see, no a civil word fr naebdy, and everyone agreed it was terrible how she'd never thought to mourn for her man, how she'd just dusted herself off as if she'd stumbled over loose paving and walked on away from his corpse, terrible so it was.

The only one with the right to make such a judgement thought so too; it was as if she despised his father for failing her in not returning from the war, and so had torn him out of the records, like Stalin ordering new histories to be made. In this new truth, Peter had never had a father; there were no photographs of him, no letters to be read, his was the first virgin birth for almost two thousand years if she was to be believed; not that she ever denied him, just that she said, will ye stoap askin aboot that bloody man? and then went into the corner again and sang gently to herself, words Peter could never make out. For years, Peter tried to put his father back together again by stealing pieces of him when she wasn't looking; memories she allowed to fall like pictures secreted in the loose leaves of an old book; he learned she'd married him for reasons of ruthless practicality, because he was in a good trade, in the shipyards, in a secured profession, which meant he didn't need to go and fight, except there was the brother he'd lost in the Spanish civil war, and he was minded to go and leather the bastard who'd helped take him when the trouble in Poland set the fuses burning all across Europe. She'd begged him, even used herself as bargaining, but he said, ye're an awful wumman, Mary Caulder, n I'll take whit ye're offern tay keep me fr the time I'm gone, but ye canny gie a bully leave tay take whit isny his, cause he'll take yir ain next. He was worse than a fool, he was a principled fool, and she'd mutter under her breath to herself when she thought Peter wasn't listening, shid niver ey merried ye, Thomas Caulder, you n yir beliefs, whit use're they tay the womenfolk n the weans? and he later began to understand that the corner she sat in was a retreat for her, like a ship in its dry dock, where she made repairs to herself whenever she was tempted to think kindly of her late husband, where she sang her smiling song to remind herself never to display grief, and where she spoke sternly to herself if ever she felt the need to indulge her sadness.

Peter constructed a hero out of the man he kept bits of like scraps of felt; it was his first artistic triumph, this absent father, and he only had his face in the mirror to go on for a clue as to how his father had appeared. Even when he was quite young, it occurred to him that if there was a blend in him of his mother and his father, then once you'd taken the likeness of his mother away you'd be left with a resemblance to the man who'd died fighting. His features were a mixture of roundness and sharpness, and he knew the roundness came from his mother; so the sharpness, the appearance of a mask made by cutting a folded profile of card, must be his father's; a kind of stark and uncompromising kind of face, and that was what he tried to follow, not his mother's softness but the smooth and welded quality he saw that was not hers.

In the meantime, Mary Caulder had found herself another man; and all because of that voice of hers that could sing and make accurate portraits of everyone she ever met to amuse Peter with when she came home from her work. She had a graceful telephone manner, able to pretend a class or two above her birth, which had landed her a secretarial position in a firm of solicitors; she had a proud typing hand and a good memory for correct spelling, and she was quick and accurate with Pitman's, which brought her to the attention of a young man who'd missed the worst of the conflict by dint of his rank, and the social position which had granted him his commission. Peter's only knowledge of his mother's friendship with this man was how she was in the evenings, cooking late dinners for her boy and singing all the while in the scullery; the music which had oppressed her husband's memory now coming out of her like the gas when you shook a bottle of ginger; and she even took her telephone voice home with her, I feel a turn in our fortunes, Peter, honest I do, settling his plate of stovies in front of him and then shimmering into the seat opposite his at the unfolded table, and Peter wondered if his mother had gone mad, if so much loneliness and work had deranged her, but he wasn't to learn the reason for it for some time yet.

She kept Peter indoors like a secret when her man came to pick her up in his car that was too rich for here; to Reginald Balfour, she said it was an empty house she was leaving, while to Peter she said there was the taxi to collect her, and neither knew of the other until she was satisfied of Balfour's honesty and decency. Peter knew she'd never dressed like this for her evening classes, but he only truly began to understand the night she revealed them to each other, turning them over like cards in a game of pontoon, though obviously one knew more than the other; Peter, this is Reginald, Peter is my son, and as young as he was, Peter understood the game now. Reginald was bearing gifts that evening, in preparation; a tablet of paper, and a tin box of watercolour paints, which Peter opened at his mother's urging while Reginald, what the hell kind of stupid name was that for a bloke, said, your mother tells me you have quite a talent for drawing, I thought you might like this, and his ma said, thank Reginald for his kindness, Peter, and away and do us a painting.

Peter sat at the unfolded table, glancing over at the settee every so often, at the properly distanced Reginald and his ma, talking to each other in voices that didn't carry to him. After a while, Reginald stood up, came around behind him and looked over Peter's shoulder at the painting.

Is that a soldier, Peter? That's awfully good.

Peter snapped shut the tin box, locking the brush inside it, held it out to Reginald; spun around in the seat so he could get a good look at the big jessie's face.

It's my faither, n ye cn huv yir effin peynts back, I'm finished wi them noo.

He said effin to Catherine as he was telling it to her, but not to Reginald. It was the first time Mary Caulder had ever given her son such a leathering, and it had to be in front of Reginald, as well; she never understood that punishment was different in houses such as Reginald's, that the child was meant to present himself, herself, for striking once a wrong had been acknowledged, rather than scurry like a rat against the skirting as Peter did. It was Reginald who begged for mercy on the child's behalf, or else she'd've gone insane and done him a dreadful harm, but this he did say to Peter once the boy was pulled to his feet and stood in front of them:

I am very sorry for your display of ill manners, Peter, because your mother invited me to your house for a very good reason, one which I'd hoped would be cause for celebration. After some time of knowing your mother, I have decided to ask her for her hand in marriage, and she has agreed to this. The paints were offered in the spirit of friendship, since I understand that you still miss your father, as is only but natural. For the sake of our mutual regard for your mother, I hope that we may become friends before too long, and I hope that you will find me a fair and accommodating man, but I am determined in this. You may keep the paints, and the paper, and with my blessing you may paint as many pictures of your father as you wish, but please bear in mind that we will be living under the same roof before long, and thus a certain shall we say arrangement must be understood between us if there is to be harmony, and that's all I'll say about it.

Peter looked him in the eye the whole time; saw the softness, the roundness of compromise in the features, a cushioned, luxurious cast to the flesh. Reginald picked the box of paints from the floor, where they'd been dropped just before the chase, when Mary's hand had flickered towards her son's jaw like the erratic reach of fire; gave it into Peter's hand, and he accepted them for a moment, weighing the tin as if to compare it to the weight of thirty pieces of silver; then went over to the hearth, and carelessly tossed the box in among the nest of flames, where it sat until the gaudy enamels suppurated and blistered in the heat, and the metal turned red.

Both of them declared their intentions that evening; and Peter was right about the softness of his mother's new man, but he was fatally mistaken about the compromise; it was a softness that took all blows and spread the force of them so there was no resulting hurt, and so for Reginald there was no deterrence in Peter's opposition. Perhaps Mary could smooth a cloth of silk over her rough-cut voice, and go in the disguise of a higher birth to meet Reginald's family; but Peter was her despair and her disgrace at the wedding, and they couldn't even go on a proper honeymoon because of him, and worse than that in her estimation, Reginald became more estranged from his family who didn't care to have their cut-crystal sensibilities scratched across by the brutal manners of what they called that little corner-boy with his sewer expressions and his mockery. The only compensation was the fact that Reginald bought them all a new house in the west end, which was really their honeymoon as they moved in almost immediately after the marriage; Peter was given his own sizeable room, and there was bugger all for him to do but paint, and think of how he'd been avoided by all his footballing chinas in his own street before the move, as if he'd been infected by the leprosy of Reginald's snobbiness, as if he could carry it to them with a touch.

So no, this was not the man to judge folk from the schemes, because he'd been made a traitor by circumstance, and he wasn't about to abandon folk of his own kind of birth because of his nature. His principles were framed like his canvases, the hardness of purpose which had kept him at war with his stepfather since the fat thing tried to suborn him against his own kind; it took some strength to keep reminding his mother of the earth she'd been pulled from when she was so enamoured of her new bed, but he knew that his true father would've approved of this hardness in him, and so he went on, soldiered on you might say, fighting the battles in his father's memory, and if it reminded his mother of her own forgotten soldier, then so much the better.

Catherine saw the march in his step as they went along the road, the constant pace that made her breathless to keep up with him, and she wondered if this was a safari or a reconnaissance he was on, a mission in more senses than just the military one.

The singing attracted him to the mouth of the close; love you, yeah, yeah, yeah; a woman's voice striking the notes like a piano. Peter stopped, then looked at Catherine; here they'd been talking about miracles, and here was a genuine one, like the close itself making music. He went before Catherine, mounting the steps, passing the doors to the ground-floor houses, out the passageway to the drying green, following the song round the back; a woman with her hair in curlers, wearing a brown cardigan and a red skirt to her knees, her bare feet in red carpet slippers, and she was thrashing the dust out of a fireside rug slumped over a clothes-line, keeping time to her own singing with strokes of a cane beater shaped like a clover leaf. She made a dance of it; one step towards the rug, swinging during the step, swiping like a tennis player and then retreating to escape the dust. Catherine wondered if the girl had a vacuum cleaner in the house, or if she was just thorough by nature. She had her back to them, didn't even notice them until Peter landed his foot on to the gravel, and then she spun on the grass, lifting her free hand to her breast and making wide eyes at them; you could see her pregnancy almost immediately as she turned, and she fell back and laughed at Catherine and then Peter.

Gied us a fright, so ye did,

she said. The moment she turned, the girl, Catherine thought she'd a trusting kind of face. She looked as if cruelty puzzled her, and would as a result be destined to attract it. She dropped the beater by her side, shifted awkwardly from foot to foot, like she'd been caught enjoying a labour given to her as a punishment. Peter stood back a little from her, afraid she'd bolt, because she was eyeing his duffel bag, and thinking the same as Catherine would've been thinking if she'd met Peter like this; that no one innocent carried a bag of that kind at a time when folk had left their houses to go to the shops, or to their work. Peter took the bag from his shoulder and held it between them.

Awfl soarry, said Peter. We jist heard yir singin. No bad, so it wis.

The girl patted her hair.

Thanks very much, she said. My husband says I've a good voaice as well.

Aye well, said Peter, he's no wrang. Tell ye why I'm here, cause I'd be lik you if some eejit wis staunnin here wi a funny-lookin bag.

He pulled the bag open, and went closer to her to allow her to see into it. The girl dipped her head to look; she was puzzled by the contents, stepped back towards her rug and brought her arms around herself, holding the beater so the clover leaf tapped against her shoulder.

I canny make my mind up if ye're the auldest schoolboay I've ever met, said the girl, or jist no right in the heid.

Catherine laughed along with her, and Peter turned around to Catherine, his mouth twisted up at one side, as if to say, thanks for the support. The girl wriggled on the spot, as if she was used to paying for her cheek, but Peter just fished in his bag for one of his sketchbooks, took it out and opened it for her, the way he'd shown Catherine when he first met her. The girl looked down as Peter turned the pages, became genuinely curious the longer she stared.

Allow me to introduce mysel, he said. I'm Peter Caulder, artist tay the masses.

You a cathlic?

Naw, no they kin ey masses. I mean, I jist draw n peynt folk dayn evryday stuff. This is my lovely assistant, Cathrin.

Catherine took her cue from Peter; twinkled with a few poses like a quiz show hostess, one hand behind her head and the other on her hip, cocking a leg. The girl looked past Peter, to her.

How'd you assist him?

I hold his bag while he does the drawing.

The girl giggled.

No much ey an assistant.

Catherine shrugged.

He can usually do it himself, but I have a day off my real work.

The girl went back to scrutinizing Peter's book, said over the top of it,

I'm Maureen. Hoosewife n cairpet beater tay the gentry, nae reasonable oaffer refused. Is this a' you day fr a livin?

Peter shut the book.

This n the brew, aye. No believe me?

Maureen tapped her lower lip with the end of the beater, thoughtfully.

I thoat artists were meant tay peynt bowls ey aipples n stuff lik thon?

Aye, shite wans, pardn my French. The best wans day peyntns ey real folk.

Should I no know you, if you're wan ey the best artists?

How, whit artists huv you heard ey?

I canny think, noo; yon blok Picasso, mebbe. Aw aye, n yon ither blok; blok tht did yon wumman, whit's the name again? Moanin Lizzie r somethn?

Mona Lisa, said Catherine, Leonardo da Vinci.

I knew that, she said, but I think she looks mare lik a moanin auld besom mysel, so I call her Moanin Lizzie.

Well, said Peter, I don't waant tay day you as a moanin auld besom, so rest assured.

Maureen brought her hand to her breast.

Why'd'ye waant tay day me?

Peter shrugged again.

Cause ye're lookin right healthy n pregnant n I think ye'd make a smashn subject. C'moan, say aye.

There was never any question she'd do it; Peter said afterwards, he'd known the moment he'd heard the voice, and then when he saw her, the way she carried herself, all the wee extravagant gestures, the clutching around her heart, the keen-to-please smile; she'd been waiting and begging God for offers like this until Peter came along, and he wasn't blaming her for it, he was just stating the case as he saw it. Catherine had to summon all her charity not to see Maureen as some wee star-struck snip; watched as Peter directed Maureen to stand beside her rug on the wire so she'd be in profile, and raise her arm as if she was giving it a hiding with the beater. As Peter noted her down in his sketchbook, Catherine said,

Mind her condition, Peter, she'll tire awful soon with standing,

talking from her own experience of being that far gone, but Maureen said,

Nae bother, if he disny take too lang wi it.

I'll day her in the foregrun first, then I cn day the backgrun wi her no staunnin. Y'awright jist noo, Maureen?

Maureen held her chin a wee bit forward.

I'll let ye know soon enough,

she said, and Catherine slung the duffel bag over her shoulder, and etched a quarter-circle in the gravel with the point of her shoe, annoyed by the waiting more than when he'd been drawing the dolls in the window; another bloody doll, she was thinking, mercilessly.

*

So, Catherine asked when they returned to the house, would Peter be making paintings out of any of the day's trophies? and he gave a wee sideways look and told her maybe, maybe not; opened his wardrobe and let her see under the laundry on the floor of it, where he kept an entire library of sketchbooks. There was where he kept the game from his safaris; early stuff before he'd lighted on a theme to his work, and which he showed her with some embarrassment, folk who wouldn't stay still long enough for him and who were gone before he could make anything out of them, buildings, which he'd tried for a time because he could at least finish work on them; the common furniture of any town, churches, civic seats in the parks, mostly empty, after long experience of folk sitting on them and then getting up to leave before he'd done. He showed her one where he'd had to erase the woman he'd been drawing, an old wifie with her trolley; you could still see her haunting the seat and a glaucous drift across the paper, and he said, efter yon I thoat, bugger this fr a caper, I'll day the seats, and he'd a good sequence of them from parks and even some installed on the bank of the Clyde, where old folk sat to watch the ships arriving at the ports as well as, if they were lucky, new builds on their way to the ocean. He showed one of those to Catherine; an elderly couple seen from behind, and she couldn't really tell from the picture if they were watching a ship going to sea or to unload cargo until Peter told her it was the north bank, meaning it was leaving dock; and then he showed her why it was one of the most dishonest pictures he'd ever drawn, or so he said anyway, when he turned back a few pages where she saw the boat on an entirely different stretch of the river, and then a picture of the two old folk, with no boat in it; and then turned the page forward to his composed scene. Catherine said, well you may blame yourself for that, because the two drawings taken separately said different things to her; the ship was optimism and adventure, since that was what her voyage had meant to her; the two old folk seem intolerably lost and blown around; together, the images were one emblem of wistfulness and forsaken opportunities, and even though he said it felt right to use them in that way, she couldn't escape the feeling that it was more a collage than a true picture, and he said that was why he never repeated it, because it'd seemed dishonest to him while he was doing it, and that was why he'd never made it into a painting.

Some of the pictures he'd done in life-drawing classes, and he'd kept them all together in one book.

You mean, like, in the altogether?

Catherine said mischievously, and he said back, aye, very funny, and opened those books accompanied by the crack of the bindings, the threads pulling loose on them, it was so long ago. For some reason, she'd thought the pages would be filled with women, and she teased him about it before he showed her properly,

That's some way for a man and a woman to meet, she said, her freezing in the what you call it, the studio, and him leering at her over an easel; would you not be better going to a dance? at least there's some mystery there.

Peter passed the book on to her,

Aw aye, he said, look at the first model I ever drew; pure in love, so I wis.

There was a frontispiece of marbled paper, stiffer than the pages inside; Catherine opened it, and then laughed at the first entry. It was a tired-looking old man, standing with his hands on his hips, his age-slackened flesh creased around his waist; to be fair to him, he'd a good head of hair, and a face with a story of past strength written in the lines, but it wasn't what she'd expected. Peter told her the young man had fought in the First World War over in France, and had taken back with him as a souvenir a love of art, but no aptitude; the elderly man was quite content to offer himself as a subject in the hope that someone would see fit to make a painting of him, but mostly he was just an exercise for the students, and that pleased him well enough. She'd expected more glamour; there were men and women of all ages and conditions, earning a wee bit of cash in hand, some reclining on sheets, others standing casually, or posed with objects, window poles, apples, whatever'd been around at the time. Catherine closed the book over, shook her head when he offered her another of them to look at.

You don't do that kind of thing now, though?

She was kneeling on the floor beside Peter, while he was sorting through his books. He spoke into the cabinet of the wardrobe, where the cloth smothered the words.

Noo n again. Tay keep in practice, jist.

Any more recent than those?

He went so far into the wardrobe, it looked as if it was going to consume him; his hair stopped her from reading his expression, lank by the side of his head.

I canny right pit my hauns oan them the noo, but I'll let ye see thm when I've fun thm.

Catherine said, all right, I'm not in any rush, but she thought he'd sounded reluctant, considered it was better not to press him. There was still a kind of tenderness about their arrangement, after all; not emotional tender, but tender like a new scar, where the lips of a wound had knitted together as best they could, and it wasn't a thing she was minded to test just yet, in case the binding between them would split. She thought, she'd leave it for now, and look at the work he was willing to show her, and be complimentary, even if she didn't like it much, and put honesty on the shelf for another day, until she was more certain the way they'd healed together would stand her true thoughts.

Ten

She only really knew Heidless by what he'd left behind; the reek in the hall, the rotten breath of his room drifting under the door; but the more she heard of him the more she knew she'd've hated him if ever she'd had the chance to meet him. On the Saturday of her weekend off, she asked Peter while he was at work on Elvis, had he thought of what they might do with the unwanted room, rent it out to another tenant or use it somehow. Peter was too busy to attend much to her; maybe, he said from behind the canvas, they could do with another rent coming in, but he wasn't minded to discuss it when he'd unfinished work pulling on his shirt. She asked him if she could see the room so she'd've some idea of what had to be done before you could ask anyone to consider living in it; Peter nodded her towards his set of keys on the table, told her the key to it wasn't on her ring, said, help yirsel, almost grateful to have her away from him.

When Catherine came out of the room five minutes later, the first place she went was the bathroom, and she felt she daren't touch the cleanliness of the ceramic tiling. She turned on the taps in the sink and soaped her hands, and rubbed them until the lather dried on her skin and she had to make it slippy again by making it wet under the hot water; and only after she'd towelled her hands dry would she reach for the bath taps. She put down the toilet seat and sat on it, waiting for the bath to fill; she was in quarantine behind the bolted door until she'd washed herself. She sat forward, rested her head in her hands; the soap's perfume helped rinse away the thought of the reek breaking over her once the key'd been turned, but the sight wouldn't be cleansed away so easily; the deliberate waste and carefully assembled disorder of the room.

Heidless's fall into dissolution was apparent in every grain of dust in the room. They could've been doing with Maureen coming round with her beater to thrash the carpet within an inch of its life, only it would've taken a team of Maureens three years working in shifts to beat all the dust out of it. As she went deeper into the room, Catherine began beating the dust out of the pile herself with her feet, drawing a mist that swirled around her ankles. The dust wouldn't've been so bad on its own; but Heidless had done all his living in this one room, working, eating, drinking, sleeping, and if the sodden patches on the carpet in the corner nearest the doorway, and the streak of lime blistering the wallpaper and the powerful territorial scent of cats were anything to go by, it'd been his lavatory as well, though he'd tried to soak up the piss with layers of brown-paper wrappers from chips. Peter'd said to her that Heidless had been knocking on the door of madness ever since he'd known him as a bursary student at the art school; it seemed she'd stepped through that door just then, into the most expressive lunacy she'd ever come across, into a madness of a kind she'd never considered giving into even during her worst moments of isolation.

The bed was indescribable, the mattress soaked through with a drunkard's incontinence. She tried not to breathe, but like a swimmer she had to at intervals; detected the smell of rusted iron among other things she preferred to ignore. In the opposite corner of the room to the lavatory, the one nearest the window, there were three dents in the carpet, which she recognized as the footprints of an easel, and behind that, all the half-bottles of whisky and cheap fortified wines clambering over each other towards the casement, and she thought for a moment there was a deliberative pattern to it, as if he'd turned the room into a museum of solitary inspiration, the drink he'd emptied into himself, the place he worked, the waste at the hind end. She couldn't help thinking of her father the longer she looked at the monument, only he'd been drinking for the company, generous to folk stupid enough to think him wise, or wise enough to tap the drink from him; she could understand that, but this seemed morbid and senseless to her, and she'd some pity for Heidless, even as she was relieved she hadn't had to live in the same house as him.

The strange thing was, the room drew her deeper in; she'd never seen ruin like it before, apart from when she'd come back after the break-in, and once she'd learned to breathe in through her mouth and out through her nose, she was taken by curiosity, studying it like one of Peter's canvases. She discovered where all the missing plates and teacups from the kitchen had gone; under the bed, colonized by mould, stacked in a pretend kind of tidiness. There was a saucer on the bedside cabinet, in which maggots of roll-ups fed on the burnt flesh of cigarettes, which explained why Codie's teacup had nowhere to rest. She looked up to the ceiling, at webs of dust spilling over the picture rail, and real webs softening the four right angles of the oak-leaf cornicing, obvious nets spun for idiot flies; now in the winter, there wasn't much food around, but you could see the spiders drumming their fingers patiently on the cables, and Catherine saw why there hadn't been a blizzard of insects as soon as she'd opened the door; the webs had enough fodder caught in them to last until well after the spring, and each of the spiders had fat, glutted hind-quarters, with enough weight on them to bend the strings in the middle.

Catherine went down on her haunches to examine more closely some of the debris on the carpet, and found they were cigarette packets torn apart and flattened into mats. There were pencil drawings on the clean sides, which had taken her interest in the first place; Peter'd told her this had been one of Heidless's habits, never buying a sketchbook, but he'd search around a pub for these cast-offs, on the rare occasions when he'd the money to leave the house for his drink, take them over to his table where he'd be drinking on his own, open them out and draw on them what he fancied. They were the only memory he had sometimes, the only evidence he'd ever left the house, but they weren't sacred to him; there were plenty of them left behind around the prints of his easel, and Catherine lifted a few which had been fastened together by Sellotape, when he'd obviously needed a wider frame. The scene was the interior of a pub, no surprise; but the lines were surer than she'd've expected, not as bold as Peter's but long and sustained, with a severe definition and little sense of roundness to them, and no texture in what they held, like the boundaries of continents on a political map. Evidently Heidless had drawn the work on several packets at once all laid out on the table to overlap like slates, and then matched them when he came home; the lines carried from one to another, sometimes looping back to the tile they'd originated from, and she thought it must've been a right puzzle to fit them together again. The entire picture showed an old man standing in profile by the wall of the pub in the foreground just near the door, and Catherine couldn't believe what she was seeing; he had his coat parted as well as the buttons of his fly, and he was making water against the wall as if he was in front of a urinal, or hidden in an alleyway. There was some good observation in how he'd made the face of a man made oblivious by the drink, but Catherine thought, he'd likely seen it often enough in the mirror to recognize it so well. The drunk took up one panel of the drawing; the rest of it was the bar, the landlord behind the counter fat with the luxury the drinkers bought for him, milling his arms in the air and with his mouth round and astonished; and the various reactions of the drinkers, some of them laughing at the farce of it, others disturbed by the way the old man was humiliating himself in the corner.

It wasn't the picture that made her want to wash herself; she thought it was quite well executed, even if she didn't much care for the scene. It was just that suddenly after a week of standing in Gianfranco's Paradise, her legs became tired, and she was shifting herself around to relieve the ache when she lost her balance and tipped backwards, losing her grip on the raft of pictures and sending it skimming through the air. She landed on her back on the carpet, feeling the crushed chip papers studded against her, raising a splash of dust. The impact of her fall drove the breath from her, and she swallowed some of the dust into her throat, making her cough; her head was clotted with the decay, and she got to her feet and ran from the lair as quickly as she could, closing the door behind her, locking herself in the bathroom, afraid of touching anything in case she printed the contagion on taps and door handles.

When the bath was full, Catherine stripped herself of her dusty clothes and put them on the linoleum, keeping her underclothing separate by placing it on the closed toilet seat. She hadn't the least notion for now how she'd get back to Peter's, race there in her underclothes, maybe. For now, though, she lowered herself into the bath and watched the blanket of hot water pull itself over her, and even before she'd begun to lather the green soap she felt cleaner, her skin sterilized by the heat, and she was grateful almost for a mess that could be ridded once and for all, that she could make more homely with a wee bit effort.

Mrs Kilsyth's had been a good training for Catherine in housework, for all that it'd been poky. Not that she'd particularly enjoyed it, but at least she was being paid fair money for the job, and the old duchess could've been much worse, although it was bad enough her reaching up from her wheelchair and sketching lines on the window sills to see if she came away with dust in the isobars of her fingers. For Francis and Cameron, it was different; that was keeping a home in good order, and she'd always been aware this was just another way of making the house safe for the wee one, just like having a decent father and a mother watching out for him, when her own experience had been of one and not the other, and she wouldn't have that repeated in her own place.

The wee local shop had a peculiar smell of firelighters to it, floor polish, and new-baked loaves, which she wasn't expecting; she caught the taste in her mouth, and wished the middle-aged man behind the counter in his red and white striped apron would gildy along the old ladies instead of sharing their news with them, of so and so who'd fallen sick and had to go to the hospital, a grand customer, he'd say, hope she'll get better soon, poor auld dear, or a woman who was away suspiciously long from her man, he says it's a holiday, said the owner to the customer after, but he's too proud ey himself tay tell, shame for the bloke. She reached the front of the queue after everyone else had filled the shopkeeper with their news.

Jist moved in round here?

he asked the cash register. Catherine reached into the pocket of her coat for her purse, opened it while he made the total jump in the window and announced the cost to her.

Sort of.

Aye, thoat I didny recognize ye. I'm awful good wi faces, see. I cn tell folk who've no been in afore. Livin round the coarner?

Top of the hill.

Fair auld hike, yon.

She snipped shut the purse and returned it to her pocket, and held out her hand so he could hook the full bag of messages on it.

And I should be starting it now, I think. Thank you very much.

She began feeling sorry for her abruptness to the shopkeeper on the road back, but she hadn't liked gossips like him over the water. When her mother had come over for the wedding, she'd told Catherine that rumours had been posted like telegrams as to why the O'Hara colleen had been so long absent; run away, they'd said, and some of the tongues had been clicking she'd been seen in the capital where no honourable girl would be standing, if it weren't for trade. Catherine had told her mother, then say the truth to them, and damn them for handing me the blame and not spreading the rumour that it was my da who did for me, or do they still think he pisses holy water when he stands over the pot? The shopkeeper wasn't as malicious as them back home, but he was of their kind, and she resolved to find another shop, no matter how far away it was.

She began wondering what the room would look like once it'd been tidied on her way up the stairs to the house; not unlike Cameron's old room in the house she'd abandoned, she was thinking; filling up with the sun at the same time of day, same kind of proportions to it, only it'd be bare and without the furniture a wee boy would expect. She wondered what Cameron thought of her after all this time without a word or a visit; and then she'd the keys to Peter's house in her hand, and she thought here was the bed she'd made, and she'd little choice but to lie on it without complaint, no matter how sick she was for Cameron, and what opportunities she saw in a clean, tidy, empty room for claiming her right to him.

It was Peter who found Heidless's drawing where Catherine had dropped it, let Codie see it, said,

No mind oan that peyntn ey his? Pure brilliant, so it wis,

and Codie nodded to agree with him. She wouldn't've known what Codie'd been thinking if he hadn't nodded; not after she'd given them dishtowels soaked in water, folded from corner to corner to wear tied around their heads and keep them all from breathing the dust. Peter'd said, I feel lik the bloody Lone Ranger wi this oan; Codie knotted his loosely, the Lone Ranger wore his mask ower his eyes, ya f, em, ya bloody eejit; and Peter said, aw aye, right enough, so he did; well then, dis that make us bandits? Catherine warned the two bandits before they started, if you've any clothes you want kept good, don't wear them now, because they'll have to go in the midden after you've been in there. The laugh was, they looked more respectable in clothes they didn't give a sniff for than the ones they wore every day; Peter wore a pale blue nylon shirt and grey trousers which looked to Catherine like woollen trousers from a suit, while Codie had on a white summer shirt and white cotton trousers, and when Catherine asked him did he want to change into something more suited to the work, Codie said, I've been waitn tay howff these in the bin since my ma gied me them fr my birthday, don't spile it fr us, and just to prove it he wiped his hands over them, dirtying them before any proper work had been done, which was fine by her, so long as he understood she wouldn't appreciate seeing them in the laundry among her clothes and Peter's. Nae danger, he said, I hate lookin lik wan ey they eejits that plays cricket.

They went in behind her like archaeologists, looking for relics; Codie found his saucer, the glaze blackened by the smoking doubts, and Peter saw Heidless's cigarette packets, remembering the paintings from them. He saw the tile of pictures almost immediately; just by the corner toilet, on a dry but stinking part of the carpet, and picked it up tenderly by the edges in case the dry Sellotape gave way. Codie came for a look over his shoulder; said,

Aye, course I mind; maist ambitious thing the big man did, if ye're askin.

Catherine put all the cleaning stuff against the wall in front of the door, brush and shovel, disinfectants, a bucket of hot soapy water, dusters, a scraper for the walls, the whole arsenal, as Codie'd said; closed the door behind them, breathing through the wet mask, and deciding where they should begin.

What's so ambitious about an old man relieving himself against a wall in front of a whole bar?

Peter and Codie both looked up at her together, as if she was daft or blind.

It wis a big big canvas,

said Peter.

No canvas; paper,

said Codie.

Aye, paper, right y'are. Big waatercolour. Wee details, jist. The faces ey the men. Smoke a' roon aboot. Jist brilliant.

He did it black n white n grey, ye see, said Codie, nae colour, like an auld photygraph. Made the auld duffer pure dark in the foregrun, n everthn else grey, lik ye were terrn through the smoke tay see it.

Catherine frowned while she looked into the bucket for the cloth.

I thought he was too busy drinking to do any painting.

Peter smiled behind the wet dishtowel.

Thon's when he did maist ey his peyntn. I widny waant naebdy telln me no tay if thon wis the routine I wis in.

Well, I still don't see what's so ambitious about it.

Aye, said Peter, cause you're thinkn it's a picture ey an auld man pishn in a bar; ye're no askn whit the picture's really aboot.

Catherine was impatient to begin.

I'm afraid I think it's kind of sordid looking. It's like he's making fun of the old man. I'm sorry, but that's how I see it.

Peter and Codie exchanged an entire conversation in a glance, deciding between themselves who should try and explain; Codie took it on, shifting himself around.

It's no jist aboot the auld man, he said. It's aboot the bloks lookin oan at him.

He took the board from Peter's hands, brought it over to her so she could see for herself.

See, the auld man pishin's no the hale thing. He's whit ye see first. But the vanishin poaint's no wi him, so he's no the focus ey it, see whit I'm sayn? It's in the middle ey the pub, n a' yir men roon aboot ur sterrn at the auld man. The vanishin poaint's wi them. They make him the focus cause they're sterrn at him, so there's really two poaints ey focus, wan ey thm natural, the vanishin poaint, a wan ey thm forced, n that's the auld man. See whit I'm sayn?

All the while, he sketched with his finger on the joined-up card, showing her where the measure of perspective ruled lines towards an off-centre on the opposite side of the old man, then where the lines of their staring tended to weight the picture towards him. Catherine frowned, tilted her head towards Codie.

So you're telling me I've chosen the wrong place to look?

No the wrang place, said Peter from across the room. Jist wan particular place. Whit're ye thinkin ey when ye're lookin at the auld man?

Catherine made herself look at the picture again.

I'm thinking of when my house was broken into, you remember. I'm looking at the corner of this room. I don't think it's funny.

Then ye're agreein wi the bloks who're no laughin, said Codie. But there's them that wid think yon wis a rerr laugh. He's no askin ye tay side wi wan r the ither. Draw yir ain conclusions.

Well, I wouldn't pay to see it in a gallery, and nor would most folk.

Peter shrugged.

There'll come a day, mark my words, when folk'll know whit the big man wis a' aboot, n they'll come fae a' five coantinents tay see his work.

And they'll be the folk who didn't have to clean up after him.

Codie laughed, but Peter didn't reply. He turned away, and looked at the corner and the bed, and let out a huge breath that swelled out his mask like a sail.

Right then, he said, where day we stert?

After seven hours' work, you wouldn't've recognized the place. The carpet was up, for one thing, exposing the bare boards, the wood scabrous with old lacquer, and the bed was away; Peter tried to argue for keeping it, but Catherine said, who in their right mind would want to sleep on that thing, and Codie went over and lifted the mattress, showing Peter the rusted mesh underneath, and the carpet under that, so there was no more arguing, away it went. The bottle monument was away as well; Codie picked it apart one bottle at a time and put them in boxes, which went out by the midden alongside the dismantled bed. Catherine watched him do it while Peter unscrewed the headboard from the frame for easier carrying; it was the most beautiful thing in the room, the way the light fired in the glass, unravelling the spectrum against the wall, and she couldn't help thinking of the vase she'd given to Cameron. They did the carpet last of all, rolling it up like a cigarette and fastening it with twine; Peter disputed that too, but Codie pointed to the mist around their ankles like the fog in an old horror film, and Catherine stamped on the pile to raise the dust and showed him that corner with its smell of cats and ammonia, the dye bleached out of it. Codie's contribution, apart from his deceptively strong arms, was to persuade Peter they couldn't leave the room as it was, and Catherine was grateful; with Codie saying the exact same as herself he had to give in, and at last Peter rolled up his sleeves to the elbows, and he was the one who fetched the screwdriver for taking the bed apart, and the twine for binding the carpet.

Once the dusting was done, Catherine opened the window. There was a breeze from outside that triggered the warning wires of the cobwebs, alerting the spiders, and Codie and Peter both stood away from them, but Catherine knew how you got rid of them; got a cup from the kitchen and ladders from the hall cupboard, and once she'd been to all four corners she'd a cupful of spiders, which she let them see. Their curiosity made them look in as she raised the lid of her hand; the four spiders were too fat and lazy to fight amongst themselves, instead clambered over each other to gain the rim, ensuring none of them escaped. Peter and Codie couldn't believe Catherine had gone up the ladders to gather the spiders in her hand; she dropped the spiders out to make a wilder living for themselves in the drying green, wondering at the strange creatures men could be at times, when they could live alongside this kind of squalor, and be feared of beasts no bigger than your fingernail.

When it was all done, Catherine and Codie stayed in the room with the tea she'd made for him and the coffee she'd made for herself; Peter'd left with his, and she thought she heard the water running in the bathroom sink, but she wasn't certain. Codie was sitting on the floor, about where the bed had been, bracing himself against the wall with his legs bent and wide apart, his arms resting on his knees and the cup in both hands, warming his hands on the china. The white outfit was even filthier than he'd hoped; from the neck down, he was like a pencil sketch of himself, in different shadings, and he pulled at the fabric, happy to see it beyond respectable wearing, winked at Catherine who made a face at him. She seemed happier herself now that the room was bare, and more than that, hygienic; she'd especially scrubbed in that corner with a solution of bleach to rid the wood of lime and urea, and the wood was damp there, but she'd sooner have the chemical smell than what had soaked into the planking.

Codie lifted his cup in a toast to their work, and she joined him; said,

And to your new room, if you want to have it.

Codie shook his head.

I like my wee coarner, Cath. My ma says I wis boarn by Caesarian section. Mind you, I've goat a wee notion ey my ain fr this place, if the perr ey ye'll jist leave it tay Codie.

Catherine shrugged.

Fine. Talk to us later about it. I'm off to bed.

She found Peter in the straight-backed chair by the table, in different clothes, his coffee beside him. At first she thought he was playing patience, dealing cards out on to the cloth, but when she came behind him, she found they were the leaves of Heidless's sketchbook, the clean sides of the cigarette packets. He'd put the one Heidless had made a painting out of in the centre, and he was dealing the others around it, from twelve to eleven o'clock. She couldn't see his face, but she could tell his despondency from the slouch of his back; put her hands on his shoulders, tilted herself towards him, saw the pictures drawn on the other white cards; stout blokes, blokes with expressionless pinched faces; one man in his work overalls, standing at the counter of the bar, stripping the notes from his wage packet, exchanging them for a pint. She couldn't see what was so ingenious about these images; Peter'd said to her once it was all to do with truth, and how real folk lived, but she couldn't see either quality in Heidless's bold cartoon hand, only a flat, insubstantial savagery. It was as if he'd bled them all as pale as corpses, and then stood them up like dummies, making these the only significant moments of their lives, standing eternally at the bar, laughing and distant with the beer.

It didn't matter what she thought; Peter dealt his cards, deriving his own meaning from them. After a while of staring at their faces, he picked them from the cloth and made a pack of them, dunting them on the table to level their edges. He stood up, and went to the bedside table; opened the drawer, put them in, closed it. He stood there for a while, and kept his eyes away from her, as if sparing her the accusation.

Codie's plan was simple. Here there were two painters in the one house, and one room spare; neither Peter nor Catherine understood what he was on about, and he was fair dancing with frustration at how slow they were, but they were both tired in their own ways; Peter too full of his images to have much room for thinking, Catherine not long back from the café, her legs aching and her head full of figures and orders. Codie stared at them both as they sat at the kitchen table with their coffees, Peter slumped over like a schoolboy defending his jotter from the copycat next to him, his chin near touching the wood, and Catherine enjoying the first real seat she'd had all day, and he was drawing out his plan on the air;

Two artists, man, he said, n wan room sperr; no ring nae wee bells r nothn?

Peter couldn't even summon up a shrug to order, and Catherine didn't have a clue; their days had wiped them clean.

Right then, said Codie; whit dis an artist need mare n anythn?

As far as Catherine was concerned, before she'd met Peter, she'd never thought an artist needed more than a canvas, paints and a brush. Peter was beginning to understand, though; lifted his head from the table, and you could see the idea was starting to come to him, displacing his exhaustion the more he thought about it. He said,

It's no awffy light, but; the sun swings roon tay it in the efternun, n the winday's awffy wee as well.

Codie smiled like a conjuror.

Leave a' yon mere details tay yir china Codie, he said. I think I cn fix it.

What the hell're you two planning now?

said Catherine, as frustrated as Codie'd been a minute or two ago.

Think aboot it, said Peter. It's no a bloody riddle. Whit wid two artists waant wi a sperr room?

So Codie went and saw Kenny, who'd been at school with him, and who said over a pint at the Minister's Stoup that he'd see what he could do, with no promises. The first Catherine knew of the arrangement, apart from Codie returning drunk the night he'd gone to meet Kenny (a pleasant kind of drunk, though, sealed up in his own wee turmoil), was the morning she went down the stairs to go to the bus-stop, and found a glazier's van pulling up outside, the sort of van with the wooden frame lashed to the hide of it, and endless panels of mirrors secured by ropes. The angle of the frame tilted them so she could see high over her head, and the reflection showed Peter through the open sash of the window upstairs, almost as if he was expecting the delivery; the man who stepped down from the cabin was tall and thin as a plank, and he was staring at Catherine from head to toe in open appreciation, as if his dinner had been brought to the table, and he was giving it a moment's study before he lifted the knife and fork. Catherine started down the hill, ignoring his attention and the eyes following her; but every so often she looked over her shoulder; saw Peter taking a number of panels up the steps to the mouth of the close; saw Codie doing the exact same thing, with the thin man standing by his van. By the time she was at the foot of the hill, Codie and Peter had a carrying chain going, one coming down to replace the other going up, and it must've been the mirrors they were carrying, from the heliograph blaze that lit up whenever they tilted the panels towards the sun. Catherine couldn't wait to think about it, or look back any longer; but it was a wee mystery she took with her to the café, distracting her enough for Gianfranco to notice.

Why would they be shifting mirrors into the house?
she said, and Gianfranco gave a huge, dramatic shrug.
Who understand artists? They no want understand, he said. They want, what you say, eh? they want admiring. You worship like God Himself, they are happy.
She smiled, for the first time all day.
Have you ever met an artist, Gianfranco?

227

Gianfranco leaned over the counter of Paradise, glancing over his shoulder towards the Inferno, peering through the ribbon curtain, dropping his voice.

My Rosa, she make art in the kitchen. I tell her, too much salt; I no worship her cooking, she go like Americans do to island, you call it, Bikini, no? boom! off in my face. Your man will be too, I think.

By the time she was on the road back, she was consumed by her curiosity, having blown on the mystery all day to keep it burning. The two men were sitting in the kitchen when she came in, looking pleased with themselves; the water was hot in the kettle, and Codie made her coffee for her while she waited for an explanation from them, but they were like weans with their wee secrets, and eventually she tired of it and asked them what the delivery had been for. Codie presented her with one of Peter's enamelled mugs, the coffee milked and sugared exactly as she liked, and said,

Tellt ye, leave it tay yir china Codie, he waves his wand n lo, it's done.

Codie went in first to turn on the light switch. She didn't think the room would be so bright, not even when she'd begun to suspect what'd been done with the mirrors; it was like the sun in her eyes. She looked away from the source, saw nothing had changed about the boards, still the same sorry-looking flaked varnish as before; but they printed on her eyes as vividly as if they'd been sanded, or freshened in some way. When she was able to see comfortably, she raised her eyes to take in the result of their day's work while Codie stood by the window, a look on his face as if, beat this, proud as a father.

She was in the exact centre of the room, underneath the bare light bulb, which she could almost feel as a heat. The mirrors had been arranged so there were no seams between them; although you could see the joins between one panel and the next. They'd put a great deal of work into it; there were blunt-headed rivets over the heads of the screws, and they'd fixed the panels from floor to ceiling, only separated by the interruption of the picture rail, and by the sashes of the bay window.

Fae a dump tay an artist's studio in wan easy step, said Codie. Whit d'ye think?

She thought again of the vase she'd given Cameron; how it put together the broken images. The closer she went to the glass, she could see flaws, scallops like chipped flint, imperfections on the panes. The vase's crystal had been purer, and it had extended your own sight, not like this relentless introversion, which was more of a room in your own head where you could ponder yourself to eternity, self-obsession without the relief of another presence. She saw her own face; she saw herself from the back just by looking over her own shoulder, in profile if she turned her head to the side, as if the room had opened out into space, you could imagine rooms beyond this one, rooms you couldn't see but with their own mirrors, projecting themselves into the box they were occupying.

Codie was explaining how he came about the mirrors, and she saw him without having to turn, on the same wall as her reflection, more of him to the side, beyond that a paper chain of Codies. They knew about his mate Kenny; well, Kenny had been friendly with this woman who was knocking on a bit (Kenny's words, Codie protested, catching Catherine's disapproval off the glass), but she still kept herself in fair shape. She'd been married to this bloke who was big in some kind of concern no one talked about, but it was known to be pretty shady stuff; lovely house in Bishopbriggs, no weans at big Marjorie's request, because she'd other fish to be frying. She'd a wee coiffure salon in the west end, this Marjorie one, and it ticked over very nicely, thank you very much, but she was aye saying to Kenny, with that studied graceful Kelvinside she affected, Ai'm very happy in mey chosen profession, Kenneth, but Ai can't help but feel an expansion to the big smoke may be called for in the near future, efter all, it's where the top people in the coiffure trade become gregarious eeventually. Her husband's death from a heart attack and the lack of heirs gave her the money to indulge herself; within a few weeks of a proper mourning time, she had a shop rented in London, north Edgware Road, but it was a foot in the door, she said, and she was back home to arrange the dismantling of her old place; which was where the mirrors had come from, blemished with peroxide spills and useless for anything else. Now, Codie's favour had been called in at a good time, because Kenny'd been trying to pass on the glass to others before he cut it into tiles and framed the pieces for bathrooms and living-rooms; he couldn't hope to sell the panes on, not without the proper contacts, and they were just so much clutter and work in his back shop; when Kenny had asked over their pint, n whit 'm I gettn oot ey this wee gift? Codie'd said, tax aff fr wan thing, n the satisfaction ey helpin oot yir mate fr another, and the deal was settled with a shake of hands and an agreement as to when the glass should be delivered.

Catherine heard it all, but listened to none of it. She was too busy with the mirror, changed her focus again, caught sight of herself between two panels, divided by the seam. She was like the doll in the window; the crack down the china face, and she remembered how uneasy she'd felt at seeing it. There was a dent in the glass like an injury on her cheek, the healing from a terrible scar, and the longer she stared, the more she was thinking it was a mark she'd carried from birth. It was exactly where her father had touched her with his thumb the first night he'd chased her ma and brother away, when he was touching her face and saying, I'll never hurt you, me love, me daughter, as if the mark had been printed on her from the time of her conception, there for her father to find, worn into her by his touch, and even when she moved away from this spot on the mirror it was still there, still visible, etched, corroded on to her skin.

She saw Peter behind her in the mirror; but it was her father reaching for her, wanting to print his claim on her, to stroke away her hair with his thick fingers that smelled of beer and leather. She didn't think she'd fainted; she could remember the floor under the soles of her shoes, solid for a few steps, the insulated softness of the carpet, then the giving-solid of linoleum, and then there was a shock as she fell on to the chair, a return to her surroundings as she became more aware of where she was. They made her drink a cup of water drawn from the tap, cold and full in her mouth. She fought away the cup when she saw they were trying to force another mouthful of water on her, and they stood back, just a little. Her throat was closed like Peter's duffel bag, and she could only make the water slip down by easing the constriction, loosening the pursed muscles through an act of will. Peter was the one holding the cup; he put it on the table for her to take if she wanted, got down on his haunches beside her so he could look properly at her; looked over her shoulder, at Codie, she thought, and she heard his steps leaving the room, traced them through the hall and into the studio, she could tell from the echo. She leaned forward on to the table, suddenly exhausted by the seizure, whatever you called it; Peter looked confused.

Ye'd'a thoat, he said, the time you take afore a mirror, ye'd be lik a fish in waater in there.

Maybe too much water, she said. I'm sorry. I wasn't quite ready to see so much of myself.

He didn't understand, but he nodded anyway.

Codie's lik a wean wi a new toay in there. He jist waants tay show it aff. Took us a' day.

Who gets first use of it?

She was talking quickly, just to hear herself.

Codie says I cn use it cause I'm in the middle ey work, but he cn use it when I'm no.

Does that mean I'm going to be in the room on my own while you're at your work?

Peter shrugged.

Ye cn sit in wi me if ye like.

Catherine thought of the tarnished mirrors; how many more marks there might be on the glass.

Then I think I might be on my own quite a lot,

she said, and picked up the cup by its ear for another drink.

Eleven

There was always cause for Colum O'Hara to lose his short temper, and one of those favourite excuses was the state of the house; Catherine's ma would be cooking and sorting out the mess the owl goat had made the night before, and Catherine would help get the place in order for her, which she didn't mind since it spared them all, her mammy especially. In the house she'd made over the water, she hadn't been cleaning for her life; it felt more like a relaxation. Francis said he didn't mind if the dust made webs on the ceiling or the cups or the dishes stayed unwashed in the sink; not that he was untidy, just that he hadn't married her for a skivvy, the way his father had his mother so there'd be someone who'd all but wipe his arse for him when he made a slutter in the house; but she did it anyway, to keep a consecrated place for making into a new home, not wanting to bring a child into a place she hadn't dedicated her time and effort to.

She was just as thorough in playing the wife for Peter. She wiped the dust from the wood and the glass and the frames of his paintings, taking special care not to polish over the canvas in case she made the paints bleed. She made certain all the used plates were taken back to the kitchen, and she laundered his clothes for him in among hers. He was always saying he didn't want her to work too hard for him, but she just gave him one of her tilted smiles in reply and thought to herself that if there was anything she'd learned of men in her time it was that they seemed to imagine surfaces repelled dust all by themselves, that the leftover bits of food on your plate healed themselves like scabs and fell away once they hardened, stains on cloth would wear away given long enough; thinking a woman would use a grown man as practice for the work of mothering.

What did you ever do before there was a woman in your life, Peter Caulder?

Peter beamed like a wean.

Daft girl thinks she's the first.

She spent some time taking the pulse of the house; after all, she wasn't long here, and she thought it'd take her a while to get used to, like with Mrs Kilsyth, and the house she'd left behind. Often she met Codie in the kitchen first thing in the morning, awake before herself and already at work on his painting, and there'd be hot water for her to share for her coffee, but just as likely he'd be asleep within his curtain, and her boiling of the kettle and its whistle would cause the drape to fly out like a sail, and she'd hear the clenching together of a zip and then he'd come out to share her hot water for his cup of tea. She thought he must lead a disciplined existence, not to be tempted into making his own nights and mornings, when he could pull the curtain to make it dark or switch on the light to make a daybreak, his life a public exhibit. She wondered if he'd seen enough of the world already, that he chose never to come back into it, except to buy food and drink the odd pint, and she was wondering what she'd do if she had the gift he'd been given; she'd want to fill that gallery so she'd have an infinite recall, travel so far and see so much that she'd obliterate everything bad. She told that to Codie over her toast and Camp one morning, and Codie simply smiled in the way of priests trying to explain the nature of vocation to those who hadn't been called; said,

Aye, it's a f, em, it's a bloody selfish wee giftie I've been gied right enough,

explained that it'd be so easy to misuse his talent as a walking sketchbook; that Grecian urn shite, beauty being truth and truth beauty. It was only when he went to the art school, and fell in with what he called a pair of bams, meaning Peter and Heidless, that he was shown how he could make the best use of his gift; like they'd handed him an instruction manual for himself, how he could make folk see that beauty and truth weren't identical things, that to print true on paper you had to be like the camera and turn light and shade around, make negatives of what folk expected of painting.

Mebbe they cried me efter a camera, he said as he smoothed the paint on to the canvas, stepped back to see the effect, but I'm no jist a f, em, I'm no jist a bloody lens; I'm the film it prints oan, n I cn poaint mysel wherr the f, em, wherr the hell I fancy.

But, said Catherine, finding a space for her enamel mug among his tubes of pigment, you can't choose where to point yourself, not completely.

Codie shrugged.

True, he said, but I cn choose whit tay mind oan.

It was time for Catherine to leave for her work; she stood up, took her cup to the sink and rinsed it under the tap, asking over her shoulder,

What happens when you run out of tramps?

There's aye folk runnin oot ey pride every day; it's how things ur that drive the poor buggers mad. I waant my work tay pile up afore folk lik boadies til they're cryn tay me tay stoap it.

Catherine had her handbag to collect from the room before she left the house, and left Codie in peace to his usual morning's work, but on the way out of the door, she turned to him and said,

Don't make the mistake of thinking everyone on the street's there because they're mad, Codie. They may have drunk themselves mad, but I'll bet they didn't start out that way.

Codie didn't even raise himself to reply; he was bent towards the canvas as close as a magnifying glass, using a needle-pointed brush to attach a thread of shading.

N you'd know, I sppose?

Catherine smiled at his back.

I'm surprised you don't have me in one of your paintings, she said, I was on the streets a while when I came here. Maybe you weren't looking hard enough.

He cried after her, heh, wait, just as she closed the door on him, went back to the room and found Peter still dead to the world. She picked up her handbag, which she'd left the night before on the table where she'd easily find it, and went over to the bed, leaned down and kissed him on the cheek, his shadow beard rough against her lips; it didn't shift him, or remind him of anything. She took a moment to examine him, as he was lying on his side towards her; wondered where was the clock that would tell him to rise and begin his work; and then she had to be going herself, still feeling the bristling on her lips as she took the stairs.

She hadn't yet got used to the notion of calling her arrival back at the house coming home, not after so little time and experience; but it had the rhythm of a home life, as well as a fixed rhythm of its own into which she felt she was intruding; they already had a backbone to their day after she left, Codie and Peter, and that was their work. He'd already told her, Peter, that she should be understanding of that, it wasn't like herself with the book-ends of waking and coming back pressing either side of her working day, they could be doing their work at any hour God sent and it was entirely up to themselves, they'd no clocks to punch and it was their own discipline that made them do it. Catherine teased him while they were finishing off the dinner she'd made; said they were every woman's dream, leaving her alone to do the tidying in peace; Peter smiled and stroked the back of his hand across her cheek, said,

Is the right answer, doll. I'm away tay day Elvis noo. Think ey me covert in iles n shite, n think ey the greater glory ey the workers' struggle while I'm away,

and then left her to take the plates through to the kitchen for washing, where she gave Codie the spare mince and tatties at the bottom of the pan, which he was grateful for.

If Peter thought it was all for his sake, this tidying and fussing while he was away in the studio, he couldn't've been more mistaken; there was a deeper comfort she took from the silence of the room. For a while it hadn't seemed right, being in another man's bed, and to be doing the tidying for him; but after a few weeks she began to turn it around so that it wasn't a favour for Peter, it was a penance for herself she was doing, the way Father Byrne used to send you into the dark at the back of the chapel to say your confessional punishment of Hail Marys, whole rosaries of them. Before he sent her away like a fish too small for the griddle, the priest spoke with his breath of mint, and said that the prayers were to be offered up to God as a sacrifice, along with her devout intention never to sin again; Catherine knelt on the raised bench in front of her, and every so often she'd tilt her head around so she could watch her father beside her, knowing he'd've been told the same as her; he was a trembling architecture of devotion before God and the altar, his hands joined and the doubled-over fingers pressed against his lips, his eyes closed the way they'd've been for a kiss, knees angled uncomfortably and his legs bent under the pew, and she was thinking, it was as if he was throwing the same strength into his prayer as he did into the work of the farm. She was thinking to herself, if he'd been told like herself to pray he never sinned again, perhaps this was what he was trying to do, to pray for that strength never to lift a glass to his mouth again and fill himself with the drink; and so the Hail Marys she said weren't for herself, she added them to the same bundle as his and formed a plea to God which she spoke after every prayer, and it was, please make my da mean it when he intends not to sin against us, through Christ our Lord amen.

It was yet another strain on her belief when the old sot couldn't seize the reins of himself despite God's help, and went off two nights later to do what he always did; another strand connecting her to God frayed through; but when she did her penance now, it was because she still believed in paying off your guilt as if it was a debt to yourself, and this was why she did the work of Peter's house without complaining; because she didn't intend to leave her mothering instincts to wither in the absence of Cameron, and she was still hoping she'd be a good mother to him some day, and that she'd make herself and the house she brought him to live in worthy of him. Peter never knew when he came back to everything in its place, the laundry done and ironed and folded, and the room smelling of freshener, that none of it was for him; and in this way Catherine kept her loyalty to the memory of Francis, and Peter got out of the bargain a beautiful clean room such as he'd never had in a while, and as long as he concerned himself with metaphors and appearances, his own stock in trade, and didn't look under the bed or the wardrobe for reasons why she'd do this for him, then both of them stayed contented with their arrangement.

*

Some nights she'd a little time after her tidying, and it was far too early to go to bed. If it was dry out on those nights she went for a walk, to the park around the back of the house, the ribbon of paving around the perimeter. It was always quiet out, and at this time in the winter dark as well. She left the house because she was forgetting what it was like outside at a time she didn't have to go to her work. The park was always closed by the time she was able to come to it, and sometimes she stood at the fence like a prisoner, pressing her face between the iron bars and feeling the warmth drawn out of her, and she'd take her hands out of her coat pockets and curve her fingers around the bars so she could touch the cold and then nest them back inside the coat again, warming them against herself.

On most of the dry nights, the sky was clear, and you could look down on the pavements and see sparks of hoar frost against the stones, and then look above you and see the mirror of them pricked into the dark; she loved the sound of her feet cracking the ice glazed over old rain, and there were two forests to be seen on her walk, to her right on the rim of the pavement the straight trunks of the lamp standards with a seed of the moon in their globes, to her left through the fence the elms, lashing in the wind; the slight drone of electricity, the sound of wind torn to rags by the branches, and she was looking for a place to escape the light because she wanted an unobstructed look up at the sky, and she knew where broken lamps spread pitch over the street, halfway around the circuit, the globes smashed by vandals.

She needed the dark, because she was looking for the hourglass of Orion, one of the two constellations she knew despite Francis's attempts to teach her the others, the rest were join-the-dots with no pictures at the end of them, and she just laughed when Francis told her the animals and heroes they were meant to be, old swirly line the Greek god, she said, and Francis nailed her with a playful look of disdain and said, class behave r I'll huv tay skelp ye. She knew Cameron would be looking at it as well, because they'd all been out together one night, walking from the bus-stop along the road through the grounds of the industrial estate on the approach to their scheme, coming back from a film the wee one had wanted to see. Francis had said, show me Orion, wee man, and Cameron had pointed to the oblong held in at the waist by its corset of three stars, there it is, and, very good, Cameron, exactly right, said Francis, turning to Catherine and he was giving off pride in his son. Catherine got the devil in her just then, said, even a fool like me knew that was Orion, and then winked at Francis. Cameron huffed out a mist in front of him, and then went on to name others, Pleiades and Camelopardus, and then he said, I know something you don't anyway, my dad told me the stars are all so far away the light takes years and years to come to your eyes, and he nodded gravely like one of those dog ornaments in the back of cars, weighed down by all the facts his head contained. She looked quickly at Francis as if to ask, is that true? and Francis nodded briefly, the wee one was right. She said, how can that be when you can see the light now? and he was away off explaining with all the authority of his dad behind him; light had a top speed, he said, just like a car or a bicycle, and it went off on a journey to reach you which meant it took time to get from where it started millions of millions of miles away to where you were standing watching, and Francis nodded and said, dead right, wee man, top ey the class, and Catherine despite herself felt a wee bit conspired against by her menfolk. She said, doesn't the light get tired having to come so far? but he just looked at her as if he'd an idiot for a mother and said, course it does, that's why they twinkle cause they're out of breath, and Francis made a face, and the wee man fa's doon at the last hurdle, and Catherine laughed, so he doesn't know everything, that's a comfort, and her two men spent the rest of the walk exchanging the true reason for the stars' fluttering like Christmas lights, and Catherine said, I like Cameron's reason better, which brought a frown from Francis.

On the clear nights, she stood in the dark and tipped her head up until she could see Orion among the scrawl of the other stars. She couldn't help wondering if Cameron was looking at it too, at the same time as herself; there were times she felt as if she wasn't just one bus ride away from him, but the distance between herself and the stars and then the distance from them to Cameron added to that, and on those nights she'd sooner have had Peter back in the room from his work when she arrived, the blood infusing her skin, looking for more comfort than she could get from a heat by the fire and a cup of hot coffee.

*

There was once a tree near where she lived over the water; Michael had told her what kind but she'd forgotten by now. One winter, before her father plied her with his stinking intimacy, there was a profound snowfall that turned the world into a clean page and locked them all in until time and heat turned the snow into rags on the ground. Owl Colum was heart sorry that he wouldn't get to see his buthies in the village, for he was sore in need of a nip of the spirits to warm him then, but he was sober for all the days while they waited for the thaw, and so Catherine had the best time of her life with a father she never recognized, who almost earned her love during his stay in the house. He let the children play in the grounds, made sure they were in their woollens before they went out to make snowballs in their hands and fashion snowmen, sure and ye're me two fleecy sheep, he said, now go and flock and come back for yer tea, and remember to watch for your own footprints if ye get yerselves lost, now, and their ma was surprised to be hearing her words coming from the old fellow's lips, but grateful as well.

Kate and Michael ran through the cold, wondering what to make of this new material with its many forms; soft like talcum, hard and brittle like glass, dirty and wet when it churned and folded itself into mud; they were wee sculptors, exploring their medium, gathering it into piles, looking for the prints of their shoes and the treads they left in it; and of course they fought with each other, picking up snow by the handful and dashing it into each other's faces before it melted in their gloves, and then making smooth cold pearls of it in their hands and throwing it at each other like cowboys shooting from cover, the trunks of trees, the swelling of a dyke over a rise, and by the time they'd chased away from the house, they were in land made unfamiliar by the white purging of feature, and the game had gone quiet in a cloth of snow that stifled their voices so they could surprise each other with another attack, and they were separated so they couldn't even hear their feet tramping the powder flat.

This was when Kate came across the tree, and she'd never seen the like in all her life; she called on Michael, Mikey, come see this, I'm not playing the game any more, I just want you to come see this, and when he appeared from behind a bush, he was carrying two eggs of snow in his hands and ready to hatch them against her if she was tricking him, but when he saw what she was looking at, he dropped them and went to stand beside her, and the vapour was caught in their throats as one looked at the other, both of them barely able to speak.

It was a tree of pure ice, seemingly, rooted as if it had the snow for its soil, had bled the ice all over itself as a kind of winter resin. Catherine went up to the tree first of all, and touched the smooth trunk of it first with her hand in its glove, and then with her bare hand; Michael said, frostbite, Kate, but Catherine ignored him, drawn by the promise of her hands gliding on it. The next thing, her hand almost froze to the trunk; as if there was a fairy spell on it, the touch of the ice had begun to turn her to ice itself, and she'd been dunce enough to fall for it, and she pulled herself back from a cold that was almost as intense as burning before the ice made a statue out of her. She looked at the skin where she'd touched the glass bark, the palm of her hand; it wasn't even as if she felt it raw, or that there was any sensation she could tell of, the blood seemed to have stopped at her wrist and when she stripped the glove off her other hand to touch it it was like when she touched the calf's liver her mammy cooked up for them sometimes, sensitive blooded flesh touching dead matter. In a moment, Michael had taken off his own gloves and began to rub his sister's dead hand in both of his, but Catherine was afraid for herself, as if the morbidity would rise inside her like the resinous ice, cold sap inside the tree, and she began to scream, Michael help me, don't let the rest of me die, and he said to her with a snap, don't be a fool, Kate, your hand's just numb, here, stand still, and after a while she felt the blood slowly animating her so she could move the fingers ever so slightly, and Michael made her laugh by saying that she'd better not cry or else the tears'd turn to jewels in her eyes and she'd be blinded as well as have to have her hand sawn off by the doctor. She was only able to laugh because she knew he was only saying it for cod, and because she had the feeling back in her hand again, enough to feel him as living; but it was a queer thing indeed, the hand for a while still never felt as if it quite belonged to her, as if she'd had her true hand amputated and another stitched on to replace it; now it was too warm inside the glove, and the flesh seemed to have slackened around the bone, worked loose by the contraction of the cold and the expansion of the heat.

When they got home, their mammy had the old tin bath ready on the kitchen floor in front of the range, the one she used for laundering the clothes as well as for laundering them. Until lately, the two of them had had their baths together, but in the past few months their mammy had judged that Michael as the elder of them had grown too big for it to be right; you must be filthy dirty, she'd say to one of them as she boiled up pots of water on the range until the air was thick with a cotton steam, but, to yer room, pet, she'd say to the other, and then call the dry one in afterwards for a soak in the milky water she warmed up with water from the reserve pans she'd put on while the first of them was bathing. Catherine got the first of the baths that evening when Michael'd explained how she nearly came to be a wee colleen of ice, and he was sent to his room; she knew he'd be noting down her stupidity in his diary while she was at her bath. She'd already asked her mammy if it was because of the sprouting of hair between her brother's legs that they were bathing separately these days; her mammy had blushed like fire and told her she was too young to be asking questions of that nature and that she'd know when she was older; Catherine had frowned, it wasn't as if an older man or woman had come to her and whispered the question into her ear, but she knew it wasn't like her father saying God knows, out of ignorance, it was just that her mammy would sooner not answer her just now, and it was a shame, because she'd other questions to ask about their bathing. She'd always wondered why Michael and her had been allowed to wash each others' backs but not their fronts, why that was a task for mammy only, spooning out the clouded water in the palm of her hand and stroking their skin as briskly as a brush; and why they were always to wash their own down-belows while their mammy knelt back and clapped the time out with her hands, hurry now, hurry now, don't dawdle, quick and clean, quick and clean, rushing to see who could be the first out of the water and into the warm towel.

Catherine was so cold after returning to the house that it never occurred to her this time to ask the questions, and her hand still felt ill-fitting as her mammy asked her to take off all her clothes which were soaking with the snow and perched them on a clothes-horse which she set before the range. She was just settling into the bath when in came her father from outside; still he hadn't made it to the pub, but Catherine's mammy gave him a knowing look, as if she knew he'd tried.

Cup of tay, if you playse,

he said; his wife watched him as he took the coat off and draped it around the back of a chair, and was about to sit down to wait for it.

Bit of daycency, if you playse, Colum, she said, yer daughter's in her bath, can't ye see?

Colum's feet were kicking the tin, so he could hardly say it was an obstacle he hadn't noticed. He stood up suddenly as Catherine shrank inside the water, apologized to her and then asked his wife if she'd bring the tea through while he went to the bedroom to read an old newspaper. He turned and went through the door, leaving Catherine to wonder what had been so fascinating about a girl having a bath that his eyes hadn't come away from her once since he'd come through the door; but she soon enough forgot as the water heated her blood, and restored her hand to her once again, as good as new.

She was thinking of the ice tree on a night that was as cold, even without the snow; a dense white frost underfoot that cracked like gravel, making twisted apparitions of the elms beyond the fences as they took the silver from the lamps and made themselves into the spirits of trees. She felt the cold of the pavement through the leather of the shoes as if she was shod in ice itself, and it was enough to deaden her feet, making them reverberate as they struck the ground. She went to her hollow of darkness around the back of the park, the back as seen from the kitchen of the house, anyway; when she looked up at the sky, it was as if the cold had made black glass of it, and the stars had condensed on the overturned bowl, had frozen, and there was a scythe of a new moon cutting into the dark so it wouldn't slip to setting at too fast a speed. She was outside because it was beautiful clear weather that made her feel clear herself, but she was out to escape Peter as well, him and his finishing of the picture of Elvis. The canvas was already done, but he was making the frame himself; cutting four lengths of wood, carving tongues and gouging slots at the right angles to make them join, and then, most painstaking of all, and a thing he had to do before he could do any of that, he had to cut beading into it and then smooth it down with sandpaper to give it warmth and roundness. She'd asked him why he couldn't just buy it ready-beaded, but he'd only looked at her as if she was being mischievous and said, a good worker dis a' the work, see; I'm in fae the stert, and he told her how he stretched the canvases and made joints for the backs, the battens, if they were needed; see, ye cn get a' yon done fr ye, but I like tay think I'm a coanscientious worker, stert tay finish. Catherine laughed and said, why not go the whole journey? weave the cloth yourself, mix your own pigments, catch your own rabbits to render down for priming? and he looked at her sadly as if she'd missed the point and said, aye right, whn I cn afford a loom, n a' the powders tay mix wi the iles, n whn I cn spend my days catchin tons ey bloody rabbits fr an ounce ey glue, mebbe then, but noo I'll huv tay make day, wid ye excuse me so I cn day my work? and away he went into the studio, and she heard the sandpaper through both doors and across the hall, and that had driven her mad enough to want to leave the house after a while.

There were four shallow walls surrounding the park, shallow because they didn't need to be high; the park had been laid on the crest of the hill and the back courts fell sharply towards the level of the houses. The houses were risen like loaves above their own walls, and when Catherine grew tired of looking up, her neck becoming stiff and sore, she looked at the speckling of lit windows, distracted by the activities of folk in their homes; families that saddened her with thoughts of her present circumstances, old folk entombed like pharaohs among their lifetimes' possessions, and there was even a boy playing keepie up with a football in his living-room. There were wives sitting in their houses alone while their men were down the boozer; a good number of those with their teles in the kitchen so the heat from the stove that was keeping their men's dinner warm would keep them warm too, having to save the money their men were wasting. The windows were all laid out in an even grid, like the canvases in Peter's gallery, and there were different qualities of light in them; the families preferred warm bulbs which gave their houses the appearance of paintings in the chapel, brightening the colours, but there were those who'd gone with the rage and had installed fluorescent strip lights which made their interiors look cold and dutiful, the wintry cast you'd find in a public lavatory. The old folks seemed to prefer lamps to overhead bulbs; maybe, Catherine was thinking, it reminded them of the softer light of their younger days, candles and gas lamps, no direct glare but the product of slow burning. There were some of the solitary wives, but some of the families as well, who sat before their teles and that was their only illumination, playing like a fire but with all the colour bled from it like the corpse of flame; and Catherine pitied those wives who were both sitting in the kitchen in the borrowed warmth of the stove, and in the dark with the ashen light of the tele, saving their money twice over; she counted three in the one block, and she was wondering if this was what they'd settle for for the rest of their lives until they became like the old folk, and she found the thought made her angry.

The windows were like the stations of the cross, the passion of ordinary folk, young mothers coddling their babies and starting the process, families where the weans had grown ambitious for themselves like the teenager with his football, or families like the women bathed in the grey flame of the tele not knowing where their men or their weans were, old age where folk were left to themselves with their pride around them, their keepsakes, even the light was funereal. The last window Catherine looked into before she started back towards the house was what drove her away eventually; one of the bright rooms, lit by lamps on shelves and by an overhead bulb, so that it seemed optimistic to look at from outside; there were furnishings that were so new she was thinking newly-wed. She had a downward vantage on the house, so she could see a woman seated in an armchair, young and with her hair drawn up into a beehive; she was reading a magazine, leafing through the photographs on the pages but reading none of the words. A young man came into the room and stood by the chair, standing with his back to Catherine; suddenly the young woman stood up and threw the magazine on to the seat, and the next thing the pair of them were yapping at each other, their mouths working at the same time like fish breathing the same ration of water; the argument drove them around in a kind of a dance so that Catherine could see their faces against each other; she wondered if she was seeing the beginning of an argument or a continuation of one, thought the continuation more likely, it'd been too quick to strike without a cause. The woman drove her face closer to his, tilted her head almost as if she was angling for a kiss; and then the man reached out his hand and grasped the woman by the crest of the beehive, and you could see the pain on her. Catherine was ready to run up the road to the house and dial nine nine nine, thinking of Bernadette, and the prizefights she used to have with her man; but she waited to see what would happen, and eventually it seemed as if the man took control of himself and released the woman, and then left the room so as not to see the woman collapse to the floor where she stood, not in a faint but in relief, and she was shaking and holding herself.

Catherine didn't know if it was relief she was feeling herself to see the woman let go like that. She didn't remember a thing until she was halfway around the spool of the road, away from the house, and by then she was wondering if she'd left because she was convinced that was the last act, or in case she'd be there for the next one. She said to herself, it was the cold which had driven her away, pure and simple, and she decided when she got back she'd pour a bath for herself, just like her mammy used to for her when she came in from the cold. The bath was so her blood would melt once she'd come back into the house, because that ridiculous wee red grin of a heater stopping up the hearth wouldn't be enough to warm her up. If you showed yourself to it, then it just made your skin crisp like bacon in the pan and left the cold deep inside you, but it was all Peter would allow for fear of the soot and ash ruining his paintings. She lay back in the water and let her hair steep like black linen; she could still hear the scraping of the work in the studio, the glass-paper on the wood, and it only seemed to emphasize the industrious silence of the house; it wasn't so much a home this place as a workshop, and she was beginning to feel as useless as an ornament the longer she stayed here, a decoration for Peter's room like a china shepherdess on the mantel.

She hadn't heard Peter leave the studio, but the drain had been swallowing over her bathwater, and she'd been paying more attention to the state of her hair at that time, so he'd probably arrived in the room then. He was sitting in his usual chair, opening and closing his fingers, blinking his hands the way a wean pretends to be a lighthouse, to relax them she supposed. He watched her come in, petting her hair through the towel; shifted his legs so she could sit on the floor in front of the fire. His irises were almost blanched by the mirrors, his hands at rest curled arthritically from pinching the glass-paper for so long.

Jesus Christ, he said, my hauns're awffy sore.

Catherine continued to pad at her hair, turned to look at him as if, I can see that. There wasn't much room for them to avoid touching each other, she leaned and rested her back against his doubled legs, and he sat back in the chair with his eyes closed. There was only the monotone of the current through the wire of the electric heater to be heard, an urgent sound like a wasp; he tired of being idle after a while, leaned forward in the seat, rested his arms against the arms of the chair; she could feel his breath warm as he stationed himself over her, descending towards her neck, stroking it at the nape.

Waant me tay day that?

She didn't even bother turning her head around.

I thought you'd got sore hands. Anyway, you've a lovely wee hair-drier sitting in your hearth.

Peter smacked her head lightly through the towel.

Ha bloody ha. You're askn fr it, my girl.

Catherine shook her head sadly.

I could have a lovely fire burning in the grate, but you and your priceless works of art . . .

It's no jist the soot n the ash, see in a room as wee as this? Ye'd waarp the frames n mebbe dry oot the iles n a'. They wid no be happy, n neether wid I be.

Them being happy be blowed; they can't complain when they're frozen.

Aye, but they'll complain when they're ower hoat.

Not one of my complaints, I must tell you. I've always been used to coal fires.

She made a pout, like she used to with her mammy when she was after bright new shoes from the shop in the village, turned it towards him so he could see, but he just grinned wider.

Listn tay her, wid ye. Well, my peyntns're no used tay bein mis-treatit, so ye cn pit that in yir hearth n set light tay it.

He leaned over and kissed her head through the wet towel, to show it was for cod. She remembered close, affectionate evenings like this between herself and Francis before she was pregnant with Cameron, only it was a proper fire, she'd be couched against him the way she was now with Peter, and sometimes she'd rise and turn off the overhead bulb so that they'd watch the fire leaping in the grate, a supple varied light, not this constant electric shining that hurt your skin like when you were dealt a smack by your mammy. To make her point, she took the towel from around her head, folded it into a kind of pillow, put it on the lip of the hearthside; bundled her hair up in her hands like shanks of wool and then threw her arms out to the side and brightened her face like the models in glamour shots, making a pose of it, came back to herself and said,

Shift your legs, you,

and then lay down on the pillow of towelling and exposed her hair to the glow of the fire, so he could see what use his wee spit of heat was.

After a while, Peter went to the wardrobe. Next he went to the bedside cabinet, obscuring it as he bent over it; she heard a percussion of objects tumbling over one another as he sorted through the screwdrivers and needles and bobbins and all the stuff he kept in the drawer; she was always on at him to keep a separate toolbox and sewing box and stationery cupboard, but he said he knew it was all in the one place and told her she was just being a fusspot, which was maybe true but it was no excuse for untidiness. Eventually he found what he was looking for; turned, went over to one of the straight-backed chairs and spun it around so it was facing towards her; sat down, and only then she saw what he'd been collecting; one of his paper tablets bound with a wire spiral threaded through the lintel, which he opened several pages in and set on his lap, pencils of different densities of lines which he put to one side on the table, except for one which he kept; a craft knife, with which he whittled the nib of the pencil he'd kept, pricking the pad of his thumb until he was pleased with how sharp it was.

I love cuttn the end ey a pincil, he said, the smell that comes aff it.

He put the craft knife on the table alongside other pencils, brushed the shavings off the page and into his hand, dispersing them on the tablecloth. He sat back and crossed his legs, supporting the tablet on them; held the point of the pencil over the paper, stopped it there, tilting his head as if waiting for her permission.

Speak noo, r frever haud yir peace.

She lifted herself on to her elbows in a kind of half-sit, as if to discourage him by moving.

What d'you want me to say?

I waant ye tay say aye if ye mean aye.

She pulled the dressing-gown around her, drew her knees close and embraced them, adjusting the gown again.

What if I mean no?

He didn't answer her. She hugged herself more tightly in confusion, as if she'd be less of a target the smaller she made herself; she was thinking, why should she allow him more intimacy than ever she'd allowed Francis, the man who'd been dearest to her? Sure and if Francis had been a painter she'd've allowed it because she owed him her love for the home they'd made together, but all she was owing to this man was the roof over her head when she'd needed it, she'd never had a child by him and she wasn't certain if she ever would. The way he told it to her, he couldn't stop himself from copying down what attracted him, like an instrument for making sense of creation, and the only choice he had in the matter was where he turned his sight, what he chose to turn free on the page in front of him.

C'moan, he said. This is no fr the masses.

Who's it for then? I thought all your work was for the masses.

Peter put the tablet on the table, slowly, afraid of alarming her, laid the pencil on top of it; eased himself on to the floor so he was kneeling down at her level, walked himself over to her on his knees. It was becoming uncomfortable and tiring to hold herself forward; it curled her back all wrong and made her tight, but she was determined she'd make a parcel of herself he couldn't open, not if he was going to pick up the tablet and the pencil again. He reached out a hand and pressed the open palm against her cheek; but she wasn't trusting him until she knew what he was after, knowing only too well what touches like that led to.

Some ey my work, he said, 'll never be fr the masses.

The pencil wood in his hand made his touch sweet and resinous, and he was close enough that she could see herself reflected in his eyes. She'd been putting on her make-up by touch ever since she'd seen her father's mark on her; it was the first time in a while since she'd seen her own face, except maybe in shop windows. She was thinking of when her and Francis saw each other like that. She'd known of the black greediness of his eyes ever since she'd met him, and there she saw herself, dark and shaded as if she'd half been swallowed by him already, it was his greed surrounding her and not the affection he pretended.

She felt a pulling around her middle, and when she tried to look down he held her face in his hand, kept her head level so she couldn't see. The cold of the room seeped in through the open front of her gown, and the cloth came away from her breasts; he was pulling gently at the knot in the gown's fastening with the hook of his finger. He hadn't looked down once, and there'd been no change in how he'd regarded her; nothing except that greed of his, which remained constant.

Ye've gied yirsel tay me already, he said. Jist a bit mare. Please.

His eyes before seemed to peel away suddenly, as if they'd held another pair of eyes inside them all along, every bit as greedy and possessive. There was a sweetness carried on another breath, the sweetness of decaying whisky stroking around a voice that was as gentle as you'd use to cajole a beast into the trap; a bit more, me love, me own, o, jist a bit more, o, ye're doin fine, me love.

Catherine lashed out as much through the years as across the distance between herself and Peter. She landed her fists on his chest, more of a shove than a blow she gave him, but him falling back on his heels purchased her the time to be up on her feet and to pull the gown more tightly around herself, and to fasten the cord around her more securely. Peter was sitting back on the floor, kicking away from her into the corner, and when she next became aware of herself his books were off the table and were scattered around, there was a crack spun like a spider's web in the bottommost pane of the window, and Peter was easing one of his pictures out of her hands, and he was saying,

I'm soarry, Cathy, leave the peyntn doon, gie it here tay me, I'm awfl soarry, I'll no ask ye agayn, I promise, jist don't brek up my canvses,

and she was so astonished at the transformation of her newly tidied room, and at the sudden pleading in eyes which had held her so easily, that she did as he asked, and let go of the frame. Peter took the picture and hooked it on the wall with a long breath of relief.

Catherine stared at her hand as if she'd been right all along; all those years ago, and another hand had grown from the end of her wrist after she'd deadened the old one with a touch of the ice tree; a raging hand that had made her upset the order she'd brought to the room. The more she thought of it, the more it made a kind of lunatic sense, like a drunkard babbling the truth by accident; it was the same hand she'd used to strike Cameron, and here she was again, losing her head but still able to direct her hand when it came to ruining things.

Catherine wouldn't let him touch her for the rest of the evening, as if she was carrying an infection she'd spread to him, as well as because she was punishing him. When the light was out, and they were in bed together, he sent his hand out and rested it on her shoulder, saying he was sorry again; but she threw it away, and pulled her share of the blankets more tightly around her, making a cleft between them, a cell of her own he couldn't enter.

Twelve

Every Sunday Agnes dressed herself with particular care to go to twelve o'clock mass, and Daniel was merciless with her over it. He lay in bed like a scruff, watching her, all he'd need to complete the picture would be a fag dreeping out of the mouth spilling ash on the sheets, and he'd have that sarky wee wise smile on him, like he was a philosopher or something who'd the unalloyed pleasure of running rings round a fool with his good brain up against the fool's wee walnut of thinking gear, and she hated that. He thought she was a hypocrite for going on about Kate and her faces, when she was a one for putting on her Sunday best; a face like a wean crayoning all the features into a circle; she'd get out a big floating dress from the wardrobe and put that on. She said he was jealous of God because she was dressing for Him and not him, but he had his reply ready for her,

It's no lik Goad's gonny ask ye fr a dance, Agnes.

Their conversations used to be like a dance, in the days before their marriage; but now she felt out of step, as if Danny was sticking out his big feet to trip her up, and she had her fear to make her step around him. She said,

Never heard ey Sunday best, Daniel? It's fr pride in yir hoose,

and then she'd go on at him about how pride meant your garden as well, meaning that wasted back garden of weeds and sticks which he should've taken responsibility for, since he lived out there most of the time; but he'd just yawn and remind her that it was all for their future, and the garden could wait as well as herself until they'd the prosperity to do it up properly, and that was meant to satisfy her, but he knew it didn't. He wouldn't help her get ready in any way, because he said that'd only be encouraging her; there were times on a Sunday when Agnes felt as if she was an ambassador sent out into the normal world of faith and belief to represent the house, and she wasn't going to hear nonsense from Daniel if she was the only one earning them their respect among folk; so she dolled herself up for God, just to make him feel that wee bit more jealous, and then left the house alone, her stilettos clopping like the hooves of the coalman's horses, preparing herself in her thoughts for the mass.

It wasn't far to the chapel along the road, and when they'd first moved into the scheme Agnes had been startled by the look of it. It seemed to be all roof and no walls; Daniel called it the tent, or when he was being cheeky he called it the Toblerone, or at least she thought he was being cheeky until he explained how it looked Swiss to him, like a chalet or something, and he had that wee crooked smile on him as he said, mebbe it's a garrison fr the local detachment ey the Swiss guerds. She struck him lightly on the shoulder for that, and told him she'd hopes he'd see the inside of it before it was too late; but that was before Francis, and she never said things like that any more, in case she was bringing on the very thing she feared. He thought the shape was meant to inspire you to consider the Blessed Trinity. There was a spindly black wrought iron crucifix that quartered the triangular vault on your way in, a kind of frieze; Jesus was an iron pipe-cleaner man suspended from the crucifix, with a smooth head like the bowl of a wooden spoon, and no hands and feet. Daniel's curiosity brought him closer, and Agnes worried at her lip with her teeth in the hope that there was a revelation coming to him, like it happened in films with the cloud splitting and beams of understanding radiating like sunshine from above; but he was only approaching to laugh at the fact that the iron Christ was pinned to the cross not by nails but by ungraceful spot welds, and he pointed out the blisters with a kind of gleeful look on him, as if it tickled him to think that this Christ had been hung up by the same kind of join that held boats together. So there was the industrial God the Son, while above his right shoulder there was another wrought-iron decoration in the stylized silhouette of a flying dove, worked so that it was sealed like a link in a chain of them, which was God the Holy Spirit, and above Jesus's left shoulder there was a kind of iron tiara of radiating lines that reminded Agnes of the ornament in the middle of the altar, on its candlestick stand, only that one seemed to be made of pure gold and this was dull like the fencing that kept you out of the park, and that was surely God the Father in his guise of the kind of sun a wean would paint in school, casting off light as a sign of his presence.

Agnes had hoped Daniel would come in to see the rest of the chapel, but the forecourt was as far as he'd go, and when Cameron came to them she was warned that there was as far as he'd go as well, unless she'd no respect for the wishes of a dead man. They argued about it for weeks, after the wee one's bedtime; Agnes said there'd be no harm in it surely as long as there wasn't a mass going on inside, maybe she'd be passing with him and she'd feel the need to pray, and surely he'd just be sitting with her, not participating, but Daniel finished it by saying sternly, ye wereny pit oan this earth tay be a missionary, Agnes, n we'll huv tay return this wee package someday the way we fun him, so nae daft thoats in that heid ey yours, right? and then he made her agree that the wishes of a living parent and the legacy of his dead father trumped her concerns as a foster mother. She didn't so much agree as hold her tongue, the way she always did when he asked her to twist herself awkwardly around the queer shapes of his beliefs and his blasphemies, keeping her peace to keep the peace of the house, and more fool Daniel for taking that as assent.

Daniel only ever saw the outside, but if he'd come in with her, swallowed into the throat of faith, then he'd've seen that the interior was square like an ordinary chapel up to a point, when it became a lean-to roof like the summit of a house of cards, buttressed by a lace of girders like the inside of a shed or a warehouse, and the windows were canted so as to make the light shine down in beams of revelation such as she'd hoped had struck Daniel, though there were fluorescent strip lights suspended on chains just in case it was overcast. There were paintings of the passion of Christ in a long gallery that led you to the altar, which Agnes didn't much like. Christ and all the figures of the disciples were as thin as you'd bring them into your house and feed them out of pity, but it wasn't a natural kind of hunger claiming

253

them, it was as if the painter saw everyone like that, and he used colours that seemed to Agnes about as elaborate as a good lick of emulsion on your wall, but they at least guided her towards the wrought-iron chandeliers on either flank of the dais, which she made straight for the moment she arrived.

Every week Agnes lit candles so her prayers might shine on God, and each one of them was a wish of hers for someone, carried along with the prayers like dust riding the light. The chandeliers were simple racks of three tiers, the candles seated like an audience at the theatre; there was a tray underneath containing a battery of candles, and a padlocked coin box with a slot in the top for your coppers, which led Daniel to remark that He was a coin-op God, like a tumble-drier at the Laundromat; like all his wee blasphemies, Agnes ignored it, but she couldn't help thinking of it every time her coppers rang in among the others, and sometimes she smiled as if participating in the blasphemy, and sometimes she smiled with a wee frown to show God she was disapproving of it.

The number of candles she lit varied with circumstances, but there was always one for Daniel, to help mitigate his offence to God, the offence of his unbelief; she reminded God he was a good man at heart, and that he wasn't deserving of the worst torments of the fire; and this she did while she was on her knees at the small devotional altar in front of the candles, separate from the dais at the centre, with an icon of the Madonna against the wall in the distance, painted by the same bloke who did the passion by the distorted looks of it. Her other wish for Daniel was that he'd come to God in his own time, once he'd learned how the world was like one of those derelict shop fronts without your faith, its windows brushed with the milk of whitewash, looking alone and beaten. For a while, there'd been another for the soul of their as-yet-unconceived wean to light its way to her belly, and on it she wished devoutly for the tearing of that damned sausage skin her man insisted on using; she blushed like fire to make such wishes in the house of God, but she was certain He'd understand her reason for asking it of Him, since it wasn't a thing He approved of, and that way she kept her conscience clear for all the times Daniel had worn it. There'd been a third for the duration of Francis's illness, one after it'd been diagnosed for his recovery, then for his easy death, and last for God's mercy on a good man with only his arrogance to keep him from eternal rest; a fourth, and then a fifth, were for Kate and Cameron to give them strength in their time of loss, and then there were only four as Agnes decided judgement on Francis would've been passed by that time, and so she guiltily discontinued the expense of that particular light.

At first, when Cameron arrived, the new arrival as Daniel said, which had pleased her no end at the time to hear it, she saw much of his mammy about him; a way he had of creasing up his nose whenever there was a puzzle in front of him, the dance of his hands whenever he was trying to explain himself; they were reminders to Agnes of the other blood in him, and it disappointed her to have the care of him and not the blood in common. As for Kate, and how she'd shirked her responsibilities to the wee one, don't get her started, as Daniel said, especially once the wean was in his bed and there was the peace of a couple of hours for her to speak out of turn without the wee one hearing. With Cameron away in his bed, Agnes loaded her magazine with ammunition and let fly. Kate was a poor mother, in her judgement; a poor mother for giving away her son, her own son for the love of God, into the care of another without a moment's thought. Well seeing she was from farming folk, she thundered away to Daniel after he'd come back from the shed and they were both sitting in front of the tele with the tea she'd made for them, they were hard-hearted folk used to rearing creatures from infancy and then selling them off to the slaughterhouse. She took pleasure in being able to show Daniel she'd more knowledge in her than he gave her credit for; that was where veal came from, she said authoritatively, calves, wee innocent weans of cattle, they were sold on by farmers when they were not long away from their mother's suck, and they never thought twice about it, not if they were to get the cash in hand for the sale of it. Daniel turned his head to the side, his eyes revolving sceptically towards her, his expression balanced halfway between a smile at how ridiculous she was being and a frown at her unfairness. She lifted her legs on to the sofa and made that self-satisfied wee curling up of herself that reminded Daniel so much of a cat secure in its own territory, her legs doubled under her and the rest of her draped over the arm of the sofa like when you couldn't be bothered hanging up a coat and threw it over the nearest furniture because it was your own house and you could tend to it later.

Oh aye, he said, gonny be servin roast tatties wi him as well?

She lifted her head, just like a cat when you interrupted its sleep with some mysterious human noise, the patient victim of insolence, lids heavy over her eyes, the lashes like a straw besom sweeping the sight of him away from her and under the carpet like dust. She didn't like this notion he carried around with him that he could steal the argument away from her and make a clean getaway because she was daft enough to let him. He could make the words in his mouth mean one thing one day and something else again the next, and it was a trick she couldn't turn back on him; he knew right enough what she meant, clever get that he was, it was just another way of disagreeing with her, why he couldn't just say that made her despair of ever having a proper conversation with him, one she could follow from start to finish. What she meant was, she filled herself with breath to signal her wish that he'd allow her to expend it all in the making of one decent observation for once, what she meant was, that country folk weren't as sentimental as folk from the towns; town folk would never think of selling on a dog they'd reared from a pup, or a cat from a kitten, but country folk were forever breeding creatures for nothing but death, or for some other kind of use, milk or wool or some product to sell, and surely that meant they were just as dispassionate about their own breeding as well. Daniel took a long drink of tea, and let her point die; he was hard up against the other arm of the sofa, and he put the cup down on the coffee table, tilted himself and crossed his legs towards her, having some rare amusement at her expense.

So toon folk'll no pit a litter ey kittens in a sack n droon them in the canal? R they'll no take a dug oot faur fae its hame n leave it tay get loast oot in the wilds? I'm that glad ye've explained it a' tay me, Agnes, I see noo why Kate's such a terrible mither tay her wee yin.

Agnes said a wee prayer into herself, that God would give her the strength and patience not to up and clout him about his righteous head and knock his sarky wee smile around the back of it. She could've cried for that wee one when he was brought here as a new arrival; the haste of the arrangement, one phone call giving Agnes a few days to make ready the room Daniel had always insisted was spare for guests, not that it needed much in the way of preparation. It'd been ready for a wean ever since the day their number came up on the council list, and Daniel always swore that when the time came for her to give birth, the time he was always saying was soon, she wouldn't go near a hospital, she'd stand astride a wee crib and strain the baby out of her without the help of doctors, so impatient she'd be to see that room filled. The room was no bother; quilt covers and matching curtains a boy like Cameron would appreciate, royal blue with stars on the fabric, most like starfish, but that didn't matter, she was thinking of what he'd like; the least wee bit dusting and vacuuming, especially around the desk Daniel had bought when he first considered working in the house, knowing her nephew was a studious one and he'd be spending most of his time there; a wipe down of the paintwork with a damp cloth, and it was all done, waiting for Cameron.

It was just the way he looked when he was standing there in the doorway with Kate when the time came; his eyes down at the carpet, avoiding everyone, they were all lights too bright to be seen directly. Kate didn't even stay for dinner; stayed for tea, though, like she'd exchanged her wee prisoner, and she was just performing the rest of her duty by socializing with the new warders for as little time as was needed. She left him with a hug and a kiss that Agnes thought was like Judas's, a traitor's kiss if ever she'd seen one; Agnes had said later to Daniel that there'd been relief about Kate when she went to the door, but Daniel said it was just that she was trying to be cheerful for the wee one's sake, and Agnes looked at him, cn ye no see the nose in front ey yir face, Danny? and Daniel turned away from her, aye I cn, Agnes, cn ye no see yir ain n no stick it intay ither folks' business? and then went away to wash the dishes as if to remind her he was tending to their own home and not anyone else's.

It became their business, though; and that was the time when Cameron was most in her prayers, for those first few weeks while he was walking through their house in silence like a beast that couldn't tell its own suffering to you. Daniel even tried helping, asking

Cameron if he'd like to come to the shed with him to see what he was working on now; old salvaged tele sets was his recent obsession, but even a prospect she'd've thought would've thrilled a wean with Cameron's kind of curiosity (which was why she'd allowed it in the first place) didn't move him any further than the room he'd been given, and Agnes was beginning to feel like a warder right enough, as if Cameron had simply exchanged gaols as well as gaolers. It was because of her despair that she'd said to Daniel that evening, for talking's sake, if there was ever a boy who needed faith it was Cameron, mourning the loss of two parents in his wee cell upstairs, grieving sorely because one of them at least had chosen to leave him. He hadn't the devotion in him to confide in the Sacred Heart, or even ask the Mother of God for succour; to Agnes, something vital had been cut out of him at birth, or even he'd been born with some dreadful handicap in the head like those poor weans you saw who weren't all there, limbs cracked in queer directions and their eyes like wells run dry. He couldn't see God in the world, had no sense of a directed will in creation, and for that she blamed Kate, though she wouldn't speak ill of the dead father, even if she knew as well as Daniel that Francis's teachings to the wean had come from reason, rather than Kate's instinctive, learned disbelief. Daniel's eyes rolled in his head like marbles knocked out of their circle by the irrational momentum of her argument;

C'moan tay grips, Agnes, whit wid you day? N don't tell me ye'd day it a' wi prayer n Goad's help, cause He husny pit in an appearance since he gied Moses the commandments, if ye're no coontn the wan that goat Himsel nailed up. Kate's jist efter her man dyin, left her wi a wean tay bring up oan her ain; a wee bit mare unnerstaunnin, if ye please.

How he turned it around so it was her fault for not understanding Kate, sooner than Kate's for not taking proper care of her son; he'd stolen it away from her again right under her nose, bugger that he was. For one who said believers were quick in their judgements of others he was never slow in judging her, but he never called it judgement, he said he was setting her straight, like she was paving laid down crooked and he had to break the stone of her wrong thinking to fit it together again the right way, throwing away all the awkward corners. She wouldn't allow him the satisfaction of sitting still in the dock before he passed sentence on her.

Aye, well, mebbe if she'd the church tay turn tay, she'd cope that wee bit better wi it, n the wee yin n a'. Whit wid you day if ye hudny merriet a daftie lik me, Daniel? Who'd ye get up oan yir high hoarse fr then?

She hated the way Daniel went whenever she talked about God and faith; as if she was prone to hallucinations, that pitying look you reserve for weans in a high fever, or mad folk. He opened his mouth, his head tilted, the cargo in it thrown to one side, and she wondered what bitter stuff was going to come out of it now, what kind of blasphemy he was going to prick her with; the sudden noise seemed to come out of his mouth and it took them both by surprise, so much so that Daniel's mouth clamped shut almost immediately as if to reassure himself that he wasn't originating the din. It was noise against the ceiling, a dunting dunting dunting like Kate said she heard above her when the two boxers were at one of their prizefights, and there was a regular pulse to it, a message beaten out in code the way prisoners were said to talk to each other after the lights had gone out. They looked at each other, the agreement coming in their silence the way it never did when they were speaking aloud; in a moment they were both out of the sofa and leaping up the stairs, Daniel taking them two at a time while Agnes in her stockinged soles trailed behind him, and by the time she'd reached Cameron's room the door was wide open, and Daniel was standing beyond the threshold, unable to move for the puzzle he was witnessing, one which held her in place as well, because she couldn't for the life of her fathom what the wee one thought he was up to.

She'd seen him playing with the town he'd made from his car boxes often enough, both when she'd come into his room in this house, as well as in his own room at Kate's; knew how he added to it with each new model car he was bought, using paste as mortar to build his walls higher, she'd even watched him do it with the few cars she'd bought herself to see if he'd come around. He'd brought his town out into the middle of the room, and he was in his pyjamas and dressing-gown; in the back of his throat he was making the drone of a wounded aeroplane from a war film as he lifted his leg over the

259

town, and then an explosion whenever he stamped it flat with his bare foot, repeating it again and again until the card was beaten thin. Agnes didn't know which frightened her more, the spiteful expression on him as he did it that made her think of devils possessing him, or that he didn't seem to have noticed them, went on with his destruction until the understanding that evaded her came to Daniel, and he went forward and stood behind his nephew, embraced him around the chest and pulled him gently away, saying,

Here, here, wee man, whit're ye dayn? Took ye years tay build yon up, lee it alane.

He must've thought he was doing his nephew a favour, that he'd realize once he'd calmed down and then cry like a baby with regret for allowing himself to be taken by stupid anger like that; but all the while Cameron was being pulled further away from the broken town, he kept pounding away at it with his feet and then at last he kicked the scraps and wreckage so they fled away under the desk and the wardrobe, and she'd never seen a look like it on the face of a wean in all her years, frustrated that he hadn't been allowed to complete his demolition. Agnes still hadn't the least notion of what she'd seen, not even after Daniel pulled him back so he'd nowhere else to go and made him fall to sit on the bed. Agnes was about to approach them both and sit beside Cameron on the other side of the bed from Daniel; even if it was a mystery to her, she could at least remind the wee one of what comfort having a kind of ma and da could bring, but Daniel hardened his face into a frown and shook his head slightly so Cameron wouldn't be alerted to it, and Agnes said she'd be away and make a cup of tea for them all, just so Daniel would know she wasn't abandoning the wee one completely, even if she did appreciate that Daniel was trying to make this into a talk between the menfolk.

By the time she came up with a tray and a teapot, three cups and milk and sugar ringing on top of it, as well as a plate of chocolate digestives for Cameron, he seemed to be calm enough to talk, and most of the talking had been done, leaving her with little else to do but offer comfort, hug him the way mothers were supposed to. She felt the resistance in him at first, all his bones hard and tending away from her, but he softened into her after a while, and his affection near took her breath away, so much like having her own wean was it. They promised to clear up the mess afterwards, and put him back in his bed; he seemed relieved that all he'd got was a talking-to for his misbehaviour, and before Agnes put out the light she looked back into the room, and saw that he'd retreated peacefully into the bedding, like an ordinary wean again rather than a storm which had broken over his model town. She asked Daniel what had been the cause of it, if he'd managed to find out while she'd been downstairs, but he only shrugged and said,

He niver tellt us, hoanest truth, Agnes; I jist says he could come oot tay the shed wi me any time he waantit, jist afore ye came in, n he wis the way ye saw us efter that.

Agnes searched Daniel for any sign of a lie, but it even sounded true. She wondered if that'd been all, a storm breaking; hoped it meant he'd be coming out of his room to make a proper family of them, and that Daniel was beginning to understand the responsibilities of a father. Maybe it'd been all to the good, this wee storm, an answer to her candle prayers in more ways than just one, having distilled the father from Daniel for a brief moment, and having given Cameron a sight of a new loving house he could call his home; and she thought she saw the purposes of a higher will being brought to bear, and from that day, she thought, Kate and her neglect of the wee one's welfare, of the spirit as well as the body, wouldn't be a matter of any more concern, except in the realm of Kate's silent conscience.

Then one week she was asked into Mr Farrell's office; at first the headmaster said it was a disciplinary matter, that young Cameron was not participating in his doctrinal lessons, and that there'd been complaints from Miss Telfer, his class teacher, about his disruptive influence on the other pupils. Cameron was there waiting for her, seated in a wean-sized chair stolen from behind one of the desks in a classroom and placed beside the more comfortable chair meant for grown-ups like her, folded in on himself like a flower that wouldn't open out. Mr Farrell was evidently minded to humiliate the child from the first.

Can you not even just learn the prayers along with the other children, Cameron? he said. You learn poetry, is that not so? Can you not just say your prayers like a poem? That's all Miss Telfer is asking of you.

Cameron silently shook his head and looked towards Agnes as if for the salvation of kin, imploring her to speak up for him; the pleading was like tears in his eyes, and she felt a coldness like a weight dropping through her belly as she knew she couldn't allow him to intervene in her conscience, that she'd have to betray him.

Ye don't huv tay believe whit ye're sayn, Cameron,

she told him, and she remembered the time Kate had turned the priest away from the door, how adamant she'd been when Agnes had said the same thing then. She didn't know if Cameron remembered as well, but he gathered himself even more tightly together, wrapping his arms around himself and bowing himself over so that he was looking at them both from under the topmost rim of his eyelids, and he turned to her and said in a small voice,

You said they wouldn't make me say prayers.

Mr Farrell leaned over his desk, hands joined over his blotter, which was wet with the grease from his palms, huge continents of discoloration leached into the capillaries of the paper from gestures like this every day.

Perhaps your aunt gave you such an undertaking, young Cameron, but this school cannot. This is Saint Bonaventure's Catholic School. We are here to ensure that Catholic children grow up strong in their faith, a faith in which I believe you were never baptized. A special dispensation was required to allow you to be educated here, alongside other children who were baptized in the Catholic Church. Already one special provision has been made for you; a second would be asking too much.

He had a trimmed moustache divided in the middle like a pair of eyebrows, while his eyebrows made a continuous frontier under his forehead, a line drawn under the sum of the thoughts inscribed deeply into his brow, like an emphatic calculation. The eyes were focused through lenses of heavy glass that burdened his wide, prominent nose, leaving red dents astride the bridge. He had a cruel look on him, as if he was used to depriving children of their wants, had become inured to it; Agnes thought she'd been right to send the wee one here, despite Daniel's complaints and her assurances that she'd tell them about Cameron's disbelieving upbringing; Farrell knew what was best for a wean, better than the wean did itself, and she trusted his judgement as an educated man over her own as an inexperienced foster parent. She was as much a pupil in the sparse room as Cameron; she had lessons to learn herself in how to keep a child away from its own fascinations, and Farrell's severe eyes, magnified by his spectacles, were as hard as the glass in front of them. Cameron withered like a plant, but he had enough courage to speak up in a voice that carried only as far as the headmaster so you could tell it was sincere inside him and not the kind of troublemaking arrogance that enjoyed filling the room with disruption,

My father wouldn't've wanted me to say things I don't believe.

Farrell didn't notice, but Agnes did; how Cameron had shut the door firmly on his father's presence, but not on his influence, and how he'd a clear understanding of the difference between the two. Farrell sat back in his seat, took his glasses off by their legs and pinched the corners of his eyes together with his fingers in a theatrical show of weariness in the face of such obstinacy; the swivel of the chair creaked under the strain as if it was his own bones, and he let out his despair in the same breath as his reply.

I take it Miss Telfer has told you what a martyr is, young Cameron?

Cameron nodded, bringing his head back to rest, his chin against his chest. Farrell came back over to lean on the desk, opening and closing the legs of his glasses; his eyes seemed weary and bloodshot.

Is that why you persist in disobedience? Do you consider yourself a martyr for the teachings of your father? Does it give you pleasure to spread this atheist's gospel your father has given to you, and to receive the belt for your troubles?

Agnes sat upright in her chair, put her handbag on the floor, the blood singing from the roots of her copper beehive to the ends of her toes.

Haud oan a minute, she said. Who's been gien him the belt? This Miss Telfer?

Farrell quickly put the glasses back on, one folded leg stumbling over his brow before he shook it loose, sat back and made his arms parallel with the arms of the chair, regarding Agnes rapidly and guiltily before looking at the blotter.

Once or twice, I believe, he said, for impertinent behaviour during doctrinal lessons.

Agnes snapped her head around to Cameron; he saw the rage in her, but knew it wasn't at him, said,

I wouldn't say prayers with them.

Farrell settled his hands in his lap and joined them there, a mandarin gesture of possession in his own office. This was a different matter for Agnes; punishment for insolence was one thing, but punishment for a thing the boy could no more help than the way he walked or the precise voice with his mother's cadence in it was another thing entirely. Farrell shrugged.

And I agree with Miss Telfer, such behaviour is impertinent, considering that the pertinence of the lesson is doctrinal. I presume one of the reasons you chose to send him to a school like ours was to end the long neglect of his spiritual education, and if he will persist in obstructing lessons, then I'm sorry, but that is impertinence. I would assume that, since all teachers are given authority by such as yourselves to act in loco parentis, and since you yourself would in all likelihood punish impertinence in a child, then we have that same right to issue the appropriate punishment.

Agnes was spun around by the words, but she was sure enough of their meaning.

Aye, she said, loco right enough, ye're a' bee ell ohoh dee why loco here by the sound ey it. Wid ye belt a wean fr bein, Goad, whit d'ye cry it whn ye're boarn n ye canny see colours right?

Colourblind,

said Cameron and Farrell at exactly the same moment; Cameron tipped his head back down again, and Farrell's clever brow near surmounted the rim of his glasses, deepening into a v. Agnes smiled briefly with pride, as if it was her own accomplishment. He leaned forward to Agnes, bringing her into his confidence almost, glancing sideways at Cameron, understanding now that a conversation in the adult cipher of long words would no longer be secure.

I cannot be seen to favour ignorance of that kind. I have to consider the example such obstruction sets for the other pupils, if they believe no punishment will be forthcoming for it.

Then take him oot the cless.

Then other pupils will wonder why they cannot be accorded the same privilege. I will not do it.

Agnes crossed her legs, made a structure of her arms on her lap to support her head, and stared constantly at this headmaster with his words that rattled briskly out of his mouth and his merciless application of the law. Finally, after taking her sounding of the man, she turned to Cameron and said,

Cameron, wait ootside the oaffice fr a wee minute.

Farrell leaned forward to the furthest tilt of his chair, which Agnes saw rocked as well as swivelled, and he was about to protest against this usurping of his authority, but it was all to do with that loco parentis rubbish he'd been talking earlier; she wasn't as green as she was cabbage-looking, was Agnes, she knew her Latin as well as anyone with a Catholic education and she knew that he derived his authority only so far as she was willing to grant it, and the look on her dared him to say different. In the end, Farrell leaned back and nodded towards Cameron.

Well, boy, he said, you may go,

trying to make it seem as if the boy was obedient to his will sooner than Agnes's, but everyone in that office, Cameron included, knew who'd given the order; Cameron smiled tightly at his aunt, grateful for her intervention, as he lifted himself from the seat and went to the door, seizing the doorknob in both hands and giving it a mighty twist before he was released into the corridor smell of polish and disinfectant. When the door was closed, Agnes turned back to Farrell in his chair, and she gave him such a frown as he'd never seen in all his years of dealing with parents, leaned forward and strayed her arm on to his desk, claiming some of his land for herself.

Mister Farrell, she said, I tellt ye whit the boay's upbringin wis when I brung him here tay begin wi. You tellt me ye'd bear it in mind, they were the very words you used tay me, ye'd bear it in mind. I thoat that meant ye'd gie him a wee bit mare, whit wid ye say, a wee bit mare rope than the rest ey the cless that were broat up in their faith. I didny think it meant ye'd gie him a beltin fr no sayn his prayers. Noo, I broat him here whn my husband, the boay's uncle, his da's brither, didny waant it, cause I tellt him it wis too faur tay go tay the nearest Protestant school, n I tellt him I'd make sure a' yous here didny make the boay learn onythn he didny waant tay learn himsel.

Farrell held up his hand like a warden halting traffic.

Strictly speaking, they're not Protestant schools, they're non-denominational schools.

She might've known; another man trying to make her feel wee and daft.

Still, they're no fr Cathlics, that no right?

Farrell spread his hands and nodded, embracing her point.

Right, well. I didny waant him gaun tay a Protestant school cause it wisny the faith his da wis broat up in afore he turned away fae it, n I wis thinkin, mebbe if he sees the faith in the right light, mebbe he'd waant tay come tay it himsel, n I've goat his nana's backin fr that.

Farrell nodded, all agreement so far.

Just so, he said, we had this conversation when he first arrived.

Agnes nodded, infuriated by all his just sos and neverthelesses and all his empty noise.

Aye, she said, jist so, like ye say. I mind sayn he could keep him in they, whit d'ye call them, doctrinal lessns, so lang as ye didny make him day nothn he didny waant tay day.

Which is tantamount to allowing him to do as he pleases as an example to the other pupils,

said Farrell, and Agnes held up her hand flat the way Farrell had done earlier, her patience near ending with this wee strutting creature.

Whit the hell is this tantamount? Cn ye no speak the wey a boady'll unnerstaun?

Farrell retreated deeper into his seat.

The same thing as. It would be the same thing as allowing him to do as he pleases.

Agnes now put both her arms on the desk.

Fine, she said, right, but here's my poaint. I waant him raised in the faith, you waant him raised in the faith, n so dis this Miss Telfer, she waants him raised in the faith bad enough tay belt him, right? Whit lessn d'you think that's teachin the boay aboot the Cathlic Church? Wid that no turn him away fae Goad, d'ye no think? N believe you me, Mister Farrell, ye couldny turn him awffy much

266

further away fae Goad than he's turnt jist noo. He wis broat up wi nae faith at a', lik I wis sayn, colourblin, he cn nae mare see Goad in creation thn you n me can see nae Goad in creation. Day you n thon Miss Telfer waant tae make him blin tay Goad, lik they poor folk wi nae eyes at a'? Cause if so, jist go oan the wey ye're gaun, n ye'll lose that wee sowl tay the faith.

Agnes fell back into her seat, which cracked under her transferred weight. Farrell heard the words as if they were the skip at the end of a record, repeating until the stylus arm was put back on its rest. He had his hand up at his mouth, defending it, his thumb following the line of his slack jaw, his forefinger under the jut of his cheekbone; his eyes were watery with indecision behind his spectacles, and he shook his head, not to say no, simply because the rhythm seemed to comfort him. At long last, he smiled, the way he'd've smiled at any unusual specimen put in front of him, and he dragged a long breath into his lungs before composing his words, letting them out with care.

I look forward to the day when you decide to take holy orders, madam; you argue like a Jesuit.

Agnes wondered if this meant she'd got the better of him, but she took it as a compliment anyway.

No hope ey that, Mister Farrell, she said. I waant tay send weans ey my ain tay this school wan day.

Farrell laughed.

And I trust they will not be born colourblind, and will prove less obstinate than your nephew.

Agnes looked down at her feet, recovered her handbag, returned it to her lap.

No if I cn help it,
she said.

Agnes had never had an excuse before to go to the shed to watch Daniel at work, until Cameron arrived. The wee one spent his evenings there, as Daniel had promised, once he'd done his homework; and Agnes every night had to fetch him out so he could return to the house and go to his bed so he wouldn't be turning up sleepy at school the following day, dreaming behind his desk when he should've been dreaming the night before. He didn't welcome her turning up at the shed, knowing what it meant; more humiliation from Miss Telfer at the end of the corridor of sleep, now that that awful woman had been forbidden her favourite means of persuasion; and it bothered Agnes that Cameron might think of her as a messenger for Miss Telfer, that she'd been given all the nagging things to do for him, brush your teeth, eat your dinner, get up bright and early for school, while Daniel got to be more like a brother to him, they even had a secret place the two of them could meet and play, a wee den to themselves, and she was thinking it was just as she'd feared, now she'd two weans to supervise. She even began wondering if Daniel had arranged it that way; he was never the one to send Cameron back to the house, oh no, muggins had to watch the clock for him, go down herself in her shoes and an extra cardigan on top of the one she wore around the house to protect herself from the cold, steal out of the back door with her feet whispering in the neglected grass when it was glassy with frost, tap lightly on the door and hope the weans hadn't conspired a secret code knock between themselves to exclude girls and strangers. That last wee thought came from bitterness, but she wouldn't've put it past Daniel to evade the responsibility of being the one to tell Cameron to come in, his time was up, so she'd be the one to enter like the wicked witch and put a damper on things; so he could turn to Cameron and give him that regretful wee look as if to say, whit cn ye day, wee man? missis moan says it's time to shoot the crow, and I'm as much at her beck and call as you are.

Agnes had had enough of Cameron looking down at the floorboards whenever she came into the shed, pacing silently with her all the way back to the house, trying to make a smile for her out of the wee crescent of a downcast mouth he had on him as she tucked the blankets under the mattress. She decided there was only one thing for it, and that was to come early to the shed; maybe then she'd become associated with reprieve, rather than the killjoy immediacy of her turning up. The first night she tried it, she went along an hour before her usual time; she crept up to the door, feeling light and giggly, Daniel's childish secrecy infecting her so she felt more like a wee girl ready to argue her way into a closed gang of boys; she pointed her knuckles and knocked on the door, one, two three four, five six, and wondered if she should wait until the door was answered for her or if she should just go in herself as she usually did. In the end, Cameron answered it; he was polite to a fault, tried not to allow his disappointment to show too much, but the corners of his mouth dropped a wee bit, and he looked over his shoulder at the back of Daniel before letting her in.

There was a curious smell in the place, more like an atmosphere, as if the air had been cleansed using some massive industrial procedure and then released back into the room with a faint acid metallic taste to it. The light overhead was warm, like all the votive candles in the chandelier from the chapel concentrated into one bulb, but there was another, harsher light which she saw came from a lamp attached to a vicious-looking clip that bit on to the edge of a shelf over Daniel's left shoulder, and which he'd directed into the back of the television set he was working on. She hadn't realized what a dreadful mess he kept the place in until now, since most of the time she collected Cameron at the door and never got to see the inside of the den. He had wires, insulated and bare copper, in open cardboard boxes like weeds; the instruments most of the house's money was being squandered on lay on the bench surface, probes that lit up when they came near current, blades fashioned into rings to strip the rubber from cables, and other whatchamacallthems Agnes couldn't recognize; to one side of where he was working, there were meters for this and that, current and voltage she supposed, as well as other quantities she couldn't imagine, their needles fluttering around half-circle calibrations; switches like on a bar fire on wooden mounts and threaded into a trap of wires and whatnot that looked to her more like an accident. It was like that film where they brought that stitched-together man to life with the help of lightning and stuff like Agnes was seeing in front of her; with Daniel hunched demented over the bench. Daniel twisted in his seat so he could see who it was, shied away from the glare of the clamp light and then shaded it with his hand, and he raised his eyebrows in surprise.

Is it no a wee bit early fr bedtime the night?

Agnes smiled towards Cameron, reached out her hand to his shoulder to gather him in.

Course it's too early, Danny. Jist here tay see whit the weans're up tay. It's no time fr bed fr oors yit.

It had the desired effect; Cameron brightened, and led Agnes over to the bench, to stand behind Daniel, while Daniel watched her suspiciously. The only thing he said, though, was she should take care not to stand in his light; she stood behind and to one side of him while Cameron sat in the passenger seat, you might say, ducking around the side of the cabinet for a better look.

If Cameron was sitting beside the driver, then Agnes was definitely in the back seat, pointing out wee curiosities off the road that the driver couldn't attend to without dividing his concentration, and Daniel treated her accordingly, saying aye or naw first of all and then,

Gie's peace, Agnes, wan wee slip here n ye might as well gie us a coat ey batter n serve us wi chips.

Agnes was about to protest, but the set wasn't connected to the supply, he was just being bee ell ohoh dee why minded, she'd bet he didn't treat Cameron that way when he was asking questions; but after a while he turned around in his seat to face her and said,

Mind I tellt ye aboot capacitors? Lik, even whn the set's aff n the plug's no in, it hauds current lik a battery, enough tay kill ye?

Agnes nodded, and then Daniel tossed something over his shoulder, which she caught instinctively like she was a girl again in the playground, those games where you stotted a rubber ball against the school wall and spun like a dancer before you had to catch it. She realized it was heavy, that it dragged down into her lap, and that it was made of tiles of metal built up in slices like a loaf of bread, the corners pressing into her palms, and it was still warm, as if it'd come out of the oven freshly baked. The moment she knew she'd caught hold of something strange, all kinds of fright lashed through her head like the charge she feared was still in it; she mistook the heat in it for electricity, and with a howl her hands fled apart, and it fell on to the tent of her skirt, and then on to the floor, where it landed solidly a little in front of her.

If you could've wired Agnes up to one of those bloody meters to one side of Daniel on the bench, there wouldn't've been a calibration fit for measuring the rage that charged through her; the needle would've caught on the pin at the end of the scale, more after Daniel went into a flight of laughter at his wee joke, and even Cameron chanced a wee smile at the expression on her as if this was his own back for being pulled out of the den night after night when he wasn't ready for going. Agnes felt her manicured nails bite into her palm, and Daniel's laughter it seemed would never end; he was beating the bench with his hand, applauding himself, and the blood was beating through her head to the same time, the pulse in her jaw leaping to see both her weans laughing at her.

That wisny funny, Daniel.

He raised a hand, like Farrell and his wee gesture of hold your horses.

I grunded it afore I gied it tay ye. Ye don't think I'd chuck a live capacitor at ye, surely tay the Goad ye believe in?

Cameron went red with embarrassment, she didn't know if he was embarrassed by her anger, or because he'd been caught laughing at her. Daniel was not the least bit repentant; she wondered if that was a thing that came with faith, if folk without God ever felt repentance for their thoughtlessness. He was wearing a face of astonishment, and she thought, it was Cameron who was behaving like an adult, while Daniel was the one acting like a wean, blindly failing to understand why she'd be so put out.

Wid it'uv been so funny tay ye, she said, if I'd no thoat that?

Daniel quietened down at that; shrugged.

Cameron knew I wisny aboot tay kill ye, did ye no, wee man? You saw me grundin the capacitor.

Cameron tilted his head down and nodded silently. It was different to taking sides with your own mother and father, and it seemed he still hadn't got over the idea he was nothing more than a guest in this house, it wasn't enough to have a room to yourself and a school chosen for you to be allowed to back one or the other. Agnes forced the breath into herself to calm herself down.

Noo ye're tellin me I've no the wit in my heid ey a ten-year-auld.

I'm tellin ye ye learn aboot things, then ye know. If thon capacitor hudny ey been grunded, no a' the faith in the world wid ey saved ye.

Jist as well I've faith in the man I merriet, then, isn't it? That he's no gonny kill me jist tay make a poaint.

Ye know why they'd pit a thing as dangerous as a capacitor inside a telly set, Agnes?

So you could play daft wee jokes?

He smiled at that, as if pleased she'd the fight in her.

See, you switch oan a telly, it draws a wee bit current fae the wa', but that's no enough tay stert it up. See this thing here?

He used the chisel end of a screwdriver as a pointer into the back of the set, to a thing like a square bell turned on its side, which sheltered all the other components; bare copper wires trailed from the end of it, rooted themselves into the boards of components. She nodded, that she'd seen the bell thing, and he went on.

Thon's whit ye ca' the cathode ray tube. That's yir screen where ye see a' the pictures. The back here,

he used the screwdriver to indicate where all the cables went in, where a bell would have all the rope fixed, a kind of cylinder capping it,

is where yir picture sterts. It makes a wee beam ey light, kin of, n there's two magnets tay bend yir beam so it covers the hale screen, but they're no important tay whit I'm sayn. Right, so tay make the beam, this bit here needs mare power than yir set cn draw fae the wa', lik I wis sayn. Where's it gonny get the power fae?

Agnes didn't know if he was asking her, or if he was proposing to answer it himself; the silence suggested she was meant to answer, which was daft if he already knew, to Agnes's way of thinking. Cameron was leaping around on his seat, the wee pupil that knew the answer and who was trying to attract teacher's attention, but Daniel flattened his hand to quieten him, and turned back to Agnes, giving her a big chance to show she wasn't a daftie after all. Agnes thought for a moment.

It'd huv tay steal it.

Daniel smiled at her, encouraged by her as well as encouraging her.

Aye, kin of, ye're oan the right track. That's whit yir capacitor does; no stealin current exactly, mare pittin it in the bank fr later. The cathode ray tube's the thievin get that raids the bank whn it needs mare current than ye cn gie it fae the wa'. Naw, mebbe ye're right; the capacitor's the thievin get stealin yir current bit by bit efter the set's turned oan, keeps haud ey it even efter the set's turned aff, n it gies it ower tay the boass man whn he asks fr it.

He tapped the bell, cathy whatchamacallit, gently with the point of the screwdriver; Agnes was surprised to hear glass, but not too surprised when she considered it was a kind of window, which would have to be made of glass if you were to see anything. A comparison came into her head, which she offered to Daniel to show she'd understood;

Lik, whit d'ye cry it, ye turn the key in a caur tay make it go . . .

Ignition,

Cameron said, and Daniel posted his broadest grin as his two pupils came good for him; that was the kind of smile she remembered from him, one that wasn't bitter with cold and clouded over with ulterior purposes; one of the things she'd married him for, when she could've listened to him for hours on all the wee things she'd never thought of, when she wore him like spectacles and he made the world clearer for her.

Jist lik that; turnin the key in the ignition's jist lik switchin oan yir telly, baith ey thm need mare power tay get thm stertit, n yir capacitor's jist lik the battery in yir caur.

He was seated sideways in his chair; suddenly he went serious, touched the point of his screwdriver against his temple as if he was fixing a loose connection in his head, and all the while he was staring at Agnes as if he couldn't finish the parable, not without stepping over the mark of his earlier cruelty and certainly not after he was pleased with her for learning something in his wee classroom; but she knew where the parable had been going, and she agreed with him that they should keep their differences away from Cameron.

It was ridiculous to her, how quickly she'd allowed her temper to pass, but she thought they were like the bits in a set, the bits of a working family, and her and her faith were the capacitor that gave power to the arrangement, her the instrument, faith the unseen force she stole to make everything light up. She'd always said to Daniel, how come he'd no faith in God because God was unseen when he'd faith in his electricity through the wires, and he'd said, because he could see the effects of it, lights coming on and tele sets working and cookers heating food; and because he knew it could kill him if he didn't watch himself, use insulation. That was what she could be to this new family, and if Cameron couldn't be persuaded towards God by argument, then he could see Him by His effects within her, warmth around him and meals on the table and soft clothes whenever he needed them, and she could remind him that she was a godly person herself, not meaning pure but meaning she was a believer and could work by example. What Daniel would've thought, if he'd imagined for one second that that was how she'd taken his parable; but there was no sense in disrupting the mood which had passed between them after he'd delivered his teachings to them, and so she picked the dead capacitor off the ground as casually as if it was a windfall apple, held it confidently in the palm of her hand, said,

Dis that mean I get tay be in the big boays' gang, then?

Whit day you think, Cameron, 'll we let her in oor gang, r 'll she be able tay keep up wi us, d'ye think?

Cameron nodded strenuously, pleased the argument had been averted; and from that evening, she represented to him time nearly up before bedtime, but at least that was better than the absolute misery she'd been before, and that first night after the wee one was put to bed, she was even happy enough not to think of the prayer she'd said over the candle on Sunday, for the splitting of that bloody skin inside her.

Thirteen

She saw Cameron in the street, walking hand in hand with Agnes, while she was out at the weekend to buy a new pair of shoes. He was wearing a new pair of shoes himself, brown leather sandals, polished so sparks of sunlight came back from them. He had a new blue anorak, quilted and stitched in diamonds. She'd even bought him a new pair of short pants, his bare legs white with the cold. Agnes was walking him by the hand, taking him to all the shops she was interested in; the windows of hardware stores with everything for the home body, clothes shops, both for himself and her; Catherine knew he was too well mannered to drag behind her as they were passing the toy dioramas, which was why she'd always let him run beside her, choose his own interests. Agnes looked new as well; she had her hair all turned copper and tall like a helmet over her scalp, the colour of it reminding Catherine of Bernadette, and she was wearing new clothes herself, a green jacket of rough wool, a plaid skirt that came to her knees, short and daring according to the fashion.

Catherine had decided to wear the new shoes, in case there was the kind of wintry rain later that came on the turning of spring; the old ones were in the box, and the box was in a paper carrier, beating against her leg as she walked along the road. They were beginning to let her know where they would most disagree with her feet in the coming days; there were aches on her left instep, and on the joint of her right big toe, and the skin was becoming tender with the start of a bruise. She was wishing she'd taken Peter's advice, and taken the old ones in for mending, but Peter had missed the whole point of today; it was a reason for her to use up time she had spare, and she'd decided she wasn't going to be staying in the house while he worked on this next big project of his after Elvis, which he'd said he was starting just now, one of the most delicate times for any new canvas; and besides, he hated shopping, making wealth for the wealthy he said, and she'd be better on her own anyway.

Until she saw Agnes and Cameron on the opposite side of the road, Catherine had been feeling happier than she had in a long time; the air was thick with burnt exhaust fumes, and the cars and buses snarled like a cage full of big cats; she hadn't gone into the town for a good while. She'd forgotten how cautiously you had to move in town, and the wee dances that came of folk breaking in the same direction as you when you were trying to avoid them; it happened with an old lady, laden down with a net shopping bag of groceries, step to the right, step to the left, step to the right again, and her and Catherine stopped before the collision, shared a laugh about it, and then Catherine kept still while the lady decided which way she'd step, to her right, into the fast flow. The old lady had a proper, dignified appearance to her, but Catherine detected the faint odour as she passed of incontinence, and as she followed her down the street with her eyes she saw her do her waltz again, with a tall man this time, step to the left, step to the right, step to the left again, and you couldn't help but wonder if loneliness had brought her to this means of raising a smile out of folk who'd otherwise pass her without notice. It was wee things like that that made Catherine glad she was out of the house; just that she was hardly ever able to see other folk around. Even daft things, like when she was going into the department store to buy her shoes, and the first place the doors opened on to was the perfumery. Catherine managed to get a day's worth of fragrance for herself by drifting towards a busy counter and then picking up a wee sample phial and tipping it on to her wrist, touching behind her ears and into the hollow of her throat before stoppering it and heading away. She felt like a comet leaving a scintillating trail of musk behind her, and while it wasn't the same stuff as Francis used to like her wearing, it was good enough, though she agreed with Peter that it was hardly worth the money for a brew of spices and crushed flowers stirred into alcohol.

She left the store with plain black shoes for her work which she expected would last her a while; had taken off her dressy pair with their high heels. The new pair was starting to cramp around her feet, but she was prepared to endure it; she went to the big chemist's store on the corner, where she bought a roll of moleskin plaster which her ma always used to swear by if you were breaking in a pair of new shoes. She'd just turned into Union Street, and was about to consider staying for a while and making an afternoon of it, when she saw Agnes and Cameron emerging from Central Station, and she stopped dead in the middle of the pavement, causing a young man in a Teddy boy outfit to run into the back of her and cry,

Heh, missis, gonny watch wherraboots ye're gaun?

Catherine hardly noticed him. She was transfixed, the breath went stale inside her, and there was a confusion that felt like madness, the bustle around her had turned inside out and she was the centre of it. The thoughts of other folks were like Tannoy announcements, folk asking what this lunatic woman was doing standing there.

Catherine couldn't even hold one of the thoughts, let one of them guide her. There were cars and buses interposing themselves with the folk inside in profile; through them she saw Agnes bending over Cameron, reaching into her jacket pocket for a paper handkerchief, wetting it with her tongue and then wiping it across the wee one's face until she'd given him a spit and a polish and his face was shining like brass and she was pleased with the result. She thought the passers-by would mistake her for Cameron's mother, but her feet wouldn't come away from the pavement, and she'd seen Cameron tilting up his face to her, submitting with his eyes closed the way you did to your first kiss, and the notion that he was allowing her caused Catherine to keep on her side of the road behind the cordon of traffic.

Catherine watched them reach the end of the pavement. Agnes held Cameron's hand at the pedestrian crossing, and waited with him. There was a leaking of folk from one side to the other before the lights changed, defying the traffic to run them over, but Agnes bent down to talk to the wee one, and Catherine knew precisely what she was telling him; always wait at the lights until they turn green for you, and never follow eejits like them who haven't the patience, just because they got away with it today didn't mean they would tomorrow as well. Catherine lost them for a while as they swarmed across. She picked them out again by the colour of Cameron's anorak, blue disappearing around the corner, and she remembered when it was her leading him safely across the streets, and wondered that Daniel wasn't out with them, unless he was back in that shed of his, avoiding the day out.

Catherine thought about chasing after them, but she'd lost her chance, and she didn't deserve to claim a mother's right to talk to her son after her timidity. The corner hid them within a few paces, and Catherine stood there relieved to have no decision to make; after a while she came back, saw she was being caught in a snare of glances from folk who thought she was mad, or thinking they might be watching the start of some kind of fit. There was an elderly man behind her in a tweed coat, wearing a clean flat cap on a long head; and he was standing as if waiting to be introduced to her.

Evrythn a' right, hen?

It's very kind of you. Thank you.

Jist, he said, I thoat ye were takin a turn tay yirsel. 'S lang as ye're fine.

She said she was fine, thanked him again for stopping. He nodded, and went around her, so that she could see his broad back, his steps slow and cautious. Catherine thought she'd made enough of a spectacle of herself, but it was still as if she was fighting against a current that drove her thoughts back; and it wasn't until she was on the bus for the house that she could tell herself she'd done the best by him, by leaving him be with a woman who was taking at least as good care of him as she would've herself, if she hadn't been crippled by Francis's death.

By the time she was in the house, she was hobbling like a granny, and her shoes were hurting like another penance; she took them off, and it was like paring away her own skin. She peeled the stockings from her legs, another skin to tear away; thought she'd been wise to buy the moleskin plaster, and she cut two squares from the roll and pressed them on the wounds. She went to the kitchen to make a cup of Camp for herself, found Codie hard at work at his canvas. She said in a kind of museum whisper that she wouldn't disturb him, and he nodded with his face still turned towards the easel; stroked the brush on each of the cobbles individually, layering the paint on them so they were prominent and dimensional, softened and polished by walking.

In a distracted moment, he looked towards her, and then at her bare feet with the pads on them; returned to his mixing on the palette without missing a beat, spoke towards the canvas while he crouched next to it.

Ye've been trampin aboot tay some tune.

Catherine waited by the hob, as much for the heat from the ring as to wait for her kettle.

New shoes, she said, just bought them today.

He shook his head in sympathy.

I hate that, he said. Yir plates ey meat get turnt intay raw liver wi a perr ey new shoes.

Plates of meat?

Yir feet. Like, ye say, china plate, ye mean yir mate. Plates ey meat, feet.

Catherine smiled, but he didn't see it.

Well, you can tell your china plate that my plates of meat hurt too much for me to make him a plate of dinner.

Codie took the brush with its blend of darker grey towards the canvas, stroked it minutely around the edges of the cobbles.

Chips the night, then.

Aye, and he's going for them, I can hardly walk. I was walking a long time around the town today, even before I bought the shoes.

The house seemed close around her. Codie's life seemed like hers, the way she was feeling just then; abbreviated, carved down to the house and the room she was in. She wanted to tell Codie she'd seen her son that day; she wanted it to be a confession, like she'd've told to Father Byrne, she'd seen Cameron across the road and she hadn't the courage to go to him, and that the injuries were rosaries of true contrition; that she'd've scoured herself raw if only she could return herself to when she was standing on the pavement, like the girl of ice she nearly became from touching the tree years back. She would've got the blood moving in her again, thought straight and true and waded through the traffic and the folk, to hell with her mother-in-law and this forbidding her to interfere with her own child, there was no interference in the love of your own flesh, leave Agnes to get a child of her own to polish like a wee ornament on the mantel.

Catherine poured herself a coffee when the water was hot, and took it through to the room. She sat down in the chair, and put the enamel mug down on to the hearthside, and then stretched out her legs so they were on the seat of the chair opposite. The carrier bag was where she'd left it, just beside her; she raised it on to her lap and took out the shoebox, inside which were the dressy shoes she'd worn into town that day. She picked them out by their heels; the leather on them was soft like cloth, and she tried to remember the last time before today they'd been on her feet; she thought it might've been when she met Bernadette in the mouth of the close, but it seemed to her she'd been wearing them the day she'd taken Cameron to his aunt and uncle's. Catherine remembered how she'd handed the wee one over to Agnes, and Daniel had said to her on the doorstep, he's faimly, Kate, we'll treat him lik faimly, and she'd kept from crying until the wee one was behind the closed door, and she'd never thought she'd see him except at Agnes and Daniel's to take him back again when she was strong enough, ready with a new, better home for him, not better than the one with his father, maybe with a man who'd have him as a son, maybe not. That was the problem, she'd never been ready for today, never thought she'd see him properly mothered and she'd be like the one stealing him. She felt so tired as the fire burned her legs, and she thought she'd rest her head against the cushion behind her, dropping the shoes on the floor, and the next thing she was away to sleep.

She was still holding the empty shoebox when she awakened; Peter was sitting in the chair by the table, since she'd put her legs up on his chair. It seemed as if he'd been sitting there for a while, and she smelled vinegar, saw that he was turning back to the table every so often to pick chips and scraps of battered fish from an open parcel of brown paper with his fingers.

Codie tellt us ye wereny up tay makin dinner, he said, so I goat us some chips fae the shoap. I pit yours in the oven. Didny waant tay wake ye, no whn ye were lookin so comfortable.

His eyes looked washed out again, red around the lids. Catherine shifted herself; her legs were stiff, and the empty box was heavy on her lap, the lid resting on the floor among the wrappings of white tissue.

I'll clean all this up after.

He shrugged; didn't matter to him.

'S the bloody weekend. Gie yirsel a rest.

Catherine stood up. Her feet ached, but she didn't show it. She picked up the tissue paper, crushed it into the box, put the lid on, slid the box into the carrier bag.

There, she said. Doesn't take much time to do.

Peter posted a morsel of fish into his mouth.

Wis that aimed oot the pulpit at me?

If the shoe fits,

she said, lifting one of her sore feet to show him.

Aye, very good, he said. If the shoes're made tay fit, whit else cn ye day but wear them?

He nodded down at her ruined feet.

D'I no tell ye, ye should ey goat they auld wans mendit?

I wanted new ones, she said. I don't know what the fuss is for.

Peter conducted another piece of fish to his mouth.

Typical. Yir decent kin ey bloks're dialectical materialists, but yir wimmn're aye ruinin it cause they're jist yir coammn r gairdn materialists. Ye'd gie cake intay the mooths ey theym that cn afford it, n steal the bried oot the mooths ey the bloks in the mendin shoaps.

He was wanting a fight, by the looks of him. Catherine sank back into the chair, to let him know she wasn't interested.

I don't want to think of your blokes just now. I let my son pass by me in the street today, and I didn't go over and talk to him. So you see, I don't care if your blokes're eating cake or gingerbread, d'you understand me?

Peter's eyebrows raised.

How'd ye no go ower n talk tay him?

He was with his aunt. Remember he's staying with her until . . .

I know, I know, till ye've fun a decent hame fr him, r till hell freezes ower. Ye'd think ye were ashamed ey him.

Of course I'm not ashamed of him, what a ridiculous thing to say.

How'd ye no go ower tay talk tay him, well?

He was with his aunt, I was on the other side of a busy road, it wasn't easy to get across.

How hard cn it be whn yir son's oan the ither side fae ye?

Leave me alone, Peter.

Whit, lik ye left him alane? Is it me ye're ashamed ey? No waant him tay see the slum his ma's in the noo? R the man she's ta'en up wi, that it?

She just wanted an end of it; stabbed him with a vicious look.

If the shoe fits.

Peter brought his hands together and rested them on his lap, as if he was remembering the comfort of prayer, of begging into emptiness. He studied her for a good long time; finally she sat forward to escape from it, turned so her back was to him, pretending to be warming her hands by holding them out to show the fire. She heard a creeling of the chair as he lifted his weight from it, paper rustling; from the door he said,

Why should I gie pity tay you? No when ye'd let yir ain son go by lik a fucken stranger, n ye know it's no right yirsel.

She turned to say to him not to dirty her with that word, but the door was closed by then, and the studio door was closing. She'd've left the house for a walk if she'd been able for it, but she couldn't even stand up without her legs hurting, and the misery of the pain magnified her discomfort and all her dissatisfactions with the house and her circumstances. With nowhere else to go, she went to find blame in herself, some action of hers to explain why she'd chosen a gaol like this to lock herself in, and she could only pull the line as far as her beating of Cameron, where all the blame in her began and ended, the guilt that had paralysed her that afternoon, that kept her here when she had the leaving of Peter any time she could draw her belongings together. But she was thinking as well, it was true what he'd said about her shame of him, and it was no way to treat a man she shared a bed with, and who'd taken her in when she'd needed it; she retreated into sleep, the way prisoners sleep away their incarceration, to release herself for a while.

*

The only other escape open to her was to occupy her time. The picture of Elvis was hanging on his wall of portraits, framed and finished, evening out the grid; all his canvases seemed to be the same size, regular as photographs. She'd watched him hanging it to square off the vacant right angle on the lower left, fussy like the curator of his own museum, making adjustments with the tips of his fingers until it was ruled evenly with the rest of them. He was the same if he saw she'd tilted any after she'd done with her dusting, and she laughed at him; he swore it wasn't vanity, but she said with a sceptical tilt to her head, all right then, mister trout on the line, back into the water with you, no need for any more of your wriggling. She did everything to reassure him it was only meant in fun, but he still went into a sulk over it that took him the whole night to get over.

The picture was hung where she could see Elvis when she opened her eyes in the morning, and he was still staring at her when she returned from the bathroom to fetch her working clothes. There were times she thought it was as if she was painted on to the same canvas as Elvis, as if he was searching into the world of depth. Peter declared it was the immediacy of him that disturbed her, said she was a bourgeois in waiting for not being inspired by Elvis's spirit of resistance, but she told him he was talking rubbish if he thought a lout leaning on a fence represented anything but himself, and after a daft accusation like that she decided then and there she'd need a project of her own to occupy her during the evenings, which was to come to her own understanding of the canvas so she'd feel easier around it.

For about a week after Elvis was finished, Catherine positioned herself closer to the canvas by sitting at the foot of the bed, just in front of where Elvis was hanging. She narrowed her focus until only Elvis was clear to her. Without Peter's guidance as to its significance as a composition it reduced itself to a feathering of brush strokes on the crop of the fabric, dense where there was substance and the black substance of shadow, lighter where there were reflections and manifestations of light. The uprights of the fence severed the light in alternations of black and gold, so it was as if Elvis was leaning against the back of a tiger. She noticed as well that the paint was thicker around Elvis, probably applied with the palette knives, so he stood out in the kind of dimensional effect she'd seen in certain religious icons folk hung in their homes; tricks she'd learned from Peter's book were called trompe-l'oeil but which they'd known about in the faith for years, with their manufactured works of the saints and the Virgin, Christ as well of course. Those were printed on boards, and none of them was original, but the boards at the backs of the pictures were swollen around the holy silhouettes, as if their sheer piety was a kind of infection of saintliness provoking an immune reaction in the flat venal world they were in, but not of. That was what Elvis was like; only she couldn't understand why he was swollen into the world, what quality Peter considered made him a presence, this spirit of resistance he seemed to value, his malevolence, or if he was just an irritation on the face of the canvas. She approached closer until Elvis became touches of pigment across the canvas, a crust like a black continent against the tiger skin. He'd used more reflective paint to represent how light played in the creases of leather; the closer she went, the more she saw shapes in the lacquered white, thorns and scythes and dagger edges like an armoury of broken glass, or the pieces of her father's broken promises. Even light made weapons on Elvis, broke into fragments against him.

She went to the face next, the flesh pale and hard, they called that kind of complexion peely wally round about here, which she'd thought funny when she first heard it from her mother-in-law. Francis had explained it meant pale as porcelain or any other kind of ceramic; wally was what they called ceramic here, wally closes, closes with tile decorations on the stairs and the landings, wally dugs, mantelpiece ornaments of dogs, even wallies, false teeth, though he'd said he didn't think they were made of ceramic any more. Peely wally; as if Elvis would've rung like bone china if you'd struck him with your fist, only there were his scars as evidence that he was made of softer material. Peter had made them out of two risen crescents of scarlet paint, scarlet right enough, the colour of scars, new moons of blood when you were close, but it was another trompe-l'oeil the further away from the canvas you went, the shadows became the hollows of Elvis's cheeks and you saw where he'd been cut open like vivid meat.

Next she looked at the hands; one insolently hooked on his jeans pocket, the other holding his payment of beer; both pale as the face, but chipped around the knuckles, where he'd burst himself open in the wars with the Mad Street team. The fingers were ruined with conflict, like dead roots you'd dig out of soil. The last thing she studied was the eyes, those bloody eyes that followed her around the room; sunk into their orbits, retreating from the blackening they'd received from the Mad Streeters. Peter had made his paint as thin as the paint Codie habitually used, giving an eggshell appearance to the whites so that even his eyes seemed to have been fired in a kiln; the bloodshot was mapped on to his eyes like veins through stone, and if it wasn't for those hands like roots you'd think he'd been tooled for aggression, constructed rather than born.

The project took her several nights, but by the time she was finished she'd begun to separate the work from its subject. She began to note how Peter had put Elvis together, and how Peter's hands had influenced the way he'd represented Elvis. It was more subjective than Codie's way of working; Elvis pressed into the foreground, away from the trap of learning behind him, the thick paint celebrating his release, the paint thinner for the school behind. She came to understand, not Elvis himself, but Peter's understanding of Elvis; and now she'd learned Peter's technique of foregrounding for emphasis, she decided to press on with understanding the rest of the gallery, because she was beginning to see that it was also a way of understanding Peter himself, and if he wouldn't speak to her while he was busy with his new work, then this would have to be her only dialogue with him, through the work that was so important to him, if she was proposing to live under the same roof as his tempers.

He knew she'd fled over the water away from her father, and that she'd never got on with her old man, but she never told him why. That would be for later, once she was sure it was safe enough for Cameron in the house he called for a joke the den of artists. He made very few jokes these days, which was why she remembered that one so clearly. Den ey iniquity, he said, den ey thieves, den ey artists, same kin ey hoorhooses. She'd said, what am I doing in a den of iniquity? and he'd laughed, you're the wan keeps us respectable, every hoorhoose hus its cleaner, n at least we're no the kin ey hoorhoose ye widny bring a wean tay stey at, and she looked sideways at him and made excuses, that they'd never live with a wean running around, they'd never have peace to do their work, and Peter nodded, aye, I suppose no.

He was never done hearing of Francis. She knew it saddened him, but it was like opening the doors to a dovecot; the words flew away from her before she could stop them, and she knew it made him despair, but she couldn't help it. In his better moods he'd smile as if she was telling him a story about a friend he only pretended to like for her sake, but if he was hurt he'd say, it's bad enough knowin yir rival, it's worse whn he's a deid man, and all she could do was coory up to him and plead for understanding; it wasn't far enough away yet, and this was the father of her son she was talking about, after all. He had to understand that Francis was still in her, that it wasn't long since she'd worn him in her eyes; all she could ask of Peter was that he forgive her for now if she needed to remember. Sometimes he said it was good she remembered her man so fondly, others he was silent. But he needed to know that she couldn't make an album of her life the way Codie could do, or even like Peter himself, with his books of folk caught in their moments; she had an ordinary man or woman's memory, fine for now but becoming less capable with age and wear, and there'd come a day when remembering Francis would be an effort, just like every other task in old age, and for now she wanted to keep Francis in easy reach, add to her memories of him the way folk saved for their infirmity, and Peter said he understood that, when his work was going well for him, and turned sullen and silent when it wasn't.

What he didn't know of her was that she wasn't quite as ignorant of picture-making as he thought. He'd wondered why she was so confident in handling the camera he'd used to demonstrate the reason for Codie's name; she'd told him about her wedding, Michael firing off the camera, but had never wondered where it had come from. It wasn't a secret; just that she hadn't thought of her Uncle Finn in years herself, having never seen him in years; meaning years before she'd run away, let alone her years of marriage and home-making. She'd always thought it strange that Uncle Finn hadn't come over to her wedding to take the pictures himself, but she'd been too busy on the day to consider why not; maybe there were too many explanations for comfort, why owl Colum hadn't been invited; after all, the house over the water had been boarded up by secrets, and Finn lived a couple of counties away, hearing not the faintest echo of it, and hadn't her da been a respectable man to begin with? His had been the first photographer's shop in the village, the first for miles around if truth be told, and it'd been open for as long as Catherine or Michael could remember. He made his money from picturing folk at their weddings, and at their fêtes and fairs; some said he made his start sneaking pictures of the time of troubles into newspapers, but they were the deeds of a daring young man, and in his settled middle age he was far happier with celebrations than with recording misery. The photograph Catherine had only ever seen once when she'd gone into her ma and da's bedroom had been by Uncle Finn, taken in his studio after the event before her mammy's dress had to go back to the shop, so even it was a lie; her white lie, her mammy called it, because she was done up with her dress white like cloud over a mount, and only later did Catherine think she might've been meaning more by it. Catherine only ever saw it once, but there were pictures of herself and Michael in the kitchen, after they'd been baptized, and the poses were the same, mother seated with a garden cloth behind her as if they were acting in a play, on a seat made out of wood pleated like wicker, with Colum standing bowed over the seat with his arms braced against the arms of the chair; the only difference between the first and the second one was that Catherine was the child in swaddling, and Michael was protected under his father's arms. Catherine always wondered why the pictures remained intact down through the years; the only reason she could come up with was that they were ideal moments in the old drunkard's life, which rendered them sacred beyond even his worst tempers, and so there was the promise made implicitly in the photographs, to protect the family, which was broken as well, so perhaps there was no reason to break them in deed when they'd already been broken in intention.

They had to plan to visit Uncle Finn every time, since he lived so far away, which was why they visited him so rarely; and there was always somebody getting married, or some church blessing or celebration in the summer, so you could only rely on him being in during the winter months, when the weather was so bad. How he ever sold a camera, Kate never understood. Not only was his shop closed most of the time, but when you did enter, and the bell over the door sang like the voice of brass, he was always in his darkroom, crying out from behind the door and the curtain that insulated him from outside, just a minute now, I'll be with you as soon as I'm able. Kate wondered if he was being clever, giving the customer the chance to read the labels and study the cameras on display without the pressure of a salesman, or if he was just a busy man, like a monk in his wee closet. His work took a wee while, but if it was taking too long, their ma would shout, come out of there, Finn, or have you no time for your sister and your niece and nephew? or are you having a nap in there? He'd shout back to let them know he was busy, but he was always pleased to hear them, and he'd come out of that evil-smelling room wiping his hands on his apron. The nap of the apron was sepia like a print developing on his belly, but he had a flashbulb grin that came and went, good day to ye all, Kate, Mickeleen, me darlin sister, what time is this? and Kate thought he lived without time, he was so long in the night that he couldn't tell you the time of day or the weather outside. For all she liked him, in her younger days she could hardly endure the stink of him; cleaning fluid, acid, a smell like the hairdresser's in town; she had to be older before he'd tell her what the smells were, when she'd enough confidence to say the names of the chemicals without tripping over them, hydrogen peroxide, sulphuric acid, words that sounded like spells, but were really just the names for the baths he dipped his papers in.

That smell convinced most folk around his village that he was mad, more even than when he first left bills in all the pubs and shops to announce its opening; what use were pictures, folk said, when everyone had tongues and ears for the spreading of stories? but Finn reminded them of deaf folk who spoke with their hands, though he only did that to be contrary. Their complaints were the same, just said for the sake of contrariness, because they honoured him for the pictures he took that told of British wrongs, and besides there wasn't a single one of them who hadn't been to his shop to ask him for pictures of their weddings, and they knew he wasn't so mad when they saw him with his cameras packed away after the mass drinking at the bar with them, enjoying the hospitality at their expense. It was that mystery of the extension to the back of the shop that made them think of him as insane; how he'd converted a greenhouse of all things into a darkroom, and the dreadful withering smells like a fart from your arse, and there was a man named O'Dowd, o awful funny, said Finn, giving him his due, but he strops the edge of his tongue along with his razor, so he does, who said, I don't have the faintest feckin clue what ye're makin in that still at the back of yer shop, Finn Corrigan, but I'll be first in line for a sip of it, and Finn, who was quick enough himself said, aye, you do that, O'Dowd, and we'll collect it out the back of ye and see the picture of ruination ye've turned yer guts into with all yer years of thirst.

Finn's hands were like two aces of spades from the silver iodide, and he wouldn't touch the children until he'd washed them, and then they turned the sepia brown of nicotine stains on a heavy smoker's fingers, or like the wipe on his apron. If the children were good, or if his sister swore they'd behaved themselves on the journey over, he'd allow them into his night room, as Kate called it, much to his delight. The smell that had only been unpleasant outside became the atmosphere of the place once the black curtain was drawn, and he made them wait by the door while he felt around for the switch that lit the safe light, the lamp coated in dense red film that made it more of a dawn room than a night room. Michael, inquisitive wee thing that he was, was all over the place on their first time, what's this, Uncle Finn? what's that? what does it all do? but Kate felt attacked by the fearsome reek, coughed as she stood by the doorway. Uncle Finn said, I'm sorry, darlin, this is no place for a colleen like yourself, but Kate became determined once he'd said that, I'll be fine, Uncle Finn, just lost me breath there, and she saw the smile carve into his thin features, that's me brave wee sowl, stay with me, so ye can see yer Uncle Finn isn't as hare-brained as they say he is.

Kate knew the difference between her uncle's madness, and her father's that came from a bottle, but her mother had sworn her to silence on that, especially in front of her uncle. What her uncle did wasn't madness; it was well organized, and it surprised both her and Michael at how much work and organization went into a print. In the blood-red light of the lamp, Finn showed them his plate developed from a film; she was astonished at the reversal of day and night on it, the inverted shadows; a couple standing before the chapel, the groom in his white suit and the bride in her black dress and the family surrounding them as if it was a funereal wedding of the dead. It was as if the whole scene had been carved out of shadow, and these pale manifestations were what you got when you cut shadow to the bone, the lustre of shadow the way light inhered in coal. Next he went to a strange contraption like a small ballot box with a concertina funnel slung underneath; took a sheet of paper that even in the dim bloody light Kate could see was shiny with a substance Finn told them was called emulsion, and slipped the sheet into the plate behind the negative, and then fixed them both underneath the funnel, taking measurements and adjusting the extension of the funnel until he was happy with the result. He reached around the side of the box, and there was a click that rang through the black metal; a pure white light exclaimed from the funnel, and he said,

This is what ye call a contact print I'm makin, won't be long now,

and he counted, one one thousand, two one thousand, under his breath until he made the count silent in his head while showing them the canister the film had had to go in to be made into a negative, which explained some of the evil smell, slopping with chemicals like stock for the devil's broth. There were three troughs on the other side of the bench and to the right of the lightbox; Finn said they could go close to smell them, but he implored them not to dip their hands into them, because they weren't full of water; the nearest was developer to bring out the image, the middle one was stopbath which prevented the image from darkening too much and making it seem as if the weddings happened at dead of night; and the last was fixer, to keep the image stable. Once he switched off the box, Kate and Michael were dazzled and rubbing their eyes, and Finn told them why the room had to be dark, how the crystals of silver iodide in the paper's emulsion darkened under light, so sensitive that the last wee leak of daylight would leave you with a picture, as Finn said, of a coalman filling your bunker. He conjured an image on to the plate he'd just exposed for her, and for Michael, of course, watch, pretty one; baptized it in the stinking waters, holding it with a tongs before washing it in the other waters, running the print under the water of the sink to wash all trace of chemicals from it, and then holding it up for her to see; the image the right way around on the paper, light and dark where they should be, and she thought it was magic from the fairy folk until he explained it.

Finn gave the photograph to her as a present, but she'd left it when she fled. She'd thought at the time of fleeing to him; the ocean was nearer, though, and there was always the risk of her da considering the notion as well. All the same, she'd fond memories of her uncle; he came into her night's prayers when she still said them; God bless me mammy and me da (there was a commandment that required her to say that last name), God bless Michael, and God bless me Uncle Finn, keep them safe from harm, and she meant it for three of them at least. She often wondered if her uncle still had his shop; it was one of the many things she wondered about what she'd left in the wake of the boat, like how her mammy had explained her sudden absence to Finn, or why she'd gone, or if the house still kept its secrets like the camera, sensitive film that would be exposed and ruined in daylight.

She had to tell Peter about her Uncle Finn to explain all the things she emptied out of the carrier bag on to the table before dinner one night, and which she placed alongside the shoebox, still not thrown out after days of sitting there empty. He wanted her to throw it out, but she told him, her mammy said you never threw out anything if it could do you a turn, and especially not boxes, because you could hold your entire life in them. Of course, in her mother's day, most items came in sturdier boxes of tin, like the one her mammy fetched from the room to show her what she meant. It had once contained grated soap for cleaning your clothes, but now it was full of treasures, daft wee keepsakes. There was a tortoiseshell hairband, bought by her sainted nana when her mammy was as old as Catherine at the time Kate left home; that's for capturin yer hair, she was told, and yer hair'll capture you the man ye'll marry some day, like a rabbit in a trap. Catherine had inherited fine black hair from her mother; her mammy tried on the band so her daughter could see how beautiful her hair had looked with her wearing it, and although some of her hair was wiry and silvered, you could still imagine her as young, the tide of it directed in a river lapping at the small of her back. There'd've been love-letters from Colum O'Hara in the box as well, if ever he'd learned his alphabet, but he'd talked a good-enough courting; the only papers were documents, purely business, legal papers, receipts and the like, anything she might need as proof in case of future dispute. Last of all, under all the adult concerns, came her child's discoveries, precious to her beyond calculation, for all they were just scallop shells found printed in the sand, and pebbles the sea had done the lapidary's work of polish and flattery upon until the water evaporated and they became misty with salt and dowdy like your owl boots. The things Kate remembered best were the last things to come out of the box; sepia photographs of a stern-looking woman and a man with a moustache in two furious skeins. They were Kate's nana, and her granda, a patriot, for all the good it did him, but they weren't what interested her; it was the copper dust frosting the emulsion of the photographs, and at first Kate thought it was the picture coming away from the backing, but her mammy told her no, that was all that was left of a treasure that hadn't lasted. She'd picked a leaf from the earth for the sake of its colour, brilliant red you'd think would bleed red if you cut its threaded veins; she was young enough to think it was ripening the way an apple ripens, but the longer it stayed in the tin, the more it became a dry old fist until one day she took it out and it splintered, taking its mysteries with it. The thing was, and she smiled to think of it, she couldn't bear to throw it out even though the tin was causing it to turn to dust, and now she kept it to remind herself of the foolishness of her years, of the girl who never thought of such things as death and passing; she thought it especially valuable, now that her hopes of a happy marriage had turned like the leaf, and that was her legacy to Kate, this reminder that all the hoping in the world would never preserve a thing that was dying to begin with.

So Peter wasn't allowed to throw out the box, because of what it might keep for her, but there was something else she planned to use the box for, keeping of a kind, and she explained it to Peter as she emptied out the carrier she'd brought home from the town while he'd been in at his work. She brought out a long, flattened box about the size of one of Peter's sketch pads, bright yellow and printed over with the same trademark Peter had half covered over with his thumb to explain Codie's nickname; and three bottles of brown glass, which you'd've thought contained liniment or the like if you didn't read the labels and see that there were warnings printed in red, that the liquids were not to be touched or drunk, and that immediate medical attention was to be sought (sought, he said, with a wee twist of his mouth, as if the word hadn't been coined for the likes of him to say with a straight face) if there was misuse of the product. He recognized what they were once he'd read the names on the labels, after all, he did have an art training, and wanted to know why she'd bought them, so she had to explain herself. It just seemed to be another excuse for talking about Francis again, but she denied that, said it was more about Cameron than Francis, and he settled down in the chair while she told him, folding his arms and crossing his legs.

The shoebox had reminded her of a time in the old house when Cameron drove everyone nearly mad with a book he'd taken from the school library; a big picture book all about light and the spectrum, and it had experiments at the end of every chapter, things to do you might say, and they were what drove everyone mad; well, Catherine mad, more like, because Francis was as much of a wean as his son about it, helping him make a colour wheel and cut it out of card, and the like. The idea of a colour wheel was this; you cut your circle, your wheel, out, and then pierced two holes in it at equal intervals from the centre opposite one another. Before doing anything else, you had to paint alternating wedges of red, yellow and blue radiating from the focus, and once that was done, you had to find a length of thread, which brought Catherine into it, since she knew where to find the needles and bobbins of thread in her seamstress's box, as well as blunt-nosed scissors the wee one could safely use. Francis was very patient with his son, knowing that this was learning in its purest form of discovery; showed him that you described the circle first with a pair of compasses and then painted it before you cut it out so you could leave tassels of excess paint over the edge which you wouldn't notice when it was separated from the card. He let Cameron thread the cotton through the holes without result for a while, before showing him how you did it without the end catching on the entry and splaying out, which only made it more difficult to push through; he said, day whit yir mammy does, n pit it through the eye ey yir needle, n then pit the needle through, see whit happens then, and of course it went through first time after that, and Francis made a wee knot to secure the loop because Cameron's fingers were too clumsy, and there was his colour wheel, ready for the experiment. Even Catherine was curious; Cameron spun the wheel until the thread was tight around his thumbs and it was braided around itself into a spiral, and then he pulled his thumbs apart so the wheel spun as the spiral unravelled and then caused the thread to tighten again, keep dayn it, said Francis, n ye'll see. The spokes of red and yellow and blue were bleached pale as the wheel gathered speed, and when it went as fast as it would go, it was the queerest thing, the wheel became blinding white and you'd think Cameron hadn't painted it at all, and Francis said, that's tay teach ye there's a' the colours in white, and Catherine looked to her husband, the delight on him as well as Cameron, even though he understood how it worked.

The next experiment needed a box of angled mirrors, with a pinhole on one side, and Catherine gave him a square of mirror glass she knew was in the house. A shoebox was ideal for the purpose, said the book, and one wasn't hard to come by, what with Cameron going through pairs of shoes at a furious rate. Cameron placed the mirror so it was angled against two of the walls of the box, and then drilled a hole in the wall opposite with a needle. He then got a battery torch, and pressed it against the outside of the box where the hole was. You were supposed to observe where the pin of light struck the inside after it'd been reflected by the mirror, but the light in the room contaminated the experiment, so Francis switched off the bulb, and went over to the hearth and used the bellows to gather a breath of smoke from the grate, and then puffed it into the box. The lesson of this experiment was that light struck the mirror at a particular angle which you could measure, called the angle of incidence. If you measured the angle on the other side of the point at which the beam was snapped like a matchstick against the face of the glass, the angle at which the beam sped away, it would be exactly the same as the angle of approach, and this was called the angle of reflection, and the whole thing was summed up, said Francis, by saying that the angle of incidence was equal to the angle of reflection. The whole experiment was a wee bit too sedate for Cameron, and after all, once it'd been done, its point had been demonstrated, and so Cameron soon enough lost interest and was waiting for the light to go back on, but Catherine came over to watch, and Francis gathered another breath of smoke in the lung of the bellows for her and scooshed it into the box so she could see what he meant; the slender straw of a beam bent against the single facet of the mirror. She said, what's the angle if your torch is directly in front of the mirror? and Francis said, no degrees at a', that's jist lik sterrn it in the eye, lik you day when ye're pittn oan the make-up, and she slapped him lightly on the shoulder for his cheek and said, so what's the use of all this? and he said, for folks like themselves with jobs and things to do, nothing, but for Cameron, with his thinking still young enough, he thought this kind of experience was priceless, because it would either help him in later years if he wanted to take his studies further, or it would become knowledge, which was never a waste in Francis's opinion.

It was one of the later experiments that proved to be a problem, because it clearly said it was for older children, and Cameron wasn't the right age for it. You needed another shoebox, and Catherine was thinking, the author of the book must've known children, how quickly they went through shoes. You needed to drill another hole in the exact centre of the narrow wall of the box, and you needed to cut a square of photographic paper to fit the wall opposite. The next stage was simple enough; point the box at an object and leave it for a few hours, and then come back and seal the hole with sticking plaster; it was the stage after that Francis wouldn't allow, which was to buy bottles of developer and fixer, and trays to pour them into, and then make a room dark and develop the image on the paper. Cameron was eager to do that experiment, and Francis knew why, he'd've been the same if he'd been Cameron's age, dangerous chemicals, working in darkness, the whole notion was so irresistibly adult, and he was half inclined to buy the stuff and allow Cameron to do the experiment up to where the picture needed tending to and then do that bit himself with Cameron's assistance, but Catherine said no, she wasn't going to let the wee one anywhere near chemicals, and neither would Francis if he'd stop being a wean for a minute. Francis agreed, even if he was disappointed for the wean, and sat Cameron down one evening and told him he wouldn't likely do the experiment before the book had to be returned, told him it'd be a few years yet before they'd allow him, and Cameron was more disappointed than Francis, but he didn't argue with his father. Francis and Catherine looked at each other and they were thinking the same thing, they were right not to allow him but they'd put down his enthusiasm like an animal, and Francis said, I hope he disny forget tay day it some day, n I'll help him then.

A few nights before, Catherine had gone into the drawer of the bedside table, and found a reel of cotton with a needle slipped between the turns of thread. There she found as well a ruler, and a pencil; she had no thoughts in her head as she drew diagonals on the narrow wall of the shoebox and pricked a hole in the intersection with the needle. Maybe it was her thinking of his birthday coming up, making a present of her permission to do the experiment. By the time she was asleep with the box all ready to take pictures, she was much more at peace than she'd been in a long time, after thinking the way other folk said their prayers last thing at night she'd have something proper for the wee one next time she went on a visit, not just pretend fussing with a handkerchief wet with spit to wipe off his face. She'd have a true gift for him, something he'd wanted and that he could remember his da by as well, and that was something Agnes could never offer; the thought was warm like the blankets over her, and Peter never even noticed that the box had been touched until she told him that day, looking over at it from his seat and seeing the lines she'd drawn on the face, the sticking-plaster shutter.

Peter shook his head sceptically all the way through the story; finally stood up and went over to the table, picking up the box first of all and turning it end over end, aware he could put a stop to it all just by crushing it in his hands, almost testing her trust in him.

Patient man, Saint Francis ey Assisi. So whit's the score wi a' this? Yir son comin tay oor hoose tay meet his new uncle, that it?

I thought I'd try it out for myself first. It's a while before his birthday yet. I was just wanting to give him, you know.

Peter nodded as he lifted the bottle of developer again, sighted through it at the window, the distortion of daylight bottled inside it.

'S an awffy thoatful wee present. A reminder ey his da. Present fr yirsel n all, that no right?

He put the developer back on to the table, settling it precisely in the ring it had left in the cloth, the dent of its weight.

I don't need reminding, Peter. Have you not noticed?

Peter went blank with judgement, contemptuous of her weakness, she thought, disgusted by her. She sat in the chair before the table, but he settled down on his haunches in front of her so she couldn't get away from it; he was lower than her, an adult's lowliness. It reminded her of her da speaking to his daughter; she brought her arms loosely across her, just in case.

A noarml ma'd buy a train set. You're gonny take wee pictures fr him.

Peter was only an amateur when it came to intimidating her; she felt able to speak up for herself,

You can't tell me what my own son would like for his birthday, Peter Caulder.

Peter's mouth twisted. He stood up slowly, and then went towards the bed, where he stripped away his jumper, up over his head, sending a reek of sweat and linseed and turpentine towards her. He flattened the jumper on to the quilt, folded its arms behind it, folded it small, and then put it on to the seat of his chair before the fire. He was wearing a vest underneath, into which paint had seeped.

Ye waant yir bed afore r efter dinner?

He pulled the vest over himself, but it'd been a while since Catherine had had any comfort in that bed with him. She shook her head deliberately, turned herself in the chair towards her day's shopping on the table.

I want dinner before bed, Peter.

He went towards the wardrobe, picking out clean clothes. She felt the frustration in him, but it was his own fault for his cheek.

Fourteen

Peter thought he knew Catherine well enough, but until the time she saw herself in the studio, he'd thought she was harder than to be disturbed by ghosts and shadows.

It wasn't as if she'd had no experience with mirrors. He'd seen her applying her make-up in the wee tile of glass he'd hung from the handle of the wardrobe. She did it every morning before she went to work while he was resting in bed. One artist recognized another, and the process genuinely fascinated him, how she dipped her hand into her cosmetics purse, a fortune of the stuff to spend on her face. When she'd finished, she'd turn to him, she'd her back to him the whole time and he didn't know what was coming, and she'd smile and say, will I do, d'you think? and she knew herself, she just knew she looked a million dollars. If all this palaver had just been pure and simple vanity, he'd've said, away wi ye, hen, away n clean that muck aff yir face, just to take her down a peg or two, but he knew there was more to it than just look at me. She primed her skin the way he primed his canvases; foundation, pale if she was wanting a blush in her cheeks, tinted if she wanted to seem affluent. She knew all the painter's tricks, how to cast a light over whatever she wanted you to notice, how to hide in shadow if she didn't want you prying, a hundred others like the proper emphasis for her eyes, how to make you notice she had a brow that was high and intellectual, even if there wasn't a thought in that smart-looking head that hadn't been put there by Saint Francis of fucking Assisi, no matter, she'd just paint herself differently to become the kind of wee girl you'd think would need teaching. She'd even learned the most difficult trick of all, and that was the knack of applying make-up so it didn't appear to be there at all; that was her true face, you would've sworn, unless you knew the woman who'd gone to the glass, so that when she turned to him, not just was it a different face, it was a different woman from the one who'd turned the morning before, and you'd know the voice, and a way of smiling, and little else. No wonder, Peter thought, Saint Francis of Assisi hadn't refused her a thing; bastard would scarcely've been able to believe his luck, he'd married a hundred women instead of just one, different enough to keep life interesting from day to day.

It took a while before Peter discovered the truth about Cathy; that her faces weren't always the simple declarations they seemed to be. If she was bringing emphasis to the brow, her bluestocking look as he called it though not to her face, it'd likely be on a day when she felt stupid and vulnerable, so she was making a canvas of herself right enough, and the work that was being executed on it wasn't a display of knowledge, it was a fear of ignorance, of giving off ignorance like other folk were minutely calibrated detectors of it, like those machines that stammered nervously over the presence of radiation. If she painted a glamour over herself, dark like a gipsy and with the mouth full-blooded with lipstick, it'd be the morning after she'd said to him she sometimes felt she was as plain as an envelope, she'd turn around to him and he'd go poker-hard under the blankets and he wouldn't want her to go to work, he'd want her to stay with him in bed; if she said she thought she looked sluttish and too available, men's eyes drilling her to mine the sex from her, then she'd go artless, would seem lacquered and beyond touch like the virgin in a pietà, beyond defilement, to be either adored or broken but never violated.

Peter couldn't help but admire her art, the knowledge that made her into a creature blending in with her worst fears of herself; but there were times when he wondered if there was a centre to her, a point to which all this experimentation with her own nature might be anchored, the way he had his ideals, his faith in the masses to anchor him. He remembered the times she'd stroll around his gallery, and she'd ask what such and such a painting meant, and he felt like when you draw your finger across a page and it slices you, and you stare at the blood and think it strange how a thing not meant for harm can turn on you like that. He went like a wean again playing that hand game for deciding arguments; paper cuts flesh but fist crushes paper, and he said, hark at the peyntit lady, and she turned solemn on him, said, it's not the same thing, that's just make-up, but he told her it was art just the same, more devious than his if anything. He couldn't make folk come to his, but her art was more like advertising on a hoarding, she was an advertisement for herself, she could be loved or hated for her face but she couldn't be ignored. So there was his art, honest in its intentions and the awareness it brought folk, hidden away like a secret, and there was her art, a whisper to herself that cried out to strangers. He said she should know that, just as she chose a face to wear, he had to choose faces for his canvases, and just as folk would judge her on her chosen face, so they would him by the faces he chose for his canvases, and he chose the face of his principles sooner than the face of his vanities.

He'd half expected a telling for that bit of cheek, even if he did believe the truth of his side of it, but she went serious and quiet for the rest of the evening, and the woman that turned to him the next morning was the one with the attention drawn to her brow, as if to remind herself as well as him how full of knowledge she was. This time she said, what d'you think? and the stylus skipped in the groove this early in the morning and he realized she meant what did he think of her and not what were his ideals and philosophies, and he said, beautiful, darlin, jist plain beautiful, and then came the smile, as if she'd been appreciated for the self she'd wanted to project to him rather than the self he knew her to be. That was when Peter first thought he had to make himself understand her, work on her the way he worked on the likes of Elvis and all his images of folk, and if there was a centre to her, a place she was anchored to, then he was the one to find it, because it was clear to Peter that, for all his unquestioning adoration of this woman, and the kind of naïve eyes that only ever saw the Madonna in her, Saint Francis of fucking Assisi hadn't ever come close.

Then she started acting funny; not long after she'd had that shock in the studio, the apparition no one else saw. The next morning after that, she went to the glass as usual. Peter was a witness to it from the bed, he'd been looking forward to the show, to guessing what was going to turn to him today; but it was as if the image in the glass had spat in her eye, she turned almost immediately and she was so pale you'd've thought she'd chosen a corpse's face for today, she was blinded to herself, couldn't even stare herself in the face, and she took the make-up purse over to the window and stared into that, into nothing, choosing this bottle, that blush, dabbing herself. When she turned, she said quickly, I have to go to work now, greased herself across his sight so he couldn't see what her final choice had been. On her way out, he told her not to worry if he wasn't in the room, he might be working in the studio this evening finishing Elvis; she listened to him from behind the door, said, all right, I'll make dinner for you when I come back, and then she left, closing the door behind her with emphasis.

He tried to take photographs of her with his eyes in the mornings, thinking if Codie could do it then why not him, so no matter how quickly she moved he'd have a picture of her to study later. He caught it one morning when she was careless; the easiest face she could manage, a bridal face, with fire in the cheeks, blue on the lids of her eyes; a recreation of innocence like a plastic doll your mammy would give your sister for her birthday. By the time she was back from her work and dinner was made, her face was beginning to erode badly; running in the heat from the coffee maker. There was darkness in her cheeks, and she was leaving half her plate uneaten, so he was becoming fat on her misery; but he knew what had to be done once he'd got Elvis out of the road, and the conviction only hardened with what he saw of her when he came in once his day's work was over. She looked like a cigarette with lipstick on the filter crushed out into an ashtray. Her morning face was rotted away by this time in the evening, the make-up gone to powder and grains, leaving welts and scars of her real flesh underneath, her mouth smeared like a wean eating strawberry ice-cream.

Peter would've felt pity for the state of her, if he hadn't been in a state himself with all the work. It was as if everything around him was pictured in stained glass like the window of a cathedral, bold forms with thick outlines like the borders of nations, thin colours barely lit from behind with candles. Mired in that kind of exhaustion, where even the skin holding you together was weary with effort, he became hard and unforgiving, and Catherine's frailty seemed to make her precious and childish to him, the kind of indulgence you'd give a wean a good shaking for giving in to.

His long hours made him as weak in his thinking as her, and he'd no one else to blame for it but himself. It was the work softening him; but he'd never felt so much like the masses before, he wasn't apart from them in a way that made them regard him as a kind of insane priest or minister or someone eaten from within by a vocation. The only thing that separated him from the working man was the wage packet, which was quite a significant separation in Catherine's mind since they'd only her income to rely on, but otherwise he was a working man; waking for the work, in his own wee workshop, and he was coming home at night with a good kind of tiredness about him to a house that was well maintained, there was a dinner on the table and a woman who was nearly his wife waiting for him when he finished the late shift; he was grateful for it, even grateful for the exhaustion that kept him apart from her. There was a kind of settled clockwork to his days now, the spinning of a perfectly circular movement, levers tripping in order and at expected times. He'd know the hour and the minute by the front door closing which meant she was home from work herself, and he'd know she was in for a half-hour when the smell of cooking seeped in under the studio door, knew that an hour had passed by her tapping, your dinner's ready, then back for more work until the tiredness made claws of his hands, and then it'd be time to go to bed after he'd rested for a while.

At least, he was thinking, it wasn't that bourgeois whoredom his mother had sold herself into; pure pipe and fucking slippers job that had been, no joke, like she was the keeper of a guest-house dedicated to the comfort of one resident. She tried new recipes for him, settled his slippers in front of the fire, had the delivered morning paper folded for him and waiting on the arm of his chair, the ashtray on the other arm fine and clean so he could manky it again with those Secret Service fags or whatever the fuck you called them. Catherine should be grateful she wasn't getting that fussy cunt Reginald as her man. He celebrated Christmases like an Englishman, trussed up in paper garlands and ribbons like he'd learned how to do it from Dickens, and he hardly celebrated Hogmanay at all, one wee sherry at the bells and that was the extent of his acknowledgement of the festival; feared of the whisky, Peter thought at the time, feared he was unwrapped to his rotten core like those gifts in paper he tried to bribe his stepson with the week before, and which were always thrown back in his face unless they were to do with painting.

He'd seen enough of the ideal marriage, the possessiveness and self-centredness that came with it, to be circumspect in his choice of women; but the day Catherine stopped wearing her different faces, and in the days that followed when her face remained the same, Peter found himself thinking maybe this place was where she'd dropped her anchor, and the notion made him feel stupidly pleased with himself. He'd thought this new face of hers, never varying from day to day, was a declaration of purpose on her part; maybe she was achieving this centredness she'd been lacking before, and he couldn't help but hope that her life with him, this almost marriage they had together, he was the centre she'd found. He even imagined she could have the wee one living here with her; he thought the two of them, him and Cameron, were much alike, both mourning still for the deaths of their fathers. He wouldn't make the mistakes Reginald had made, of bribery and outright replacement; he'd be a friend to the wee one, his newest china, he'd be understanding of the wee one's predicament, and in time he could maybe be a teacher in the manner of Saint Francis. He wouldn't try to rub out the lessons of his blood father, because that would be a certain way to turn the wee one against him, but he'd remind the wee one that there were other ways of seeing the world. Maybe Cameron could have Marx as a scripture, and when he'd grown up maybe he could explain it to his dottery old stepfather, since for all Peter recognized the greatness of old Karl's work, he'd never ventured further than a couple of chapters into it.

There was once, that Reginald and his mother had come to his final-year exhibition of work at the art school, before Reginald had bought him the house; he couldn't stop them, since it was a public show, but he wanted them to come, so they could read the messages in the pictures and understand finally how much he hated all their graces. Reginald and his mother went from work to work, not just his but the others as well; Reginald pretended to cover his eyes like see no evil when he stopped at the works of students who'd chosen as their influences the abstract painters flinging paint in your eyes, and Peter never liked him more than when he realized that Reginald hated the sterile modernity of them as much as he did himself. Finally they came to Peter's works; they soared over his mother's head like a flight of eagles, but Reginald stood back from them, gave them the dignity of his full attention, came closer to them as if they were whispering truths in his ear. At last they were finished; Reginald and his mother came over to him, his mother looking at him from under her toque hat and through her veil, they're awful good, son, but Reginald took a long draw on his fag, and he breathed it out all over Peter, I never realized what an evangelist you are, my boy, but I suppose it makes sense, you always were disdainful of worldly goods, perhaps there's more of God in you than you realize yourself. Peter asked him how he'd derived that from the paintings, and Reginald smiled; his hands were fastened behind his back in a gentlemanly manner, until he had to bring his hand around to place the cigarette between his lips and draw from it. You cannot share a house with anyone, he said, even one who spent most of the time imprisoned in his own room, without coming to some sort of understanding of them. You will never know, or appreciate, how much I admire the strength of will and the discipline you have shown through the years, even as you will never know how much it pains a man whose work revolves around keeping his clients out of gaol to find that he can barely persuade his stepson to give himself time off a sentence of his own choosing for good behaviour. However, there is much of you that I recognize in your work, which is hardly surprising to me. You were always concerned with the poor, most especially when I gave you gifts which you deemed too expensive; I always used to say to your mother that there were two occasions I could look forward to a good sermon, and those were when we went as a family to the church, and when you were displeased at some purchase I had made which you considered to be excessive. (Reginald smiled at that, obviously a joke by the way he judged things; the curious thing was, Peter smiled too, despite himself, more at the memory.) I must say that you have taken the gifts your father gave to you by the circumstances of your birth sooner than those I offered through the circumstances of affluence, and made excellent use of them, and I believe that if he were here in my place he would have been very proud to have had a son who expressed himself with such clarity and depth of passion.

At the time, Peter was quite moved, even if it had been said in the manner of a solicitor closing an argument, thanked Reginald genuinely for the first time ever, but it was a kind of formal admission on both their parts, like heads of conflicting states agreeing a temporary truce; the war began in earnest not long after, but Peter quite fondly remembered that moment of peace when the weapons were laid aside and he discovered that, in his cups when they went to the bar afterwards, Reginald could be halfway decent, even as Peter's mother was shocked by the joking man the modest amount of drink liberated from her husband. Peter resolved that, as Reginald had conducted himself on that day, so he'd be with Cameron the whole time, honest and affectionate, talking to an equal sooner than he'd come the substitute father with him; and Reginald had been right about his stepson, there was something of the preacher in him, as much as Peter suspected there'd been a wee bit of the college lecturer in Saint Francis, and Peter made this promise to himself and to Catherine, that the wean's moral education would be his as well as hers, so when the wee man was birthed from the house, from his home rather, he'd enter the world a confident adult from whom no secrets had been kept, and who'd know that world for the corrupt place it was, and what was to be done about it.

Except he never got the chance to tell Cathy any of his wishes for her and Cameron, because it became apparent after not too long that if this constant face of hers was a bride's, then the man for whom she'd composed it was dead and buried, and it was sure as fuck not Peter.

He caught her with a note of paper on her lap; his eyes were too tired to see properly what it was, but after a time he became accustomed to the dark, and anyway she turned it to him; the nearly dissolved image of her wedding day, the flayed emulsion on which you could still make her out in monochrome, Francis standing beside her in an unaccustomed suit, and she said,

Francis hated wearing that suit; said he felt like a lunatic in a strait-jacket,

and she was smiling all across her smeared mouth, and Peter tried to smile with her, but she'd cut him again, the daft bitch, and she was all innocence about it. In bed, he cooried up to her, needing her to let him know that she was still aware of his wants, but she threw him away and turned on her side away from him, said she was tired and had to have some sleep so she could be up for work tomorrow; only there was no work tomorrow, it was a Saturday and she wouldn't be needed unless Gianfranco had an emergency. Peter turned his back on her, one bad turn deserving another, and in the darkness Peter thought he'd have to die himself before he'd ever be considered a tenth as kindly as Saint fucking Francis. He went to sleep thinking that this centre to her was still evading him, that maybe she was like a concave lens with its centre of focus away from the eye instead of within it; that maybe Francis had been her centre and now she was blind to what she had in front of her. He had this plague of thoughts before he went to sleep, and when he wakened the next morning, she was already in the kitchen, with not a wipe of make-up on, frying rashers of bacon, two for each of them arranged like quotation marks in the pan and cracking eggs into the centre of them in an exclamation of hot fat, while Codie worked on the picture that might be his last work the rate he was going at it. Peter sat at the table and thought she was running like a tram on its rails, remembering services she performed for Saint Francis and which now she performed for him as if the altar had burned down and her best means of accepting the fact was to undertake the same rites in another parish, making do with him.

And then came this business of the pinhole camera, not long after she'd refused to model for him; Peter hadn't the least fucking clue what she thought she was playing at. Why she couldn't just use a Kodak, or even the Kodak he had in his wardrobe, like everyone else, Peter couldn't understand; she said that wasn't the point, the picture wasn't the whole reason why she was doing it, and Peter threw up his hands and said, Well, whit is yir reason fr dayn it? and all she could do was sit and make a wean's moony eyes at him, as if he'd asked a thing beyond her present understanding, but that she'd be able to answer in a year or two, once she'd remembered it and her comprehension had matured enough for her to draw the right meaning from his question.

By this time, Peter had another canvas to work on. By its very nature he had to keep it behind closed doors, and he'd persuaded Codie to forgo his studio time with a promise that Codie'd get two pictures' worth out of his next shift. Codie'd been hoping for a shot at the room he'd made possible, but at the speed he worked he'd make those two canvases last until the end of the year, and the immediacy Peter needed to make this work a success would be lost. It would completely upset the symmetry of his gallery once it was finished, but that didn't matter to him; this was a work of dedication he was embarking on, and better yet it might even be heading in a direction that would please MacHenery, that he could settle on top of his desk in his wee gallery office and say, there, ya fat pig, sell that, n tell me that's derivative ey fucken genre peyntn.

In the meantime, he'd this obsession of hers to come home to every night. The problem was, she'd told Codie all about it once when she was in the kitchen making dinner, and he was already beginning to fall for the charms of her wee experiment, as Peter called it; trust one fucking camera to seduce another. Peter waited until she was away at her work before he stole into the kitchen and gave Codie into trouble for supporting her, but Codie looked up at the ceiling, said, look, man, you're fuck all company fr her the way y'are jist noo, n I think it's a brilliant idea, so gie her a fucken brek n lee her somethn tay day wi her evenins, and Peter thought they'd all been touched by the same kind of madness that drives moths to burn themselves against light bulbs, and hoped he wouldn't be next to catch it.

And then the weekend came; the house was awful quiet for most of the day, and Peter heard voices as giggly as weans taking their first secret draw off a fag from outside in the hall when the light was beginning to fail and he had to switch on the overhead bulb so he could see what he was doing. He didn't want them spoiling his attention on the canvas; he worked until he couldn't tell the time, and his hands were in an old biddy's arthritic clutch, aching with being seized around brush and palette. He couldn't even tell the time reliably from the amount of work he'd done; some effects took long repetitions to accomplish and others a wee dash of the brush, and he was so tired he couldn't remember how long ago or in what order. The only thing he could think of at this time was his bed, and he went through his usual ritual of protecting the canvas, cleaning the brushes, covering the palette, and when he switched out the light, he could've pictured himself in bed already, dreaming of being up on his feet, so weary that he was dreaming of wakefulness.

Codie and Catherine were in the room together when he entered, and immediately he came in their talking stopped as abruptly as if they'd been planning his murder. Peter halted at the door; he began to feel like a prisoner newly come out of the gaol, not knowing if he still had a wife and weans or not. He began to search around the room, and all he could see were Codie in his chair, with his hands on his lap and the fingers steepled as if he'd cause for satisfaction, and Catherine in her usual place, turning herself around so she could see him coming in, and she was smiling for the first time in ages. The air in the room tasted of vinegar, and Peter wondered if they'd gone to the chip shop for their dinner; he realized he hadn't eaten himself for hours, and as if his belly had just realized too it made a wild sounding roar, which made Codie fall back into the chair with a farting laugh, and which caused Catherine to roll in her seat with glee, wiping the hair from her face. Peter felt excluded, like the ill-fitting wean in a playground, the one always kept away from secrets and jokes so he could be a joke to everyone else, and he couldn't've been less in a mood for it, hungry and tired as he was.

Whit huv the weans been playn at while I've been away? he said. No at keepn hoose, that's fr bloody sure, else I'd'uv hud my dinner by noo.

Peter stood over by his chair, staring down on Codie until the signal was transmitted, the insistence of it received and understood, roger and fucking out, that he was expecting his seat back. Codie stood up from it, passed around the front of Peter. Catherine kicked her legs under the legs of her chair to allow him past, and Codie

308

negotiated his way around them both towards the straight-backed chair, turning it around to face them both, more towards Catherine than Peter.

Heh, I'm soarry, big man, he said. Jist, there wis some good work bein done, we've no eaten oorsels. Here's yir dinner.

Codie reached behind him to gather an apple, sitting on top of one of the smaller books from his library, perched at the very end of the table nearest the window. The next thing, Codie tossed it like a rubber ball for Peter to play catch with, and Peter flailed out a hand; missed completely, blunted by tiredness, and it beat against his leg, lodged itself in his lap. Peter picked the apple out of his lap by its stem, held it up and stared at it, and that set Codie and Catherine off again, to see him consider how it'd landed there.

He aimed it so it would reflect off her shoulder, and the world was all sound after that; the hard contact of it against her, the dunt it made as it fell into the pen of the hearthside tiling, her yelping and the hand over her mouth clutching herself where she'd been hit. It had the proper sobering effect he'd been after; Catherine turned small and wary in her seat, and Codie tightened, making fists and sitting up straighter in his chair, that daft wee grin abolished, and Peter sat taller with the sense of discipline returning to his court. He brought his eyes around to Catherine; her hair was all over her face, her head bent low, and he thought he saw that her make-up was intact, for a wonder. She was looking sullenly into her lap, and he was thinking he'd no pity to waste on folk who pitied themselves so much that they hadn't enough to spare for the rest of the world.

A proapr fucken dinner, I'm meanin, he said, no food fr fucken hoarses. Whit the fuck kin ey work wis it ye'd miss yir ain dinner fr, leave alane mine n all?

He ate the apple while Codie guided him towards the gallery Catherine had made over the headboard; Catherine sat in the chair, still tending to her arm. She'd already put up her wee performance of being offended by his rotten tongue, and he'd apologized immediately, for that and for chucking the apple at her; but when he discovered he'd thrown the object of her first still-life exercise at her, realizing as soon as Codie brought him over to the pictures above the bed, he went back to the hearth and picked it up, polished it against his shirt, fixed her in the eye and said,

Thanks fr dinner, Codie man,

and deliberately ate a bite from it; the hair was a black hood over her, and from under it she managed to look murderous and fearful, as if she was seeing something else mapped on to him, a different man maybe. Peter followed behind Codie until he was standing near this pathetic wee gallery which was made up of three prints of the apple, all formed into a triangle. Nothing seemed to be supporting them on the wall except Catherine's wish for him to see them, but Codie said it was just Sellotape doubled on itself. He pointed to the first of them, on the left base of the triangle; Peter took a big scooping bite out of the apple, you could hear him tear into it, and tilted his head. It looked like the image had been scorched into the emulsion, the apple served on the photograph charred black as if there'd been heat along with the light of exposure. Peter laughed, said,

Aye, there wis somethn burnin in the oven right enough, n it wisny my dinner.

Codie looked over to the chair, said shut it to Peter with his mouth but not with his voice; Peter shrugged, no matter to him what he said in his own room, but from behind him came a wee voice,

I hope that's the last I hear about your bloody dinner tonight, Peter Caulder.

At last she knew how it felt, when you said something offhand and folk got hurt by it; Peter threw his reply over his shoulder:

Gie us peace, you. Be mare ey a wife tay a man, n no so much ey a bloody hobby hoarse.

He winked to Codie, out of sight of Catherine; Codie shook his head, and moved him on to the next of the prints, to the right of the triangle. This one, he explained, had been wrong the other way, too cautious, and Peter had to bend close to see anything in it at all. He thought it must've been taken while there was still daylight, from the way the shadow was clutched around the back of the apple; the apple itself was so ghostly you'd imagine that if you stared hard enough you'd make out the seeds in the core. It was flat and empty like Peter's first sketches as a boy, and he forced the air from the side of his mouth to show he wasn't impressed. Catherine came around by the bed to sit on the mattress by Peter's side, said,

That one was just, what d'you call it, like a test.

Yir sense ey coamposition's shite, by the way.

That'll come later, I hope. You can be a critic later as well, when I start doing this seriously.

Peter looked down at her; took another bite from the apple, showed her not long to go before it was eaten down to the hourglass of the core.

Fine, I'll mind that. I'm no gonny go easy oan ye, mark my words. Right, so this wan wisny cookt right. Next.

This wan, said Codie, came oot the oven right enough. Feast yir f, em, feast yir eyes oan this, ya cheeky c, em, ya cheeky bugger ye, n shut the f, em, shut the hell up aboot yir fat belly lik the lady tells ye tay.

At least you could tell what this one was meant to be. To Peter's eye, it seemed almost as if the image had been painted on to the emulsion; there were no harsh edges like you'd expect from a photograph taken the usual way. If this had been done by a painter, he'd've said without hesitation that whoever it was he was a sloppy workman, or at least one who was enthused by everything he saw, there was no discernment between the differing elements of the composition, nothing to show the camera's interest in a particular object to the unfocused exclusion of all else; it had the democratic interest of the painter's eye, this box of tricks of hers, but there was nothing sharp in the foreground, everything was a monument but nothing was monumental, the same weight and emphasis had been brought equally to bear on the apple, the book, the table, the grid of the window, and this made the whole execution seem curiously flat to him, with no sense of layering by which you could tell the distance from the apple to the window, or from the window to the sky outside. He drew his finger over the print to illustrate with lines of his own, scrawling his authority over her work, and then pinched the core of the apple between his thumb and forefinger and took the last bite out of it that revealed the seeds, staring at Catherine as if to dare her to say he of all people was wrong.

Catherine stood up from the bed, slowly, with a look on her as if it'd been a beating he'd just handed out to her. She stood opposite him, but he wasn't going to indulge her with pity or favours, not if she was fishing for them. Finally she went to the door, and then shut it with a crash that reverberated around the house and knocked several of his pictures out of square. Peter laughed, looked sideways at Codie as if, what was that all about, and then leaned over to arrange his pictures back to true; when he turned round, Codie was on the boil, looking Peter up and down slowly and analytically, like the box taking the picture of a bastard.

Go you the fuck oot ey this room n talk tay her,

he said. Peter wondered if this was another crisis in the house, of the kind that'd led to Heidless's leaving.

R else whit? he said. Whit's gonny happen?

R else, said Codie, gently, ye're gonny huv wan big hoose tay yirsel.

How, you gonny run away wi her?

Codie shook his head this time, as much in pity as denial.

I vowed tay mysel I'd niver stey in anither hoose wherr a wummn gets treatit lik shite again.

It wis jist a fucken aipple I chuckt at her, man.

Gie yir excuses tay her, no me. Aw aye; n sayn soarry widny go amiss neether, ye no think so yirsel?

Peter didn't know what she was going to be like. He was half feared she'd be waiting for him behind the kitchen door with a knife, or worse that she'd be sitting at the table crying her eyes out; didn't know if he'd be hardening himself against her or defending himself against her, and he hesitated before going in, but Codie might've mistaken that for him believing himself in the wrong. He thought he'd get the apology over with as quickly as possible so they could all get to their beds, and he might even deliver a wee compliment to her about how much work she'd put into it, though he was fucked if he was going to encourage her to waste her time on it, the way Codie had. He opened the door, but the kitchen was dark, and there wasn't the least sign of her, although he made sure by putting on the light. Codie said,

I know wherr she'll be, you've no been there but I huv,

and led Peter to the bathroom, stood to one side, nodded towards the handle; this was his job, after all, not Codie's. Peter gripped the handle and pushed open the door, went forward again even as he saw no light on in the room,

Doot she's no here neether, Codie,

he said, and then suddenly the darkness wrapped itself around him, and he felt like one of the treasury of insects in the webs Cathy tore away in Heidless's room, caught in strands and pulling away for his life. By the time he realized he'd walked into a black woollen curtain, Codie was helping him pull it to one side, here ya eejit, and the light inside the bathroom revealed the extent of the changes in making a darkroom of it, as well as Catherine sitting on the lavvy pan, and he was thinking, at least he hadn't caught her making use of the amenities.

There were three trays of hard black plastic in the bath, upside down like tortoiseshells after having been rinsed. There was a light fixed to the wall near the door, dark red like a blood blister, and it was fixed into the plaster by four screws, with a cable down the wall to where it coiled at the foot of the bath; alongside the cable was another one, and then the antique lightbox which was on an elongated crane to make it look down at the prints, and then another cable belonging to an extension lead to which the whole cluster, Peter supposed, was fixed, drawing electricity from the socket in the hall. The smell which had reminded him of vinegar was more powerful in the confines of the bathroom, like a breath of glass dust, and it was more chemical in nature, making quite the wee laboratory out of the place. There wasn't just the one curtain in the room; there was another over the window behind the porcelain throne, cut to fit over the casement, held by drawing-pins; he turned to look behind him, at the curtain he hadn't been able to tell from lights out, and saw that it had been nailed into the lintel to keep the room lightfast. Catherine was seated on the throne, glowering at him as he came to her along the avenue behind the bath and the wall.

Peter genuflected in front of her on one knee the way Catholic folk blessed themselves before the Virgin in chapel. It was a false supplication, because he was still convinced she was on the wrong road, but he was too tired for any more argument with her or Codie.

He thought she might've been afflicted by a passing madness; he just needed enough peace in the house to allow him to finish the canvas in the studio, and then he could show her what all the exhaustion and the long hours had been for. Codie could have the room then, and he'd have the time and the patience to explain to her why there was nothing of value to be seen through the eye of her camera; he'd explain it kindly to her, the way Saint Francis had explained things to her son, that pictures that excluded folk because they were too slow to print on the film were a debasement of all he believed was truthful in art, and she was engaged in art right enough, even if she didn't know it herself. He'd take the camera out of her hands, as gently as you'd strip a knife from the hands of a wean, and tell her that it was dangerous and a lie because it made a virtue of stone, and made invisible the folk that gave the stone meaning; treated them like lice that infested towns and cities, rather than builders and makers of communities. He'd comb through her hair with his fingers, and tell her it was all right, he understood she was only trying to bring Cameron closer to her, there was no shame in wishing your son was near you, but this wasn't how it was done, not by demonstrations to yourself of how you'd let him do now what you'd denied him in the past, and he'd tell her there'd be a day when Codie might be after a place to himself, and the bed in the kitchen would be waiting for her to collect the wee one. All this he'd tell her later, once his work on that fucking canvas was completed, but for now he reached out to touch her hands, and tried to let her see in his eyes that there were reasons for his concerns, that it wasn't just cruelty for the sake of it, and that he was sorry for his behaviour.

Come tay bed, Cathy.

Catherine pulled her hands away from him, held herself in her arms, excluding him again.

I was a wife to a man, Peter Caulder, she said, don't you forget it, because I'm no wife to you. Leave me be, and I'll come to bed when I'm ready.

Peter bowed his head, looked down to the linoleum, the green dappled pattern like the sun through branches. If he'd known which cemetery Saint Francis was resting in, he'd've gone there with a hammer that very moment, broken the grave marker into dust and gravel, defiled it with his pish. Catherine's hair was all he could see of her, black as the curtain he'd stumbled over on his way in. He stood up, and went to the end of the room, hearing his own feet solid on the floor. Codie was holding the black cloth to one side so he could leave, closed the door behind him once he was through.

Efter the night, said Codie, it's a fucken miracle she's comin tay ye at a'.

Go you tay yir fucken bed, said Peter. If it wisny fr you, there widny be the need fr fucken miracles.

Codie stood firm, his eyes level on Peter. At last he turned, and went to the kitchen. Peter leaned against the jamb of the bathroom door, and he was thinking, she'd her own studio now, dark where his was bright, and he wondered if he'd ever see her outside of it, now she'd learned to make pictures for herself.

Fifteen

Agnes had almost forgotten Kate, outside of her prayers, when she saw her through the window that Sunday afternoon. The smell of the roast was prowling around the house, and she'd read as much as she cared to of the Sunday paper. Cameron was in his room, doing his homework for the day after; Daniel was in the shed, getting to grips with his tele, had this idea in his head that he could turn it into something else with just a wee bit application, and she couldn't even pronounce what he was planning to make of it. That left the daftie to sit around, not even able to do the front garden; some weeds had woven themselves into her beds of daffodils and crocuses, but the ground would be thick with wet so she wouldn't be able to pick them out, which left her to read the Sunday Post so hated by Daniel. Whit's the voaice ey the kirk n the damned Tories sayn the day? he'd sigh if he caught her looking at it, but Cameron liked the cartoons of Oor Wullie and The Broons, even if he didn't like the stories. Weans were like that, they loved pictures, and Cameron won the paper its reprieve, and besides she thought Daniel secretly enjoyed reading it so he could tear his fingers across the wee itch it gave him.

So she'd finished the paper, and she was crossing to the living-room window just to see if the rain had slackened. The cloud was torn across in places like an old sheet, giving her hope she could fetch the trowel from the cupboard and claw out the weeds before they throttled the life out of her spring plantings. She saw the woman coming along the road and thought she had a familiar kind of high-heeled practice to her walk, and it wasn't until she got close enough for Agnes to see that it wasn't a black hood over her head, but black hair with water pouring over her shoulders, that Agnes came to think, Kate never did suit her hair long; and she realized it wasn't a memory of Kate, it was Kate herself, and Agnes took a step away from the window so quickly you'd've thought Daniel had electrified the frame.

Agnes splintered into pieces with all the things she wanted to do before Kate arrived. She made for the sofa, to settle the cushions upright and plump them; cancelled it as she remembered the kitchen, wondering if she'd cleared away all the scraps and peels; cancelled that to feint to the bathroom, to see if the porcelain was clean; she was rooted to the spot by the futility of doing anything when Kate would be here in a few steps. She wondered if Kate had seen her at the window, thinking if not then she might have time to run upstairs and tell Cameron to come down, but she couldn't even make herself do that. The moment passed as she began to wonder why the hair oil she should feel so small in comparison to a woman who'd left her son and then disappeared for months on end, when the apology should be on the other foot, you might say. She hardened herself, decided the only thing she'd have time to prepare was her own appearance, and looked in the mirror over the settee, to see what kind of state she was in.

Agnes worked her hands through her hair, the copper beehive she'd recently had done after seeing it on a girl on the tele. She'd lacquered it earlier in the day for going to church, so a quick brushing up with the tips of her fingers did the trick. She looked down herself, to the brown sweater she'd changed into after returning from mass, and the black slacks; flicked away lint and oose, looked past herself to the floor, to see if there was dust on it. The last thing she did was to take a long breath, closing her eyes and praying hard that it wasn't Kate after all, God forgive her. If it was, then she prayed that no secrets would come up in the conversation, and that Kate would have no suspicions that Agnes knew anything about the reason for their mother-in-law's visit early in the new year.

A while ago, Agnes had bought new door chimes with Daniel's discount from the electrical store he worked at. She'd brought Cameron along with her the Saturday she went to buy it, so she could kill two birds with one stone: Cameron could see where his uncle worked and she could choose a nicer sound for answering the door. Cameron had gone to the wall, where you'd think the entire store was built out of the luminous bricks of tele sets. The three channels were repeated over and over, but the multiplied pictures fascinated Cameron, and one out of every three pictures was in colour, even if those sets were only displaying a test pattern. When he came back to the counter, he had a pleading face on him, and she knew he was too young to understand the notion of working to save money. To distract him, she asked him which of the chimes fixed to a pegboard display on the counter he preferred, and Daniel lofted him so he could sit on the counter beside them and press the buttons. The one she chose was different from his choice; they all played different songs on tubular bells, but she liked the one that sounded like Big Ben, the beginning of the hour being rung, and he liked one that sounded as bad as the one she was getting rid of. Cameron asked Daniel, had he made all the tele sets and the gramophone cabinets in the shop, and that made Daniel laugh; no, he said, but he could make more than that if he was given enough time in the shed. He put the bell in on the Sunday, and got Cameron to help him sort out the screws to fix the stud on the outside, and the wee croquet hoops, as he called them, for keeping the cable from the button to the chimes flush against the jamb and the skirting. That was the best weekend Agnes remembered since Cameron had arrived, because she'd felt as if they weren't just a pretend family; Cameron laughed with her and his uncle, and although Daniel hated the bell, and said he was only doing it for a quiet life, the main thing was he still did it for her, and when the job was finished he made Cameron fetch her from the kitchen so she could hear it being rung properly for the first time, which he did himself, so she could answer the door to him, and he could say, there y'are, madam satisfied noo?

The chimes sounded now and when the notes died away, it was like a choir losing its breath. Agnes looked around her living-room to see if it was fit for visitors, and decided that since she'd only tidied it yesterday, it would stand the competition with anyone else's. If Kate had the brazen cheek in her to take her to task for anything to do with Cameron's upbringing, then she'd have to tell a good story as to why as a mother she'd gone from her old address and left no word of where she'd be staying; and if they each had wrongs to tell the other, then at least both of them would be sure-footed in their grievances. All that bothered Agnes was that if they both went to confession to report their sins, then she knew which of them would find herself with a longer penance to say, and it surely to God wouldn't be her, when the steps she'd taken herself were for the good of Cameron's soul, which was more than you could say for Kate.

Kate even looked different on the threshold; she'd lost her touch with the make-up. Agnes would even've gone so far as to say she was looking whorish, trying to cover over misery with a wee bit lick of paint. The long black coat Agnes recognized, dusty and creased; the black leather handbag was fat with too much stuff, a present for Cameron maybe. Her hair was dealt over her shoulders like a mourning shawl, and the light rain was like dew through it; but her eyes had a kind of penetrating accusation that made Agnes shiver just to look at her. She'd brought funny smells to visit with her; the cinnamon perfume that Francis had liked, probably for Cameron's sake; but there was one that reminded Agnes of decorating, and she wondered if Kate had flitted to a new house, if she had the room maybe for Cameron now, the last bit of furniture she'd need to finish it.

Agnes felt the water close over her, a long drowning fall into evenings with the tele for company, no reason to go to the shed any more; more prayers said over candles for a wean to make a home inside her, and then make the house into more than just a billet. She stood determined she'd wait for the kind of civility you'd expect from a woman who'd as good as abandoned her child, who should've been approaching humble, before she'd stand out of her way.

Kate, she said, we huvny heard fae you in ages. How're ye keepin?

She seemed healthy enough; but you could cover any sins with paint that thick.

My house was burgled, said Kate, in case you were looking for me. I'm staying somewhere else for now.

I'm soarry tay hear that. Whit did they take?

Nothing, but they smashed everything that would break.

Did ye no call the polis?

What for? It wasn't fit for staying in anyway.

Did ye no think tay call us? We'd ey helped ye tidy things up.

You'd only have put it back together the way it was before. Anyway, I didn't think you wanted to hear from me. I thought first-footers were meant to wish you well for the New Year.

Agnes wished she could've maintained the indignation she'd felt before she'd heard her story, but she was guilty of too many things. She was guilty of keeping Kate away from her son; guilty of wanting Cameron to stay with them in a childless house, when he'd already helped bring her the glimpses of a father in Daniel; guilty, worst of all, of conversations with her mother-in-law behind Kate's back, and although she wouldn't be condemned in the next world for encouraging a spiritual education in the boy, she knew that in this world she'd have to answer to Kate for it.

Agnes stood to one side to allow Kate through. Kate cast around a while through the open door to the living-room while Agnes stood behind her.

I'll make us a cup ey tea n ye cn gie me yir coat. The wee yin's up the stair, dayn his homework.

Kate didn't move, either back so she could be helped out of her coat or forward into the living-room. Her face was in profile to Agnes, peering beyond her shawl of hair. Agnes had heard of folk walking around as if they were in a dream, but she'd never known the proper meaning of it until then. Kate carried a wee frown around with her, as if she'd just found herself here.

Do you have coffee?

Only her lips moved, red with lipstick. Agnes was beginning to feel afraid.

I don't, Kate, I'm that soarry, jist tea.

Kate gave a slight nod.

There's not many folk drink coffee, she said. I just began drinking it recently myself.

Agnes was beginning to wonder if Kate had gone away to have a nervous breakdown; if this was Kate back together again, glued into some kind of sane order but with chips in her nothing could fix right. She was saying things you couldn't answer back to; Agnes began to wonder if she was right in the head.

Where's Daniel?

Aye, mebbe ye'd be better keepin yir coat oan; he'd in the shed, ye know him n his wee hoabby. Ye waant me tay take tea oot tay ye r wid ye sooner see the wee yin first? I cn take tea up tay ye there, if ye waant.

Agnes took Kate through the kitchen to the back door, and opened it for her as if her sister-in-law was a child incapable of patience. Kate stepped over the threshold, and then paused for a moment, remembering what she'd wanted to say since she'd come here. She half turned, and said in that dreaming voice,

I will have him back, Agnes, and you can tell our mother-in-law that from me. Actually, I've told her already, but I've told you now, and you can tell her again, just so she knows I mean it.

Agnes watched her go towards the shed, and a memory came to her; of the day not long after Kate had been wed to Francis when Agnes found herself watching her sister-in-law burning clothes at the end of the garden, and thought she was mad then. Afterwards, she made tea for them all, and Kate offered to help wash the dishes, and while the men were away and in another room, Agnes asked her in a roundabout way what had been the meaning of it all, why burn good clothes when God knew they cost enough to buy in the shops? Kate shrugged, and explained; the cotton dress, she said, was the one she'd arrived in from over the water, and that meant she could never return home exactly the way she'd left it, and she'd been wearing the corset under her wedding dress on the day she'd been married, but the dress had been hired, and she'd never have got her deposit back if she'd burned that. Kate flushed the grit of tea-leaves into the sink from the bowl of the cup she'd been given, and seemed faintly exasperated that Agnes couldn't see what she meant. It was another journey, she said, from one place to another, or one state to another, and she didn't want to be able to pick up an object from before then and say, this is the way I was and here it is with me now; she wanted the object gone from her, and the clothes she had on were the most obvious signs because they took your shape so that folk thought of you in a particular way, a stupid wee colleen, or a bride. Agnes still didn't see why Kate couldn't've just put the clothes on the midden and let the dustmen dispose of them for her, but then Kate shrugged

321

again and said, because you can see them burning in front of you, and the warmth is their last gift before they pass from you, staring at Agnes as if she was some kind of defective for not seeing it without her help.

Agnes watched Kate knocking on the shed door from the window over the sink; filled the kettle from the tap, and wondered why Kate going mad should surprise her so much. A godless, mad woman, coming looking for her wean; Agnes thought maybe she'd reveal herself to Daniel, and then he'd have to agree the wee one could never be trusted with her again. She just wished that God hadn't answered her prayers through Kate's suffering, but then, maybe that was Kate's fault for having no God to stand in front of the blows that seemed to land on her one after the other, and for not learning to trust His judgements, and His mercy. Agnes's ma used to say that you'd have no luck at all if you turned away from God; she thought, maybe Kate had been sent to earth as proof of that, as she put the kettle on the ring of the electric cooker, and spun the dial halfway round so she wouldn't have to take the tea out too soon.

The last thing Daniel expected when the knock at the shed door came was that he'd open it on Kate. He thought it would be Agnes with a cup of tea, or Cameron to report that he'd finished his homework. He should've known it wasn't either Agnes or Cameron, because they'd've been in the shed by now. He showed her to the seat Cameron usually took; relieved to see her at last, briefly angry at her for making him invent all kinds of reasons for Cameron's sake why she hadn't come round, hadn't called on the phone even, and because he'd been worried himself. Kate knew it was only concern; Daniel would've sworn she was almost relieved to hear him raise his voice to her, as if she was waiting to confess all her sins to someone.

You look so like him, Danny, only you have the temper, and he had the patience of a saint. I wonder how that happens in families?

Daniel had never seen her so tired, wilting as if she'd had a short time of flourishing and then had only seen darkness after that, growing crooked for the want of something to lean against. Frankie had never said why she'd run so far from home, but there'd been enough in his reluctance to fill books for Daniel, and he felt like he was meeting

Kate the way she'd been before she and Frankie met, running and miserable and looking for any kindness.

Huv ye been up tay see the wee man yet?

Kate tightened her hands around her handbag settled on her lap.

I don't know, Danny. No, I mean I haven't. How's Agnes been treating him? I don't even know if he wants me as his mother.

Don't be daft, Kate, he said. Agnes is treatn him fine, but she's no his mither.

D'you think he'd rather have her as a mother?

I think I've spent lang enough tellin the wee man ye're fine, n then no bein able tay tell him how I know that. Whit the bloody hell were ye thinkin ey yirsel, Kate?

Daniel was never so relieved to hear anger in a voice; at least she was capable of being stirred.

Why don't you ask your own mother that, Danny? She seemed to think Cameron was better off under Agnes's care than mine.

He'd always told Agnes, not very original but still true, that fitting components to making a working circuit was like putting together a jigsaw; if the pieces weren't meant to go together, then the arrangement made nonsense and nothing would light up. He'd had a laugh to himself when Agnes said, but jigsaws don't light up, and she put on a wee look as if to say, there, I'm no so daft as you at times, and he said, ye know whit I mean, Agnes, jigsaws'll no make sense n circuits'll no light up if ye've no goat yir pieces right. His ma had left them to go to Kate's at New Year, and it was New Year when Kate stopped visiting the house. The light came on, and Daniel wiped his hand over his face to clean the dust from his eyes.

I could strangle thon bloody wummn sometimes, so I could. Huv I her tay blame fr cuttn yir phone wires as well?

Kate told him about the burglary. Daniel asked the same kind of things as Agnes, only he meant it; and when she told him where she'd been staying in the meantime, his hand came down over his eyes like a shutter, as if, good night, shop closed for the evening, and when he lifted it she wouldn't be sitting beside him, it'd be a brand new day and he've dreamt her coming here and telling him of all this shite happening to her. He didn't want to hear about this artist bloke who'd taken her in, didn't believe her when she said there was a room spare in the house and noticed she was careful not to say if she stayed in it or not; the first thing he said when he took his hand away and held it out to her in a pleading kind of fashion was,

Huv ye tellt Agnes this?

because he was thinking they'd never prise the wee man away from her if she even got the least wee odour of Kate living in sin with a bloke, whether it was that sort of arrangement or not. When Kate shook her head and said no, Daniel let out a breath and told her to keep it like that; something occurred to Daniel the more he learned about her circumstances, other lights coming on.

Is he a good kin ey blok, wid ye say, Kate, this Peter? Ye know Frankie wis never expectin ye tay go intay a coanvent efter, ye know, efter, but he widny'uv waantit ye fa'en in wi a mad kin ey blok neether, forgive me if it's nane ey my business.

Kate took strands of her hair in her fingers and spun them around in long black spirals. She stared directly at Danny, as if seeing him through a barbed-wire fence. By now Daniel was convinced she was needing help; and then she went into her handbag, coming away with what seemed to be postcards, which she dealt on to the bench in front of him, one after the other, sitting back as if he'd find the answer written on them.

I brought them for Cameron, she said. Tell me honestly what you think.

Catherine stood before the door, and found her hand going dead, the way it had when she'd touched the glass bark of the tree so long ago. She was wondering if she'd managed to wash the reek of chemicals from her hands, as well as the reek of Peter's touch, and before she knocked at the door she brought her hand up to smell it. She couldn't smell a thing, but she'd heard you became used to a smell so you could be living among it and not notice. She gathered the material of her coat; still nothing, and by this time she was wondering where Peter's influence on her had gone. Her breath was coming to her in short draughts the longer she waited by the door, and she stood in front of it for a long time, listening to the other side. She'd had to swallow over breath like pills that wouldn't stop falling into her mouth all the way up the stairs. She'd Daniel's reassurance that the wee one had been asking him for weeks on end if she'd been heard from, and the steps of that carried her to the room. She wondered if he could tell her feet from his aunt's or his uncle's, if she was warning him of her coming just by mounting the stairs. She used to ask to come into his room when he'd the door closed with a special knock, three quick beats, a pause and then the same three quick beats, and she thought she might do that now, just to let him know, but she decided against it, not so much afraid it would disturb him as more afraid that it wouldn't.

Cameron was sitting at the desk, boosted up by the pillows from his bed, when Catherine went in, and she wondered for a moment why her and Francis had never bought a desk for him. Catherine thought maybe she should've said something through the door, or even should've allowed Agnes to lead her, even if she didn't want Agnes coming away with the idea that a visit with her son was a privilege. He was sitting over the desk like his uncle at his bench, his fingers clawed around a pencil jutting as big as a pole beyond his hand, and she could hear the stop and start of the lead on the paper. The room appeared different since she and Francis had used it to stay over. It was softly carpeted, and the bed had a quilt cover with stars on it; the walls were newly papered with patterns of gold stars, Agnes's choice. She went further into the room, closed the door behind her, and Cameron turned to see who it was that wouldn't speak.

She was thinking, she should've noticed the black hooks around his ears from behind as soon as she came in; the way his head was tilted to see her caused gold leaf to be spread over the lenses, the reflection from the light above, and she couldn't see beyond it, making her feel doubly estranged from him. She wondered why neither Agnes nor Daniel had bothered to mention it; unless Agnes had wanted to emphasize how little she knew about her own son these days, and Daniel had been too busy worrying about her. The new spectacles were thick rectangular windows, like the spectacles you'd draw for mischief on an advertising hoarding, and the glass was only dense around his left eye. She went to the bed to sit on it; over his shoulder something sparked, drawing her attention, and she saw it was the vase placed so it was always in front of him while he was studying.

She wondered how close to his eyes he could bring it with the glasses in the way, assuming he still played with it like that; and she felt easier for seeing it there.

Catherine didn't know how she felt; guilty she hadn't been the one to notice, grateful to Agnes that she'd been so quick off the mark when the need became apparent, pleased he was at least seeing right. She bent down and gave him the hug he was expecting, and a kiss on the cheek; he clutched around her, and despite her own stern instructions to herself before she arrived that she'd keep the cork in the bottle, she felt a warmth running from her towards him. She held his head so close to her that she felt the leg of the spectacles hard against her temple; he went tight with a wee boy's embarrassment at giving in to a woman's kind of softness in himself, but his arms were more truthful, and they were like that for a while, her on her knees and him resting comfortably against her, until their coming back to each other had become established as plain as any of Francis's facts, like the spinning of the world or gravity, and Catherine held the wee one a little away from her and filled her eyes with him, the strangeness of him with the glasses on mattering nothing because he was still the same behind them.

He explained the glasses to her; the nurse coming to the school, and he'd been fine in every other way, only he hadn't been able to read below the third line of the chart after she'd covered over his right eye with her hand, the descending letters becoming a churn of lost focus, until they were obliterated by the time he'd reached the foundation of the chart. Agnes and Daniel had been informed, and he was at the optician's the first weekend after she'd received word through the post. Catherine smiled as he looked down at the floor and said in a wee voice,

I didn't like these glasses, but Aunt Agnes said they were all right. Can you see me better through them?

Cameron pushed the glasses closer to his eyes with a finger on the bridge, and then gave her his hand again. He peered at her, squinted his head to approach her differently, went nearer and then withdrew; at last he declared,

I can see you better further away. The optician said I could see things close to me without the glasses. Your hair looks different.

I haven't had it done any different.

No, I mean I see it different; I can see all the hairs. And your nose looks . . .

He hadn't the words to explain, so he put his hand in front of his face as if he was stroking a muzzle, or a beak. Catherine frowned.

I hope you're not saying I've got a big nose.

He laughed, shook his head.

No, but I can see it sticking out more. I can see everybody's nose sticking out more.

How did you see them before?

I don't know, flat, I suppose. I just didn't see them sticking out until I started wearing glasses.

Catherine laughed, and she let go of his hands, the laughter with him making her feel secure enough to leave him be, like something keeping her afloat. She was thinking, stupidly, that all her make-up would've been ruined by the crying she'd done, the mascara running in black tears on her face, but there wasn't a mirror in the room; it was a wee boy's room, with the toys familiar from home under the sideboard, and no vanities about the place that hadn't been put there by Agnes. She lifted herself back to sit on the bed, took a paper handkerchief from her handbag and tried to dab away at her eyes, but she was thinking she'd have to deal with it before she left. In a strange way, she was glad Cameron's defective eyesight hadn't been noticed before she'd given him to Agnes; almost as if he hadn't got a good look at her while she was her grieving self. She returned the handkerchief to her bag; it was streaked with black along the nap of it, but she saw the pictures in her bag, reminding her, and she said,

Remember the time you and your da and me did those things with light? From that book you brought home from school? The shoebox, remember? Your torch and the mirror?

Cameron thought for a moment; there was a wee pain in him as he brought his da to mind, but it went quickly enough, and he nodded. Catherine brought out the pictures and held them secretly towards her.

D'you remember the camera? All the palaver with the chemicals?

Cameron nodded again. Catherine stood up over him, behind him, and laid the photographs on the table of the desk over his shoulder, as she'd done earlier with Daniel, like when you play patience; he turned in his seat, watched as she put them down in order. She arranged them under his open arithmetic exercise book, tattered by previous ownership, and his jotter; he bent over them but didn't touch any, and as she went down on her haunches to see what he was thinking, she noticed that the grey daylight from the window was glazing both the pictures and his lenses, so you'd've thought it was a blind wee boy staring at blank paper.

His first question was about the black circle that girdled all of the prints. She explained it was caused by the limits of the pinprick in the face of the box; she was like Francis all of a sudden, explaining things to him, and his presence came to her like a shock, as if the separation between them had folded one on to the other, mapping Francis on to her. He liked the picture of the apple; she told him, that had been taken in the house she was staying in just now, and he angled his head towards her and frowned, the lenses clear so she couldn't take refuge behind the glare; trust him not to miss that.

Are you not staying at home? How not?

She told him bad men had come into the house and made it so it wasn't nice to live in any more, and she was staying in another house for now; told him nothing of Peter or Codie, in case he thought she'd replaced his da with another man like a piece you'd taken from a draughts board, simply said it was too wee for him to come and live with her. Cameron looked as if he was ready for tears after she'd told him, but she laid a hand on his arm and said,

There'll be another house, Cameron; come on now, what d'you think of your mammy's pictures?

She was distracting herself as much as Cameron; he turned to the other prints, and rested his elbows on the desk, his head in his hands, studied them with care, looking for his own distractions. He asked her what the next one was; the place she worked, she said, remembering Gianfranco watching her sit the box on the counter after she'd finished her work one morning when the place was empty, sighting along the long edge in such a finicky way. What you do, Catherine? he asked, his face that cloudy way when he was confused at something, and once she'd told him he smiled, ah, capisco, like Leonardo da Vinci, the camera obscura, only he use to draw and you use to take photo, and she nodded even though she didn't understand what he was meaning. She needed to take more than one before she got it perfect, just like with the apple, days it took but Gianfranco wanted to see every one of them, you say which best, he said, and I frame. She kept the most satisfactory print, the second was here with Cameron, and the third Gianfranco got for himself, hung by a chain from the shelf of the library of sweetie jars in Paradise, so that it swung back and forth every time she served a wean a poke of candy balls or soor plooms. Cameron seemed fascinated by the inside of the café; the ironing-board tables and cane seats, the frosted mirrors, even the curtain of strips that laced together and so became indistinct in the hot wind from the kitchen, spoke to him of ice-creams and cream soda floats and the kinds of treats you're bought when you've been good. She told him what Gianfranco had said, that one day she'd have to take him in for a special knickerbocker glory, and that made him sit up in anticipation, like she'd just told him the purpose for her visit that afternoon, but he'd never been a selfish wee boy, and when she told him it was three bus rides away on the other side of town he shrugged as if it didn't matter, the promise had been made and he wouldn't forget, and Catherine was thinking that was another promise she'd have to keep, apart from the one to herself about collecting him from Agnes some day.

The subjects of the next two prints, both of them taken outdoors, weren't of much interest to Cameron; the first was a church along Great Western Road, or at least as much as the box had seen of it, excluding the tall spike of the spire; the second was of the City Chambers, seen from the opposite edge of George Square, and they might have interested him more if he'd become involved in the process of gathering the image with her, but they were only pictures of buildings as far as he was concerned, and she was thinking wryly to herself that he and Peter shared that much. What did interest him, though, were the pleated smears across the faces of the prints, and he asked her what they were. She told him they were people and cars made slippery on the glossy paper like your fingers on damp ice. She asked if he remembered what the book had said about that, and he thought for a moment and then recited it back to her, that it wouldn't be a good camera for taking portraits of folk unless you used real photographic film, since they wouldn't be still long enough for the box to notice them as anything other than ghosts. You could even tell it'd been a windy day when she'd taken the picture of the City Chambers by the trees on the bordering gardens of the concourse, how the branches were whipped glassy like harp strings, and she let him in on a wee secret of its taking, that she'd put the box on the plinth of one of the statues of great men on the periphery of the square and weighed it down with a book in case it was blown away, and folk looked at her as if she was mental while she did it, all the men and women going on about their business, and the drunks who lived in the open, which made Cameron laugh, gleeful that she'd fooled all those folk into thinking she was mad when she'd a purpose in mind beyond their understanding, it quite appealed to his alienated way of thinking.

Catherine asked which of them he'd like to keep; he surveyed them one after the other, said,

All of them,

and then told her why; the apple, because he could see something of where she was staying in it; the café, to remind him he'd been promised a knickerbocker glory by her; and the two pictures from outside, because he loved the patterns folk made before the lens, the kinds of waves they made as they walked, rising and falling as they pushed off the ground on one leg and handed on the other, and Catherine knew what he meant, she'd liked that herself once the images had developed, as if folk were leaving themselves behind in the medium through which they were travelling, like aspirin dissolving in water. She reached around him and then gathered them together, dunting their edges on the table and then placing them into the palm of his hand before telling him they were all his if he wanted them, warning him against touching the emulsion surface.

That would never do, she told him, after all the hard work your mammy had taking those pictures,

and he nodded gravely, and took care of them as he took them by their blind side, and slid them on to the table.

Would you like to come with me sometime on one of my wee safaris out in the wilds? And you can help me develop the pictures afterwards, would you like that?

she said, explaining what she meant by safari, and he nodded strenuously.

Today?

he said, but Catherine shook her head. She was thinking about the house she'd come from, Peter and his jealousy of the box, his disdain for her competing gallery over the headboard, his complaining at the state of the toilet now it'd become a darkroom as well.

Soon enough, Cameron,

she said, meaning either when Peter came back from his obsession or she found another place, she didn't rightly know herself for now.

Catherine sat in the Cinerama seat of the Sunday-quiet bus, and thought back to how she'd left Cameron on the front step of the house. The rain had stopped by then, and the sun was showing through the cloud, sending down an apology of light to make up for its late arrival. Agnes stood behind Cameron so Catherine could approach him without feeling she was leaving dust all over Agnes's prized possession; and Daniel stood beside his wife to keep an eye on her, but she seemed to be subdued enough, if not in that tongue of hers.

Ye could gie us a ring next time ye're comin, n I'll make enough dinner fr us a'; r mebbe ye could gie me yir phone number, if ye've goat wan wherr ye're steyn.

Daniel looked as if he could've kicked her shins for her. He confined himself to rolling his eyes when he knew Kate was looking. They were waiting for her to make her goodbyes to Cameron, who was standing down on the path in front of her; she knew she was going to put her arms around him again, and she made it quick so she wouldn't be tempted to close the embrace around him and hoist him away, and she was gratified by the way he leaned into her again, and she couldn't resist staring up at Agnes while his head was resting on her shoulder, just to remind her to mark this date in her diary, the day she finally learned who was the right mother of the wean lodging in her house. She was still holding on to Cameron's hand when Daniel came forward and touched her arm, and said quietly,

If ye're needn someplace tay stey, mind oan here; if I cn use a shed fr a workshoap, you cn surely use oor bathroom tay develop yir

331

pictures in. Gie Agnes somethn tay day wi hersel, cleanin up efter ye.

He winked out of sight of Agnes, but Catherine could see Agnes bending towards them, her arms folded across her, her expression all made up of tight straight lines, even her eyes ruled narrow. Cameron pulled on her arm.

Remember, you promised, I can go with you when you take photos, and you have to buy me a knickerbocker glory,

and everyone laughed, except for Agnes, who saw Daniel lightening in mood now Catherine had kept up her claim on the wee one. She gave a sour wee turn of the lips as if she didn't want them to think she was dour and humourless. Catherine punctuated her leaving with a kiss on Cameron's forehead and a promise she wouldn't be so long before seeing him next time, but Cameron ran the length of the path as she clipped the gate shut behind her, and wasn't satisfied with her turning away from him, insisted on waving her out of sight around the corner towards the bus-stop.

The bus made a steep turn, tilted on its suspension, and bore Catherine towards the window, just as she was thinking of Cameron, and his new glasses, how serious they made him look. She wondered who'd given him the faulty eyes, her or Francis, and tried to remember who she'd met in either of their families who'd worn glasses; her mother-in-law, but that was the fault of age, there was no one else except for her. She wondered if it could be her own fault, since she'd never been to an optician in her life; to think she might've been imagining her sight to be perfect for all these years, when it was as Cameron said, he hadn't known any better until he'd put on the glasses in the shop.

Now she was on the bus, it was as if Catherine was sharing in Cameron's clear sight; she couldn't imagine for the life of her why she was going back to the house. It wasn't quite like living with a drunkard; but it was as if the work was affecting Peter the same as drink, the way she'd seen drink affect her father. If Peter had as much as raised a finger to her, then she wouldn't've been on this bus going back, so it wasn't a true comparison between him and her da; but they both had unpredictability, a kind of moodiness that was like a climate in the house. There were even three persons in Peter, like

Father Byrne said there were in God; three men who came in from the studio, left behind once everything of value had been spent on their work. The optimist asked for her patience, spoke as if he wanted to be healed of his isolation, pleaded with her to wait and see, the work would sell, she could give up her job at the café because he'd be earning enough for them both soon. He took both her hands in his, stared at her in a way that didn't make her feel as if she was in opposition to him, and Catherine took the assurance from him, said, then this had better be worth all the waiting and the secrecy, and he said, aye, jist trust me, Cathy, please tay Goad trust me. If she was lucky, she'd get a few nights in this one's company, a kind of flying visit before the next one would appear; if her luck wasn't holding, the optimist would be gone overnight, as if he'd got lost in the woods, but however long it took, the angry one came back from the studio eventually, and she knew him by his stunted walk, the way he settled into the chair like a king on the throne. His voice was rough like wood, all thorns and splinters, and he'd say things like, ye're impressin naebdy wi thon bastard pictures ey yours; he'd tell her she was extolling the virtues of stone and silence over movement and life, and when she asked what he meant he said, cn ye no see, fr Christ's sake? ye canny pit folk in they pictures tay tell their stories, so ye've goat tay day buildins, n the folk're no there, they're lik a dod ey mud ye've pullt ower the photy, it's lik they're makin it manky r somethn, ach! and he'd tell her she should be minding her home instead of obliterating the very thing that made art worthwhile in the first place. Days later, that would burn itself out, and the maudlin one would turn up, slump forward in his seat and tell her that all he wanted was a home where the wife was loyal to her man, that he thought more highly of loyalty in a woman than any other thing, and then she'd be comforting him; if there was anything about his moods she hated, it was how they changed her as well, from being an optimist like himself to being a wean cowering before his temper, and from that to being a mother to him, she'd never seen a man behave like this before who hadn't been stinking of ale and whisky.

Catherine felt the engine straining under her feet as the bus climbed a hill, shaking everyone inside until you'd think the old bus was held together by rivets of determination. She caught sight of herself in the panel of the window, and she turned her face one way and then the other, decided that she'd made a good job of repairing her spoiled make-up in Agnes's bathroom, in the mirror of new silver glass on a medicine cabinet she hadn't seen before. Cameron had been standing behind the door, watching her, and every so often she'd bounce a smile off the mirror towards him; she washed the black tears from her cheeks, and used tissue paper to wipe off the mess she'd put on before she'd left the house that day, without a mirror to help her. She brought the emergency cosmetics out of her bag, and let him watch as she powdered her face, stroked the mascara over her lashes, brushed rouge on her cheeks, drawing a mouth on herself, and then turning to him and saying,

Will I do, d'you think?

Cameron was staring at her as if he'd had a blindfold taken from him. He came close to her, tilted his head up, and she turned her head from side to side, the way she was doing for the glass in front of her just now, so he could see the effect. She wondered how the glasses were changing her in his sight, if he was more critical of her now he could see her with more definition; but at last he smiled, and nodded firmly, and Catherine clipped the bag shut.

Catherine recognized the woman in the window of the bus, sitting opposite her. It wasn't the woman she'd seen in the studio, afraid of the prints of a touch on her long ago, and it wasn't the timid woman who'd hidden from the darkness of the old house when the door had been forced open. She was the mother of a child, and she'd kept several promises that day, and made others she'd have to redeem soon; but there was strength in that face that made Catherine believe those promises would be kept. She didn't need any grand reasons for taking pictures, when the walls around her were full of them; didn't need any explanation other than, it was for Cameron's sake, and the sake of her husband because he wasn't there to do it for Cameron.

Catherine and the woman in the window were in complete agreement; that she'd return to the house and to hell with Peter's moods, and she sat up straight as the bus turned so that the light struck her in the side, making it seem as if she was sitting beside herself.

Sixteen

Catherine wouldn't've been able to bear Peter if it hadn't been for Codie, his help and advice with her wee hobby, as Peter would dismiss it. He was always willing to put down his brush and come through to see how she was getting along. His only complaint was the reek in the darkroom, even with the window open behind the curtain, and she looked at him as if she'd just been called black by the kettle, what with all the oil and turps he anointed himself with during his work; but he was just warning her in his own way to be careful. She understood his concern; she'd've been gassed to sleep if the window hadn't been open, burns would've spread like an empire over her hands, and in case she was looking for proof of how risky this wee hobby of hers could be, the enamel of the bath was growing cancers of discoloration from the mordancy of her developer and fixer and stopping solution. Peter said he'd rather pish in a bucket than have to use the toilet when she was in the middle of her developing; it was just as well, because she couldn't spare him the time to make water while she was busy, no more than he could seem to spare the time for her. Of the two of them, Peter trying to put her off with his complaints, and Codie asking her to look out for her own safety while encouraging her by telling her all workers had to worry for their own safety, she knew which kind of concern she preferred. Codie always wrinkled his nose whenever he came into the room, the dim red safe light making a wean's irritation into a damned sort of grimace put together out of broken tiles of red glass, all sharp edges and angles.

N ye're proposin the wee yin, yir wee boay, helps ye tay day this? I widny let a wee boay near it if I were you.

Catherine showed him the things she'd allow her wee boy to do. The process of making a contact print was easy enough; the only harm that might come to him there was if the holder that clipped the negative image to a fresh sheet of emulsion paper bit his hand while he was undoing the wingnuts to make it adapt to the size of the sheet, or if the clips pinched his fingers, and she thought that was unlikely. She'd let him count the right number of seconds for the exposure, maybe give him a watch with a second hand; but she'd do the next part herself, bathing the exposed print in the three vital solutions, and let him count the time so he'd still be contributing. She turned to Codie, tilted her head to coerce approval from him, and he shrugged,

Fair enough; lang as ye've goat it a' planned oot, n he's no gonny baptize himsel in they f, em, in they foants ey yours, nae boather,

and she asked lightly how long he'd wanted to be a father, enjoying the embarrassment that made him shift on the lavvy seat.

Once she'd taken a variety of exposures, the box shown its subject for different lengths of time, they brought the prints through to the room to see them in a better light; she relied on his more acute sense of depth and tone. He always sat by the table to study the prints, and hunched himself forward over them with the chair turned to her and towards the overhead bulb, cradling the prints underneath on the points of his fingers like a waiter holding a tray, while they were still wet from rinsing. He'd say, this one was too dark, too light, good but not quite there, wee bit more time or less time; would point out to her what it was that made a good print, reminding her she'd never get pictures as clean-edged as if she'd taken them with a proper camera, which she knew anyway from Cameron's book, but Codie telling her the obvious wasn't as bad as Peter doing it somehow. She was as much grateful for the company as the advice; even listening to him go mm hm was preferable to being alone. She wondered how much of his own work he'd been getting done lately since he'd started coming in to help her; how much of his bothering with her work was a kindred interest in preserving the vitality of images, less immediate than his own means maybe but still a kind of memory.

The gallery over the headboard of the bed grew more like the

336

scrapbook Francesca kept of articles about her favourite groups than like Peter's regimented gallery. Every day if she could she made a point of contributing something new to the scrapbook; even if it was only another interior of the café, if say she wakened up exhausted and knew she wouldn't be bothered later going out to chase images. It was as if she'd been granted a gift like Cameron's new sight, or like Peter's that never allowed you a minute's peace and always followed you around.

She began thinking like the box. She could never go anywhere now without imagining a picture, or searching for a place she might settle the box even if she didn't have it with her. She could sit places for hours at a time and notice say a truck which had been parked for a while suddenly come alive with ignition and drive away, and she could almost see it still inscribed on the air. Folk became unbearably fast, jets in formation leaving their passing behind them like vapour trails; their conversations like the argument of music you get when neighbours on opposite sides of the landing turn up their gramophones. In slowing her down, the box had restored something she'd forgotten from her time across the water, quarried out of memory by the fear of her father; and that was how she'd responded to the rhythm of an entirely different clock in those days, waking as she pleased and kicking from here to there without any special hurry. The box loaned her its understanding of time as well as the images it gave her; folk that stopped it would notice for a while, as if they were calling its attention to them; folk waiting for friends or their other halves, made to slow down by the need to wait; old folk slowed down by infirmity, making more pronounced streaks across the paper as if their ungainly daunnering was unbearable speed; drunks with no particular place to go, clutching their paper-wrapped bottles of fortified wines close to their chests, and you could tell them on the print by how easily they seemed to be blown off course.

Codie usually left the room to finish his work before Peter arrived, leaving her with some encouragement because he knew she wouldn't receive any once Peter came in. The first thing Peter did before he settled himself down before the fire was to go over to the headboard to see the latest bulletin; he'd make a sceptical noise deep in his chest, and then tell her he hoped the bathroom was cleaned and aired after her developing shenanigans; poisnin the hoose, by Christ, he said, wi yer daft wee hoabby. He'd point out where someone had persisted in the box's vision, and there'd be a triumph on his face, there y'are, he said, ye'll no wipe oot folk so easy as thon, as if the rats infesting her prints had refused her poisoned dish of silence and invisibility. She'd tried for long enough to make Peter see that it wasn't herself wishing folk away from her prints; it was folk themselves who wouldn't accommodate to the box's understanding of time, thrashing about from here to there like mice hurrying for the skirting. She spoke up for the box but the more he saw of her gallery, the more he seemed to think it was pernicious in its intention, no longer just herself trying out an experiment for her son but a movement like his own, trespassing on his land without a map or the sense to keep to the worn paths, and after weeks of trying to justify herself she realized he wanted to think ill of it, and found that the only defence against him was none at all, when all his accusations just fled past her like the folk that never left their mark on her prints, and if he made the mistake of believing she was listening to a word he said, just because she was saying nothing in reply, then more fool him.

Peter had a number of his canvases lodged in a gallery owned by a fat suited effort called MacHenery who fancied art the way some folk fancied pigeons, a wee hobby he kept to the side, away from his other interests. He was a mean-minded bastard who put up all kinds for sale, those whirling confections by art school students, pretend Pollocks and Rileys for folk as well-to-do as himself who wanted a wee bit jewellery for the house but who weren't rich enough to buy the real things; and he had a profitable line in those tweedy paintings of deer estates and Highland cattle mowing the grass by the side of a loch for envious bastards with more aspirations than taste. MacHenery smoked thick cigars he claimed he had imported from Havana, breathed out his smoke like a chimney-stack from a vile industrial concern, and met all the artists he displayed personally; wore black velvet jackets and silk ties wild with Paisley patterns as if he was a work of op art himself. He was all for a good profit, but being a fancier of the arts, he didn't expect anything great of his wee public service, as he called the gallery, and was quite pleased if it paid the wages of the art students he engaged to help with the running of the place. He had the studied good manners of the new arrival, a man who'd learned a thing or two, the first of them being compromise; no compromise with his workers, you'll note, but with his origins, no sign of it anywhere in his voice, more likely you'd look for it in his enjoyment of luxuries, the drinks cabinet he kept in his wee office, the balloons he filled with brandy for all the artists he invited, no whisky for the bastard, all his pleasures had to be imported to be worth a damn.

Peter hated him down to his shiny boots, hated the very notion that he had to deal with folk like this to get his paintings sold or even noticed.

He'd brought Peter into that office the first time, sat him in front of a thick mahogany desk in a chair that embraced him like a whore leeching for custom, poured him one of those brandies and set the balloon on Peter's side of the desk, a wee pish of a drink in a vessel that could've held a bottle's worth. He saw Peter pick up the glass under the stem, said,

The volume of the glass, Mr Caulder, is out of proportion to the volume of the drink within for a very good reason.

Peter just said, aw aye, to show his lack of interest, but the fat thing went on,

One of the pleasures of a good brandy is the aroma of it, the bouquet, one might say. The glass is blown so that the vapours may collect on top, like cream, and you may inhale them before you drink.

Peter smelled the bloom, just to oblige him; like burning sugar, sweet and fiery, briefly enough to show he wasn't impressed; he hated talking with folk who were trying to beat you over the head with how much they knew more than yourself. You had to show them it was business you were after, not enlightenment.

I'd sooner huv a good malt,

said Peter, and MacHenery smiled, rolled the drink in the balloon until it became just a skin against the glass, brought the rim to his nose and drew in the vapours like he was inhaling gas at the dentist's before taking the smallest nip from it. He let the brandy roam around his mouth for a while before allowing it to drain into his throat, and then sat back at the experience of his sacrament; his leather chair cracked under the weight of his satisfaction.

A malt would not be the right drink for an occasion such as this. Now then, Mr Caulder, you wish me to display your dismal wee derivatives of genre painting on my walls, am I correct in so supposing?

This was more to Peter's liking; he had more taste for the thought of disputation with this cushioned bastard than he had for the drink in the huge glass bucket he'd been given. He finished his glass in one just to show MacHenery what he thought of his wee bit pish of hospitality, rested the balloon on the very edge of the desk, sat back himself.

So I tellt yir flunkey oan the phone, aye.

MacHenery laughed, rested his elbows on the arms of his chair and made a temple of his fingers.

So many artists speak their minds like yourself, I find it quite invigorating after the insincerity of proper business folk. You do understand, do you not, Mr Caulder, that your work could hardly be described as original? That it has a centuries-long tradition behind it and that there is unlikely to be any call for it among my particular and discerning clients? Given these facts, why should I disturb the balance of my gallery to make room for your drivel?

Peter tried to look comfortable in the wealthy seat, but after years of chairs that gave like railway shunts when you committed your weight to them, the inventory furniture of private tenancies, he wasn't used to sitting in fine moulds like this. He grinned viciously in reply to the criticism, and sat forward, as if at an arm's length from the throat of this moneyed get of folk who could've been his neighbours at one time.

Ye mean, cut a wee gap fr me in a' they Riley derivatives, n Pollock derivatives, n Monarch ey the Glen derivatives? That wid be an awfl shame, noo, widn't it?

Have you ever studied totalitarian art, Mr Caulder? The paintings approved by the National Socialists during their time in office, or those commissioned by the Soviet Union to this very day? I'm sure they were intended to be very uplifting for those who shared the visions of the bodies who approved them, but are they worth a farthing as art?

Peter glared at MacHenery across his desk as if the brandy's vapours had finally ignited in his gut.

You callin me a fucken Nazi?

Immediately MacHenery raised his hand to settle Peter back down, made a lullaby of his voice.

I'm calling you nothing of the sort, Mr Caulder. I simply wish to make the point that fervently held beliefs do not necessarily bring forth great art, or even good art. I make no apologies for the fact that this establishment is little more than a market stall for those who wish some fashion of superior ornament to brighten their homes. My clients receive singular and original works of art, imitations perhaps of shall we say better-known artists, homages might be a more agreeable word to express it, but original nonetheless.

Then they're no original, ur they?

I would urge you to be cautious, Mr Caulder; from which particular glasshouse are you casting that rather pointed stone? They are original, in so far as they are works by an artist who has not copied or forged. They are derivative, in so far as the artist is wearing the clothes of a better-known talent, for the purpose of earning money to support himself while he finishes his apprenticeship, as it were. If you find such conduct dishonourable, then, Mr Caulder, please return to me once you discover a gallery in this town that doesn't sell the latest in off-the-peg imitations, and tell me I am grievously mistaken.

Bastard knew the score well enough; Peter listened to the fluting Kelvingrove voice, he was far from his home right enough, you'd never've known from the fine leather of his expensive shoes that shoes were a new encumbrance for him, that in his young days the only blackening on his feet was the dirt he picked from the cobbles.

So, ur ye gonny take my canvases r no? 'M I wasten my time here?

MacHenery slumped back into his chair, wearied you'd think by the conversation. He placed one arm across his belly, while with the forefinger of the other hand he stroked his fat lips like a wean searching for the tit, straightening the finger once he was done and aiming it at Peter.

I think we can make room among all our other imitations for yours, Mr Caulder. I will tell you my commission, which will not be negotiable, and remember that I am afraid your work will be here on what will amount to a permanent exhibition, since I fear there will be no call for it. I do this favour for you, because despite my misgivings I believe your work to have some merit, and rest assured that I will draw the attention of those of my clients as I believe will find your work of interest to your canvases. If you find this satisfactory, then we will choose which of your paintings I will hang. There's the deal, Mr Caulder; do you find it acceptable?

He didn't; but there being no other choice, he offered his limp hand into MacHenery's wet envelope of a grasp, and drank another of MacHenery's meagre share of spirits to finish the bargain.

For weeks, fuck all happened; no sales, no interest from any of MacHenery's clients; they said Peter's work was too dreary and pessimistic, if they wanted to see old folk struggling along in the rain with their messages all they had to do was look out the windows, and they wanted the children from the schemes playing in ruins with broken prams to remain in the schemes, thank you very much, not come to live on their walls. After months of fuck all, Peter was ready to withdraw the whole lot from the gallery; your bastard clients don't waant the truth, he raged in MacHenery's office, coughing away the smoke that purled from the cinder of MacHenery's latest Cuban pleasure, they jist waant tay be hypnotized oot their heids wi they swirlin things, that r they're jist efter a winday oot oan a nicer place than they've goat the noo, I'm no gonny make a broon penny oot ey this, might as well fucken chalk Rembrandts oot oan the pavement fr a' ye're making fr me, and MacHenery just sat behind his desk with his brandy and his cigar and let Peter discharge his wee tantrum into the air, and when Peter was finished he let the crackling of Peter's annoyance settle and said,

I can fully understand your frustration, Mr Caulder, because I share it; in trying to sell your works, I have noted a distinct lack of enthusiasm on the part of my clients for them. I've even tried to locate your work in the great tradition of Dutch genre painting, but they still won't take that as bait. One of them even went so far as to say that they were perhaps not critical of paintings, but, and I quote, they knew rubbish when they saw it. Many have suggested that I have taken leave of my senses in promoting your work. What would you have me say to them, Mr Caulder? That you are a misunderstood genius?

Peter sat back into the chair; was becoming used to its shape behind him.

I never says I wis a genius.

MacHenery stood up from the desk, noted that Peter's balloon was empty; collected it, went to the cabinet and pulled the crystal stopper from his decanter.

Oh, come now, Mr Caulder. Every artist considers himself a genius, unless he's fallen for that communist folly of genius as being an expression of bourgeois individualism. What perfect arrogance, to believe that your work does so much as turn a single wheel in the arrangement of the world among the heavens. Surely that's a belief in your own genius, is it not?

For the first time, Peter noticed the slackness about MacHenery's perfectly combed silver hair.

Get thee behind me, ya baldy arse ye,

said Peter, but MacHenery only laughed and brought over the drink, settled it on the desk in front of Peter, went round to his leather throne and sat in it.

My point is still well made, Mr Caulder, that you will go to your grave believing that it was your political commitment that kept you in poverty, rather than the awful truth that it was your grinding mediocrity, coupled with your principled inflexibility, and no amount of faith in your own genius will alter that. The question I must now ask is, how are you prepared to tackle these shortcomings in your approach? Because the truth is, you have talent, but no genius, and you could manage quite comfortably if you were only to allow yourself to consider a change in subject, which would further allow you the time for your own private work. I offer it as a suggestion for now, but I hope you'll give it a reasonable amount of thought. Consider it an act of childbirth, in which we share the parentage, my suggestion and your undoubted artistic vigour coming together in one creation, so to speak; far better than your present course of intellectual onanism, where your seed spills forth on barren ground.

He let out a thick release of smoke into the air, which spun around Peter while he tapped a stump of cohesive ash into a crystal dish to one side of him on the desk, and he was smiling as if the cause for amusement was larger inside him than this slight manifestation of it. Peter drank the brandy, again in one; let the balloon down on the desk with a loud ring that caused MacHenery to recoil for a fraction of a second, and then stood up, leaned on both hands so he was levered halfway over the desk.

Aye, fucken childbirth, ya fat pregnant wee bastart ye. You tellt me you'd sell they peyntns I gied ye tay sell. Fucken sell them.

MacHenery wasn't impressed by the show of temper.

For the good of the masses?

he said, the wee smile curling up one side of his mouth. Peter launched himself away from the desk before he committed a murder.

Fr the good ey my welfare n all, n well ye know it, ya connivin shite,

he said, and left lit up with rage, crashing shut the office door and then the door to the gallery, running up the steps from the basement to street level, needing cold air in him just then.

Well, the plain truth was, as MacHenery well knew, Peter needed his services; and in the following months Peter had been thinking of a way of giving him this wean he was after, a work that MacHenery could deliver into his gallery that wouldn't upset this balance of his, but that Peter wouldn't disown out of shame. It wouldn't be a wean conceived during an act of whoring, not if he could help it. It'd have to flatter MacHenery's jumped-up sense of refinement, but be insolent as well, like the seeds of the bourgeoisie's destruction bred from within its own ranks. He was after a kind of subtle unsettling, a beauty that poisoned itself the longer it was looked at, drawing the eye and then repelling it in an act of cruelty that more resembled the disfigured world Peter understood than all the pastoral nonsense and paint marked on canvas like a wean playing in its own shite.

About one week before Peter thought he was ready to finish his canvas, he took the snapshot camera into the studio, framed the work carefully in the viewfinder. He didn't need a flash; there was enough light in the room to make ten days' worth. The film was ready on the Saturday, as they'd told him it would be in the chemist's, and once he'd collected it he went straight down to MacHenery's and smacked the paper envelope containing the prints on to the desk, watching MacHenery chewing on the end of his cigar. MacHenery lifted the purse of photographs and settled it on his lap while he opened it, shuffled through the deck one by one, his eyebrows raising in slight increments as if they were measuring his surprise.

This is a welcome change in emphasis, Peter.

He dropped the photographs on to the desk, and raised himself from his seat to go to the drinks cabinet; the chair and the polished floorboards he trod on howled under his weight. He pished a wee drop of brandy from his decanter into the two balloons, smiled over his shoulder as if it was a ritual by now between friends, came back over and landed a glass on the desk in front of Peter, sat back down into his chair, raised his own glass as high as his head. Peter wondered if the bastard was ever sober, from all the drinks he offered folk.

Dare I propose a toast, he said, to a new spirit of pragmatism? A realistic assessment of the market? The eventual dawning of the fact that we serve a small parish, and that as such we should not be painting solely for the approval of the shade of Karl Marx?

His lips were drawn out thin, and he twisted his amusement into Peter's guts once too often. Peter took the balloon and emptied it out all over MacHenery's grinning face, for all the wee splash it made, a spit in the eye and no more, landed the balloon exactly where MacHenery had put it, with a quiet ring of the glass against the wood.

That, he said, wis fr makin me day that fucken picture, ya fat baldy cunt ye.

MacHenery took the cotton handkerchief from his lapel pocket, and began to mop the drink away from around his eyes. He was about to restore the handkerchief to the pocket when he raised it to his nose; it was reeking with the brandy, and he placed it carefully on the desk in front of him, where it began to blossom and unfold, half darkened by the moisture. All trace of the usual indestructible bonhomie with which he greeted Peter's slights and insults had been washed away by the brandy; he leaned forward on the desk, his eyes narrowed, the fat around them pressed into severe creases.

You may think yourself to be as rare as diamond, Mr Caulder, but you are as cheap and as plentiful as coal, and it is the illusion of my industry that I must dupe others into taking you for diamond when

I know otherwise. Be grateful that I am still prepared to grant you the favour of a display in my gallery even after this stupidity. Leave my office now, and pray I don't think better of my decision in the days before you are due to deliver this painting to me.

Outside the gallery, Peter felt light and exultant. He took an unaccustomed drink of cold air into himself; it was as if the spell of his work had been broken, not so urgent now they were so far away from him. He minded on the bar, only a few streets away, where Codie, Heidless and him had drunk away their time at the art school; it was a more hospitable thought than home, Cathy and those fucking capers of hers with the box, Codie turned against him, helping her when he should've been thinking of his china. He'd a thirst on him that was a thirst for the fire in the drink sooner than the water, and his feet took him to the source as if he'd no say in the decision.

The only thing different about the bar was the folk serving, like you'd expect. The wood panelling was painted in varnish as black as treacle, and the bar counter was a long parenthesis between you and the drink. There was a sprinkling of sawdust over the lino, so as to mop up spills from pints and from customers, and there was a yeasty, contained smell of yesterday's ale. Most of the circular tables were empty, but you could always rely on two kinds of folk to be here this early, both of them with the same kind of thirst as Peter was carrying with him the now; old folk, solitary pensioners who welcomed the sleep the drunkenness brought to them like a wee practice for their coming deaths, and alkies, tanning their livers inside them until they were like offcuts from a hide of leather, wishing their deaths on themselves sooner. You could tell between them because the old folk took their time with their drink, knowing they'd still be there by closing time and in the perfect state for returning home and collapsing gutted like fish on to the slabs of their beds, experience teaching them caution; while the alkies were hammering one drink after another until they'd bend over like nails struck out of true, beating themselves too often, too hard, and they'd have to be thrown on to the pavement when they'd punished themselves more than they were able for.

And then there was Peter, taking in the familiar smell of rolling tobacco and sawdust, nodding to the polite old folk who'd nodded at him first from their tables, studying the alkies to see which of them were maybe going to be trouble. There was the mirror behind the gantry he remembered, you could see your face as you asked for your poison, as well as the back of the bartender, the wee buckle on the adjusting strap of his waistcoat. The bloke was standing there with his arms wide apart braced on the counter; he had thinning hair scored across his head, and Peter saw it was thickened and blackened with boot polish, so that Peter could grant him the favour of pretending not to notice in return for his drink.

Whit's yir pleasure?

Peter nearly laughed.

Y'only sell drinks here.

Thon's good enough fr maist folk that come intay a bar.

Maist folk, aye, said Peter, and then, Gie us a whisky tay begin wi.

Catherine went to the studio by way of the darkroom; she was just looking for a comfortable place to sleep that night, and she couldn't knock on Codie's door after what had happened. Everywhere in the house was dark as if her darkroom had unfolded into the whole house leaving her with intimations of the house's true geography. The darkroom seemed like the best refuge for her, a place with its own lock, somewhere away from the imitation of her father sleeping in Peter's bed.

The journey to the darkroom seemed to take hours; there was nowhere she could get comfortable, nowhere that cradled her the same as the bed she'd left at the beginning of her travels. In that bed, you could imagine yourself back inside your mammy, and the dark was the same, close but not suffocating because your air was coming from somewhere else; you could sleep at peace and never have to waken. On the good nights, Peter would leave her to lie in peace with the covers over her; but there were the nights like tonight when he was expecting favours of her, and he wouldn't leave her be until she'd granted them. That was a lie; there hadn't been a night like this one before in all her months of staying here. She'd never given in to him before tonight out of fear; indifference maybe, a wish to be sooner asleep and the knowledge that he'd be pleased enough once he'd had his wee fit to himself. There'd be a week go by before he'd ask anything of her, too tired maybe after his time in the studio, and then there'd be one evening he'd press himself against her so she could feel him aroused, and she'd allow it just to get it done. She'd been long used to pawning herself in exchange for peace before she'd ever met Peter, and if truth be told there'd been worse done by the man who was meant to be blood to her. She wasn't afraid of it, it was just a bargain you struck with your circumstances, at least until this night, when she couldn't've stayed in the bed with him any longer, not after what he'd done.

Tonight, she smelled the drink off Peter's breath, the smell of the brewery in the sweetness off him, the distillery in the sharpness, and there was a stink like milk on the turn behind it, as if he was manufacturing sourness in his mouth. This time, he'd been looking for new favours, favours he hadn't dared to ask when he was sober; only they weren't favours, they were demands, with threats behind them like the light she shut out of her darkroom. He could hardly balance himself; his legs were solid enough on the ground, but from the waist up he swithered like a man in disturbed water, waves knocking him this way and that. He waited until Catherine was in her nightshirt with the light still on before he approached her; stood opposing her and stopping her from going to her bed, saying nothing for the longest time, his eyes clouded with the drink but still fierce with his desires, like a light you see burning in a window to guide you through the dark and the mist, inviting her to make the journey to him, angry when she wouldn't take the first step.

The fact that Peter wasn't to know was no excuse for Catherine; she'd've told him the way she'd told Francis if she'd trusted him enough. Maybe tonight wouldn't've happened at all if maybe she had trusted him with knowing of her father. Peter tilted himself forward and gripped the hem of her nightgown in both his hands; and suddenly there wasn't a width of water between herself and her submission, it was here in front of her, another drunken man, and all her remembered capitulations came back to her as the fear of one drunk became a fear of the other. All his clothes reeked of smoke and beer, the air of all the pubs he'd gone to between MacHenery's and home mantled around him. He drew himself level with her, the pub smell clotting in her head so as to make her obedient enough to lift her arms and make it easier for him to undress her again; it was more like the memory of obedience, a clockwork surrender tripped again after years as if he'd touched the lever by accident, through his not knowing. He drew the cloth over his head, crushed it and threw it to one side, on to the chair she thought; she folded her arms over herself, not just for shame but because her father had liked that expression of innocence about her before he set about the work of traducing it, and she thought it might save her now, that and the apprehension ringing through her, making her shake enough for him to see.

Peter's expression changed the moment he saw her naked in front of him; softened, as if he'd recovered a lost faith, a tendency to worship wasted with disuse, and she remembered where she'd seen a look like that before; Francis, their wedding night in the hotel, after she'd allowed him to take the dress off her. She hadn't been afraid then, she'd made all the running; but now she didn't know what was being asked of her, if anything would be asked of her or if it'd be forced on her, she was turned in on herself, defending herself almost, everything was stirred up and clouded, and the uncertainty was like the cold in the room, an atmosphere in which you could almost see the spores of your breath. Peter landed heavily on his knees, bringing him inches away from her but down at the height of a child; his head was tilted up, and he was staring at her as if he was expecting to receive a sacrament from her, the way old biddies approached the altar and put out their tongues hungry for the Saviour at Communion, and she nearly leapt back at the expectation he put on her, the weight of his desires.

Peter took her waist in his hands, danced them around until he was facing the bed and her back was to it; she might've laughed at his awkward gait on his knees if things had been different, but as it was she complied with him until she was standing where he wanted, and he let her go.

Cn ye no see me?

he said, and Catherine didn't know if she was meant to reply; she was looking down on him as she would at Cameron, but all the power in the room was in him. There was a kind of pleading to him, and his arms were wide apart like a penitent. Catherine came to understand that her safety lay in her silence; she had nothing to say to him, after what he'd just done, and before what he might do, but he brought his arms back towards himself and then, a curious thing, he began to trace the shape of her with the palms of his hands, keeping them apart from her and closing his eyes which she saw were filling with tears. It was so cold that the heat was radiant against her skin from his palms; if she'd closed her own eyes she'd've known just where he was on her from the warmth of him, but she didn't dare take her eyes off him for a minute, still afraid that this was leading to a punishment like those punishments of her father's, the old jealous god himself, in the days before he learned another use for her.

'M I gaun too fast fr ye?

He cupped his hands around her shoulders, and she could feel his breath warm against her ribs; she was shaking now with the fear of being devoured, her own breath stammered coldly in her throat, and she wanted to run, out of the room, away from the house, the town, but her father had her trained like a sheepdog, she held her place, waited.

Next, she was falling, back towards the bed, on to the mattress, into the litter of her prints he'd torn off the walls pressing against her skin, cold and sharp; the cry of shock followed her down, landed with her, was driven deep into her by the stop, and she'd only the time to recover the position of her arms, her only defence, before she felt the bed dented by him approaching, crouching over her.

When'll ye see me?

After he'd pulled away from her, he lifted himself off; she wondered if he was going to dress himself again, leave for more drinking, but he was only allowing her to lift the blankets from under him, so she could go to bed. She said,

Am I going to be left in peace to sleep?

and tried not to sound afraid; she wasn't as frightened as before, when it'd only been a possibility, it was done now, and even the peace that came after was familiar to her, he might've thought he was powerful, but he was only following a design she recognized, and it kept her strong, the knowledge that his tyranny was no different from anyone else's. He looked as if he was going to cry again, as if she'd carelessly thrown aside his gift, but he nodded, at least with the decency in him now to leave her be. Quickly she got under the blankets, sweeping the prints on to the floor and not caring how they landed or if they were bent, made that wee cell between herself and the rest of the bed she'd become used to constructing out of the hollow mattress and the sheets folded under her.

I'd like you to put out the light now, Peter,

she said, and felt the creeping of his spit between her legs as he did as he was told, and then weighed her down towards the centre of the bed with his coming in beside her.

Why Catherine chose another place inside the same house to sleep, rather than filling her case as quietly as she could, and then making for Agnes's and Daniel's; unless it was to spare Cameron the worry over his mammy, or maybe it was the refugee's shock at being displaced so suddenly. She waited until Peter's breath became level and rested, herself unable to even think of sleep, while he went away like a wean, drugged by his pints and bottles, before easing herself out of the bed and finding her nightdress by touch, where it'd fallen to the floor in front of the heater, slipping it over herself.

Once the door to the room was closed behind her, it felt like the start of a journey; her feet cautious on the carpet, carrying her in the dark to the bathroom door. She thought she'd feel more protected there, and there was always the bolt, just in case. The room stank, but it was the air she'd been breathing for the past few weeks; it cleaned away the bar smell he'd rubbed on to her, and she took it in deeply, more welcomely than she'd taken him into herself. She let herself down on the floor between the bath and the wall, and used two of the thick white bathtowels as blankets. With the door bolted, and a secure darkness around her, she laid her head down at an awkward, unpillowed angle, and in starts, like a climb down ledges, she fell asleep.

When she next wakened up, the darkness was so complete she could hardly tell it from the sleep; but she was coughing as the chemicals in the air lacerated the back of her throat. She was without a proper sense of when in the morning it was, and more than that, she hardly had a proper sense of herself, as if she'd become identical to the darkness. Her neck was sore where her spine had been bent by lying on her side, and she rubbed it to nurse some flexibility into it. When she finally got up, it was like the darkness itself testing its limits; an infinite field of the absence of light, and yet there were obstructions, the cold enamel of the bath pressing against the backs of her legs, the wall alongside it that guided her to her feet, the floor underneath her. She felt liquid inside her unsettled by her change to standing upright; she coughed to bring it up, used her hands on the wall and brief steps to find her way to the wash-basin and then the toilet pan, disposed of it in a way she'd never have done so freely if she hadn't been protected by the dark; she heard the water take it, swallowing it the way she'd refused to, and she felt better for emptying it from herself.

She'd been sleeping lightly; her thoughts had become identical to dreams, without the distraction of a light outside her, she could see them more purely than if she'd had to bother with stumbling through the world of objects and surfaces. When he'd just newly come back, and she'd become aware of the state he was in, Peter asked her if she was determined to do to folk what'd been done to the paddies by his own people; she frowned, but she was afraid of this game of drunkards, long familiar to her, to make you say what most displeased them, like that game on the tele where you hadn't to use yes or no as a reply, when all the questions were meant to make you say it. She told him she didn't understand, because she really didn't, knew she was in for a storm of all kinds of mad blatherings, wondered if this was truly Peter, truer than the man who'd come into the café all those months ago; at this stage in his game of argument, anything could've happened to her, but he sat by the fire and she'd never seen anything like it before, he seemed to be tormented by a dreadful pain, like a burning that injures you without breaking the skin, and he was writhing around on the chair as if to escape it.

You're takin pictures ey buildns n nae folk roon aboot, he said. Cn ye no see, this toun wis built up by the sweat ey the workers; d'ye no see noo?

Catherine kept herself out of the game by pleading silence; shook her head while Peter hunched himself over, his eyes fixed on the floor between them.

Jesus Christ almighty, Cathy, this you obliteratin me noo? This you wipin me oot the picture?

That was when she'd started dressing for bed, taking refuge in saying nothing to provoke him, lead him anywhere. Now she was in the dark, she began wondering all kinds of things she hadn't let herself think then: if this was where folk she obliterated went, into a limbo of blackness where everything of them dissolved, if this obliteration was the world's forgetfulness, where lost or stolen memory was kept like books on shelves.

She shook her head, felt her neck tighten as she tried to throw the daze off herself; it was the overwhelming burning of the chemicals in her that was draining the air from her, and she thought it was better for her to find another place, somewhere with a lock she could turn for her own protection, just in case Peter woke from his sleep.

She locked the studio door as soon as she was inside, and opened the window sash so as to rid the room of the settled reek of Peter's work that made her cough almost as bad as it'd been in the darkroom. She thought maybe here she'd get some peace; she'd been so keen to escape that she'd forgotten her darkroom was also the bathroom, that folk might've needed to use it, maybe Peter; but she didn't feel much safer here, even with the key turned. At least the smell was more irritating than poisonous; and the light was as bright as day after her confinement in the darkroom, the mercury vapour lamps interrupted by the clutch of elm branches between them and the window. The breeze that exchanged the turps and oil for fresh air from outside lashed at the trees and braided together the light and the branches, weaving jewellery out of the thin wires of the moon. Her shadow was printed on each of the mirrors, a famine that wore her shape, and when she looked to the floor, she found that her shadow stood astride the room as if she herself negated the fluorescence, and there was a conference of shadows where her other reflections tended towards the centre, where Peter's easel was, turned edge on towards the long wall on the other side from the window.

Catherine approached the easel from the side, expecting to see it in a room that annihilated darkness the same way as her darkroom annihilated light; but the canvas didn't want to be seen, hooded by a cloth over it, and she remembered Peter saying he covered it over every night to protect it from dust. His work table was nudged against the wall opposite the canvas; she could make out the shapes of the jars, the brushes jutting out where he'd left them the day before, and the palette, another cloth over that, the one he kept dampened so the paints wouldn't dry out. There were papers held on the walls, more than just the one he used as a guide when he came to making a canvas; the breeze lifted them, and in her curiosity she bent closer to see. If she changed her focus on the wall beyond the papers, she could see something like the roots of a tree on each of them, but she was also dazzled by a constellation of lamp heads, the same lamp shown to one facet of the room and multiplied until it could've been anywhere around her, every wall had a window to the same outside, like one of those mad drawings in one of Peter's books where two dimensions allowed you to commit absurdities in three dimensions, up slopes that went down and the like.

Catherine stared at the papers for ages, but nothing resolved on them. She was taken by a new exhaustion, thought that if she couldn't see properly what was on the papers, she'd surely not see what he'd done with the canvas. She'd brought the towels with her, and looked around for a place to nest; there, in the bay of the window, it was cold but she needed the fresh air pouring in through the sash to rid herself of the chemicals she'd breathed in earlier.

It was much like her time on the streets when she'd first come over; she felt just as much abandoned, but then she'd had the security of distance where now she'd the lock between her and what was troubling her. At least when she'd arrived here like an orphan, she'd never acted on her blood; for all the times folk on the streets had offered her a drink of their fire-water, she'd kept her optimism at the bottom of her carpet-bag with her clean clothes, refused them politely, no matter how much of a thirst came over her, and when it turned out well, like when she saw Mrs Kilsyth's advertisement in the cast-aside newspaper, she knew it was because she'd never given up to the drink, and she felt stronger for it. Now she felt deceived by Peter; as if he'd been hiding her da inside him all this time, and it'd only be a matter of time before more of her father would seep through the cracks, and he'd be saying to her, I won't do it again, until the next test he had to go through. Her last thoughts while she was settling herself down, arranging the towels so that one lapped over the other to keep her legs warm, were of escaping, that or she'd confront Peter with what he'd done, maybe even trust him with her reason for running from home so she could make him see why she had to leave him in the bed by himself; but she was too tired to persuade herself of either course of action for now, and this time there was no climbing down to sleep, she dropped her head and her eyes closed in the dark covert under the window, and she was gone before the second breath.

She wakened because her weight crushed her against the floor and brought on cramps; she had to turn on to her back to escape them, pull at her hair which seized up underneath her, making a kind of pillow which she gathered into her arms. There was early morning light in the window-panes, and reflected in tiles against the mirrors; the containing of the light making the room seem brighter than it was outside, even though the sun wasn't high enough yet to fire the room properly.

She saw the papers when she was lifting her head, when the discomfort of the hard floor made her back stiff and lifeless like a string of cotton reels. The sight of them stood her on her feet to approach the wall, the towel around her chest turned into a robe, the other dropping to the floor like a mat. It was like seeing herself in the mirrors that first time she'd come to the studio; the shock of not recognizing herself. She could see now the structures she'd imagined were roots in the dark were limbs, thrown carelessly over the mattress in sleep, with no thought for how you seemed; you never thought there were eyes on you when you strayed your arm out, or crooked one leg across the other, and so you were natural to yourself, as natural as you'd be in death. There were more papers on the table, and they were all dated in the corner so she could tell when they'd been done; the earliest were not long after she'd told him she didn't want him to draw her, days after that just, and she wondered that she hadn't felt the blankets peeled away from her, or been aware of the light suddenly in the room, from his Anglepoise if she'd learned anything from him about how shadows were cast, too stark to be natural light, too sharp an edge on them. She picked up the papers

355

one by one; the table was more of a mess than she'd been able to see earlier, rags crushed and wet, a kind of livid soft palette swollen with the oils, and she noticed how the colours soaking into the protecting cloth were the same as those staining the front of his shirt after he came into their room from work, pale flesh colours like open gutted salmon.

Catherine unveiled the painting, stood back so she could better see herself. She could've looked beyond the canvas and seen herself as she was; trembling the way she'd done last night with him kneeling in front of her; but she couldn't look anywhere else, she was thinking, this was truer than words because it was how he regarded her, his explanation of her. He'd used a sketch in which she'd been turned away from him, but he could've chosen a hundred others; her gathered into herself, her on her back, her limbs afloat on the mattress, both towards and away from him; he had a complete record of her movement while she was asleep, taken over several mornings. She wondered why he'd chosen that one over others until she approached the canvas more closely, saw the fiction in his paintings; a full-length mirror, as big inside the painting as the canvas was to her outside of it, on the other side of her as if it was always in the room. She was reflected in it, her nakedness from the front as she slept, and Catherine began to make dry spasms the more she followed the topology of herself in the canvas. It wasn't just that he'd violated her as grievously as ever her da had after she'd told him not to, it was what he'd done to her; how he'd mutilated her so that her eyes were black caverns, how he'd cut the eyes out of her and left her blind to herself, with a leak of blood that reminded her of the drops from the crown of thorns piercing the Sacred Heart. She spilled the papers on the floor, found her legs weaken under her, and the next she knew she was kneeling among the papers, the easel standing over her the way she remembered her father used to when she was little, and on her knees she crept towards the door, the way she remembered cowering from him, her eyes wet and blinding her in a different way to the woman on the canvas.

The thought she'd had the night before, of reasoning with Peter to stop his drinking, had gone; she was thinking, never again, all the way as she left the room on her knees.

*

She crawled towards the darkroom, opening the door and pulling aside her curtain, closing it, shooting the bolt through its stay in the jamb and drawing the curtain shut behind her. She breathed as slowly as she could, drew in the vapours of her developing chemicals as if she was bringing an image of herself to substance with each breath; she sat back against the wall, and it was strange how safe she felt. With her legs at full stretch and her back straight she measured the distance between the wall and the bath like a set square. She remembered her home over the water, how in the mornings after her father first began his touching Michael found her in her room, on top of the bedclothes, her hands overlapped on her breast, and when he asked what she was doing she'd said to him, still lying on her back in her nightgown and her eyes closed, don't they lie dead people out like this, Michael? and he slipped his hand underneath her back and prised her away from the mattress and said, yes, they do, Kate, but not fine young women of your age, and she knew then that he'd the right notion of why she was bringing death on herself, and she'd laughed and when he asked why, she said she didn't know because none of it was funny only it was mad, your father loving you the way husbands were meant to.

She was thinking that just now as she measured the right angle with her legs and her back stiffened; it was mad when you were hiding from the man you shared a bed with, it was mad when he blinded you in his imagination, because you couldn't say for sure that wasn't in his thoughts, it wasn't right to be doubting your own safety so close to your own belongings.

Catherine lay like that for a while, paralysed. She'd no means of telling the time as easily as when she'd been in the studio, but after a time she thought she heard a rattling at the door handle, and when she turned her head to the side, she felt a wind of opening that must've made the curtain swell out like a sail. The hand that pulled the curtain to one side was lower than she'd've expected, but she remembered the light well; it was the hall light from the old house, casting itself over the darkness the way shadow cuts across light, and there was a wee shadow within it. She wet her lips with her tongue, and said to the wee one to come in, but he stayed where he was, on the threshold, the curtain in his hand, and she had the feeling he'd asked these questions before, but that she'd given him different answers. She told him he shouldn't be afraid of this, because it was what you did when you were feared of the man you lived with, that you should never be afraid to hide from the madness of your elders, because folk weren't always as loving as they made out at first. She told him, sometimes you had to discover and it wasn't your fault, and you should never live as if it were your fault, because that way brought you to madness when it was the madness of another infecting you, and you needed the strength to know when it was their madness and not yours that was causing these fevers, these doubts and spasms. She told him to say it back to her as she'd said it as proof that he'd understood, and he was word-perfect, and so she let him go and turned her head away from him fixing the curtain back and closing the door, still pinned against the wall, and was satisfied enough to allow herself to go to sleep.

As soon as she wakened for the fourth time, she thought she'd gone blind. She'd tipped over on to her side during her sleep; for all she knew, the darkness could've been tight around her, like the closeness of a burial casket, or it could've been as wide as a field; it was so complete a darkness that there wasn't the least margin of light to give a definition to her surroundings. She thought it was time to be up, but she'd forgotten how she'd come to be here. For a terrible moment she thought the eyes had been plucked from her head, one of those mad thoughts that you bring into the new day; she lifted herself into a half-kneeling position, and then she thought to press on her eyes with her knuckles. That brought out the prints of red gold and tarnished copper she'd expect if she was properly sighted, and that was another relief; she had a compass of up and down, and when she breathed in she had a chemical flavour in the back of her throat, so she even had a place for herself, knowing it was the developer and the fixer, and a memory of the night before came to her, of what she'd come here to escape.

She felt for the rim of the bath like a cripple hoisting herself to her feet. She felt all her muscles on her right side fused into one inflexible mass; the blood warmed the choked pipes of the veins and arteries on the side she'd been lying, heated the mortified flesh until she could open out her fingers like petals. She reached out with her hand; the curtain wrapped itself around her fist; with the door open, she began to feel cold, and she remembered the towel which had come with her, thrown aside during her sleep, saw it on the floor when she looked back over her shoulder, and made a shawl of it to keep the cold from her, thinking she must look like a beggar in her raggedy clothes and the corners of the towel clipped around her by her fingers.

Once she'd closed the door to the bathroom, it was as if she'd lost her cover, she felt apprehensive and exposed. Her eyes went from the door to Peter's room to the kitchen; and she was thinking, it was a choice she'd always had to make since she'd come here, weaving from one to the other; Codie who'd been the listener of the two, Peter who'd first caught her fancy, she'd been sent back and forth, to one of them for mending, and to the other who snapped her like thread, until now, when there was too great a job of mending to be done. She could see that Codie for all his kindness was how Peter kept his little oppressions going for so long, and she was thinking to herself, no, she wouldn't go in and tell Codie about any of this, because he'd just try to make her better and send her back to Peter, and she was looking for more in the way of condemnation from anyone she thought of as a friend at that time.

Catherine thought of how she'd entered her brother's room as she was entering Peter's, because there was so much alike about how she approached them both; creeping on her bare feet, although there'd been no carpet over the water, bare boards your feet played like piano keys, a door with brass hinges that sang like a choir but squealed like a waxed string if you took the opening slowly. The first night she went to him, it was to say how sorry she was that Michael had been chased away from the kitchen at the end of a broom as if he was a mouse at the skirting; to see as well if he'd been hurt by the beating. She'd thought it was wrong then that her brother should've been hit when she'd escaped it, and she was feeling bad as well because the dirty old lout had made pleasure come to her and called it his gift to her, like the promises he gave her mother, another of his gifts with no permanence to them. She walked as if punishment was at the end of the hall, which it surely would've been if she'd been caught; she was thinking of now, when she was avoiding wakening the one in the bed, when at the time she came to Michael she'd been concerned with avoiding wakening the one up the hall, listening for a change in his breathing which sounded in the close darkness like a millstone grinding seeds of air into a powder fine enough to pass through his funnel of a throat. It was the same with Peter now; sleeping off his drink, unaware of the violation he'd committed, or maybe like her da he was innocent of it, only in the sense that he didn't know it for a wrong; there'd been no presumption because they hadn't thought she had any right of refusal, her father and Peter; her da nursing his parent's right to command, Peter assuming his right to make an image of her, no difference to the pair of them, book-ends on either side of her.

As she was gathering her clothes from the wardrobe, she was remembering that other time when it'd been so important not to waken a sleeping drunkard; when the door to Michael's room came sweetly open, and she could hear the gentler breathing of him on the bed; at right angles to the door to please their mother, who thought it was terrible luck to have your feet pointing out the way you'd be taken out of the room if you were to be carried away in your casket. She could steer herself by the crucifix on the wall, because her mother had put one high on the wall opposite the bed in her room as well; the tin Christ gleaming in the moonlight like a compass rose, his suffering head to the north and his doubled feet to the south, his pinned hands out to east and west; when she'd been losing her faith, she'd wondered how Christ could be with them both, and her mother said it was just to let Our Lord know that he was honoured in this house, and being in her adolescence, but still full of a child's questions, she asked, is He coming then? and her ma laughed warmly and said, sure, me darlin, n He'll be wantin a cup o' tay from us and look around our home, and won't He be best playsed to see Himself on the wall? That night, though, he was white as the marble ornament on a grave marker, polished silver by the moon outside, and underneath it lay Michael in the earthy darkness that permeated the entire house, as if at night the house was covered over by the soil it attended, so that night was a burial for the house, and she had to claw her way through to get to her brother; still creeping, as she was just now in taking her clothes to the suitcase, until she fell into the shelter of

Michael's bed, reaching to him through the dark as if to expose him from under the suffocating earth.

She was watching Peter all the time she was collecting her things and putting them into the suitcase; clear yellow sunlight came through the curtains as if all the impurities had been kept back, and she was thinking, he'd taken the sleeping image of her, and she'd never even noticed him getting up, never heard the scrape of the pencil, or his breath. She felt robbed by him, the way folk said that when you took an image of a person, with the appearance came the essence; and it was as if he owned her eyes, had taken them for himself, and she had a rage about her she hadn't felt since her father had come in on her and Michael. She clipped shut the suitcase when it was full of everything, her clothes, her toiletries, her make-up palettes and her own pigments, and it was like when she'd left her home across the water all over again; a rush for her belongings, her eyes, her true eyes full of sight and life skinned for the least movement, her ears alert for the least wee noise. There was a thing she'd never even told Francis, for all he knew of how her da had used her; that she'd been the one who'd spread her father's corruption to her brother, the way rot spreads like fire over a field. She'd been the one guiding his hands when he hesitated, who made him fret at her where their da had been only hours before, saying gently, I don't want his rotten gifts, filthy owl beast that he is, I don't love him and I don't want him to love me like me ma does, and Michael responded to the snap in her voice, even when he thought he was causing her pain, until she made a cry deep in her throat, held in so it wouldn't flee outside the door and bring their ma and their da running, and in the quiet afterwards she held on to him and said, if you've sinned, Michael, our da's sinned a thousand times over, I hate him, but I don't hate you.

She looked around the room she was in now; there was no compass, no Christ on the walls to steer by, only endless windows of Peter's own making, and she was thinking, they were all full of pity for folk he'd never known, like the stations of the cross on the walls of the church back home, folk quietly bearing their poverty like mules, but they were all there as signifiers of his own goodness, his own capacity for pity, like her father's promises to her ma meaning sorry and never staying intact for long enough to be worth a damn, and she'd've torn

361

down the windows on his hypocrisy if she wasn't about to commit another of her escapes, her possessions packed away and ready for another destination.

She was remembering a thing Michael had said to her when she was in the bed beside him one morning, when her coming into his room had become as routine as her da's using of her; she'd asked him, without looking for an answer, why'd our ma marry a man like him, Michael? and she'd thought that even then, back before either of them had been born, the old man had frightened their ma into it, making her fear for the consequences of a refusal. Michael told her that on the first night Catherine had been kept behind in the kitchen, it'd been told him by their ma, that their father hadn't always been a drunkard; he'd had the mild aspect of when the year turns towards summer when she'd first known him, and she'd been alone after the death of her father, and her mother was old and infirm; along came a man who lifted her mother out of her bed and took her through to the kitchen to sit in front of the range for the heat, who'd help with the dishes and the other jobs of a farm, then he seemed as constant as the hills, strong and responsible, an ideal father of children. It was after her mother died that the stitching of him loosened, as if it'd all been a show for the old woman, all the carrying and fetching he'd done, the piety that had made him bring Father Byrne to the house to administer the host to her; he began to take walks in the night, and she could smell the very little whisky from him as a vapour on his breath, and she'd thought there must've been a flask about him somewhere from which he'd been taking secret nips on his way along the road when he'd said he was taking the air. It was after the birth of Michael, when she'd been spending all her time with the new babeen, that he took even further to the road, declaring, I'll not get in your way while the little one's taking up so much of your time, and he wasn't coming home drunk exactly, he was walking to and from the village to the pub and didn't have the time for a good long drink, and he began to say things like, sure, there's a grown man here who's workin hard for his wife, and is he not deservin of your attention once in a while? and if there was a warning, she ignored it, because she made light of it, and a woman's job is to take care of her wee man as well as her grown one, Colum, and who was the one gave me the wee man in the first place? it wasn't the fairy folk, that's for sure.

It was Catherine's arrival that sealed him in the barrel with his drink; two more mouths to feed, and no time for himself. He was always on about getting a motor car, until their ma directed him to the books and showed him that his drawings for his wee gallivants into the village were bleeding the money from the house; if he could steal one away from his dreams when no one was looking, then he'd be the proud owner of one of those beasts, but until the day that became likely, he'd have to be watching himself and his own habits, because it wasn't the children who were strangling his wishes, and she said, if this is so ye can drive to the village and then drive back filled up with the whisky and the ale whenever ye please, then I'd say there were better things to be spendin yer money on, wouldn't ye be saying so yerself? But he was a man who knew his own wants, and if he couldn't be having what he was after, then he'd settle for the next best, which was why he left the farm for a day and came back with a new horse and cart, declaring he'd saved them money, for if he'd had a car like he'd wanted, they'd've been even deeper out of pocket, and that night Mary O'Hara locked the door against him, and told him he wouldn't be coming back unless the horse and cart were returned to the farrier's, and she watched out the window with wee Kate gathered to her and Michael barely able to reach to see over the sill, while Colum O'Hara sat on the board of the cart and trotted the black horse down the road, his head low and despondent on his shoulders.

That was when he was sober, and filled with good intentions, but after he'd stopped off at the pub, it was the drink that filled him, displacing the man who might have listened to his wife. She could lock the front door, but it was his farm they were on, and he knew all the hidden entries, windows left open, so that when she'd begun to worry at the lateness of the hour, she wasn't listening for the return of a cart, she was thinking he was wandering lost in the utter darkness, or that he'd been robbed of the money the farrier had put back into his hand. She wasn't expecting him to turn up in the kitchen, from another door of the house, loosening the belt from around his waist, saying, so ye'd tell a man how to be spendin his fockin money, bitch that y'are, another mouth to feed, this horse, is it? Well, I'm not the one that brought the other mouths into this house, and ye'll heed me from now on, woman, by God ye will, or else ye'll feel me belt across you like ye will this night!

Their ma sacrificed herself that night for the children, becoming their shelter; drawing him away into the bedroom they shared; Kate had no memory of it, but Michael did, and that night they were together in the bed, she learned of the first time her mother was beaten by their da, and she cried to hear of it. Michael said, that's how our mammy never knew; d'ye think she'd've married the devil if she'd seen the hooves on him? and as she was gathering herself together to leave Peter now, that was what she was thinking to herself, she was damned if she was going to allow herself to wait until she was rooted in this house the way her mammy was in hers; she'd had plenty of warnings, and now was the time to cut the thread of continuance from her mammy to herself, if ever there was a time.

She found the carpet-bag last of all, under the bed where she'd stowed it; she had to reach close to where Peter was sleeping on his side, his mouth open and the brewery smell driven towards her with his breath. She collected it quickly, and looked around to see if there was anything she'd forgotten; her pictures over the floor, squares of glossy paper, some looking as if they'd been fed too much shadow, others as if they'd been starved of it. She gathered them together, put them into her bag, looked over her shoulder towards the table and saw the box there, sitting on top of the tablet of photographic paper. She was about to collect them as well, when something made her put down her carpet-bag and pick up and box and the tablet; it was mad, because she'd still to put on the clothes she'd laid out over the chair, but she knew she'd have a while before leaving for Agnes's and Daniel's; she was thinking she'd have to draw all the money she'd left out of the bank, but she'd have to do that tomorrow when it was open, and she'd have to tell Gianfranco she was leaving, because she couldn't stay here, and she wasn't meaning this house, she was meaning this town.

She took the box and the tablet of paper into the darkroom, and cut an oblong out of one of the sheets using scissors she left in the dark where she knew to find them; opened the lid and secured the paper opposite the shutter. Once she'd made the box ready, she took it through to the studio, and tried to avoid a look at herself on the canvas, but she made herself look at the box as if she was a child wishing on a birthday cake, preparing to blow out the candles. There was only one place he'd never see it, and that was outside the window, where she'd have to settle it on top of some books, and even place a book on top of it to weigh it down, in case of the wind. Once she was prepared, and the sash was down, it was as if she'd wakened from sleepwalking, the job done according to another's instruction, Francis whispering in her ear maybe, she didn't know why she'd be after a picture of him, other than a feeling that some good might come of it beyond its value as a souvenir, and that was all she thought of it before she'd have to get weaving.

Catherine went back to the room, and put on her blouse and her skirt and her coat before taking five books from his library, and carrying the box carefully on top of them, in case it fell and exposed the paper. She returned to the window, opened the sash and made a stack of three of the books on the sill outside, put the box on them, angling it so it would get a proper look at the canvas and the mirrors, crowning it with two of the books once she was satisfied. She pulled the sash down, went back to the room, gathered her suitcase and the carpet-bag, and put them in the cupboard, at the very back; she didn't want anything to announce her leaving to Peter, or to Codie if it came to that, and she didn't want to be weighed down by luggage. She unlocked the door as quietly as she could, turning the key slowly, and then went down the stairs, wondering where she'd go to spend the hours before she'd have to come back to collect the rest of her things.

Seventeen

Catherine didn't bother watching over Cameron when they were on the boat; she thought he'd appreciate being trusted enough to know not to go too near to the railings, and besides, this was strange for her, too. She saw him going close to the prow of the ship to see the ocean being pared away by the bow, and then to the stern to see the water healing over, and the scar of their wake. Apart from Cameron, she'd her carpet-bag and suitcase and his case of clothes and toys to watch, all of which she kept seized between her ankles; she was remembering the journey the other way about, so many years ago, away from torment, and she'd felt ridiculously optimistic for someone who hadn't a clue as to where to go or what to do after she reached harbour. She'd small fears of what would become of her, she hadn't known about money or accommodation or jobs in those days, but if she had known she'd've weighed them against other fears, of what she had to return to, the consequences of discovery, and she'd still've found her feet were taking her away.

Catherine looked along the deck to where Cameron was, and thought she could see excitement in him where there'd been trepidation before. Journeys did that to children, they loved travelling because there were always things to be seen, seagulls describing spirals overhead, crying out from deep in their throats, that cry she'd always thought was partly a bleat like a lamb new birthed, partly exultation, high and sharp. There were rags of seaweed torn away from the hull, gathered from the harbour in all likelihood, lost from the shore and drifting, bottle green against the dull water. They were caught between two shores for a while, and she had that feeling she remembered from her first journey, of being on an island without stone to anchor it, and remembered it was a feeling of being secure in herself, having no needs or wants, no fears. Cameron was feeling the same as well, she was thinking, and she hoped that might be forgiveness in him, because she knew herself, and how she could be when she was wronged.

The land came to meet the ship; first they were doll's structures like Cameron's model town on the fringe of the green, and then as the hills drew in their sight the harbour with its wooden jetties and its port became squarer and more solid. Catherine called out,

We're here, Cameron, come over beside me,

and he pulled himself away from the railings as the ship cut into the embrace of the harbour, and Catherine urged the wee one alongside so they could wait for the gangplank to be erected, and they could go down to land.

Catherine could see that the passengers opposite on the train were enchanted by Cameron; there was an old lady with a headscarf, and she was saying to the old flat-capped man next to her, sure and couldn't you just eat him all up, and Catherine smiled and wondered what Cameron would've made of that, if he'd been paying attention to it. He was fixed to the window-pane, the pads of his fingers flattened and his face so close that he was making a pig's snout against the glass; she didn't know what it was attracting him, whether it was the speed of the train or the scenery, more like the speed given the kinds of things he liked. The carpet-bag was still between her ankles. The old man opposite was smoking a rolled-up cigarette; he was thin and bony in appearance, and he was knocking the ash on to the board of the aisle, but some folk had their quarter-light windows open, and the currents took the flakes and swirled them like leaves in a river, depositing some of them on Catherine's dress. She'd worn a bright summery thing for the journey, white cotton, a floral print of yellow roses; the old man's ash smeared across the fabric when she tried to brush it off, leaving dark fragments like the scales off a moth's wings, and she took to pursing her lips and blowing them away instead.

Catherine looked at the old man while he was staring at Cameron; the elderly face leathered by age and the winds, and the eyes soft and dimmed with the years, blue and dusty as if they'd been described in pastel chalks. The beard on him would've been pure white, if he'd allowed it to grow, but he'd shaved that morning, even though she could still see the white quills through the skin, growing around scabs left by an old razor, brief red wounds grown over with barnacles of dried blood. His eyes were fixed on Cameron as if he could see something of himself in the wean's antics; she caught herself, wean, a word from her old home; there was much that her experience had cut into her, it was easier for her thoughts to run along like the train on its rails sooner than resist. His wife next to him was fixed on Cameron as well, but it was different for her; she had an old woman's beard of threads drawn from her chin, and she had a milder expression than her husband, memories of carriage perhaps, of having contained a life like the wee one's, of being a vessel for the likes of him. They were wanting to begin a conversation with Catherine, but Catherine severed it by looking away out the window of the train, coughing to show her displeasure at the old man's cigarette, even though none of the smoke was catching in her throat; these were town things she'd learned, how not to find yourself laced into talking with another, minding your own business and encouraging folk to mind theirs. She was thinking, it was a beautiful day for arriving; there were torn clouds like stuffing raked out of the sky, the trailing ends of the cloud they'd left to bother the town with rain or the threat of it, and every so often a small fleece would wipe over the sun and then it'd come up bright and polished; and she was thinking, in the town she'd never bothered with the climate, it was all furnishing like the houses and the lampposts and the coverings on the manholes, either the lights were on and you'd be filled with an optimism you couldn't explain to yourself, or the lights were out and you'd be miserable along with the rest of the world, worse if the sky was leaking rain.

Cameron knelt on the seat to see the hills better, and the sheep mowing the grass on the backs of them; Catherine turned to him.

Cameron, sit nice, don't put your feet on the seat like that.

The elderly woman smiled; her teeth were old, eaten away by wear.

Boys will be boys, is that not right?

Catherine smiled, just to make the reply, and then returned to staring out the window, not caring if they thought she was a surly bitch.

She was looking for Michael the moment she cleared the station, and hoped the letter had been enough of a warning for them. She hadn't written much, only that things had gone wrong at home, just to make clear how she considered the house over the water as digs or lodgings for the time being, and she'd be bringing her wee boy to meet them, but she still emerged with apprehension, holding Cameron's hand in hers and seizing the carpet-bag in her free hand, and cast around to see. There were cars on the cobbled streets, but not many of them, more horses and carts; Cameron was fascinated by the difference between the village and where he was used to, the houses lower to the ground and with shallow roofs, the paving round and silver and irregular under your feet, you could feel them through the soles of your shoes, the hard mounts of stone. He said,

Is this a village?

and Catherine said yes, this was a village, while she was looking around. There was a man standing by the kerb, holding the reins of a horse which was taking oats from the palm of his hand, soothing it so it wouldn't run off with the cart; he was wearing a flat cap on his head, and he was taller than her, but the eyes were recognizable at once, green as the sea, they were her own eyes, eyes she'd seen herself in many a time, and the face was older than she minded on but not much. Catherine went over to the man and said the name; he said hers back, and then she was home, not the thing of stone miles up the road but in an embrace like the ship coming into harbour, although he was holding her awkwardly, as if he'd no right to do it after so long a time. The next thing he did was to release her, keeping one arm around her shoulder, and guided her to where Cameron was standing; he released the horse's reins and held out a hand to be shaken, like one adult to another, said,

This must be the wee one you were telling me about. You must be Cameron. I'm Michael, and if I hear any of that uncle rot off you, ye're walking the miles to the farm, and I'll give you directions meself.

369

Cameron smiled, took the hand; Michael could just about make a fist around his.

Mum never said I'd an uncle.

I'm sure there's a deal yer mum never told ye about her home. Have ye ever been in a cart afore?

Cameron shook his head. Michael turned to look at Catherine.

I'm thinking it's not your tongue he has in his head, Kate; begod, he's a quiet one.

She hadn't heard Kate from his lips since the wedding night; the kiss on her forehead, goodnight, Kate, and take my thoughts with you.

There's a lot of his father in him. His tongue, maybe; the shape of his face.

Michael frowned.

He didn't leave ye, did he? I didn't think he was a man like that.

Kate tilted her head in the direction of the boy, begged him with her eyes.

Later, Michael, please. But no, he didn't leave me, not the way you're thinking.

Michael read the plea from her; nodded, then released her and took a step closer to Cameron.

And here we are; d'ye not get fed up with these bloody adults talking over yer head most of the time, and they think you can't hear them just cause you're smaller than they are? I know I did when I was your age.

Cameron laughed, nodded furiously, looked towards Kate as if to blame her, but not seriously. Michael took him by the hand, and led him over to meet the horse, allowed him to stroke its fine coat of chestnut hairs, gave him a pile of oats from out of his pocket and urged him to feed it, told him the name was Jackie; Catherine hadn't met Jackie before, and she thought here was a measure of how long she'd been away, the lifetime of a horse, and there was a greying in Jackie's mane as well. While Cameron was busy making friends, Michael approached Catherine, looked down at the carpet-bag she was still holding, her fists closed around the wooden handles at the top.

Came the way you left, I see. A better class of dress, though. Nicer shoes. You're a lady from the town now; you'll be looking for a chipper on every corner, and you'll probably think the less of us cause we haven't a phone in the house. We've a letterbox, mind you, but that hasn't been troubled much till very recently.

It was just a tease, Michael's way, but she was wondering what there was behind it. She said,

Is himself still up to his tricks?

Michael looked to the cobbles, fretted at a loose one with the point of his shoe.

Himself is in no state to be up to any tricks, let alone the owl ones. You'll see. Now let me have yer bag and yer cases, and we'll be on our way.

On the last of the journey, Michael wanted to know what kind of nephew he had, so he asked Cameron about his interests; but his father's quiet tongue got the better of him, and Kate said, he liked to read about space flight, and going to the moon, like the men had a few weeks before. Cameron sat between them on the board of the cart; he was watching his uncle make adjustments to their road with slight tugs on the reins, and Michael looked over to him, smiled and crooked his eyebrow at the same time.

Space, is it, Cameron? Sure and what is there up there but a load of candles?

Kate laughed, because she knew what'd happen next. That was another thing he'd inherited from his father; he was off like a wee teacher, lost in explanations, finding his tongue; each candle was a star, like our sun, only they were so far away that light from them reached us on the ground at different times, which then meant he had to explain the speed of light to his poor uncle, as Michael called himself when he was lagging in his understanding. The nearest star, said Cameron with authority, was Proxima Centauri, which was four light years away, which meant that light came to us from it four years after it had been shed by Proxima; Michael grinned to Kate.

Your boyeen there's on first-name terms with these stars o' his; a few years and he'll be out for a drink with his owl buthy Proxy; a few light years, I'll bet,

but Cameron shook his head and made tsking sounds in the back of his throat, like the kinds of sounds Michael made to gee up old Jackie; light years weren't a measure of time, they were a measure of distance, and he'd such a serious wee mouth on him that Michael immediately went sober and said,

Well, my heartfelt apologies to your friend Proxy; I suppose that's like when you say a place is three days away, when ye're meanin a number o' miles and three days o' travellin there?

Cameron thought about it, then nodded. Michael looked forward and pulled gently on the rein to urge Jackie to start on a slight swerve in the road.

And what's all this space palaver anyway? I was readin in me paper that you'd only need one hole in that tin can they were up in and all their air'ud be lost, and they'd fly off into the blackness. At least if you were at sea and yer boat hit the rocks you'd have a chance at swimming for land.

Catherine tried to catch Michael's eye to stop him from teasing, but he saw her and then stared at Cameron anyway, waiting for his question to be answered.

They have spacesuits.

Aye, spacesuits and no way to come home; sure and wasn't I reading as well things burn up when they come in to land from this space of yours.

Again Cameron nodded. Michael nodded to echo it.

Well, if it's all the same t'ye, young one, I think I'll be keepin me feet on level ground. Maybe one day you can drop me a postcard from the moon, and I'll write back and say, here's yer owl Uncle Michael, perfectly happy knowin his air's all around him, there for the breathin, and I'll be looking to the sky and hopin me nephew lands in the world again without burnin up like an owl match.

Catherine saw the house from the distance, as she'd seen it before on the way back from masses and journeys to the village, and it'd always meant the same thing to her as it did now: a gaol, and her at the beckoning of the warders, bargaining for her peace. Michael was quiet and swollen with the need to comfort her, but the child between them kept him still, and all he would say was,

Are ye fine, Kate?

to which she nodded, and then she put her arm around Cameron; comfort for herself as much as protection. There'd been rain here recently, perhaps the rain yesterday which had settled over the town on the day of their leaving; ditches were brimming with water, half-moon prints of hooves on the unpaved road filled like moulds with cooling metal, ruts sliced in the earth while it'd been soft. As Jackie pulled them closer, Catherine was thinking of what Michael had said about the old man, knew it hadn't been explained to her because of Cameron, and now she was gaining on the house she was thinking of how she'd seen it over her shoulder while she'd been running from it and watching it dissolve into the hills as she raised her pace. She'd thought then of the relief of cutting it out of her, like a growth on her which had been causing her dreadful pain while it was still her own flesh, but even while she'd been away those years she'd known it was still here, and she remembered what the doctor had said in the hospital when she'd asked him to explain cancer to her, that it could go away, remission he said, without any cause or reason sometimes, but it was never wholly gone, and now she was coming back she minded on the feeling that the house was still in the world somewhere, as if her years with Francis had been her remission, her time of cruelty to Cameron her relapse, now the operation to come. Jackie's coming towards the house was at a slower, more deliberate pace than her leaving of it, and she was thinking it was the way she'd've approached the house if she'd been on foot herself, taking all her time before she was within the compass of the house, not just its grounds but its influence, settling down her instinct to leap from the cart and make again the run she'd made when she was in her old dress, carrying the carpet-bag, with boots instead of fine shoes to leave their prints behind on the earth.

Their mammy was wearing her apron, and an old black dress of the kind she wore when Kate left, and she tore out of the house with her arms out to welcome; Kate filled them, and thought the old girl was smaller than she remembered, oppressed by mothering two men. If she'd any bitterness over Kate's leaving, then it wasn't to be seen about her; but it hadn't been there at the wedding either, and there was a child to be considered now as well. She made a grandmotherly fuss over Cameron, hoisting him in her arms although he was really too big for it, as if to make up for all the times she couldn't do it, but Cameron didn't seem to mind, accepting the kindness for what it was worth, and when Kate introduced the woman smelling of the kitchen and yeast and onions as his grandmother, he peered into the close-by face like it was the moon in a telescope, reading it for familiar signs, and smiled, perhaps seeing his mother in it, Kate didn't know. She took the carpet-bag from Michael when he gave it to her; saw her mother looking down, and couldn't tell if she was examining the carpet-bag or her town shoes slathered in muck from the yard, the heels stabbing into the welter and levelling her feet; another example of Kate thinking like a woman from the town, considering the start of her journey but not the ending of it. Her mammy had lost teeth with the years, and Kate couldn't help but wonder if it was to the rot or to her husband; fine down one side of her mouth, but the rest were fallen like the uprights of an old fence, and there were still pieces left under the curve of the lip, and Kate was afraid for a moment. The first thing she said before her mammy turned to the door to let them in was,

How's himself? As usual, is he?

Just as she'd caught the look at her town shoes, her mammy caught her looking at her mouth; looked briefly at Cameron, then at Michael, before turning to face her, and she said,

He's not himself, Kate, sure and he isn't. I don't know what Michael's been telling you.

Michael shook his head, took off his cap in anticipation of entering the house. Kate looked full into her mother's eyes, as if to assure her she was prepared for it, tilted her head towards Cameron, to make sure she understood why.

Not a thing, mammy, just what you said yourself.

The look on her mammy puzzled Kate; as if grieving had come early to her. She tightened her mouth, and paced back towards the house.

Well, there's things you haven't told me, like why you're not here with that man o' yours. You can tell me over a cup of tea, but I think it's best if you meet himself first, and I'll give a fruit scone to the wee one while you're with him.

*

Michael took her to the door of their parents' bedroom, and before she stepped in, she was feeling small and childish, because her mammy had made her take off her muddy shoes and put them in front of the fireplace so the mud would dry into a shell and could then be cracked off sooner than dirty the sink. The house had the warm smell of peat about it, and there was a savour of celebration cooking about the place, a meal to mark her coming, as well as the arrival of the never seen wee one; and she'd baked scones for them, and a fruit bread, which Kate always thought of as consolation, about the only one the house ever had to offer. She was feeling the niches and crevasses in the floorboards more intimately through her stockinged soles, and it was a reminder to her of the way the house felt in her bare feet, when she'd walk around swaddled in a towel after a bath, or the times she'd steal into Michael's room at night, maybe that was another of her consolations, even after they'd taken their affection beyond play. She couldn't help wondering just then if Michael had ever seen the corruption of her by their father as spreading to him by her hand, but it was a brief thought, and she never thought of what she and Michael had done as corrupt, sure and hadn't her father taught her it was what you did for one you loved, and she'd loved Michael and not the one who'd taught her, and she'd never blame herself for that. She was thinking, it was like how Father Byrne said you should approach the altar of God for communion, in all humility and with a knowledge of His perfect love for you as well as an understanding of His perfect judgement, and the fear that understanding could inspire; like that, except it was his love she feared as well as his judgement, and she began to feel the cold the longer she waited, and Michael saw it and she remembered the look he gave her and the time he stood outside another door, the kiss to let her go, only now she was minding it was on the lips and not on the forehead as she'd pictured it before, and she'd opened to him; she wondered why she'd remembered it different the last time it'd come to mind.

Michael rapped on the door three times, and no one answered. He undid the latch, opened it and looked round; there was a smell not unlike that she remembered from Heidless's room, a smell of unwashed flesh but without the contempt for cleanliness; the smell of clothes worn for days on end. He said,

Da, someone to visit you; it's Kate.

There was still no answer. Michael widened the door, and let Kate by, stood on the threshold; Kate rounded him, listened to the breath that came from the corner, secrets without words.

She remembered the chair from the kitchen, four straight blunted pins for legs, an arch at the back from which the arms grew and battened themselves to the seat. There was a cushion under him, made and stuffed by her mother from old rags by the look of it. He was wearing a beaten-looking cardigan, the elbows penetrated and frayed by the cutting edges of his, and under it was a linen shirt which had been white once but which was now smeared with dropped food, meats and the brown gravies they'd been cooked in. His trousers were elderly work trousers, the lap darkened with spills, and the boots he'd shone like the reputation he had with the other chapel-goers were scraped and neglected. His hands fell over the arms of the chair, and when she traced them past the shoulders, to the head he'd held so proud in sobriety as if he'd nothing to fear of God's judgement landed on that day, she saw the old face was slack with idiocy, the head bowed over as if he was continually saying prayers into himself, and his eyes were drawn into their wells. The chair had been placed so as to give him a view out of the window of the property he'd tended all his married life, but it could've been a portrait of somewhere he'd never seen for all the attention he paid it; his eyes had been turned about in his head so that all he could see were the lights shining through and the grains of dust spinning in the beams, and he never even regarded Kate when she approached the chair and went down on her knees to interrupt his staring; she was thinking, it was like genuflecting in the chapel, or how Peter had knelt to her the night he'd put fear in her, and it was disturbing her how she'd lost her faith but the journey had brought her to this mockery of worship before the one she truly believed made her sooner than God almighty.

Da, she said, it's Kate. I'm back.

She was thinking, she'd prepared for this since she'd left the house with only Codie in it over the water, and since she'd claimed her rights over Cameron. She'd watched the ocean cut open by the boat over, and she'd tried to see herself in the broken ocean, imagined the turbulence was her own head and then looked away from where she could see her own image to the flat water; saw waves pleating the cloth of it and thought there was purpose to them, a drive towards shore, and she imagined she'd learned their lessons and knew the purpose of her journey was to stand in accusation of her father, explain to him the way she was always asking for explanations from others even if he wasn't looking to hear it. She'd wanted him to understand his legacy wasn't the property, or even what promises he hadn't broken in his rages, it was the rage itself he'd planted in her, placated for a while when she went looking for a mild man, breaking surface when she'd Cameron to take care of by herself; she'd even made up the words in her head she'd use to express it, memorized like the prayers in a mass, she knew them as well as she knew her Hail Mary and the Magnificat. Now she knelt in front of him, and she was feeling small and cheated, because here he was, appearing frail and she couldn't help thinking of Francis in his last days around the house. She reached out and put her hand on his, waiting for him to look up and his eyes to turn outwards, to see her and then for him to say her name; but there wasn't any ignition, and he was looking at her for certain, but he might as well have met her on the street for all he recognized of her, and when he opened his lips, he said,

Where's Kate? Away with ye, girl, ye're too owl to be Kate, ye're fockin ravin in me ears,

and then he became agitated and writhed in the seat, turning away from her as if she'd been a devil sent to lead him to temptation, or a light he couldn't stare into for too long without being blinded.

Kate could tell Michael had rehearsed it before with their mother what they were to do in the event of Kate being distraught about the old fellow, and once Michael had pacified her father they executed the arrangement perfectly; it was a consequence of being brought up in a house of preparing for contingencies, they had their signals, and Kate read them as if she'd been here all along. Michael came back into the kitchen, and nodded towards Cameron, who was eating a warm scone filled with butter and bleeding with jam and sitting across the dinner table from Kate, and then looked up at their mother and nodded towards the door; that was her signal to wipe her hands on her apron and approach Cameron from behind, touch him lightly on the shoulder and bend close to him,

Would ye like to come and help me feed the horse, and then I can show you the farm while we're about it?

Cameron nodded, dropped the half-eaten scone on to the plate underneath, but he asked Kate for permission first; she was as keen to have him away as Michael was. Her mammy took him over to the fire first of all, so he could lace himself into his muddy shoes, and then guided him towards the door with a gentle hand on his back, and before she closed it, she looked towards Kate in understanding, and then left them both to it. Michael went over to the range, where the teapot had been left to warm, took a cup and poured some for himself, took it to the table for milking and sugaring, and sat opposite Kate, in the seat Cameron had left.

He's mad with the drink, Kate; or rather, he's drunk himself mad, and he'll never be right again.

Kate was picking her finger along the tablecloth, as if to undo the stitching, unravel it along with her imagination of how she'd meet her father, how it'd be between them. She noticed all of a sudden what was different about the house; a sense of weariness which had settled on them all, Michael especially, as if it was heavier to walk around here than before, gravity increasing and tethering them to the earth more intimately than anywhere else in the world. He drank the tea, didn't use a saucer, unlike herself or Cameron, put the cup directly on to the cloth alongside Cameron's; she wondered if that meant they were considered to be visitors here, her and her son, or was it just a sign their coming was thought of as an occasion worthy of celebration by the use of the best china.

How mad, Michael? What d'you mean, mad?

Michael shrugged, the only thing to be done before a mystery like it.

I mean, he's not like he was, Kate. His memory's going. He thinks this is the place he was born sometimes. He thinks I'm his da sometimes, and he thinks our mammy's his mammy. Lord alone knows what he makes of you.

Does he remember none of it?

Now and again, now and again. He could do the work at first, he could harvest and plant, but he lost the will when he stopped recognizing the place. Why should he, he was saying, when we're nothing to him.

I'll bet he remembers the public house, right enough.

Not even that, Kate. Oh, he still looks around here for the drink, but we don't keep a drop of it here, so there's a black mark on us. The doctor says it was the drink made him like this, dried out his brains, made him demented. He says he'll forget more and more until he dies with his head wiped clean like a blackboard. Until then, it's like taking care of a baby, only he can strike back if you don't give him his suck.

Kate shook her head.

How's it for our mammy?

Michael picked up Cameron's unfinished scone, examined the bites from it, the jam slavering from the trap of the two shut halves, dropped it back on to the plate.

She thinks she's managing. She says it's no different to how he was when he'd all his faculties, but maybe she tells it different in confession. She at least has the man she married when he was sober. She prays a lot to Saint Anthony with her rosary, praying he recovers his brains.

Kate reached across the table with her hand, placed it on top of his; hoping he wouldn't be shamed by this touch of hers, wondering if after so long it could ever just be the touch of a sister again.

And yourself?

Michael looked to her hand, looked up at her; but the weariness interfered with the closeness he was after, and he spoke gently.

I didn't want the farm like this, Kate. I've to protect our mammy from a man who's as good as drunk all the days of his life. I've to lift him to clean him, and take him to his bed. I've to tell him we're not trying to kill him when he accuses us of it. I've to do everything without his thanks, and I don't have our mammy's trust in God to keep me from thinking about those times I'd've sooner bled him like a pig than dress him like a babeen. I wouldn't say this to our mammy, Kate, but I wish he'd hurry up and die; his bloody brains're withering, but his body's as strong as ever. D'you know, Kate, the first thing he forgot was that you'd left the house? He went out looking for you, dead of night, didn't say a word to me nor yer mammy until I chase after him and says to him, where d'ye think ye're going, da? and he says back, where's Kate, Michael? I want Kate, and I thinks to meself, it's the drink and I tells him, she's left, da, not remember? she's a husband now, and a wee boy to herself, and he looks at me like I'm lyin to him. So like I say, I'm thinking it's the whisky making him forget, but he's as sober as a judge two days later at breakfast and he says, it's not like Kate to be late up in the morning, Michael, go through and waken her, and I tells him again, and he says, oh aye, ye were at the wedding a while ago, and that's the last we hear of it until a few mornings later, he asks again, why's Kate not at the table? and then he calls us liars, and goes through to your room and doesn't find you, and we had to show him the pictures I took, remember all those pictures? before he took Jackie to the village to report it to the Gardai. I wouldn't swear an oath to it, Kate, but I think it was your leaving that broke his mind, because he's not been the same man since. He's been losing the time of day, the time of year, the bloody seasons, Kate, like you can't tell the difference between spring and winter, and now he's lost everything. Oh, it drifts back to him from time to time, he'll ask how you and the wee one are getting on, and I've to tell him you won't write to us but as far as we know you've married a good man who'd surely write if anything had happened, and he says she's my darlin daughter and he wouldn't wish anything but kindness and happiness on her, and I'm chokin on it, Kate, I'm wanting to tell him well, you should've shown her the kindness when your brains were still well enough, but give him half an hour and he's back to starin out the window like he doesn't know the road home. If he was sick like a beast, Kate, I'd take the double barreller and put us all out of his misery, but yer mammy says that's for God to do; but sure and would God not see it as evenin the score?

Kate curled her fingers under his, took his hand instead of pressing it, and he gripped her hand in his strong fingers and she could see the weariness was taking him over, the responsibilities he'd been bequeathed even before the earth had closed over their father. If it'd been an exhaustion that had just been brought on by work, she could've ordered him at once to bed, wakened early to make his breakfast, shared the running for as long as she could stay; but you just had to look at him to see he was tired of his passions and resentments, and not all the sleep in the world would cure that.

I'll help for as long as I can, Michael, she said, but I can give you the biggest help of all if you'll give me a few days.

Kate slept with Cameron alongside her; her belly was full of her mammy's best cooking, and the bed was as she remembered it. His glasses were off, folded on the cabinet by the side of the bed, and it was like seeing him as he was before Agnes had taken him. Her mammy was in bed with her husband for the first time, Michael told her, since Kate had left; just that she'd been practical enough to think there was a room begging, and she couldn't bear to sleep beside this incestuous lout any longer, but he was a different man now, and it was as if she was performing some memorial duty to the one she'd married, rather than the man she'd ended up with. Cameron had found it disturbing when Kate snuffed the lamp; not like going to sleep at home, where you'd the sodium lamps burning yellow outside and diffusing against the curtain, this was a different night to the kind he was used to, black as cloth, and he was afraid of how you couldn't put your hand up the way you could in the town and still see it as if you'd the eyes of a cat. It made her think of when she'd first arrived in the town, sleeping in lanes at the backs of the shops, like trying to fall asleep in daylight, as strange to her as this overwhelming darkness was to Cameron.

She was wondering when, or even if, she would bring Cameron to meet her father. It seemed important to her to introduce them, even if they wouldn't know each other. He hadn't even been brought to the table when they were having their dinner; Michael went through after they were finished and fed him stew from a bowl, and Kate went with him, watched while Michael loaded a spoon with meat and vegetables and lifted them to his mouth; new stains appeared on the breast of his shirt and his lap. He complained, why'm I being fed now, ye daft boyeen, I'm not hungry, but Michael made him swallow the food, tilted the spoon over if the old man opened his lips and forced him to take the stew in or else splash it over himself, and Kate thought it was like when she'd fed Cameron as a baby, and you'd think they'd tied him to the chair the way he avoided the spoon when it came to him, lifting his head to the ceiling or shaking it from side to side to emphasize no to the idea of being fed in this way. She could see as well what this was costing Michael in patience, you knew he'd sooner grip the old man by the hair and keep his head still than have to do it by persuasion, and more than once he said, damn ye, da, take the stew, or starve, it's up to you, and Kate was thinking, it wasn't worth it, let the old bugger starve, it was only what he deserved for coming in at all hours and demanding a hot plate he couldn't stay for when everyone else was taking their dinner; let him eat it cold when the emptiness knifed him in the belly. The pity of it was he was making her brother and her mammy share in his penance. She was thinking, it was another long wasting death like Francis's, and she hadn't the charity in her to make it easier for him.

Cameron shifted in the bed, prodded a knee against her back; she thought he'd not been sleeping since she'd come in beside him, and she asked softly if he was awake, so softly he'd think it was a breeze from outside if he wasn't. He said,

I can't get to sleep. The bed's so hard.

The down had had the life crushed out of it in time; it was like lying on bones, you could feel the wooden ribs of the frame under you, but it was still comforting to her, in a curious way; when her father dismissed her after she'd paid for her keep, there'd been this bed to return to, it meant being away from him, all she had to do was endure and she'd see her own bed.

Monks sleep on beds like this, she said. Nuns as well.

She could just imagine Cameron's expression just then; the frown to show he was thinking, the pout when he wasn't quite understanding.

You don't want me becoming a monk, though.

There's another reason. You don't want a sore back for the rest of your life, now, do you?

She felt him shaking his head against the pillow, until he remembered she couldn't see him, and then he said no. He was quiet for a while, and then he said,

Aunt Agnes said I should come to chapel with her, just to see if I liked it.

Did you?

Uncle Danny wouldn't let me.

Did you want to go?

Only because I'd never been before. Would my dad have minded? Kate thought for a moment.

Not if you wanted to do it for yourself. He wanted you to make your own mind up, always.

Cameron was quiet for a long time, and then he expelled a breath.

I went into the chapel Aunt Agnes goes to. I only went once on my way back from school. There wasn't a mass on or anything.

What did you think of it?

I didn't like it.

Kate gave him a hug for that, under the sheets, and then told him he should go to sleep. He rested against her, and then she felt his breathing become steady, warm on the cloth of her nightgown. She was remembering when she'd collected her debt from Daniel of a room when she needed it, as well as the debt of her son; she'd slept beside Cameron then, more content than she'd been in a long while. Daniel brought her down to the shed with the wee one so she could see what it was he did in there all night; he explained to her what the screen of a tele did, and she made a face and said, you're as bad as, bit it off because it wasn't what she meant, started again, you're as good as your brother was, and Daniel knew what she meant, even when she'd said it wrong, smiled to let her know he'd take either of them as an honour. Agnes kept out of her road, in mourning that she'd to give up the boy at last, but sure and she hadn't lost a thing that was hers to begin with, and Kate hadn't the time to waste in pitying her, not when she'd plans to make.

On the day Kate and Cameron went for their train, she took them by way of Gianfranco's, to keep her promise to both of them, and Cameron watched from behind the counter while Gianfranco made one of his knickerbocker glories, coddling the scoops of ice-cream into the tall lily-petal glass, drizzling raspberry syrup in between each of them, crowning it with a spiral of cream and a glacé cherry. He made a cappuccino for Kate, and wouldn't take a penny from her, friend today, he said, no customer, and pointed to the print swaying on the shelf of the sweetie library, I pay for my photo, is equal. Rosa came out of the kitchen and spoke through her husband's lips, saying, you right to leave bad man who no marry, and Kate shrugged, maybe; Rosa gave Cameron a big mother's hug, from which he came away reeking of basil and garlic, but he didn't seem to mind, though later he rubbed his chest and asked her what the smell was, and Kate said, the most delicious things you could imagine, but they hadn't had the time to eat the dinner Rosa offered them, which was a shame. Kate had been to the café on Sunday to tell Gianfranco she was leaving before going over to Agnes's and Daniel's; then she'd said goodbye to Francesca and Beatrice and promised them she'd write from wherever she ended up; she made the same promise to Gianfranco now, and he said now what he'd said then, is sad, my Paradise no have an angel, and Kate said now what she'd said then, that there were plenty of angels desperate for the money, but she said it lightly, respecting the truth of it as his eyes filled up, and allowed him to embrace her before they left, and Rosa too, who, for all she'd said nothing the whole time of Kate's employment, was just as sad as her husband on the occasion.

The last thing they did before they went to the station was to meet Daniel at the cemetery, so Kate could keep the promise she'd made a shamefully long time ago. He took the heavy cases from each of them, leaving Kate with the carpet-bag; they walked the groves as they were lashed by the wind, and though Kate hadn't been there since the day of Francis's burial, she guided them exactly to the plot, hard up against the surrounding wall where a tide of the dead lapped against its harbour, the wind calmed around it. She hadn't brought flowers, because Francis had told her when he was still in his right mind he didn't want her living by the side of the grave, like those widows who kidded themselves they'd be meeting their husbands in the hereafter but gave the lie to it by tethering themselves almost to the headstone, and flowers were part of their deception; but there were roses already there, fresh red roses, and there was a card tied around the stems. Catherine bent down to read the wavering elderly hand written on the face of it; it said, God have mercy on my son, with a flourish underneath, in fountain-pen ink. Daniel had a yellow biro in his pocket, which he found after Kate asked for it; on the other, blank face of the card, she wrote, using the arch of the headstone to lean on, Never far from us, all my love, and then made her initial K on it, and inscribed a cross beside it, giving it over to Cameron so he could put his initial on it. She replaced the tribute by the headstone, and then stood along with Cameron, thinking, she hadn't broken her promise to Francis, they weren't her flowers. She'd often wondered how she'd be when she returned here, maybe touched by the temporary insanities of bereavement that cause folk to cast blame into the grave along with the soil, holding the dead responsible as if they'd turned their backs on those left to carry the absence with them; but the truth was, she felt calm and stronger for having been here, and when they left together, she was the one comforting Cameron when his face twisted with the effort of pretending not to cry, as if she'd Francis's comfort to offer him as well.

One thing that Kate insisted was that she shouldn't be kept out of the chores to do with her father, insisted on taking her turn with the rest of them; guilt at running away and leaving Michael and their mammy to it for all those years, maybe, she didn't know. Michael had told her the old fellow most hated being fed, and that was often when he was at his most malicious; he'd allow you to spoonfeed him, or so you'd think, he'd take the food in and chew it properly, and you'd imagine he was enjoying his meal grand style when suddenly he'd open his mouth and all the pulp would roll out, splash down his front and on to his lap, and if he was feeling especially impish he'd spit it at you, just to show he was no child needing fed or milked at the pap. He'd leave the tea on the low table and say he'd drink it later, and when he finally did, hours after, he'd cry out at the top of his lungs and then you'd come through thinking he was in some distress and he'd say, me fockin tea's got ice on the top of it, I'm needin a warm cup; he was a frustrating patient, and there was once, Michael told her, when he'd been frustrated into retaliating, not over tea, but over a feeding.

It wasn't long after his father, their father, had begun to sit in the bedroom quietly for hours on end, and Michael was thinking it was time to be taking on labour to help them make up for the absence of his da's strong arms during the time of the harvest. They alternated the feedings, Michael and his mammy, one giving him breakfast and the other his dinner; they thought he'd grow fat on immobility, but he stayed as thin as straw, and they'd been advised by Dr Flynn that, if they had the money, they'd be better sending him to a home where he could be looked after by nuns practised in tending to the elderly and infirm, but they hadn't the money, and besides their mammy wasn't for the notion of strangers looking after him, even if they could've paid others to labour over him. So Michael took his turns, and this one day, he was bringing a stew to the old fellow, in a bowl so it wouldn't be so easily up-ended. He sat on the end of the bed, alongside the chair, and their da turned his head to look at Michael, his expression loose and confused, and he looked at the bowl of stew with the spoon leaning into it on Michael's lap as if wondering for a moment why this stranger had brought his dinner in here to feed himself with. Michael dug out some meat and vegetables from the bowl, said to his father it was time for his dinner, conducted the spoon towards the ruined old mouth and said, eat now, da, we've had our dinner, now it's time for yours, but the old fellow just stared at him; it seemed to be the boy calling him da that stirred his head around, as if his thoughts were cold and clear like water in a pot and nothing would infuse among them, not the recognition of the boy sitting on the bed, nor any reason why he should be eating at this time of day. Here's me not even hungry, now, a drop of the whisky and ye could be temptin me, sure and you could, but I'm not in the need of your fockin woeful stew, take it away afore I'm up and leatherin ye one, said the old man, but Michael told him it'd been made by his wife, and again the idea of him being married ploughed lines into his brow, and wouldn't even begin to trouble him. At last Michael said, look, da, I'm not sitting here until this turns cold, if he won't eat it then ye'll have to be fed it, and bloody swallow it this time; and the old boy did open his mouth a crack like a pillar-box inviting the post, and Michael delivered the meal inside and watched the old boy work his jaws, watched the swell of the Adam's apple. He'd loaded the spoon again, and pressed it against the thin lips, when the old boy opened his mouth insolently and then let fall the mash of the last spoonful, turning his head away so it spilled all down the shirt and settled in the crack of his lap, leaving a trail behind it. Michael hoped to shame him into accepting the next mouthful, ye filthy owl sloven, me mammy'll have to launder that shirt for ye, anyone'd think it was torture to eat, now take this and swallow it or begod I'll be leavin the bowl til it gets cold, but despite the talking-to, maybe because of it knowing the contrary old bugger, he did exactly the same with the next two mouthfuls. The last straw was when old Colum chewed his food, and then spat it out into Michael's eye; it caused Michael to fall over backwards, turning over the bowl and dealing the contents like slops over his shirt and his trousers and over the bedlinen. Michael wiped the pulp from his face, stood up and looked down at himself, painted in the brown of the gravy and the solids dropping to the floorboards; the old man was sitting there, and he uttered a laugh that Michael well remembered from the times he'd come home blazing with the drink and he'd be doing his mischief, breaking his promises once again, turning on his wife, their mammy, if his dinner didn't come to him hot and freshly made, and he was thinking of Kate as well, what she'd to suffer by him.

His arm drew back and drove forward, and contacted his father's face between nose and mouth; during the swing, he'd made a fist. The old boy's head was thrown back against the arch of the chair, you could hear the impact and it sounded like the collision of two wooden things, one solid and the other hollowed out, the emptiness where his memories had been eaten away like rotten wood. Michael stood upright and said, ye'll starve, then, you ungrateful owl bollix, and if ye do that again to either me or me mammy I'll serve on ye the tenth o' the beatin ye gave to her and your daughter in yer lifetime, and that should be enough to kill ye. The old boy had his face hidden behind the clasps of his hands; when he revealed himself at last, he was crying, and the tears were running along the channels cut into the skin by the years, pronounced lines where anger would express itself, diluting the blood which had sprung from his nose, and there was a terrible grief about him, and recognition at last as if he'd been an old radio set that was only needing to be struck to start working again. He said, oh sweet Saviour, I'll die at the hands o' me own flesh and blood, and the Almighty'll turn ye aside at the gates of heaven and send ye down to burn for all eternity in hell. If he thought it would scare Michael into mercy, he was mistaken, because now Michael knew the old fellow's brains had been jarred into life, he took the opportunity of the lucid moment to drop to his haunches in front of the chair and say back to his face, tell me, da, just tell me what corner of heaven God's reserved for a man who'd beat his wife and his son and violate his daughter in a way the Church won't even allow for couples who're not married? if I'm to burn for killin you, then I'll be roastin on a spit next to yourself, and I'll have the consolation of knowin ye were given as good as ye gave, so don't you dare to give our mammy any bother when she's showin ye more kindness in yer infirmity than a dirty bastard like you deserves.

Michael regretted afterwards how brutal he'd turned, leaving the old man to his crocodile tears and marching past his mammy in the kitchen and out into the yard. He told his mammy on the way out he'd clean up after himself, but when he returned she was boiling up some water for laundry, had the tin bath out ready for the linen and his father's clothing, and she told him she'd even mopped the floor, because she couldn't be abiding the mess in the room. Michael felt as powerful as if he could reach up and pick the full moon out of its orbit like an apple from the branch, but it was a despotic kind of power that left him tainted by the exercising of it, and he'd never truly left the Church as Kate had, so he was feeling sorry for his actions; the thought that he could use this new power to torment the old boy to his death filled him with dread, and he remembered once a long while ago when the old boy was sober and making the effort to be fatherly, showing him the use of the big double-barreller that rested on his shoulders like a cannon on a trestle, and he thought of the times when he'd almost found himself sleepwalking into his parents' room to find the keys to the house, to test every lock and find the gun the old man kept hidden from them.

He was actually all right with Kate; never spat out his food once for her, and although she wouldn't dress him in the morning, she still tended to him to give Michael and her mammy a rest from the chore he'd become. She asked him again and again, d'you know who I am? and every time he'd say, ye're something to me, I know that, ye're an O'Hara, but I can't right place ye, and she went on with the feeding. There were times she'd just sit with him, resting on the bed and waiting for him to ask for something, a cup of tea, a read at the paper, anything at all; if you'd told her before she made this journey she'd be a nurse to him, she'd've laughed, but then she'd not expected to see him so frail. She did laugh anyway to hear some of his antics; you could give him the same paper time and again, for one thing, and he'd read it from cover to cover, and her mother told her this and finished by saying, ah, God love him.

Kate even allowed Cameron in to see him, and this brightened him; he recognized at least family about his face, and she introduced the wee one as his grandson, but the old boy wasn't listening. He wanted the boyeen up on his knee. Kate wasn't having that, so Cameron sat beside her on the bed, and old Colum O'Hara looked fondly on him as if he was a trophy on the mantel. She told him the wee one had been brought up in the town, and wasn't quite used to life away from it yet; he was always looking for a television set to be staring at, and he was missing his favourite programmes; Colum O'Hara listened to him, smiled. She knew he wouldn't know a television from a window if you put it in front of him. She was thinking, she'd rather have this old man with his infirmity of mind than the father she'd been dealt through her childhood and the growing that came after; and then he turned to Cameron and said,

Where about's yer sister, Michael? Is she out in the yard, is that whereabouts she'll be found?

and Kate felt as if the old down mattress was pressing up against her, and she wondered who on earth he thought she was to him if he didn't know her as his daughter.

God love him.

One night he came back to himself, briefly, as if he was returned for a visit. He was all set for dressing himself for the pub; stood on his hind legs, which had atrophied to sticks with all the sitting around idle. If he recognized Kate at all, and he did seem to, it was from her wedding photographs. She didn't know if time had come back to him with his memories, an appreciation of what he'd missed, or whether he'd wakened from a long sleep, forgetting she'd been a married woman with a house to herself and a child, or never knowing. She took him by the shoulders and guided him back towards his seat; he didn't have the resistance in him to push against her, it was like exhaustion, and he sat down again, and this time his eyes were full of a hot glare, he was smelling sulphurous, and he'd the bony hands clutched around the arms of the chair until the rounds of the knuckles were bleached white from lack of blood. He said,

When'd ye come back, Kate? Are ye just arrived? Are ye come to make certain I don't quench me thirst, is that what ye're fockin here for?

She was sitting on the edge of the bed, and she was thinking of the times she'd asked her questions of him, and he'd said, God knows; she was ready to serve it back to him now. She said,

You're ill, da. I've been here near a week, and you haven't known it was me.

Colum O'Hara stared at her as if she was asking those daft questions of hers. He released the arms of the chair and kneaded the air in front of him like the dough for soda bread, like their mammy in the kitchen; it was as if he'd made substance of his thoughts, and he was working that elastic substance into giving shapes, modelling it.

Are ye tellin me I don't know me own daughter when she's in front o' me? Don't be making a fool out o' the owl man, Kate, I'm not as soft about the head as ye're thinking I am; oh Kate, oh, Jaysis our Saviour, I've missed ye terrible, and ye've come to me, it's a miracle, so it is, a rotten fockin miracle for sure.

Kate was paralysed. Seeing him frail and emptied out like an old sack had made her feel tender towards him, but now he was full of the life she remembered, like seeing an abandoned old cottage with the lamps glittering hard in the window, one good breath and they'd be extinguished again and the pall of dereliction would return to it. She was afraid for herself, and she tried to push herself away from him, but she couldn't. She said,

My husband is dead of the cancer, da. I'd nowhere else to go.

She lied by omission the way she'd've told it to God, if she'd believed in Him; she wouldn't have him knowing his daughter had lived in sin, or else he'd be screaming for her to be taken to the Magdalen Home, where the nuns made you work for your penance and kept fallen young colleens until they were old and beyond sin, as if he hadn't done enough himself to make her a candidate for it. She thought she was sparing him, and she was thinking, hadn't they all spared him over the years, not telling him what the drink made of him; their mammy had said, he wasn't in his right mind, when it was just beatings and breakages, though she stopped saying that when it was, stay with me, Kate, the rest of ye can fock off away from it. Colum O'Hara looked down at himself as if only now becoming aware of the body he'd been sealed into like a man awakening in a sepulchre; stopped wringing his hands, placing one on the arm of the chair and the one nearest to Kate resting across the other arm, suspended between them, frozen in its intention.

So ye're here, Kate, he said. I've treasured those pictures o' me only daughter on her weddin day. Why'd ye never invite me over, Kate? Why do such a hurt to yer owl da like that?

Did you not hear, my husband died?

Aye, but the weddin, Kate. It was a mortal hurt to me. I wouldn't've been any trouble to ye, Kate, I swear I wouldn't. Me heart was breakin, to think I'd never see me daughter marry. Was he a good man, Kate? Was he good to ye?

He hurried the questions, before the time of clear remembrance passed.

Aye, he was. He was gentle, and he wasn't a drinker. He took fine care of me and the boy.

The boy? A wee boy? Is he here with ye? Is he your son?

I brought him through to you, not the other day.

The old man brought his hand to his forehead, as if he'd reach into his head and pull the memory out of it, but there was nothing there to find.

Damn me and me head; fock this bloody wretched head o' mine, d'ye know I've no recall of it. So ye'd a good man, then, he gave ye a beautiful child, I tell ye, I'd've been over the water to fockin rattle him into next week if he wasn't a daycent man by ye, ye know that, don't ye, Kate?

You weren't needed, she said. Everything would've been fine if he hadn't got the cancer.

Aye, ye were saying, the cancer. I'm heart sorry for ye, Kate; ye know I only wanted happiness for ye, ye know that.

I knew nothing of the sort, da. You were always wanting something from me, never anything for me.

Ah, now, that's not true, Kate.

Are you forgetting why I ran away in the first place? Fine well did ye choose the illness that'll claim you, da, if it allows you to forget what you did to me.

Colum O'Hara brought the hand that was held between them to life; reached it towards her leg, seized her knee, rode it until it was near the inside of her thigh, intending to stroke her there.

Ye know yer da loves ye, he said, ye know he's the only true love o' yer life.

Kate found the strength to move away at last; got to her feet, took his manky old paw from her leg, threw it back at him so that it landed on his lap, among the stains of his spilled food. The rage of his drunkenness came back to him as well, he was staring at her like a light shone through ice, and he said,

Fock t'ye, then, ye ungrateful little bitch! Ye'll not turn yer da aside again, I'll mind on this night and I'll make ye sorry for it, so I will, by God and all his angels!

Kate went to the door. She heard him speak her name as she was about to leave, and it had a whimper in it, that old voice of his, as if she'd beaten him. She went through to her old room, and sat in the chair by her bed, and she began to cry, the way she had before she and Michael found their comfort with each other.

The next morning, Kate wakened after a night of disturbed sleep, and she was alert for the sound of her mammy and her da leaving their room, for her mammy to take the old man to the kitchen so she could boil up a bath for him. She wakened Cameron with her getting up, as quiet as it was; she went to the door of the room on her bare feet, unclipped the latch and opened the door as wide as her eye, to see her mother guiding the old boy along the passage towards the kitchen. He appeared sad for some reason, as if he knew where they were going and why; her mammy had said he knew what to do once he was in the tin bath, it was just cajoling him there that set her the problem. She always told him it was for breakfast they were going in the mornings, and then showed him the bath, and the water boiling in the vast crock which Michael left on the range when he went out early to do the work of the farm, and she'd say to him, d'ye not remember ye were telling me to leave a bath out for ye? She'd become practised in turning his pride against him, and he wouldn't say a word as he undressed and then settled himself into the water, which she made blood temperature for him. The nightgown lapped his feet, advancing with him as he took his wee steps, and she heard him muttering to himself as he passed the door,

Why'm I not dressed for breakfast? Tell me woman, I must've been drinking to some tune last night, I know that, but surely I wasn't as bad as I can't mind on where I was or who I was with,

and her mammy was busy deceiving him,

Ye'll be fine after ye've had yer ham and eggs, Colum.

Kate went to the carpet-bag when the kitchen door had closed, and hoisted it on to the bed. She took out the clothes she'd packed, carefully, dresses she'd recovered from the break-in, and laid them out in their folds until at the bottom of the bag she found the shoebox, and the lightfast bag of linen. Cameron was watching her from the bed, seated on the angled pillows; he never once asked what she was doing when she closed over the curtains until the whole room was as black as tar, and didn't know why he was holding the carpet-bag closed for her so she could bring the box into the linen bag. She felt around the box with her free hand, finding the shutter of sticking-plaster on the narrow side as if it was a message in braille, lifted the lid and put the paper inside, using her fingernails to prise the sheet away from the floor of the box and secure it opposite the pinhole, and then, when she was done, she closed the lid of the box and took it out of both the lightfast bag and the carpet-bag, and pulled back the thick woollen curtains. She smiled at Cameron as he flinched against the light thrown against his face like a ball he hadn't been ready to catch, and then left, quietly, padding against the floorboards and thinking how well she knew this house, when she could plan her steps along the boards so that she wouldn't trigger any of the creaks or squalls she knew were hidden among the planks.

Finding a good place for the box was more tricky than with Peter, because there was no table in the room apart from the one at the bedside, and she didn't want to be shifting it in case he'd notice, or more likely her mammy would. The only really good place for it was the window-ledge, but that was too narrow to hold it, unless she opened the window sash and put it on to the sill outside; which she did, with difficulty. The frame and the sash were tight-lipped with disuse, and she had to work herself under the frame and press up with her legs to lever it; the two separated with a sound like the way you heard a tooth coming away from its anchors inside your head. She opened the window as high as the box was tall, and fixed the box in place, and once she'd done that, she left the room, and went back into her own, telling Cameron to prepare himself for the bath once their da had used it.

She waited for her father to finish his bathing; she could hear him, calling at her mother, wondering why she was in the room with him, but it wasn't unusual, he'd been like that ever since they'd arrived. She'd never understand how he could claim modesty now, after all he'd done in his time. At last, she heard him leave the kitchen, heard their feet on the floor, her mammy clumping in her boots, him soft and padding along, triggering all the noisy boards Kate had avoided. Her mammy had said she could get away with much more in the morning with him, because there was a time of confusion just as he awakened out of sleep, maybe him trying to fathom whether this was just a lunatic imagining of a home, or if it was a thing to be touched with the waking senses; he was more willing to be guided, as much as he'd complain about it, as if she was an apparition spun from memories tattered in his head, made out of unravelled threads of other folk. So she took him to his bath, and back from it, and Kate heard the unsettling of the boards next door to her, they played the planks with their feet like the wee man from their parish whose name she could never remember and who stamped on the bass pedals of the wind organ every Sunday when they went to Father Byrne's nine o'clock mass, and she could almost map their route from the songs of the flooring, could almost place them exactly from the sounds she was hearing, and when she heard her mammy leave the room to go back to the kitchen, she knew where her father was, where she'd find him when she went next door.

He was settled in the chair as content as ever; meaning he was watching the window, and she thought, it was like Peter when he stared for hours on end at a sized canvas, composing the picture before taking the charcoal stick to it. Once she'd asked Peter, can you ever change something if you're not pleased with it when you've put the paint on? like you can erase the pencil in a sketch, can you do something like that with paint? He'd smiled, said, ye cn try n rub it aff wi turps n a cloath, but ye'll mess up whit's aroon it; best jist tay work ower it, or aroon it, see, Cathy, if ye wanted tay destroay a peyntn, it's dead easy.

Kate went over to the box, and took the sticking-plaster from in front of the pinhole, and then quickly, before she decided against it, she left the room, to come back to Cameron, and then remembered he was in the kitchen, having his bath.

It would be a slow process, she remembered that much from her experience with Peter. She'd decided on this morning because the moment she'd wakened, she'd become aware of the sun being up, there was the sun striking the window, and then loaning the heat to the curtains, which smelled of the heat, settled odours being revived by it; smoke from bonfires, old cooking, her own touch from years ago. She knew she had enough light for the box to see him by, and that was when she drew aside the curtains and saw no cloud to interrupt the supply of light the box would need to frame a picture, and that was when she decided, the time was perfect, and there mightn't be another day like this one for a while. There were other reasons for her decision; nights spent in the kitchen, when her mother would take a seat by the table after dishes were washed, and she'd rub her hands over her face and you'd see the wedding band, a ring of gold around her finger; and then she'd take it off to give her hand a rest and Kate saw the trench it cut just into the flesh above the knuckle, pale and white. Her fingers had fattened in the time since it'd been given to her. She put the band on to the table, and stared at its narrow golden orbit as if to find objects at its centre; rubbed at her finger to remove the impression it left, and then after a few moments she picked it up again and threaded her finger through its eye, smiled at Kate and said nothing, not even aware she'd done it. She was thinking about Michael as well, wedded to the farm as much as her mother was to the old goat in his room; a troublesome enough marriage in its way, with just himself and whoever he could persuade to work for him during the months of sowing and harvest, they were pissing away the money on occasional helpers so they'd hardly any left for themselves, and of course there was your man, another mouth to feed, and if it'd been any other father they'd had, like Francis had been to Cameron maybe, then you'd've said it was owed to him, but he was nothing but a weight now, strapped on to the back of the land, and the more she saw of Michael, the more she knew she had to help, and not just by sharing the familiar work while she was there.

And there were her own reasons, of course; but she didn't need to give them a second's thought, any more than she had with Peter.

Underneath the photograph of Peter were the photos she'd recovered from the break-in; her wedding, the sort of christening they'd had for Cameron. She ran her fingers over the surface of them, the gloss of developing made ragged by the splinters from the broken frames. She remembered picking them from the floor of her home, and feeling nothing to see them almost erased, and keeping them anyway. She began to wonder if her da's inheritance would be this forgetfulness of his, and she was thinking it might even be a relief in her old age, if she could find rooms in her head locked against her; she might only have these pictures to look at, and she'd wonder why herself in her dress and herself with a child in her arms was with this man, and why the pictures were nearly stripped of their images like an old wall with the paint coming away from it. She could see herself, in a chair like her father and burdening someone like Cameron, or another child if that was to happen to her, asking them, why are there no pictures of me before this wedding? why's there nothing to remind me? and her being told, because you told us yourself, if you'd had a camera then, they'd've been pictures of you and your da and Michael and your mammy, smiling as if nothing was wrong, and those pictures would've been lies, pure and simple; d'you not remember telling us that?

Kate put the pictures tenderly back into the carpet-bag, and waited for Cameron to come back from having his bath. She found herself wondering more about the nature of light on the photographic frame, how it was as if light had become solid, until you developed the pictures yourself, when you discovered that the skin of the retrieved light was thinner even than your own skin. She came to think of a thing Francis had said, that some day all the buildings and monumental structures in the world would be empty and abandoned by folk, because it was just in the way of things to live out their time and then fade, and then the buildings would erode like any other formation of stone, cliffs or mountains and the like. She could hear herself saying to him, Christ, you're cheerful, Francis, and he said to her, don't swear by whit ye don't believe in, no mind? but for him this way of thinking was optimistic, mebbe somethn'll come up in oor place n no make such a mess ey it next time. And now she had the pictures to do with whatever she wanted, keep and look at, destroy if she no longer wanted the reminder; she could take the decision out of the hands of accident and make sure no one but her ever saw them.

It was his own fault really, for sitting there like an old statue with the lichens growing over it and the lime from the arses of the pigeons spattered on it. If he'd only kept moving, instead of thinking pity on himself, but then he'd always been the centre of gravity around which they'd all spun; it was a good day when owl Colum O'Hara said it was, and they'd his permission to do as they wanted, and it wasn't when the moods took him to the pub, and he bought friends with rounds of stout, bribery for company, and came back surly, because he knew they'd only been there, his only true friends, for the porter. Kate left him for that, and she was surprised that Michael wasn't blaming her for her desertion; but then, Michael had prompted her to go, and even though they were young when he'd said it, he uttered not a word of regret or accusation, less than Kate had to herself after her return. Selfish bitch, he could've said, as bad as our da, for allowing the old man to waste and us to have the looking after of him. Not now.

So it was his bloody fault for being paralysed with the contemplation of his own grief and misery, in mourning for the loss of his brains, because he'd never have printed if he hadn't just sat there. He could've started out of his bloody chair and got moving again before it was too late, but he didn't, so there was no question of it being a murder, like she'd thought of before she left, the kitchen knives that could pare away the skin from a rabbit; he was as much complicit as she was guilty. There were times she'd walk in on him and he'd raise his hand; the first time, he was becoming translucent, and he stared at his glassy hand as if he wasn't the least bit surprised, as if it was happening because he was forgetting himself, his own existence in the world, you'd think his substantial nature for all these years had been maintained by an effort of will, and he said,

I am. I am. Oh, sweet Jaysus, I am,

but it was like meeting himself on the road to town, and Kate thought, he'd always been dreadful with names.

The next time, he was haunting his own house, and him not dead yet; the bones of the chair were visible through him, but he was still sitting on it, and she thought it must be the same for him, the house fading like a picture exposed to the sun, and perhaps he was mistaking it for death, only if she'd been him she'd've been expecting darkness, the opposite extreme of the spectrum. He was looking around himself, and he saw Kate standing by the door; he said,

Am I dying, Kate? I can't seem to draw a good breath,

and it was as if the words had been accidents of wind through the branches, forming the likeness of words, the way tree bark or flames in a hearth could resemble faces sometimes. Kate stood over him; his transparency took the edge off her shadow, and it fell over him with a little darkness to spare for what was behind him.

She never rightly saw it happening to Peter, because she'd been too busy preparing for leaving him. She'd gone to Gianfranco's, knowing he'd be opening to catch the custom from the twelve o'clock mass who'd fasted before receiving the Eucharist in their mouths, and might be hungry after it, or for children who'd been promised an ice-cream if they sat nice in the pews for their mammies. On the bus back from town towards the house, she'd been preparing herself for what she'd say to Peter once she'd confronted him in the studio, developing a picture of it the way she developed a picture in her darkroom. He'd be surprised at her coming in, and he'd wonder why; she'd go to the window, pick up the box and tell him what she'd just done, she'd just made a keepsake of him and she'd either develop it just then, before she went to pack away her darkroom things, or she'd develop it later if he made leaving troublesome for her. She'd made herself ready for what might happen next; his indifference, because he'd got her on the canvas and didn't need her any more; a hypocrite's outrage, a fight for the box, the picture torn from it or even the box itself destroyed, it was only cardboard after all; pleading that last night wouldn't happen again, and she'd be ready for that one, it'll never happen again, Peter, because I won't be here to allow it, now leave me be. She was hoping Codie would help if Peter turned on her, but in the event she didn't seem to need any help. Peter didn't answer her knocking, and when she went in, there was no sign of him, other than a sable brush on the floor leaking deep red, and a tell-tale of paint glistening on the boards that seemed to describe a fall, a spin away, and then a long smeared landing; and his palette, dropped like a slice of bread butter side down, the pigment radiating in a chromatic explosion from the point of impact. She stood before the painting, but she couldn't quite see what he'd been working on before he left; there were feather strokes on the canvas that were brighter and more glossy than the rest of the pigment, round about the empty eyes in the image of her, but nothing else seemed to have been touched. She hoped it was guilt that made him leave it, went to the window and sealed the sticking-plaster shutter over to blind the box, laying the books on the work table as a paperweight on top of all the sketches, and then decided she'd have time after all to develop what was inside the box before she'd leave a note to him.

Kate watched the print consolidate on the emulsion paper under the red safe light. He'd printed more clearly around the middle of the photograph, just in front of the canvas, but the small movements he'd been making had blurred him into a gaseous shape, without definition, and while the arm outstretched to the canvas was quite still, the hand holding the brush was severed at the wrist. The next clearest images were of him standing back from the canvas, his arms folded, and he was likely surveying the result of his brush strokes, standing in the same place for a while; but he was smeared across the field there as well. The last, and most peaceful image, was of him in the chair in the corner, and Kate thought there was an appearance of resignation about him, as if he was surrendering to a long illness. He was almost vapour by then, contained by the memory of a shape, and he had three distinct heads on him; one staring at the door, as if considering escape; one looking over his shoulder, to the mirrors, as if to see the trail of substance he'd left behind him; and one fainter than the others, staring at the floorboards, defeat, she was thinking.

He was copied on to the mirrors as well; the cloud of him in front of the canvas, the multiplied figures standing away from the picture, the three-headed creature in the chair, guarding the room. The last detail she noticed was the brush, on the floor where she'd found it, and the palette, exactly where it would've been dropped if it'd slipped out of his fingers while he was standing in front of the canvas; and Kate knew where he'd gone as if Francis was beside her explaining it to her. While the print was drying, she gathered together all her developing things and put them into the suitcase, wrapping them around in clothes so they wouldn't break, and even before she'd left for Agnes's and Daniel's, she knew two things for certain. The first was that she couldn't wish goodbye to Codie as she'd hoped, and thank him for his help, because he'd never believe there hadn't been a murder. The second was that, if she was right, the best place for her to go once she'd collected Cameron was the one place she could think of where there was another who deserved to be forgotten so completely, and here she was now, seeing happening before her what she'd only guessed had happened to Peter.

No, da, she said, you're not dying, you're just being forgotten.

She brought Michael in for the last of it, because she thought at least one of them should know. Michael came towards the glassy remains of his da; reached out a hand, and passed it through the film, across the shoulders and piercing the other side of his chest, said to her it was like the touch of water, the slight resistance you feel and the knowledge of warmth it contains, but otherwise it was as if nothing was there. She told him that she thought this last transition, from vapour to nothing, took the longest, because there wasn't much light left in him for the plate to absorb. The curious thing was how well Michael understood, remembering the times they went to visit their Uncle Finn, when you could believe anything of light and images on the film. She hadn't known what he'd think, but she'd hoped he'd at least understand she'd done it so he could have his first rest in a long while, and so her mammy wouldn't any longer have to wake thinking of bathing the old man, or feeding him; so that her first thoughts on waking would be of herself, and how neither of them need now consider running the farm.

What'll we do if we haven't the farm?

said Michael, but Kate had an answer for him:

Anything you bloody like, Michael,

she said, and she wondered if the old man could hear them, talking about picking apart his legacy, while there was nothing he could do about it.

She wasn't going to keep secrets from their mammy after she'd run from a secret so long ago; their mammy stood with them, and of the three of them, she was the least understanding; she clapped her hands to her cheeks and said,

Merciful God, what's this? Has he died and come back as a spirit already?

Kate told her the reason behind it; how it was her doing, in a way she didn't completely fathom yet, but she pointed to the box, how it gathered the light from unmoving objects, and how she thought that was how her father was disappearing. She did lie to her mother, though; said she'd just wanted a picture of him for a keepsake, and much to her surprise her mammy didn't blame her for it, saw God's work in the miracle of a painless release for them all, himself included, and Kate thought it must be the relief she'd never tell to another soul, the burden of him off her back. He seemed perfectly substantial to himself; his hands were tearing at his ghost flesh, where he was itching no doubt, and Kate wondered if it was just a translation, if he was being drawn through the lens of the pinhole, becoming another kind of substance. If Francis were here, he'd've tried an explanation for her; but then, if Francis were here, that is, alive and with her, present in the world, then she wouldn't've been here at all, unless it'd been for old Colum O'Hara's death, and she'd've watched his blind casket falling into the ground and she'd hardly've been more exultant than she was now.

Let's leave him,

she said. Their mammy insisted she stay until he was dissolved properly, and from the looks of her Kate thought it wasn't so much her saying goodbye to the old goat as making sure the process wouldn't turn about and bring him back to life again. Kate warned her to stay on the opposite side of the room, just in case, told her that if she was thinking of holding his hand there was no point to it; her mammy nodded, and went to the kitchen to find a chair so she could spectate, since that was all she could do at this time; and Kate thought her ma seemed to be gaining in substance even as it was stolen away from the old man, and if she thought it was an answering to her prayers, and thought of it as a miracle, then it was as good an explanation as any for what was occurring.

There was little mourning after her mammy came through and told them it was the end of him; there was confusion between her and Michael, as if the house had been left in ruins. Michael, practical as ever, said they'd send the Gardai if they thought it'd been anything but a natural death, or by misadventure. Kate said,

Let them find a body, if they're so certain it was murder, and who're you meanin they, anyway? None of them talked of his treatment of us when he was living.

Kate went past Michael and her mammy, into the room. She went over to the window-sill, took the box from it and put it on the bed, before closing the window. She carried the box out of the room, and closed the door gently, as if your man was still in there not wanting to be disturbed. She took it to the kitchen, and put it on the table, in front of Michael and their mammy, and sat between them for a moment. Their mammy looked at it as if it was a coffin, and Kate was thinking, that was exactly what it was, containing the old man's earthly remains, the memory of him. Kate said,

Did you ever use that camera you took to my wedding to take a picture of him?

Their mammy looked up at Michael, as if he was speaking for them both.

Never. I've a good enough picture of him where I'll never lose it.

Kate nodded. She raised the lid of the box and took out the emulsion paper from the rear of it. She showed them all what she'd done; the image of him in his chair, burned into the paper in the exact reverse of living shades, black and white turned about so that she said if she used that as a negative, then she could make a picture of him in a darkroom, with all the things she'd brought with her. Their ma asked her what had taken her to think of it, and then remembered her

402

brother, but Kate told her, that wasn't exactly it, told her of the experiment Cameron had never been allowed, how she'd come to decide to do it for herself; it was beyond their ma's understanding, but she nodded politely and asked Kate what she'd do with the picture now that she had it. Kate looked over at Michael, and in this house of signals, they passed agreement from one to the other, Kate flexing her hand around the print to bend it at the edges, and Michael urging her, go on, with his eyes, giving her the final confidence to crush it into her palm, and then take it over to the grate of the range and toss it in along with the peat and the dry, dead wood. The paper blackened quickly, withered until the petals turned in on themselves, until there was nothing left but ash remembering the shape of the untouched paper, and they were all brightened by the last flare it gave out before it shrank, warmed briefly by the little heat it made. Kate put the box down on the table, the lid beside it, and found the poker by the side of the range; broke the remains into pieces, watched as they fled alongside the ashes from the peat, drawn up by the currents of the flue. Michael caught his sister smiling for a moment, asked her why; she said,

Just wondering what Francis would've made of this. He was always explaining things to me.

Kate was about to use the poker to close the port of the range when she saw the mirror, sitting over the mantle, now wholly taken by the disease of silver. She never thought twice about swinging the poker at it, dashing the glass into blades; the frame tumbled and fell on to the boards, and diligently she smashed the teeth out of it, the last of the glass fixed to the silver.

Your da bought that for me as a wedding present,

said her mammy.

I'll buy another glass for it,

said Kate, and then she returned the poker to its rest, and sat down at the table.

Their mammy fretted about what they'd say to Father Byrne when he came on Sunday to deliver Communion to his best parishioner, but Kate had an explanation for it; that he'd wandered off in the night, like demented folk often do, and they hadn't seen him since, and Michael nodded, and they even made a conspirator of their mammy, who said she'd never tell in confession, but she'd pray for forgiveness in her night's private prayers. Kate cleaned up the glass of the blighted mirror in case any of them trod on the sharp edges, the way her mammy had tidied up all of owl Colum's broken promises, and consigned that to the fire too; as convinced as she was that there was neither a heaven nor a hell, she could understand God's satisfaction in burning unrepentant souls, and she watched as the tarnished silver blistered on the nest of the peat. The last thing she did was to tear apart the box, neatly along its edges, and feed that into the grate, watching the banquet the fire made of it. Michael never stopped her, but once it was charred and brittle and she'd closed over the grate, he said,

Were ye not after givin the wee one a shot of that? Did ye not promise him?

Kate shrugged, and her shoulders felt lighter than in ages.

It's not far to Uncle Finn's, she said, and besides, any owl box'll do.

After the confusion came silence, and Michael made tea for himself and his mammy; Kate declined it, asked where Cameron was; playing in the stable, Michael said, last he'd seen, and so Kate left them to talk and went to find Cameron.

He was on his haunches next to the resting horse, petting its flanks and talking to it, good horse, there's a good horse; he'd told Kate earlier he didn't like the sound of the name, Jackie, so he didn't use it. Jackie seemed quite contented to be worshipped and not worked to death; he was looking over his shoulder at the little boyeen and then at Kate, trying to place her almost, not coming up with anything. Kate had put on her tall-heeled shoes to go out, since the earth was dry; they made a sound on the stable floor like shod hooves, and Cameron looked up at the same time as Jackie, pulled to attention by the same string. Kate went into the stall by the open gate, stood next to Cameron, avoiding the mounds of dung that smelled lively in the close air of the stable. He asked if they could have a horse, like you'd beg for any toy you saw in the shop if you were his age, but Kate said,

Where on earth would you put a horse, Cameron?

Cameron had found oats in a nosebag hanging alongside the reins that linked Jackie to the cart, and he brought his hand up to Jackie's muzzle, seeming to like the rough lips brushing against the serving dish he was making out of his palm.

In a stable,

he said, as if his mother was being daft. Kate smiled.

They don't build houses in town with stables, you eejit.

Cameron went suddenly grave, frowned.

Are we not staying here?

Kate brought herself down to his height, sitting on her heels. She was thinking, the house might as well be abandoned now, without himself holding it together, but it wouldn't be her decision.

I don't know, Cameron. I don't think so. Why, d'you like it here?

Jackie rummaged around in Cameron's hand for the last of the oats, and Cameron withdrew, because the horse was beginning to bite, little nips of his teeth. The horse's muzzle followed, but Cameron shook the remaining flakes on to the straw, so Jackie could chase after them there.

There's more stars here,

he said. He looked at his hand; the thick tablets of Jackie's teeth had left dents in him, and Kate took his hand, examined it, didn't think they'd bruise. She kept hold of the hand for longer than necessary, as if to warm it, closed her other hand over it.

We don't need to stay here, she said. There's plenty of other places we can go.

Cameron shrugged.

I'd like it better if there was a telly.

Catherine looked at him through the panes of his glasses; saw herself doubly reflected in them. She ruffled his hair, and thought, it was a big world when you didn't know where to be in it; but there was plenty of time to make those kinds of decisions. There was only one place she wanted to see before she'd have a calm think about it, and that was Uncle Finn's, where Michael had had the wedding film developed; she was beginning to remember the kind of pace that the box would understand and forgive, and she was thinking maybe it was time Cameron learned of another, less instant existence than he'd been used to, the kinds of lessons she could teach a child.

We'll go see your great-uncle tomorrow, she said. You'll see all the pictures you'd ever want to see there.